GET A CAMERA
GET SOME STOCK
GO SHOOT A MOVIE ...

The Guerilla Film Makers Movie Blueprint

Dedicated to my grandfather, John Holland, whose vision and wisdom I still feel today.

For Simon and Angie, their courage has been my inspiration.

Continuum

The Tower Building
11 York Road
London SE1 7NX,
UK

370 Lexington Avenue
New York 10017-6503
USA

www.continuumbooks.com

British Library Cataloguing-in-Publication Data

A catalogue record for this book is available from the British Library

ISBN 0 8264 1453 2

Layout and design by Chris Jones.
Cover design by Peter Mundy with Chris Jones and Jim Loomis
Printed and bound in Great Britain by Biddles Ltd, www.biddles.co.uk

The
Guerilla Film
Makers Movie
Blueprint

By
Chris Jones

Assisted by Jonathan Newman
Production managed by Cara Williams

continuum
LONDON • NEW YORK

Acknowledgements

I would like to thank all the contributors to this book for sharing their experience and expertise, helping to shed light on the way parts of the British film industry works. I would also like to thank everyone who has helped Living Spirit produce its first three feature films: The Runner, White Angel and Urban Ghost Story, especially those who have supported Living Spirit financially and emotionally. Thanks Mum and Dad, for explaining to me at a very early age that . . . 'the surest way to succeed is to be determined not to fail'.

Thank you Catherine for championing me and keeping my best interests at heart.

Thank you Genevieve for being my partner in crime, my constant inspiration and best friend.

Thanks also to David Wilkinson, Phil Mathews, Toby White, Lucia Landino, Bex Callas, Stuart Roweth, SImon Pickup, Sue Bamford and Simon Cox.

Special thanks must be extended to the other creative people who helped make this book a reality!

Cara Williams

Thank you Cara for your tireless editing, typing and genuine friendship during the darkest and toughest time of my life. The days have been long, the journey even longer, but we have got here. And I couldn't have made it without you.

Jonathan Newman

Thank you JJ for all the box outs and microviews you conducted for the book, and for persuading the sponsors that this would be a great publication with which to be associated. You have become a true friend and I would like to acknowledge that.

Jim Loomis

What can I say Jim, you're a tireless star! Over-worked, underpaid but let me be your champion. Thanks for creating Jo Jo, our young film maker, and for your amazing drawings. www.loomisimages.com

Eddie Hamilton

Thank you Eddster for your amazing and insightful knowledge and boxout text, and for your quite staggering proof reading. You are the man!

David Barker

Thank you for your understanding when I let deadline after deadline slip by. You are the best publisher I could ever hope for, encouraging, pragmatic and you never lose your temper. You are soooooo cool!

Fiona DeSouza

Thanks for your amazing work in creating the Avid XpressDV tutorial. Your contribution will help many new film makers and I can't wait to see YOUR first feature! Go girl! Make it happen!

Steve Simmons

Thanks Steve for your fantastic storyboards. Not only are the beautifully crafted, but you did them so quickly! Hire this man! www.airworksart.com

Claire Trevor-Roper

Thank you Claire for your help early on, and I am sorry for our brief intermission, but happy that the main feature is back on track. Thanks for your amazing interviews and boxouts.

Jon Walker

Thank you Jon for being there when I needed you most. And for writing the amazing software available on the website, not to mention your boxout contributions and proof reading.

Jay and Nat of Oval Pictures

Thanks guys for stepping into the breach when the walls were tumbling about me. Great work guys!

Preface

When I began this book it seemed like a good idea! Kind of like making a film. Writing a new book about film making, incorporating everything I had learned from the other books, wow, that sounded like a great project. But like any other major endeavour, book or film, the constant process of 'turning a stone' to find two problems instead of the expected one, of everything taking twice as long as planned, of things costing more and generally being, well er, BIGGER than expected . . . well it all just made everything take longer and cost more. Again, just like making a low budget movie.

The face of low budget film making has changed radically since my last book, The Guerilla Film Makers Handbook, as DV has become a major player. Now everyone and their brother calls themselves film makers. And while there's nothing wrong with that, it doesn't mean they will make a great, good, or even watchable movie. No. On the whole, DV is a red herring. It's just a tool. Great movies are still entirely about a great screenplay that has been done justice through the various disciplines – direction, photography, sound, production design, make-up, costume, acting, editing etc . . . SCRIPT! SCRIPT! SCRIPT! Get the great script and you'd need to be a fool to mess it up. Get a duff script and you'd need to be a genius just to make it passable.

What I have tried to do in this book is detail the whole process, from start to end, in as much practical detail as I could muster. Yes many people will disagree with what I have said and there is always someone who will tell me it's either impossible, OR, that they have done it for half as much and it's twice as good! Takes all sorts! And for those of you out there who feel the need to write to me about the huge amount of spelling mistakes in the book, first I apologise. I took the proof reading budget for the book and spent it on creating an extra 100 pages. I thought that would be more useful than checking that every 'i' has been dotted and every 't' has been crossed . . .

For now I look forward to getting back to what I love most. Making movies. It's been a long time and I hope to have another flick chalked up sooner rather than later. So if you are interested, watch this space, or at least, the web site at www.livingspirit.com. Feel free to join our newsgroup if you want updates on new books, courses, movies and software. And of course, feel free to drop me a line with your thoughts.

Chris Jones
Film maker and writer
mail@livingspirit.com
Ealing Studios
1.22 am, March 28th 2003

The Guerilla Film Makers Movie Blueprint Sponsors Include

 Avid.

 EALING STUDIOS

National Film + Television School

 www.movietools.com

FUJIFILM

 Sargent-Disc Ltd

Entertainment Partners' **Movie Magic** Scheduling

 DOLBY®

 media and entertainment

ARRI MEDIA

 EXTREME MUSIC

Screen INTERNATIONAL

 BRITISH COUNCIL

Shooting People

SPOTLIGHT CASTING DIRECTORY STAGE AND SCREEN

 GUERILLA FILMS

Nando's Chicken Restaurants www.nandos.co.uk

SOHO IMAGES FILM LABORATORY DIGITAL POST

Diva Pictures LTD

 MIDNIGHT TRANSFER

Contents

Expert Microviews

The Guerilla Film Makers Movie Blueprint
LEGAL DISCLAIMER

READ THIS FIRST!

Nothing in this book should be construed as legal advice. The information provided and the sample contracts and documents are not a substitute for consulting with an experienced entertainment lawyer and receiving counsel based on the facts and circumstances of a particular transaction. Furthermore case law and statutes and European and International law and industry practice are subject to change, and differ from country to country.

The copyright in and to the sample contracts and documents in this book is owned and retained by the originator of the work ('the Owner'). These sample contracts and documents have been created for your general information only. The Owner, the authors of this book and the publishers cannot therefore be held responsible for any losses or claims howsoever arising from any use or reproduction.

Blueprint
Overview

Low budget film making is and should always be professional film making with reduced or no salaries and compromised production techniques. It is not amateur, it is just not made through the normal routes. It represents both an exciting opportunity as well as a terrifying challenge. There is really only one hurdle to overcome . . . not 'do I have enough money?', 'is the script any good?', 'should I quit my job?', 'what if I can't sell it?'. . . These are just problems that you will solve. The real problem is YOU — have you really made the decision to do this? Because if you have, it's a long and bumpy road, but you will get there, and upon reflection, these will be some of the best days of your life. So are you ready to rise to the challenge?

A movie is made, or rather re-made, three times in three distinct phases . . .

ACT 1 – The script

This is the first envisioning of your story, limited only by idea and perceived budget. The maker of this first stage will be the writer (aided and abetted by the producer and possibly the director if they are on board yet. The writer, the original architect of the story, will always be overshadowed by the mighty director).

ACT 2 – The shoot

This is the second envisioning of your story, where actors put a face onto the characters and cameras capture their performances. The maker of this second stage will be the director (aided and abetted by a talented crew and cast whose input will always be underestimated).

ACT 3 – The edit

This is the final envisioning of your story, where the sound and picture that was shot on set is stitched together in the most appropriate and stimulating way. The maker of this final third stage will be the editor (aided and abetted by the producer and director and possibly a test audience reaction).

Blueprint Overview

So you want to make a movie?

Contrary to popular belief, it isn't hard. Any fool can make ninety minutes of picture and sound and call it a movie. Goodness knows, we've all been there, sat in a darkened theatre, wondering why on earth we spent £5 on this rubbish. What is difficult however, is the making of a good film, never mind a great film. The other problem is surviving the manufacturing process without it crippling you. It's no fun making a film if you then have to spend five years working yourself out of debt.

If this were a movie . . .

'The Writer's Journey', a book written by Christopher Vogler, analyses the structure of great stories and breaks them down into broad, thematic strokes and stages. If your life were a movie about you *'making a movie'*, then you would be the hero about to embark upon the hero's journey. Spookily, your quest, and the adventures you will take whilst making your movie, will often mirror the journey of the hero or heroine *in your movie!*

Here's the deal. This is *your* story . . . You know where you want to go, you know the rough route you plan to take, but you fear the unknown and with good reason. For there are hurdles to overcome, mistakes to put right, wickedness to overcome . . . and all in the pursuit of your holy grail, your movie. At first you will 'refuse the call to adventure', preferring to sit in pubs with friends and stay in that pension and mortgage paying job. *'Oh, it's too risky . . . '* But over time you will confront your fear and take your first step on the adventure.

Quickly your old life of security and routine will seem but a distant memory. As you pass through these new, strange and foreign lands, it will often feel like all hope is lost. The quest is surely impossible. But as long as you stay true to your quest, the goal will seem closer. At your very lowest moments, allies will unexpectedly appear, joining you on the journey, helping you overcome all manner of obstacles . . .

And before you know it, you will be in the *'belly of the beast'*, and shooting your film. The battle will be won, but only just . . . and there will be many casualties, some creative, some professional, many personal. Worse still,

Making a low budget movie is like running a marathon. It's a long, long way from the start line, you know you will go through hell, but as long as you stay the course, you will get there . . . And hopefully, run another as soon as you are recovered.

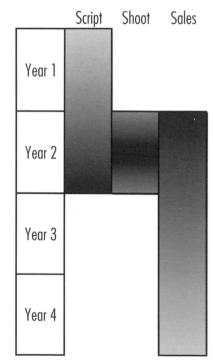

The long haul

The time scales over which most low budget films are made is often a shock to new film makers. It will usually take about a year to get up and running, the script developed etc. Then another year during which the film is made. Then another couple of years during which you will try and get the movie sold, attend festivals, and perhaps start working on the next. Yes, it's a long haul. This model is for the year of production and will show you just where and when there are flurries of activity within each department.

The shoot takes place from week 21 to week 24 (inclusive). There are re-shoots in weeks 29 and 34. The first screening for sales agents and distributors will take place in week 50.

Business – *you will be running your business all the way through the shoot, primarily dealing with money and accounts.*

Script – *you should have at least a year's script development under your belt, followed by another six months before the shoot. All the way through post you will have flurries of script rewrites for the re-shoots.*

Pre production – *the actual preparation for shooting. Note there will be additional pre production for the re-shoots.*

Production – *the weeks you actually spend shooting, on set or location, with a camera, cast and crew, no matter how small.*

Post – *the editing and general technical completion of your film to industry standards. Note in this model a trailer will be cut in week 50.*

Sales – *at various points there will be flurries of activity as you attempt to get sales agents and distributors excited about the film. Note that you will NOT show your film until it is completed (week 50).*

Investment – *you will never have enough money so never stop looking for money. By the end of post production and the start of sales you will still be looking for money for the huge amount of outstanding bills that need paying.*

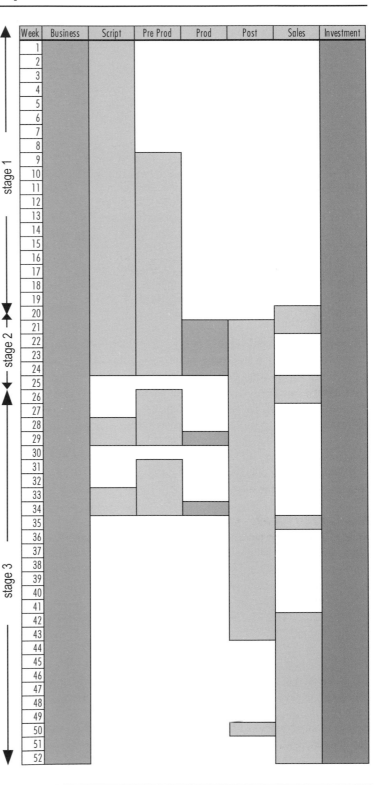

Win an Oscar when you're sixty

One of the problems facing new film makers is the pressure exerted by other first time film makers who have gained incredible success. The myths (and half truths) are aplenty . . . Spielberg directing 'Jaws' in his mid-twenties, Tarantino directing 'Resevoir Dogs' whilst holding down a video shop job, Rodriguez selling his body to science to make 'El Mariachi' . . . These tales will serve to both inspire and also to set you up for disappointment and disaster. We can't all be an instant genius. Sure, hope and aim for it but if and when you fail, don't let it crush you. There is plenty of time for you to succeed.

During the making of your film, you will inevitably 'talk it up', but beware of talking it up so much that you buy your own lines. In the words of Tony Montana from Scarface, 'don't get high on your own supply'. The truth is, that outside one in one thousand, your film will fail to achieve your own personal sky high standards. In time, you will look back at your film with fondness and realise that it was much better than you thought at the time, that it did win some awards at film festivals, that you did make some sales, that it did appear in the video shop and on TV, that you did get some good reviews . . . you just didn't win an Oscar. Crucially, it was also a stepping stone to making that elusive second feature film.

For me, I was gutted when I realised that I wouldn't get an Oscar nomination for my first film. In retrospect, it's a ridiculous concept, but at the time, it's what kept me working until 4am, and would then get me out of bed at 7am . . . month after month. Use your aspiration as a tool to achieve the seemingly impossible, but resist wholly believing it.

you will now realise that this, the shooting of your movie, was just a skirmish, and it's not the final confrontation you thought it would be. No, you must regroup in the editing, before mounting the real and final assault on the fortress that is *'success . . . '* your only real nemesis awaits you there, its claws sharpened, teeth drooling and breath bated . . . and its name strikes horror into all, for it is called *'sales and distribution . . . '*

All but the most unlucky will succeed in their goal of making a movie . . . But you, I hope and trust, WILL make it. Perhaps even succeed through the sales and distribution where most of us fall.

A warrior reflects

Whilst reflecting at the premiere, exhausted, battle weary yet heady from victory, you will realise that whilst you have made your movie and won the *'prize'*, the movie itself is not your reward, it is not the holy grail that you thought you sought. No. Your true reward IS THE JOURNEY, the one you began so many months, possibly years ago . . . It is the fears that you faced, and the character that you displayed when it mattered most. This is your true and just reward. This experience is the steel in your hand that will be your trusted and powerful weapon and ally on your next great adventure . . .

The undertaking of this journey and the rewards you receive are why I feel it is most important to make your movie *now!* Not necessarily the movie you want to make, but the movie you can afford to make. So that when the real challenge appears (that Hollywood deal for instance), you will stand your ground and fight the true and just fight in the name of cinematic excellence. How else

Many new film makers just make the one film, then give up. It's too hard. Prepare for this and try and stay the distance. If you get past movie number two, you are probably a film maker for life. There is no shame in choosing a different path, just be sure you do so for the right reasons.

does a great warrior become great, but by fighting many wars and living to tell tales of extraordinary valour.

The real world

The world is filled with film makers who have several exciting projects in development. None of which will ever see the light of day. And if by chance or fortune they do, the film maker who spent years putting it together will probably be asked to leave the project, or muscled out because they have no experience. Low budget film making is *film school for the real world*.

Get on with it then

Some people have no problem in getting on with it. For better or worse, I am one such person. I tend to recklessly go and do something and then deal with the fallout later. Not entirely smart, but useful for getting things going. If you are the kind of person who finds it hard to take that all important and possibly terrifying first 'real' step – *'I quit my job', 'I've cashed that investment cheque', 'I've set a shoot date'* – then close your eyes, take a deep breath and just go for it. Don't look at things too closely, there is plenty of time to deal with detail much later, but for now, what's most important is that you decide that you are going to be a film maker. Announce it to the world, you will feel better and more confident with it out in the open . . . *'I am going to make my movie!'*

It's a big step and many friends and relatives will probably ridicule you, or worse still, treat you as a mental patient. Film making in most people's eyes is akin to magic, it only ever happens in Hollywood, it is the preserve of the rich and famous, and the director will usually marry a supermodel or rock star. Is that you? Of course not. They look at you and see the kid who they used to hang around on street corners with the office temp, the weird geek without a girlfriend, the pretty assistant who is no more than eye candy . . .

The law of breaking the laws

aka – 'If it can go wrong, it will . . . twice!'

Picture this. You go to a restaurant for dinner and are seated by the waiter who gives you the menu. Moments later, you see that a table by the window has become available, and as it is more pleasant than the one at which you are sat, you decide to move. From that point on, the probability of 'screw-up' increases dramatically. The waiter doesn't know where you are so your order gets taken late, and then accidentally assigned to the wrong table, gets given to a different customer, returned to the kitchen, back to you cold . . . in essence, you have bucked the system and chaos often ensues. This is entirely what low-budget film making is about – bucking the system – not doing it the way you are supposed to do it, avoiding convention, re-inventing the wheel – hence, the capacity for everything to go wrong (repeatedly) is enormous . . .

If it can go wrong...
It will go wrong...
TWICE!
THINK AHEAD!

The smart producer will have conceived a project that is small and contained from a production perspective, yet large and exciting in emotional content. But because it is a small, contained production, the possibility for screw-up is reduced, at least contained. It'll still go wrong, but dealing with it and fixing it will be easier. I know it's a broad and terrifying concept, but you just have to prepare for the unexpected and always listen to your paranoid, nagging little voice . . .

Buy the books

I am big on books. They are the cheapest advice you can buy, they are detailed, you can consume them whenever you want to do so (and at your own pace), and they are always there for reference. In short, they are about the best investment you could make prior to making your film. There are a number of books I recommend throughout this book. You may already have some of them, and you'll probably have some I haven't recommended, probably because I haven't come across them. Aside from one or two books, most of the 'how to make . . .', 'how to write . . .', 'how I made . . .' etc. books are very good and you will always get something new from any of them. Some books are of course, excellent, hence the recommendations here. Reading these books will have an unexpected reward too, they will crystallise what you already know, or suspect. They are the tales that will inspire and the manual that will prepare . . . just don't put off making your movie in favour of reading every book ever written on the subject!

Top Hollywood screenwriter William Goldman's two, now legendary, books Adventures In The Screen Trade and Which Lie Did I Tell are both essential reading for any film maker who wants an insight into Hollywood film making as well as some fundamental, hard learnt home truths about the art and craft of storytelling. It doesn't get much better than these two books, as they are both fun AND informative in equal measure.

'Making Movies' by Sidney Lumet is an intelligent and extremely readable insight into the entire process of Hollywood movie making from the earliest stages of script development to the film's release, with excellent sections on directing actors, using the camera, and successful editing. Not strictly about low-budgets but an absolute must-read for any first time director nonetheless.

Robert Rodriguez's book, Rebel Without A Crew, has become the myth that has spurned a thousand careers. If you want inspiration you'll get it in spades here. After reading from cover to cover, I felt like dashing out to make my movie, but then . . . there are not too many 'real' or 'useful' insights, although the tales are entertaining. This is the book you read to brace yourself before going into battle, not the book you read to help form your detailed plan of attack.

What They Don't Teach You At Film School by Camille Landau and Tiare White is a slim volume of almost philosophical contemplation's on how to approach the madness that is low budget film making. More than any other book, I found myself nodding and saying 'that's so true . . .' Not too much practical information though, but it does manage to tackle head on lots of stuff you don't really think of until you are there and dealing with it.

Independent Feature Film Production by Gregory Goodell, is a thick and cheap and possibly the best book on the subject. The information is comprehensive, (unlike so many other books) and also extremely detailed, and his approach is pragmatic and enlightening whilst never frivolous. It is US orientated (which is a shame for us here in the UK, but hey, he is American), and perhaps better suited to bigger budget productions, but nonetheless it's a tenner well invested.

The Guerilla Film Makers Handbook written by, er, me and Genevieve Jolliffe. Ruthless self promotion? You bet. It's half interviews with experts, half inspirational and cautionary case studies of other film makers. It's been adopted by many new UK film makers as THE reference and comes with a CD with some software and contracts. Mid 2003 will see a new USA edition on the streets too! Cool!

The magnificent seven

There are seven primary qualities, or characteristics (not necessarily people), that should be present in any team attempting to make a low budget film. You may not have them all, but you may, for instance, find six in you and your partner, and a seventh in a close crew member.

The artist or craftsperson
The characteristic that empowers through a consummate understanding, or at the very least, a fearlessness of the whole film making process. Often they are either a craftsperson OR an artist (geek or luvvie), rarely the two combined. Their knowledge and love of the process is what will help seal the illusion that this is NOT a mad caper for the fool hardy.

The Leader
This is the characteristic that makes it all happen, the person whose belief in the idea and project is so strong that others will follow, even if the pathway looks dangerous or even stupid! They will see obstacles as a challenge, perhaps even as opportunities to be exploited. They will not understand the phrase 'it can't be done' and will be a constant source of inspiration and encouragement for the whole team. This person is often the driven director of the film.

The opportunist
This is the characteristic that takes a problem and turns it into an advantage. Lateral thinkers and crafty buggers are all good at this. Essentially it is the ability to look at a problem and see a solution that no one else sees. Or perhaps a way to avoid the problem altogether. They will also look around and see all manner of possibilities in the strangest of places.

The deal maker
This is the characteristic that seals the deal or opportunities created by the Leader and the Opportunist. It's all well and good breaking the doors down, but you need a person to pick up the pieces and make everything 'all right'. Tough at negotiation and firm in their needs and budget. Must, at all costs, be able to close a deal that is in the favour of the team and project.

The flirt
The characteristic that will open doors through the power of flirtation. Usually a phone person who likes to talk and can ask for things without sounding desperate or demanding. Usually this is a people person who for some reason has the guts to shamelessly ask for the impossible (not usually a quality found in a 'people person').

The organiser
The characteristic that likes to take all the facts and note them down, putting the information in neat files, alphabetically listed, numerically indexed . . . The accountant, the bookkeeper, the contract interpreter, the cool and calm organisational force. Must not be flustered too easily.

The pragmatist
The characteristic that allows the team to break through obstacles by questioning the course of action proposed. Often the Pragmatist and Leader can be in conflict so a healthy respect for each other should be present. Often the Pragmatist will suggest alternatives that will in time be seen as a flash of creative inspiration.

One way of surviving financially is by making corporate videos, but they can often become quite embroiling. Wedding videos are often a much easier job, stressful sure, 'cos you can never do take two (!) but fundamentally easy and well paid. Place an add in the yellow pages now and start looking for jobs. In six months time when you are REALLY broke, jobs will start to appear. Remember Spring is wedding fever season so plan ahead. You can charge extra for a properly edited version, even put it onto DVD for the client.

they do not see the successful and rewarded film maker that is desperate to escape the mundanity of their existence. So are you ready? *To answer the call to adventure . . . ?*

Preparations

For some time, you will flirt with the idea of your adventure. Close friends and believers will encourage you – *listen to them . . .* others will mock – *ignore them . . .* As the day of the first step approaches, so will your excitement and trepidation. Just go for it. Before you know it you will be on your way. And trust me on this, YOU WILL NEVER LOOK BACK!

Unfair advantages of others

One of the most distressing things you will encounter is the unfair advantages that other film makers have. Broadly speaking, these advantages fall into two categories. Nepotism and personal wealth. I mention them here only because so many new film makers use other people and their experiences as benchmarks for their own success. This is a useful tool but it's important not to become disheartened because other film makers (who have unfair advantages) appear to get much further, much faster, and often produce work of questionable quality.

If you have bought this book then you probably want to be one of the following – director, producer, writer, lighting cameraperson, editor etc. And I will bet you don't want to be in sales and distribution? Who wants to do that? I want to make movies, not sell them! Yet if you look at the overall process, sales and distribution represents at least half of the overall journey you will take. This fundamental disinterest is what will lay you open to exploitation and abuse, so do your research, meet sales agents, go to markets . . .

Nepotism. Is it any wonder a particular film maker is already making their first feature at the age of twenty-six when you consider that mummy was a BAFTA award winning costume designer and daddy was a stuntman on Bond pictures? At the age of seven, they'd have been hanging out behind the scenes, at age eleven they'd be pretending to help out in the costume department, age seventeen they get their first job as a runner or third AD . . . And all this after having already spent most of their life hanging out on set, with actors and crew (at age seventeen, I was hanging around a chippy, dreaming of kissing girls and making Super 8mm zombie horror movies). Is it any wonder that these people have a head start? Many a young film maker that explodes on the scene will have these kind of connections.

Personal wealth. Film making is expensive, but even more of a problem is *'how does one survive during the very long development, production, post-production, sales and distribution of a movie?'* No matter who the film maker, if they have managed to make a low-budget film, they will have solved this problem in one of a number of ways. Most common is that mummy and daddy are rich and can pay the rent and upkeep whilst you make the film. Almost all new film makers that I know of are someway intertwined in the property business, which usually means they or their parents have acquired a flat in which they can live for free. Failing personal wealth, the rest of us invariably end up either leaning on mum and dad and staying at home well

Shoot for the stars

You'll probably miss and hit next door's greenhouse, but at least you aspired to greatness. This is a fundamental part of your psyche and film makers who don't aim high enough will recount their regrets at the premiere. Here's an example. You have £10k and an interesting script, but because you already have a DV camera, you decide to shoot it on Mini DV. The production gears up, grows in momentum, the script attracts a good cast, you find a bit more money but still shoot on miniDV because that is your mindset – the lowest technical format acceptable. The film looks rubbish and goes nowhere or . . . You have £10k and an interesting script and you decide to put your miniDV camera in the closet (to be used only for some behind-the-scenes footage later on). The production gears up and you aim to shoot on film (knowing in the worst case scenario, you still have your DV camera in the closet). Because you're now shooting on film, you get a better cast and incredible DP. This in turn inspires one or two other people to stump up some cash and your budget expands. When you shoot the movie, you get increased professionalism and better performances because you are doing it properly. All because you chose the more difficult option in pursuit of a higher dream. Now apply this philosophy to every aspect of your film.

beyond the time most sane people will have flown the roost, or leaning on partners and their well paid jobs, or most contentiously, employing the executive producer known as the good old DHSS.

Why low budget?

Contrary to the accusations I often receive from certain members of the established film world (who believe that low-budget film making somehow erodes quality, exploits crew members or even takes jobs away from other crew members – yes, they're protecting their over paid jobs) . . . I don't want to make low-budget films, I never have. I don't know anybody that does. But if it's a toss up between making films on a low budget or not making films at all then it's a no-brainer. The films I have made have all begun life in an attempt to attract multi-million dollar budgets, but for one reason or another have been unsuccessful in attracting that kind of finance, so I've made them with whatever resources I could muster. This isn't necessarily smart, but I have had the pleasure of making three features, all of which have made it to the big screen and received international distribution, two of which also received UK cinema releases.

Many of my peers have chosen to wait for finance, joining the cappuccino clan of Soho who spend their days discussing their numerous projects in development and generally talking it up – but get nothing made. On the whole, very few of them have had any success, although one or two of them have managed to make bigger and better movies than the ones I have made (and have been paid well to do so). They chose one route, the industry route, I chose another route, one that is outside the established industry. And all too late I have discovered that the British Film Industry kind of despises 'upstart' film makers who dare to just go and do it. Not so in Hollywood and I can see that my days here in the UK are becoming numbered. Genevieve, my film making partner on my first three feature films has already given up the ghost and now lives in sunny California!

Clearly, it's up to you which route you feel best suits your temperament. Just remember it is an extraordinarily competitive industry. It IS glamorous (the worst job on any film is better than stocking shelves at the supermarket any day of the week), it is well paid when you get in, it is fun and rewarding at almost any level . . . It is a dream factory. Who wouldn't want to do it?

Maintaining a relationship while making a film is tough. You are rarely present in body as you work such long hours, and when you are there, your mind is usually on production problems, or hanging out with the characters in your story as you quietly brainstorm with yourself. Hopefully your partner will understand, and ideally they will have their own all consuming career too. Just be aware, making a movie can be the breaking of your relationship.

Other bad films

One of the big problems facing you as an independent film maker is that whenever Joe public goes to the cinema to watch, or rents, a low budget movie, they are all too often very disappointed. It's an unpopular thing to say, but many, no let's be honest here, the vast majority of low budget films are at best dull, and

What kind of movie do you want to make?

The type of movie you choose to make will clearly impact on the next five years of your life. So you'd better love it to bits. There are two basic philosophies that have a very large grey area in-between – a movie made for love, that is, it is unique and is designed to be a calling card for your talents . . . OR a movie that is made for the profit, designed for a perceived market place to bring financial reward to the film makers and investors.

The closer you are to the centre, the greater your chances of mega success (think 'Blair Witch', an experimental and arty film but still a horror movie, or 'Human Traffic' a personal film, commercial in its style and approach but marginal in the story and the people for whom it was designed). As your chances of mega-success increase, so do your chances of falling between two stools, and if you get it wrong, you could end up with a dog's dinner that satisfies no one.

In it for the money

This is probably a production that is similar to mainstream Hollywood movies, strong in plot, simple characters with a clear goal. Anyone who has been to Cannes will have seen companies in the Noga Hilton Hotel trading these kind of movies. Production value is very important, these movies must look slick (so get shots that look expensive, smoke machines and blue light for instance). The title should be strong and simple and the production should hire the best cast possible (as big a name as you can afford). No one makes these movies for love so you will find fewer actors and crew flocking to be part of it. Critics will slate the film as a cheap clone (which it probably is).

On both my first and second films, The Runner and White Angel respectively, we attempted to make movies for a perceived market. The first, an out and out action adventure thriller, the second a serial killer thriller. The Runner was a disaster, possibly the worst film ever made, but boy were lots of lessons learnt the hard way! But White Angel is pretty good, and whilst The Runner was shamelessly 'In it for the money', White Angel was starting to lean further into the middle grey area and toward the 'In it for the credit'. Consequently it fell between two stools and failed to satisfy the critics and festivals or the serial killer thriller fans (although a lot of people really liked it). It did well at some festivals but ultimately we were disappointed by how the project performed.

In it for the credit

This is a movie that is probably quite personal and unique, perhaps even 'arty'. It is designed to get you an agent who will get you work in the future. It should open doors at production companies and may even lead on to 'output' or 'first look' deals with huge companies. All of which will give you some security as a film maker. It will be strong in story and character, perhaps displaying an interesting visual flair – although how the film looks is not as important as in the earlier model. This film is always about a unique story told in a unique way. Essentially, platforming a new film maker with a 'unique voice'. These movies are loved by film festival audiences, win lots of awards and generally receive favourable notices by reviewers, mainly because the film makers are trying to do something fresh and new (even if they have failed in some ways).

On my third movie, Urban Ghost Story, we went directly for the credit. We believed that the best way to success was through good reviews, festival awards etc. We had also failed at two commercial films and quite frankly, just wanted to make something that we felt a strong affinity for. Urban Ghost Story was that movie, and it opened doors, got agents, got Hollywood execs frantically fighting over prints to view in their private LA screening theatres and did good business worldwide. It did the job and still managed to lean toward the grey middle area (especially with the strong genre title). Most people are surprised when they see the movie. It isn't what they expect and quite unlike any other movie (although it does have echoes of other films that deal with a similar subject matter).

Keep it contained

Almost all successful low-budget films have told very simple, small scale stories. Usually, they are centered around a single location, with a handful of characters and with a plot that twists and turns. I learnt a very hard lesson on my first feature. Moving a cast and crew between A and B is expensive time spent NOT shooting your movie. Construct a story that, where possible, can be told in a single location. Then find the best, most interesting, most accessible location you can take over for the duration of your shoot.

'Reservoir Dogs' did it beautifully with little more than a down-town LA warehouse (that doesn't mean make a gangster film though!). This limitation of story scale will force you to conceive and work out a more intricate and intriguing plot, and also to focus on more interesting characters – both of which will result in a much better movie.

at worst, amateurish and unwatchable. Whilst you may feel *your movie* is different, you can't escape the fact that you will be tarred with the *low budget and independent equals crap* brush. This also extends to the industry. Most industry folk have an extraordinarily dim view of indie films, and those of them who are interested in rummaging around to find a hidden gem will base their decisions on the first few minutes of the movie (so have a great opening). Very rarely will a professional film person invest an hour and a half in your film, unless it grabs them (or they have a personal connection to you or are offering assistance). All this preconceived prejudice means that you have to try and make a film that is extra good. So every time you say (at whatever part of the film making process) *'oh we'll get away with that'*, ask yourself *'what would that top critic or my favourite film director say about it?'*

Mystique of the business

Throughout the film making process, you will come across many people who will attempt to perpetuate the public myth that film making is in some way magical. This is illustrated by the DP (the lighting cameraperson) who might swan around set waving a light meter in the air, announcing that they are creating a *'wonderful work of art that has been sculpted in light'*. Dear lord, what on earth does that mean? In reality, they are going to set up a couple of lights, measure the quantity of light with the light meter, set the exposure on the camera, frame it up, focus, press the 'on' button, follow the action of the actors and press the 'off' button when the director calls *'cut'*. There is absolutely no magic and it is certainly not rocket science.

Watch as many movies as you can. Anything you like, re-watch, but the second time round pay particular attention to the choice of shots, the pace of story, the choice of cutting points, the use of sound, the use of music etc. Diversify the films you watch. You are not going to learn much from watching Star Wars *over and over, but you will become more knowledgeable if you seek out obscure yet critically acclaimed foreign films. Even if watching films you wouldn't normally choose ends up being an unpleasant or negative experience, you are at the very least broadening your knowledge base and you will better understand your own tastes and choices. Essentially, this is one of the very important and valuable things that a film school can offer. So why not run your own home film school by watching three movies a week with a diverse group of movie lovers?*

The reason I mention this mystical quality here is that it will be used to keep you *out of the business* . . . *'Gosh, I don't understand how it all works, it looks terribly complicated'*. If you are intimidated or terrified by your lack of understanding about how these 'magicians' orchestrate their illusions, you are never going to attempt to get on stage with them. Of course, once you are on that stage, you will see all the sticky tape and string holding the illusions together and then wonder why on earth you were afraid of it in the first place.

Let me put it very simply. How to make a film. Write a script, hire some actors, film the script, edit the footage, put it on a screen in front of an audience. No magic, no mystery, no rocket science. I once interviewed an up-and-coming producer, who is now successfully entrenched in Hollywood, who said about my previous book, *'The Guerilla Film Makers Handbook'*, *'Don't tell them everything, or they'll figure out just how easy it is and then we'll all be out of a job'*.

Dov S-S Simens
Film Guru

Prejudice

This is contentious and I hope that you can take it in the spirit of empowerment, but . . . the British film industry, that is the people who control the money (but not the people who actually make films and service that industry) are xenophobic and sexist. Talent, whatever sex or ethnic background, will always shine through and rise to the top. However, talent is an extraordinarily rare commodity that most of us do not have. Now when I say talent, I'm sure we are all very confident because we are already thinking of making a film (which requires enormous self confidence and a large ego), and maybe our friends, spouse, siblings, parents all believe in us, they may even call us a genius. But that is talent on a 'local' *down the pub* scale. The kind of talent I'm talking about is international and irrepressible.

I'm not saying that you do not have talent. Clearly, I don't know you so can't comment. I'm just saying the statistical odds are against you having real talent. What you probably do have though is moments of genius, tenacity, drive, ambition, guts . . . and you have it in spades. These are all qualities that will aid you in the making of your film, but they are not qualities that people in the British film industry will champion. Anyone can have those qualities, and in fact they are very common and therefore not particularly attractive or elusive. So they'll take a look at you and judge you on an entirely different level. All too often (and I feel very sad about this) it comes down to things like if you know about ordering the right bottle of wine at dinner, being able to chat to the waiter in French, which public school you were educated at, whether you can speak the bullshit lingo, whether you are a member of the right clubs, what kind of movies you love and can't stop talking about, your accent which might imply a degree of unsophistication, your sex (*'Girls? They are just assistants, they can't direct'*), your ethnic background . . . It's brutal and certainly not PC. Please believe, I do not agree with any of these prejudices, but I have been on the receiving end of some and have seen other talented film makers on the receiving end of all of the others. Nor can I offer a fix for this problem, aside from encouraging you to use the qualities that you have and simply keep going. Eventually, you will make a breakthrough, but it's hard not to be disheartened when you see other film makers, who are not worthy of *'the break'*, getting the fast track in to the business.

Shut up and do it. The UK, for some reason, has a long tradition of making short films. Short films won't do anything for you. You can't sell a short and it won't progress your career. Make a feature film. The Brits are also fond of complaining. Come out to Hollywood for a while – you'll see that we don't have any lottery money, and we don't have any tax incentives. It's a business.

You wanna know how to make a Hollywood film for $50 million? First make a $2 million film. Before that make a $200k film. Before that make a $10k film. Walk before you can run. $10k is entirely possible to raise for a film. You wanna know where you get it from? Dentists. Hire a cinema, show the DP's showreel, and get them to commit some money there and then. They give to the ballet, why not a feature film? You only need to write 35 cheques to make your feature film. If you've shot on DV, you can make a feature film for $500. If you've shot on S16mm, you can shoot and deliver it for $20k. If you've shot on 35mm, then the 35 cheques you write will add up to $30k. That's it.

Now you wanna get your film noticed? You screen it at a festival where you know all the acquisition executives will attend. You invite them to the screening, they see how well the first 10 minutes plays in front of an audience, and they pick up your film. If you haven't sold your first film, perhaps you should consider that it's not very good. You tried kid, well done. But you failed. Now go to law school, make your mom happy and make shit loads of money.

How to prepare

If you are new to this lark, there are a number of things you should do in order to gain a broad understanding of the film making process. Of course it's not essential but no matter how many books you read or courses you attend, you'll never get a true feeling for what it's really like in script development, on set when the shit hits the fan or in post-production when the cut isn't working . . . unless of course, you've actually been present. To paraphrase a great scene in 'Good Will Hunting', 'you may know everything about the Sistine chapel, but you can't tell me what it smells like because you haven't been there'.

1. Make a short film

If you really want to know what it is like making a film, then make one. Just a really tiny one. Minimum investment, maximum experience. The making of a two minute short, shot on Super 16mm film, with a crew of twenty, shot over a weekend and costing say £1k in total will teach you more in a compressed 48 hour space than any other experience in your life. Making a short film in this way is, from a manufacturing point-of-view, very similar to making a feature film. Sure, one is ninety seconds, the other is ninety minutes, but you will still have to organise stuff, do your paperwork, hire the equipment, buy the film stock, audition actors, run a set, find an edit suite, edit and re-edit, mix the sound, finish and master the film and then put it in front of an audience. This kind of exercise will teach you all about the mechanism of film making but it may lull you into a false sense of security about the artistic and narrative aspect of film making. Telling a story in ninety seconds is very different to telling a story in ninety minutes.

2. Work as a PA

Other people's films are a fantastic way of getting valuable experience at someone else's expense. In essence, you can use their film as a trial run for your film. You can make all the simple and common mistakes without it impacting on your production. Everyone, no matter which discipline they plan to enter, acting, camera, sound, directing etc. should work on at least one film as a production assistant. Not a runner, but essentially somebody who is directly involved in the production process, whose job it is to solve the logistical and production problems thrown up by the screenplay, and also the often whimsical problems generated by the creatives of the film . . . 'could we just paint all of that wall green?', 'I feel we need three elephants instead of two', 'I said brown bread, not white bread, and I don't care If it's going to take all day to get brown bread'. Doing this job will teach you so much about the background mechanics of production and whenever you are on the other side of this job and on set (on your film), you will perhaps be a little more appreciative and less demanding of the (never thanked) production team.

3. Do some editing

Every director must edit at least once. It is inconceivable to me as a director who does edit that any director would be unable to do this job. Film makers, especially directors, can often blame everyone else for their shortcomings. The editor sometimes takes the brunt of this frustration and aggression because the edit is when the film gets to the sharp end of the wedge. If the director didn't get the right shots to make the scenes work, then no matter how much they blame the editor, they cannot escape the truth – they screwed up. Cutting material, any material, will teach a film maker about coverage and shots. Essentially, this is the language of cinema and there is no greater classroom than an Avid edit suite with a project, based on an exciting screenplay with great actors, but helmed by a duff director whose choice of shots is poor who didn't get enough coverage (shots). Being able to use an edit tool such as Avid is also a very valuable feather in your cap.

4. Network with others

Stop hanging out with your Friday night drinking buddies (as they'll depress the hell out of you with their 'can't do, won't do, just buy another drink' attitude). Forge friendships & alliances with other aspiring film makers and movie lovers. Part of making your first film is about convincing yourself that you can do it. Hanging out with a movie gang will bolster your confidence, because they'll want to do it too. Their tastes will differ from yours and they'll challenge your choices whilst you can learn from their tastes.

5. Go to Cannes

So many film courses, books, schools etc., forget, or worse still, ignore the whole second half of the film making process which is sales and distribution. It is complete folly to embark on any high investment (both personal and financial) venture without having at the very least a rudimentary appreciation of the market place. The quickest, easiest and most brutal way to learn heaps in a matter of days is to attend the Cannes film market (held in May each year). But don't go alone and have (in advance) several chats with other film makers who have been. Hey, why not go with your new found movie gang? You could also take a copy of that short film you made last weekend. What do you know! You've already made a film, forged new friendships and now sit on a beach at the Cannes Film Festival, sipping wine and hob-nobbing with the industry about your exciting project for next year!

A four year adventure?

The time scales involved in the making of any low-budget film can be epic. Roughly, you'll spend about a year messing around, flirting with the idea, asking questions, reading books, doing courses and writing your script. The second year you'll spend actually making the movie, a very intensive and exciting twelve months. The next few years you will spend embroiled in film festivals, film markets and the all important sales and distribution process. On average, it's a four year adventure.

Why does it take so long? Partly because you don't know what you're doing (even though you think you do) and you are learning on a daily basis by taking baby steps. Wherever you make a major mistake, you can go back and fix it but of course this just takes time. The other reason is that there is only you responsible for this film, which means you have to do everything, be that completing the accounts, directing the actors, working with the editor, designing the poster, negotiating with sales agents, attending film festivals etc. In the words of Bilbo Baggins, you will feel like 'butter that is spread too thin', all of which leads on to the next point . . .

How are you going to survive?

Over the duration of this great adventure, and especially for the second and intensive year of 'production', the awful issue of *'how will I survive?'* will hover like an unwelcome spectre. If you don't have personal wealth, can't lean on friends and relatives and don't want to sign on for the dole, then you are left with very few options. Of course, you could attempt to live for next to nothing, which is certainly more doable than you might think – you'll be surprised how many people will buy you food, pay for the occasional cinema ticket, donate a couple of reams of paper for printing your script etc. You could get a part-time job, which in some ways is counter-productive because you should be spending every waking hour on your movie . . . which leads to an inevitable conclusion.

You are going to have to pay yourself out of the budget of the film.

You may be uncomfortable with this concept because you feel every penny should be spent on something in front of the camera, or that you've asked your cast and crew to work for next to nothing (whilst your rent and food expenses are covered). But remember this, you are the project leader, who needs to be available 100% of the time. You can ask a cast or crew member to invest a couple of weeks, perhaps even a month or so without real pay. But no one can work for free for a year or more AND run a household.

It's also incumbent on you to maximise the investment made by others – the cash from your various investors and the work invested by your cast and crew. You are no use to either group if you have to spend most of your time delivering pizzas. In essence, your survival should be a prioritised and an

Simon Beaufoy
Film Maker

'On my first low-budget film, 'This is Not a Love Song', we decided to see how far we could push DV. We workshopped the film with the actors, wrote it in a week and shot it in a week. We pushed it to its absurd limit to see what works and what doesn't work in that timescale, although we did eventually discover that a week is slightly too short to shoot a feature.

Low-budget film making is about working fast and using everything to your advantage. So you should know it's going to be low budget even before your write, so that you can tailor your script to the budget. For instance, we planned that we would have only two actors, we knew we weren't going to light the shots so that we could shoot quickly, and that we would even get the locations confirmed – all before I started writing. Workshopping the film with actors was an essential part of the process as we didn't have time to waste in front of the camera and on location – the actors turned up on day one and knew exactly who their characters were. Find the cast and then write the script rather than the opposite way round. That way the actors can genuinely contribute to the character.

There is great pleasure in making low budget films. What I found most exciting was being able to write exactly what I wanted as no one was breathing down my neck saying it wasn't possible. It also makes you very inventive. Perhaps the best indicator of how much fun and how creative a process it was is that as a writer I feel that no one changed a single word of the script, except to make it better!'

essential budgetary requirement. How much you take is obviously up to you. For instance, on *Urban Ghost Story*, Genevieve and myself shared a flat and took £1k a month (between us) to pay for our rent, food, clothing and recreation (what recreation?). On *White Angel* it was considerably less (although I was signing on, which ultimately led to a short trip at Her Majesty's Pleasure!)

Baby steps

No matter how complicated the film making process seems, you have a year or two in which to do it all. You'll always have time to *'figure it out'*, and if you can't, you'll find someone who can. Don't fear the process. It's all much easier than you'd think . . . But keeping within a budget, that is tough. And telling a great story? That is even tougher. No, it's mythical!

And finally . . . the script

In the haze of battle, as you try to find a way to make your film, it's easy to become obsessed with the victory of actually making the film (often at all costs). A wise film maker would always take a step backwards and ask, *'is this story worthy of the battle?'* All too often, new film makers fixate on production values, casting contacts and the simple attainment of that first feature film credit – usually at the expense of the screenplay.

No matter who you talk to, if they have made a film, they will tell you one thing is important above all others . . . GET THE GREAT SCRIPT. I could wax lyrical about how important the screenplay is, how it is the foundation of your film, how it is the inspiration, the aspiration, the work upon which all other work is based. But the truth is, so many new film makers will just ignore this.

Wherever possible, invest as much creative time and energy into the development and refinement of your script. It will pay you back handsomely. The simple truth is, you will more than likely be in denial about the shortcomings of your screenplay, but you will find out about these shortcomings on set, in the cutting room or in a worst case scenario, at the premiere. Just remember this mantra . . .

The very first step can be terrifying and many new film makers spend their lives debating the ins and outs, the pros the cons, film or video, blah blah blah. The only way to become a film maker is to actually make your film, be it good, bad or indifferent. So stop procrastinating, and if you are going to do it, get on with it!

Old life, Old job / Make a MOVIE

IF MY SCRIPT IS POOR, MY MOVIE WILL BE EVEN WORSE!
(and I am in denial about just how poor my script actually is)

So are you ready for the adventure? Good. Read on then.

Company Set-up Blueprint

media and entertainment insurance services ltd

www.media-ent.com
pdc-media@netway.co.uk

Most new film makers makers are unaware of the corporate responsibilities that come with running a production company. Accounts, insurance, returns, VAT . . . All need to be considered, and in many ways, are anti-film making as they are dull, boring, but 100% essential. In short, you need to be aware of, and live up to the responsibilities of being the company director of your own production entity.

There will be three 'suits' who will feature in your business dealings.

Bank manager

An ideal source of free advice and always your first point of contact at the bank. Build a good strong relationship here, always do what you say you are going to do, and call them as soon as you have any problems. The worst thing you can do with your bank manager is remain silent when you have crisis.

Solicitor

You are probably going to need a media lawyer, but you won't need one straight away. Listen to your common sense, if a deal is too good to be true, it probably isn't true. Find a solicitor who will give you a little free advice and maybe check one or two contracts, for which you will pay a nominal fee (and promise them your next fully paid production when it happens). However, if there's one contract you must get a solicitor to vet, it is when it comes to the sales and distribution agreement. Do not sign any distribution or sales agreement without a solicitor reading it over first.

Accountant

No need for a high powered media accountant just yet, your average high street variety will do. They will do your end of year accounts, and depending on your budget, they may even do your book keeping (although that is unlikely just yet). Beware of just getting on the phone to ask a few questions as they may charge you for their time.

Company Set-up

Film making is a serious business. It can come as a bit of a shock if you have been used to running around with your mates, DV camera in hand, and shooting short films from the hip. But this is different. You're about to play with the big boys. One of your ultimate aims is to have your movie screening in a multiplex cinema, competing against and hopefully beating multi-million dollar Hollywood movies. It's no longer a Saturday night premiere for your family members who are going to be amazed that your little movie has sound and is in colour, but a Friday night opening against a major Hollywood movie. You are going to need to be a 'proper' company for this.

Unfortunately, running a company, even if it is a 'film company', is dull as ditch water. Worse. It's actually anti-film making. It is however a necessary and a begrudgingly undertaken evil.

It's all in a name

Before you start your company, you'll probably want to think of a name. Resist the usual British small mindedness and don't call yourself *'Garage films'* or *'Miniature movies'*. You are about to enter a world market place that won't be impressed by colloquial in jokes, so think accordingly. What about *'XYZ International Pictures'* or *'XYZ Film Holdings'* or *'XYZ Film International'*. These names all sound big, they sure sound like they would have glass fronted corporate offices and long oak board meeting tables. But, it could also be a spotty teenager working from his mum's garden shed. One of the great things about the film industry is that most of the time you will go to meet people at *their* offices, or in a café, and the only contact that they will have with you at your office will be via phone, fax, post or e-mail. Whatever name you choose, you are going to live with for a very long time, so choose carefully.

Start as you mean to finish

To handle the making of your film, you will start a company. This company will trade, that is it will receive funds from many sources (investors, loans, sales, jobs etc.,) it will distribute it's funds (spend money on film production, equipment hire and purchase, salaries etc.) and any balance

You will need to start a limited company to make your film, giving you legal status, protection and some street cred, especially if you are trading from your bedroom!

There are numerous accounts programs, but beware, most are simply too complicated for most people, especially us filmy creative types. Quicken is one of the simplest, and even then it's a bit of a head screw. You may find it easier to create your own simple spreadsheet in MS Excel, or even do the books by hand in . . . er, books!

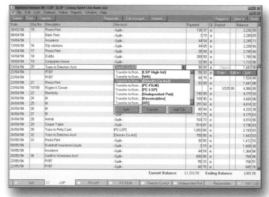

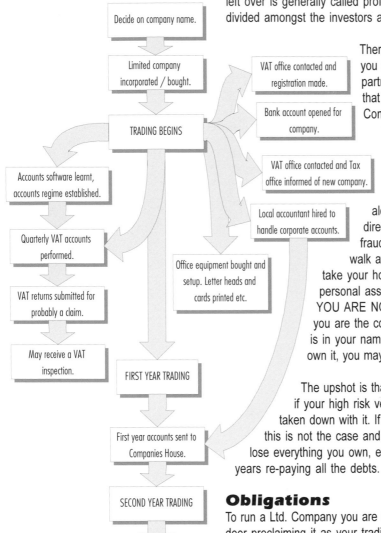

Decide on company name.

Limited company incorporated / bought.

VAT office contacted and registration made.

TRADING BEGINS

Bank account opened for company.

VAT office contacted and Tax office informed of new company.

Accounts software learnt, accounts regime established.

Local accountant hired to handle corporate accounts.

Quarterly VAT accounts performed.

Office equipment bought and setup. Letter heads and cards printed etc.

VAT returns submitted for probably a claim.

May receive a VAT inspection.

FIRST YEAR TRADING

First year accounts sent to Companies House.

SECOND YEAR TRADING

Company set-up flow chart

left over is generally called profit. Any profit you make will probably be divided amongst the investors and you, the film makers.

There are several types of companies that you could run, such as a sole trader, partnership, co-operative etc., but the entity that you are going to use is called a 'Limited Company'. As it's name suggests, it is 'Limited'. That is limited in liability. For instance if (for reasons beyond your control) your company is forced into bankruptcy, any outstanding debts that the company has will go down the toilet along with everything else, but you, the director of the company (in the absence of fraud or serious negligence) will be able to walk away from it intact. They won't be able to take your house, your DVD collection or any of your personal assets because . . . and let this sink in . . . YOU ARE NOT THE COMPANY. You may feel like you are the company, but a limited company (even if it is in your name) is an entirely separate entity. You may own it, you may be employed by it, but you are not it.

The upshot is that you get to sleep at night because even if your high risk venture goes belly up, you will not be taken down with it. If you were a sole trader or a partnership, this is not the case and if disaster struck, you could stand to lose everything you own, even the shirt off your back, and spend years re-paying all the debts.

Obligations

To run a Ltd. Company you are supposed to put a plaque on your office door proclaiming it as your trading address. You also need an address for your registered office (most people use their accountant's address). Your stationary should also display the registered office address and company number, plus you will need to file end of year accounts.

Who's in the company?

On the whole, small film companies are either one dedicated person going at it alone, or two people working together. Clearly, if there is only one person, they will be the sole owner of the limited company. But if there are two or even more people in the company, you need to be sure you are comfortable with how it's value is divided. Usually, if there are two of you, that would be 50/50. At this level, and in this model, you are not going to sell your shares in this company to raise investment.

Limited company ups and downs

Up side	Down side
If all goes wrong, you can walk away from it and even start a new limited company (in the absence of fraud or serious negligence).	You have to buy it, which will cost you money.
	You have to file end of year accounts, which should be completed by an accountant, which will cost you money.
There is some perceived kudos in being a limited company, although not as much as some people think.	Other people can access your previous years trading accounts through Companies House.
	To pay yourself a salary you will have to operate a PAYE scheme, which is somewhat tiresome.
	You are supposed to hold board meetings and take minutes at those meetings.
You would be forgiven for thinking that the running of a limited company is more trouble than it is worth, but it's true value lies in the fact that if all goes wrong, the damage is 'limited' to the company assets and YOU can walk away scott free.	You may find yourself liable for losses (for instance the bank may only loan money to the limited company if you personally guarantee it, negating the point of limited liability for that money.

Incorporation

How do you get your own limited company? There are two ways. You can buy a company that has already been incorporated (usually by a person whose job it is to incorporate companies to sell on to people like you), or you can pay a person, (usually an accountant or lawyer) to incorporate one for you. If you buy a limited company *'off the shelf'* (that is already incorporated) it will not have your company name and you will probably want to change it (although you do not need to, as you could keep the limited company name but have a different trading name. You will need to include this information in all your paperwork, for instance *'XYZ Film International is trading as Blah Blah Blah Ltd'*). Probably, the best way to tackle this is to find a small company who specialise in incorporating limited companies and ask them to incorporate one for you with the name that you want.

Multiple companies

One of the great advantages of a limited company is it's self-contained status. If you make your film and then sell it through this limited company you will always enjoy the benefit of the limited liability protection. Ahh, *'but what happens'* I hear you say, *'when we want to make another film?'* Assuming you have investors in your first film and investors in your second film, neither group will want to carry the burden of the other production. Putting it another way, if you make both films through the same limited company and your first film was a financial failure and your second a

Why not integrate your name into the company name. Much of what you do is often simple self-promotion and what better way to get your name known than to slap it on the front of your movie, your letterheads, your business cards, your website . . .

Cheap advice

Running your own company, be it a film company or a greengrocers, is fundamentally the same. Sure there are some big differences, but it's the same beast. If you want more information, go to your bookshop and buy the thinnest and simplest book on running a small business that you can find. Don't buy a big book, it will scare the hell out of you. Another free and excellent source of information is your bank manager. Plunder them as an advisory resource, they can often give you pragmatic, experienced and sophisticated advice on all aspects of your business. Unlike an accountant who will charge you for the privilege.

Other small business people will also be happy to advise and help on running accounts, doing your VAT returns, issuing invoices etc. Ask around family and friends, you'll be surprised about who has experience or knows someone who could help. Don't get too caught up in all this legal stuff, just build the company mechanism and get on with your film.

left – the book I bought, Small Business Guide by Sara Williams.

success, the investors in the second film may find their profits going to pay off the losses of the earlier failed venture (your first film).

The way around this is to start a second company solely for the production of your second film. And then a third company for your third film and so on. This will ensure that each failure or success is not contaminated by the others failure or success. The down side is clear. You may end up running multiple companies with multiple end of year accounts and multiple VAT returns. Thankfully, most people either give up the film making lark or have *'made it'* by then and this kind of crap is dealt with by the suits whilst you get on with making your movie.

How much and how long?

It should take a couple of weeks to incorporate your company and cost anywhere between £75 – £200. One member of your team will be nominated as the company director, another will be the secretary (sometimes your accountant can be the secretary). You'll need to supply a trading address and registered office address and make sure that the memorandum and articles are appropriate. These documents (memorandum and articles) are a kind of broad description of what your company has been set up to do. Most of the time the wording is so broad that you could pretty much do anything you wanted through your company. Just be aware that they exist and make sure that you aren't agreeing to things that you don't want.

If you can afford it, it may be worth joining one or two exclusive clubs, so that you have a venue to which you can invite important people for meetings. That way, they will never see your offices - or lack of!

Shares

We've all heard of a *corporate take over* and the *buying and selling of shares* – but what does that actually mean? When you incorporate a company, you issue a number of shares which are sold to raise money. In your case you will probably issue two shares and sell them for £1 each – one for each of the two team members (and company directors). The company then has a share holding of two, meaning that each person owns 50% of the company. Later, you may decide (but we wouldn't recommend it) to sell shares to raise money. For instance you could sell (or try to sell) 25,000 shares at £1 each to raise £25k, but unless you own over 12,501 shares, you are not a majority shareholder and you could be bought out and sacked. Remember, you are not the company. This is a pretty unlikely scenario because the most valuable asset that the company owns is of course you. You are the drive, the idea factory, the ambition, the graft, the tenacity that makes your company an attractive proposition. Ultimately though, it's unlikely you're ever going to sell shares, certainly not yet and absolutely not without expert and costly advice. Stick to one share each, for each of the company directors.

Trading begins

Isn't it exciting! You are now the director of a film production company. But before you get on with making your film, there's a whole bunch of niggling things that you'll need to deal with.

Bank

You're going to need a bank account from which you can run the finances of your film company. It doesn't really matter which bank you choose, but it's a good idea to try and find a bank manager with whom you can strike up an energetic conversation about business and film making. On the whole, they'll be running the bank accounts for newsagents, laundrettes, grocers, even branches of large conglomerates etc. Your business, no matter how small *you* know it is, may seem glamorous and exciting to the bored business banker. It will seem even more attractive when you tell them about the premiere and how you will make sure they get tickets.

You'll start an account in the name of your limited company and you (and/or your partners) will be signatories on the account, which means you can write cheques. Most banks will offer you free banking for the first year, which will save you several hundred pounds. A week or so after meeting the manager and filling out the forms, the paying in book and cheque book will arrive in the post, as will your first bank statement.

Nominate a drawer in your office for your accounts, financial paperwork and 'books'. This is where all your chequebooks and paying in books etc. will live. You may want to put a lock on it but I've never got round to that. You'll also need a lever arch file for your bank statements. Fastidious organisation is the key to stress free accounting, so get organised and stay organised. Always file paperwork in the right order, in the right place, make copious notes if needed, and keep everything tidy.

Paul Cable
M and E Insurance Services

'There are certain compulsory insurances you must have, like employers liability and motor insurance if you're hiring action vehicles. Often with regards to motor insurance it's easier to hire the vehicle with insurance but there can be problems when hiring cars from private owners as they don't cover film duties. In terms of low budget productions, many of the facility houses provide equipment free or at low cost, BUT, they will insist that you are responsible for providing insurance. What you should do when setting up is try to get the facilities house to insure the equipment for you, and they usually charge 15% of the hire fee. Remember, the lab doesn't take responsibility when developing your negative, so it may be wise to buy neg. insurance. With videotape and a smaller crew, it may be more economical to not buy the insurance and simply re-shoot if there are problems. Public liability is important, especially if you are filming at open locations. When you are budgeting your film you should contact a broker to discuss costs as prices have risen post 9/11. If you start negotiating with a full insurance package, certain parts of that package may not be required and you may be able to strike a deal with the broker and drop them for a reduction. Producers often contact brokers too late to arrange the cover or don't allow enough money in the budget for insurance. If you are distributing your film abroad, you will normally need Errors & Omissions insurance too, although you may not need to purchase this until a sale is in place. With recent legislation, health and safety has become a major factor in this section and use of risk assessment forms has now become paramount.'
t:020 8460 4484   www.media-ent.com

Company paperwork

In your office there will be two places where you will keep your company stuff (as well as occasionally sending it off to the accountant or archiving into your filing cabinet / system). There will be a drawer for stuff and bits, and a big lever arch folder for paperwork. You may choose to have one folder per year to keep things straight in your head. Use clear and accurate dividers to keep things separate. Remember the key words here – clear, organised, concise, did I mention organised?

Bank statements
These are the statements for your company account. For the year you make the film you should request weekly statements, thereafter you can drop down to fortnightly or even monthly to reduce paperwork.

VAT returns
Each quarter you will complete a VAT return. You will send the original off to the VAT office and make a photocopied backup for your files.

Quarterly books
A print out of your books from your software. You could do any period for your print out, but quarterly to match your VAT returns makes a lot of sense.

Invoices
When you do a job (maybe you do occasional freelance work) or sell your film, you will issue an invoice (a bill). You need to keep copies of all these documents for inspection by a VAT office. You will subdivide your invoices into Paid and Unpaid sections.

Annual accounts
Each year your accountant will produce an end of year 'corporate accounts' document that will be sent to and filed at companies house. They will also send you copies which you can store here.

Other stuff
Any other important correspondence, perhaps from the bank, tax office, accountants etc. Keep it all here.

Backup disk
Every time you do your accounts on your computer, make a backup of your files and save it on a floppy, then store the disk in an envelope in the lever arch file.

Memorandum and Articles
A copy of the limited company memorandum and articles for easy access whenever anyone asks to see them (usually the bank when they set up a new account).

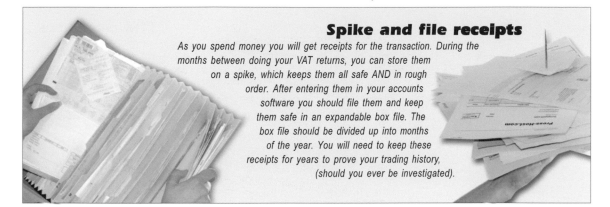

Spike and file receipts

As you spend money you will get receipts for the transaction. During the months between doing your VAT returns, you can store them on a spike, which keeps them all safe AND in rough order. After entering them in your accounts software you should file them and keep them safe in an expandable box file. The box file should be divided up into months of the year. You will need to keep these receipts for years to prove your trading history, (should you ever be investigated).

Insurance

During the bank manager meeting, they will probably ask you if you have engaged the services of an accountant (which we'll get to in a moment) but also about insurance. I'm not a big fan of insurance as clearly the profit margin is in their favour and that (outside of absolute disaster) I reckon I save more money by not insuring than what I pay out when something is damaged. However, there are two sets of insurance that you are obliged to purchase by law – Public Liability and Employers Liability. Public Liability protects the public should an accident occur and Employers Liability covers you and your staff. Other insurances will be specific to production requirements and so you don't need to deal with them right now.

Accountant

Wherever possible, you should do as much of your own accountancy as possible so that you better control, manage and appreciate your financial position (as well as save money). But it does mean (big yawn) you will have to do your own book keeping.

When looking for an accountant, ask around local businesses for the names and numbers of accountants who are efficient, fast, clear, non-scary and ideally cheap. Go and meet with these companies and follow your instincts. You want an accountant with whom you will have a healthy rapport, who won't charge you for the occasional brief phone call when you need advice, and who is hopefully into movies. Don't fall into the trap of employing the services of top media accountants as your bills might well cost more than your entire goddamn movie! Believe it or not, your business is not that special. Yes I know this is a shock, you are thinking *'hey, I'm the director of a film company . . . '* Your accounts will probably be simpler and considerably smaller than your average high street TV repair shop or plumber.

Don't spend money on fancy letterheads and cards, simple, elegant and clear business stationary will do the job. You can even set up MS Word to print your letterheads for you, so you don't even need to pay to have letterheads made up.

The accounts drawer

Somewhere in your office you should have an accounts drawer for accounts bits and bobs. There will be cash in it so you might want to put a lock on it.

Petty cash book
A log of all the money that is spent from petty cash so that you can make sure your dosh is not going walkies.

Cheque book
For writing cheques for the company. When you order one from the bank ask for the thick one, not the small thirty page book. You don't want to run out of cheques mid shoot.

Chequebook stubs
Keep these for your accountant to verify your transactions. When writing a cheque, be explicit about the details on the stub, it's amazing what you will forget when you come to look at them in six months time.

Paying In book
For paying cash into the company. Again, ask for the thick one.

Petty cash
A small box or compartment for notes and coins.

The deal you will strike with your accountant will probably fall into one of two broad models. Either they will do everything which means book keeping, VAT returns, Companies House accounts etc., for which they will probably charge you an estimated but fixed fee (probably somewhere between £1.5k–2k). Or you will do your own book keeping and VAT returns and they will take care of just the Companies House/end of year returns (which will probably cost you somewhere between £600–£1k). Personally, I choose the latter as I like to know exactly where my company stands each month, but it does mean that I lose one day every three months to VAT return nightmares. I just hate accounts!

VAT

Most accounts software will make backup copies each time you use it. Get into the habit of making copies, labelling clearly, and storing them someplace away from your office, so that if your computer is nicked or the office burns down you are not screwed. Losing your accounts data is one of the biggest headaches and time wasters you can imagine.

Value added tax, (VAT) is the sales tax that we use in the UK. It's currently set at 17.5%, and works like this. If you buy a TV for £200 from a shop, the actual cost of the TV is £170.21 with £29.79 added on as VAT. The people who you bought the TV from will then pass on this £29.79 to the Government via HM Customs and Excise. So every time you buy something that has VAT (as not everything has – see list) whatever it costs, 17.5% is VAT. The company who you bought the TV from probably bought it from a supplier and it cost say £100, plus VAT, which means it actually cost them £117.50. The company is then allowed to re-claim that £17.50 from the Government. This means that all their sales are off set by their purchases, and if they only ever sold one TV, then they would owe the Government £29.79, and the Government would owe them £17.50 which would give a balance of £12.29 (to be paid to the Government). Still with me?

Now blow that single transaction into several hundred transactions, they bought hundreds of TVs and sold hundreds of TVs. The sales will be off set by the purchases which will create a balance. Essentially, if they sold more TVs than they bought, and made profit, they will probably be in a position where they have to pay the VAT man. If they made a loss and didn't sell enough TVs, then they may be in a position where they can re-claim from the VAT man.

So essentially, VAT is a kind of UK sales and profit tax for companies. And here's the silver lining. Your film company will spend a lot of money bringing a single product to market (your movie) which may or may not sell in the UK (VAT does not apply outside of the UK). So if it takes you two years to make the film, for the first two years of trading you will not make any profit, and will be in a constant loss situation which means you will regularly be re-claiming VAT from HM Customs and Excise. If and when you eventually sell the film in the UK, say for instance £20k to a TV channel, you will invoice the TV company for £20k plus VAT which equals £23,500, the £3.5k VAT element being paid to the VAT man (of course, you will still off set your purchases against this sale).

You will probably do your VAT accounts once every three months, usually referred to in accounting circles as a VAT quarter. Depending on your personality, the last few paragraphs may have confirmed what you already know, or . . . it will have struck the fear of God into you. If you are the latter, don't worry. Trust me, it isn't as complicated as it sounds, but you do have to do it and you must do it properly. Customs and Excise do not mess around, they will fine you if you are repeatedly late and they have the power to arrest you on the spot if you've been doing dodgy dealings. If there is one time to lock away the producer in you, it's during meetings with VAT officers. They do not understand or tolerate the common currency you usually trade in, also known as bullshit.

Still confused? Get together with a friend who runs their own company and ask them to explain it to you in detail. It will eventually sink it, it's just that so many of us go cold at the thought of accounts, glaze over and slip into a coma. Is it any wonder we don't understand or remember?

Registering for VAT

As soon as you have your company set up and your bank account, you should register for VAT. You can do this by contacting the VAT office or going to their website at www.hmce.gov.uk. Once registered, you will

Phil Alberstat
Lawyer

'It's important to isolate your rights. For example to own some intellectual property rights over a book that you want to make into a film, or the screenplay itself. Film makers often don't acquire the rights properly. If you're going to buy a house, you get the essential paperwork. Film makers don't pay enough attention to this contractual detail and it slows things down when it comes to closing a deal.

You're about to close a deal and then the bank's lawyers realise there's a flaw with their chain of title. A lot of times, film makers rely on their lawyer to raise money for them. The lawyer can be helpful in introducing them to contacts but not actually raising the finance themselves. Some do, in which case they take an executive producer credit.

Producers shouldn't cut corners. They need to be professional. Often they don't think about their budget, nor do they budget properly. Most don't have proper contracts in place and there can be repercussions. Whether it's a low or high budget film, you have the same issues in that they deal with actors and locations etc., and you need to have proper agreements in place. The basic agreements are the same and there are always lawyers out there who will represent young and emerging talent with the hope that when the next film is made they can charge retail.

Producers have to be direct with the people with whom they deal. Many producers are afraid to say no. If they haven't got a lot of money they have to say they haven't got a lot of money. Be honest about what you have and what you're trying to accomplish, you will actually get further faster.'

If a friend, relative or parent is able or inclined to do so, ask them to take care of your bookkeeping. Mum is always a good and cheap option.

start to receive quarterly green forms (these are your VAT returns). Every three months you will be required to do your accounts and balance your sales against your purchases to calculate how much VAT you have to pay or re-claim. In this instance, it's almost certainly going to be re-claim. Starting the efficient running of your accounts this early is a good idea because you don't want the stress of learning all about this anti-film crap when you're in production.

The VAT officer calls

Because you will be making regular and probably quite large claims, you will almost certainly be contacted by the VAT office and informed that they are going to come in and inspect your books. This can be a terrifying prospect at the best of times. You will need to have several things ready and in good order, such as your bank statements, a print-out of your accounts, all your receipts, and copies of any invoices you may have issued. They will check through everything and make sure you haven't made any mistakes. On the whole, they are quite humane and understand that you can make minor mistakes but take a very dim view of major or repeated mistakes that cause a major inaccuracy within your accounts. Hopefully (and probably) this is not the case.

VAT officers (in my experience) fall into two categories. Nice people who do their job humanely and with minimum fuss, and not so nice people who frankly appear to be on some ego-maniacal power trip (dear lord, I know I will pay for that comment in my next VAT inspection). But the bottom line is simple, if your accounts are in good order, and you have

LEGAL & ACCOUNTS ALERT

VAT or no VAT

Not everything carries VAT, but then a lot of stuff does. Here's a list of some of the more common items and their VAT implications . . . If you are in doubt about the VAT status of any purchase, contact the VAT office and they will tell you.

THE VAT GUIDE

Without VAT	With VAT
Food and drinks.	Most stuff.
Train and transport in general, even flights.	Hire of equipment.
Some crew and actors (depends on their status)	Stock such as tapes and film.
Vehicle (does include VAT but is not reclaimable as a purchase, only rental)	Cinema tickets and DVDs (research!)
	Some crew and actors (depends on their status)
Kids clothing (costumes).	Stationery and office consumables.
Bank charges.	Computers and copiers.
Postage.	Clothing rentals, which means costumes.
Overseas purchases (although they may be vatable upon importation)	Delivery companies.
	Software.
	Adult clothing (costumes)
Books.	Pretty much any piece of equipment.

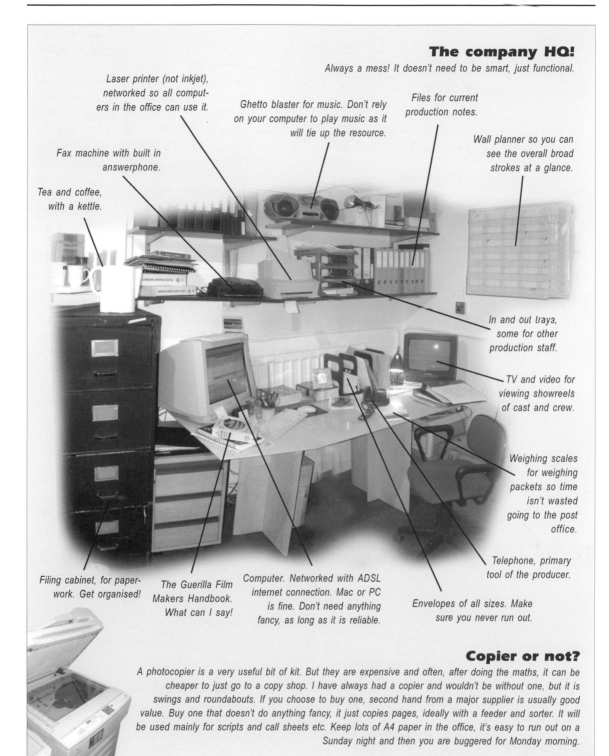

The company HQ!

Always a mess! It doesn't need to be smart, just functional.

Laser printer (not inkjet), networked so all computers in the office can use it.

Ghetto blaster for music. Don't rely on your computer to play music as it will tie up the resource.

Files for current production notes.

Wall planner so you can see the overall broad strokes at a glance.

Fax machine with built in answerphone.

Tea and coffee, with a kettle.

In and out trays, some for other production staff.

TV and video for viewing showreels of cast and crew.

Weighing scales for weighing packets so time isn't wasted going to the post office.

Telephone, primary tool of the producer.

Filing cabinet, for paperwork. Get organised!

The Guerilla Film Makers Handbook. What can I say!

Computer. Networked with ADSL internet connection. Mac or PC is fine. Don't need anything fancy, as long as it is reliable.

Envelopes of all sizes. Make sure you never run out.

Copier or not?

A photocopier is a very useful bit of kit. But they are expensive and often, after doing the maths, it can be cheaper to just go to a copy shop. I have always had a copier and wouldn't be without one, but it is swings and roundabouts. If you choose to buy one, second hand from a major supplier is usually good value. Buy one that doesn't do anything fancy, it just copies pages, ideally with a feeder and sorter. It will be used mainly for scripts and call sheets etc. Keep lots of A4 paper in the office, it's easy to run out on a Sunday night and then you are buggered for Monday morning.

Free software

Thanks to the NatWest bank, one of the simplest and most powerful software accounts tools is available for download to their customers. They don't check if you are a customer so there is no reason why you can't just go and download it. I don't know how long the link will stay up, so download it now! It's a very simple but powerful program that will even do you VAT return for you. Go to www.natwest.com, follow the links to the Small Business section, then Tips and Guidance, then Tools and Downloads, then NatWest Bookkeeper.

never done anything dodgy, no matter how nervous you get, you've done nothing wrong and so have nothing to fear.

The main pain in the arse with your VAT returns is that you can bet your bottom dollar that your VAT return will land slap bang in the middle of your shoot. You do have four weeks in which to finalise your VAT return and there's no reason why you couldn't have done most of it before the shoot (although you probably won't have because casting, looking at locations, re-writing the script etc. is so much more fun and feels considerably more pressing). If disaster struck and you were several weeks late for your VAT return, you may well get away with just a caution and at worst, a small fine.

First year accounts

After the first year of trading (and remember, you may not yet have made your film!) your accountant will contact you to tell you that they need to prepare your accounts. There are several sets of accounts that need to be dealt with.

Companies House – A special set of limited company accounts will be prepared and sent to Companies House. If you are late, you get fined. If you are very late, you get very heavily fined.

During the shoot you will rip through huge amounts of cheques. To avoid running out, which could lead you to big problems and major time wasting, order five extra chequebooks before the first day of principal photography.

Corporate Accounts – Accounts that have been prepared for the tax office. If you have made profit, you may well be liable to pay some tax.

Personal Accounts – Depending on how you have run your personal affairs, you may well need to produce personal accounts. Again, depending on how much money you have taken and from where, you may be liable to pay some tax.

Paying yourself

Getting money out of a limited company to pay yourself can be a pain. To do it you will need to operate a PAYE scheme and deal with tax and National Insurance (maybe even on a monthly basis!). This is why many film makers end up operating an extra company, which is a sole trader or partnership. This company runs all their affairs and is designed to be a stable and reliable entity for years, unlike the limited companies, that produce the films.

In summary

Running a company is a necessary evil. It is time consuming, costly and above all, dull. Yes it truly is anti-film making. But we all have to do it. If there is a person in your family who has a leaning towards accountancy, then get them on board from the start and let them deal with all your nightmarish bits of paper. The VAT office, the bank manager, the tax office, and small business books are all either free or very cheap sources of information, so take advantage of them. Once you fundamentally have your head around how companies work, then most of the fear you may feel will disappear. So get your head around it as quickly as you can and then move on to the more important problems. Such as writing the great script.

Screenplay Blueprint

SCREENPLAY & BUDGET

simple and cost effective software tools
for the budget conscious film maker.
www.movietools.com

To say the 'script is everything' is an understatement. Behind every great movie is a great, or more likely, greater script. As George Lucas says, 'You start with a great script and then it's downhill from there.' So it makes sense to get this 'cheap' stage right, or as close as possible. Think about all the films you have ever seen that you hated – bad story, dull characters, pre-visible plot . . . and then the ones you loved – great story, interesting characters, surprising plot . . . Good story telling. Nothing to do with great actors, cool shots, funky music. Just a great script. If we, the audience, don't form a strong empathic bond with the characters in the story, then you, the film makers, are lost . . .

Horror works . . .
Every so often a low budget horror movie breaks through. 'Texas Chainsaw . . . ', 'Evil Dead', 'Blair Witch . . . ' but timing and ferocious originality are everything.

Big budget clones work . . .
. . . but only for the 'B' movie market. Making a copy of your favourite movies will not open doors for you. You may find yourself pariahed by industry and critics alike for daring to do it.

Comedy can work . . .
American low budget comedies can break through but Brit humour doesn't travel too well. If you are referring to it as a quirky comedy, that might also mean a comedy that no-one else outside the UK will find funny.

Out there . . . is a big risk . . .
Then there are the movies that kind of defy genre or style and content. They are crazy and unique. Beware though, you could think it's a masterpiece, but everyone else thinks it's a turkey.

Science fiction may work . . .
With post production tools getting very cheap, sci-fi becomes a very credible possibility. Sci-Fi will all too often be let down by film makers high on what bangs and whistles they can do, and not what story they are telling.

Other stuff . . .
Then there is the really great story . . . The genre doesn't matter, as long as the audience gets swept away in the story.

Screenplay Blueprint

If I knew how to write a great script, trust me, I wouldn't have written this book, I'd be sat in Hollywood on the porch of my beach front Malibu hut, pounding the keyboard of my brand spanking new laptop computer. But of course, I don't know how to write a great script (just yet). But like most of us, I do know the difference between a good story told well, and a duff story told badly. It's patently obvious after the fact, but before words of action and dialogue are committed to celluloid, judging their quality, style and content is a deeply difficult thing to do. I'm not sure why this is the case, but do know that when you read a really great script, it jumps off the page, grabs you by the throat and forces you to read into the wee hours, your thumb aching from the frantic page turning. And THAT'S the kind of script you want.

This chapter is not about how to write a great script. Frankly, many other people have written the most excellent books on the subject, some of whom also run intensive courses. Go and read their books and if you can afford the cash, and do their courses, it can be truly enlightening. What I am going to focus on in this chapter is the elements that have a direct impact on how well you can tell your story whilst working on a micro or low budget.

Research and development

Planning is key. Research is key. Through research, you will find reality in your characters and plot. Your skill as a writer will be your ability to fuse your imagination and own personal experiences with the lives, words and stories of the people you research.

With all the films I have made, more research and more planning would have simply made a better film.

Research will put truthful, poignant dialogue in the mouths of the characters you imagine and will bring honesty to the story you tell . . . and truth and honesty are the emotional foundations on which characters and audiences connect. And once there is a connection, you can send your characters to hell and back and the audience will vicariously live that adventure with them.

> The screenplay is the most important element of your entire project, the foundation on which all other creative decisions are based. Get this right, and the rest is almost painting by numbers.

Drew's Script-O-Rama (www.script-o-rama.com) is THE place to go to download screenplays for movies. They are often typed in by fans so not always 100% accurate, nor are you really ever sure what draft or version you are reading, but considering it is free, and when you see how many titles there are, you just can't knock it. Look for early drafts of screenplays, and shooting scripts. Don't bother with transcripts, you might as well watch the movie instead. New writers will feel like they have just found the keys to the sweetie shop!

Christopher Vogler
Author

For a long time, I worked in the studio system, where the script is a selling tool. It's different in the indie world where you might not have so many masters to please. Financiers may read the script but you don't have to be as artful, clever or sneaky. The imperative in the studio world is to make it fly, and for it to be as compact and efficient as possible.

The mistake people make is to over explain things. Good screenwriting is compact and should be efficient. This mistake is due to a lack of confidence in the writer. You know what you're trying to say and you don't need to waste words. Recently I executive produced Steve Guttenberg's independent film "PS, YOUR CAT IS DEAD", based on the play by James Kirkwood (A Chorus Line). The thing I learnt most during this film is how the writing process continues into the editing room and beyond. It's a great lab for learning to write. I spent four months cutting the film with Steve. I looked at the script beforehand and gave my notes, and also gave notes while they were shooting. Shooting is a writing process – choosing whose point of view is represented, the tone, the genre, whether to lean on the comedy or dramatic side. Writing doesn't stop when you hand in the script. I learnt things on that film that can be applied backwards into the process.

Strive to make the characters as different and as contrasting as possible. Contrast is an underrated artistic principle. The tendency is to write in the same voice and, as a result, all the characters sound alike, such as in a Woody Allen film, they all sound like Woody. Strive for that unique voice.

A simple plan

As a story forms in your mind, you should start researching the elements around it. Speak to experts who have direct experience in the world of your story. You will pick up detail and get ideas you would never have sitting in front of a blank screen trying to imagine it. For instance, much of Robert Shaw's abrasive dialogue in Spielberg's classic *'Jaws'* was taken by one of the writers, Carl Gottlieb, from the mouth of an equally abrasive local fisherman. Gottlieb didn't imagine these words, he experienced them firsthand, and then put them into the mouth of an imaginary character.

Alongside the research, you'll probably start to actually write. Don't launch into the script just yet. Write a one page synopsis, covering the arc of your story, then expand it into two or three pages. Ask film maker friends to read it and listen to their comments. Integrate new ideas discovered through research. Re-write and expand to ten pages, twenty pages. It's now a treatment. Again, ask your film maker friends to read and criticise. Re-write, re-write, re-write. If you get your treatment right, the first draft of your screenplay will be simple, quick and painless.

Watch the movie, read the script

If you have time, watch and re-watch movies that you feel are great, that speak to you, that are an inspiration etc. Then if you can, track down a copy of the shooting script (not a transcript), read it and compare it to the final edit that you watched and hold so high. You will see what was written, shot and then dropped in the cutting room – this is even on the biggest movies with experienced directors and 'A' list writers.

There are lots of resources on the internet where screenplays are freely downloadable. Read as much as you can and pay particular attention to the way in which good writing reflects rather than tells, how a character may be talking about one thing but subtextually they are reflecting an entirely different story. Keep an eye out for succinct writing, how great writers can say so much with so few words, and occasionally without any words at all! Study structure (reading the books will help you identify structure too) and notice how characters' aspirations and goals change as the plot (structure) turns and moves in different directions.

Write, write, write

There is no greater way to becoming a better writer than to write, read, reflect, re-write. It makes sense really. If you want to become good at anything, you need to practice. And in a profession as competitive as screenwriting, even the very best need to practice all the time. Don't be phased by young or new screenwriters who appear to come from nowhere and produce work of breathtaking brilliance. The truth is, not everyone can be a genius, and even if they are a genius, you can bet your bottom dollar

Read the books

There are so many screenwriting books available, and almost all of them have something to offer. Keep these books by the side of your word processor, on your bedside cabinet, in your briefcase for travelling to work, in your loo. You'll probably read them in little snippets, often as a lubricant for writer's block. Think of them as cheap and freely available mentors and tutors. They can help but you have to do the hard stuff.

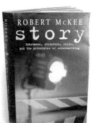

Story *by Robert McKee*

A breathtaking tome that verges on philosophical rocket science for screenwriters. I find it hard to read more than a page at a time because the information is so dense and in depth. It's not to everyone's taste and is probably the most advanced book written on the subject. Buy it now.

Teach Yourself Screenwriting *by Raymond G Frensham*

A slender volume that is crammed with bullet points and simple to digest concepts. This is the book to keep in your back pocket. In many ways it covers most of the areas tackled by almost every good book. It's also the cheapest book and an excellent first buy.

The Writer's Journey *by Christopher Vogler*

In essence, a much lighter, re-envisioning of the hero's journey that is examined in 'The Hero With A Thousand Faces' by Joseph Campbell. Vogler has studied innumerable movies and discovered common patterns and characters that appear in almost all. It's an enlightening read.

Any book by Syd Field . . .

. . . and he's written quite a few, including Screenplay, The Screenwriter's Problem Solver, The Screenwriter's Workbook amongst others. More lightweight than McKee, but nonetheless extremely informative and easier to consume. Buy all his books.

On Writing *by Stephen King*

Stephen King has written an excellent book about being a writer called On Writing. More than any book I've read on the subject, this one directly connected with me on a number of very difficult to describe levels. It's not so much about how to write a great piece of work, it's more about what it is like to be a writer, with some creative tips. And of course it's about what it is like to be Stephen King. It's lightweight, easy to read and I felt like writing Stephen King a very long thank you letter after I put it down.

After reading this, you probably think that I have shares in these books. I don't, but I do think that the £100 you might spend on buying all these books is about the best £100 you could ever spend. Penny for penny, the knowledge that you are buying is the cheapest way to get a handle on the difference between a good movie and a great movie.

Copyright

Many new writers get worried about copyright, 'how do I register my script for copyright?' The truth is, if you write a script, by law, you own the copyright. You don't need to register it or do anything. It's yours. You own it. However, proving that you are the copyright owner in the event of somebody disputing that is the important point.

Straight off the bat, let me just say I don't believe screenplays get ripped off very often. Why would a multi-million dollar company steal your idea when they can buy it off you and avoid losing millions in a future law suit? More likely, there is a commonality of ideas. If you are sitting on a great idea, it's quite possible somebody else has had that great idea too, entirely independently of you and without breaching your copyright or confidence.

If the issue of copyright does keep you awake at night, then there are a couple of things you can do. Give a copy to your vicar. He would be a very credible witness should you go to court to prove ownership. Fill out form PA (downloadable from www.loc.gov/copyright/forms) to register for copyright in the USA and send a copy of your script with the $30 handling fee to Washington DC (international sales agents may require this later anyway). Or you could register your script at one of the commercial organisations such as the Writers Copyright Association (www.wcauk.com). Now get on with re-writing and making your movie.

that their bedroom closet will be propped up by a pile of unpublished, unmakeable and perhaps even unreadable scripts that they have written on the journey to their current work. Write, write, write.

Writing in solitude is hard work because it is very difficult to analyse your own work. If you can form alliances with a group of other film makers and writers with whom you can regularly meet and criticise each others work, you will get access to good advice for free (or at least in return for reading and criticising their work). Remember, there is no *'right or wrong'*, there really isn't even *'good or bad'*, there is simply *'I like, I don't like'*. And if a lot of people are telling you *'I don't like it'*, you need to listen to them. Write, write, write. What are you reading this for? Go and write!

How to do it

Everyone has a different way of working, so there really isn't any 'proper' way to do it. However, I would suggest that you are going to do better writing when you aren't exhausted, so that means not after work (although that might be unavoidable). Whilst creative clarity may appear in the evenings or late at night, this is probably because there are no distractions. So turn off your phone, put a sign on the door saying *'do not disturb'* and write during sensible hours so you do not screw up your other lives (professional and personal).

Many new film makers think of the screenplay as just one of the production problems, a job that needs to be done. But it is so much more than that. Whilst you may be itching to get to set, you may paint yourself into a corner and spend a year editing and re-shooting trying to make it work. I have one friend who is still editing a film for which the script was never really completed. And he shot it eight years ago!

Set goals. I'm not so sure anyone can write with consistent quality for more than a couple of hours so set aside a given amount of time and make sure you write five pages (or whatever your goal is) during that time. Consider getting up early. Many successful writers get up at the crack of dawn and have their most important work of the day done before the newspaper is even delivered (I have to say this doesn't work for me, but then I'm not yet a great writer!) Try and avoid editing and re-writing until the first draft of work is done. It's emotionally safer to go back and tweak than to boldly thrash through the unknown undergrowth to find the end of your movie. So be bold and never look back until you get to the end of your first draft.

Your constraints . . .

Making a low budget movie is all about maximising resources, which means when devising your story and writing your script, you need to consider *'the production'* of the story, and ideally make all your negatives work for you. For instance in *White Angel*, my second film, we decided to set the whole film in one house so that we never had to move the cast or crew. We could then spend all our time shooting. We devised a story that would actually use the disadvantages of only having one location and intentionally tried to make the film claustrophobic in atmosphere. The production limitation became a creative advantage.

Some of the constraints you need to consider are . . .

Keep it contained

Keeping your story in one major location will mean that you don't lose time moving from A to B. You'll be astonished at just how long it takes to pack up a cast and crew, move three hundred yards, unpack, shoot and pack up again to move someplace else. On all three of my films, I used this philosophy – *The Runner* was set in the woods, *White Angel* was set in a three-up, two-down suburban house and *Urban Ghost Story,* whilst much bigger and more ambitious, was set in a Glaswegian tower block (which was built on a film stage and not on location).

At the same time as keeping your drama in as few locations as possible, you can also engineer smaller locations which could be constructed, built or dressed in the primary location where you are based. We call these micro-sets and flag them up in the script even as we write. More often than not, a micro set would be a corner of a room that is dressed to look like something else – in *White Angel* we build a crime scene lab for instance. These micro sets would be used for very small contained scenes that were needed to make the plot work, but didn't need to be extravagant in scale. Whilst this philosophy is starting to move towards production problem solving, if you can keep it in mind during the writing, it will make life easier later on.

Keep characters minimal

In an ideal world, you would keep the story centered around the fewest characters possible. Usually, this is two or three leads with two or three supporting actors and a bunch of one or two day small bit parts. Keeping characters minimized gives you flexibility when shooting because, on the whole, all your primary characters are always available so that if there are any sudden schedule changes, you will be able to deal with it. In the writing,

Show, don't tell

When you write, you will probably feel a great urge to emotionally charge your action descriptions. This, I feel, can be a mistake because you shouldn't write anything that you cannot film. For instance, 'Jane looks at Bill with profound and deep jealousy' emotes a whole heap to the reader but just how are you going to show 'profound and deep', perhaps even 'jealousy'? Sure, the audience might get it, but it's not something that can be 'acted' or 'photographed literally'. It is an interpretation of the characters, acting, direction, story, dialogue etc.

Whilst researching this chapter, I just happened to glance at my copy of 'Jaws' and after reading the last scene of the script I was struck by It's simplicity, brevity and confidence. This is how it reads (and this is the entire scene!)

> `'The two tiny, miserable`
> `heroes, swimming from the`
> `debris.'`

It doesn't say, as I, a lesser writer might have penned it . . .

> `'The two tiny, miserable`
> `heroes, saddened by their loss,`
> `yet elated by their victory,`
> `swim from the debris'.`

This is the kind of confident writing that I aspire to. Write, write, write. Don't fear the waste basket. Write, read, reflect, rewrite, improve . . . and did I mention, read the books?!

The road map analogy

If your story were a road map, it would start at point A on the left hand side of the map and over ninety minutes, would move to point B on the right, whilst twisting and turning at various points. This main story would be a motorway on the map. Alongside this motorway there will be a number of smaller 'B roads', some of them narrower and shorter than others, but all starting close to point A and ending as close to point B as possible, whilst occasionally crossing the motorway along the way. These B roads are your sub-plots, inextricably linked to your motorway, crossing and impacting on the main road story at various points and wherever possible, coming to a resolution at the same time and point as the main story.

If you think of yourself as the architect of this road map, then you should think of your audience as bored children sat in a car on the journey you're taking them on. You need to keep them occupied and interested or they will fall asleep or start to moan. Not that I am suggesting that your film should pander to the lowest common denominator, but do keep in mind that you have a responsibility to captivate your audience.

The trick with your road is to keep the passengers kind of aware of which direction they are going so they don't feel utterly confused, but at the same time, you need to disguise or hide whatever story, events or character twists lie just around the corner so they are constantly surprised. Disaster strikes when you, the architect, think you have told a story clearly enough to keep the audience on the road map, but when you check in to see how they are doing, they have left the road, are driving cross country and to coin a phrase, 'have lost the plot'. This doesn't happen too often, and as long as you have enough test screenings during the editing, you should pick up on most of the misdirection in your story and be able to fix it.

To really understand this analogy, ask yourself if you have ever seen a film that other people raved about, but you just didn't 'get it'. Essentially, you became lost on the ride and became bored. For whatever reason, that film didn't work for you but it did for others. The trick is to make the film work for as many people as possible without stooping down to the lowest common denominator. That, I believe, is what great story telling is about.

choosing minimal characters will force you to create unique and interesting people for your story, which in turn will attract a higher calibre of actor. Essentially, low budget movies tend to be about talking more than doing. This isn't ideal because, essentially, movies are about doing and not talking. However, needs must. This is going to mean that you're going to have to try and write sparkling, witty, intriguing and profound dialogue.

Keep extras minimal

People cost money. You might get extras for free, but they still need to be fed, have their travelling expenses paid, and their mere presence will eat up valuable resources with make-up and costume. Make sure you absolutely need every extra before you write them into a scene.

As William Goldman says in his book 'Adventures In The Screentrade', and to paraphrase, 'get into the scene as late as you can, and get out of the scene as quickly as you can.' If you keep this tip close to your heart, you run less chance of becoming ponderous or dull, and therefore boring.

Keep nights and atmos minimal

It's obvious really. During the day, everyone can see what they're doing and

sometimes you won't even need to light scenes as the sun will provide enough illumination. At night, no one can see what they are doing and every single shot needs to be meticulously lit (if you rush it, it will look rubbish and you will have to re-shoot). So it's no surprise that if you set your film at night, then it's going to take much longer to shoot. Wherever possible, write DAY in the slugline of your scenes and not NIGHT.

On the same wavelength, if in your screenplay it ever says something like . . . *'dense mist shrouds Jack as he walks deeper into the woods . . .'* or *'. . . rain spatters Jack as he walks deeper into the woods . . .'* delete the words *'dense mist'* and *'rain spatters'* unless the plot of your movie hangs on such atmosphere's presence.

It is of course possible to re-create atmospheric conditions on a low budget film, but unless you do it properly, which means lots of large smoke machines for mist, a full rig for rain and huge turbines for wind, it will stand out like a sore thumb and look exactly like what it is . . . a grip spraying a hosepipe or a runner just out of shot thrusting a desk fan into the actresses face. You won't get away with it and you will end up abandoning or re-shooting. Either way, it's a waste of a very precious resource in pursuit of something that has no profound impact on the telling of a good story.

In the business, companies employ readers to read 'spec scripts' such as yours – that is, written without any finance or deal in place. The reader will produce a report called 'coverage' which is a kind of critique of the script. It will include a detailed synopsis of the story, plus a couple of pages of comments on the strengths and weaknesses, and a final yes, no, maybe appraisal. It's hard to get hold of this 'coverage' as production companies are reluctant to share it with you, but if you can, it will give you another professional opinion.

Which means you will need

Working with all these restrictions means that you can't rely on any of the luxuries and the bangs and whistles that bigger budget movies can take for granted.

A strong story

Make your life easy by choosing a story that will naturally throw up an enormous amount of intriguing, mysterious and dynamic situations as possible. For instance, my second film, *'White Angel'*, is about a serial killer who is blackmailing a top crime writer to write his biography. He moves in with her and the story follows her attempts to outwit him whilst he tries to keep her where he wants her . . . and all the time they are talking in depth about murder. There is a lot of potential here which made for an easier writing experience.

A common mistake made by new writers is that not enough happens in their story, and that their characters are never quite in enough jeopardy. So try and keep your story moving and wherever possible, ask yourself *'how could I possibly make it worse – better – harder etc. for my characters?'*. In essence, how can you raise the stakes so that the characters have to struggle to jump higher, carrying with them the emotionally connected audience.

Your script will probably be around 100 pages in length. To read it is going to take about two to three hours, depending on how fast and how fully it is read. So asking anyone who knows what they are talking about to read your script is asking a big investment. Getting good readers who can offer insight is very hard.

Personally, whilst I recognise characters and dialogue are the fabric of the story, I sometimes feel that film makers fall a little too in love with them and forget that the most important thing is that it is a good story. Sure, it is your characters and dialogue that tell the story, just don't fall in love with them so much that you allow them to ramble aimlessly and end up boring the audience.

KISS - Keep It Simple Stupid. Obvious advice, but the best movies are often the simplest stories, just told very well, through engaging and entertaining characters, with an interesting plot full of surprises. But there's nothing REALLY new in of itself. It's still boy meets girl, boy loses girl, boy gets girl back . . . Don't try to reinvent the wheel, just use the wheel that works and do the best job you can.

Twists & turns are your buddy

Everyone remembers the end of *The Sixth Sense,* mainly because of its superbly executed twist that most people didn't see coming. Without that twist, the movie would have been a thoughtful and sensitive study of a child psychologist looking for answers and a child looking for a way to escape his fears. Pretty interesting but the movie shifted from *pretty interesting* to *must see* with the twist. Wherever possible, twist and turn your plot so that the audience are kept on their toes and engaged in the intrigue. Keep your plot as thick and dense as possible, but never so cryptic or impenetrable that the audience loses the plot, loses interest and therefore nods off.

Make 'em laugh

It's taken me a long time to understand this, but almost without exception, if you can make people laugh, you are onto a winner. I'm not talking about comedy (which doesn't travel well abroad), but about moments where the audience chuckle in recognition at a characters actions or comments. This kind of humour is often remembered by the audience because it made them feel good and it built an empathic bond between the characters in the film and themselves. It somehow rang home.

While I do feel I should add the caveat that there are moments when humour is inappropriate, I can't really think of any instance that wouldn't be improved by a witty, profound and illuminating moment. Whether the audience is crying or screaming (or worse still bored!), they will thank you for a little honest chuckle. Humour is one of the hardest things to achieve and is very individual. So beware, just because you think it's funny, it doesn't mean anyone else will.

Interesting characters

If you write a story whose lead character is intrinsically interesting, then you are making your life easier. Imagine a film about Oscar Wilde, who is magically reincarnated into our world. With the right research, you could write page after page of interesting and enlightening 'stuff'. It doesn't necessarily make a good story but it does mean that one of the vessels through which your story is told (Oscar Wilde) will leap off the page and engage the audience. As I said earlier about my second film *White Angel,* the serial killer character had plenty to say that was gripping and captivating. Some of the best scenes in the film are simply the reminiscing of a killer (almost all pure research) where the character literally talks to the camera for five minutes at a time.

An interesting setting

Like interesting characters, an interesting setting is just going to make your life easier. This almost always leads on from *'I know someone who has . . . this great castle, old hotel, private wood, keys to an abandoned asylum'* etc.

Common mistakes

Aside from a huge amount of purely creative and structural mistakes that are made on almost every project – there's no such thing as the perfect script – there are a few rudimentary things that we all do from time to time (sometimes without noticing).

Over written

Screenplays written by new film makers are almost always over written, which makes the read that bit more boring. As boredom is your nemesis, you can help yourself a great deal by re-writing and always asking yourself 'how can I say this more succinctly and hopefully with more profundity?' It's very hard for YOU to see the overwritten parts of your script, and ultimately it may be that you do the cuts needed in the edit suite. Not ideal because you have wasted resources shooting material that wasn't needed, but one could argue that this is part of the creative journey and needed for the manufacturing process. Film making by nature is a very lossy and inefficient process.

Fixation on dialogue

Too many film makers get stressed out over dialogue. Don't get me wrong, having crisp, sharp, original, truthful, witty dialogue is a major advantage, but characters are defined by what they do and not by what they say. For my money, a great story which is told through dynamic character actions (with fairly duff dialogue) will always win out over characters spouting great dialogue but in a film that has a dull story. If you are not good on dialogue, then spend more time refining and re-writing it, perhaps even asking a colleague to re-interpret the dialogue. In the business this is sometime called a 'polish'.

Derivative

This is often the crime of the young film maker, whose life experience is almost always dominated by movies. They have yet to have their heart broken, have a child, their parents die, lose a loved one to cancer etc. and therefore their only true emotional highs and lows have been experienced in the cinema. Is it any wonder that their work is derivative? If you are such a person, don't beat yourself up about it. In time, your voice will become wiser with experience and the stories you want to tell will change. But if you are going to be derivative and steal, in the words of another great film maker 'make sure you steal from the best'.

Fixation on format

If I had a penny for every conversation I have had with a new film maker who is in search of 'the Holy grail of the perfect format' I would be rich and able to fund my own films on the proceeds. It's essential to get the physical format of your script right, but there are so many slight variations and contradictions in the way in which you should format your script, and myths about great scripts being binned because they weren't perfectly formatted, that people actually lose sleep over this. Just get the format kind of right (see diagram). The only really important thing are the words on the page. Correct formatting just says 'I am a professional and know what I am doing, so read on'.

Haven't used the books

I know I have mentioned the screenwriting books and courses, but I feel compelled to bang on about it. The screenplay is such an important foundation for your movie that it is foolish to turn your back on exceptionally good advice and guidance when it can come with a £10 price tag. Buy as many screenwriting books as you can and repeatedly read them all. None will turn you into a great writer but they will help you find a better writer inside yourself.

It's a production consideration of course, but if you can secure any fascinating and ideally large locations, it will add so much to the story you tell with your limited resources. Look on your own doorstep too, you'll be surprised what you don't notice on a daily basis, that would be interesting to an audience who have never been where you live. American films so often suffer from looking like they were shot within 100 miles of LA.

Keep it mysterious but not too cryptic . . .

There is no better way to hook, and then keep that audience, than through mystery . . . *'what on earth is going to happen next?'* From a writing point of view, mystery is often hard to get right in the script because one often ends up

Slug line, all upper case, abbreviated into INT (for interior), EXT (for exterior), followed DAY or NIGHT, followed the scene location. Slug line followed by a line break.

Script title (optional).

Script edge, 1" from the top of the page.

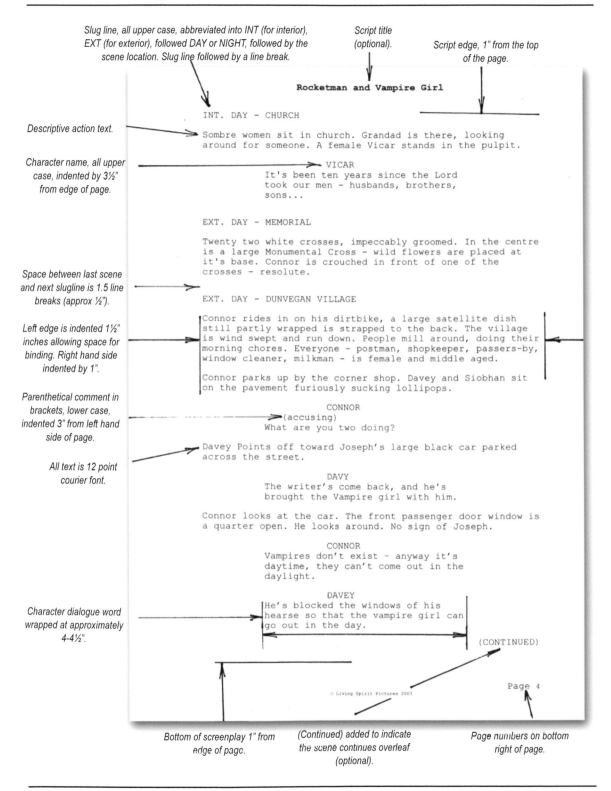

Rocketman and Vampire Girl

INT. DAY - CHURCH

Descriptive action text.

Sombre women sit in church. Grandad is there, looking around for someone. A female Vicar stands in the pulpit.

Character name, all upper case, indented by 3½" from edge of page.

                    VICAR
          It's been ten years since the Lord
          took our men - husbands, brothers,
          sons...

EXT. DAY - MEMORIAL

Twenty two white crosses, impeccably groomed. In the centre is a large Monumental Cross - wild flowers are placed at it's base. Connor is crouched in front of one of the crosses - resolute.

Space between last scene and next slugline is 1.5 line breaks (approx ½").

EXT. DAY - DUNVEGAN VILLAGE

Left edge is indented 1½" inches allowing space for binding. Right hand side indented by 1".

Connor rides in on his dirtbike, a large satellite dish still partly wrapped is strapped to the back. The village is wind swept and run down. People mill around, doing their morning chores. Everyone - postman, shopkeeper, passers-by, window cleaner, milkman - is female and middle aged.

Connor parks up by the corner shop. Davey and Siobhan sit on the pavement furiously sucking lollipops.

                    CONNOR

Parenthetical comment in brackets, lower case, indented 3" from left hand side of page.

          (accusing)
          What are you two doing?

Davey Points off toward Joseph's large black car parked across the street.

All text is 12 point courier font.

                    DAVY
          The writer's come back, and he's
          brought the Vampire girl with him.

Connor looks at the car. The front passenger door window is a quarter open. He looks around. No sign of Joseph.

                    CONNOR
          Vampires don't exist - anyway it's
          daytime, they can't come out in the
          daylight.

                    DAVEY
Character dialogue word wrapped at approximately 4-4½".

          He's blocked the windows of his
          hearse so that the vampire girl can
          go out in the day.

                                        (CONTINUED)

© Living Spirit Pictures 2003

                                        Page 4

Bottom of screenplay 1" from edge of page.

(Continued) added to indicate the scene continues overleaf (optional).

Page numbers on bottom right of page.

The Hollywood spec script market

Screenwriting is one of the best ways to break into Hollywood. If you have talent and are aggressive about networking (along with a great idea that is well executed and a large spattering of good old fashioned luck) there is no reason why you couldn't do that killer deal. And when I say killer deal, I mean earning so much cash that you might never need worry again about the big problem we all face, putting a roof over your head and food on the table. That could then mean that you can dedicate your life to your own projects, free to develop at your own pace . . .

In Hollywood, this is called the spec script market. That is, a script that is written without any cash or a deal in place. It's then touted by agents and sold to the highest bidder (or most appropriate bidder). Of course, the overwhelming majority of spec scripts go nowhere, probably because they are not very good. But if you do have that great 'Hollywood idea', a six month investment in front of your word processor could be a good career move. That first deal could also lead onto other highly paid writing assignments, perhaps even directing if you are tenacious enough. Getting through these doors is by no means easy, and in most cases you are going to need an agent. Maybe not an LA based agent, but that would help. A good UK agent should also open doors.

There's a great book about writing these kinds of screenplays, it's called '500 Ways To Beat The Hollywood Script Reader' by Jennifer Lerch. It's just a long list of insightful and helpful tips to help you use what you already have.

giving the reader a little more than the viewer of the finished film will get. That's OK though, because you will always have more than you need in the cutting room and can remove material (story / dialogue etc.) that will improve the story by its absence.

You will find that by dropping the occasional line in the cutting room, the audience will be left wondering but not confused. Cutting the ends off scenes can have an even more profound impact on the mystery of your film. Consider this obvious example. If you have made a romantic comedy, and the whole film has built up to the male lead asking the female lead if she will marry him. The question is asked in one of the last scenes of the movie . . . *'will you marry me . . . ?'* – the audience is on the edge of their seats – and with tears in her eyes she says *'yes'*. But what if you cut before she has a chance to say *'yes'*, leaving the audience hanging, screaming *'what did she say?'*. Of course, the next scene will probably answer the question (cut to the church etc.) but for a few extra moments you had them in the palm of your hand, desperate for more.

Great ending

No matter how bad the movie, if you have great ending, you will be forgiven for a myriad of sins. I think it was Alan Parker who said (paraphrasing) *'all you need to do is get the last five seconds right . . . '* Great plot twists that really get a gasp in the audience always make for a smiling audience walking out of the theatre, chattering about how they didn't see it coming, and not talking about how *'I was bored in the middle . . . '*, or *'wasn't the acting bad?'* It's not rocket science but it makes a lot of sense. Get the great ending!

The industry convention states that one page equals one minute. Because your script will be a bit baggy, after aggressive editing in the cutting room, it will probably be less than this. From script to screen, a 100 page shooting script will probably give you, the first time film maker, an 85 minute film. Once you drop below 85 ish minutes, you can start to get problems with distributors and sales agents who can't sell it because it is too short. 80 minutes is the absolute cusp.

The basics of screenwriting . . .

Characters need conflicting desires

So we as the audience aren't sure which way they will go. If a character or your story is predictable it's because you haven't built up the possibilities of your character doing the opposite of what they say they are going to do. Even do-gooder Superman has conflicting desires and therefore a strong dilemma. Will he A: give up his super powers for the love of Lois Lane or B: retain his powers but be forever lonely? You character's dilemma is what the audience latches onto and invests their concentration in. 'What would I do given the character's dilemma?' If your central character hasn't got a credible dilemma then their story and your script is inherently dull.

Characters need to desire tangible things

You have to be able to visually represent what a character desires. If their desires are abstract like love or happiness etc., you need something visual to represent and equate what that desire means to your character.

Characters aren't self-aware

They should not articulate their predicament verbally or reflect on it philosophically. This is a fundamental mistake. If a character is self-aware then they have no journey to go on, no story and no discovery to make. Characters are only given the briefest glimpse of self-awareness at the end of act climaxes, when they have the chance to make a decision based on a difficult dilemma. These acts alone illustrate their self-awareness, and they are just that, actions. For actions alone illuminate a character's fundamental desires. Not dialogue, remember talk is cheap.

Characters need to struggle in pursuit of their goal

It doesn't matter if they fail or succeed, but they must struggle to the end. If your characters don't make an effort why should an audience? Put them in situations they've never been in before, if a character doubts their ability to achieve their goal then the audience doubts too, and you have them hooked. If we know a character can handle a situation, then as an audience we don't care because we don't doubt they'll succeed. Always stack up the odds. The more an audience doubts a character's ability, the more they want to see if they can beat the odds.

Give your central character a trait you don't like

Because protagonists are really the writer living out their own fantasy, what happens is you protect and cushion them, so everything they do is great or cool, and they escape conflict and any real jeopardy. You've effectively engineered audience indifference. If your central character avoids conflict then their story isn't worth telling. Give your central character annoying traits that detach you, the writer, from the character, so they're not so precious, and you can allow them to struggle and suffer in pursuit of their goal.

Make the Audience work

Exposition has to be given to the audience to enable them to understand the rules of the world, the predicaments of the characters etc. but generally this is always done far too clumsily. Try and give information visually. In 'Unbreakable' Bruce Willis' character sits on a train and sees an attractive woman. He takes off his wedding ring. In an easy visual statement we know he's married and probably unhappily so.

Don't spoon-feed an audience what you think they need to know. Handing information to an audience on a plate stops them having to intellectually engage with your story and offers them the opportunity to catch forty winks. Back-story and flashbacks need to have the same amount of potency and active questions as the story in the present so they each affect the other. Active questions keep an audience engaged and you need to capitalize on them.

Dialogue is your enemy

Everyone knows the adage 'Show don't tell!' but very few apply it. If you want your characters to talk and talk, and you think your dialogue is great, then look for a career in television. If you believe your story is cinematic then tell it through images. Try and imagine how your script plays without the dialogue. If you're not telling the story through visuals then why are you making a film? Drop the camera description and the prose style of writing. If an audience can't literally see what you're describing, then why waste the space on the page and delude yourself it'll translate to the screen. It won't.

Genre

Recognise and apply the rules of the genre you're working in. Then push the genre conventions further. B-movies are purely derivative. To avoid this you need to understand the genre your idea sits best in and find a way to meet and then exceed the genre expectations. To break out of formula you need to set up traditional expectations and then deliver in ways that are unexpected but plausible with hindsight. Most 'original' films successfully combine two or more genre frameworks or consistently exceed expectations. Don't rely on presumptions when it comes to genre. Research well. They're always in motion. Look at the Horror Genre, in little over five years we've gone from the Post-Modern 'Scream' to the Parody 'Scary Movie' back to the played straight 'Ring' and it'll change again.

Phil Mathews is a screenwriter, script editor and Lecturer at the London Institute, South Bank University and Goldsmiths College.

Screenplay by movie tools

You can download the latest version of Screenplay *from* www.movietools.com. *This version requires* MSWord, *part of the MS Office suite. It kind of sits on top of Word, so you get a slick screenplay formatter working through a multi-million dollar piece of software that everyone seems to have. It works with all versions of* MSWord *(including* Word 95, Word 97, Word 2000 *and* Word XP *for the PC and* Word 98, Word 2000 *and* Word X *for the Mac). This shareware version is fully functional, the only restriction is that it will print the word 'unregistered' at the top of your script. So if that doesn't bother you, it's a free tool. You can of course load the shareware version on as many computers as you like. If you register and buy the passcode, when you format your script the next time, the word 'unregistered' won't appear. Cool huh?*

Installation is pretty simple, just follow the instructions on the web site and in the files you download.

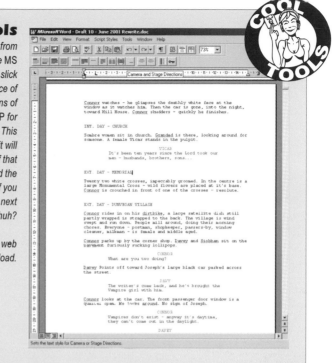

Start that great script

OK so you have installed it. Time to run it for the first time. Start MSWord *and go to the* File Menu *and select* New. *The* New Document *dialogue box will pop up. Depending on how you have set up your computer there will be a number of* MSWord *templates displayed, one of which should be* Screenplay. *Double click the* Screenplay *one and a new, blank screenplay will appear, the words* FADE IN *at the top. You might also notice that there is a new tool bar at the top, and new menus on the menu bar. We shall get to these later.* Screenplay *will create its own title page later so you don't need to create one at the head of this document, you can just get on with writing that great script.*

First words

If you don't want to start your script with a: FADE IN *you can delete it. The first thing you need to write is a slug line. Write something like* INT. DAY – JOHN'S FLAT, *then go to the* Script Styles *menu and select* Slug Line *(or you can use the keyboard shortcut of* ALT+S). *The text will turn blue (and upper case) which means that* Screenplay *knows that this is a slug line. Hit the* Enter *Key and you will drop down onto the next line. If you start typing you will see that the text is now dark blue, this is* ACTION *text (which you can easily get to by going to the* Script Styles *menu or by hitting the* ALT+A *keys). Hit* Enter *after a sentence and type a name, then go to the* Script Styles *menu and select* Character *(or hit the* ALT+C *keys). The text will change to uppercase, centered and red, denoting that it is a character's name. And so you can work through your screenplay using these simple shortcuts, never worrying about the formatting as you know the software will do it all for you. This is about as technical as it needs to get.* Screenplay *can do much more, but if this is all you want, then write on.*

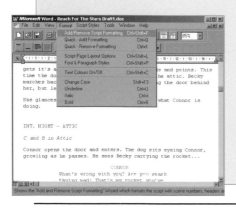

Different styles

Screenplay can handle a number of different script styles, all available from the Script Styles *menu, the* Toolbar, *or by using hotkeys. These are . . .*

Slugline *(appears blue) – this is the start to every scene, telling the film makers if it is day or night, interior or exterior and the location (keyboard shortcut is* ALT+ S). *When you enter a slugline,* Screenplay *will automatically setup the next line to be* Action.

Action *(appears dark blue) – this is descriptive text such as 'Jack enters the room' or 'Peter runs down the street' (keyboard shortcut is* ALT+ A).

Character *(appears red) – this is the name of the character when they are about to talk (keyboard shortcut is* ALT+ C). *When you enter a character's name,* Screenplay *will automatically setup the next line to be* Dialogue.

Dialogue *(appears purple) – this is when a character talks (keyboard shortcut is* ALT+ D). *When you enter dialogue,* Screenplay *will automatically setup the next line to be a* Character *name.*

Parallel dialogue *– a special format for when two characters talk at the same time, not used too often in most scripts (keyboard shortcut is* ALT+ R). *Write the two characters and lines one after another, select them both and apply the* Parallel Dialogue *style.*

Action in dialogue / Parenthetical *(appears dark blue) – this is when you add a little action to dialogue, such as (angrily) or (whilst leaving) etc. Always appears in brackets (keyboard shortcut is* ALT+ O).

Camera / Stage directions *(appears green) – used on the rare occasion when you need to convey something important about the camera, such as 'Craning up' or 'Fade out' (keyboard shortcut is* ALT+ M).

Scene notes *(appears brown) – these are notes that you can write in your script for yourself, notes that can be switched on and off in the final formatting stages of your screenplay. These notes are never supposed to be printed or be a part of the screenplay. (keyboard shortcut is* ALT+ N)

First format

Go ahead and write a few pages and get used to using the different script styles. If you discipline yourself to use the keyboard shortcuts and not the menus or buttons, you will write much faster. Once you have a couple of pages down, you are ready to do your first test format. Normally you wouldn't bother formatting your script until you had finished, but we can just do a test for now.

Go to the Format Menu *and select* Add/Remove Script Formatting. *The* Script Formatting wizard *will start. This is a simple question driven, step by step quick process that will help you format your script the way you want it.*

Cover page

The first page of the wizard is all about your title page and is all pretty obvious. Fill in the different sections – Title, Written by, Contact, Copyright etc – and select the style you want. Once you have everything, click the next button to take you to the next step of the wizard.

Notes, shortcuts and database

So far we haven't used the advanced features such as the Short Cuts Database or Script Notes so you can just ignore this page and click the Next button.

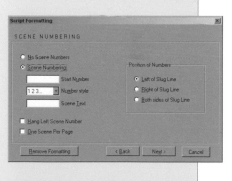

Scene numbers

This page deals with scene numbers. As this isn't a shooting script you probably wouldn't bother putting scene numbers in, but if you wanted to do so just click on Scene Numbering and select the styles you want. Click Next.

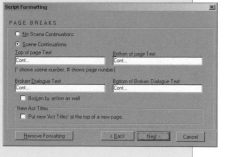

Page breaks

This deals with what happens when your script breaks from one page to the next – for instance, what if the page break is in the middle of some dialogue? For now, leave all the defaults which will add little notes at the top and bottom of pages to let the reader know if any text has been broken over pages. You can also put New Act titles into your project here, but as this isn't a stage play you won't be bothered with this option.

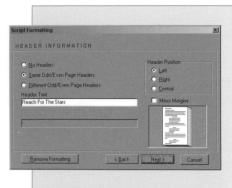

Header information

Using this you can place a header at the top of each page, usually the title of the screenplay. You can also modify the way it appears (left, right, alternate pages etc.)

Footer information

Pretty much the same as the Header Information and can be used for copyright information.

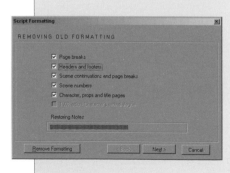

Page number and printer setup

This is the section used to add page numbers and where you want them on the page. Bottom right or centered are the best place.

Script protection

This final screen tells you that you're about to format your screenplay. Hit the Format button and the process will begin. It should take a few seconds, on long scripts with an older computer that could be up to a minute or so. Once formatted you will see how your completed screenplay would look. A pretty cool and exciting moment for any writer.

The script is now locked which means that you can no longer write in it. If you do want to make any new changes you should strip out the formatting, rewrite and then reformat. To strip out the formatting go to the Format Menu then Quick – Remove Formatting and Screenplay will take you back to where you were just moments ago, with a screenplay ready to be either formatted or continue writing.

Director's
Blueprint

www.ealingstudios.co.uk

The director is the creative head of the film. In essence, they manage and enhance all of the various talents, ideas and concepts of the cast and crew, and then impose an overall controlling idea of their own in order to find the best way to take advantage of these resources in the telling of the story. That is, of course, how it's supposed to work, but more often than not, the inexperienced director does not attempt to draw out the best in their cast and crew and simply imposes their own tyranny.

Which are you?

There are many types of directorial strengths, but most directors tend to fall into two very broad categories . . . Geeks and Luvvies. Of course, there is tremendous crossover between these two types.

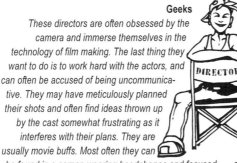

Geeks

These directors are often obsessed by the camera and immerse themselves in the technology of film making. The last thing they want to do is to work hard with the actors, and can often be accused of being uncommunicative. They may have meticulously planned their shots and often find ideas thrown up by the cast somewhat frustrating as it interferes with their plans. They are usually movie buffs. Most often they can be found in a corner, wearing headphones and focused on the video assist monitor.

Strengths – *The film will be technically accomplished.*

Weaknesses – *The performances may be flat and unexciting. The story may suffer due to obsession with technical excellence.*

Luvvies

These directors are often obsessed by performance and immerse themselves in the emotive world of the actors. Often, they will rely heavily on the camera team to handle much of the technology of film making, whilst they bond and connect with the performers. They often hail from a theatrical or fine art background, and often have very little knowledge of popular movies. Most often they will talk to actors during takes, ignore technical problems and restrictions, and command the set as though it were a stage.

Strengths – *The performances should be more exciting and perhaps even dangerous.*

Weaknesses – *Their technical film making may be uninspired and sometimes even incohesive. Story and plot may suffer as the artist in the director strives to find nuance and meaning in the performances where the audience may never see it.*

Director's Blueprint

Dirccting a low budget film is a bit like painting a watercolour in the rain. Whatever you do, external influences so radically modify and change your concepts that your overall vision can quickly and brutally get lost in the confusion of ideas, opinions, mistakes and problems.

The smart, first time film maker would, therefore, choose to paint a very small painting, and paint it very quickly, then cunningly remember to pack an umbrella too. The painting is the story you choose. A story whose execution will be contained, quick to realise, modest in scale yet extraordinarily ambitious in terms of character journey and story. The rain in this analogy is the 'crap' that happens – you've run out of time or budget, the locations have fallen through and you need to completely re-think how you are going to tell the story. The lead actor has quit because they have just got a paid job and you weren't very nice to them last week . . . In essence, directing at this level is all about creative damage control. You will lose almost every battle but that doesn't matter if you win the overall war and manage to make a movie that is a good story well told. Maybe not the best it could be, but is it ever? – *'there are no completed movies, just abandoned films'*.

Plan, plan, plan

The way to get the most out of your first time directing opportunity is to plan all your creative elements and decisions as far ahead and as realistically as the budget and time will allow. This, of course starts with the screenplay. There's just no point in writing a story that is going to stretch you to snapping point. Just to repeat, because this one is very important – **think small in scale but big in emotion and story**. A small story well told is always going to be better than a big story poorly told. Check out most recent Hollywood blockbusters and you'll know what I mean.

When writing, think about the production and schedule. Wherever possible, if you see there is something that is going to be difficult to achieve, ask yourself if, right here right now, you can choose to tell the story in a more modest way without having any impact on the story itself. For instance, does the hero need to drive a motorbike (which might be harder to film and you'll need to find an actor who can do it too)? Or can the hero turn up in a car? Maybe that choice would have no impact on the story, maybe it would have a tremendous

Everyone who wants to be in movies will secretly harbour the desire to direct. Just like everyone who wants to be in a rock and roll band wants to play lead guitar. It's just 'where it's at'.

Be secure in your own gut feelings. If take one is OK, go with it, although you might want to do a second take for insurance purposes.

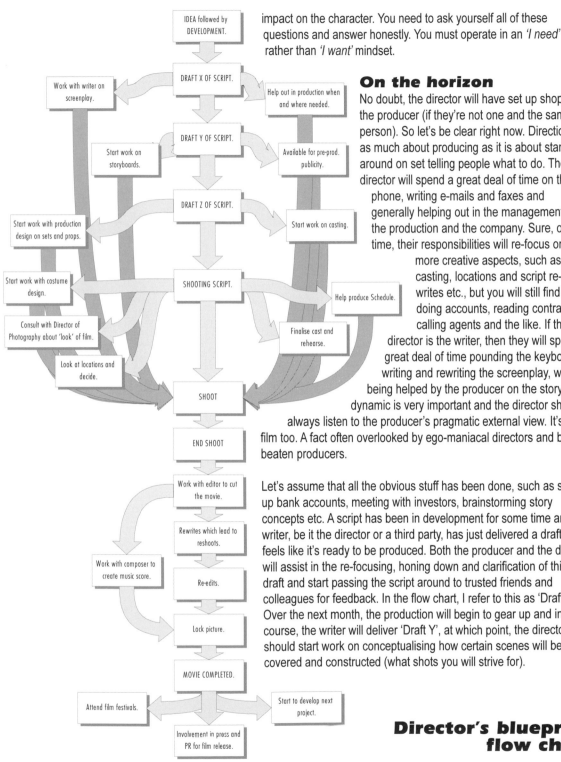

IDEA followed by DEVELOPMENT.

Work with writer on screenplay.

DRAFT X OF SCRIPT.

Help out in production when and where needed.

DRAFT Y OF SCRIPT.

Start work on storyboards.

Available for pre-prod. publicity.

DRAFT Z OF SCRIPT.

Start work with production design on sets and props.

Start work on casting.

Start work with costume design.

SHOOTING SCRIPT.

Help produce Schedule.

Consult with Director of Photography about 'look' of film.

Finalise cast and rehearse.

Look at locations and decide.

SHOOT

END SHOOT

Work with editor to cut the movie.

Rewrites which lead to reshoots.

Work with composer to create music score.

Re-edits.

Lock picture.

MOVIE COMPLETED.

Attend film festivals.

Start to develop next project.

Involvement in press and PR for film release.

impact on the character. You need to ask yourself all of these questions and answer honestly. You must operate in an *'I need'* rather than *'I want'* mindset.

On the horizon

No doubt, the director will have set up shop with the producer (if they're not one and the same person). So let's be clear right now. Direction is as much about producing as it is about standing around on set telling people what to do. The director will spend a great deal of time on the phone, writing e-mails and faxes and generally helping out in the management of the production and the company. Sure, over time, their responsibilities will re-focus on more creative aspects, such as casting, locations and script re-writes etc., but you will still find them doing accounts, reading contracts, calling agents and the like. If the director is the writer, then they will spend a great deal of time pounding the keyboard, writing and rewriting the screenplay, while being helped by the producer on the story. This dynamic is very important and the director should always listen to the producer's pragmatic external view. It's their film too. A fact often overlooked by ego-maniacal directors and brow-beaten producers.

Let's assume that all the obvious stuff has been done, such as setting up bank accounts, meeting with investors, brainstorming story concepts etc. A script has been in development for some time and the writer, be it the director or a third party, has just delivered a draft that feels like it's ready to be produced. Both the producer and the director will assist in the re-focusing, honing down and clarification of this draft and start passing the script around to trusted friends and colleagues for feedback. In the flow chart, I refer to this as 'Draft X'. Over the next month, the production will begin to gear up and in due course, the writer will deliver 'Draft Y', at which point, the director should start work on conceptualising how certain scenes will be covered and constructed (what shots you will strive for).

Director's blueprint flow chart

Storyboards

Most new film makers are so involved in their film that they forget that at some point, they are going to have to stand on set, tell the actors where to stand and tell the DP where to put the camera. Quite literally, they have to call the shots. You will always have your favourite scenes, which you will have visualised for months, but these are not a problem. It's all the other stuff. Page after page of dialogue and action for which you have no original and creative ideas. How are you going to cover this story? What shots are you going to choose? How are they going to be different from other shots and scenes? Why are they different? How are they going to enhance the performances? Are there too many to achieve? These are questions that are best answered sat at a table with a pencil in one hand and a cup of hot chocolate in the other. Ideally, you'd also have a purring cat on your knee too. The worst place to tackle these questions is on set, when you're behind schedule and everyone is screaming at you that they need to know what to do next. Decisions will get made that way, but not well thought out and inspired ones.

This is where storyboarding comes in. If you can't afford a storyboard artist then just do the sketches yourself, no matter how bad they look. You may never show these boards to anyone, but they will give you the opportunity to consider the most effective, creative and efficient way of telling your story. Rather than just directing from the hip, this planning will allow you to weave creative themes, visual styles, pacing in coverage (shots) etc. All of which will make your film stand out. Of course, once you get on set, you may have to throw all your plans away for a number of reasons beyond your control. But even then, by having thought about each and every scene in depth, you will be in a better position to come up with a new idea for how to cover the scene rather than saying to the DP 'just put it on the tripod and we'll shoot it in one wide shot'.

How much time and energy you spend on storyboarding is up to you, but no matter how much it is, it won't be enough.

More, more, more . . .

Over the next month, there will be more script development that will lead to 'Draft Z' of the screenplay, at which point things will feel like they are in full swing. The director will now start work on the casting, perhaps working with a casting director, or perhaps just on their own. They'll also start working with a production designer, discussing issues such as locations, sets, set dressing and props etc. You can see how a director might quickly become over stretched and suffer an attack of creative snow-blindness.

Shooting script

Over the next four weeks or so, the writer will deliver the final shooting script. Just to recap, the director will already have been working with the

Julian Richards
Director

'I began making films by emulating the films that inspired me, which taught me technique, but if you want to be a film maker you need more, you need a voice that's unique or original. New film makers should try to make something that is unique to themselves, stay true to that vision and not try to copy other films. Many first films are too ambitious and fail because of that. Also, they don't get the key ingredients, that is script and cast and often jump in prematurely without enough script development. They need to trouble shoot the whole script in incredible detail before even starting. Then you have to do that script the service of casting it properly. A movie is only as good as its worst performance. I don't know why they are always so eager to get their toys out! I guess script and casting are dull in comparison. But if you get the script and cast right, the rest is a production line.

Something I learnt late is the business side of sales and distribution, how aggressive and shark infested it is. Before you make your film you should at least know it's true market value – often dictated by the budget, cast and genre, and fully understand how the money from sales will trickle back to the producer, if at all! It's important to appreciate that the market is very conservative, always demanding last years big hit, where you may want to come up with something original, which has the potential to take the market by storm. This is much harder to do of course, but also more rewarding and will open doors where the 'movie clones' won't.

I've been described as being 'unstoppable'. I believe that this is the key ingredient to a long term career in the film business. It's about persistence and the ability to ALWAYS take advantage of every opportunity that presents itself. And maintaining that position and goal is a full time job in itself!

Asif Kapadia
Director and Writer

'The first script I wrote took a year of my life and was not very good. I didn't really know what I was trying to write and each draft got worse. I was treating it like a short film and thought that if I increase the font it will get bigger and finally be a feature film. With a feature film you learn you need to plan it all out. Keep the document as short as possible and work out the story line first and see how it develops. I sent out my first screenplay too early which was a mistake. Keep it close to your chest until it's definitely done. My first script was dead before it went out.

It's good to talk ideas through with a co-writer. Say them out loud and figure out whether it's a good story or not. If you can't tell it you probably don't know what it is yet. I was quite naïve when I made 'The Warrior'. When you are trying to make your first film it's not about how much you are going to get paid, it's about getting the film made. We delivered the sricpt to Film 4 and within 3 days they came on board. Because we didn't show it to anyone, people started contacting me as they heard about the screenplay. Before I shot The Warrior, I spoke to everyone I knew who had made a feature film and asked what went right and what went wrong.

Distribution is key. You want to do is be in the right cinemas – it's quality over quantity. You may play to a full house in an art house cinema but empty in a multiplex. The main battle is that for films like mine, that don't have stars, it's about hanging in long enough to build the word of mouth. The next struggle is to find the next project. I've made one movie and I got lucky. I need to make many more features before I understand the form.'

production team / producer, working on storyboards and shot lists, working with the writer (if they are not the writer themselves), working with the production designer and now, as there are only a few weeks left, they will also start to work with the costume designer, the DP (to agree the look of the film and style of coverage). They will also be interviewing actors and hopefully locking actors in before holding final and hurried rehearsals. There may be script re-writes and tweaks and a large part of their time will also be eaten up in producing the schedule. Remember, all of this with perhaps only a couple of weeks before you begin shooting. Let's not even consider how much hell this would feel like if the producer was a bit flaky, or if you didn't have all the money in place that you expected.

On your marks, get set . . .

This is an endurance test and, like any marathon, it's vital to pace yourself so that you will make it over the finish line and not drop dead of a heart attack halfway through. As the days count down to the first day of the shoot, a number of feelings will start to pump through your veins. Excitement and exhilaration at the prospect, fear and trepidation at the responsibility, stress due to an inability to lock things down, fear that you are losing control, exhaustion due to simple fatigue . . . All you can do is get on with it. This is what film making is all about.

Tips for survival

A couple of personal health tips. Remember to drink water as you can get so distracted and forget to drink that you become dehydrated. The same is true of eating. Buy yourself a walkman so you can listen to music and take yourself away from the noisy, distracting world of the production whenever you need a creative clearing. Wherever you are, look for a place to sit down so that you can conserve energy (do not underestimate this, or you may end up collapsing). Buy your thermal underwear in advance (if you are shooting in winter). If you are shooting in summer, make sure you have enough clean T-shirts and underwear to last through the entire shoot as you will soak them through with sweat on a daily basis. Avoid booze and too much coffee. Whenever possible, get to bed as quickly as you can and sleep in as long as you can, even if it means getting a production assistant to make your breakfast in order that you can have an extra ten minutes snooze. Make no mistake, no one will work harder than the director. Don't be a hero. What-ever can be done to make life easier should be done. And of course, the one we all know, wear comfortable shoes.

Before you know it . . .

. . . you'll be on set and directing. And before you know it, it'll be the end of the first day and five pages (or thereabouts) of script that you have agonised over for the last months (or even years) have now been shot and you cannot go back and tweak any more! Depending on how much work and prepara-tion you had put into it beforehand, you'll be either smiling confidently or

blo...   thi...
and pulls out a huge ... rifle, considers it, ...en
dumps it. He retrieves two plastic walkie-talkies and
camouflaged plastic binoculars. There is a thump from
downstairs - DAVEY looks out to see CONNOR riding away
- DAVEY races for the door to exit.

Script planning

In an ideal world you'd have the time to plan every shot, and to do storyboards for the entire movie. But low budget film making is far from ideal and often you just don't have time or budget to do storyboards. Worse still, you are often forced to reconsider your plans because a location or prop is lost and replaced by something entirely different. In which case you might need to abandon all your plans and direct from the hip. These four examples show you how much information you could offer in four different levels of planning for this one shot in a scene – from a simple shot list, all the way through to a fully illustrated storyboard.

149 - High angle shot looking down through window as Connor rides through shot from bottom left to top right.

Shot list
(worst case)

A simple description of the shot that relates the action. It's quick to do and is often forced upon you when locations fall through and you need to rethink your plans quickly.

2. Plan

If you are not too good with drawing, sketch out an overhead camera plan (illustrating much like an architects blueprint would) the camera position, lens, and actors actions.

3. Director's storyboard

Drawn by the director and limited by the directors own artistic abilities. Often this is drawn and re-interpreted later by the storyboard artist.

4. Full storyboard
(best case)

A wonderful and expressive illustrated storyboard drawn by a dedicated artist. If you have time and money to do this it will give you the opportunity to direct the camera before you even get to set.

(more likely) holding your head in your hands, commiserating with yourself before descending into a blind panic as you realise that another five pages are coming at you in seven hours time (yes, you over shot and went over schedule, so you're not going to get enough sleep either). You're now going to feel quite stupid about all those times you chose to have a drink instead of working on the script, or to watch a bit of TV instead of sifting through the actors' CV's a little longer, or being emotionally blackmailed to see your boyfriend or girlfriend instead of working that bit harder on the schedule to find a more efficient way to shoot the film. We're all human and there truly is only so much you can do, but unless you have done all that you can do, you will look back with regret. And there is so little you can do now as you're on the rollercoaster of your shoot. There is no time to get off to reconsider, restructure, re-plan, re-storyboard, rehearse . . .

As a creative person, I feel uncomfortable about writing anything that purports to tell you *'how to direct'*. It is so personal and creative that I think it is important to find your own personal voice. I'd advise practicing by making short films and videos. Workshop with actors so that you are comfortable in their presence, as you may find them and the way they work a bit of a shock to the system. Teach yourself about simple coverage so that when you have to throw your shot list of five shots away because there is only time to do

Storyboard to Shot

In the months running up to the shooting of my third film, Urban Ghost Story, *there was a lot of planning at the storyboard level. Much of the time, the discussions between myself and Genevieve, the director, would begin with Genevieve producing a shot list with seven shots that she wanted in order to cover the scene. We'd talk about it and come to a realisation that we couldn't accommodate all seven shots as we didn't have enough time or money. This limitation would then become the mother of invention. Free from the stress and strain of having to deal with this kind of decision making 'on set' and 'in the moment', we were able to brainstorm and consider much more creative and interesting ways of covering a scene.*

Halfway through the movie, there is a page and a half scene where the main character, Lizzie, talks to another character about her near death experience and how she then had a profoundly spiritual encounter. Here's how it read . . .

```
102 INT. KERRIES FLAT – DAY (SD8)

The room is illuminated by hundreds of candles.
LIZZIE and KERRIE lie in the centre of the room,
LIZZIE looking at the ceiling – relaxed and calm.

                    LIZZIE
          I couldn't do it KERRIE – in case there
IS a hell and I'm going there . . . (scene cont . . .)
```

Genevieve's opening plan involved the character's moving around the room, from one angle and shot to another, which would mean multiple camera set ups. It was a fine and excellent plan, but not possible within our constraints. So we brainstormed until Genevieve came up with the idea of doing the whole scene in one overhead shot with a slow zoom in. It wouldn't be too hard to achieve this shot and would allow us to do a page and a half of script in one hit.

Then we worked on the subtext of the shot – it wasn't just recording the drama, but was 'saying something too'. The design of the shot was intended to have an ethereal and spiritual feel, the position of the girls echoing Renaissance religious paintings, the angle high and floating implying an out of the body feeling, the set dressed with candles to provide a visual echo of stars, heaven and religion.

This shooting plan began with a one line description, which was then followed by a detailed storyboard of the shot. On set it was executed quickly and efficiently, helping us to stay on schedule whilst delivering a sequence with greater profundity than the one initially conceived, or the one that would have been made up in haste on the day if plans had not been made in advance, or if plans were abandoned due to production problems.

Storyboards

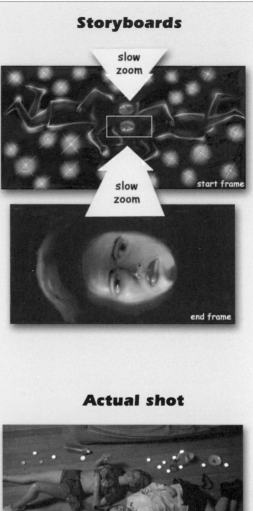

Actual shot

one or maybe two, you will have some idea of how to tackle the problem on the fly. Edit other people's work, as there is no better way to find out how not to shoot a scene!

Feel the fear

Everyone on your crew will probably be youngish and relatively inexperienced. This means that you are the captain of the boat and you probably won't be challenged, even if you are young and inexperienced yourself. Of course, if you are challenged, you need to deal with it swiftly and decisively. Common mutineers include the DP (who thinks they know better), the frustrated 1st AD (who thinks they would make a better director), the angry writer (who thinks the director is screwing it all up), and A.N.Other crew member (whose particular gripes have not been heard and they are spreading dissention among the ranks).

By far, the most terrifying person to step onto set is the older or more experienced actor. How are you going to feel when you realise that you, a first timer, are going to be directing an actor that has made perhaps fifty movies, won a BAFTA in 1977, is married to a top director themselves and seven years ago, got an Oscar nomination? FEAR. Feel it! In truth, you don't need to be too terrified, but you do need to listen to them as they probably have a much better idea of how to direct a movie than you do! Not that I am suggesting you hand over the reigns either. Just listen, learn and make the best judgements that you can make without allowing the ego to interfere.

Them and us

Your film making comrades are divided into two distinct groups. The cast and the crew. Each group has very different dynamics and needs. Some crew members will slip into the actor's world on a regular basis and the actors will slip into the crew's world whenever they step in front of the camera. Make no mistake, you might think that you have one team, but really you have two, just like a general may run a war with two armies, one British and one French for instance. United by the common enemy but at the same time cautious, divided and in need of different things. The director is one of the main conduits between these two groups and must at all times act as a peacekeeper and if needed, a *'tough love'* parent.

A typical problem goes like this . . . The crew are wrapping a location after shooting for twelve hours. It's cold and raining. And as they pack the lights in the back of a van, they notice a couple of actors sat in the front of a car, the heater on, drinking hot chocolate and reading the script for tomorrow, or even snoozing! You can easily see why any crew member would be pissed off, *'why don't they help us pack the vans so we can all go home earlier?'* Conversely, an actor may be uncomfortable acting an intimate scene with a couple of tattooed, hairy and smelly guys holding lights in position. Filmmaking is not an ideal situation. It is chaos with as much control as can

Judith Weston
Acting Coach

'It's remarkable that the acting is often the worst thing in low-budget films. Finding rehearsal time need not cost any money at all, but directors are often afraid of rehearsal because they don't know how to do it. They need to chain themselves to the acting process in order to understand the characters through the subtext and connect with the actors. The subtext is the realm in which they can speak to the actors. There's so much written about film making and writing and so much is very 'surface' – about fixing something in a script – what I call 'the result area.' Whereas the 'process area' (the subtext area) is what needs looking at. The first thing is to have directors take an acting class in order to appreciate subtext and the problems for actors. Next is to apply this to their rehearsal techniques where they can connect to the actors on this level of the script.

A director's role is to tell the story. An actor's role is to stay in the moment. There is a tug/contradiction between these two roles – a creative tension. The language of intention, subtext, images, situation and emotional event are ways to guide the actor in a performance that tells the story without sacrificing their ability to stay in the moment. Directors stray from the job at hand by calling attention to the result of the performance, like 'be angry' or 'it needs to be funny' rather then creating behaviour that has to do with the situation and event of the scene.

A lot of directors are terribly insensitive and treat actors like furniture and are suddenly surprised when the actor loses energy and commitment. What constitutes authority? It's more than telling people what to do. Genuine authority is built on trust and trust is an intimate relationship.'

Directing Actors by Judith Weston is one of the best books on the subject of directors getting the most out of their actors. It's full of insights, many of which we directors feel uncomfortable confronting head on, but there is a truthful resonance in her writing and a genuine desire to empower directors, and therefore actors, so that work of exceptional value and quality is produced. If you can, read and consume, then work with actors on something that isn't too drastic, a short film perhaps, to flex your muscles and put into practice what you have uncovered.

be brought to bear. If everyone in both camps can be coerced, asked, begged or even ordered to behave and fully appreciate that everyone is there to do their job and no more, then the shoot should be a more pleasurable experience all round. Mutual respect is the key. Any actor who thinks the crew is lazy should haul some lights, and any crew member who thinks acting is easy should act out an orgasm in front of a crew. Whatever happens though, work as hard as you can to avoid a *'them'* and *'us'* situation developing, as it is very destructive and time wasting.

Lead, don't rule

Common sense, but you have no money to pay people and if you persist in barking orders, people will leave. If you inspire people through compassionate leadership, they will follow you to the ends of the earth and forgive you for all *your* human mistakes. Unquestionably, leading a cast and crew will always result in a better working environment, which will mean better film making, than if you wreak the tyranny of being a ruler upon them.

How many takes?

It's obvious that you're going to try and shoot as few takes on any shot as possible (to save stock and time). However, an insecure and searching director may end up doing twelve takes of a shot, eating up an extra twenty minutes on-set time, when in fact, take three was adequate. Let go of the pursuit of perfection. There's plenty of time in your career a few years down the line to do that. Right now, you're fighting a war of coverage. You never have enough shots. So take three will be fine unless there is a serious

Typical day for a director

When you consider how much work the director actually puts into a film, it's a wonder any ever survive. Perhaps the hardest thing to do is to stay sane during the whole adventure, so that you can answer questions in the best way . . . It's a grueling day. Every day. And the questions are relentless. Should it be blue or green? Should I cut that line? Do I stand here? Have you read the new script rewrites? Can I wear the red hat in this scene? Which lens? Track or legs? Is the gun loaded or not in this scene? Do you need another coffee? Argggghhh! Sit down whenever you can, and of course, wear comfortable shoes!

6am	Get out of bed, shower and eat.
6.30am	Read through script, check notes etc.
7.30am	Arrive at set, meet AD, go through day, plan first shot.
8.00am	Start shooting. Work relentlessly…
12.30pm	Break for lunch. View yesterday's rushes with lunch on knee.
1.00pm	Meet with AD and discuss afternoon shoot.
1.30pm	Start afternoon shoot. Work relentlessly…
6.30.pm	Break for dinner or snacks. Work on problems after dropping behind.
7.00pm	A little bit of a break, although the questions will keep coming.
7.30pm	Evening shoot to catch up on schedule. Work relentlessly
8.30pm	Wrap. Discuss next day with AD. Replan and regroup.
9.30pm	Cutting room to view the day's editing.
10.30pm	More food. You need it. Planning next day's shots.
12.01am	Time for bed… unless you need to do some more plans!

The 'line' of action

The 'line of action' is most commonly referred to on set when there is a problem and someone announces, usually the camera team, editor or director, that the shot may be 'breaking the line'. This kind of mistake is rudimentary film making, but it's still easy to screw up, even on big features with experienced directors.

The line of action helps a director understand when two shots, if cut together, would work or not. The two examples illustrate this simply, and in this context, it's fairly easy to understand. It gets more complicated when there are multiple characters in a scene, or when the two shots are filmed several weeks apart and your memory is failing ('was he looking left to right or right to left in the other shot?'). Either way, it's essential you get your head around it. If you can't understand this, grab a camcorder and shoot some scenes and cut them together. Go out of your way to break the line and see how it looks when edited. You will soon understand. If you are to direct quickly and efficiently under pressure, you must completely grasp this concept. The audience's view of the world, and that of the story, is in part based on this spatial awareness and film geometry.

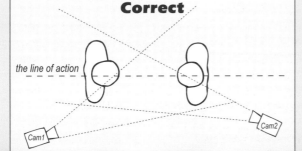

In this first example, the line remains unbroken. Note how the two resulting shots give the impression that the two characters are facing each other. Look at the Camera 1 shot and then the Camera 2 shot, imagining that they are shots in a sequence. The two look appropriate. Note how both cameras are situated on the same side of 'the line'.

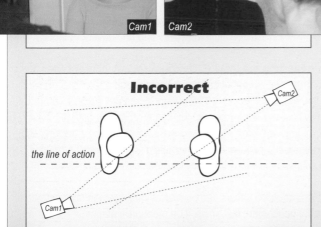

In this second example, Camera 2 has now moved across the line of action, 'breaking the line'. Remember, the actors are still standing in exactly the same place, but now look at the resulting shots and how they no longer 'feel right', almost as though the characters are not looking at each other.

problem. Low budget film making is always about getting what you need and not about getting what you want. There just isn't time or money, even if the will is plentiful. A number of things will suggest to the director that *'we need to do another take'*. Commonly, these include . . . an actor who feels they could give more (by take twelve you realise what they felt and what they could give are two different things that have just wasted time and stock), a DP who is obsessive about framing or focus (when experience tells you that you will get away with it), a continuity error that is spotted on-set, when in fact no one would ever notice it in the film (unless of course, the story and film making is so dull that the eyes of a bored audience start to wander around the frame, looking for mistakes). Whatever the reason, it's up to the director to know the difference between a compromise and a genuine problem. Don't waste time pursuing perfection.

Camera tricks

Every director wants to use a track and dolly – the equipment that is used to move the camera smoothly through a scene. It's a kind of heavy trolley mounted on strong steel tracks, it's weight creating the inertia needed to ensure smooth moving shots when pushed up and down the track. The only problem is that it can take ages to set up and just as long to execute the shot (as it can be technically challenging). Wherever possible, the director should ask themselves about the validity of using a track and dolly. Can they do it another way? Will a slow creeping zoom (which is an optical movement as opposed to a physical movement) do the same job, but in half the time and expense? Can the shot be done hand held, negating any need for a track and dolly at all? Can you just forgo this one and do it on a tripod?

The same is true for crane shots. Every director wants them. Are they really needed? Will they be cut out because whilst they look pretty, they may end up simply slowing down the story. Understand one truth. Audiences are not impressed by flashy shots (or at least the flashy shots you can do). They want a good story well told. Often an obsession with crane or tracking shots is saying more about the insecurities of the film makers than the needs of the drama – *'look at this shot, it's so cool, it looks like a real movie!'*

Consider the production values and budget of your average car commercial. That is the benchmark that you will be measured against. And you won't win, so don't waste time in the pursuit of what you think is visual splendour which will really be interpreted (by the viewer) as a boring moment to be endured as they wait for the story to continue. If you really must use a crane, then consider a cherry picker as a cheap alternative (trucks with raisable platforms that are used to change streetlights for instance).

Try to learn and remember everybody's name, especially the actors. If you find yourself on set about to shout 'you over there, could you stand three feet to your right please . . . !' Stop before you open your mouth and replace the word 'you' with their name. Failing that, fall back on the old director favourite of 'darling'.

Directing is editing

At the most basic level, the director needs to provide the editor

Shots

It's pretty tough to illustrate the choice of shots you have in a book as film making is almost always about movement – both the movement of the frame and the movement of the subject. But let's have a go anyway. The shots you choose should always serve the story. Sometimes that will mean a selection of creative angles that tell the story in an interesting way, other times that may mean just setting the camera back and allowing the actors to do their thing. More often, the compromise of budget and time will limit the choice of shots, so be sure of what you want and why. The choice of lenses can also change the way the shot looks (especially shooting close ups of actors on a wide angle lens or a long lens – see the camera section for more examples).

Wide shot (W/S)

This wide shot (not too wide here) is wide enough to capture all the action and environment. Often these shots are used to start scenes as it can clearly establish the geometry of the elements, who is where for instance. On DV formats wide shots are hard to accommodate as the CCD chip in the camera can limit the width of angle, which means you need to get the camera further away for wider shots, which means you need to get a bigger location! Wides are also often used for establishing shots of mountains, cities, buildings etc.

Mid shot (M/S)

Still wide enough to see the world around the subject, and in this case, it accommodates two actors. Note how they are not facing each other so that the whole scene could be shot in one, a simple way to cover a dialogue scene quickly without needing to shoot reverse angles.

Close up (C/U)

Well chosen close ups can have a dramatic impact, it's like the audience is thrust right into the face of an actor at the right moment. It's easy to overuse close up shots, so be selective. Actors need to be aware that a close up might mean they can move around less in the scene as the camera would need to follow them. It's common to shoot a wide or mid shot and then 'crash in' for a close up of the same angle, but for selected portions of the scene only. This means that minimal re-lighting will be needed and the camera may not even need to be moved. All that would happen is the zoom lens would be 'zoomed in' or a prime lens is swapped for a longer lens to get the close up shot.

Extreme close up (EC/U)

An extreme close up shot is usually a tricksy or effect shot, the actor's eyes as the killer approaches for instance. It can also be used for information too, a shot of a name in a telephone directory, the bullet going into the gun chamber, the number flashing on a mobile phone for instance. Depending on the camera and lenses used, you may not be able to get as close up as you might expect and an additional filter may need to be hired (or you could buy a cheap Cokin Close Up filter which would do the same for a tenner).

Dutch angle

Normally the camera team spend a great deal of time making sure the camera is levelled off so that verticals and horizontals in a scene match the edge of frames. However, a Dutch angle can have a different effect and it's often used to make moments feel a little weird or crazy. The camera could tilt into a Dutch angle, or you could simply cut to the Dutch angle. Either way, the excessive tilt can have an unsettling effect on the viewer.

Pan and tilt

The ability to move the camera from side to side (panning) or up and down (tilting), usually to follow an actor or to reveal something. The quality of the camera movement is dependent on the experience of the camera operator, but mostly on the quality of the tripod head (so rent the best you can afford). The longer the lens the more difficult it is to pan and tilt as even the slightest camera movement can have a dramatic effect. Panning and tilting is often combined with other camera moves such as dollying or zooms. Of course, hand holding the camera will give the operator even more freedom of movement, but potentially at the expense of camera steadiness (although camera shake can also be desirable for creative reasons).

Zoom

Anyone who has used a camcorder knows what a zoom lens can do, it moves from wide angle to close up and back again, at the speed the operator chooses. The advantages are that you can reframe within a shot, and because the camera is not moving, there will be no need to refocus. The down sides are that to get a smooth zoom you will need to hire a special zoom control motor, and that zoom shots often look a little odd. This is perhaps because we cannot zoom our eyes and so our brain knows that this is a trick effect. Either way, it's not too desirable, but if used when needed, or for slow creeping zooms (when a track is impossible for time reasons) it can do the trick. NEVER allow an operator to perform a zoom manually, it must always be motorised.

Track and dolly

Used to physically move the camera smoothly in a scene. Backward and forward (in and out as in the picture) is called dollying, moving left and right is called crabbing. Every director loves a dolly shot as it is very dramatic, but it can take a huge amount of setup so chose your shots wisely. Dollying shots can be enhanced by using a little zoom at the same time (which means your track could be shorter). Cranes can also be used to get sweeping up and down shots, but now we are slipping out of low budget world and into properly financed film making.

High angle / low angle

Keeping the camera high or low can have a dramatic impact on the subject. High angles looking down can dominate, low angles looking up can imply power. Beware though, use of these shots can often mean hidden production problems. Looking up might shoot 'off the set' or shooting against a bright sky may mean extra lighting, or special equipment may be needed to mount the camera on the floor (it may even need a trench to be dug or the actor to stand on a platform).

Watch the movies

Watch your favourite movies and examine each and every shot. How do the shots make you feel? Ask yourself what it is saying to you. Has the director subtly added to the story or performance by the choice of shots? Some film makers, such as Hitchcock, are very obvious and clear in their intent and execution. Others aren't so obvious, but you can bet if it's a great film, a thoughtful director has made creative choices along the way. Analyse how these shots might have been achieved (technically). Look at the shots before and after, how do they cut together? Look at the lighting. Look at the framing. Look at the emphasis of the image and how that was achieved through lighting, focus, production design etc.

Wide or long?

From a directorial perspective, the choice of lens with which to shoot an actor can have a dramatic effect. The wide end of the lens (left) tends to distort the face and much of the background becomes visible and messy. It's an uncomfortable look for my money. However, the same style of frame, shot on the long end of the lens (right) does not distort the actor, and the background is crushed down and softer making for a more attractive image. Technically, the wide angle shot (left) was shot from only a few feet away, whereas the long lens shot (right) was taken from twenty feet away or so. Clearly this has an impact as not all locations can accommodate the camera being set so far back. One advantage of the camera being further away is that there is less chance of camera noise bleeding into the dialogue.

with enough shots that cover the story and action, so that the story can actually be told on the screen. These shots should also be structured in such a way that they will edit together seamlessly. This isn't too hard to get your head around, but some directors are much better than others. I would urge any inexperienced director to learn how to edit and then edit either their own work or somebody else's. There are a whole pile of simple mistakes and tricks to be learnt and getting it wrong on your first feature film is not the best way to educate yourself. This is one area where making a short film before embarking on a first feature will really reap rewards that are of true value.

Second unit

An inexperienced director may resist the idea of having a second unit director and camera team. This is their insecurity speaking, it's a kind of 'control freak' mentality that can manifest. But understand this, no matter who does what, no matter who shoots or creates the material and footage, the director will get ALL the credit. If they don't like the shots that have been provided by the second unit, they can ditch them in the edit. The major benefit of having an active second unit is that you can potentially increase (massively) the quantity of shots that you have available to tell your story. Whether it's specific shots or sequences, commonly close ups of inanimate objects or establishing shots of buildings (shots that do not feature the actors), or whether it's shots grabbed on set where a second camera roams around looking for interesting and alternative angles while the main unit shoots the primary shots. This footage can be a scene saver, much cheaper than re-shoots, and better than being forced into unwanted re-cuts or even dropping scenes through a lack of coverage. This second

If you want to get an extremely low angle shot of an actor for instance, why not shoot into a high quality mirror on the ground? You don't need to stand anyone on a box then, or dig a hole, although the actor will be mirrored for continuity – but would anyone notice?

Keep it simple and tell your story in the most clear way. Audiences do not remember flashy shots, but they do remember a good story well told. There will be time to play with your story and shots on later films . . . THIS IS THE FIRST OF MANY, IT IS NOT YOUR LAST FILM!

camera on set, means that potentially, for example, for every wide shot of a scene you could also have a mid or a close up of the same scene without wasting any time messing around and doing another set up. Of course, it also means that you will shoot much more film stock, but in the grand scheme of costs, this is very good value for money.

Blocking

The concept of 'blocking' a scene is where the director will work with the actors and heads of departments, such as camera, sound, production design etc. and quickly work through the shot or shots within a scene. This blocking process, which happens as you prepare each scene, will flag up potential problems as varied as actors not feeling comfortable delivering a line in a certain place, to the camera team discovering their lights would appear in shot. Blocking is not rehearsing, as the actors won't 'give' very much. It's about discovering the physical geometry of the action and the shots. The camera team may even follow actors, watching where they stand, then marking the floor with tape (which is where the phrase *'hitting your mark'* comes from). Under pressure, you'll be tempted to drop this blocking in favour of saving time. Occasionally, this may be appropriate, but on the whole, five minutes spent blocking a scene before everything is set up will often save you twenty minutes messing around. Quite simply (and literally), everyone will know where they *stand*.

Get through the script

The most essential job for the director is to make sure that you have actually filmed the entire script by the end of the shoot. This pressure can cause flare ups for creatives who value excellence over completeness. Perfectionists (be it the director, DP or actor etc.) can sometimes insist on doing shots and scenes a certain way or performing multiple takes above and beyond what is needed (remember, needed not wanted). It's up to the director to decide by using the schedule as a guide. It's essential that you do not fall behind schedule too far or you may get to the end of the shoot with large chunks of screenplay simply not filmed. Clearly, this will not result in a complete movie. Many new or first time directors fixate on detail and artistic integrity at the cost of coverage. You don't need it great, you just need it good, and you need all of it.

As a shining example, on every film I have made, there have been numerous shots that have been a real problem to get right. Normally, I would end up doing eight, ten, sixteen, even twenty takes to get it right, or what I perceived or insisted was *'right'*. Yet once the footage was in the cutting room, somehow pretty much every shot would be adequate (and I would end up using take three for instance!) This is where experience and confidence can be a great ally.

The director's script

The director will, of course, have their own screenplay. It will become dog eared very quickly, often covered in little reminder notes about minor modifications to one scene which will have a minor impact on another (that would otherwise be forgotten, only to be rediscovered later in the cutting room). The director will also probably mark up their script to show where shots will start and end, with notes on the shot and (ideally) a reference back to a storyboard. These are represented by lines to graphically illustrate where these shots start and end.

The example here, from the film I am proposing to do next, shows a simple scene and the directorial choices I have made for it. It is a scene between the hero of the story, Connor, his little sister and her young friend. All three are walking up to Hill House, the legendary home of the 'vampire'. Connor is old enough to know better and no longer believes that the girl in the story is a vampire, but the kids are afraid for Connor who has been summoned to do some work. The scene plays as they slowly walk up to the house.

It begins with a wide shot, establishing the house in the distance, and the three small figures walking toward it. The dialogue would start over this shot, although on the day we would shoot this shot mute and use the dialogue from the next few shots.

I then chose to play the bulk of the scene on a tracking shot, moving alongside the kids. I would use this track four times, shooting a wide of the scene (making sure I get an attractive background). I would probably shoot this one last as I would want to see the sun setting in the background. I would also shoot a close up of the entire scene on each character. This would mean that I am really getting the most from the long setup time for the track, and it would also give me plenty of material for the cutting room. Because the camera is running parallel with the kids, there will be little or no focus problems as the cast and camera are always the same distance apart – that will make life easier, especially in the fading light in which I want to shoot.

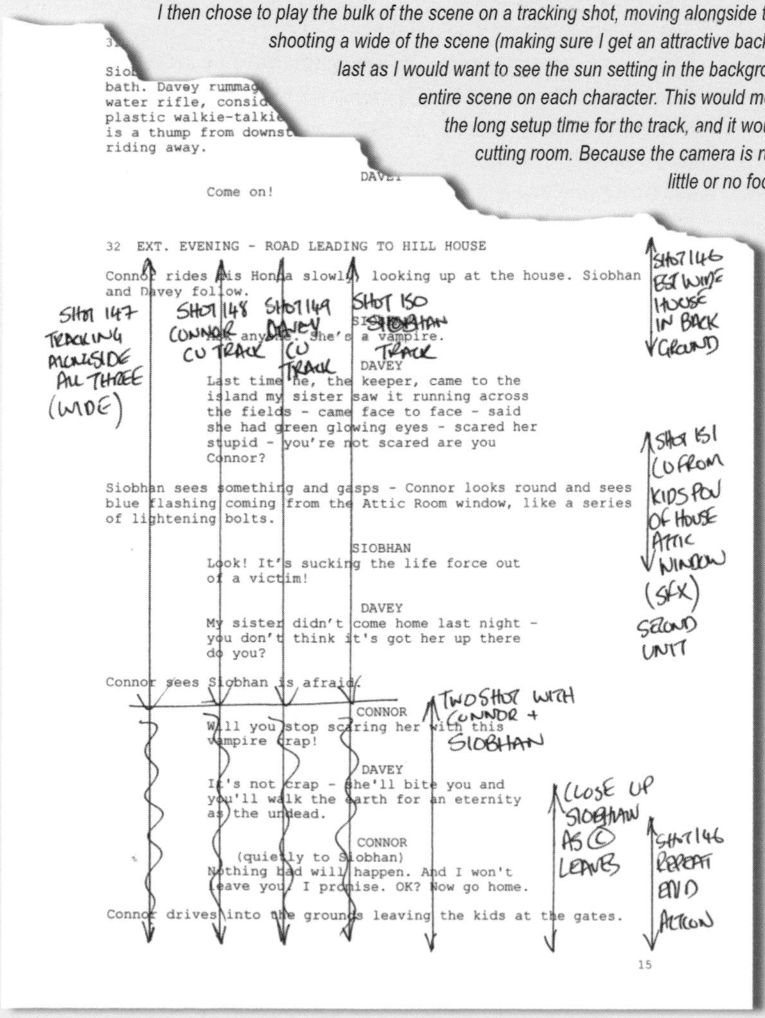

Toward the end of the scene I would grab a two shot close up of Connor and his little sister, and a big close up as he reassures her that it's going to be OK. These new close up shots will be static and give more weight to the moment because it is so different from the last shots. It will also give the actor playing Connor a moment to pause, find the peace in the moment, in order that he can reassure her . . . it's going to be OK. Finally, we would reprise the wide shot of the house as Connor leaves the kids and makes his way up the hill.

In the middle of the scene there is a shot of the attic window from which blue lights flash. This would be a long lens shot with lots of setup time because of the special effects, even though they are not too complex (blue flashing lights). This shot would almost certainly be given to a second unit team, freeing me to keep on schedule.

Script excerpt (marked-up director's script):

Sio[...]
bath. Davey rumma[...]
water rifle, consid[...]
plastic walkie-talkie[...]
is a thump from downst[...]
riding away.

                    DAVEY
    Come on!

32 EXT. EVENING - ROAD LEADING TO HILL HOUSE

Connor rides his Honda slowly looking up at the house. Siobhan
and Davey follow.

                    CONNOR
    anyway she's a vampire.

                    DAVEY
    Last time the, the keeper, came to the
    island my sister saw it running across
    the fields - came face to face - said
    she had green glowing eyes - scared her
    stupid - you're not scared are you
    Connor?

Siobhan sees something and gasps - Connor looks round and sees
blue flashing coming from the Attic Room window, like a series
of lightening bolts.

                    SIOBHAN
    Look! It's sucking the life force out
    of a victim!

                    DAVEY
    My sister didn't come home last night -
    you don't think it's got her up there
    do you?

Connor sees Siobhan is afraid.

                    CONNOR
    Will you stop scaring her with this
    vampire crap!

                    DAVEY
    It's not crap - she'll bite you and
    you'll walk the earth for an eternity
    as the undead.

                    CONNOR
    (quietly to Siobhan)
    Nothing bad will happen. And I won't
    leave you, I promise. OK? Now go home.

Connor drives into the grounds leaving the kids at the gates.

                                              15

Handwritten notes on script:

- SHOT 146 EST WIDE HOUSE IN BACKGROUND
- SHOT 147 TRACKING ALONGSIDE ALL THREE (WIDE)
- SHOT 148 CONNOR CU TRACK
- SHOT 149 DAVEY CU TRACK
- SHOT 150 SIOBHAN CU TRACK
- SHOT 151 CU FROM KIDS POV OF HOUSE ATTIC WINDOW (SFX) SECOND UNIT
- TWO SHOT WITH CONNOR + SIOBHAN
- CLOSE UP SIOBHAN AS C LEAVES
- SHOT 146 REPEAT END ACTION

Surviving the shoot

Getting through to the end of the shoot is grueling. On a daily basis, you'll feel that you didn't get enough shots, that what you did get wasn't as good as you'd hoped for, you'll have dropped behind schedule which will force cuts in the script, and when plans fall through and you're forced to direct from the hip, you'll feel upset at your lack of creativity . . . on top of which, you will be utterly exhausted. You're going to make mistakes and probably lots of them. In the moment, don't worry about error or poor creative judgement, just learn from the experience and keep going. Never look back, never stop, never self-indulgently self-doubt. As long as you shoot every page of the script, you'll have made a movie. It may not be great, but it's a movie.

Cutting room

After the shoot wraps, you'll take a break before getting into the cutting room and begin to re-discover your movie. Now is the time to let go of all your preconceptions, your aches and pains, your cunning interpretations and attempt to make an entirely new movie out of all the bits you managed to film. It's going to be a long process of editing and re-editing, but it is one of the most rewarding stages of the process. It will probably lead to re-shoots, where you'll have an opportunity to create new stories and characters or modify and adjust what you had previously shot by re-shooting it in a different way.

Upon reflection, you'll be filled with an overwhelming feeling that if you could do it all over again, you'd do it all differently. That's what the next movie is for, to take what you learnt on this one, and apply it to a new project.

Producer's Blueprint

National
Film +
Television
School

The producer will run the business of the film. Whenever a problem appears, it will more than likely work its way to the producer, who will then have to fix it. After their first film, most producers say *'if I'd known what I know now, I would have never done it'.* Still, take comfort in the fact that they tend to go and do it all over again. The job of a producer on a low budget film is more like that of a production manager. It's all about organisation and getting the most out of every penny. One of the key skills a producer needs is the ability to negotiate the very best out of every situation. Some people are extremely skilled at this and can seem to pull off the most incredible deals. There are a number of tricks that you can use to get what you want.

Flirtation – *One of the reasons there are so many females in production is that they have a better chance of getting 'the great deal' because when they ring to ask, more often than not, they are greeted by a bored middle aged man. Yes it's sexist I know but it's amazing what a flirtatious telephone manner can pull off.*

Get it in writing – *Whatever deal you get, try and get the supplier or company to send you an e-mail, letter or fax confirming prices and dates. Sometimes, people are sacked, leave or move on to other companies and you may find yourself without a deal unless you had it in writing.*

Cash up front – *If you are going to get an amazing deal, the last thing the person who has offered you that bargain wants to do is chase you for months for payment. So if you can offer cash up front, you will always be in a better position to close the deal.*

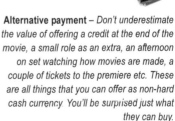

Go in hard – *Whatever money you have, always offer less. This will give you room to improve your position by offering more later on, or not (in which case you've saved money). It's a simple negotiation technique that frankly I'm staggered people fall for, but hey, I guess we're all human. If your budget really is pitiful, you may have to offer everything up front and beg for mercy.*

Never say never – *During negotiations, if it looks like you aren't going to get what you want, don't close the door. Even if you can't agree, it's essential that you don't say, 'well this isn't going to work, so let's not bother', but leave it on something like 'well we can't agree now but I'm sure we could come to an agreement. Maybe we should think about it and look at some alternatives. I'll call you in a few days'. Never close the door.*

Alternative payment – *Don't underestimate the value of offering a credit at the end of the movie, a small role as an extra, an afternoon on set watching how movies are made, a couple of tickets to the premiere etc. These are all things that you can offer as non-hard cash currency. You'll be surprised just what they can buy.*

Producer's Blueprint

A good producer is also an artist. Not a frustrated director, but a kind of business minded reflection of the director. They know what a great movie is and they will strive for it. They will always have the best interests of the movie at heart (and not their ego), they are pragmatic and at best, can work with the director to make the most of this opportunity (opposed to in conflict, and that also means that the conflict doesn't come from the director too).

A thankless task

Producing a low budget film is a thankless task. You have no money. You have no real creative control. You're inexperienced, so you make lots of mistakes that eat into your non-existent budget. Most cast and crew distrust you at best, and at worst, downright hate you! And to add insult to injury, no matter how hard you work on the film, no matter how much of your creative influence is embodied in the film, no matter whether you mortgaged your grandmother to pay for it, the director will get ALL the glory. Get used to it. No-one knows or cares who the producer is and people perceive the director as the entire creator of the work. If you want to drown your sorrows in a drink over this, go to your local bar and you'll probably find the writer there too, having had the same treatment. The director is god, everyone else made coffee (except the camera person and actors). At least that's the way 99.9% of the world will view it.

So why do it? It's a good question. The truth is, I'm not sure. Yes, a low budget film can be a stepping stone to bigger and better things, but more often than not, it isn't quite that. The experience can be invaluable, but so can the life changing experience you would no doubt get from a car wreck. I guess it comes down to this. You just really want to do it and the challenge alone is sufficient fuel for the journey and the respect and acknowledgement of your very close peers who know *'the truth'* will give you the measure of glory that you will be *'cheated out of'*. And without doubt, there is a heady sense of achievement from attending the premiere for your movie, or the opening night of your theatrical release, or by renting it from your local video shop, and by finally ringing round all your friends to tell them that your movie is on TV next week.

But what really is the job?

The producer is the most powerful person in the film crew. They are

> *The producer is the business head of the film, the person who assembles all the pieces of the jigsaw, be they the script, actors, cash, director . . .*
>
> *And a good producer is also a creative person who may not know how to 'do it', but knows 'what needs to be done and why . . .'*

Screen Daily, the electronic and free version of Screen International, is the main source of up to date movie information. It is read by film makers, agents, distributors and anyone else connected to the business. And yes, it's FREE!

Put together a business plan outlining your overall strategy, timescales, cashflow, statistics, targets, short and long term goals, plot synopsis, storyboards, casting ideas etc. This will help when you speak to bank managers, accountants and investors. It will also force you to consider the long term issues faced by you and your business.

the business and management head of the production. Whatever the problem, the buck will stop with the producer. Ultimately, they are the people who have the power to sign cheques, and hire or fire. But there's so much more to it, most of which is downright unpleasant, except for the pathologically optimistic career motivated *'I want to be a producer'* types. Fundamentally, producing can often be about as far away from film making as you could possibly get whilst remaining theoretically within a film crew. You never get to hang out where the action is at, or ever get near to a camera or actors. The producer's primary tool is a telephone, not a camera.

Throughout the whole process, from conception to completion, a producer will regularly say *'no we can't afford that, think of a new way of doing it but differently.'* The most skilled low budget producers will work with the creative team to find the very best way to tell the story with the limited resources available.

The blueprint

Let's assume for the purpose of this chapter that there is a film making team that is a producer and a director, and together they are the writers. The director is perhaps the more talented writer, the producer being good at creative broad strokes and criticism. Nonetheless, together they are considerably stronger together than they would be alone (a fact that can often be forgotten). When it all goes horribly wrong and someone has to do the dirty work, probably YOU . . . YOU will feel like quitting because YOU feel you are doing much more than your partner(s). Will you be better off alone? No, you won't I fear. Stick it out. Keep the peace. Build bridges.

Whilst the director is working on the screenplay, the producer will no doubt be juggling a number of balls . . . they'll be seeking money from investors, looking at the feasibility of basing the production in certain locations, figuring out how to attack massive production problems, working on a budget so that they can better figure out the best way to squeeze as much as they can from the money that they expect to become available, supporting the director with script development meetings, and of course, manning the office so that to the outside world, their little film company could appear like a major player *of tomorrow*. There'll be months of this kind of preparatory work before the screenplay is ready to be shown to anyone else.

Think on

So much of producing is just good old common sense. Look at the script. How are you going to do it? Can you do it? Make calls and see if what appears to be impossible is actually possible. Ask other film makers about their problems. Ask professionals for advice and help. If you make the right approach (polite and flattering) you will almost always get good free advice.

Ideas into reality

When writing the script, the writer and director might say 'hey, we've got this great idea. What if . . . ' It's obvious really, but everything that is in the screenplay needs to be found, arranged, hired, begged borrowed or stolen by the producer or a member of the production team. Consequently, there is normally a degree of friction and antagonism between the creatives and the producers. Hang out in the creative camp and you will hear 'don't they understand that the whole of act two rests on Bill seeing the three elephants?' Hang out in the production camp and you'll hear 'have you heard the latest? Now they want three elephants. How the f**k do they think we're going to get three elephants?' On your average low budget there would then be a rewrite that would start with 'maybe it could be two elephants, or why not just the one?' And it will end up at 'we're not going to have any goddamn elephants, so find another way!' Of course, it's the job of the producer to know whether the elephants are worth the trouble and expense. Like any good general, the producer should know which battles are worth fighting and which should be walked away from.

And remember, there will always be a rift between the creatives and the production. Look at it this way, how would you feel if every day, you were expected to achieve the unachievable. And then, on a whim, (or at least it's perceived as a whim, even if it isn't) the creatives pile a whole new and unexpected production nightmare on to your plate. A good producer will always strive to get the staff to appreciate each others problems and to keep the peace.

Purse strings tight

Money. You never have enough of it. Not even on big budget movies. Having said that, working with a normal budget would afford the producer the luxury of being able to buy themselves out of most problems. On a low budget, you do not have that luxury, so must avoid costly mistakes wherever possible. This is obviously a bit of a problem because you are inexperienced and will therefore make simple mistakes. Add to that the fact that what you are doing in the first place, working outside of the system and in an unorthodox manner, is a direct invitation to unforeseen problems. Still, you have to get through it. Just think ahead. Always consider *'what will happen if . . . '*

It will be the producer's job to keep a tight grip on the financial reins. Wherever possible, you should seek to avoid payment of anything (bills etc.) until after the shoot. Whatever your budget, I would lie about it and claim it is less. Everyone involved will base their calculations on your budget – what they think they or their equipment is worth, or how much budget their department should have. Understand that you will run out of money and that not all debts will stop you dead in your tracks. It's not a popular thing to say, but if push comes to shove, you want to be paying the people who stand in the way of completing your film and pay in second position the people who are just complaining that they have not been paid but can't do anything about it. This is financial crisis management. It will happen. Please don't send me angry e-mails about this. I am not suggesting it as a cunning way to do crafty business, it is an observation of what will probably happen and the best way to deal with it for all concerned.

The primary tool of the producer is the telephone. It's amazing just what you can get for free if you make the right approach. Always be courteous, professional, cheeky and respectful, and follow up any help with at the very least a thank you letter.

Simple techno models

Most producers fall over because they don't sort out their technology. So if you want some simple rock solid 'it's gonna work' models, here they are . . .

If shooting on film, shoot at 25fps (no matter what anyone tells you), shoot sound at 48khz. Post production will then be very simple. Do not shoot at 24fps!

If shooting on DV shoot in 4:3 (not 16:9 unless you have a true 16:9 CCD, which you almost certainly won't), and record sound at 48khz. Do not use frame modes (the film 'look' will be applied in post.)

If shooting DigiBeta, shoot in true 16:9, with sound at 48khz. If HiDef, shoot at 25P (progressive scan) and NOT 24P.

Do it all or delegate?

There are two kinds of producers. Those who choose to take the weight of the production on their own personal shoulders, and there are those who choose to delegate.

Those who choose to do everything may have been forced to do so because there is no one to help or they simply don't trust anyone else to do the job properly. The advantage of this is that the producer will have intimate knowledge of all aspects of production, and if anything goes wrong, they can't really blame it on anyone else. The downside is that this producer can quickly become exhausted through sheer overwork, and more importantly, they get drawn into dealing with the mundane and relatively trivial production problems that occur daily.

On the other hand, whilst focusing on the bigger picture (things like casting and script) the producer who delegates can run the risk of things not getting done as efficiently and cost effectively as if they did it themselves, as not everyone in the production team may be as dedicated, tenacious or as experienced. However, if you do have a top rate production team who are organised and resourceful, it's a smart move to delegate as much as possible of the *'crap'* that lands on a producers desk. This frees the producer to step back and manage the production from a more objective viewpoint and not to stretch them to the point of exhaustion. This is the approach that I took on the last film I made, *'Urban Ghost Story'*. I had a team of three people who I could implicitly trust and I delegated absolutely everything I could to these guys. Consequently, I was freed to contribute creatively to the production.

Fix a start date. And stick to it. If you make the decision that come hell or high water, you will be shooting by a given date, you will stand a much better chance of actually getting it done. You will be more motivated, you won't put things off, others will see this and rise to your higher standards and energy levels. You will also talk about the movie with real conviction, and before you shoot, the movie is just an idea in your head, it isn't a reality yet, but by setting a shoot date, the movie becomes a reality in the minds of others.

Decision making

A curious thing happens when you make a movie. Occasionally, small groups of actors and crew amass around you, each with absolutely *'essential and pressing'* questions. Whilst they do need an answer, most of the time these are unimportant questions that could be dealt with by assistants or empowered production staff. Wherever possible, ask people to seek answers elsewhere and come to the producer as a last resort. There will of course be occasions when you are forced to make difficult choices to which there are simply no right or wrongs, or worse still, you just don't know! So when the production designer screams at you, *'I need a decision is it blue or green?'*, you will have to answer.

This dilemma is one of the most horrific things you'll have to deal with. It's one of the reasons why you must have an intimate knowledge of the screenplay, of the director's approach and intentions, of the casting, the schedule, the production team's problems, locations etc. It's really no use blaming other people for your lack of knowledge in these areas. You are the producer! Leadership and power come at a very high price. You need to know everything about everything, which means you will probably get less sleep than anyone. Only with this kind of omnipotent knowledge will you be empowered to make the best decisions quickly. Michael Winner has a great saying about film making, *'the hardest thing about making a film is staying awake for three months'*.

Choose people wisely

Whoever you choose for your cast and crew, ask yourself *'would I be happy going on holiday with these people?'* If the answer is no, find some other people. You're looking for a happy team who will work long hours without complaint and endure dreadful conditions without losing it. The biggest problem is always about being valued and personal ego. The director of photography on many low budget films is regularly the source of headaches. They often have inflated egos and perceive themselves to be more important than the rest of the crew. If it's a tough shoot, this arrogance and inflexibility is going to result in at best, tension, at worst, complete breakdown. Of course, attitude problems and ego are not limited to or necessarily present in the camera department and can sometimes spring up in the strangest of places. Value each and every crew member equally.

Therapist on set

During the shoot tensions will run high. It's not surprising as everyone is asked to do the impossible on an almost hourly basis. On the whole, most battles will be lost. Each crew members vision, including the directors, will rarely (if ever) be fully realised. This can create the impression that nothing is ever going right. That isn't necessarily the case as even on big films, the director rarely gets what they want. The question is more often, *'did I get what I need'*, or putting it another way, *'can I get away with what I've got?'*

Daniel San
Producer

'Don't make a film that you can't afford to make on your budget. Thrillers and comedies are good genres, whereas action films on a low-budget will look cheap. My film was a comedy with young people and looks grungy but it suits the film.

If you're making a microbudget film below half a million, that is, making a film independent of a distributor, it's like being an ethnic minority – you have to try twice as hard and be twice as good. If a distributor has put money in a film they are gonna distribute it even if it's mediocre. For a distributor to make an acquisition, the film has to be exceptional. It's hard to break even on a film with no distribution attached. The key is not to think of making a profit but to take steps to minimise the downside. For example, make a sellable genre, get a name, shoot it on a format that suits the film, and make something that separates your film from the other 500 films made that year. It's not so easy.

With my first feature I tried to sell it myself. I took a stand in the British pavilion in Cannes and stood bored for 11 days. Do not try to sell your own film because you have no idea of the buyers and they'll eat you alive. I made money on our film on UK video where we shipped 3000 units and made a nice profit. We also made a TV sale through our UK distributor. We had the choice of theatrical or straight to video, and the costs on paper were better to release on video only, so we dispensed with ego. The common mistakes made by new film makers are that the script is shit, the actors are shit and that they think that 90 minutes of just having a film makes a good film. The competition is huge, anyone can pick up a video camera now and call themselves a director. If everyone is telling you the script is bad, it probably is. If the film doesn't make money, live with it and move on.'

Hold regular production meetings with your production team, keeping your eye on all the balls, even if you aren't dealing with problems directly. Keep meetings as short as possible, except the very late night ones which will inevitably turn into production team de-stressing chill-outs.

This constant failure on set can get spirits down, and when the pressure increases, so the sparks can fly. During the shoot, some cast and crew members will crack. If the producer sees this happening, they should get that person off set and calmed down. More often than not, a group hug and a chat along the lines of '*I know you're doing the impossible, I know it hasn't gone to plan, but we're all in this together, I wouldn't have anyone else doing your job. I know that you will do your best, which is good enough for all of us. There, there, there*', the crew member cries on your shoulder, they calm down, and you send them back to the front line.

Don't PANIC!

Other people on the cast and crew will have good reason to panic. Almost anything conceivable could screw up and cause all manner of headaches, which combined with extraordinary pressure, exhaustion and dreadful working conditions could easily lead to panic or a flair up on set. Whatever happens, the producer (and for that matter the director too), should never lose it. This is not a multi-million dollar film where you can stomp your feet and throw your weight around. If you do, next morning, you'll find yourself a couple of actors and crew members short. The cast and crew, much like troops in battle, must always feel that the people at the top are completely in charge and know exactly what they are doing. And like the military, if you feel the need to complain, moan or blow off steam, do not do this with any cast or crew member, '*always complain upwards in the chain of command*'. Call a friend or relative and moan to them. The editor can also be a good confidante and therapist for the director and producer as they are not directly involved in the on-set manufacturing process. You may well get used to eating your lunch sat in front of an Avid, watching yesterday's rushes, but really you are having a whinge about . . . '*blah blah blah . . .*'

Second director

One of the most valuable things the producer can bring to the project is that of a second level of creative veneer. The producer is not a direct '*creative*' but is one of the only crew members who will have a '*higher*' view of everything. Assuming the producer hasn't been sucked into dealing with the day to day trivia of production, they should be hanging out on set, checking rushes, speaking to actors when the director isn't talking to them, encouraging other creative crew members and wherever possible, clarifying and refining stuff. An eagle eyed producer is likely to spot a fundamental story telling mistake that is esoteric in nature. For example, in the last feature I produced, a character turned up on set wearing a costume that I felt was inappropriate. It wasn't a big problem but it did have a fairly major impact on the characterisation. No-one else saw this as a problem and it would have gone unnoticed had I not raised my concerns (remember I was not in the forest so could see the wood). When we all looked closely at '*the problem*', everyone agreed that it was a not quite right and it was quickly dealt with.

Remember, this stuff is rarely 'black and white' and mostly about ideas in the grey area of interpretation and vision, etc.

If the director isn't available for off-set creative consultation (because they're on set working their arse off), then the creative producer can step into the role of secondary director. Not all producers are comfortable with this as some people are simply motivated by the organisation and business end of film making. Personally (at this level) I feel that many roles, while still distinct, tend to merge. The producer may end up doing a bit of directing, the director will certainly do some producing, the editor may record sound for a day, everyone is to some degree interchangeable. That's one of the reasons why I prefer the term *'film maker'* than labelling myself as director, producer, editor, visual effects supervisor, writer etc. (all of which I, and many other low budget film makers I know, have been paid to professionally do).

Stroking the luvvies

One very important job that a producer can perform is that of ego massage for the cast. Some actors require a quite staggering amount of attention. The producer, being one of the only crew members without a specific minute by minute, hour by hour job can help here. A quick drink, chat in the cutting room or late night dinner with an actor can turn around a difficult problem. One thing that I am a great advocate of (that many other film makers shy away from) is that of showing the cast and crew portions of the edited film as we go. We all understand the fundamentals of film making but there is no greater motivator than to show people the individual shots cut together with a few sound effects and music to create the illusion of a movie. There is genuine magic here. Any actor who has had doubts because of the apparent *'incompetence'* that they may have experienced during the shoot, will be charmed by this magical illusion. On rare occasions, actors who are particularly worried about their appearance or are overly self-critical will not enjoy these screenings and it's best to keep them out.

Of course, the director will be the biggest problem when showing the cast and crew the clips (as they will feel very exposed). It's up to the producer to convince the director that even though they may feel uncomfortable, it's going to result in a more motivated and excited cast and crew.

Overload danger

A big problem for both the producer and the director is that of losing direction and focus through a kind of overload, be it organisational, financial or creative. This is one of the reasons why in the real world, films are often shot in slightly more sensible hours and sometimes only five days a week. There is no real answer to this problem aside from rest and relaxation (which you can't have!) or by delegating. On every film I have made so far, whether I or my business partner, Genevieve,

Try and avoid drinking to relax, you will pay for it the next day. You can't be late. You can't pull a sickie. You are the leader and must always be seen to lead by example. Sleep is the drug of choice so get as much of it as you can, whenever you can.

Alice Dawson
Line Producer

'My job is to help organise to shoot the film the director wants to shoot, but within the budget the producer has provided. Within this equation there is an inherent conflict, which is part of the fun of the job. Above all we must get the film shot. Half a film is no film! But then it's important to strive to understand the director's vision. Clearly there is plenty of opportunity for confrontation, especially when something goes wrong, but you must always move forward. Never allocate blame. It doesn't matter what happened, it's how it will be fixed. There is always a way to get on with it, something will always mess things up and you just have to deal with it. Ironically, good things will often come out of disaster as people are forced to be more creative.

Reading the script and doing the breakdown will help you get intimate with every aspect of the story and characters contained within it. After all, you are not the director or writer, but it's still essential your knowledge of the screenplay is as great. It's about getting to know the story intimately and its ramifications. In reading and creating the breakdown, lots of questions will be prompted which in turn will force you to find out exactly HOW you will do it.

Don't waste time shooting stuff you know won't make it to the final cut. This is the greatest sin. Everyone on the cast and crew will sense that the work is not needed, their energy will be sapped and time and money will be wasted. All in the pursuit of what is most commonly a trivial whim of a powerful cast or crew member.'

was directing, there would be a time when overload was hit and the director's reigns were temporarily handed over to someone else for a morning or afternoon (whilst batteries were recharged by lying down in a dark room and listening to some music). I guess the trick is to realise when you are in overload and immediately stop and delegate rather than flap around like a headless chicken, which will help no one or the project.

Accounts nightmare

In the weeks running up to the shoot and during the shoot itself, there will be no time to prepare your accounts for a VAT quarter. You'll know in advance when your VAT return is due and can plan your shoot to miss it, or you may be able to convince the VAT office that you will be unable to do your return on time. Whatever happens, do not plan to do your accounts during the shoot, as it simply will not happen.

Inevitable re-writes

When the shit hits the fan on set, the creative producer can perform a very important job. Typically, some kind of disaster on set could force a re-write. It could be caused by dropping behind schedule and four pages of script need to be condensed to a half page, or something just didn't play out in front of the camera as it was expected to when it was written etc. Whatever the problem, a re-write will be needed. The creative producer who has had their finger in all the pies – script, schedule, casting, editing, etc. – will be the best person to either perform this re-write or oversee it with the writer. Remember, you won't have much time, perhaps even only an hour over lunch before it is re-shot or integrated into the schedule. It's a quickening moment when you realise that all those months (perhaps years) of poring over your screenplay are now going to be subject to a slash and burn followed by a brutal quick-fix. This is why you must know everything intimately – characters, character motivations, character histories, as well as actor availability, scheduling clashes, etc.

In the cutting room

Each morning, the editor digitises and begins assembly of the previous day's material. This is a terrific opportunity for the producer to spend a little time examining the footage to see where improvements can be made – be it in photography, sound, production design, acting, direction and of course the all important coverage (are there enough shots?). If problems arise, the producer should have the creative ability to work with the editor to find the best way to quickly, efficiently and most importantly appropriately (from a creative perspective) fix problems. Often, these sessions will result in a shot list that will be given to the director, or the producer will act as a second unit director and do these shots independently (assuming they are minor shots).

The producer acting as second unit director is an excellent idea (assuming the producer has managed to delegate the majority of the mundane production issues and has an understanding of the film making process). Lunchtimes are an ideal time to catch up as the main unit will not be using the equipment. As long as the director can grab either a bold camera assistant or a camera operator, one or two quick shots can often be knocked off. There will always be resistance to this, especially from the AD department and the lighting camera person. However, you are fighting a battle of coverage and you have equipment, locations and actors at your disposal. If it can be done, it should be done.

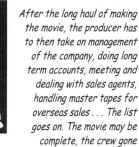

After the long haul of making the movie, the producer has to then take on management of the company, doing long term accounts, meeting and dealing with sales agents, handling master tapes for overseas sales . . . The list goes on. The movie may be complete, the crew gone home, but the producer is still going to be working hard.

After the shoot

Most real problems start after the shoot. You've run out of money. You owe too much money. The shoot went badly and you will need extra shoots for which there is no money. Nightmare. Now is the time to cut a promo and start seeking more cash, starting with all your existing investors who you can tempt into parting with a bit more. There are no tricks or quick fixes, you just have to get through it. This is a very tough time for the producer. Get on the phone and keep talking, it's the best way to convince people that there are no serious problems.

Premiere

After the film is completed, the producer will probably organise a premiere. Many low budget film makers fob their cast and crew off with a special screening, often on a Sunday morning, at a central London cinema. Personally, I believe everyone has worked so long and hard to make the movie that a glitzy premiere is in order. Yes I know you have run out of budget, but this is a one time only deal, and I look at it as something like a wedding where friends, family, cast and crew can all dress up in posh frocks and DJ's, have some drinks and generally applaud each other. Saturday night at BAFTA, 195 Piccadilly, has so far been my preferred venue. Yes it's expensive but I have always found someone who has been able to help me with the bill.

More than anyone, you the film maker deserve this moment of glory. So find a venue, get some booze, rent the posh clobber and wallow in the glory of what you have achieved, even if it is only for one evening. Remember, you have a lot of work ahead of you in sales and distribution, so enjoy and remember this moment.

The Crew Blueprint

FUJIFILM

The size of your crew will be defined by your budget. No matter how many people offer to work for free, they will always need to travel and eat food, so they are NEVER free. The budget breaks here are to help you figure out just how many people you should be working with. Remember, hire the most enthusiastic and experienced people you can find. These are my 'terms', not the industry's — speak to anyone in the film business and they'll tell you that 'low budget' means under two million quid!

Core group

These are the people who make the film happen, a director (who may or may not be a writer) and a producer. Sometimes, a production assistant will slip into this group too. All will need to work for free to get the project up and running.

Crew of tenish

Ultra micro budget, probably a digital film shooting for £10-20kish, for between one and two weeks or a number of weekends. Department heads only with all hands on deck, all of the time. Hard work but short and sweet.

Crew of twentyish

Micro budget, £20-50kish, probably shooting on Super16mm or digital for between two and three weeks, with a number of re-shoots later down the line. Same team, with a few extras to help all round. Mean and lean but susceptible to acute fatigue.

Crew of thirtyish

Low budget, £50-200kish, shooting on S16mm or 35mm for between four and six weeks, with re-shoots and pick-ups later. Same team, just more again. Now starting to work like a well oiled machine rather than the over-stretched teams for the micro budgeted movies.

Crew of fortyish

Medium low budget, £200-£600kish . . .OK, everyone is taking a pay cut but this is how the industry would make a fully financed film. Shooting for six to seven weeks, on 35mm . . . what on earth would they do with all that cash?

Above and beyond

It does happen, a new film maker finds themselves behind the wheel of a monstrous budget, working with an experienced and older crew . . . more often than not, they will be invited to leave . . . or more likely, unceremoniously booted out.

The Crew Blueprint

The crew are the creative labourers who operate the mechanics of your film making machine – be that the camera, sound and lighting equipment . . . or making the actors look good, the set convincing, the location appropriately dressed . . . or working on the support mechanisms by supplying the crew with paperwork, information, food and drinks.

The guys and gals whose tireless labour, skill and energy helps make the movie what it is – good or bad!

This section contains a number of production models for crews of different sizes and budgets. As a general rule, as the budget grows so does the size of crew, which will create more professional shooting conditions, which in turn will produce more professional results . . . but always at a slower pace. Let's be clear though. More 'professional' does not in any way mean better story telling by default. A great script on a £10k budget will almost certainly make a better film than a poor script on a £10m budget (which does not mean your £10k film will do better business, see the section on sales and distribution. But it may open other doors to new opportunities).

Right person for the right job

As the film maker at the top, producer and director, it's your job to hire the best people for the job. That doesn't mean the most experienced. Experience can sometimes come with intolerable ego and continual dissention over working conditions and the budget. A dedicated, eager wannabe who is unproven but you get the positive vibe that they could pull it off, whatever job they will do, is preferable to a talented, established, experienced professional who has reluctantly agreed to do your film and will spend most of the time complaining. Clearly as the budget increases so this particular problem diminishes (conditions and pay improve).

Shootingpeople.org, a network and community especially useful for new film makers. An ideal starting point to find eager crew.

The core group of your film will be the producer, writer and director (often the writer and director are the same person). Over time, others will be adopted into this inner sanctum of your film family, usually people like the production manager/assistant and editor, as they will be around the production so long (and not necessarily during the glorious shoot phase) that they will fully experience the unending hell

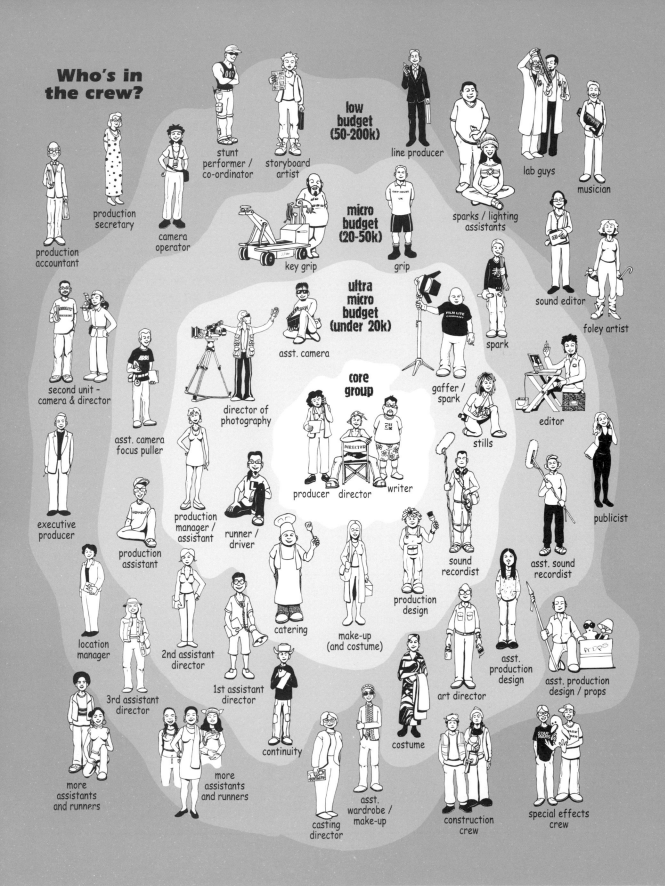

Who's in the crew?

low budget (50-200k)

micro budget (20-50k)

ultra micro budget (under 20k)

core group

production accountant

production secretary

camera operator

stunt performer / co-ordinator

storyboard artist

line producer

sparks / lighting assistants

lab guys

musician

key grip

grip

sound editor

foley artist

asst. camera

spark

gaffer / spark

editor

second unit – camera & director

asst. camera focus puller

director of photography

stills

executive producer

production manager / assistant

runner / driver

producer

director

writer

sound recordist

asst. sound recordist

publicist

production assistant

catering

make-up (and costume)

production design

location manager

2nd assistant director

asst. production design

art director

asst. production design / props

3rd assistant director

1st assistant director

continuity

costume

more assistants and runners

more assistants and runners

casting director

asst. wardrobe / make-up

construction crew

special effects crew

that is low budget film making. Many late nights will be spent consuming far too many takeaways and too much booze.

Finding the crew

Finding and hiring the best people for the job is both easy and hard. About 70% of the positions on your crew will be filled without much difficulty (camera, runners, musicians, editors, etc.) but the remaining 30% will always be tough to find – there are just some jobs that are not much fun to do, are often thankless, and you can't risk hiring completely inexperienced people (gaffer, sound recordist etc.) The best place to find your crew is under the recommendation of other film makers who have made low budget films.

You're not looking to hire the most talented people (but it does help if they are very talented), you're going to be looking for folk with team spirit, hard workers, good communicators, optimistic disposition, unfussy and crucially, not in any way doing it for the money. Once you hire one or two crew members, they will probably know other crew who know other crew . . . and so you can follow the chain of recommendations and invite people to join your 'motley crew'.

There are agencies that represent crew members but you can forget them because you are not paying. There are several internet resources where crew, both experienced and inexperienced, keep a look out for jobs – mandy.com and shootingpeople.org for instance. Even the dedicated actors newsletters such as PCR and SBS will result in crew members contacting you (as film making is such a hot bed of heightened emotion it's not surprising that many actors are romantically partnered to crew members).

How long?

Each crew member will be needed for a unique amount of time. Some starting early (such as the production manager/assistant), some starting on the first day of the shoot (such as the sound recordist), others finishing months after the shoot (such as the editor).

On the whole, people are never given enough time to do their job properly, something that can lead to considerable stress. On a day to day basis, especially during the shoot, its essential not to over work the crew to the point of exhaustion as it will lead to complete breakdown. Avoid shooting more than 12 hours a day and 6 days a week. Remember people have to get to and from location/set which may add an extra hour and a half to their shooting day, and they also need to deal with things like paying the rent, doing their laundry etc. Everyone needs time between shooting days, so you can't have a midnight wrap and a 6 a.m. call the next day. The production does not own the crew, they are welcome and helpful guests.

Who's in the crew?

The plan to the left outlines rough groups for the four budgets – starting with the core crew in the middle, then moving out through the different levels. These are NOT absolute – stories, directors, producers etc. may suggest different crew structures. These models represent the simplest ways I would do it, and have done it, at the various budget breaks. Some crew members are possibly multi functional – director as writer, editor as sound editor, director as composer etc.

Rather distressingly, you will launch careers whilst your own appears to stand still, or crawl along. As other crew members move onto bigger and better things, you will be left holding the baby – arguing with sales agents, pacifying investors, doing accounts - none of which is actually the making of films!

Brian Shemmings
Health and Safety

'Overall there is an awareness amongst most producers to ensure they do the right thing in terms of health and safety. If there is no H&S officer on a low/no budget film, there should really be someone on the crew who has taken a health and safety course, like the 1ˢᵗ AD – because they're on the floor all the time. There's no use having someone from the prod office as your H&S officer because they're in the office all the time. One needs to pay special attention when working in old buildings and at heights and roofs, that's where you need your specialist advice. Ok, in a field or main studio floor, in the main it's straightforward as Health and Safety is 90% common sense, 10% technical, like using mobile elevated platforms such as scissor lifts or erecting camera platforms.

With things like fire effects and explosive effects, I urge you to use a properly qualified technician. Films that employ car stunts, leaping from roof tops and heights should use a stunt co-ordinator. Don't be frightened to ask H&S officers to come to work on your film, no matter what the budget. If something happens, then the small budget goes through the window.

If an accident happens on set, it's in the hands of the insurers in terms of any possible claim. Serious accidents are investigated and the producer is then duty bound to submit a report to the H&S officer if a crew or artist is absent for more than 3 days. In the end it's about common sense. Don't take undue risks. It's silly to do so. Create a safe film set. Don't get carried away. At the end of the day it's only a film.'

How much?

How much you pay your crew is up to you, but the less you pay them, the more difficult it will be for them to validate (to partners, debtors, bank managers etc) why they are doing it. If they can't afford to exist, they can't do your film. This is one of the reasons why so many crew members tend to be quite young – they are happy to rough it like students, or better still they live at home with their parents which keeps their personal overheads so low that they can afford to take time off to do the movie. I would also recommend that whatever you pay your crew, you pay everyone the same amount, be they the toilet cleaning floor runner or the visionary DP.

In essence, everyone is doing the film for free, you are just greasing their palm with a small payment to cover their expenses with just enough left for beer and fags. For example, on my second film, 'White Angel' which was made using the second model here (£20k–£50k budget), we paid crew members £50 a week, plus everyone was also offered a one month tube pass. On my third film, 'Urban Ghost Story' which was produced on the third model (£50k-£200k), the crew were paid £100 a week and given expenses. In both instances, nobody complained about the pay. Everyone was there because they wanted to be part of this opportunity and experience.

Big break

The big bargaining tool you can offer to all crew members is that of experience. A professional camera operator may choose to do your film if they are bumped up to director of photography (DP), a sound assistant may do your film if they get to record sound instead of holding the boom. These are career breaks that professionals find hard to get, but once they have that oh–so–important credit on their CV, and a clip on their show reel, they may find themselves getting jobs on films that prior to your project, they would not have got.

Many crew members will see the small investment of a couple of weeks work, maybe even as much as a couple of months, as a sound investment from moving up from set dresser who was previously paid £500 a week to production designer who will now be paid £1500 a week, so don't feel bad or apologetic about working conditions and pay. You are offering a very big break, and ultimately we're all grown ups and you're not holding a gun to anybody's head. They are free to say 'no thanks'.

Of course, there is a flip side. You need to be completely professional. This is not an amateur shoot. This is a fully professional feature film, except, everyone working on it is an investor in spirit. If you behave unprofessionally, you will be pulled up on it.

As examples of this 'big break for free work deal', each and every film that I have made has been crewed by younger and less experienced people than

Stop the rot before it spreads

If you find you have some rotten apples in your barrel, typically people who consistently complain about conditions and pay, or people who are frustrated creatives in the belief that it is their divine right to be in control and do nothing but criticise and undermine other creatives (most commonly the director) then you maybe forced to remove them.

No one likes to fire a crew member and the crew don't like having one of their colleagues removed, but sometimes it's essential to stop the rot from spreading. And make no mistake, stressed and exhausted leadership, over working, bad working conditions, poor food . . . all common to low budget films . . . is a fertile environment for dissention, rumour mills and if not treated swiftly, mutiny!

the fully professional version would have been. Whenever I move to the next film, I of course would like to hire the same crew but almost always find that the talented people I previously worked with don't need the break anymore. Whilst they might want to do the film for old times sake, they are unable to do so because they now carry the trappings of wealth, such as a new car, mortgage, perhaps even partner with children. Those who do come back, almost invariably take a step up the ladder – for instance, Stuart Roweth was a spark on my second film 'White Angel', was camera operator on 'Urban Ghost Story' and is now a professional DP. Harry Gregson Williams wrote the score for 'White Angel', his first film. He then went on to do little films like 'Armageddon', 'Enemy of the State', 'Chicken Run' . . .

Lead not rule

On a philosophical point, you the film maker, the creative and business head of the production, should seek at all times to lead and not rule. It's a subtle distinction. Like the stories of great generals of the Roman Empire, you must always be seen to fearlessly fight on the front line, eating with the grunts and generally inspiring the crew through limitless enthusiasm, appreciation of hard work, tolerance of genuine error and at all times a exude a cool, even tempered, unflappable impression that you are in complete control.

If you choose to rule your crew, very quickly people will quit. No one will be barked at to do a dull, overworked, underpaid and thankless task. If you want to rule, get your chequebook out. It's the only way they will stay. Leadership comes easily to some people; a crew can sense it in the director almost immediately. If you do not have such a temperament, you'll need to work on it before you get to set.

Cock-ups

Everyone makes mistakes. In light of the fact that you are not paying people and they are often being asked to do jobs they are not used to, you have to accept that there will be a number of silly mistakes. Generally, you don't need to give any crew

Every crew member must be responsible for their accounting to you. Without a valid receipt, you cannot give people their expenses or costs as that money will simply not exist in your accounts. No receipt, no money. Be tough or you will pay at the end.

LIVING SPIRIT

● Living Spirit Pictures Limited, Ealing Film Studios, Ealing Green, Ealing, London, W5 5EP ●
● Tel 020 8758 8544 ● Fax/Messages 020 8758 8559 ● mail@livingspirit.com ● www.livingspirit.com ●

GENERAL CREW AGREEMENT

FROM: Living Spirit Pictures Limited
TO: JOHN DOE
DATED: 12/03/2004

Dear John Doe,

Re Rocket Boy ("the Film")

This is to confirm your engagement by this Company on the following terms and conditions: -

1. We hereby engage and you hereby agree to render your services as (*Crew Member's position*) in connection with the film (**"the Film"**).

2. Your total fee for all services rendered by you and for all rights granted to us hereunder shall be £100. The said fee shall constitute full compensation for the exploitation of the products of your services hereunder in all media worldwide. No further pay shall be due. The said fee shall cover all overtime, any no-meal breaks in time, or petty cash in lieu of meal breaks. It will cover all payments for night work, and this fee is inclusive of payment for holiday credits. It will not cover pre-approved expenses, which will be paid at the end of the contract on production of receipts.

3. Your engagement will commence on the 1st day of April 2004 and terminate on the 7th day of April 2004.

4. We shall be entitled to your exclusive services throughout the period of your engagement and you agree to render your services to the best of your skill and ability at such times and wherever we may require and in accordance with our instructions. We shall not without your approval (not to be unreasonably withheld) require you to work more than a 12 hour day from arrival on set to release on set.

5. All rights in your services and any products thereof are and shall remain our absolute property and copyright or that of our assignees. You hereby by way of present assignment of both present and future copyright, assign with full guarantee all such products to us to hold throughout the world for the full period of copyright and all renewals and extensions thereof. You further irrevocably waive the benefits of any rights under Sections 77-85 inclusive of the Copyright Designs and Patents Act 1988 and any provision of law known as "Moral Rights" or any similar laws under any jurisdiction now or hereinafter enacted. You hereby confirm that the above assignment includes an assignment of all rental and lending rights and the compensation payable under this agreement is full and equitable consideration for such rights.

If you are in agreement with the foregoing, kindly sign the enclosed copy of this letter and return it to us at the above address, your payment will then be sent by return of post.

Yours sincerely,   Accepted and Agreed

....
For and on behalf of Living Spirit Pictures Limited   For and on behalf of *John Doe*

This crew contract was composed for and used by Amulet films on their 35mm films, 'Ghosthunter' and 'Moth'. www.amuletfilms.com

NOTE – THIS CONTRACT IS PRINTED HERE AS A GUIDELINE ONLY AND SHOULD NOT BE RELIED UPON WITHOUT TAKING LEGAL ADVICE.

---

member a hard time about this, as they will feel terribly guilty and rather stupid for doing it in the first place. Just make sure they don't keep doing it.

Production meetings

At the end of each day it's good to hold a very brief 2-3 minute production meeting for the crew. Remember that they are investors in the film as well and should be treated with respect. Use the meeting to keep them informed as to how much was shot or dropped in the day, what you'll be shooting tomorrow, what you have just been editing and how good it looks etc. The AD department will also use this time to pass out call sheets for the next day.

Wherever possible, congratulate a crew member whose hard work generally goes unnoticed and (if appropriate) give them a little round of applause. It's a bit happy clappy I know but everyone leaves set with a goofy grin and the person whose hard work was recognised will work that bit harder the next day.

Producer on set

During the shoot, a smart producer will take a moment every so often to visit the crew members that perform the worst and most unappreciated jobs. Taking a cup of tea to a stressed out production runner, who would normally take a cup of tea to the producer is sending a strong and simple message – 'the most important person on the film (the producer) values the contribution of the least important person on the production (me)'. Result? The 'valued' crew member works as hard as they can due to 'inspiring' leadership.

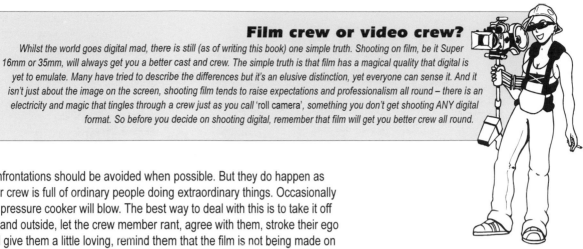

Film crew or video crew?

Whilst the world goes digital mad, there is still (as of writing this book) one simple truth. Shooting on film, be it Super 16mm or 35mm, will always get you a better cast and crew. The simple truth is that film has a magical quality that digital is yet to emulate. Many have tried to describe the differences but it's an elusive distinction, yet everyone can sense it. And it isn't just about the image on the screen, shooting film tends to raise expectations and professionalism all round – there is an electricity and magic that tingles through a crew just as you call 'roll camera', something you don't get shooting ANY digital format. So before you decide on shooting digital, remember that film will get you better crew all round.

Confrontations should be avoided when possible. But they do happen as your crew is full of ordinary people doing extraordinary things. Occasionally the pressure cooker will blow. The best way to deal with this is to take it off set and outside, let the crew member rant, agree with them, stroke their ego and give them a little loving, remind them that the film is not being made on a low budget out of choice and that everyone is under pressure . . . most of all, ensure that they know that you understand and sympathise. *'It's alright to make mistakes, just do your best . . .'* Then send them back into the furnace.

Crew of 10ish Ultra Micro Budget

Ultra micro budget . . . Under 20k and probably shot on Digi-beta or minDV in 2 weeks or over a number of weekends. Shot with a minimal crew of around 10ish.

How much is your crew going to cost you? You're going to be working with ex-film school students and inexperienced wannabes, with an occasional pro getting a big break (camera assistant doing lighting etc). This is going to be a big break for them so they'll work for little or no pay. If you get someone who wants to be paid more, ditch them and find somebody else. They will just complain about working conditions, bad food and that the whole production is 'below them'. They will make your life hell.

Shooting for two weeks with a crew of around ten, paying them £50 a week for just the duration of the shoot will blow 10% of a £10k budget. Some will need to work weeks in advance, burdening the budget yet more. £50 a week is about as little as you can get away with as all it really covers is fags, transport, and an occasional beer. You're going to be shooting on a digital tape format, ideally digital BetaCam and in a worst case scenario, miniDV.

Working with a crew this size means you'll travel light. There isn't much equipment and at a push, you can get your cast, crew and kit in two cars and a van. You will be able to shoot quickly but the shots will be 'from the hip' and rougher than a slower shoot with bigger crew. There will be little or no control of your shooting environment and in many ways, you will have to go with whatever happens in front of the camera. What most crews call 'necessities', you'll call 'luxuries'.

Everyone will be expected to look after themselves, even the actors. Some actors will buy into this and embrace it, turning in spontaneous performances and enjoying the adventure. Others will see it as 'amateurish', 'slap-dash' and 'below them'. They'll complain about working conditions, catering, having to wear their own clothes blah blah . Cast enthusiastic and friendly actors. In auditions, be explicit about the way in which they will be expected to work . . . So who is on the crew?

Director

We're all familiar with what the director generally does and more than likely it is you or your business partner who is directing.

Shooting a 90-minute feature in 2 weeks is a massive creative accomplishment. You will be forced to direct from the hip, making compromises left, right and centre. Very quickly, the director can develop a kind of creative blindness and suffer panic attacks – *'all my shots are the same', 'I'm not getting enough shots', 'the locations were all wrong', 'the actors were rubbish'* etc. Try and keep production problems away from the director, keep them on a need to know basis. Buy them a Walkman and so they can listen to music when thinking about what to do next otherwise everyone will continually ask them questions. You'll constantly slip behind schedule and look forward to those scenes where you realise you can do two pages of dialogue in one shot. Fatigue is a problem as the director will be unable to stop and rest during the weeks leading up to and including the shoot.

'What do you mean there isn't time to do it in three shots? And where are the crew? We've only been shooting for twenty hours. What's their problem?"

In brief . . .
The creative head of the film, possibly the writer and editor too. Driven, blinkered and egomaniacal, the director is the accelerator of the production . . .

Needs to be able to hold the whole film in their head, to make fast decisions, to inspire and get the best out of people, and at all costs, to look utterly in control.

Unfortunately, the director will also have to assist (AD) themselves, keeping cast and crew aware of what is happening next. You may pull on the services of a production manager or runner to help out but they're not the exclusive property of the director. The producer should also stand in as a surrogate AD where possible, but this is infrequent as the producer is constantly fixing problems.

At this budget level, the director will probably be the editor as well. You can take a view on this but at the end of the day, there will be no budget to pay someone for the 3-6 months you need to edit your film.

Producer

Producing a feature film for under £10k is arguably the worst job on the planet. It can and has been done many times, but there will be a steady stream of people who will confidently and knowingly tell you *'it's impossible', 'you're mad', 'get a real job'* etc. Ignore them, most likely they are jealous that you are living the dream while they are stacking shelves at the local supermarket. The other issue at this level is that of 'problem overload'. There are simply so many problems to be dealt with that the producer will become swamped.

On micro budgets, the producer isn't really a producer either, they are a production manager / line producer. They fix the problems that come out of the 'manufacturing' process of film making. The biggest problem facing this producer is stress and fatigue. Very quickly the joy and excitement of making the film will be replaced by a dread of phone calls and the realisation that the film making process for you is little more than a production assault course and endurance test.

'I am sorry but I have a problem called producer's cramp, it prevents me from signing cheques"

In brief . . .
The controlling force of the business end of the film who has to find solutions to truly impossible problems. Rarely thanked or recognised, the micro budget producer seldom dashes out to do it again. If the director is the accelerator of the production, the producer is the brake . . .

Not a job for the faint hearted and best suited to the stubborn pragmatist who knows when to stand their ground, and when to run like hell. Needs the desire to make the film at all 'non financial' costs. Should be good at finding solutions rather than being right. Will become part crew therapist, part accountant, part solicitor, part negotiator . . . oh and a small part film maker.

Production manager/assistant/AD

A friendly, helpful, multifunctional assistant who should start early in the process, giving them a month or two to help prep. Get them to break down the script and start finding creative and alternative ways to fix myriad problems thrown up by this process. Locations, props, production consumables, special costumes (uniforms like police, nurses, army, men in black etc), general production equipment (vans and cars are always a big problem), film production equipment etc – all need to be dealt with. Given enough time, a plucky, polite and endearing telephone manner, followed by a brief, well worded letter will solve almost any problem . . . *'Hi . . . yes I need three elephants tomorrow morning, can you help . . .?'* I don't want to be sexist but the majority of decision makers that this production assistant will bump into in their quest for 'the impossible for free' will undoubtedly be bored, middle-aged men. Not surprising then that a young, flirtatious, engaging female voice will usually get better results. Sorry about this, my e-mail is chris@livingspirit.com if you feel the need to send me some hate mail.

"We've done so much, for so little, for so long, that we're now qualified to do anything for nothing!"

In brief . . .
The production fixer, whatever it is, they will hopefully find a way of getting it done / found / acquired / borrowed / nicked . . .

Needs the ability to take any problem and find a cheap solution. People skills (especially on the phone) and organisational skills essential. Must drive and be able to push a computer, specifically Word and Excel, to the limits. Supports the producer first, then anyone else can make requests. Directly oversees the runners.

A close relationship will develop between the producer and production assistant, often resulting in a good cop / bad cop scenario, or the PA softening before the producer hits hard etc. This person must have a full, clean driving licence, ideally own their own car (although they may be able to blag a free car) and must be able to use a computer to the fullest. If the assistant has any friends who are also good on the phone or with computers, they may well find themselves invited into the furnace. In the run up to the shoot, the director will also do their fair share of production managing, although they will lean toward creative tasks such as casting and locations.

Case Study – 'Being Considered'

Jonathon Newman's 'Being Considered' was shot on S16mm and edited for under £10k! It's available to buy or rent on both VHS and DVD so its quality was high enough to bring it to market. It's a simple light hearted comedy starring James Dreyfus, Saeed Jaffrey and a bunch of other new actors. It was shot over 21 days, spread over four weeks, with a crew of around ten . . .

'I directed and produced as well as assistant directed myself which was hard work. Everyone worked for expenses only, it was the only way I could get it done for the money. It would have been great to be able to pay the crew but this isn't possible on a no-budgeter. Inevitably this means that you begin with young, eager and enthusiastic crew members (who volunteered in the first place) who by the end of the shoot, end up resenting you and the production – they feel used and taken advantage of. You don't go into the process intending to hurt or upset anybody, but this is one of the pitfalls of low budget film making. The crew consisted of myself as director, AD, producer and writer, then there was a three person camera / lighting team (as I was shooting on film I needed more people than I might if I was shooting digitally), a make-up girl who also handled wardrobe (who was assisted by a friend), two runners, a sound recordist and boom operator, a production manager / assistant who began working on the film weeks before the shoot, a production designer with an assistant to do props (who would also pull in a few friends for the occasional bigger scenes) and a person shooting stills. 'Catering was handled by my mom. Just before the shoot we went to the local supermarket and bought a pile of food which she then cooked, sealed in plastic food boxes, and put in the freezer. Each day we would defrost, reheat and enjoy real home made food! That was the best part for the crew, great food and it only cost 20p a head!'

Camera and lighting team

Traditionally, you have a large camera team, each with their own defined job. On this shoot, you have a camera person, assistant camera and a spark / gaffer. Everyone will be interchangeable and often do each others jobs. To help lift the pressure, the director may even operate camera on occasion.

Lighting camera (DP)

This person is the most important crew member, not because they are a great artist, but because the speed at which they work will define the speed at which the whole production runs. Hire a slow and ponderous DP (director of photography) and you'll quickly slip behind schedule. It's their job to light and shoot the film, but it's the director's job to tell them where they want the camera, what they want the camera to do (hand held, on legs – that's industry speak for a tripod – or even a track and dolly shot). Prior to the shoot there should have been creative discussions about the look of the film and it's a good idea for the Director and DP to spend some time watching a few movies that have a look that is similar to what you are after.

The DP will decide on the exact equipment needed (though the producer and director will have already decided on a format – DV, DigiBeta or S16mm even – yes it's possible) which will include cameras, lights, track and dolly, cranes, stands, clamps, drapes etc. But on this budget you are going to get very little. A camera, tripod and head, and a few lights . . .

On the day the DP will work with the gaffer/spark on the placement of the lights, the assistant camera in loading film / tapes, and the director in the placing and lining up of shots etc. The big problem is that three people just aren't enough as the process is so physically demanding. It's possible that the camera team could grind to a halt through simple physical exhaustion.

You should get between 20-40 shots a day, and that's going some. Any more and you're not taking enough care and attention. Fundamentally, the most important thing to do is to shoot the action so that the audience understands what is happening in the drama. If the shit hits the fan you may be forced to step back and shoot the scene in one 'wide angle' shot . . . *'I know you want to do it in seven shots but we only have time for one . . . so pull wide and go!'*

The director should always be planning ahead, thinking about the next few shots and warning the DP of anything weird or difficult. When looking for a DP ask the important question . . . *'do you have an estate car so we don't need to hire another van . . . ?'* A large estate car will comfortably house the camera department kit (and maybe one or two small lights), but not the main lights and grips (if you have any).

'Vell you zee, I am an artiste. I sculpt vis light'

*In brief . . .
Controls the look of the image. Often competes with the director for creative supremacy and can be extraordinarily arrogant and stubborn.*

Needs to be part artist, part technician, part sergeant major. Overall head of camera department, often with several people below them. Often asked to make scenes look amazing when only lit with three cheap lights. Ideally should be good at making the cast feel secure. No-one should work harder than them, their team being the first on set and the last to go home.

'Do I look cool with my bat belt?'

In brief . . .
Assist the DoP in all aspects, pull focus, change magazines / swap tapes, log shots and generally keep the department organised.

Must be a consummate technician. Always a couple of steps ahead of where you are currently at. Usually keeps to themselves, quietly doing their job efficiently. Usually go unrecognised for their exceptional skills.

Assistant Camera

This person will take care of managing the camera kit, ensuring the camera is always loaded, writing out report sheets, pulling focus during shots (when needed), checking the camera gate, and generally doing whatever the DoP needs to help get the shot in the can, or, er, on the miniDV tape!

Gaffer / spark

This person will look after the lights and the rigging of the lights. You don't have too many lights but this is an exhausting job, so before you yell at a spark to hurry, remember they've been hauling lights all day. If you can manage to get them an unpaid assistant or trainee, that will help. Much of this job isn't rocket science and there is always a piece of kit to be carried, a stand to be supported, a switch to be flicked at the appropriate moment etc.

'Where d'ya want it guvnor?'

In brief . . .
Rugged and hard working, it's their job to set up the lights after the DoP has told them what is needed. Always hard to find good sparks to work for low pay. Gaffer is at the top, with sparks below. Physical strength and endurance are needed, and don't think that means muscles. Should have an understanding of electrical wiring, and lighting techniques.

Lighting and water don't go well together, whether that's a swimming pool or rainy night, you are just asking for problems. The overwhelmingly huge problem for the lighting team is always *'where do I get my power'* (you can't afford a generator). Most lights can't just be plugged into the wall (they have different plugs), so at this budget level, you need to ensure that everything is terminated in a standard wall plug . . . AND . . . that if you plug it in and switch it on you won't blow the ring main wherever you are shooting! (beware of high powered HMI lights . . .) Allied to *'where am I going to get power'* is, do *'I have an extension cable long enough?'* Get hold of as many 13 amp, long and flexible extension leads as you can lay your hands on. Production assistants regularly spend time knocking on doors asking if they can plug an extension into the neighbours power! Cheeky and ridiculous, I know, but they almost always find a sympathetic household / pub / restaurant etc. If there are any tracking shots it's going to be all hands on deck to manage the track and dolly, but on this size crew you really are pushing it.

'I know it's supposed to be a space ship, and yes of course I know it's three cardboard boxes, but if you look at it from this angle right here . . . '

In brief . . .
To make sure that everything in front of the camera is at best, thought about and designed, at worst, just appropriate.

A tough task as there is no budget or time to even prepare the most rudimentary designs. The more people on this team, the better. Things like wardrobes, cars, the simplest of props, can quickly become nightmare problems.

Design

As there is no budget, the job of the designer is more about managing what is to hand than actually creating a look. In front of the camera, the designer should focus on keeping the background to shots as interesting as possible. One dead give-away of a low budget is 'white wall syndrome' where all the walls look the same and are empty. Pictures in frames, vases, plants . . . in fact anything to break up the background will help. Keep actors as far away from the wall as possible, to create a more detailed background and impression of depth. The designer should also work with whoever is looking after locations so that the most interesting places in which to shoot are selected. It will be the designer's job to go through the screenplay and detail all the unique props that will feature in the drama, then work with

a production assistant on getting them all in a box in the office. When shooting, the designer should be allowed to see the shot and take a moment to arrange things to maximise the 'look' of whatever is in front of the camera.

They will probably come onboard a few weeks prior to shooting, assuming the production team have already taken care of major design issues such as main locations etc.

Make-up / costume

As with all other departments, it's more about management than creativity. Actors will be asked to wear their own clothes, whilst the production manager will help find special costumes (and blag for free). Keeping actors in fundamentally the same clothes throughout the story will minimise costume changes and speed up shooting. Outside of a few high impact examples, very few audience members will even notice what the actors are wearing, as long as it is appropriate to the story.

Make-up, managed by the same person, frankly, will be non existent, except for special makeup like cuts, or when a character needs a 'look'. You are going to have to go for the natural look. Thankfully most actors are extremely aware of how they look and will happily groom themselves. Make sure the DP regularly comments on how good they look.

Make-up / wardrobe should pay particular attention to continuity and the actors should be encouraged to keep an eye on this too. The space that is used for actors to wait and rest in-between takes (The green room, or in this case car / kitchen / toilet etc.) will be where Make-up / wardrobe will spend most of their time. They will need to take lots of stills for continuity so blag a free digital video camera and printer.

This person will also be a spy for production as they are the only crew member actors will feel comfortable moaning to. Keep a good channel of communication open between producer / director / make-up / wardrobe so that you can monitor potential actor problems.

Sound recordist

This is the person who records the sound, and most importantly, the dialogue of the actors. Normally they would have an assistant but you can't afford one, so they will have to muddle through it alone. This will be the hardest position to fill. At the best of times, sound is looked down upon by many crew members, and when there is no pay or an assistant, it's going to be a hard sell. They will record the sound on DAT (digital audio tape) and use various microphones, sometimes on a boom, sometimes tie clip. If you are shooting on DV

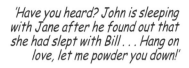

'Have you heard? John is sleeping with Jane after he found out that she had slept with Bill . . . Hang on love, let me powder you down!'

In brief . . .
Exists in the twilight world between the luvvies and the crew and can act as a conduit between the two during tough times. Takes care of the actors appearance, what they wear on their face and on their body. Spends a great deal of time making people look beautiful, a fact often overlooked by some cast members.

Must be relaxed and fun. Should help get actors 'up' so that when they leave the dressing room they are already feeling good. Need to be fastidiously organised from a continuity point of view.

'Is there any way to turn off that boiler?'

In brief . . .
It's their job to record the sound, that is, record the dialogue as 'clean' and 'crisply' as possible. Ideally, they would be assisted. Unfortunately, they are seen as a poor cousin to the camera department and often maligned as they only seem to pipe up to interfere with the actors, 'more volume love . . .' or the crew, 'could you move the generator 100 yards up the mountain path?'

Hard to find a sound recordist, never mind a good one! Get your sound wrong and you'll spend months in post trying to fix it. Needs patience, technical excellence and a keen instinct for where to place the microphone. Usually comes with own kit. Learn to record sound yourself as a backup.

or DigiBeta you may plumb the microphone directly into the camera, negating the need for a DAT machine at all (although you may need a small portable mixer instead). They should fill out sound report sheets throughout the day, something that would normally be done by the assistant sound recordist, so it may occasionally go by the wayside. If pushed, the director should be capable of filling in the job of the sound recordist as you may find yourself without one every so often – which may lead on to you considering buying a DAT recorder and a microphone or two.

The sound recordist will want to record all manner of extra sounds and wildtracks. You don't need them at this level, only get actors' voices (or wildtracks of their voices if there is a problem on set). Don't worry about recording doors, cars, footsteps and atmospheres etc. You can replace all of these later.

'. . . can I get you a cup of coffee?'

In brief . . .
Whatever is needed, off set, by the production, they go and get it. Becomes everyone's best friend when they announce they are going on a chocolate run at 11pm on a winter's night.

Young, enthusiastic and bright, a runner is often a director / producer in the making. Considered the lowest job on set, yet can hold up shooting at almost any given moment, so treat with respect. Should have their own car.

Runner / driver

The runner is simply a person who will do whatever is needed of the production – get the DP some tea, drop off the film stock, find a loo within 100 yards, buy some sandwiches, stop the traffic, stall that copper etc. It really is a thankless and relentless task. Ideally they should be able to drive and own their own car (watch out for excessive petrol receipts).

On most films the runner is the lowest of low jobs. On this film they will often be elevated to production manager status and be given breaks they would never get anywhere else. Still, it is a crap job that is essential, so producers, thank the runner(s) regularly. More than likely you will end up with more than one runner as there is always an extra cup of coffee to be made.

Stills

'OK, just hold that for 30 seconds please . . .' click click click' . . . just another 30 seconds . . . 'click click click' . . . almost there . . .' click click click

. . . .

In brief . . .
They take the photographs that will be used in publicity, often only coming in for a couple of days for key scenes and actors.

Often considered an interfering outsider as they are an infrequent visitor to the set who demands time to take their pictures. Needs to be patient but firm, and FAST! Get a pro for a couple of days and your overworked assistant camera to click off a few shots when they can

It's vital to the production that you get some good stills and it's advisable to get an experienced photographer who has done movie stills before – even if you have to pay them. They may only need to come in for a couple of days, shooting their stills on 35mm colour film and focusing on key scenes. Everyone will hate the stills photographer because they will interrupt the natural flow of production and no one, but no one, thinks that the stills are important. Trust me, without them you can't sell your movie. They'll do their shooting after each major setup, asking the cast and crew to wait for a couple of minutes whilst they shoot pics of the actors in place. They will use the lighting used by the crew so there won't be any time wasted putting up flash lighting. They should also click off a few 'crew' shots and pose a single shot of the director, er, directing. Get hold of an additional 35mm camera and a few rolls of stock and thrust it into the hands of a crew member who expresses an interest in taking some shots. Ask them to watch what the pro does, then every so often do the same themselves.

Caterer

Feeding your cast and crew is one of the biggest production headaches. You can't get away without doing it and it always costs money. On this budget, find a person who isn't a pro caterer – friends, relatives, siblings are all good candidates. Lunch can often be a large baguette and lots of fruit, with dinner being heaps of hot food such as chilli or pasta. Quantity is more important than quality. Ask your caterer to make up a six day menu and then rotate that. You will probably need to cater for veggies / vegans, so factor that in.

If possible, make as much food as you can in advance. Buy a couple of large second hand fridge/freezers and stock up prior to shooting so catering can sometimes be just a matter of reheating food. If you are shooting in a location make sure everyone eats outside, unless you can cope with spillages, which will happen (and no smoking inside either!) Plastic cutlery, paper plates and cups, and black bin bags should always be to hand. Tea and coffee is easy to deal with inside – get a free two week hot and cold water cooler trial and then cast and crew can help themselves whenever they want. Outside you will need to get hold of a couple of catering flasks with taps. Keep tabs on the tea / coffee, cups, sugar, milk, waste bins situation as it can often lead to revolt.

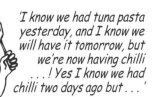

'I know we had tuna pasta yesterday, and I know we will have it tomorrow, but we're now having chilli . . . ! Yes I know we had chilli two days ago but . . . '

In brief . . .
It's their job to keep everyone fully fed and watered, breakfast, lunch, dinner, supper, snacks, tea and coffee, whatever is needed. Prepare and clean up with minimum fuss.

Usually a friend or relative. Order of business is quantity first, quality second. Think field chef near a battlefield and you are pretty close to the job. If they are doing their job, they are everyone's friend . . . If not, you have problems. Will need a space to prepare and serve, often hijacking a runner or production assistant for an hour and a half around feeding times.

The writer

The writer could appear at any budget level, but at lower budgets, it's likely that the director / producer / lead actors etc. are the writers. The screenplay will probably come from one of two different philosophies – written for this project, or written over some time and finally found its way to this project. Either way, the screenplay probably isn't as good as it could be (or someone with real cash would have optioned it) which all makes for tough film making. If the screenplay was custom written for this project, it's likely to be over wordy and under developed. If it is a long held dream script that hasn't found backing elsewhere, there are probably some flaws with it. Either way, that's all moot now, 'cos you're gonna make it anyway!

The writer will probably be a frustrated creative, desperate to direct but for some reason hasn't made it, or doesn't have the guts, ego, temperament, desire etc.), but by the time they are through with this experience it's almost certain they won't let another director screw around with their material ever again. Having the writer close to hand is a double edged sword. On the one hand it's terrific to have the story and character expert to hand. Their advice on forced or quick scene or dialogue changes (and their implications on the overall story) is invaluable, as is the ability to have that quick scene rewrite over lunch. The down side is the possibility of an ever present moaning presence . . . *'that's not what it means . . . '*, *'why did you cut that line . . . '*, *'she said her lines too quickly . . . too slow . . . '* etc. If push comes to shove,

'No. no, no . . . That's not what it means! What do you mean it's been cut . . . And who is that? What do you mean he is now a she . . . Don't you understand the character arc?'

In brief . . .
The always under-credited and unappreci-ated original 'creator' of the work on which everything else is based. It's their job to write the story, create the settings, put words into the mouths of the characters
. . .

Good writers are like hen's teeth and on low budget films, the writing often becomes a collaboration between writer / director / producer / actors etc. Beware of blindly believing in the creative talents of any one individual, if you are doubting, listen to those nagging voices - especially relevant to charismatic, confident writer / directors.

'I know you have looked forward to shooting that scene for two years, that it took three days to shoot, that it cost a huge amount of the budget . . . but it has to go . . . '

In brief . . .
It's the editors job to edit the pictures and sound, then oversee a certain amount of the final post production stages – ideally all the way through to the premiere and sales delivery.

The editor is the second 'director' of the film, looking at and re-interpreting the footage to make the best possible edit of all the material. Even tempered and enthusiastic, the editor should also be a movie buff of encyclopedic knowledge who has studied the 'form'. Instinct is also very important, they should know how to make a good cut.

producers may need to ban the writer from set. Encourage your writer to be pragmatic – everyone is doing the best and it's up to them to keep the creative possibilities as high as possible and to make the most of a once in a lifetime opportunity. If it works out well, the writer could be a secondary creative 'director', sat in the background, continually consulting with the director about character arcs, character subtlety and other less obvious story elements that may have been lost or forgotten or misinterpreted. But . . . the director has authority and must NEVER be challenged, at least not in front of cast and crew.

Editor

If you can get an editor it is a tremendous advantage as they should be employed to start editing from day two of the shoot (although to cut costs, the director may edit). By the end of the shoot you should have a rough cut of your movie, a major creative tool to help you judge what scenes need more work. Re-shoots are easier to do mid shoot as you have your cast, crew and locations available – not so two months after you wrap and your editor delivers the first assembly with some fundamental creative flaws.

Editing kit used to be a problem but now with the advent of Avid Xpress DV it isn't really an issue. Blag, borrow or steal an Avid Xpress DV system and set up a cutting room somewhere convenient (or an old Avid Media or Film Composer). Spare bedrooms and living-rooms have been home to post production on many low budget movies. Nothing fancy, just functional. If you are shooting film (16mm or 35mm) you must shoot at 25fps if you want a hassle free post production. The editor should know all this, if they don't, find someone who does. Don't hire the first person who offers to do it, find someone who is on your wavelength – there are a lot of people out there who can cut your movie, so find the best person.

Look for someone with editorial flair AND technical expertise. They should act as your post production supervisor and should know all about frame rates, SMPTE timecode, VITC, BITC, frame overlaps, digital transfers, safe title areas, neg. cutting etc. If they don't know about it, you'd better know it all or you will end up in post production hell, writing cheques for huge amounts of money you aren't even sure you need to spend. Prior to the shoot, get the camera team, sound team and lab guys all in one room and talk through the whole post production process. Then write it out and give a copy to everyone. The editor will become an integral cog in your team, along with producer, director, writer and the production manager. Many reckless take-outs will be ordered and there will be frequent late night drinking sessions that will be regretted the following day. The editor will need to commit for anywhere between three to six months. How much can you pay them? As usual, as little as you can and as much as you need to . . . but few people can afford to work for peanuts for six months, even if it is a big break.

Crew of 10ish – Weekly Workout

This model, whilst a crew of tenish, forces crew members to combine jobs as there just aren't enough people available. For instance it's likely that the producer and director will also take on the jobs of editor and writer. It's assumed that there has been a good six months or more working on and rewriting the screenplay. Weeks 1 to 12 will be the producer and director working alone in the office (aka, shed / garage / bedroom etc.), working on the script, calling agents and dealing with major production concepts (to make sure everything is actually possible). As the weeks go by, the script will become tighter and problems seem more solvable. By week 13 a production assistant will start (ideally earlier). They will take much of the day to day workload off the producer and director who should now focus on locations, actors, story-boards (or just shot lists) and of course, the script. Soon after the PA joins the team, so will a designer, giving them time to find and build props, as well as recceing locations with the team. Most of their time will be spent trying to get things for free, their job not so much design but more production management for design. Of course, the PA will help out here. Nothing is simple. Everything is bigger, heavier, further away etc. than you expect.

By week 17 the producer and director should have locked the script and be completing the schedule. They will also be meeting actors and other crew members who are about to join the team. To help with the workload a runner/driver will also join, doing and fetching whatever is needed by whoever. Week 18 and Make-up/costume come on board, giving them only a couple of weeks to make sure every scene and every actor is considered. Week 19, the week before the shoot and the rest of the crew comes on board. The DP will finalise the lighting and camera equipment, and meet the assistant camera and gaffer. As there are so many people knocking around, catering will also need to kick in, a full week before the shoot has even started.

Week 20 and the shoot starts, sound and stills appearing for the first time too. Ideally the editor would also start now, but if the editor is also the director, editing will need to wait until after the shoot. Week 23 and the shoot wraps, behind schedule and over budget. Most of the crew will be involved for a few more days, picking up the pieces, clearing up, returning equipment etc., you just can't cut and run. The PA will hang around longest as they will need to make sure everything has been accounted for so no unforeseen bills for lost or damaged stuff turns up.

The edit will be in full swing by now and the producer and director will spend much of their time in the cutting room. In week 32 there will be a minor re-shoot, picking up lots of missing shots, usually small props that weren't good enough during the main shoot. This will be with a very small crew, mainly producer, director, camera and PA. A few weeks later there will be a much bigger re-shoot, tackling more profound problems with the edit, probably getting actors back and make-up/costume too.

Over the rest of the year the edit will complete and work on the sound will be carried out, before in week 47 the PA will return to help with the workload again as the film gears up for that first screening to distributors, from a DV tape (not film). The editor will also have completed their work so may well scurry off to a real and properly paid job now, although such a strong bond may have formed that they will hang around and help out.

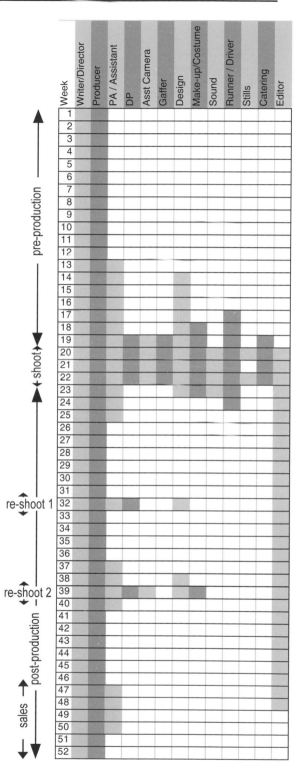

Crew of 20ish
. . . Micro Budget

Micro budget . . . 20-50k and probably shot on DigiBeta, Hi- Def or Super 16mm film (possibly even 35mm), over a period of two to four weeks. Shot with a crew of around twentyish

As per the last budget level, you are probably going to be working with inexperienced people, but one or two pros may be tempted to do the short two to three week shoot as you might be shooting film – and that represents a real opportunity. Shooting on film will generally get you a better crew than shooting on digital formats.

Shooting for two to three weeks with a few pickup weekends is your aim, and at this level, you are still on micro-pay . . . £50 a week with twenty crew members is going to set you back £3k, then there are the usual prep and wrap people, and the editor . . . that'll all set you back another couple of grand. So that's about £5k – pay them £100 a week and that will double to £10k. Cut your cloth accordingly and do your deals. Remember, everyone wants more money as it makes life easier for them, but fundamentally, they are not there for the cash. Your real pay is their experience at your expense, and a credit on what you hope will be a successful movie. You have so little money that you must ensure that every penny ends up on the screen.

Working with this size crew will start to slow down the whole process – more people, more paperwork, more organisation, more decisions, more potential mistakes . . . Ironically, you'd probably get more shots on a £10k movie in two weeks than a £50k movie in three weeks . . . But the shots on the £50k movie will be much better. At this level, the cogs of your 'skeleton' crew will start to turn much as they would at bigger budget levels. This is the budget level I believe will get the best results for least investment.

First assistant director (1stAD)

The major break for the director at this budget level is that they will get an AD. This isn't someone who massages their neck and gets coffee. It's possibly the most important organisational job on the crew! The 1st AD, or 'First' should start a couple of weeks before the shoot and work with the producer / director on the schedule. They will then take on the organisation of ALL elements, making sure that all heads of department are clear about what they need to do and prepare (production design, costume, make-up, special effects etc.). This will free the director to work on creative issues such as casting, locations and script rewrites (which the AD will hate as they will have nightmarish rescheduling ramifications).

During the shoot they'll manage the set, always two steps ahead of everyone, communicating what needs to be done and by when to individual department heads / crew members, and generally making sure everything stays on schedule. A layman might think that the 1st AD is the director as they spend most of the time shouting messages . . . 'Quiet on set . . .', 'Roll cameras . . .' etc., and on the walkie talkie . . . 'Bill, I need Jane down in full costume in three . . .' This is no easy job and getting a good 1st AD who can keep people on track and motivate without pissing them off is a tall order. Most inexperienced ADs stomp around, barking orders until either someone clocks them one or everyone develops AD deafness . . . 'I didn't hear you . . . even though you are yelling and standing right next to me . . .'

Beware of frustrated directors acting as an AD – sure they can offer alternatives or object on the grounds of it being *undoable* . . . but it should never challenge or undermine the creative leadership of the director.

'OK . . . Quiet please, we're going for a take . . . Will someone shoot that damn dog!'

In brief . . .
The sergeant major of your shoot, relaying orders to the troops. Always seen to be in control, firm yet reasonable in the face of impossible requests. Ideally motivates rather than demands.

A good First is hard to find and experience is essential. Speak to directors with whom they have worked if you want a brutal appraisal. Beware of wannabe directors who will challenge on a creative level, that way leads to ruin.

'Did you get the call sheet?'

In brief . . .
Back-up for the First AD and primary creator of the day to day production paperwork that informs and organises the cast and crew.

Needs to be cool and organised and not be phased by talking to actors. Also needs to be tough as they will always be the first to hear about, and deal with, people being late.

Second assistant director (2nd AD)

Not so much an assistant to the First, more a distinct and separate job answerable to the First. The second assistant director spends much of their time in the production office preparing the next days elements, making sure actors know what they are doing (and when), that locations are cleared, major props arranged etc. They will modify the schedule if and when needed (based on the days shoot). Toward the end of each day they will finalise the call sheet for the next shooting day, handing it out to all cast and crew members (and faxing it to those not present). The call sheet is a list of the next days call and wrap times, and a brief plan of the scenes to be shot with notes on locations and by what time they should be completed.

The Second may spend so much time in the production office preparing and printing paperwork that they may need their own computer workspace, often an uncomfortable shock to the production team who need to make a new space in their already overcrowded and noisy office. Often they will take the space that the director leaves, assuming the director spent much time in the production office in the first place! Along with the First AD, when shooting in large locations with lots of extras, the Second may be pulled in to 'direct' the background action.

'Yes, I wonder if you can help me, we're making this low-budget film and we need 200 rolls of toilet paper for free. Yes we can give you credit and you can come to the premiere'

In brief . . .
Brought on early to aid the production department in solving whatever issues are at hand. Often young and inexperienced, this secondary production assistant is often little more than an empowered runner.

Production assistant

This PA will be younger and less experienced than the other PA. Most of what they do will be legwork and menial tasks for the production department. Not quite a runner but certainly encompassing the remit of the gofer. Even on the smallest, uncomplicated production there seems to be a limitless amount of things to do.

It's simply a question of manpower, do you have enough people to get on the phone and deal with getting for free, blagging, borrowing, stealing the vast quantity of stuff thrown up by the screenplay. Ideally this person would be brought in a couple of months early in order that they start to deal with non essential but still important production problems.

'We were on the 25mm lens, shooting from here, John had a glass in his left hand and was facing slightly to his right . . .'

In brief . . .
It's the continuity person's job to check that nothing is accidentally omitted from the screenplay during the shoot. They will also keep tabs on what is being shot so that they can advise on issues of continuity.

This person should be bright and observant, anal in their note-taking, diplomatic and discreet in conference.

Continuity / script supervisor

Often referred to as and the *'continuity girl'*, this genderless job often leads to a degree of problems and angst. Their job is two fold. Firstly they should ensure that what happens on set is actually what is written in the screenplay. It's easy for the director and the actors to forget a seemingly trivial line of dialogue or action in the script only to discover that this omission has serious ramifications several scenes later on (sometimes this might even result in a costly re-shoot). The continuity person should watch and listen to what happens on set and check that against the screenplay, notifying the director whenever changes occur. Very quickly the continuity person

A valued crew is a happy crew

Having worked on numerous low-budget films and having been in touch with various low-budget film makers, I now believe there is an equation to help you deal with scaling your pay. It's a bit radical but hear me out. Everyone gets paid the same. Yep, from the floor runner to the DOP, from assistant wardrobe to assistant director. Whatever their job title, they get paid the same. Whether its £50 a week, £100 a week or even £200 a week. When you get into a budget in excess of £300k you could start to scale your pay, but under £300k, it's tough. Why pay everyone the same? Quite simply, whatever you're paying is less than what they're worth. Nobody is there for the money. They are there for the experience, the contacts, the career break, the credits, the showreel etc. If they are there for the money, you don't want them as there will be complaints about conditions, working hours, pay, inexperience, 'it's below me . . . ' blah blah. You want people who are just desperate to be part of the opportunity you have created. If you pay the Runner £50 a week and the DoP £75 a week, it will make little difference to their bank accounts, but it sends a profound message that one is worth half as much as the other. Think of their fee as nothing more than beer and fags money and that they are doing the film for free.

and director will work out a simple and effective channel of communication so that the continuity person does not need to pester the director about each and every minor modification to the screenplay. The second part of their job is to watch between shots and takes to make sure there are no continuity errors. They will probably make copious notes for each shot, frantically scribbling down camera positions and lenses, lighting set-up, dialogue covered and physical facts (such as the actor was holding the pen in the left-hand) etc. They will mark up a screenplay with lines indicating which shots covered which parts of the scene (later used in editing).

Depending on budget and experience, many continuity errors are allowed to slip through as on the whole audiences do not spot continuity mistakes, and if they do then they are not engrossed in the story and you have bigger fish to fry. Most continuity errors will actually be created in post-production where scenes will be chopped and changed and lines of dialogue dropped creating what appears to be a continuity error.

During the shoot when the continuity person spots an error, it shouldn't be announced for everyone to hear, relay the information to the director so that there is an opportunity to say *'no we don't need to re-shoot'*. If actors find out about ANY continuity error they will be unhappy unless the scene is completely re-shot, even if the continuity error occurs out of shot or the director knows that it simply will not play during the scene. By the end of the shoot the continuity person will have a thick file of notes which they will regularly cross reference to check facts – such as *'was the actor holding the gun in the left hand'* as they walked out of the previous scene and in to the scene that is currently being shot? Make-up and wardrobe should take care of the continuity for their respective departments.

Sound assistant

Now we have moved up a budget level the sound recordist can have an assistant. This person will have one distinct duty aside from general assistance. They will *'swing boom'*. That is they will hold the microphone, usually extended out on the end of a very long boom pole, getting the microphone into the best possible place to record the sound. This frees the sound recordist to concentrate on the recording levels, and perhaps even recording sound from several different microphones (such as additional radio microphones). Swinging boom is a specialised job and takes some body strength, as well as patience to hold the microphone steady, often for several minutes at a time.

'Where's my edge? Out . . . Out . . . Out . . . Out . . . OK I'm in?'

In brief . . .
The sound assistant is usually a recordist in the making. They assist the sound recordist and hold the microphone, usually on the end of the very long boom.

Patience, an understanding of actors, overall fitness, and terrific upper-body and arm strength are all needed.

Prior to going for a take on set, the assistant sound recordist will often bob the microphone above the actors and ask the camera operator for an edge of frame. It's their job to get the microphone as close to the actors as possible, thereby recording clean dialogue, but at the same time keeping the microphone out of shots so the microphone is not seen by the camera and therefore the audience. Anyone who has ever swung boom will have sympathy for film makers who occasionally allow a shot through where the mic dips into frame – they know just how hard it is to get 'that close' yet always be 'out of frame'.

Make-up and costume

Previously, the duties of both make-up and costume were handled by one person. Now there are two! Whilst make-up and costume are very different jobs, they do tend to work in each other's pockets and therefore there is some convergence and resource sharing.

'You see I saw you in blue denim . . . not pink angora!'

In brief . . .
Make-up makes the luvvies look beautiful and appropriate for the story. Costume puts the shirt on their backs, hopefully with creative flair and originality.

Talkie, touchy, feely folk are always good as they will keep the cast happy. Beware of over doing the make-up, unless appropriate, and keep the costumes simple.

The costume designer should be brought onboard a good couple of weeks prior to shooting. You still have no budget to speak of so actors will, on the whole, be wearing their own clothes. The costume designer will contact the actors prior to shooting to discuss the costumes, and ensure that every actor is happy to relinquish their clothing for the duration of the shoot. The costume designer will need to keep hold of all costumes at all times (including the actors' own clothes) as you can't rely on your luvvies to remember to bring them each day. Plus the schedule may unexpectedly change or there may be unexpected re-shoots and pickup shots with body doubles. Once they have all the costumes they can organise the 'frocks' onto hangers and rails, and prepare detailed notes on what characters are wearing during each story day.

Assuming there are no special requirements of the make-up department, they can come on board a matter of days before shooting begins. They

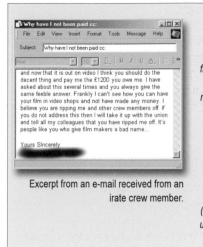

Why have I not been paid cc:

File   Edit   View   Insert   Format   Tools   Message   Help

Subject: Why have I not been paid cc:

and now that it is out on video I think you should do the decent thing and pay me the £1200 you owe me. I have asked about this several times and you always give the same feeble answer. Frankly I can't see how you can have your film in video shops and not have made any money. I believe you are ripping me and other crew members off. If you do not address this then I will take it up with the union and tell all my colleagues that you have ripped me off. It's people like you who give film makers a bad name...

Yours Sincerely

Excerpt from an e-mail received from an irate crew member.

Don't do deferrals

The phrase 'deferrals' means that cast and crew members defer their fees until after the film has been sold. The reality of this process is that no one ever gets paid. This isn't because the film makers are crooks but because the project will almost certainly never make enough money to pay the deferrals. The upshot is that films made with deferrals end up with irate crew members calling and writing letters threatening action, often many years after the film has been finished. You can understand their point of view. They don't know the hell you have had to go through, the amount of money you have spent and the pittance you may have been rewarded in order to get your film on a cinema screen or in a video shop. No matter how certain you are of success, the statistics paint a grim picture. 'Ah but . . . ' I can hear you say "we're different . . . ". I hope you're right, but I would urge you to consider asking people to do the film for whatever money you can offer them up-front with no deferrals. After all, they are getting a break and only investing a few weeks work after which they can move on into fully paid work (with a new impressive credit on their CV). On the other hand, you'll work for years, unpaid and unrewarded. Put simply, you will never be able to honour the deferred fee, so be honest upfront and don't lose friends.

will need a small budget to purchase make-up in advance and will need a space in which to work, almost certainly with a washbasin and large mirror. On low-budget films make-up and costume will, more often than not, inhabit the same room. It can get a little crowded and chaotic so you need to keep all non-essential people out of that space.

The make-up and costume room often doubles as the actors' green room so a walkie-talkie permanently lives in there.

Grips

Your budget can now accommodate equipment that facilitates the fluid movement of the camera. Normally this would be kit such as a track and dolly, or a crane . . . equipment that is operated and maintained by crew members called grips. At the top of the pile is the key grip, older and more experienced, assisted by a younger grip who may have little or no experience, just muscles and a will to use them in pursuit of the film making dream. Occasionally, camera team members may help out with the grips, and the grips may occasionally lend their muscle to hauling lights.

Track and dolly is the most common form of grip equipment. It's a bit like a large and heavy metal trolley onto which the camera is mounted. Sometimes the dolly will run on metal tracks which are laid out on the floor, or if the floor surface is smooth enough, just on rubber wheels. The grips will then move the dolly up and down the track as the director instructs them, following the actors movements and allowing the camera to move fluidly within the scene. Track and dolly equipment isn't too expensive to hire but you will need at least two very strong people to handle it, and it will need its own van for transportation.

'So you want twenty foot of track so that you can slowly creep the camera up on the actor . . . '

In brief . . .
These guys are responsible for operating and maintaining equipment like track and dolly.

It is a physically demanding job and will require an extra van which one of the grips should be able to drive. At least one of them should be experienced with grips equipment.

The lord of darkness . . . and light

The lighting camera person is, for some bizarre reason, seen as the demi-god of your film shoot. They swan around, light meter in hand, tools swinging from their 'bat belt', discussing beautiful imagery and generally 'sculpting with light'. It must come from the top, and that means you, that the camera team is in no way more or less important than any other crew member. Don't be seduced by promise and pursuit of wonderful imagery. You need lots of good shots, not a few great shots. You need quantity with acceptable quality. If you don't get enough shots, you don't have a movie, no matter how good they look.

I'm not saying go out of your way to make your movie look crap, but from a visual point-of-view, you're competing with commercials that cost £1m for 30 seconds. You will never win. No one will be impressed by how your film looks. They will simply be impressed by a good story told well. If it happens to be attractively framed and shot then that's a bonus, but it is absolutely, fundamentally secondary to the story telling.

'I thought the movie business was glamorous . . . Still I've got bigger muscles than I had three weeks ago!'

In brief . . .
Does whatever the gaffer tells them, usually moving, setting up and taking down lights, as well as cable bashing (moving power cables).

Will probably be a wannabe. As long as they have the attitude, strength and stamina they will do just fine.

Cranes are another toy that film makers enjoy using, but they are extremely expensive to hire, dangerous and, on the whole they waste time in the pursuits of frivolous shots that add nothing of genuine dramatic relevance to a low-budget film. Remember, it's a war of coverage, one shot in two hours is not time well spent, no matter how pretty.

Sparks

More lights means bigger lighting team means more sparks. As long as the gaffer (the person in charge of the lighting team) is experienced, relatively inexperienced people are capable of doing the job of a spark – carrying, assembling, positioning, disassembling and wrapping lights. Much like most of the other assistants coming onboard the shoot, this person will probably be inexperienced, perhaps on a film set for the first time. However, this isn't a job for the feeble. Resilience, stamina and strength are essential.

Focus puller / camera assistant

With the move from digital (video) to film, so the complexity and 'fussiness' of both the camera team and the camera equipment increases. Film cameras are tough as nails, but they need looking after and an additional camera team member is always welcome. The camera team is composed of a DP who will also operate the camera (that is look through the eyepiece and point the camera), an assistant camera who will deal with changing magazines, writing reports and maintaining the kit, and now a new addition to help out. Their primary role will probably be that of focus pulling, that is constantly re-focusing the camera so that actors never go out of focus. They may also mark up the clapper board as well as a whole heap of other camera team stuff.

'Depth of field is down to an inch and you want me to keep the actors' eyes in focus as they drive past at sixty!'

In brief . . .
Another addition to the camera team whose duties will be quickly decided by the group. Focusing camera, marking the clapper, calculating depth of field, cleaning lenses, checking the gate . . . etc . . .

Usually a DP in the making, young and eager. Not too hard to find this person.

On the whole the camera team will self organise and quickly delegate the jobs amongst the members. It's usually one of the best oiled machines on set – hence their often aloof cliques. Unlike almost any other department, you'll rarely have trouble putting together a camera team. It's those shades and the utility belts – feeds the geek in us all.

Art director & asst. production design

Production design, formerly a job (in the last budget range) that allowed the designer little more control than moving the plant pot to the left or the right in a shot, now blossoms into a department worthy of the title 'production design'. At the top is the overall creative influence of the production designer. All creative decisions about the look of whatever is in front of the camera will filter through this person. There still isn't much to control because of the lack of budget, but given enough prep time, the combination of designer, art director and assistant, can work miracles.

The art director will take care of many of the finer details such as selecting props and the dressing of sets, whereas the designer will handle the broader strokes of the production and look at locations too. The assistant will, not surprisingly, assist, but may also handle the management of the props, a job in its own right. Ideally this team should come on board as early as possible – you can get pretty much everything you need for free or next to nothing, but you need time to break down the script, make the calls, send the letters, look at stuff, collect it and store it someplace ready for the shoot. Your story will contain a lot of 'stuff', mostly props which will simply be dropped on the day of the shoot if you haven't given the team enough time to prepare. A gun will become a knife, a helicopter will become a sound effect, photos of the victims body will be shot from the back so you can't see them etc . . . all of which doesn't help you fool anyone into thinking you are making this with a real budget.

Good creative people are hard to find as they often fall into two groups – practical but inartistic, or artistic and impractical! Phew, what a pain. Get an artistic production designer and practical art director and assistant. There might be tension, may even be tears, but you'll get a better chance at something interesting in front of the camera.

No. No. No. Green! Green! We MUST paint the walls green . . . !'

In brief . . .
The newly expanded production design team now has a chance of putting something in front of the camera worthy of shooting. Breaking down the script, getting everything in one place, all within a tight time frame and ridiculous budget is the challenge.

Look for an artistic designer who will work with a practical art director and assistant. Should have access to a van, and will need a space to work and store props. Give them as much lead time as possible.

What's the pay . . .?

When hiring crew, if you find yourself selling hard to get a crew member on board, it may be wise to pass on them before you even get to set. You want to surround yourself with crew who are there because they're desperate for the opportunity and appreciate your offer of the work and career break. This especially relates to money. The cash you can offer is a token of appreciation of their hard work and not representative of what the crew member is actually worth. Anyone doing it for the money is a time bomb of trouble waiting to go off at the most inopportune moment.

Crew of Twentyish – weekly workout

In this model, as with all the others, it's assumed there has been a protracted period of screenplay development – but now the job of writing has been taken out of the director's hands and put firmly into the creative hands of a writer. The writer/director/producer team will have creatively spearheaded the production and at the appropriate moment have kicked off pre-production in week one. The budget, which is now somewhere between £20k -£50k is still minuscule, but it does mean that the crew can be paid a tiny amount and that each and every department will have some budget, no matter how meagre. The production will be run from a convenient front room and for the first couple of months the producer and director will man the office alone. In week 8, a production assistant will join the team. Their job will be to find, fix, beg, blag, borrow, and steal as much as they can. By week 12, a second production assistant (more of a runner) will come onboard to help with the workload.

The production designer will also join the team now, giving them a couple of month's prep time to make sure all props and locations are found/created/checked and signed off. The designer could start later but you run the risk of inferior props and dressings. And it only takes one dreadful prop in your movie to let the whole thing down. By week 14, the art director and assistant to the art team joins to help build several micro sets which you will use to avoid moving cast and crew to numerous locations. You'll probably get a good cast, good DP but what will let your film down is poor, unplanned and badly executed production design. So get the guys in early.

By week 16, a runner/driver will join and in week 18, the costume designer, with only 2 weeks prep will also join. Costume will have a very tight budget and most of their job will be looking at the actor's own clothes to make appropriate selections that fill the needs of the story. By now, the producer and director will be neck deep in scheduling the film, just as the 1st AD joins to help planning and examine the screenplay in detail.

Week 19, with only one week to go, and the production machine moves into the final stages of prep. There are so many people involved now that catering will begin, make up will have joined the team and be working through the screenplay, considering how they will attack the job. The camera team will be having meetings with the camera hire facilities, labs and checking locations. The 2nd AD will have joined and have begun work on the paperwork for the shoot, whilst backing up the 1st AD.

This 4 week shoot will be arduous, but unlike the previous model, there will be a degree of creativity to the way in which it is shot as you have slightly more time and budget. At the end of week 23 the film will wrap. Various crew members will linger for the next few days to help return equipment and clean the mess. The producer and director will take a short break before entering the cutting room where the editor, who has been working since the beginning of the shoot will have a 1st assembly of the material. At various points during the edit, the writer will return to re-write scenes that have been isolated as problems (in the edit) and these scenes will be re-shot in weeks 32 and 39. For each of these re-shoots, various crew members will return forming a crew of around 5-8 people (depending on the complexity of the re-shoot). By week 47, the editing will be drawing to a close and work on the sound will have begun (the editor will have also cut promos and trailers for distributors).

The production will now set up screenings for distributors and sales agents in week 50. For this sales push, the production assistant will return to help out in the office.

Lets look at the time-scales here, six months writing and brainstorming, one year in prep, shoot and post, then two years or more in sales and distribution . . . How are you and your partners going to survive?

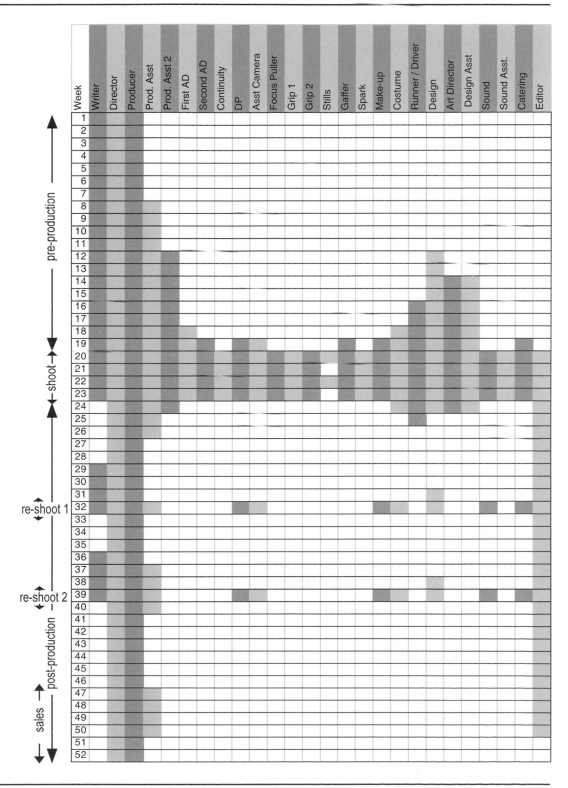

Crew of 30ish . . . Low Budget

Low budget . . . 50k-200k and probably shot on Super 16mm or 35mm over a period of four to six weeks with several pickup weekends and a seperate second unit camera and director team. Shot with a crew of around thirtyish.

As the budget jumps over £50k (possibly up to £200k), so the crew expands again. On the whole, this crew behaves like a full pro crew, heads of department are no longer helming alone but have people below them doing specific jobs, some of whom have assistants and runners helping them! If you had £1m, you'd hire a few more crew, and perhaps more experienced people, but on the whole it wouldn't be much different from what you have here. You still don't have much cash to play with, but it's enough to raise you above the beer and fags salary you have previously been paying – don't go mad though, you want as much of that cash up on the screen as possible.

They will be completely liberated to just deal with the creative aspects of the film – no matter the task, there's someone to help – casting director for actors, storyboard artists for planning shots, location manager to help find the right place to shoot, PAs to get you coffee . . . In essence your production has moved out of the 'I will shoot what I am dealt on the day' into 'I will create and manipulate the world to fit what the story and production needs.' You may feel there is excessive wastage in this more lumbering production – many people seem to stand around doing nothing a great deal of time – just remember, it's just the nature of the beast . . . all you can do is ensure that you are shooting as quickly and efficiently as the machine of your crew will allow. You should be getting anywhere between 15 and 25 shots a day.

You may use a second unit, a two person team who will pick up loads of extra shots and sequences. This is a very cost effective way to add a huge amount of shots to your movie, although the main unit director may be reluctant to release control. Just remind them that they will get all the credit, and if they don't like the shots, they don't have to be used. In post production, the director will regularly kiss the second unit director for all those great shots that regularly save the scene, then take all the credit at the premiere.

Executive producer

Not so much a film maker, more a financier. The exec. producer at this level is almost certainly either a private investor who has lumped a huge amount of personal dosh into the project, or a professional such as an accountant or lawyer, who has lubricated the elements (usually a bunch of investors) which resulted in the cash becoming available. Either way, they are here for the ride and can offer no real technical or creative expertise. Their presence can be a little uncomfortable on some shoots (especially if they start to meddle with the script and direction), on others they are a welcome member of the team. No matter who they are in the real world, if they are taking up set space and eating their slice of the catering budget, put them to work – keeping the actors happy, making production phone calls, painting a wall – whatever they are good at. If it is their money on the line, they should be happy to contribute on any level they can. They often have age and personal wealth, which means they can bring authority to the mix, so use that also – delinquent crew and cast members may tow the line quicker if asked to do so by an older, authoritative person who has paid for the whole thing in the first place.

'Last week I was the successful MD of a decorating company. I invest my life savings, become a movie producer . . . why then am I still painting?'

In brief . . .
Probably the person who invested their cash, or a lawyer / accountant type who found the cash for you.

Most execs negotiate their way into the credit using their chequebook (or clients chequebook!) as currency.

More production assistants & runners

Now the crew is getting bigger, so the support team expands. New, young and eager PAs will be brought in to help with whatever needs to be done. Catering will almost certainly earmark one person whose duties will also cover dealing with afternoon snacks, tea and coffee. These people will probably be young and inexperienced, so much so that many will quit as they thought film making was something else – some will get with the program, quickly assume responsibility and be trusted with increasingly important jobs.

'How can we help? What needs to be done? Where do you want it?'

In brief . . .
More of the same, do what ever they are asked of, and generally support the whole team. They will be very green and many will fall by the wayside, but some will shine as superstars for your next film.

*'We'd like to film in your garden . . .
The only problem is that we need to
dig it up to make a world war two
trench . . . Oh and did I mention
the pyrotechnics . . . But you'll
hardly know we are there . . . '*

*In brief . . .
This person will find locations, recce them
with the creative team, get permissions,
organise logistics and co-ordinate the clear
up. They should be brought in a month
beforehand.*

*Any person with good production skills should
be good at this job, indeed production
assistants will be shanghaied in to helping out,
both finding locations, but also managing during
the shoot.*

Location manager

As the scope of your production broadens, so does the aspiration of the story telling – one result is that you will try to tell your story in many more and increasingly interesting locations. Until now, your story will probably have centred around a single location to keep production problems limited – now you might be sprawling into a whole pile of new places. Wherever you want to shoot you should (ideally) get permission. This isn't always possible and there is a school of thought that says 'if you are lean and mean and think you can get in and out without anyone noticing, then why wake the sleeping dogs?' I would go along with that philosophy most of the time. If you plan to do something naughty, listen to your instincts – if the alarm bells start to ring in your head, go ask permission.

It's the job of the location manager to deal with finding locations, then find out how feasible it is as a location, recce it with the director and seek permission if needed. During the shoot, they will get to the location ahead of time to make sure everything is OK, and usually they will be the last person to leave!

Typical problems include inadequate parking (or parking that disappears on the day), facilities such as loos and a place to sit and eat (although a cheeky production manager can often help here), power (if needed), traffic (if it needs to be stopped – yes ask the police!), using dangerous props (explosives or guns for example), clearing up and not trashing a location ('cos you will need to go back for a re-shoot in two months time!), and of course, getting the damn location for free in the first place.

This person should be efficient and politely pushy, ideally with a good knowledge of the area to be used for shooting. They will need their own car and should be brought in a few weeks before shooting, ideally a month. Encourage the director and location manager to look for 'compromise locations' where the camera can be pointed in one direction to accommodate one story location, but if turned around, the camera sees something entirely different – for example, a car park next to a forest, two distinct locations but in one place. The golden rule is always move the cast and crew as little as possible. The crew has grown to such a size that it's no longer 'lets jump in the car and go do it . . . ' more 'clear the roads we're coming through . . . '

The location manager will work with the Second AD and supply a 'movement order' for every location. A photocopied map with directions marked in highlighter pen, and written directions. Their mobile number should also be written at the top, just in case – many an hour has been lost as the person driving the lead actor got lost on the way to set.

Crew with kit

*Some crew will come to you with kit, usually
the sound or camera departments. You
need to take a view as to whether you can
afford to pay them some more 'to hire' their
equipment instead of hiring from a facilities
house (whose kit may be maintained more
efficiently). Often this is an ideal situation as
the crewmember will get something towards
their monthly repayments for their
equipment and you get a one-stop shop.
Beware, have a plan B in waiting should
your crewmember spontaneously combust
after a vehement argument with the first AD,
or their kit fail (they probably won't have a
back up). Other crew members used to
bigger budget productions will try it on,
offering to hire you their van, hairdryer,
widget etc. or other obscure piece of tackle.
Wherever possible, politely decline and you
will either lose the crew member or get a
crew member with some kit for free.*

Camera operator

The camera team gets yet another addition, a dedicated camera operator. This is the person who will spend the whole shoot looking through the camera lens, framing the shots and moving the camera with the actors. This is a highly skilled job and whilst a huge amount of experience isn't absolutely necessary, you MUST view their work.

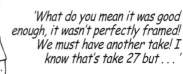

A duff operator can all but ruin the look of your film and move the director several notches closer to complete mental breakdown. You may choose to use a video assist, that is, have a TV monitor on set for the director to watch. This will give you an instant idea of how the camera operator is doing. If they aren't up to it, give them a chance to pull their socks up, if they still can't deliver the goods you must say goodbye. And not weeks, or even days into the shoot – within 24 hours! At the end of the day, there really is no excuse for poor operating, even if actors never hit their spot and are erratic, the operator should cope. They will have an assistant to turn the camera on and off, and a focus puller to deal with re-focusing during a shot, they'll even get rehearsals . . . They should get almost every take spot on, or near as damn it. On the other hand, some shots are tough to achieve, so when you know it's a hard one, cut them some slack.

Camera operators can be anal. They will always want another take, in fact as many takes as they can until they get it perfect – they probably won't even notice if the performance of the actor was good or not (by far the most important element of any shot), just if they were in focus and in frame. It's up to the director to know when the shot is good enough, 'cos it's never perfect.

'What do you mean it was good enough, it wasn't perfectly framed! We must have another take! I know that's take 27 but . . . '

*In brief . . .
Assisted by the focus puller, the camera operator will take care of pointing the camera at the right place and moving it as directed.*

Hire someone who is affable, and take a long hard look at their showreel (and a chat with a director with whom they have worked). They must be able to stay cool as a cucumber, even when they are exposed to extraordinary pressure on set.

Casting director

This person will work with the director to find the best possible cast for the movie. On the whole, there is no point employing an inexperienced person to act as a full blown casting director as what you are really getting with a pro is their knowledge, contacts and clout. Experienced casting directors probably won't work from your office but from their own as they will be doing six other projects at the same time. They will make a list of all characters in the screenplay and start making suggestions, then phone calls as they put together the best possible cast you can reach and/or afford.

If you can't convince a pro casting director to help you out, even for a modest fee (that will probably be much larger than any other crew members) then you could ask an actor who has a leaning toward production to help out. They won't bring the clout, contacts or experience, but they will have the right temperament to talk to actors and agents. At the very least they will relieve the director of the task of wading through 5000 photos and CVs for twenty or so bit parts. Get them onboard well in advance.

'Darling it's a simply wonderful part . . . and yes you do have lines . . . well you say Urghhh before your character dies in the hero's arms . . . '

*In brief . . .
Will handle the legwork for finding and attracting the best cast for your film. May also deal with all the bit parts in the story.*

Pro casting directors can offer a huge amount and are possibly the best money you could spend on any one person.

'That bottle of whiskey I asked you to get was a prop – what do you mean the actors just drank it . . . ?'

In brief . . .
Assistants dedicated to creative departments to ease workload. As ever, look for bright, enthusiastic and energetic people.

Production design assistant (Props) & costume assistant

More props and more costumes mean more people to handle the workload. Production design will probably get a dedicated props master, someone whose sole job is to make sure each and every prop is prepared and ready for every scene, before being lovingly stored away for future use.

The make-up and wardrobe department will also get an assistant who will act more like a dedicated runner for the department. Often they will spend much of their time running errands for the actors and generally keeping people happy. Keep an eye on this so that it doesn't get too out of hand.

'Yes, he will be on set in three minutes . . . He's just, er, well . . . (flush) . . . on his way'

In brief . . .
Keeps tabs on the actors, interfacing between the set, production office, car park, green room, behind the bike sheds – anywhere actors will loiter . . . Look for a people person, someone who can be firm yet fun with it. A film set is a pressure cooker and a third will often be sent to find stressed out cast and crew, and the last thing they want is to be barked at.

Third assistant director

Yes, another one. More of an assistant this time, doing whatever is needed, but also looking after actors, making sure they get to and from set on time and when called.

The First AD is usually on set calling out orders, the Second AD is in the production office co-ordinating tomorrow, the Third is usually loitering around the set waiting for that order or to quickly ferry an actor to wardrobe for a quick costume change, making sure they don't spend too much time wandering around, chatting, phoning their boyfriend etc. on the way.

Storyboard artist

At lower budget levels the director will work by the seat of their pants. Now there's time to reflect and refine the coverage that they want. Most directors can scribble stick men diagrams but a storyboard artist will flesh these out into clearer images. It's important that the director and storyboard artist work together as early as possible, often months before the shoot – any later and more pressing production problems overshadow this creative and contemplative planning process. The producer should keep an eye on the storyboards as the director will always want more shots than will be possible within the budget and schedule. Storyboards are a tremendous opportunity to have a first crack at directing the film – ideas can be played with and rejected, and the most effective (both creative and financially) coverage can be conceived, something you can't do when you are on set and people are screaming. You might not need to board everything, just key or difficult scenes. As boards are 'signed off', so they can be collated and copied for the production design and the camera departments. This will help them plan the most efficient way of achieving the shots. Storyboards should convey the motion in the shot as well as the geometry of the actors, props and locations. In an ideal world, the director would also draw an overhead camera plan for each scene / shot.

'failing to plan is planning to fail . . . '

In brief . . .
Storyboard artists are extremely talented crafts people who can work very quickly. It's their job to work with the director to help them realise the shots they want before they even get on set.

Start early, many months before the shoot. Don't let a director work completely unsupervised with a storyboard artist, unless you want your schedule of 400 shots to change into 1200 shots! Equally, never let a storyboard artist come up with the shots on their own, they are not the director.

Second unit

Usually a camera operator with lighting experience and a director with sound recording experience. The job of the second unit is to pick up the balls dropped by the main unit by shooting cutaways, extra shots, extra coverage during scenes and additional shots and sequences that have been ear marked for second unit during the preparation of the schedule. An active second unit can almost double the amount of shots in a film and as low budget film making is often a war of coverage, this is a very desirable team to hire (although their may be ego problems / friction with the main unit director and DP).

Typically they'll shoot cutaways for a scene, such as a newspaper headline or a close up of a door handle turning etc . . . In fact, anything that can be done without a large crew, and usually without the involvement of the actors (although an appropriately dressed stand in will provide hands and shoulders etc.) They will also wait on set, the second unit director watching rehearsals, looking for attractive or useful shots / angles that the main unit won't shoot but that may be useful in the edit. These shots are pure icing sugar on the production cake as they are entirely unplanned. During editing, only one in ten of them may be used, but the one that is used will usually save a scene. Second unit will also take care of small scenes or shots that have been designated for them in the schedule, usually stuff like establishing shots of a building, street, or a montage of shots to bring in a scene etc.

Second unit should be a free roaming entity, separate from main unit. This way they can maximise the situation, shooting on the main set over the lunch period for instance, as they can break for lunch later. They may occasionally corral in a few assistants to help and often plunder the camera department for lenses and filters. On the whole, second unit will usually be seen as a nuisance by main unit, especially the assistant directors team who just HATE having new and unscheduled shots thrust upon them.

The first port of call each morning for second unit will be the cutting room where the editor will give them a short list of shots that are needed to make sequences work. Usually these are bridging shots – two shots when cut together don't really work, so a new shot is filmed and will be placed between them to hide the uncomfortable edit.

The only equipment they will definitely need is a tripod, head, camera body, one good lens (ideally access to all the lenses in the camera department too) and possibly a microphone and cheap DAT machine (a minidisk recorder would suffice for the occasional sync sound or line of dialogue). Due to their free roaming status they will need their own vehicle too.

'Second unit . . . we get all the best shots! AND we don't have to work with actors . . . !'

In brief . . .
A two person free roaming team of director and camera whose job is to pick up dropped shots, cutaways without actors, establishing shots and any other shots they can sneak in without anyone noticing.

Both people need to be very experienced, the camera person confident to operate, load, pull focus, light etc., and the director must have editing experience and understand why (from an editorial perspective) shots are needed.

A night to remember

Everyone has worked so hard making the film that at the very least, reward them with a premiere to remember. The British Academy of Film and Television Arts (BAFTA) at 195 Piccadilly, central London is a superb venue. It's prestigious, relatively cheap if you can strike a deal, available most of the time and has a bar. What more could you ask? Cast and crew may only get one chance to see your film properly and this is it.

(Above, the premiere of Urban Ghost Story photo Nick Wall)

Crew of thirtyish – weekly workout

As usual, no budget here for script development or sales after the fact – just the year of production. The writer, director and producer have all been working on the project for some time and a proper office with all the trappings – phones, fax, copier etc – will be in place. There will probably be some kind of Executive Producer too, the person with the chequebook who will drip feed payments into the production as and when needed. They will bob in and out, keeping tabs on things all the way through the whole process.

Early on a casting director will be employed to help pull in those great names who will be so important to the sales and distribution stages. The casting director will work sporadically up until the shoot, helping fill holes when actors drop out or fail to confirm until the eleventh hour. In week 6, the director, free from production issues, will begin storyboarding with an artist. This will continue until the shoot starts (sometimes off and on though). Week 7 and a Production Assistant will join the team to help with the producers workload, starting on breaking down the script and getting all the usual stuff as cheaply as possible. Week 11 and a second PA will join – there is a much greater workload due to the inflated size of production – more scripts to copy and send, more calls to make, more paperwork to file . . .

Week 11 also sees the first creatives join the team. The production designer and location manager. They will work together when viewing possible locations and the designer will struggle to find an overall cohesive look for the film, as well as considering props and dressings. The design department will soon fill out with an art director and assistant to the department whose job it is to help get things for free and pick up and drop off.

Very quickly the whole crew will appear, a much bigger machine, everyone doing their job. Ideally no one should be regularly stretched to the point of snapping as the workload is more evenly spread out. Don't get me wrong, it's still all hard work, but whilst the machine of your crew will move more slowly, it will be efficient and to a large extent self maintaining. Often a producer can have a crisis at this level as they can quickly appear to be a little redundant. They are not, they are a creative and should keep an eye on elements such as casting, locations, props, storyboards, even the on set direction and coverage. They are a second level of directorial control and should be seen as a welcome safety net for the director.

The shoot will being in week 20 and shockingly, you won't know the name of everyone. You will very soon, but it is odd to walk out on set and see a bunch of people you may have never met. Hopefully you will get great coverage – better shots as they are more thought out and well lit. You can shoot more footage too which means there will be more in the cutting room to help make difficult scenes work.

By week 25 the shoot will end, a few people lingering as usual to help clear the mess.

Time and money . . . Just to pay the crew means writing out forty cheques, or getting the cash from the bank (which you will need to arrange before hand) and putting that carefully in envelopes and handing out - how long will that take to do each and every week? Who will do it? Especially when all the creatives are on set doing their thing, possibly including the producer.

Post production will be in full swing and there will be the obligatory re-shoots to fix problems discovered in the edit. The writer may come back to help pen new scenes although they will usually be written by the editor and director – it's usually pretty brutal stuff, explanatory dialogue to make your scene work (problems you may have found in test screenings where the audience just didn't understand what was happening) . . . 'we have to get out of the building in two minutes 'cos the bomb will blow then . . .' Yikes, that's never gonna win an Oscar but it will make your movie make sense.

Toward the end of the year the PA will return as usual to help start the push to find the right sales agents and distributors.

crew pay cheques

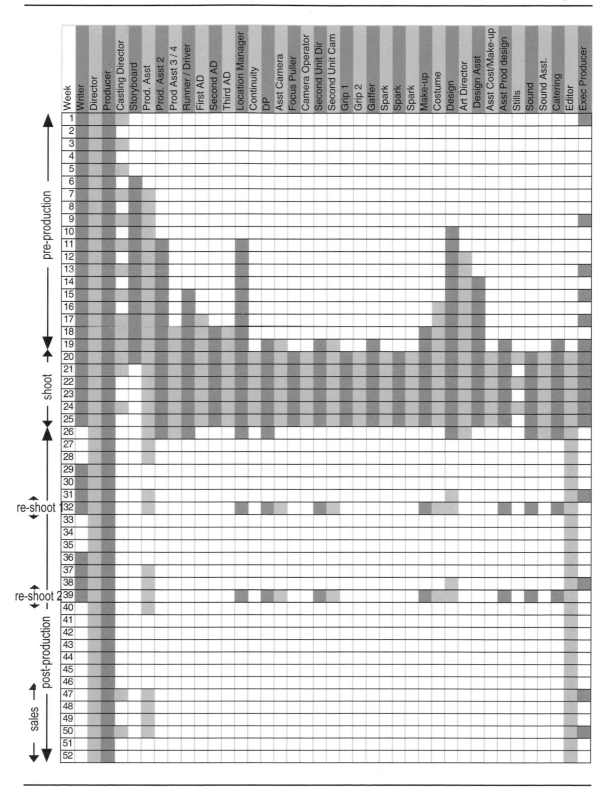

Crew of 40ish . . .

Industry Low Budget

Industry Low budget . . . 200k — 800k and almost certainly shot on 35mm over a period of six to ten weeks. Shot with a crew of around fortyish.

As ever, more assistants, runners, drivers . . . And also more sparks for the lighting department.

Now we are wandering into what I would call 'fully funded film making'. The industry still considers it 'low budget' but hell, give me £800k and I could give you three top notch movies or one cracker. At this level you are doing everything properly, crew members still on the lower end of the pro scale salaries, but hell, the wages are more per day than a person stocking shelves at the local supermarket would get in a week. And that all starts with you blabbing about the budget – whatever you have, someone else will want a slice of it. Ironically, compared to the last budget scenario, there isn't that much difference in the way you will do things except – you will get cabs instead of the bus, eat better food, do power lunch, generally waste money. You'll also pay people more . . . three, four, five, eight, ten, fifteen times as much . . . or that's what they will drive for. So keep a lid on the real budget. You want to spend it all on a great cast and production value. That's what will make your film a success, not paying everyone silly amounts of money.

As you'll see from the additional crew members, there are now a few people involved who can, and probably will pull rank – suits! Very quickly, unless you are consummately savvy and tough, your film will become their film. The director may get sacked, the producer may get sacked . . . Five years to put together, five minutes to lose. It can happen. It has happened. Contract or not, they will find a way of removing you, if they want to . . . so if push comes to shove, make them use their chequebook. On the upside, you'll be paid a salary. Not so much money that you can put in an order for that yacht you always wanted, but enough for a new car, deposit on a flat, or to pay off big debts. Either way, it's a welcome change. But don't get too comfy. Keep focused. You have NOT arrived yet. Study the UK Box office charts in this book, many films have been made on much bigger budgets and then taken pennies at the box office. You will still have to work incredibly hard to make the most of this opportunity. Screw it up and this might be your last film, so there's no room for complacency.

The length of time you shoot could be as much as ten weeks, and undeniably you'll be working on 35mm. Almost every task will be efficiently performed by someone else, as long as you hire the right people and delegate appropriately. If you are lucky enough to get a budget at this level, let other people worry about the small stuff, focus on the script, the storyboards and the casting, whilst keeping a hand in production design, stunts / effects, make-up and costume. It's unlikely you will find yourself at the helm of this kind of beast early in your career . . . but stranger things . . . etc etc. Be prepared for the unexpected.

Line producer

This person is hired to do what a producer would do on a lower budget. They'll cut all the deals with suppliers, crew and hire companies etc., manage those deals and keep their hands firmly on the purse strings. There will be a fundamental change in the way you approach the business of film making . . . instead of *'we have no money, can you help, please, you are a very nice person, go on please . . . '* the line will be, *'we don't have much money, but we have some, we can pay this much and want these things . . . '* It's incredible just how many problems go away when you can get your chequebook out. Ah the joy of having a budget. There is a down side though. It is perceived that you are a cash pot that is somewhat bottomless, so everyone will try it on, attempting to get more money, more resources, more fees etc. This is where a tough line producer is worth their weight in gold. They will know what must be paid / bought, and what is bullshit. During the shoot they will keep a constant eye on the budget and schedule, taking action where needed.

The only problem with an experienced line producer is that they're used to

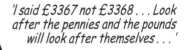

'I said £3367 not £3368 . . . Look after the pennies and the pounds will look after themselves . . . '

In brief . . .
The line producer will cut all the deals with suppliers, crew, hire companies etc., manage the cash and generally do the day to day job of the producer.

Friction can occur if you hire an old dog, reluctant to play the new tricks that you may be used to. Find a broke new film maker with a feature under their belt and pay them, they will be on your side at all times.

doing things a certain way, and you may be used to breaking all the rules. These are two diametrically opposed viewpoints which can result in conflict. A broke, low budget feature film maker with a movie under their belt will often make an excellent line producer. They know the best way to get the GREAT deal and they'll still entertain your crazy money saving concepts.

Production accountant

Managing the books for your film is no longer the painful and depressing job of the producer, but the production accountant. Many films at this budget level have specialised accountants. I would suggest that you cut a deal with a local high street accountant, or even just a bookkeeper. They will do pretty much the same job and cost you heaps less. However, depending on where your budget came from, the experienced film production accountant may or may not be a requirement. Don't be phased or blinded by accountant speak *'Oh you need to be careful about your* – accountant jargon goes here – *or you could find yourself in serious trouble with the revenue / bank / VAT office etc . . . '* Financial terminology is as bad as legal jargon, especially if this kind of thing sends you into an instant coma. At the end of the day, they're just adding numbers, making sure everything tallies. Don't fear it or be blinded into hiring someone you think is good 'cos they ain't cheap, have a nice suit and know the *'speak'*. These people drive expensive cars which you pay for.

It will be their job to keep tabs on what has been spent and what is going to be spent, as well as make sure paperwork is in order, cashflow around problems and deal with VAT and reclaiming it during the shoot. Due to the sensitive nature of accounts, you may wish to give your accountant their own dedicated laptop computer if they don't already come with their own. This job, like so many others on a film, is not rocket science. But it is dull with a capital D. On lower budget films, if you have a bookkeeper in the family (or a relative you trust could do a competent job) get them to enter all the details into your accounts books. Do not, under any circumstances, just leave this till the end of the shoot. You do not ever want to open a shoe box to find three thousand receipts and have to piece that jigsaw together.

Production secretary

Your production company will no longer be faking it from your front room, you'll have real offices, and a secretary. The jobs of a traditional secretary and a production secretary are similar so it makes sense to combine the two and whoever has been assisting you in the office up until now will probably slide into the job of production secretary . . . simple office work, writing letters, copying, paying bills etc. The advantage of using someone who has been working with you for some time is that you will be able to trust them and they will already know the ropes. If this person has some production experience it will help as there is jargon and odd production requests to deal with regularly. Ideally, this person should have an

'What do you mean that plastic bag is your accounting system . . . ?'

In brief . . .
An accountant's job is to keep the books during the shoot, to make sure every penny is accounted for, to cashflow the production and to warn when over spending occurs.

A competent high street accountant could do this job, as could a bookkeeper – especially one who is interested in movies! The professional film production accountant may come as part of your budget package, it makes investors happy.

'how many copies of the script? Yes. Sent to where? Yes. By when? OK, consider it done . . . '

In brief . . .
A secretary for the whole production covering much the same area as a traditional secretary.

Look for efficiency and people skills. Ideally hire the person who has been working with you for some time as they know the ropes and you can trust them (as long as they are up to the job).

excellent telephone manner, good English (able to spot your spelling mistakes in letters), be discreet, efficient and self organising.

Stunt co-ordinator / performer

Whether you need a stunt person or co-ordinator is largely dependent on the story you are telling, but even the most mundane of tales may well require some form of physical acting. If your budget is tight and before seeking a stunt co-ordinator, ask yourself – do I really need this scene / sequence – can it be done another way? Clearly if you are making a thriller, part of the deal is that you will 'thrill', but other genres would allow you to tell the story through a sound effect, actors' reaction, comment, fast cutting etc., anything to avoid an expensive sequence. For instance, if you made a film about someone whose partner was killed in a car crash, instead of seeing the crash, you could do it only with a sound effect. On low budgets, film making is all 'content' and little 'form'. And with your budget, whatever you put up on-screen is probably going to look like a pale imitation of a run-of-the-mill Hollywood actioner.

The very lowest level of 'stunt' is physical acting, which many actors can handle – but beware, even the simplest 'trip' or fall in a scene could lead to a broken ankle. If you need a fight sequence, either rehearse extensively with

'So the bomb blast throws me through the window, whilst I am still on fire, and down three floors where I land in the lake . . . OK . . . And what's for lunch?'

In brief . . .
It's their job to oversee, choreograph and perhaps even perform the extreme physical actions required by the story.

Hire the best. Stunt performers love to work so ring around and ask for help, you'll probably get it. Beware of working with amateurs who think they can do the same job. Even the experts get injured and killed, it can be that dangerous. Hire lots of cameras and shoot in slow motion.

Case study – 'Urban Ghost Story'

My third feature film, Urban Ghost Story, was made at this level – £240k to be exact. Considerable time was spent on the script, although in hindsight we did shoot too early. The movie was storyboarded which made a tremendous difference and many many months were spent on finding the right and best cast for our story.

It was a four week shoot, with several major re-shoots later on. One re-shoot we knew would be a nightmare (a car crash that we wanted to be jaw dropping) so it was left for a few months and picked up later in the year with it's own pre production, planning, storyboards etc.

The main crew were all paid £100 a week and that worked out fine. The actors were hired on the PACT / Equity registered low budget model. All in all, it all ran very smoothly. We shot on a set built at Ealing Film Studios, actually is was just a bloody huge shed which was a pain when planes flew over, but it did mean that we had control over lighting and conditions.

The cutting room was in an office adjacent, so at lunch and after the days wrap we could all look at scenes and rushes. A major advantage. The crew were all given a food allowance and they could either bring sandwiches and keep the money, or go to the onsite canteen. We also had a production office 100 yards from set, green rooms for the actors, full make-up and costume departments, loos etc . . . It was by all accounts (except for the wages) a proper shoot.

All in all it went very smoothly. Whether that is something that is reflected in the film I cannot say as I have no objectivity whatsoever. It gets like that after watching your movie several hundred times!

A deal is a deal . . .

As so many members of your crew have worked on your film for the credit, it's important to live up to your end of the deal and give them the materials they need to move up the ladder, focus puller to DP, set dresser to production designer etc. You'll be asked to supply VHS tapes, DVDs or Beta clips for show reels, and transparencies, prints or digital photos for portfolios and websites. Crew are often happy to pay the cost of making or duplicating these materials, but it's up to you to give them access to the masters in the first place.

actors, or get a co-ordinator in. Falling down stairs, out of a window, crashing a car, catching fire, being hit by bullets, falling through glass . . . we've all seen these stunts and shots in movies a million times, but to do it well and safely will need a professional.

You may think you can get away with just a stunt person who can perform a minor stunt, but as sequences grow in scale (as they do in the writing) and complexity (which may include multiple performers) so you may need a co-ordinator. The co-ordinator may bring in other people – specialised companies that hire stunt equipment like air bags, people who rig cars to roll or explode, cable and wire experts etc . . . It's all very expensive and time consuming to get right. This complexity and time consumption is the primary reason why stunts often slip into the realm of the second unit.

If you must have that breathtaking moment in your movie, then you must really go for it. Break the sequence out of your main shoot (if possible), take your time planning and setting up and hire as many cameras as you can (which will run in slow motion). Don't make the common mistake of filming at normal speed, an event that may be over in a second. And don't treat it like just another shot on set. Always shoot slow motion with lots of cameras. It's the best way. One tip, ring around all the camera people you know who own a camera and ask them if they want to come and film this 'big stunt' just for the kick. You may end up with a number of free cameras with operators. Stunt performers and co-ordinators are members of the actors union, Equity, and their hiring will be subject to the same rules etc. Spotlight publishes a book called the *Stunt Performers Registry* which will give you contact details.

Stunts (which often go hand in hand with practical effects) are just plain expensive, time consuming and dangerous, so be absolutely sure you really need 'it' before you write 'it' into your screenplay. And a last word of warning, be very careful about asking a non professional to help out – just because they think they can drive really well, are a kick boxing tutor or just want to be a stunt performer doesn't make them so. Lives can be at risk!

'Coool - yeah we can make his head explode . . . '

*In brief . . .
Will create, co-ordinate and where needed perform, all manner of visual effects. You'll know when you need effects guys 'cos you won't know how to do 'it', whatever it is in the screenplay, without an effects team.*

Don't spend too long trying to create amazing effects. We are used to multi-million dollar effects and whatever you come up with will be second rate. You'll spend all that time and money, then cut it out as it is rubbish after all.

Special effects team

Visual effects fall into two broad categories – practical and digital. Practical effects are things that actually happen on set and in front of the camera, such as rain, snow, mist, wind, bullet hits, sugar glass windows (that are safe to break), rubber knives, forced perspective models, animatronic creatures, gore etc. Digital effects almost always take place in post-production, but they need to be planned extensively and prepared during production, such as shooting bluc or green screen (for compositing effects later), asking actors to react to something that will be placed in the shot later, duplicating crowds to turn 100 extras into 1000 etc.

Effects guys are usually geeks who are in love with the sleight of hand that is film making. They simply love the illusion. Depending on your budget, you may hire a professional company to handle your effects or a young and talented wannabe who can take 3 yards of string, a roll of tape, 2 cardboard boxes and somehow turn that into a spaceship. Low budget effects are notoriously awful and often the best, cheapest and most effective solution is to create the impression through sound, actor reaction, lighting and editing rather than actually seeing. Of course as digital effects get cheaper and easier to produce, so the possibilities for low budget film makers expand.

Inexperienced actors often react badly to low tech, low cost visual effects because on the day it looks, er, well it looks completely rubbish. Reassure them and tell them that when they see it properly lit on film, edited and with sound effects, the illusion will be sealed. They are just afraid that they will look stupid reacting to the monster when the monster is quite clearly a production assistant wearing a rubber mask.

Construction team

If your budget can stretch to it, you may be able to shoot in a studio and build sets. If you do, you will need to hire a construction team, which will probably consist of chippies, carpenters, painters and plasterers etc. These people will collectively build the sets in accordance with the plans of the production designer. It can be expensive to build the sets but the advantages to shooting on a set are enormous. You have no crippling space limitations – you can remove walls for instance and put lights above actors. You have total control over the lighting – every light on set is there because your DP put it there, so there's no nasty uncontrollable sunshine. You don't have to find the right location – you make it how you want it. You have facilities – ideally it will be sound proofed and have loos, catering, changing rooms, green rooms, wow, what a breeze! Beware though, you may not have ceilings on your sets so you need to make the walls high (or hire short actors!). The sets will need to be painstakingly decorated and dressed – which costs money. And like any builders, the construction team will work slower than you hope and cost more than you can afford.

Ideally, make detailed plans of all angles you expect to shoot in your sets. This may reveal an entire wall or perhaps half the set that needn't exist, and therefore does not need to be built – think about Monica's flat in 'Friends', there is one wall we never see, and therefore does not need to be built.

Your production designer will take care of who needs to be hired, but essentially there will be a foreman / production manager who will hire and fire labour as needed. Get your chequebook ready.

'No, no, no, don't worry guvnor - we'll have it before lunch - lovely bit of MDF - just whack it and smack it up . . .

In brief . . .
The team responsible for the manufacture of your sets.

The more inexperienced builders cost less but tend to take longer as they don't realise it only needs to look good, it doesn't actually need to be built like a house. It will go over schedule and over budget.

The others . . .

Not needed for all shoots but should always be considered, a mixed bag of crew you might have forgotten about.

Aside from the actors and extras – and there could be heaps of them under the banner of acting – including child minders, groupies, partners etc – there are a few other people to consider. You may not need all of them, but you will probably consider most of them and work with some of them at the very least. Some people, like stuntmen and a special effects team just won't factor in a kitchen sink drama for instance, but most of us will want music to be composed (although not all!) and sound editing will need to be done by someone.

Others are professionals you will simply bump into on the journey. Accountant, solicitor, lab technicians, telecine operator etc . . . So enjoy this mixed bag and enjoy as you pick and mix.

Publicist

'Yes darling, it's simply wonderful . . . It's a kung fu horror movie with a slash of romance . . . And you'll never guess who's in it . . . ?'

In brief . . .
The person who will get you into / onto papers, magazines, radio, TV etc.

Pro publicists are expensive but deals can be done. Given enough time, most film makers can do this themselves, although they will always have to take the long way round to get anything done. It's all about contacts.

Throughout the making of your film (if you can afford it) you will have hired a publicist. It's their job to make sure enough photographs have been taken, that interviews with the lead actors and director are done and typed up, and perhaps even oversee the production of the electronic press kit (EPK). The most important job that they will do will be to get journalists, publications, shows etc, interested in your movie and giving it exposure at the relevant time.

There are two usual windows in which to seek PR – during the shoot which is usually aimed at the business, and the release of the film which is aimed at the public. Professional PR companies are not cheap and it maybe wise to off-load the production / management of the EPK, stills, interviews and press kit etc. onto a production assistant and just hire the publicist for the launch of the movie.

Lab Guy

If you are shooting on film, you will be using a laboratory to process the footage and deal with all the other post-production stages that will follow. It's important that department heads including camera, sound and editing, meet with the laboratory contacts before the shoot, so that everyone can hammer out and agree on the production route you will take. If you don't, you may find yourself spending money to fix simple mistakes later on down the line. When you cut a deal with most laboratories, you will be assigned a lab contact. This person will probably be a mix of account manager and laboratory expert and should be able to hold your hand through every stage of post-production – which will include processing and sound synching, negative cutting, answer prints, optical sound transfers etc.

'Well you see I think that the latitude of the 250 is better than the 125, and the grain structure . . . don't even get me started!'

In brief . . .
Your contact at the laboratory who should hold your hand all the way the through production and post production.

They are sometimes hard to get hold of, as often, they start work at 5am! So if you want to have a conversation, call early.

During the shoot you will get lab reports faxed to you telling you about how your negative from yesterday looks. If there is a real problem, such as a scratch or camera failure (that the camera team hasn't spotted) you'll get a frantic phone call. Whenever you push to get the job done more quickly, the lab contact will invariably say 'ooh, I don't know mate, its going to take a while'. Whatever you do at the labs, it always takes longer than you expect. And you can't push too hard either, as you do not want them to make mistakes. Remember that this is the stage at which a blade comes into contact with your original camera negative.

The most important creative in the lab is the colour grader or colour timer. It's this person's job to slightly modify the colour of the shots so that they look like they were all shot at the same time – two reverse shots of two actors talking to each other may have been shot weeks apart but the grader will make them match – and also to modify the image in accordance with the wishes of the DP and director. Film grading is NOT like using Photoshop. There is little flexibility to do ANY effects, merely warm up, cool off, rebalance colours. Anything else is an effect.

If you shoot digitally and want to distribute theatrically (as of writing this book) digital video projection is not yet a wide spread technology used in cinemas, therefore you will have to make a 35mm print from your digital tape. And so you will meet a different set of lab guys who will be experts at taking your digital images and converting them to film. Yet another slow and staggeringly expensive process. Lab guys are geeks who enjoy what they do and get off on 'the image'. They are also happy to take you out for lunch and down more than a pint in the local next to the lab. You won't pay a fee for these lab guys as their services will be included in the overall cost of working with the laboratory.

'So my left foot is the prostitute, my right the builder . . . Can you pass me that orange and the cucumber darling?'

In brief . . .
A highly skilled performer who can recreate quickly and expertly, all the human sounds of the actors on screen.

There are only a few Foley artists and they work most of the time. Hire the best you can get. Ask at the dubbing theatre if they would recommend a particular Foley artist.

Foley artist / footsteps

If you listen to a film whilst turning off the picture, you'll become aware of the quite detailed and clear sound of things like doors, footsteps, clothes rustling, keys in pocket etc. Creating these 'human' noises is the job of the Foley artist. This person is an expert at recreating (in a sound studio) the noises of the actors on the screen. You need this level of sound detail in order to sell a version of your film for to foreign countries where they will be dubbed.

It will take one very long day in a pro studio to do the job efficiently and quickly. The Foley artist will come to the studio with a bag of shoes, different fabrics and materials (which they will use to make various sounds). Hopefully, the studio will be used to Foley work and will have different surfaces (concrete slab, wooden floorboard, bags of salt for snow etc), doors and props. The studio will record the foley artist as they watch the film and act out the movements of the actor(s). Later, these effects will be cut into the movie. Professional Foley artists are excellent at their job, and whilst they may cost you a couple of hundred pounds for a day's session, they will add acoustic depth and richness to the texture of your soundtrack, and do it both quickly and efficiently. This in turn will save you days, perhaps weeks, track laying sound effects. Spend money to save money.

'For the top of the building scene we can have either heavy arctic wind, or er, very heavy arctic wind . . . My bet is on the second!'

In brief . . .
They will clean up dialogue tracks, add sound effects and atmospheres and organise and prepare everything for the final mix or 'dub'.

Look for a geek who understands technology, has their own kit and gets off on sound in movies. Give this stage enough time and you could double your production values for virtually no cost.

Sound Editor

As well as editing and cleaning up the dialogue tracks, this person will look at the pictures and add appropriate sound effects and atmospheres to create a rich, dynamic and varied soundtrack for your film. It's possible that they may well be the editor as well, and the producer or director may well pitch in during the final stages of track-laying sound effects. Most of the sound editing process is just about the graft – car doors, doorbells, gunshots, body falls, police sirens etc. They all need to be sourced or recorded and individually edited onto the unmixed soundtrack for your film. As a rough guide you may find you need anywhere between 1000 – 3000 individual effects, all of which should be unique. Anything less and you maybe compromising the audio canvas for your film.

Most sound effects will be pulled off CD or downloaded from one of the new SFX internet websites. Others that are more peculiar to your story or action will need to be custom recorded, probably on DAT or Minidisk, before being track laid into the film. The sound editor will need a quiet space in which to work, where they can also set up a computer running their sound editing software with a couple of whopping speakers – they must be able to monitor how the effects will actually sound, and as they will work all hours, it's best not to situate them next to the kid's room! To fully tracklay the movie will take anywhere between four to eight weeks. Don't make the usual mistake of limiting sound effects to doors and gunshots, be imaginative and create an acoustic world that supports the story and enhances the performances.

Depending on your budget and whether you can cut a deal you might be able to farm this entire process out to a professional audio company. Whoever your sound editor is, they should have a profound love of sound and really get off on acoustic detail. They will probably be a geek, as the technological hurdles through which they will have to jump, can be a little complicated.

Musician

The composer of the music in your movie will be brought in too late, have little or no budget and be expected to deliver an Oscar winning score to help prop up your dodgy movie. Tall order huh? Their job is to write the music for the film, probably perform it and master it to tape, CD or a digital file that can be dropped into the final mix.

Composers are easy to find now, technology has empowered a huge amount of creative people and even the most challenged have exceptional bedroom recording studios. Shooting people is always a good placc to start looking. Try and get them onboard as early as possible, even if they can't start composing to picture, they can start working on themes and ideas. Common mistakes include hiring composers who are not talented, and then asking for too much music (which will dilute the impact of the music on the drama and stretch the composer to create more music in the same amount of time). But the biggie is simply leaving it too late in the day to get the job done well.

'I feel we should climax here . . . before sweeping down with these heart-aching strings . . . Or we could just use your idea of the drum and bass . . .'

In brief . . .
The composer will write custom music, timed to picture, for your movie.

Hire the talent, not the technology, and give them enough time to do the job well. Beware of using too much music, thereby stretching the composer and their resources, and also diluting the impact of the score.

Dubbing mixer

This job is much like the producer or mixer in the music world. They take all the individual tracks that your sound editor has carefully compiled and edited and they mix them into one long version of the film that can be played back in cinemas or on TV, video and DVD etc. Normally the choice of dubbing mixer will be dictated by the audio facility or dubbing theatre that you have chosen for your final mix. The geeks out there may feel confident that they could probably do their final mix themselves on Avid Xpress DV, and whilst you may get partway there, sound mixing is a very specialised craft and is one of the only areas where it is true folly to try and do it ALL yourself. There is no greater give away that your movie is low budget than that of dreadful sound.

Whatever way you get your final tracks to the dubbing theatre, be it off digital tape or disk, the dubbing mixer will perform a number of premixes to get everything at roughly the right level, all cleaned up, with appropriate reverb and echo added etc. Once done, they will take the

'Do you want more out of the neck cracking or was that enough?'

In brief . . .
They take all the sounds, dialogue, effects, foley, atmospheres and music, and combine them into one final mix.

Mixers are technical whizzes, consummate peace keepers (it can get pretty heated in the mix) and audiophiles who love and respect excellence and detail. Ask to see the CV of the mixer you will use at the dubbing theatre you have chosen.

pre-mixes and combine them in the final mix. After doing this final mix, they will almost certainly do a second mix called a music and effects mix (M&E). Doing these mixes at full speed (and with significant but not intolerable creative compromise) will take around two to three days. Doing the job properly will take at least a week. How long you'll get will depend on how good a deal the producer gets, but often rates come in at around £1000 a day, although getting entirely free mixes is definitely possible.

Neg cutter

'Yeah don't worry man, everything is cool. It's coming along nicely . . .'

In brief . . .
They will cut your master negative into pieces then stick it all together to match the cuts you made on the Avid.

Always hire the best company, irrespective of cost. A mistake here could cost huge amounts to fix. Ask the lab for advice then they cannot blame the neg cutters when errors occur at the lab.

This is the person who will take your edit decision list (EDL) from your 'offline' Avid edit and cut up your camera negative to match it. Clearly, an extraordinarily important stage. All hopes, dreams, aspirations and investments are encapsulated in that master camera negative.

Every film maker experiences terror when they realise their negative is going to be cut up. But neg cutters are good at making you relax and they'll quickly put you at ease. After all, the technology has existed for decades and they have probably been doing it for just as long. They rarely make mistakes. Unless of course you have hired the cheapest negative cutter with least experience. Obviously, it is worth hiring the best. If you shot on S16mm you need to check that they have cut this format before and never suffered joins jumping on the edit (kicking in the gate – a common problem with cheap cutters). If you go with the best company, you'll get sterling service. If you have used one of the better labs, they will already have a deal with one of the top neg cutters such as Sylvia Wheeler or Tru Cut. It will take the neg cutter about two to three weeks to do the job. When you call for updates, it's always worth asking to speak to the person who is actually cutting your negative or you may end up speaking to an intermediary. Don't put the negative cutters under any pressure. Ever.

TK operator

'Yeah, I will try and get more out of the blacks, bring some detail to the image . . . Oh, what do you want for lunch?'

In brief . . .
The expert operator who drives the telecine machine to copy your film onto a videotape.

Look for someone with experience in grading feature films, not TV. Also try and get the best machine in the facility, even if that means waiting and working in odd hours.

TK, also know as telecine, is the process where film is copied onto videotape. In of itself, the process is very simple. Film is loaded into a telecine machine, a bit like a film projector with a video camera built in, and it is recorded onto videotape, usually onto DigiBeta (if you are mastering). The equipment is very high tech and the ability to modify the image is almost endless.

Most new film makers make the mistake of doing a cheap, quick and dirty telecine, and then six months down the line are forced to redo it by the sales agent (as the quality isn't good enough). Telecine operators are a bit like dubbing mixers. You get whomever the facility assigns to the job. However, it is worth pushing for somebody with considerable experience in feature film grading as they will know just how far you can push the re-grading of the image. Remember, this version is to be seen on a TV screen and not in a darkened cinema, so it will be brighter. Telecine operators are normally geeks with a happy disposition. They have expensive kit to play with and spend all day pushing it, and their knowledge, in the pursuit of image excellence. Pretty cool if that lights your fire.

It will normally take a day to do a fully graded telecine, and that is working at top speed. Any less, and it often turns into the producer saying 'oh sod it, that will do' which also means 'I will see you in six months when I come back to redo it all again and spend time doing it properly'. Telecine facilities are often darkened rooms with big leather sofas and young trendy production assistants who will happily get you anything you want for lunch.

Sales agents

Whilst on the periphery of the crew, sales agents and distributors will be part of your post-production process whether you like it or not. It's their job to take your completed film (often advising about re-editing before the film is completed) to market and sell on the international market place. At best, sales agents are scheming, vicious, money orientated, inartistic, pit bull terriers . . . but if they are YOUR pit-bull terrier, that's a good thing. At worst, they are incompetent car salesmen who were sacked from the forecourt because they couldn't even get rid of a cheap GTI to a boy racer.

Sales agents are always good at the 'talk' and will seduce you and buyers (to whom they are trying to sell the film) with outrageous promises and positive statements of questionable fact.

They will need a number of items from you to sell your film, which you will find hard to deliver as you have run out of time, money and budget. But somehow, you'll muddle through. The kind of sales agent you are looking for is someone who sells similar movies to yours, who is happy to give you the numbers of other film makers whose films they have sold (so you can call them and ask awkward questions), who won't lock you into a long contract period, who will openly share all accounts and contracts for your film with you, but most of all, a person who returns your calls and you can talk to. Unfortunately, like any dysfunctional relationship, the sales agent will probably seduce you into bed before screwing you and then disappearing in the morning never to return a single call. That's why you want a short contract period.

'Yeah, your movie is wonderful, you are so talented, you are going to be rich beyond your wildest dreams . . . Just sign here . . .'

In brief . . .
They sell the movie around the world in return for their expenses and a commission.

Look for an agent or distributor who is recommended by other film makers (a very rare breed). Consider selling yourself so you don't need this person. Insist on that 'get out' clause in the contract.

The Budget
Blueprint

Sargent-Disc Ltd

Entertainment Partners'
Movie Magic®

Sargent/Disc, Pinewood Studios, Pinewood Road, Iver, Bucks, England, SL00NH
P:01753.630.300 F: 01753.655.881 www.sargent-disc.com

The budget is the financial blueprint for your movie project. It details how much money you have and where you plan to spend it. It's a good idea to keep quiet about your budget as many people in the business will judge your film by its budget, and who wants to go see a cheap movie? I don't! Resist the urge to scream from the rooftops about how you managed to move heaven and earth for a pittance — this could damage your future business plans for the film and essentially, no one is interested in your budget (except other new film makers who will use you as a yardstick, and sales agents who want to know how much they can rip you off). The only thing that truly matters is the movie
. . . 'Is it a good story told well?'

Be warned, these budget templates are VERY rough guides. Every film is different. Every budget is different. Some people will get amazing deals where others will not. The time of year can play a significant role in the kind of deals you get, as will personal relationships already established. Just because certain figures are printed here does not mean that YOU will get this good a deal. At the same time, you could improve on the figures too. There are no rules. Cut your cloth accordingly. Make the calls and get your own quotes.

DO NOT TAKE MY WORD FOR IT!

Budget Blueprint

The most common question I am asked by new film makers is *'how much does it cost to make a low-budget film?'* The answer, of course, is very simple. It isn't *'how much will it cost?'*, it's *'how much have you got?'* You cut your cloth according to that figure. Whenever I have loftily announced that I believe 'X' to be the lowest budget one could possibly make a professional standard film, someone comes out of the woodwork and announces that they have done it for £3k less!

Let's be clear here. Any fool with a camera can shoot 90 minutes of material and call it a feature film. What I am talking about is doing it professionally, but without paying for a whole pile of things. Essentially, getting as close to the way the real film industry works by stretching one's money. In this book, I've proposed four rough budgets with four different crew sizes. These are *under £20k* (with a crew of around ten), *£20-£50k* (with a crew of around twenty), *£50-£200k* (with a crew of around thirty) and *£200-£800k* (with a crew of around forty). For simplicity within these models, we're going to make some assumptions about the shooting format. The *under £20k* budget will be for a production shot on miniDV. The *£20-£50k* budget will be for a production shot on DigiBeta. The *£50-£200k* budget will be for a production shot on S16mm. The *£200-£800k* budget will be for a production shot on 35mm.

But first . . .

Let me just say that no matter how low the budget, I will show you a film maker who has shot their movie for that amount of money . . . AND ON FILM! Yes, I could reel off a list of film makers who have shot on both S16mm and 35mm for under £20k. Hang on a minute, some of them did it for under £10k. Hang on a minute, one of them did it for under £5k. So aim high and no matter what your budget, try, try, try and shoot on film. Unless of course the subject matter would benefit from being shot on a digital format (think of any of the *'Dogme'* films, *'My Little Eye'* etc).

You also need to recognise that, currently, if your film is going to *'get out there'* you are going to need a 35mm internegative from which you can make cheap 35mm prints. Accordingly, these

> The budget for your film is usually calculated by the producer or a line producer. But for you, the question isn't 'how much will it cost?', but 'how much have I got?'

Movie Magic is the heavyweight budgeting tool used by big movies, but for low budget pictures, it's a bit complicated and over featured. You'd do better to look at doing your own spreadsheet or by using some of the cheaper tools out there.

ID	Name	Description	Equation	Units	P	Value
S	Shoot Weeks	LocWks+DistWks	Weeks		5
LocWks	Local Weeks (5-day)	2	Weeks		2
DistWks	Distant Weeks (5-Day)	3	Weeks		3
PP	Post Production Weeks	5	Weeks		5
UPM	UPM Weekly	2500			2500
AD1	First A.D. Weekly	1250			1250
AD2	Second AD Weekly	750			750
PA	Prod. Asst. Weekly	300			300
LocHrs	Local Hours (5-Day week)	70	Hours		70
DistHrs	Distant Hours (6-Day Week)	88	Hours		88
TECH1	Department Head Hourly	15			15
TECH2	Dept. 2nd Man Hourly	12.50			12.50
TECH3	Dept. Worker Hourly	7.50			7.50
T1	Dept. Head Weekly Local	TECH1*LocHrs			1050
T2	Dept. Head Weekly Distant	TECH1*DistHrs			1320
T3	2nd Man Weekly Local	TECH2*LocHrs			875.00
T4	2nd Man Weekly Distant	TECH2*DistHrs			1100.00
T5	Dept. Worker Weekly Local	TECH3*LocHrs			525.00
T6	Dept. Worker Weekly Distant	TECH3*DistHrs			660.00
SEC	Secretary Weekly	750			750
LocDrHrs	Local Drivers Hours	77.5	Hours		77.5

following budgets do not include the very final 35mm stage (there is a separate generic budget for this).

Don't worry too much about the cost of this conversion / blow-up to 35mm, if your film is any good, you will somehow find the money to do it. Beware though, there is a low budget industry myth that the distributors will, out of *exuberance, charity, delight at your project, pragmatism . . .* give you the money to do your final blow-up. This does not happen. In the extraordinarily rare occasion where it does happen, they do not give you the money, they advance you enough cash to do the blow-up, screw you in the deal because you are in a weak position, re-coup their money so they are not out of pocket, make enough money to give them some profits, but spookily enough, there's never quite enough money in the pot to write you, the film maker, a cheque.

So in essence, you need just enough money to develop and shoot your movie, then get through the editing and final sound mix before halting and attempting to find some more money. Of course, there is no better advertisement for raising money than being able to show an investor an exciting trailer, or inviting them into the cutting room to watch the first ten minutes. Obviously, you couldn't do that if you had waited for the whole budget instead of recklessly raising just what you needed in order to get it shot.

Post-production

Editing used to be a major problem for independent film makers. Now as everyone and their brother seems to have an Avid or at least be able to get access to an Avid, editing your movie should now just be a minor production problem, followed by intense and protracted creative work. So much technology is available and so many deals can be done that you should be able to complete your movie to a broadcast, fully graded videotape version without having to endure the final and extraordinarily expensive stages of 35mm conversion / blow-up. The upshot is that you should be able to present your film to sales agents and distributors in a format that is 95% complete without having to carry the burden of a huge and expensive final stage. You also have the benefit of being able to modify your film, should sales agents and distributors suggest re-cuts (which they will because your film will be too long and slow).

Don't listen to people who say 'It can't be done . . .', 'you are mad . . .', 'get a real job . . .', 'who do you thing you are, Steven Spielberg?' These people are usually jealous that you are out living the dream and they are in no way qualified to advise you. Ask a mountaineer who has climbed Mount Everest if they think you are mad and they will probably say, 'Well, do you think you can do it?' . . . and there's your answer!

Some funny figures

Some of the budgeted amounts proposed here will seem ridiculous . . . *'How can the costume budget be £100!'* They are not ridiculous, they are the answer to a *'needs must'* situation. The best way to keep your budget down is to refuse to pay for anything. Not that I'm suggesting that you buy or rent something and then don't pay the bill, but I am suggesting that you find a way of legitimately acquiring what you need without having to pay for it in the first place. Most professional producers make problems go away with their chequebook. You cannot do this so you will have to rely on a huge amount of leg work, letter writing, phone flirting, lateral brain storming, blagging, press ganging family and friends . . . and somehow you will find a way to achieve the impossible.

Every department will want more - more equipment, more stock, more money, more space, more time . . . And on the whole, they won't care too much about any other department who also needs more . . . It's your job to slice up the pie and try and keep everyone as happy as possible, but there will be endless complaints about impossible requests and a complete lack of resources. Keep your head down and just get through it. Keep focused on the goal and encourage people to do their very best. No one can ask for more.

Cash flow

There are two important mechanisms that you can implement that will radically improve your ability to produce your film and reduce stress.

First, offer cash. If a camera hire company gives you a quote for £20k to hire their kit, go back and say *'really sorry but we can only afford £200'*. They'll probably tell you where to go, or . . . but then they may say *'OK. You're shooting in February when we don't hire much of our equipment. We like your project and your enthusiasm, we like your DP, so we'll do a deal on the understanding that on your next film when you DO have a budget, you come to us. Of course we're going to have to modify the equipment list you gave us and you're going to get our oldest cameras, but they are still terrific'*. So they give you a bill for £200 for this amazing deal. How are they going to feel if you don't pay and their accounts department has to spend time and energy chasing you for such a paltry amount? It's a slap in the face for them. So offer to pay up-front. You'll get the kit you need and they get a token

Debt Management

If disaster strikes . . . You've found yourself over budget with no way of paying, the bills piling up, the phone ringing . . . You need to take action. DO NOT OSTRICH! That is, stick your head in the ground and hope they'll go away. They won't. Everyone has cashflow problems and as long as you are honest, sincere, and sound like you will be able to pay eventually, people will give you time and often work with you to work out your problems.

But take action straight away. Call your creditors, find out who you will talk to about your inability to pay (usually credit control) and explain you have had a problem. You want them to know that you are always available to talk, that you have prioritised their debt, that you will pay as soon as you can, that you feel terrible about this. Ideally send them a cheque straight away, even if it is only for 10% of what you owe them. Don't send them a post-dated cheque for the whole amount (which they will ask for) unless you know that it will clear. Set up a mechanism where you send them cheques in dribs and drabs, as much as you can spare. They won't like it. You won't like it. But YOU went over budget and they supplied you with a product or service in good faith. You are the bad guy here, so do whatever they ask.

Occasionally you might get a credit controller who gives you the 'I'm going to sue you . . . ' line. Usually this is a threat. They don't want to spend lots of money to sue you, which will then force you to go bankrupt, which in turn means they never get paid . . . AND it cost them a fortune to sue you in the first place! So they probably won't sue you. A wise friend of mine once said 'If you owe the bank £1000 YOU have a problem. If you owe the bank £50,000 THEY have a problem'. Perversely, the more you owe the less of an immediate problem you will have. It's the small creditors who will really make life hell.

payment (that will just about cover the cost of the assistant who will book the equipment in and out for you). Make sure you follow up with a bottle of whiskey or flowers for the person who did this deal for you. And make sure they get tickets to the premiere. Remember too that in four months time, you're going to be ringing them again to ask for some camera equipment for your re-shoots, and you really don't have any money this time! So don't burn your bridges.

There's a basic amount of 'stuff' that you are going to need to find, blag, borrow, steal or worse, buy! This is stuff for your office such as fax, phones, computers, printers, photocopiers, filing cabinet . . . Friends and family, their extended friends family, and colleagues are a good place to start. Someone always has an old fax or photocopier that they'll happily donate in turn for that very sexy premiere ticket promise.

The second thing you can do to make life easier is that once you are in the thick of the shoot, try and avoid paying any bills or invoices until a week or so after the film has wrapped. Most people will happily wait four weeks for payment. If disaster has struck and you have sky-rocketed over budget, you want to make sure that you spend your limited funds on paying the bills that could potentially shut you down and not on the first bill that drops through your letter box. This is not an ideal situation, but it can and does happen, and the best way of moving forward so that everyone is happy is by finishing your movie, not shutting down the production because you didn't pay the laboratory and they won't release your rushes. Prioritise your debt.

Movie model

For the purposes of these budget models, we're going to use the story for 'White Angel'. Here's the pitch . . . London is in the grip of a serial killer. Real crime writer, Ellen Carter, ends up killing her abusive husband in an accident that she knows will look like murder. In an attempt to conceal the crime, she hides the body . . . but serial killer Leslie Steckler figures this out . . . and as he has just left a clue at the scene of a murder, which he knows will lead the police back to him, he decides to blackmail Carter into writing his biography before he is apprehended.

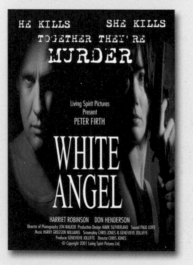

The bulk of the movie takes place in one house as these two characters play a deadly game of cat and mouse, attempting to outwit each other at every turn, whilst exploring the dark psyche of a serial killer and a writer guilty of manslaughter.

The cast is small, the two leads, a housemate, a police officer, a few smaller parts and a bunch of extras. Over 80% of the story takes place in this single 'house' location.

My production company, Living Spirit Pictures actually made 'White Angel' on a budget of £17k up-front, shooting on S16mm. It cost an additional £13k to complete post-production and ultimately the budget ended up at around £80k, which appeared in dribs and drabs over a two year period and included everything such as posters, final 35mm blow-up and the Dolby Stereo sound mix.

Development

Story & scripts	£87.50
	£87.50

Pre-production

Main fixed crew	£3,000.00
Production and office	£3,750.00
	£6,750.00

Production

Principal cast	£1,450.00
Crew	£3,550.00
Equipment hire	£1,945.00
Design, costume and make-up	£708.00
Location & set facilities	£2,350.00
Accommodation & catering	£1,537.50
Transport	£2,850.00
Stock	£270.00
	£14,660.50

Post production

Editing and Post (first phase)	£3,800.00
	£3,800.00

Sub total	**£25,298.00**
Contingency (2%)	**£505.96**
Insurance (2%)	**£516.08**
Grand Total	**£26,320.04**

Budget summary for ultra micro budget movie at £20k-ish shot on miniDV

OK I hear you say, you said it was under £20k, why then is it over £26k? Well I wrestled long and hard but decided I needed to put more that you might need into this budget so everything is listed – you can delete it or get it for free, thereby dropping the budget (you could easily save £1k by getting the edit equipment for free for instance).

This model also works on a three week shoot when you could easily drop to a two week shoot, saving a huge amount. It also includes limited company incorporation and accounts at the end of the year, which wouldn't normally be part of the budget, but hey, someone is going to have to pay – and that someone is YOU!

This budget does not include the final grading and blow up to 35mm film, but it should get you to a pretty damn hot looking miniDV master (or BetaSP) with fully mixed soundtrack and music. In essence, it is completed, you just haven't gone through the very final and expensive blow-up phase.

The VAT return in the quarter directly after the shoot will give you a welcome chunk of cash, usually around 15% of the amount of money you have spent (remember not all purchases have VAT). So if you spent £20k, you could be looking at a cheque dropping on your door mat for around £3k ish from the VAT man. Certainly enough to keep some of the wolves at bay. Don't use it to pay off one debt, pay a little toward a lot of debts.

Budget breakdown for ultra micro budget movie at £20k-ish

Story rights

Normally this would be the fee the writer is paid, but for here and now, that'll be a big fat zero. You should register your screenplay in the US, using form PA1 (see Screenplay section) which costs £25, and be aware that just making copies of your script will carry a cost. Find someone who works in the copy room of a major corporation and ask them to stay late and do 100 copies for you.

Story rights	Quantity	Unit cost	No. Units	Definition	COST
Story rights	1	£0.00	1		
US Copyright	1	£25.00	1		£25.00
Screenplay Duplication & Binding	50	£1.25	1	each	£62.50
					£87.50

Main fixed crew

That's you and the other long haul staff, namely the producer, director, writer and editor. These are token payments and frankly shouldn't even be made (except to the editor). It would save £1,500 if D/P/W were not paid, but then you have to ask, how are you going to survive over the coming months? Mums and Dads and the good old DHS have all acted as unwitting exec producers on many a low budget film.

Main Fixed Crew	Quantity	Unit cost	No. Units	Definition	COST
Producer	1	£500.00	1	fixed	£500.00
Director	1	£500.00	1	fixed	£500.00
Writer	1	£500.00	1	fixed	£500.00
Editor	1	£50.00	30	weeks	£1,500.00
					£3,000.00

Production and office

It's going to cost something to set up your Limited company, ideally less than the £150 here, and by law you need Public Liability and Employers Liability insurance, so there is a cost there too. Ideally you work from home so no office rent is paid, but you will need to buy occasional office supplies. Blag as much as you can from self employed family and friends. You'll place an ad for your cast, probably in PCR or SBS. Running your vehicles for the year will also cost a lot and there is no way around expensive petrol, you can't walk – can you? Borrow a bike! The phone and fax are another whopper of an expense, as are mobile phones which ideally you need to ban. The accountancy fees are for the year end accounts which strictly speaking wouldn't be part of the budget, but you do need to pay them and can't get out of it – unless your brother in law is a book-keeper?

Production and Office	Quantity	Unit cost	No. Units	Definition	COST
Company incorporation	1	£150.00	1	each	£150.00
Insurance (PL and CL)	1	£250.00	1	year	£250.00
Office rent	1	£0.00	52	weeks	
Office supplies	1	£200.00	1	approx	£200.00
Cast advertising	0	£50.00	1	each	£50.00
Vehicle fuel for production team	2	£200.00	1	approx	£400.00
Phone and fax	1	£750.00	1	approx	£750.00
Accountancy fees	1	£1,000.00	1	approx	£1,000.00
					£3,750.00

Principal cast	Quantity	Unit cost	No. Units	Definition	COST
Steckler	1	£100.00	3	weeks	£300.00
Carter	1	£100.00	3	weeks	£300.00
Mik (friend)	1	£100.00	1	weeks	£100.00
Taylor (cop)	1	£100.00	2	days	£200.00
Dezrae (minor role)	1	£25.00	2	days	£50.00
Carter's husband	1	£0.00	1	days	
Dead girl in park	1	£0.00	1	days	
TV host	1	£25.00	1	days	£25.00
TV reporter	1	£25.00	1	days	£25.00
Inspector Forrester	1	£0.00	1	weeks	
Witnesses	2	£25.00	1	days	£50.00
Forensic expert	1	£25.00	1	days	£25.00
Gangster	1	£25.00	2	days	£50.00
Café extras	3	£0.00	1	days	
Prostitute	1	£100.00	1	days	£100.00
Secretary	1	£25.00	1	days	£25.00
Gansters daughter	1	£0.00	1	days	
Stecklers wife	1	£25.00	1	days	£25.00
Husband of victim	1	£25.00	1	days	£25.00
Stecklers assistant	1	£25.00	1	days	£25.00
Prostitute 2	1	£100.00	1	days	£100.00
Bank Manager	1	£25.00	1	days	£25.00
Park crime scene extras	4	£0.00	1	days	
Hunting montage extras	6	£0.00	1	days	
Second crime scene extras	3	£0.00	1	days	
Gangster party extras	6	£0.00	1	days	
TV show extras	2	£0.00	1	days	
Police arrest extras	5	£0.00	1	days	
					£1,450.00

Crew	Quantity	Unit cost	No. Units	Definition	COST
Production manager /assistant	1	£50.00	22	weeks	£1,100.00
DP	1	£50.00	6	weeks	£300.00
Assistant camera	1	£50.00	5	weeks	£250.00
Gaffer / spark	1	£50.00	4	weeks	£200.00
Costume / make-up	1	£50.00	7	weeks	£350.00
Production design / set / props	1	£50.00	13	weeks	£650.00
Sound recordist	1	£50.00	4	weeks	£200.00
Stills camera	1	£50.00	2	days	£100.00
Runner driver	1	£50.00	8	weeks	£400.00
					£3,550.00

Cast

In this budget I have decided to pay all the actors £100 a week or £25 a day, with a few exceptions. One of the big problems in preparing a budget is that you only have an idea of what is going to happen and don't know just how far you will go over schedule (and you will), so you never know how accurate your budget will be. The payment exceptions I suggest are that the Cop character (for which one would try to get a bigger name) would have more money budgeted (in reality I think you would pay a lot more than £200 for the two days, but it would be money well spent and you would borrow from Peter to pay Paul in order to accommodate this).

The actresses who would play the prostitutes would need to be paid more as there is nothing in their role for them to get excited about, except to look dead and take off their clothes. Almost all extras, kids and even one or two small characters would be doubled up from friends, family, wannabe actors and crew. Hardly ideal but certainly cost effective. The main problem with extras is getting them in appropriate costume, and the allied cost implications of doing that.

Crew

Boy this is a small crew! Everyone is on the same money, £50 a week. Little more than a token payment. I have heard of people paying £25 a week, even nothing at all. It's up to you, but people have bills and can't work for absolutely nothing. Can they? Also I have budgeted for a three week shoot, which would probably come down to two when the crunch came. There is a lot of prep time which also might get the snip, but people can work miracles if given enough time to do so.

£20k-ish

Equipment hire

The kit you hire will fall into four groups – camera, sound, lights and production extras. You're shooting miniDV, probably the Canon XL1, which you already own or can blag, so no cost there. The lens on this camera is good, but hiring a better TV camera lens will improve the results significantly. You're going to need a tripod and fluid head (don't cut corners here), some plastic filters which you can buy from your local camera shop (Cokin filters are about £10 each – don't rent, buy). Finally there are consumables such as camera tape, gaffer tape etc. Beware of a sticky tape happy crew, this stuff is VERY expensive.

The sound department is basically a DAT machine, some mics, a boom pole and cables. Don't skimp on the mics – Sennheiser 416 and 816 mics are old, but excellent quality and good value to rent. Ideally your sound recordist would have their own kit which you might get for free, but that also means if they quit, you lose your kit. You might want to rent a couple of radio mics too, although they can be pricey and are the lazy way to record sound. For my money, a boom and overhead mic (or cunningly placed and hidden mic) will always give more natural sound.

This lighting kit isn't extensive but it's enough to light all but very wide night exteriors. I'd look for a negotiable deal (both price and kit content) rather than sticking rigidly to this, or any list. This really is a bargain deal and you may not achieve it. Remember, a broken HMI bulb can run into the £hundreds, so don't drop 'em! Watch out for liberal use of gel, trace and spun. This is the stuff the lighting team clip over lights to alter the type of light emitted – colour balance, diffusion etc. It's damn expensive so make sure everyone knows that they must save and re-use. Practical bulbs are like normal light bulbs only they burn at a higher wattage and therefore brighter, usually 275w. They're ideal for quick and simple lighting but can melt plastic fittings, so only use metal fixtures or for short periods. Lastly you might want to hire a smoke machine as they are always handy.

Equipment hire	Quantity	Unit cost	No. Units	Definition	COST
Camera Department					
Camera kit (includes body,mag,filters etc.)	1	£0.00	1	own	
Zoom lens	1	£75.00	3	weeks	£225.00
Tripod legs and head	1	£50.00	3	weeks	£150.00
Cokin camera filters	2	£10.00	1	each	£20.00
Camera tape, gaffer tape, consumables	1	£50.00	1	approx	£50.00
Sound Department					
DAT recorder	1	£50.00	3	weeks	£150.00
Microphones - wide	1	£25.00	3	weeks	£75.00
Microphones - narrow	1	£25.00	3	weeks	£75.00
Microphones - tie clip radio mics	2	£25.00	3	weeks	£150.00
Boom pole & wind shield	1	£15.00	3	weeks	£45.00
Misc accessories and cables	1	£15.00	3	weeks	£45.00
Lighting Department					
4k HMI	1		3	weeks	
1.2k HMI	1		3	weeks	
2k Blonde	2		3	weeks	
1k Redhead	4		3	weeks	
Inky Dinks	4		3	weeks	
Mizar	2		3	weeks	
Stands & tripods	1		3	weeks	
All in lighting hire deal	1	£500.00	1	all in	£500.00
Gels/ trace/ spun	1	£100.00	1	approx	£100.00
Practical light bulbs	15	£4.00	1	each	£60.00
Smoke machine	1	£150.00	1	approx	£150.00
Production equipment					
Walkie talkies	1	£150.00	1	approx	£150.00
					£1,945.00

Design, Costume and Make-up	Quantity	Unit cost	No. Units	Definition	COST
Production design budget	1	£250.00	1	approx	£250.00
Props (make and buy)	1	£150.00	1	approx	£150.00
Costume budget	1	£100.00	1	approx	£100.00
Make-up budget	1	£100.00	1	approx	£100.00
Continuity Polaroids	6	£18.00	1	films	£108.00
					£708.00

Location & Set Facilities	Quantity	Unit cost	No. Units	Definition	COST
Location Fees (house rental)	1	£1,000.00	2	months	£2,000.00
Location power	1	£350.00	1	approx	£350.00
					£2,350.00

Accommodation & Catering	Quantity	Unit cost	No. Units	Definition	COST
Catering Cast (approx)	1	£2.50	360	meals	£900.00
Catering Crew (approx)	1	£2.50	175	meals	£437.50
Caterer fees	1	£50.00	4	weeks	£200.00
					£1,537.50

Transport	Quantity	Unit cost	No. Units	Definition	COST
Cast Travel	1	£500.00	1	approx	£500.00
Crew Travel	15	£25.00	4	weeks	£1,500.00
Vehicle Rentals - Lighting	1	£250.00	3	weeks	£750.00
Parking	1	£100.00	1	approx	£100.00
					£2,850.00

Design

Normally these sections would be separate, production design, make-up and costume, but as everything is so close to the edge, it's easier to just lock it all together, agree a silly budget and hold people to it. Most people like to read the script and submit a budget. Here, you are going to give them such a small amount that it's really just basic expenses for finding stuff for free or next to nothing.

Location and set facilities

In essence, you are just going to pay for the hire of a house for two months, sleep one or two crew members there for security, store equipment in one room, have a production office in another, and use a bedroom with the bathroom for make-up and costume. The rest of the house, which isn't much, will be used for locations, dressing and redressing rooms to be different rooms within the story. Ideally there would be a garden and garage for extra space, useful at meal times.

Accommodation and catering

Hard but true. You are going to shoot in a major city so that everyone, cast and crew, can live at home. You cannot afford to house a single person, unless they will rough it on the floor of the rented house (location). Catering has been set at a staggeringly low £2.50 per person per day, so you'll need to study the recipes in the book and find all new ones to keep food cheap, filling, hot, as healthy as possible, and varied.

Transport

On the whole, cast members will either get themselves to set / location, or they will want to be collected and dropped off (by a production manager or other crew member). The crew has been budgeted at £25 a week traveling, enough for local trains / tubes / cars etc. Just. Well not really. But that's all you can give. The camera team will carry the cameras in a car, but the lights will need a van, probably a Luton size but possibly a Transit. It's best to avoid parking expenses but there will always be an unexpected time when you'll need to feed the meter.

£20k-ish

Stock

The materials used in the production of your film, just DV and DAT tapes, with a second lot of DV tapes so that you can clone (make a back-up) your tapes at the end of each day.

Stock	Quantity	Unit cost	No. Units	Definition	COST
DV stock	1	£3.00	30	each	£90.00
Sound Stock (Nagra or DAT)	1	£3.00	30	each	£90.00
DV backup stock (clone rushes)	1	£3.00	30	each	£90.00
					£270.00

Editing

Not too much money for the cutting room, but somehow you will find an Avid XpressDV, or perhaps you may be forced to use Final Cut Pro (which may have implications later). There is £200 budgeted for a Foley artist and £500 for a studio – that's going to be tough but will be worth it's weight in gold to the sound of your film. The final mix is where all the sound effects are mixed together and is very expensive as you can see, but this will give you a properly balanced fully professional sound mix. Unfortunately, you and the editor will have been the sound editors as there is no budget to hire one. That's going to take you a month at the best. Lastly is the music – £100, what a joke – but it can be done if you find the right composer.

Editing and Post (first phase)	Quantity	Unit cost	No. Units	Definition	COST
Cutting room hire (plus equipment)	1	£1,000.00	1	all in	£1,000.00
Foley Artist	1	£200.00	1	day	£200.00
Foley studio	1	£500.00	1	day	£500.00
Final Mix	1	£1,000.00	2	days	£2,000.00
Music	1	£100.00	1	fee	£100.00
					£3,800.00

Digital to film

Currently, if you want to shoot digitally and then go to a theatrical release, or even reach ALL film festivals, you are going to need to convert your master DV edit tape (or whatever final videotape format you have chosen) to a 35mm print. This is no mean feat as you are converting digital information into a photochemical / mechanical format. It is MUCH more complicated than copying from one tape format to another. And it's very expensive too. There are several processes, the cheapest and roughest simply involves kind of shooting a 35mm camera that is pointed at a high resolution computer monitor. It works, but it isn't the best solution. The problem is, to get the best results, you need to spend the most money . . . And here's the rub . . . by the time you have spent all that extra money on blowing your digital movie up to 35mm, it may actually have cost the same as if you had shot on S16mm or even 35mm in the first place. That's the end figure remember, not what you started with, and you may not have had access to all that cash up front. Low budget film making is about cash flowing. Raise a little dosh, shoot a little, raise some more, edit some more, raise a bit, blow up to 35mm and so on.

So how much will it cost to blow up from a digital format to 35mm film? It's hard to put an accurate figure on it as the technology is changing, getting cheaper, better and faster. But as a rough guide, think in the region of £30k . . . yes that's right, £30k(!) for a combined optical 35mm negative ready to make multiple release prints.

Development	
Story & scripts	£150.00
	£150.00

Pre-production	
Main fixed crew	£3,300.00
Production and office	£5,764.00
	£9,064.00

Production	
Principal cast	£2,470.00
Crew	£6,100.00
Equipment hire	£6,440.00
Design, costume and make-up	£1,630.00
Location & set facilities	£3,000.00
Accommodation & catering	£3,025.00
Transport	£4,975.00
Stock	£4,315.00
	£31,955.00

Post production	
Editing and Post (first phase)	£9,850.00
	£9,850.00

Sub total	**£51,019.00**
Contingency (2%)	**£1,020.38**
Insurance (2%)	**£1,040.79**
Grand total	**£53,080.17**

Budget summary for micro budget movie at £50k-ish shot on Super 16mm

Even though this budget has more than doubled the £20k-ish model, it's still very similar. The main differences are the crew almost doubling, the fact that it is now shot on Super 16mm film, and the shoot has extended by a week. Most departments also get a little extra cash, but in essence, it's the same shoot. What is shocking is how little the production is altered by having more than twice as much cash!!

This budget does not include the final grading and blow up to 35mm film, but it should get you to a pretty damn hot looking miniDV master (or BetaSP) with fully mixed soundtrack and music. In essence, it is completed, you just haven't gone through the very final and expensive blow-up phase.

NOTE – PLEASE REFER BACK TO THE £20K-ISH MODEL AS THIS £50K-ISH MODEL SHARES SO MUCH IN COMMON.

The figures quoted here do not mean you will get these deals, just that these deals and sometimes even better, are do-able . . . But there are no guarantees and NEVER tell a supplier that 'I should get this deal 'cos it was in that book . . . '

£50k-ish

Budget breakdown for micro budget movie at £50k-ish

Story rights

Still no payment for the writer and just the fees for US copyright registration. Bigger film, means bigger crew means more copies of the screenplay, so there's an increase in copying charges.

Story & scripts	Quantity	Unit cost	No. Units	Definition	COST
Story rights	1	0.00	1		
US copyright	1	25.00	1		25.00
Screenplay duplication & binding	100	1.25	1	each	125.00
					150.00

Main fixed crew

Same payments here as the last budget (remember you could slice £1.5k off your budget by not paying the W/D/P), and really these are just token payments to help with the rent. The editor has an increase in pay from £50 a week to £75 per week.

Main Fixed Crew	Quantity	Unit cost	No. Units	Definition	COST
Producer	1	500.00	1	fixed	500.00
Director	1	500.00	1	fixed	500.00
Writer	1	500.00	1	fixed	500.00
Editor	1	75.00	24	weeks	1,800.00
					3,300.00

Production and office

In short, exactly the same as the £20k-ish model – see earlier!

Production and Office	Quantity	Unit cost	No. Units	Definition	COST
Company incorporation	1	150.00	1	each	150.00
Insurance (PL and EL)	1	250.00	1	year	250.00
Office rent	1	75.00	8	weeks	600.00
Office supplies	1	500.00	1	approx	500.00
Office power	1	100.00	1	year	100.00
Vehicle fuel for production team	2	400.00	1	approx	800.00
Phone and fax	1	750.00	1	approx	750.00
Toner / Inkjet carts	1	200.00	1	approx	200.00
DSL connection	1	22.00	12	months	264.00
					5,764.00

Crew

The crew has more than doubled in numbers, a clear and obvious cost increase. The shoot is also four weeks and not three now, another 25% increase, although everyone is still working for peanuts! This size crew will behave much like a fully pro crew and if you oil the machine, it should run very smoothly. Everyone is stretched but there are enough people to do the job. There is still plenty of prep time in this model which could easily get the snip if push came to shove. Departments are now fully populated, and whole new departments, such as grips, have now appeared.

Crew	Quantity	Unit cost	No. Units	Definition	COST
Production manager / assistant	1	50.00	22	weeks	1,100.00
1st AD	1	50.00	5	weeks	250.00
2nd AD	1	50.00	4	weeks	200.00
Continuity	1	50.00	4	weeks	200.00
DP	1	50.00	6	weeks	300.00
Assistant camera	1	50.00	4	weeks	200.00
Focus puller / asst camera	1	50.00	4	weeks	200.00
Gaffer / spark	1	50.00	4	weeks	200.00
Spark	1	50.00	4	weeks	200.00
Grip 1	1	50.00	4	weeks	200.00
Grip 2	1	50.00	4	weeks	200.00
Costume	1	50.00	7	weeks	350.00
Make-up	1	50.00	4	weeks	200.00
Production design	1	50.00	13	weeks	650.00
Art director	1	50.00	5	weeks	250.00
Props master	1	50.00	5	weeks	250.00
Sound recordist	1	50.00	4	weeks	200.00
Asst sound recordist	1	50.00	4	weeks	200.00
Stills camera	1	50.00	2	days	100.00
Runner driver	1	50.00	8	weeks	400.00
Production Assistant	1	50.00	5	weeks	250.00
					6,100.00

Principal cast	Quantity	Unit cost	No. Units	Definition	COST
Steckler	1	100.00	4	weeks	400.00
Carter	1	100.00	4	weeks	400.00
Mik (friend)	1	100.00	2	weeks	200.00
Taylor (Cop)	1	100.00	2	days	200.00
Dezrae (minor role)	1	25.00	2	days	50.00
Carter's husband	1	0.00	1	days	
Dead girl in park	1	0.00	1	days	
TV host	1	25.00	1	days	25.00
TV reporter	1	25.00	1	days	25.00
Inspector Forrester	1	0.00	1	weeks	
Witnesses	2	25.00	1	days	50.00
Forensic expert	1	25.00	1	days	25.00
Gangster	1	25.00	2	days	50.00
Café extras	3	0.00	1	days	
Prostitute	1	100.00	1	days	100.00
Secretary	1	25.00	1	days	25.00
Gansters daughter	1	0.00	1	days	
Steckler's wife	1	25.00	1	days	25.00
Husband of victim	1	25.00	1	days	25.00
Steckler's assistant	1	25.00	1	days	25.00
Prostitute 2	1	100.00	1	days	100.00
Bank Manager	1	25.00	1	days	25.00
Park crime scene extras	6	20.00	1	days	120.00
Hunting montage extras	8	20.00	1	days	160.00
Second crime scene extras	5	20.00	1	days	100.00
Gangster party extras	8	20.00	1	days	160.00
TV show extras	2	20.00	1	days	40.00
Police arrest extras	7	20.00	1	days	140.00
					2,470.00

Equipment hire	Quantity	Unit cost	No. Units	Definition	COST
Camera department					
Arri camera kit inc lenses (prime and zoom)	1	700.00	4	weeks	2,800.00
Tripod legs and head	1	50.00	4	weeks	200.00
Cokin camera filters	2	10.00	1	each	20.00
Camera tape, gaffer tape, consumables	1	150.00	1	approx	150.00
Sound department					
DAT recorder	1	50.00	4	weeks	200.00
Microphones - wide	1	25.00	4	weeks	100.00
Microphones - narrow	1	25.00	4	weeks	100.00
Microphones - tie clip radio mics	2	25.00	4	weeks	200.00
Boom pole & wind shield	1	15.00	4	weeks	60.00
Misc accessories and cables	1	15.00	4	weeks	60.00
Grips					
Track and dolly	1		4		
Six straights, two curves, wedges etc.	1		4		
All in grips deal	1	250.00	4	weeks	1,000.00
Lighting department					
4k HMI	2		4	weeks	
1.2k HMI	2		4	weeks	
2k Blonde	3		4	weeks	
1k Redhead	4		4	weeks	
Inky Dinks	4		4	weeks	
Mizar	3		4	weeks	
Other lights	1		4		
Stands, tripods and cables	1		4	weeks	
All in lighting hire deal	1	1,000.00	1	all in	1,000.00
Gels/ Trace/ Spun	1	100.00	1	approx	100.00
Practical light bulbs	25	4.00	1	each	100.00
Smoke machine	1	150.00	1	approx	150.00
Production equipment					
Walkie Talkies	1	200.00	1	approx	200.00
					6,440.00

Cast

Much the same budget except because the shoot is a week longer, the actors are needed for longer periods (read fuller notes in £20k-ish model on page 149).

Equipment hire

The main modifications between the £20k-ish budget and this £50k-ish budget is that there are now film cameras, a new Grips department, more lights and a week longer hire period. Film cameras are much more involved than a miniDV camera and comes in heavy flight cases. There are several cameras to choose from but it will almost certainly be an Aaton or Arriflex SRII or SRIII, all excellent cameras. The deal here is pretty damn good but do-able.

Grips, a whole new department, will only include the basics. Some track, a dolly and a box of wooden wedges. You can't ask for much more, nor do you really need it. Forget cranes and the likes for now. This kit is very large and heavy so you will need strong grips and a large vehicle to transport it. Lighting has increased too. More lights means more cables, more crew, bigger truck, more power, longer setup times . . . but it will mean your images should look better.

Sound and production equipment are largely the same except for longer hire periods. (read fuller notes in £20k-ish model on page 150).

£50k-ish

Design

The design / make-up / costume budgets have more than doubled in an attempt to put more on the screen. Still a pitiful amount though so the production team are going to have to work very hard to get stuff for free.

Design, costume and make-up	Quantity	Unit cost	No. Units	Definition	COST
Production design budget	1	500.00	1	approx	500.00
Props (make and buy)	1	400.00	1	approx	400.00
Costume budget	1	400.00	1	approx	400.00
Make-up budget	1	150.00	1	approx	150.00
Continuity polaroids	10	18.00	1	films	180.00
					1,630.00

Location and set facilities

No change here from the £20k-ish budget.

Location & Set Facilities	Quantity	Unit cost	No. Units	Definition	COST
Location Fees (house rental)	1	1,250.00	2	months	2,500.00
Location power	1	500.00	1	approx	500.00
					3,000.00

Accommodation and catering

Pretty much the same as the £20k-ish budget (page 153) except there are more shooting days and so the budget has risen.

Accommodation & Catering	Quantity	Unit cost	No. Units	Definition	COST
Catering Cast (approx)	1	3.50	450	meals	1,575.00
Catering Crew (approx)	1	3.50	300	meals	1,050.00
Caterer fees	1	100.00	4	weeks	400.00
					3,025.00

Transport

Still much the same as the £20k-ish budget (page 153) except longer hire times etc. The van for equipment will be filled to the brim now there are extra lights AND grip's equipment. If push comes to shove you may end up needing to hire a second van.

Transport	Quantity	Unit cost	No. Units	Definition	COST
Cast Travel	1	750.00	1	approx	750.00
Crew Travel	25	25.00	5	weeks	3,125.00
Vehicle Rentals - Lighting / grips	1	250.00	4	weeks	1,000.00
Parking	1	100.00	1	approx	100.00
					4,975.00

Stock

Stock has now risen sharply as you are shooting on S16mm film, the budget is no longer in the £hundreds, but £thousands. Sound remains essentially the same.

Stock	Quantity	Unit cost	No. Units	Definition	COST
S16mm Film Stock	1	65.00	65	each	4,225.00
Sound Stock (Nagra or DAT)	1	3.00	30	each	90.00
					4,315.00

Editing and post (first phase)	Quantity	Unit cost	No. Units	Definition	COST
S16mm developing inc TK	1	0.21	25000	feet	5,250.00
Cutting room hire (plus equipment)	1	1,000.00	1	all in	1,000.00
Foley artist	1	200.00	1	day	200.00
Foley studio	1	500.00	1	day	500.00
Final Mix	1	1,250.00	2	days	2,500.00
Music	1	400.00	1	fee	400.00
					9,850.00

Editing

A big increase here is the lab fees to process the film and telecine it onto videotape (either DV or Beta). You will still have to work hard to find a cutting room for the pitiful budget but you will get something sorted. There is a little more money for the final mix and more for the music too.

£50k-ish

Budget and schedule are golden

Once the crew understand and 'buy into' your budgetary restrictions, you shouldn't have too many problems, unless of course you have seriously miscalculated some elements of your story. The real problem facing you is the inevitability of dropping behind schedule, how you deal with it, how much it might cost (and remember you have no more money). It will happen. You will fall behind.

The issue here is how your director chooses to behave in the light of forced creative compromise. Inexperienced directors will often complain and stick their head in the sand, refusing to modify their vision, after all they've heard stories of Hollywood directors sticking to their creative guns and producing a masterpiece . . . But those people would always have a financial safety net, which YOU don't have. What could happen to your production is that you run out of budget and time leaving large chunks of the script unshot. That's a serious problem as you don't have enough footage to make a movie! Sure you can do re-shoots, but these extra shoots are usually designed to plug story holes and pickup up missing shots, not to create all new foundations!

The smart director will recognise that if they overshoot tonight, they will be forced to shoot less tomorrow – they would consider in advance what would need to be dropped and weigh that up against what they need to shoot now that will force them behind schedule. It's always a juggling act that is essentially about creative priority . . . 'can scene x be shot in a single wide shot instead of the three shots planned so that scene y can be shot correctly – as scene y is a very important scene. Or can scene x be rewritten to be shorter and sweeter? Can we drop scene x altogether?' These are very tough questions especially when you are on set, on the front lines, being bombarded by questions, comments and decisions. Whatever happens, keep the golden rule in mind . . . 'Never go over budget and never drop behind schedule'.

DIRECTOR

Item	Quantity	Unit Cost	No.Units	Definition	COST
Negative cutting	1	£2,500.00	1	each	£2,500.00
First trial print (S16mm)	1	£0.23	3600	feet	£828.00
Interpositive (S16mm)	1	£0.60	3600	feet	£2,160.00
Internegative blow up (35mm)	1	£0.80	9200	feet	£7,360.00
Optical sound transfer	1	£0.25	9200	feet	£2,300.00
Com/Opt answer print	1	£0.15	9600	feet	£1,440.00
Titles	1	£750.00	1	each	£750.00
Opticals	1	£750.00	1	each	£750.00
Show print	3	£800.00	1	each	£2,400.00
Low contrast TK print	1	£1,200.00	1	each	£1,200.00
Telecine PAL	1	£1,500.00	1	each	£1,500.00
NTSC dupe	1	£350.00	1	each	£350.00
Telecine clones	1	£200.00	3	each	£600.00
Telecine stock (Digibeta)	1	£30.00	5	each	£150.00
					£24,288.00

Final post stages – Super 16mm to 35mm blow up

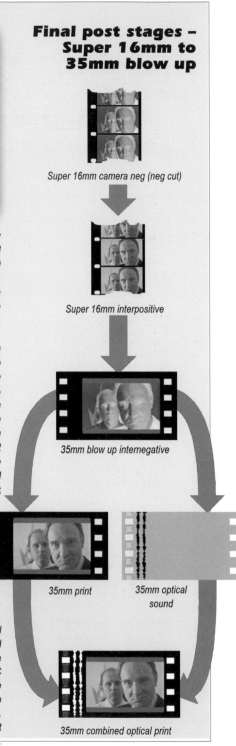

Super 16mm camera neg (neg cut)

Super 16mm interpositive

35mm blow up internegative

35mm print

35mm optical sound

35mm combined optical print

Scary propeller head time I'm afraid. Film post production is rather complicated, especially for the videotape generation who expect everything 'now and cheap'. This model is based on a movie shot at 25fps, on Super 16mm film, to be blown up to 35mm and running 90 minutes (at 25fps). OK, so you shot on Super 16mm negative (at 25fps), cut on an Avid, locked picture, broke the project down into sub 18 minute reels, sent the EDL off to the neg cutter who has checked it and given you the OK. You are now ready to go through the final and most expensive phase.

The neg cut should cost around £2500. You'll get cheaper quotes but I'd always go with the best neg cutters such as Sylvia Wheeler or Tru Cut. They're competitive yes, cheap no, but they'll get it right. The first trail print is a print made from the cut neg – this is the first time you will see it projected on film (without sound). This first copy will be about 80% right in terms of grading (colour balance) but you will need to make more attempts (with the lab guys), which you shouldn't be paying for as this is a one off price. Once you have all your grading correct (which may take three of four passes), you can do the S16mm Interpositive, a simple low contrast 'positive' (opposed to negative) copy of the neg without any joins (as it is no longer cut up from the master camera negative). Next is the expensive bit, the blow up to 35mm . . . and it could set you back upwards of £7k . . . All those times in the cutting room when you kept the shot long . . . 'It's a beautiful shot, let it breathe, let it breathe . . .' will now have a direct cost implication, about £150 per minute, or £3 per second . . . pause for thought huh? The optical sound transfer is a copy of your final sound mix transferred (through a special process) onto 35mm film (make sure they know you shot and mixed at 25fps). The titles and opticals are rough estimates, but if you keep them simple you could come in under this budget (white titles on a black background only please). The Com/Opt answer print is the first copy of your film, fully graded, with titles and opticals and a full sound mix. Hoorah! Subsequent prints should be made at the show print rate of around £800.

The final stages are the transfer of the film to video, known as Telecine (TK). I would always pay for the best, and £1500 isn't much for this. Call around top Soho facilities and ask to get the best grader . . . 'and we'll be happy to work around whenever you have down time'. It should take a long day to do this properly. Later you can make an NTSC dupe of this TK at another facility (for international sales). You'll also want to make some DibiBeta clones of your final TK for safety and your own personal archive. One way to keep costs down is to buy raw stock from a place like Stanley Productions in Wardour St., and take those to the TK (or they'll charge you £80 for their stock, as opposed to £30 at Stanleys).

Divisions	Cost
Development	
Story & Scripts	1,275.00
	1,275.00
Pre-Production	
Producers Fee	2,000.00
Production Office	5,850.00
	7,850.00
Production	
Principal Cast	20,530.00
Production Crew	28,900.00
Equipment Hire	12,000.00
Costume Design	2,000.00
Make-up and Hair	1,000.00
Production Design	16,000.00
Stunts	15,000.00
Location & Set Facilities	9,200.00
Accommodation & Catering	8,800.00
Transport	10,100.00
Stock	6,295.00
	129,825.00
Post Production	
Lab & Processing (Trailer)	1,675.00
Lab & Processing	30,910.00
Editing	18,650.00
Music	3,000.00
Professional fees	2,000.00
	56,235.00
Completion	
Publicity	1,725.00
Delivery	1,810.00
	3,535.00
Sub Total	**198,720.00**
Contingency (1%)	**1,987.20**
Insurance (1%)	**2,007.07**
Completion Bond (0%)	**0.00**

Budget summary for low budget movie at £200k-ish shot on Super 16mm

The £200k-ish budget here is one of the pre production budgets I actually prepared for 'Urban Ghost Story', my third feature film. I also did budgets at other price breaks, including £850k and £1.5m. It was shot on Super 16mm and blown up to 35mm (which is also included in the budget). The movie was set in a high rise tower block flat which we decided to build on a stage at Ealing Film Studios, and included a major stunt sequence with a high fall from the building and a spectacular car crash. Sound was an important issue too, so a large amount was budgeted there too.

The cast were all drawn from London, where the film was shot (even though it was set in Scotland), with only one or two actors being shipped down from North of the border.

Here's the truth . . . No matter how much you have, it's never enough! However, more money does mean you can pay yourself a little AND other problems can become easier to solve as you can simply write a cheque! Even though you may have more money, keep your story and production contained and focus on that great story told well.

Budget Breakdown for Low Budget Movie at £200k-ish

Story rights

The fee, which is nominal here, simply covers rent. There's the usual US Copyright office fee and £250 for copies as the plan is now to get hold of an old copier and do copies in house.

Story & scripts	Quantity	Unit cost	No. Units	Definition	COST
Writers fee (Draft 1)	1	1,000.00	1	each	1,000.00
US copyright	1	25.00	1	each	25.00
Screenplay duplication & binding	1	250.00	1	all in	250.00
					1,275.00

Main fixed crew

It's not gonna go far but a grand each will help with the rent. If you have an alternative income, that will make a massive difference.

Producer's fee	Quantity	Unit cost	No. Units	Definition	COST
Producer's fee	1	1,000.00	1	each	1,000.00
Diretor's fee	1	1,000.00	1	each	1,000.00
					2,000.00

Production and office

A limited company had already been incorporated so there was no additional cost there (as well as all the usual insurance policies). Running the office is expensive, especially as it included office space at a major studio and a nominal fee for a production assistant to help from pretty much the project inception.

Production office	Quantity	Unit cost	No. Units	Definition	COST
Office rent	1	100.00	16	weeks	1,600.00
Office supplies	1	300.00	1	each	300.00
Post / delivery	1	1,000.00	1	each	1,000.00
Misc pre production expenses	1	500.00	1	each	500.00
Cast advertising	1	150.00	1	each	150.00
Vehicle fuel for production team	1	500.00	1	each	500.00
Photocopying and printing	1	300.00	1	each	300.00
Secretary / PA	1	1,500.00	1	each	1,500.00
					5,850.00

Location and set

There's a bunch of costs here that are pretty obvious, but the main cost is for the stage, a grand a week. This is a major deal and would include green rooms and production offices. There are stages out there and when there isn't much happening, studios will often do amazing deals. Remember you will need to factor in build and strike (breaking down) times.

Location & set facilities	Quantity	Unit cost	No. Units	Definition	COST
Location fees	1	500.00	1	each	500.00
Location power	1	100.00	1	each	100.00
Location tea & coffee	1	500.00	1	each	500.00
Location repairs	1	100.00	1	each	100.00
Studio / stage hire	1	1,000.00	8	weeks	8,000.00
					9,200.00

Accommodation and catering

All the cast lived in London (hire actors who do not need accommodating!) except for the lead girl who was from Glasgow, and her mother who acted as a minder. We needed to hire a flat for them. Catering was even easier. As we were based at a studio, we gave everyone £5 a day to buy food from the canteen. If they wanted they could pocket the money and bring a packed lunch. And some did! (we didn't provide breakfast)

Accommodation & catering	Quantity	Unit cost	No. Units	Definition	COST
Accommodation	3	1,200.00	1	est	3,600.00
Catering (Misc)	40	5.00	26	each	5,200.00
					8,800.00

Principal cast	Quantity	Unit cost	No. Units	Definition	COST
Kate	1	80.00	30	days	2,400.00
John	1	80.00	25	days	2,000.00
Lizzie	1	80.00	30	days	2,400.00
Lizzie Minder	1	80.00	30	days	2,400.00
Alex	1	80.00	20	days	1,600.00
Alex Minder	1	80.00	20	days	1,600.00
ER Crew Man 2	1	80.00	1	days	80.00
Dr Davis	1	80.00	5	days	400.00
Kerrie	1	80.00	5	days	400.00
Baby	1	150.00	1	each	150.00
Police Officer #1	1	80.00	1	days	80.00
Police Officer #2	1	80.00	1	days	80.00
Police Officer #3	1	80.00	1	days	80.00
Kevins Mum	1	80.00	2	days	160.00
Shop Keeper #1	1	80.00	1	days	80.00
Shop Keeper #2	1	80.00	1	days	80.00
George	1	80.00	2	days	160.00
Magistrate	1	80.00	1	days	80.00
Kevins Dad	1	80.00	1	days	80.00
Helen (Social Worker)	1	80.00	3	days	240.00
Crowd	1	200.00	1	days	200.00
Kevin	1	80.00	2	days	160.00
Kevin Minder	1	80.00	2	days	160.00
Loan Shark	1	80.00	2	days	160.00
Henchman #1	1	80.00	2	days	160.00
Henchman #2	1	80.00	2	days	160.00
DC Goodwin	1	80.00	1	days	80.00
WPC Tomkins	1	80.00	1	days	80.00
Grant	1	80.00	1	days	80.00
Editor	1	80.00	2	days	160.00
Journalist	1	80.00	1	days	80.00
Journalists	1	100.00	1	days	100.00
School Girl #1	1	80.00	1	days	80.00
School Girl #2	1	80.00	1	days	80.00
School Girl #3	1	80.00	1	days	80.00
Vicar	1	80.00	2	days	160.00
Quinn	1	80.00	10	days	800.00
Smart	1	80.00	7	days	560.00
Extra Scientists	1	250.00	1	days	250.00
Mrs Ash	1	80.00	1	days	80.00
Mr Ash	1	80.00	1	days	80.00
Shop Keeper (heist)	1	80.00	1	days	80.00
School Teacher	1	80.00	1	days	80.00
Student	1	80.00	1	days	80.00
Doctor	1	80.00	1	days	80.00
Doctor 2	1	80.00	1	days	80.00
PA Woman	1	80.00	1	days	80.00
Police Officer #1	1	80.00	1	days	80.00
DC Mansell	1	80.00	2	days	160.00
Extra Police	1	100.00	1	days	100.00
Hospital Extras	1	250.00	1	days	250.00
Solicitor	1	80.00	1	days	80.00
Alex (child)	1	50.00	20	days	1,000.00
					20,530.00

Cast

To my horror, the cast bill came to over £20k! After this budget we did a rewrite and combined and pruned out some characters keeping the budget down. We planned to pay everyone £80 a day which we thought was fair. We actually ended up paying Equity minimum rates which, believe it or not, actually reduced the budget we had planned! In the script stage always ask yourself, do I need that extra character? 'Cos you know and I know that if you don't NEED them, they will be pruned out in the final pre shoot rewrite. Beware of kids too as you may need to hire an expensive tutor chaperone.

Transport	Quantity	Unit cost	No. Units	Definition	COST
Cast Travel	1	2,000.00	1	est	2,000.00
Crew Travel					
Vehicle Rentals - Camera	1	400.00	5	weeks	2,000.00
Vehicle Rentals - Grips	1	400.00	5	weeks	2,000.00
Vehicle Rentals - Lighting	1	400.00	5	weeks	2,000.00
Taxis		100.00	1	each	100.00
Fuel		2,000.00	1	each	2,000.00
					10,100.00

Transport

We planned to do a deal with a cab company to ferry the cast around, for which we budgeted £2k. The crew were asked to get themselves to and from set under their own steam. We hired three vans, for Lighting, Camera and Grips, each for five weeks, and of course, vans guzzle petrol too!

Crew

As you see, we had planned for a HUGE crew, or it felt like that to me at the time! Rather unconventionally we planned to pay everyone the same amount of money, £100 a week, just a token to say thanks, so no one felt more or less important than anyone else. This worked really well. The only people who got more were the child minder who came from an agency, and the editor at £150 as he had to work for many months and simply could not give up that amount of time for so little money.

Production crew	Quantity	Unit cost	No. Units	Definition	COST
Production manager	1	100.00	8	w	800.00
Line producer	1	100.00	7	w	700.00
Director	1	100.00	5	w	500.00
Production co-ordinator	1	100.00	8	w	800.00
Production asst	1	100.00	7	w	700.00
Production accountant	1	100.00	6	w	600.00
Location manager	1	100.00	7	w	700.00
1st assistant director	1	100.00	5	w	500.00
2nd assistant director	1	100.00	5	w	500.00
3rd assistant director	1	100.00	5	w	500.00
Script continuity	1	100.00	5	w	500.00
Story board artist	1	100.00	2	w	200.00
Director of photography	1	100.00	5	w	500.00
Camera operator	1	100.00	5	w	500.00
Camera operator (2nd cam)	1	100.00	1	w	100.00
Focus puller / camera asst	1	100.00	5	w	500.00
Clapper loader / camera asst	1	100.00	5	w	500.00
Gaffer	1	100.00	5	w	500.00
Best boy	1	100.00	5	w	500.00
Key grip	1	100.00	5	w	500.00
Dolly grip	1	100.00	5	w	500.00
Production sound recordist	1	100.00	5	w	500.00
Asst sound / boom ops	1	100.00	5	w	500.00
Costume designer	1	100.00	7	w	700.00
Costume asst / wardrobe	1	100.00	6	w	600.00
Make-up artist / hair stylist	1	100.00	5	w	500.00
Make-up assistant	1	100.00	5	w	500.00
Production designer	1	100.00	9	w	900.00
Art director / set director	1	100.00	9	w	900.00
Set dresser	1	100.00	7	w	700.00
Prop master	1	100.00	7	w	700.00
Construction manager	1	100.00	7	w	700.00
Carpenter	1	100.00	7	w	700.00
Painter	1	100.00	7	w	700.00
Runner	1	100.00	6	w	600.00
Stills photographer	1	100.00	4	w	400.00
Unit publicist	1	100.00	1	w	100.00
Casting director	1	100.00	1	w	100.00
Child minder	1	600.00	5	w	3,000.00
Driver	1	100.00	5	w	500.00
2nd unit crew					
Director	1	100.00	1	w	100.00
Production manager	1	100.00	1	w	100.00
Director of photography / operator	1	100.00	1	w	100.00
Sound recordist / boom operator	1	100.00	1	w	100.00
Extra crew as needed					
Editor	1	150.00	22	w	3,300.00
Sound Editor	1	100.00	8	w	800.00
					28,900.00

Costume

We had planned to keep everything simple from a costume point, characters wearing pretty much the same throughout the film. Most of this budget was eaten up on a few well chosen costumes as well as hiring uniforms (such as police etc.)

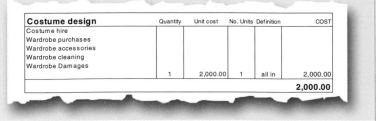

Costume design	Quantity	Unit cost	No. Units	Definition	COST
Costume hire					
Wardrobe purchases					
Wardrobe accessories					
Wardrobe cleaning					
Wardrobe Damages					
	1	2,000.00	1	all in	2,000.00
					2,000.00

Equipment hire	Quantity	Unit cost	No. Units	Definition	COST
Camera department					
Camera kit (includes body,mag,filters etc.)					
Zoom lens					
Prime lenses					
Tripod legs - short/tall					
Tripod head					
Camera filters					
Steadicam & operator					
Video assist					
Camera tape					
Gaffer tape					
Air cannister					
Additional accessories					
Lost or damaged equipment					
	1	5,000.00	1	all in	5,000.00
Grips department					
Dolly					
Bowl for camera head					
Straight track					
Curved track					
Wedges and blocks					
Snake arm					
Jib - to attach to dolly					
Remote head					
Car mount					
Camera vehicle					
Camera rig (misc)					
Grip truck					
Large crane plus operator					
Lost or damaged equipment					
	1	3,000.00	1	all in	3,000.00
Sound department					
DAT recorder time coded					
Microphones - wide					
Microphones - narrow					
Microphones - tie clip radio mics					
Boom pole & wind shield					
Mixing desk					
Misc accessories					
Lost or damaged equipment					
	1	1,000.00	1	all in	1,000.00
Lighting department					
12k HMI					
6k HMI					
4k HMI					
1.2k HMI					
5k Tungsten					
2k Blonde					
1k Redhead					
Inky Dinks					
Mizar					
sungun and batteries					
Generator					
Generator fuel					
Stands & tripods					
Gels/ trace/ spun					
Misc accessories					
Lost or damaged equipment					
Generator Operator					
	1	3,000.00	1	all in	3,000.00

Equipment hire
Rather than negotiating back and forth with the hire companies, we decided what equipment we wanted and what we could afford, and then presented that list to them. On the whole, with some little modifications, we always got what we wanted (the minor modifications were often an improvement or had no real impact).

The S16mm Cameras came from Arri Media. Eventually we got two SRIII camera bodies and shared the lenses, allowing for an ever present second camera / unit. We eventually dropped the video assist from the list which saved time and money.

The grips were the same kind of deal, although we very quickly dropped the crane shots as they were truly impractical – eventually we did hire a cherry picker crane for one of the end shots though.

Sound was even easier! It all came with our sound recordist. We hired it from him for much less than we had budgeted. He was happy. We were happy. Everyone wins.

Lighting was tougher and we had to make a lot of compromises. We dropped the generator as we ended up not needing it. One HMI bulb was accidentally broken too, which cost a knee trembling £500!

£200K-ish

Make-up

As there were so many actors, some special make-up (scars, gashes and one bloody sequence) plus stunt doubles who would need wigs, this department was more costly than I would have liked.

Make-up and hair	Quantity	Unit cost	No. Units	Definition	COST
Wig hire / purchases					
Make-up purchase					
Special make-up					
	1	1,000.00	1	all in	1,000.00
					1,000.00

Production design

This department was always going to be the biggest problem as there was a huge set that needed to be built, plus all the props to dress it. All manner of curious and new ways of building a set were devised and what was achieved was astonishing. One simple modification was to build the set only seven feet in height, opposed to eight! As it stands, the movie looks as good as it does largely due to the efforts of the whole production design team rather than as a result of simply spending money. Boy did they put their time and elbow grease into it!

Production design	Quantity	Unit cost	No. Units	Definition	COST
Set construction					
Construction equipment hire					
Construction consumables					
Materials					
Set strike / skips					
Props					
Continuity polaroids					
	1	16,000.00	1	all in	16,000.00
					16,000.00

Stunts

The plan was to hire a top stunt co-ordinator and get them to do the whole job for a fixed price. And that's what happened. There are so many hidden costs with stunts that it is almost its own little separate production – fire engines, paramedics, airbags, special rigging, production design to hide rigging, pyrotechnics, extra cameras . . . Boy it mounts up.

Stunts	Quantity	Unit cost	No. Units	Definition	COST
Stunt equipment					
Accessories					
Co-ordinator	1	15,000.00	1	est	15,000.00
					15,000.00

Stock

All stock was considered, S16mm film stock, audio stock, stills, etc. Clones of all master telecine tapes were budgeted for too, so that if the master was ever damaged there would be a backup.

Stock	Quantity	Unit cost	No. Units	Definition	COST
Film stock (S16mm rolls)	80	65.00	1	each	5,200.00
Sound stock (Nagra or DAT)	80	4.00	1	each	320.00
Master telecine stock (VT)	1	200.00	1	each	200.00
Dupe of telecine stock (VT)	1	200.00	1	each	200.00
NTSC dupe for sales agent stock (VT)	1	200.00	1	each	200.00
35mm stills stock	30	2.50	1	each	75.00
Batteries	1	100.00	1	est	100.00
					6,295.00

Editing	Quantity	Unit cost	No. Units	Definition	COST
Cutting room hire (plus equipment)	1	2,500.00	1	all in	2,500.00
Foley studio hire	1	500.00	1	each	500.00
Foley artist	1	200.00	1	each	200.00
Sound effects	1	1,000.00	1	each	1,000.00
ADR	1	250.00	1	each	250.00
Final mix / M&E mix	1	7,500.00	1	est	7,500.00
Dolby Digital fees	1	3,200.00	1	each	3,200.00
CGI effects	1	2,000.00	1	each	2,000.00
Retakes and pickups (inc possible cast & crew)	1	1,500.00	1	est	1,500.00
					18,650.00

Editing

The cutting room budget is £2.5k, hardly enough but do-able. Foley is much the same as other budgets but there is also £1k for the purchase of a sound effects library as the sound in the movie was going to play a crucial role. The importance of sound is also reflected in the much larger final mix fees, still too small really, plus a Dolby Digital licence. The movie also opens with a long CGI effect which needed to be custom made, so £2k was budgeted (the final effect was done for £2k but should have cost £20k). Finally there is £1.5k for re-shoots and pickup shoots for new shots and sequences that were devised in the cutting room, after the main shoot.

Lab & processing	Quantity	Unit cost	No. Units	Definition	COST
Negative processing and tape tansfer inc betas,TC, sync, clone dats & VHS	1	0.22	40000	foot	8,800.00
Negative cutting (cost per cut or per reel)	1	3.00	800	roll	2,400.00
S16 grading copy	1	0.23	3600	foot	810.00
Super 16mm IP	1	0.60	3600	foot	2,160.00
35mm blow up IN	1	0.80	9000	foot	7,200.00
Optical track - stereo	1	0.25	9000	foot	2,250.00
35mm check print	1	0.15	9600	foot	1,440.00
Low con print	1	800.00	1	each	800.00
Titles and opticals	1	1,250.00	1	each	1,250.00
Telecine to Broadcast Tape	1	3,500.00	1	each	3,500.00
Dupe Of Telecine	1	300.00	1	each	300.00
					30,910.00

Labs

Shooting on film and post producing traditionally is a complicated and messy business. Here's the budget drawn up for Urban Ghost Story but there is a more detailed version on page 158.

Lab & processing (trailer)	Quantity	Unit cost	No. Units	Definition	COST
Negative cutting		500.00	1		500.00
Trial print (can also be used for mixing)		150.00	1		150.00
Optical sound transfer		150.00	1		150.00
Titles		150.00	1		150.00
Textless titles backgrounds		50.00	1		50.00
Opticals		200.00	1		200.00
First answer print		75.00	1		75.00
Show print		75.00	1		75.00
Low contrast telecine print		75.00	1		75.00
Telecine to broadcast tape		100.00	1		100.00
Dupe of telecine		50.00	1		50.00
NTSC (or alternate standards dupe copy)		100.00	1		100.00
					1,675.00

Trailer post production

A separate budget for the production of a trailer was created so that it would not be overlooked until the final stages of production. The trailer is the most important point of sale that a film maker has, so it was imperative to get it right. Essentially, making a trailer is much like a mini version of the main post production process.

Music

The budget for music is, as usual, too small. Music is a minefield so I eventually opted to get the composer to do all the rights clearing himself. As he was the composer and performer (or if other performers were used they were his friends) this became much easier than it could have been.

Music	Quantity	Unit cost	No. Units	Definition	COST
Composer fees (inc relevant rights)					
Performers fees (inc relevant rights)					
Orchestra fees (inc relevant rights)					
Recording studio fees					
Incidental / library music					
Music supervisor (if possible)					
Existing recordings (inc relevant rights)					
Licenses					
Music all in deal (prefered)	1	3,000.00	1	all in	3,000.00
					3,000.00

Professional fees

This is an estimate for the lawyers and accountants. Beware of picking up that phone to ask a question as it can quickly mount up.

Professional fees	Quantity	Unit cost	No. Units	Definition	COST
Legal fees					
Accountant fees					
Production audit					
Bank charges					
	1	2,000.00	1	each	2,000.00
					2,000.00

Publicity

A publicity campaign was planned, not just for the film, but the film makers too. This campaign was aimed not just at the public, but also at the film business to get sales agents, talent agents and production companies to notice the film and the film makers.

Publicity	Quantity	Unit cost	No. Units	Definition	COST
Promotional material (press pack/stills dup	1	500.00	1	each	500.00
EPK - Elctronic press kit (Beta)	1	200.00	1	each	200.00
Clips tape (Beta)	3	25.00	1	each	75.00
Preview theatre (screenings)	1	150.00	3	each	450.00
Miscellaneous expenses / Fees		500.00	1	each	500.00
					1,725.00

Delivery

These are the final items that will be passed on to the sales agent so that they can actually sell and then 'deliver' your film to the buyers. It's a fairly self explanatory list, and the sales agent will want much more, but this is a good bare minimum. See 'Sales and distribution' later in the book.

Delivery	Quantity	Unit cost	No. Units	Definition	COST
Video dupe of master movie (inc M&E)	1	300.00	1	each	300.00
Video dupe of master trailer (inc M&E)	1	100.00	1	each	100.00
Copies of all legal documents	1	10.00	1	each	10.00
Dupes of master stills	1	200.00	1	each	200.00
VHS copies	1	100.00	1	each	100.00
35mm print (release)	1	800.00	1		800.00
35mm print (release) of trailer	1	100.00	1		100.00
Posters (if available)					
A4 one sheets (If available)					
Transcript (typed)	1	100.00	1	each	100.00
Misc certificates (origin, authorship, nationa	1	100.00	1	each	100.00
					1,810.00

BUDGET by Movie Tools

This budget template, produced by Movie Tools (www.movietools.com) was designed to allow you to quickly compile a budget for a new film, making changes and updating with the minimum of fuss whilst allowing you to present the budget in an easy to understand manner. First and most important is that it's drop dead easy to use. It requires Microsoft Excel to work.

First things first

Download the demo version and follow the setup instructions. When you open a new Budget spreadsheet you'll see that it has already been partially filled in. You can change anything you see and the quickest way to learn how is to experiment for a while. The main page of Budget shows all the sub-categories for the budget. There's the budgets name, the various main categories and sub-categories and then at the bottom you can add various percentage categories that act on the whole budget. At the very bottom is the painful truth; what you are going to have to shell out!

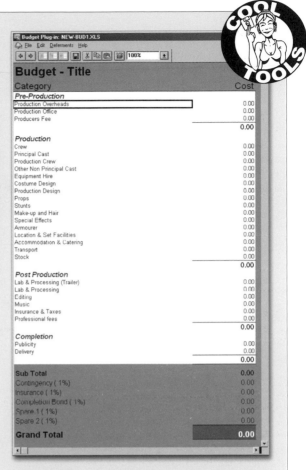

A few principles

If you right click your mouse on the budget (ctrl + click on a Mac), a small menu will appear giving you various options (the options will produce different results depending on what you clicked on). If nothing happens when you click on an option then it is disabled. Change will always do something; if you right clicked on a sub-category it will take you through to that sub-category. Add, Delete and Insert Line allow you to make new sub-categories. Cut and Insert Paste let you move sub-categories around. Insert, Delete and Move Category let you manage the main categories.

The Toolbar (at the top left of the screen) also has controls that allow you to navigate and manage budget as well.

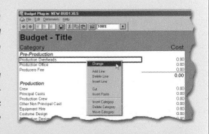

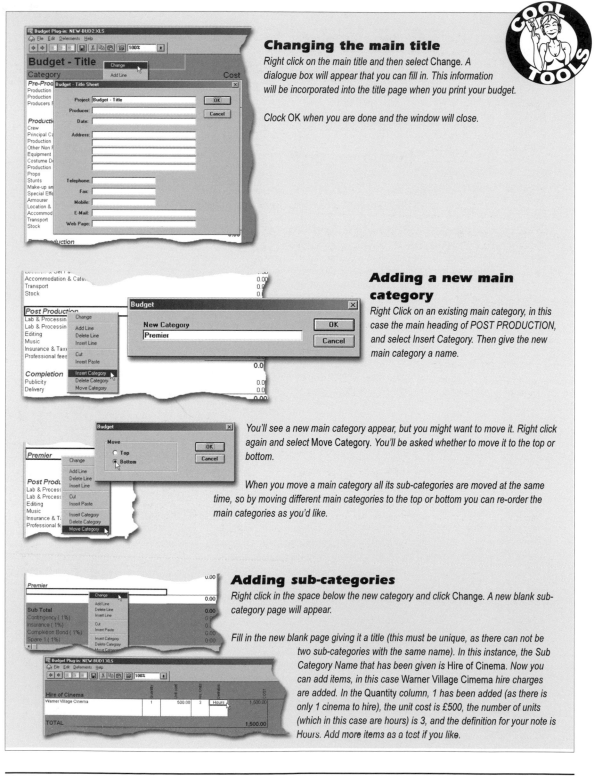

Changing the main title

Right click on the main title and then select Change. A dialogue box will appear that you can fill in. This information will be incorporated into the title page when you print your budget.

Clock OK when you are done and the window will close.

Adding a new main category

Right Click on an existing main category, in this case the main heading of POST PRODUCTION, and select Insert Category. Then give the new main category a name.

You'll see a new main category appear, but you might want to move it. Right click again and select Move Category. You'll be asked whether to move it to the top or bottom.

When you move a main category all its sub-categories are moved at the same time, so by moving different main categories to the top or bottom you can re-order the main categories as you'd like.

Adding sub-categories

Right click in the space below the new category and click Change. A new blank sub-category page will appear.

Fill in the new blank page giving it a title (this must be unique, as there can not be two sub-categories with the same name). In this instance, the Sub Category Name that has been given is Hire of Cinema. Now you can add items, in this case Warner Village Cimema hire charges are added. In the Quantity column, 1 has been added (as there is only 1 cinema to hire), the unit cost is £500, the number of units (which in this case are hours) is 3, and the definition for your note is Hours. Add more items as a test if you like.

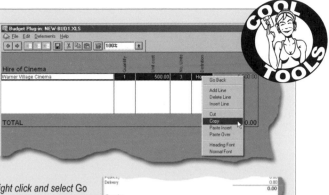

Adding and copying

Right clicking on the sub-category page lets you add and delete, copy and paste items. Play around with this for a moment to get your head around it.

To add more items just keep filing in the blank form. When you run out of spaces, use the right click and Add Line to add a blank line. When you get up to speed you will see that his is about as complicated as Budget actually gets, and almost everything is controlled by right clicking on the mouse.

When you've finished organising and filling in the page, either right click and select Go Back of click on the Go Back button.

You will now see that on the main front page of the budget, a new main category and sub-category have been created, AND already calculated and totalled! How easy is that!

Percentage categories

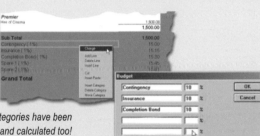

At the bottom of the main front Budget page are various customisable categories that apply a percentage to the whole budget. To customise them right click on the mouse and select Change and then fill in the dialogue box that appears.

If you leave a percentage category empty it will not appear on the budget. Click OK and you will see that these new percentage categories have been added and calculated too!

Printing a budget

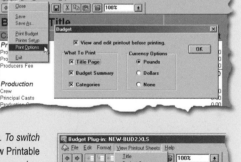

You can print a budget in a number of ways. First select which information you want to print out by going to the File Menu then Print options. If you just want to print out the budget summary (the budget main page), de-select the other options. If you want the whole budget, select Categories too. For now select everything.

Hit OK and your budget will then be analysed to produce the printable pages. To switch between the three – Title, Budget Summary and Categories – go to the View Printable Sheets on the menu bar.

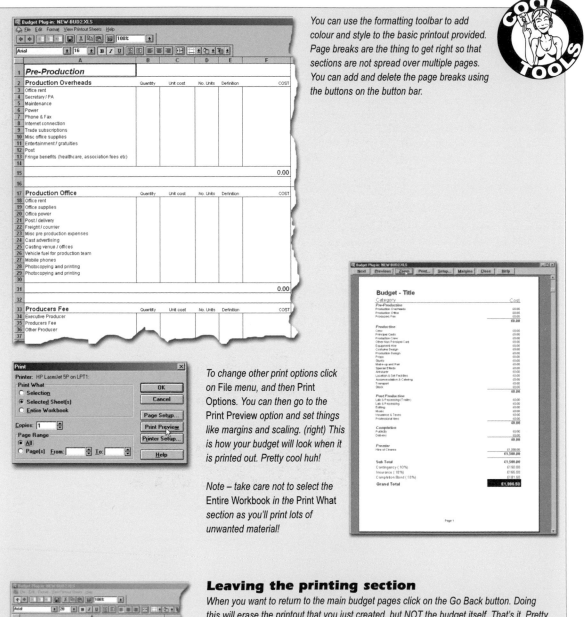

You can use the formatting toolbar to add colour and style to the basic printout provided. Page breaks are the thing to get right so that sections are not spread over multiple pages. You can add and delete the page breaks using the buttons on the button bar.

To change other print options click on File *menu,* and then Print Options. *You can then go to the* Print Preview *option and set things like margins and scaling. (right) This is how your budget will look when it is printed out. Pretty cool huh!*

Note – take care not to select the Entire Workbook *in the* Print What *section as you'll print lots of unwanted material!*

Leaving the printing section

When you want to return to the main budget pages click on the Go Back button. Doing this will erase the printout that you just created, but NOT the budget itself. That's it. Pretty easy huh?

Casting and Actors' Blueprint

THE SPOTLIGHT®

7 Leicester Place | London WC2H 7RJ

t +44 (0)20 7437 7631 | f +44 (0)20 7437 5881

e info@spotlightcd.com | www.spotlightcd.com

New film makers often overlook the importance of casting. Cameras, editing software, website design etc . . . all are fun areas of film making that DON'T argue back, nor do they have agents who ask awkward questions . . . and they never insist on vegan catering! Consequently, casting gets put on the back burner, friends are hired rather than pro actors, the phrase 'they will do . . . ' is often overheard in the production office and the result is an inferior level of acting . . . And an inferior movie.

Actors – Inexperienced, and often young

Generally you want to avoid these actors for the main roles unless you find a superstar in the making, your film is about very young people, or you have exhausted all other opportunities and have no budget.

Actors – Experienced and familiar

Generally, these are actors who have anywhere between a few TV credits and a shed load of movie credits. Often they're excellent performers but for some reason, have not had their 'break' and remain vaguely familiar but unknown. This talent pool is a fantastic resource for new film makers as you can offer somebody with amazing experience and skill a lead role that they will eat up.

Actors – Experienced and known

Generally, these are actors whose names you will recognise. This doesn't mean they are superstars, but on the whole, Joe public recognises them and often says 'oh, that's whatsitsface from that thingy I saw last week.' International sales will also be boosted by their involvement because their track record is used as a kind of currency during negotiations in selling your film.

Friends and relatives

Must never give them lead roles unless they are trained and professional, and even then it can be a bad idea as personal entanglements can get in the way. Good for extras, especially relatives for older extras. Beware of everyone in your film being young, a dead giveaway that the film was made by young people.

Kids

Using kids is a pain as they are unpredictable, usually bad performers and need supervision. By law there are limitations with how many hours they can work, and you may need to hire a professional tutor and chaperone. Write them out of your script!

Extras

The folk wandering around in the background. Signs of a low budget movie are . . . Not enough extras. Extras are consistently too young. Extras who occasionally slip into small parts and cannot act. Extras who are dressed inappropriately.

Casting and Actors' Blueprint

How do you go about casting your film? The first thing to understand is that there are two very distinct and separate parts when working with actors. The first is all business, it's when you approach agents, interview actors and invite them to be part of your film, then negotiate contracts and conditions etc. The second part is purely craft and art and involves the actor doing what they were hired to do – to bring heart, soul and a physical body to what was once merely words on a page.

The actors are the emotional vessel through which your story is told. Getting the right cast is as essential as having that great screenplay.

Slash and burn early

When you write your screenplay, you will undoubtedly have written without major consideration of the budget. Upon completion of what you consider to be the 'first draft' of your screenplay, a draft that you will be happy to present to actors, ask yourself a simple question – *'can I cut down the amount of characters in the film?'* Actors cost money, servicing the actors costs money, dealing with actors eats up valuable emotional and intellectual energy. In short, you want as few actors as possible. You might resist this notion, believing that all your characters are individual, unique and necessary, but it's a guaranteed fact that wherever it is possible to merge characters and reduce the number of characters, you will do so before you shoot – probably the night before! So why not do it now when you can think clearly and are not under pressure?

Typically, some secondary characters serve the same purpose in the story. You will be surprised that more often than not, your screenplay will be improved by merging these characters. Another simple slash and burn would be if your lead character is attacked and beaten up by four men. Ask yourself, can this be three men or even two? Budget saved!

Shopping list

Once you have completed this new leaner draft of your screenplay, you can begin the casting process. This does not, however, mean that you can rest on your laurels and you can stop writing, you must continue to develop your screenplay, each and every day by re-writing.

Take your screenplay and break it down, making a list of every single character who will appear on your screen. You should have three lists . . . Primary, Secondary and Tertiary characters.

Whenever you talk about your film, the second thing you will be asked (first is what's it about) is 'Who is in it . . . ?' You don't want to say my brother-in-law, my mates, etc. Don't short change your dreams by using unknown and untalented actors off the bat. You may be forced to go there, but don't start there.

Casting and actors flow chart Part 1

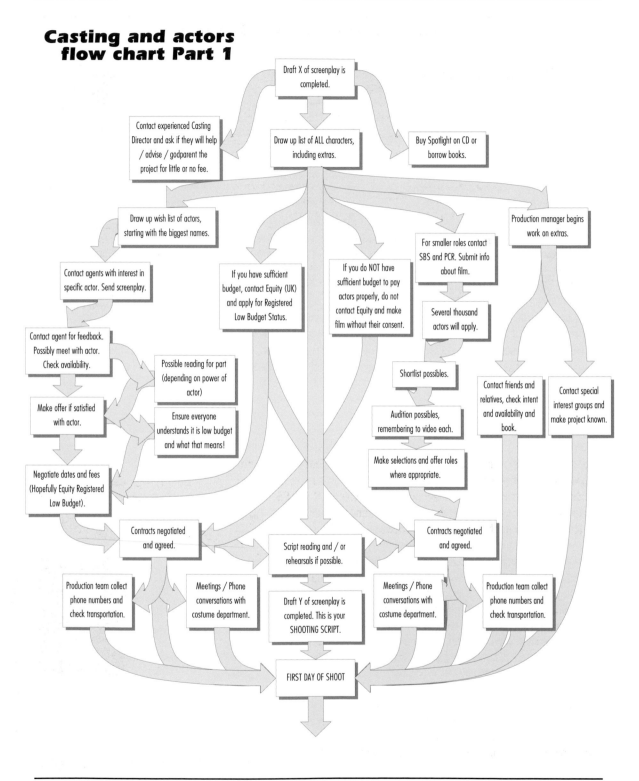

Draft X of screenplay is completed.

Contact experienced Casting Director and ask if they will help / advise / godparent the project for little or no fee.

Draw up list of ALL characters, including extras.

Buy Spotlight on CD or borrow books.

Draw up wish list of actors, starting with the biggest names.

Production manager begins work on extras.

Contact agents with interest in specific actor. Send screenplay.

If you have sufficient budget, contact Equity (UK) and apply for Registered Low Budget Status.

If you do NOT have sufficient budget to pay actors properly, do not contact Equity and make film without their consent.

For smaller roles contact SBS and PCR. Submit info about film.

Contact agent for feedback. Possibly meet with actor. Check availability.

Possible reading for part (depending on power of actor)

Several thousand actors will apply.

Make offer if satisfied with actor.

Ensure everyone understands it is low budget and what that means!

Shortlist possibles.

Contact friends and relatives, check intent and availability and book.

Contact special interest groups and make project known.

Audition possibles, remembering to video each.

Negotiate dates and fees (Hopefully Equity Registered Low Budget).

Make selections and offer roles where appropriate.

Contracts negotiated and agreed.

Script reading and / or rehearsals if possible.

Contracts negotiated and agreed.

Production team collect phone numbers and check transportation.

Meetings / Phone conversations with costume department.

Draft Y of screenplay is completed. This is your SHOOTING SCRIPT.

Meetings / Phone conversations with costume department.

Production team collect phone numbers and check transportation.

FIRST DAY OF SHOOT

Jaws – the three cast types

Primary characters	Secondary characters	Tertiary characters and extras
The main characters in your story, of which there will be three or four. In Jaws this would be Chief Brody, Matt Hooper and Quint. These characters are often the antagonists and protagonists. It will be tough to get famous actors for these roles but not impossible. They will be needed for most of your shoot.	*Characters that bob in and out of the story, but still have significant roles to play. In Jaws this would be Brody's wife, the Mayor etc. Often these characters play friends, partners, allies and gatekeepers to the next level of the story. For low budget films, these characters offer the best opportunity of attracting a name as you can offer a strong, pivotal character that could be shootable in a couple of days.*	*Characters that at best will have a line or two of dialogue (don't underestimate how one truly awful actor with one line can shatter the illusion you have so lovingly built). In Jaws this would be the town folk, Brody's kids, even the girl who gets eaten at the beginning. She's not a major character, but a catalyst to the plot, and her terrifying performance sets the tone.*

Once you have these three lists, you can begin the casting process. If during this process, you have one mantra, it should be . . . 'I WILL HIRE THE BEST ACTOR I CAN FIND FOR EVERY PART'

The tools you will use . . .

There are a number of resources that you will tap into.

PCR (Professional Casting Report) and **SBS** (Script Breakdown Service) are both weekly newsletters that are sent primarily to actors, casting directors and agents, letting them know of imminent productions. Both PCR and SBS will ask you to supply them with a list of characters, dates and other information and they will publish it in their weekly newsletter.

Spotlight now publishes their books on the web. Check out www.spotlightcd.com.

Spotlight is an independent publishing company that databases professional actors in directories (books) and the internet. You can either buy the directories or subscribe online via Spotlight Interactive. A three-month subscription is less than £50. Most industry professionals use both. The upre-shoot is whenever anyone suggests an actor, you can instantly see a photo, recent credits and skills. It's an essential tool in the casting process. To subscribe online, visit www.spotlight.com.

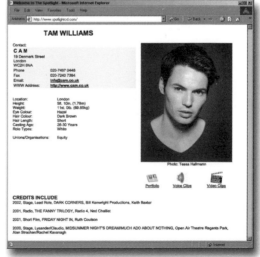

Casting directors are people who have access to actors and agents, often on a first name basis, they know who's hot and up-and-coming and can often open doors that you don't even get the opportunity to knock on. They know who's who, who's right for the

PACT / Equity Registered Low Budget Scheme

This little known or understood scheme is an absolute godsend for micro budget film makers. Hiring actors has always been a problem due to agents, contracts, negotiations etc., it all eats up valuable production time, but this scheme streamlines the process, taking away a huge amount of stress. There are a number of hoops to jump through and depending on your budget, it might just end up being impossible. On the other hand, there are tremendous benefits.

OPTION – A

There are two routes you can take with this scheme, but by far the best for you is 'Option A' (budgets under £1m) – you pay minimum Equity rates, plus 50% for a 'rest of the world buy out'. When you run into profit you will also have to share out 2% of profits with the cast. When you run into 2.5 times the budget being recouped then there would be some more additional use fees to pay (what do you care, you are in serious profit!).

Advantages are . . . *There's no need for a contract with the actors, just a pink employment form. Everyone gets paid the same (favored nations is the term agents will use). Agents like this as they feel it's fair and they don't have to wade through long contracts for a film that is paying very little . . . You will be able to say to agents straight off the bat, it's an Equity production. This will make them easier to deal with . . . The whole process of employing actors is streamlined.*

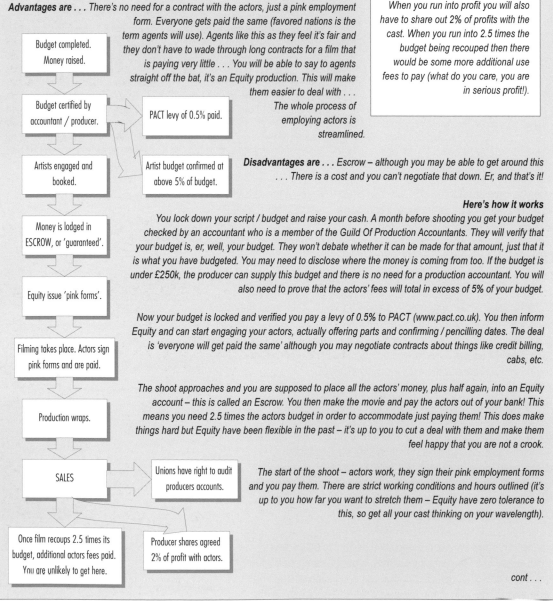

Budget completed. Money raised.

Budget certified by accountant / producer.

PACT levy of 0.5% paid.

Artists engaged and booked.

Artist budget confirmed at above 5% of budget.

Money is lodged in ESCROW, or 'guaranteed'.

Equity issue 'pink forms'.

Filming takes place. Actors sign pink forms and are paid.

Production wraps.

SALES

Unions have right to audit producers accounts.

Once film recoups 2.5 times its budget, additional actors fees paid. You are unlikely to get here.

Producer shares agreed 2% of profit with actors.

Disadvantages are . . . *Escrow – although you may be able to get around this . . . There is a cost and you can't negotiate that down. Er, and that's it!*

Here's how it works

You lock down your script / budget and raise your cash. A month before shooting you get your budget checked by an accountant who is a member of the Guild Of Production Accountants. They will verify that your budget is, er, well, your budget. They won't debate whether it can be made for that amount, just that it is what you have budgeted. You may need to disclose where the money is coming from too. If the budget is under £250k, the producer can supply this budget and there is no need for a production accountant. You will also need to prove that the actors' fees will total in excess of 5% of your budget.

Now your budget is locked and verified you pay a levy of 0.5% to PACT (www.pact.co.uk). You then inform Equity and can start engaging your actors, actually offering parts and confirming / pencilling dates. The deal is 'everyone will get paid the same' although you may negotiate contracts about things like credit billing, cabs, etc.

The shoot approaches and you are supposed to place all the actors' money, plus half again, into an Equity account – this is called an Escrow. You then make the movie and pay the actors out of your bank! This means you need 2.5 times the actors budget in order to accommodate just paying them! This does make things hard but Equity have been flexible in the past – it's up to you to cut a deal with them and make them feel happy that you are not a crook.

The start of the shoot – actors work, they sign their pink employment forms and you pay them. There are strict working conditions and hours outlined (it's up to you how far you want to stretch them – Equity have zero tolerance to this, so get all your cast thinking on your wavelength).

cont . . .

PACT / Equity cont . . .

How much do you pay?

Currently, every speaking actor or main actor should be paid minimum Equity rates of £95 p.d. (plus 50% for the world buyout making it £135 p.d.) or £380 p.w. (plus 50% for the world buyout making it £570 p.w.). Every actor will be on this deal. No one gets less or more. Everyone should be an Equity member. Kids and extras don't fall under this agreement so you can deal with that as you see fit (extras have a separate agreement but there is no requirement to use it). Do the maths on your film. For Urban Ghost Story we spent about £15k on the cast but the budget at that point was estimated to be around £190k.

At the end of the shoot you will have a pile of pink forms and a completed movie. You then sell it and if you ever recoup the cost and run into profit, you will have to share 2% of that profit with the actors. If you ever run into 2.5 times the budget in profit, then there are further fees to pay. It's very unlikely this will happen, no matter how confident you are. The unions will retain the right to audit your books too, just to make sure you aren't being a little dodgy.

Speaking to Equity may stress the hell out of you so start by having a chat with the Producers Rights Association on 020 7830 6600. They are a lot less scary.

(Note the terms of this agreement may have changed)

part, and who might do it. The only problem is that they're not cheap. Try contacting some experienced casting directors and ask them if they may be kind enough to help you with advice and perhaps by making an occasional phone call on your behalf. You may want to offer them some money as a token of your gratitude. If your budget can afford them, then hire them, they're worth every penny. Many casting directors have assistants who will work hard for little money in return for the experience and credit.

Agents are the people who represent the financial interests of an actor. It's their job to pitch for projects, to screen out inappropriate projects, manage availability, deal with payments and negotiate terms and conditions. Some agents are truly evil but on the whole most are reasonable, honest, tough and would rather see their actor working on a quirky, low budget film than staying at home watching daytime TV. Many new film makers think of agents as enemies. They are not – they are the gatekeepers who if treated with respect and integrity, can become allies.

Equity is the actors union in the UK (although they do not represent child actors). On the whole, Equity is vehemently opposed to any production that does not involve them and their strict codes. And this means you. They just hate low-budget films and will often threaten, scream, and generally worry you halfway to your grave. If you cannot afford to pay minimum Equity rates, (see later in this chapter), don't under any circumstances make the call to Equity to tell them that you are making a film. If they contact you and it is not your intention to work with Equity, get an assistant to constantly make excuses as to why you cannot speak to them and assure them you are not going to make the film. Then go ahead and make it anyway. However, if you can pay minimum Equity rates, you should, primarily because of the advantages you will enjoy (see later).

A major problem is that of letting actors know that you don't want them. Firstly you might have 2000 photos and CVs to return. Even if they sent a stamped and addressed return envelope it's a monumental task for a resource starved production. It's hard to make a call to someone who came in for an audition and say no because you just aren't sure. What if all else falls through? So you end up doing nothing and keeping everything up in the air. Not the best way to do things and not what you would want, but it just kind of happens.

Actors – how much can they cost you?

Actors' fees	How much you pay them. Minimum Pact / Equity scheme for 1 week is £570, 1 day is £135. If you are not paying Equity it's up to you how much you pay, if anything.
Transport / Cabs	Actors need to get to and from set. You may need to arrange cabs or at the very least pay petrol expenses / train / tube. Actors often work better when they don't have to drive to work.
Per diem	A small amount of money in their pocket each day, often paid tax free. If you cannot afford a fee, then a £5 a day per diem will make the pain somewhat less – at least they can buy drinks and fags.
Accommodation	If you're on location you can't ask the cast to rough it with the crew. They need space to pamper themselves. Remember you want them to look good, even if you look like you haven't showered for a month!
Costume	If they are going to wear their own clothes you will have to replace them when they get damaged - and they will get damaged. Good idea to avoid actors wearing their own clothes if possible.
Catering	On the whole, actors are slightly fussier eaters than the crew. Prepare for vegetarian, even vegan requests. Also, they will rarely eat junk food. Remember, it's their job to look good.

Working with kids

If your story contains children, then you're going to have to find some kids to play those parts. Of course if you're smart you will write the kids out of your script! If you can't then there are a number of issues you're going to have to deal with. By law, if you are employing a child, you need to apply to your local council for a licence. Depending on the age of the child, there are a number of limitations – in general, the younger the child, the fewer hours they will be able to work each day. Also, you may need to employ a tutor / chaperone to look after them and teach them during the hours when they are not on set (sometimes a parent can act as a tutor/chaperone).

If you can shoot during school holidays then you may not need to employ a tutor/chaperone. The best way around all of the headaches surrounding working with kids is to get the kids of relatives or friends to play these parts. Unlike adults, you cannot push kids to the edge. You'll quickly get a feel for when they are tired, at which point it's best to quit while you're ahead. Using kids in your film will inevitably add to your production schedule which needs factoring in when preparing a schedule and budget.

Make sure your actors can actually do what is needed of them - ride a horse, drive a car, swim underwater etc. If they can't, it's a serious production problem that will cost you money. Don't take their casual word for it, be firm and check with the agent.

The wheat from the chaff

So you've sent out your primary and secondary cast list to SBS and PCR and received about 3000 responses in the first week. Normally most will send you a 10" x 8" glossy B&W photograph with a CV, and one in a hundred will send a VHS showreel. Go through the applicants and sort them into two piles – has film or TV experience, does not have film or TV experience. Put the ones with no experience in a box on your top shelf. These people can form a catalogue from which you can draw some extras and one liners (beware, some actors will not appreciate applying for a lead role and then be offered that of a glorified extra).

Take the pile of experienced actors and start sorting them into piles for each of the characters, and a pile for those who simply do not fit a role in your film. Start selecting actors based on their physical appropriateness for the character and their experience. Then make some calls, ideally directly to the actor, and invite them to a venue for an audition. During this call it's essential that you explain about your level of experience, the budget and what that will mean with regard to working conditions. It will probably be a grim shoot, as you have no money, little experience and the crew will be underpaid, inexperienced and often grumpy because of it. There will be long hours, poor food . . . you get the picture. However, what you can offer is a role, perhaps even a major role in a feature film. Regardless of the career opportunities that may open because of it, your movie represents an amazing learning experience for them. And don't talk up the ' . . . it's going to be big hit with a major release . . . ' or you will raise expectations too high and pay the price a couple of years down the line when irate cast and crew members berate you. Also check their availability as they may have a holiday, job, other production, other commitment, that they cannot or are not willing to move.

Continuity is very important to actors. They feel that if there is a continuity error, this makes them look stupid. Make sure that if you have a continuity person, they pay particular attention to the actors, and make them feel someone is looking out for them.

If they're not phased by your low / no money situation then send them a synopsis and a few pages of dialogue that you want them to read.

Auditions

In order to audition your actors, you will need a venue – a small room will do, ideally quiet, tranquil and bright, with another room or waiting area adjacent. Draw up a list of times, starting at 9am with breaks every twenty minutes. Start filling these twenty-minute segments with actors until your day (or days) are full.

Have a pile of business cards ready and a DV camera with a good mic. At 9am your first actor should turn up. Invite them in, tell them about the film, ask them if they have any questions, then ask them to read for you. After one or two readings, you may want to videotape their performance. If you do, ask them to say their name, phone number, agent (if they have one) and agent's number at the start of their taping. If you don't, you'll forget who they are (you will be astonished how actors rarely look like their photos) as everyone quickly merges into a sea of faces.

Don't be afraid to direct – it's your job! Actors respond to direction and it's a good chance for you to practice. Look for interesting actors, people who have something before they open their mouths, and avoid casting people who look similar as this can cause confusion for the viewer.

During this audition, your 9.20 interviewee may turn up. In an ideal world, you'll have somebody outside offering tea and generally keeping people happy as it's inevitable that you will fall behind schedule. Don't audition too

The schedule and call sheets are the interface between the production and the cast. Actors need time to read, learn lines and rehearse. Often they will prepare the night before. So if there are any changes to your schedule, it's vital to let them know asap. One of the things actors hate most about low budget films is disorganisation. They don't want to come to work only to be told to wait, then do something they are not prepared for. Remember, acting isn't like moving lights, it's a necessarily emotional job.

Beth Charkham
Casting Director

'When approaching a casting director be clear as to whether you are offering them the job or if you're talking to other casting directors. Everyone knows everyone else and they will find out. If the film is very low budget, pay the casting director a small fee up-front to cover expenses. If your casting director is asked to work for no money they will prioritise the paying job, meaning you will get put to the bottom of the pile.

A problem I face regularly is that of dishonest film makers who lie about whether they have finance in place and about their budget. In the past I have approached agents / actors on behalf of some film makers only to be left with egg on my face because the finance was not actually in place. Honesty is the best policy. The truth will always comes out and no one, especially agents and actors, appreciate being lied too. This business is small and we have all heard every 'line' a new producer thinks of.

Another problem is actually getting well known actors to consider doing a part. The casting director can approach an agent regarding a well known actor but it is the actor's choice if they want to do the job. Also, agents and actors can take a long time reading scripts and coming back with an answer, and whilst the casting director can chase them, the answer is often ambiguous or no answer at all. The casting director then has the producer chasing them for an answer they cannot give!'

late into the evening as the process is extraordinarily draining. After a couple of days of this you might lose your voice and certainly will have a sore throat from all the talking.

Keep the production line of your auditions rolling and avoid letting the actors interview you! You don't have time. During these auditions you may well be seeing actors who you have directly requested from an agent (who did not apply to you through PCR and SBS). They will have come to you via the alternative route of an agent . . .

Agents

Most primary actors will either come to you via an agent, and if not, they will probably have an agent. Either way you'll have to deal with agents!

Assuming you have found (in Spotlight or through a recommendation) an actor who you would like to talk to about one of the leads in your film, you'll need to call the agent, tell them about yourself, the movie, your budget and ask about the actor's availability. Most of the time the agent will respond with 'Is this an Equity film?' You have to be honest here and it's one of the reasons it is better to work with Equity. However, Equity may simply be an impossible budgetary restriction, so be honest. Some agents will flatly refuse non-Equity micro-budget films. Others, assuming your project is interesting, you're offering a good role and you have been courteous and sincere on the telephone, may well consider it. If they do, you have passed the first hurdle and you can get your script to the actor. You will probably end up sending anywhere between 20-100 screenplays in the post, which has a significant budgetary impact. Each script will cost about £1 to print / copy and £2.50 for P&P. Do the maths!

Once the script has been sent to the agent, politely chase them. Make sure it has been passed onto the actor and isn't sitting in someone's in-tray. Be enthusiastic. Don't fax or e-mail a feature script.

Secret but flawed weapon

Oddly enough, one of the weapons in your arsenal is your far from perfect screenplay. Probably . . . it will be a bit baggy, mistructured and generally quirky. To an actor who is regularly offered run-of-the-mill commercial work, this kind of screenplay can seem like a breath of fresh air. Here's another thought. Why not write a movie with a strong female lead? Most actresses, even at the top of their profession, regularly get offered girlfriend of, best friend of, heroine running behind hero kind of roles until they hit their thirties. Then they enter a wasteland for work. Eventually, when they hit their mid-fifties they become mother of, best friend's mother, grandmother with a lot of make-up etc. Present any good actress with a strong, dimensional, female role they can get their teeth into and you will find yourself accessing a talent pool you would be refused if the sexes were reversed.

Dealing with extras

Extras are the 'actors' who have no lines but appear in front of the camera and therefore need the ability, no matter how small, to act and not over-act. Pulling extras out of your applicants from PCR and SBS is a good idea, as is using friends and relatives and even investors. For financial reasons, you may be obliged to use an investor as an extra, just make sure they have no lines and if they insist on lines, write a few that you know you can cut out. Look for people with interesting faces, perhaps even ugly 'real' people – they will add texture and reality to the background of your film.

Be aware that extras are very badly paid and doing possibly the dullest and least rewarding job imaginable. Accordingly, many won't turn up on the day so have B plans in the wings, extra extras, so to say.

One of your production managers or assistant directors should be given the task of managing the extras, making sure that they know shoot times and dates and that they are dressed appropriately. In advance of the shoot, send out a letter with a synopsis of the movie, a release form (see elsewhere in this book) and the list of points that they need to keep in mind, which should include . . .

Dress appropriately for the character that you are playing.

Prepare for bad weather and long periods of waiting.

Bring a packed lunch and flask of coffee/tea (if appropriate).

Please bring and sign the enclosed release form (this is a simple, one page legal document that allows you to use their performance in the film).

Try to avoid unnecessarily watching the actors during a take, unless so directed. Remember, whilst your character is incidental to the story, you are playing a real person in a real world with a real life.

Try to avoid accidentally looking at the camera. (This is often called 'flashing camera').

CASTING COUCH

Doing the deal . . .

Eventually, the dam will breach and you will have to make decisions, at which point you will enter a negotiation stage. Whether you have found your actor through PCR or SBS or an agent, there are a number of contractual points that will be negotiated, which include . . .

Rate of pay and overtime – *You don't want to agree to overtime, it's one fee to do the film or you're working within Equity's registered low-budget scheme.*

Per diem – *Are you going to give one and how much? The per diem is a tax free daily payment that is supposed to cover expenses. Often this is used by agents to get extra fees for their actors. On low budget films it could be £5 a day, or none at all.*

Credit billing – *Who gets top billing? Whose name is biggest on the poster? Always go for alphabetical billing of your principal cast, unless of course you have a major actor whose status vastly overshadows the others.*

Approval – *Some agents may try to insist upon some kind of editorial approval. Flatly decline this. Others may argue for approval of stills, which you may want to give.*

Points – *Or to the rest of the world, percentages. What percentage will they get of the profits? They will want gross which you cannot give them, so they will have to settle for net. Never offer more than a couple of per cent at the most and ideally, agree to none.*

Nudity – *Some actors are rightly cautious about exploitation film making. Understand that this may be a very serious make or break issue for some actors.*

Now in your favour, you might want to add that they will be contractually obliged to . . .

Re-shoots and ADR – *If you need to re-shoot a scene or you need your actor to record some ADR (replacement or extra lines of dialogue) you need to know that they will be contractually obliged to do it even if they fall out with you during the shoot.*

Movie release – *Make sure they will support the release of the film by doing press interviews etc.*

Andrew Manson
Actor's Agent

'We do deals with independent film makers, both those with low budgets and others that are working on deferments, we even have a special department that deals specifically with shorts and student films. We actively encourage our new clients to work on shorts or low / no budget films as it's is a way of promoting our clients and also gives them a showreel.

I'm amazed how many actors leave drama school and don't have a showreel. Some agents are against their clients doing this type of work, but I feel it's a showcase and a way for our clients to gain valuable experience. If I have a new client that takes part in a 'deferred' film, I always stress that they will not see any money from the film. Everyone has to start somewhere and low budget films are as good a place as any.

With regard to our more high profile clients, we always show them interesting scripts, regardless of budget. Recently, Michael York (who we represent) participated in a film called Borstal Boys, which he thoroughly enjoyed. However, when it comes to 'deferred' films, the project would need to be very strong before I would show my high profile clients a script, as it's obvious that deferred films basically mean that the actor will never see any money, no matter what the contract says'.

Script in hand

Once the script is with an actor, nine out of ten will read it almost straight away, one in ten will never get round to it. Those who have read it will then (via their agent) contact you if they are interested and you will probably meet. Now it's up to you to decide if they are right for the part. Don't be bullied by agents who insist on having an answer right now, and try to get a feel for the actor in terms of how right they will be for the part, their enthusiasm and how easy they will be to work with. You may also want to ask the actor for a reading, which you will, of course, videotape.

If you do manage to attract a very famous actor, they may be available on certain dates only. Accordingly you may need to reschedule or even cancel the shoot for a time to accommodate them. Beware though, unless they are contractually obliged, they may change their minds at the last minute and decide to go to Spain for a break instead.

Balls in the air

The awful thing about casting is that it is a horrifying juggling act, where actors don't want to commit until the last moment (in case they are offered a bigger and better job) and you don't want to commit until the last minute (because you've offered it to a bigger and better actor who still hasn't deigned to look at your script). As the out-of-control freight train that is your movie in pre-production approaches the first day of shooting, you will find yourself lying awake in bed staring at the ceiling and worrying that you are less than 100 hours away from shooting and you still don't even have your primary cast confirmed.

Investment of your time

Don't underestimate the importance of casting. It cannot be squeezed into a few intense days if you are truly looking for the best cast for your film. Sure you can find a bunch of half decent actors in a day, but the right people for your movie are considerably more elusive or may need an extended courtship to induce them. You will probably be seeing and interviewing actors right up to the first day of shooting, even during the shoot! In short, casting will probably run all the way from the first day of pre-production to potentially the penultimate day of shooting.

Group therapy

Once you have your cast, it's advisable to hold a reading of the screenplay. Many people talk about extensive rehearsals, which some people think is a good idea, and others don't (as spontaneity may be lost when it comes to the shoot). It's all rendered moot due to the fact that you don't have time, you don't have a cast with enough time prior to the shoot, and you can't afford to pay them (and if they are doing the film for little money or free they will resist extensive rehearsals). You'll be doing well to get everyone into one room for even a single day, which really amounts to a reading.

This reading is essential as you will come across all sorts of minor dialogue niggles, dialogue that can be dropped, or sequences that simply just don't make sense and need to be written. You'll even come across dialogue attributed to the wrong character, which is a simple typo, but can throw everybody if it goes unspotted. You may also get a vibe for a new and exciting dynamic between certain actors, which in turn may give you ideas that you might want to filter through and incorporate. The actors themselves may come up with ideas, but beware, they are always looking for more lines for their character (you know you are working with a pro when they suggest you remove some of their lines). Once you have isolated these screenplay problems, you can adjust them and print out a new and final shooting script.

This reading will also be an opportunity for all the actors to meet, and for you to meet them as a group, to build up an idea of how the group dynamic will work. If you can afford it, take everyone out for dinner that night, or at the very least have a drink. One of the most important aspects is to build a bond of trust and honesty between the actors and the director. Actors are often thought of as pieces of moveable furniture on a set. In fact they are trained, hopefully experienced, emotional, dynamic and physical human beings that work best when a director is able to move past pleasantries and connect on a truly profound and deep emotional level. Your luvvie alarm may be ringing right now, but actors are luvvies for a good reason and the best way to get the most out of them is for the director to become a luvvie too . . . Oh darling!

Of course when actors are not present the director will take off the luvvie hat and put on the crew hat and probably indulge in sexist, dirty jokes. Cast and crew are like chalk and cheese.

Production – First contact

At some point before the shoot begins, a production manager will contact each and every actor and take phone numbers, addresses, faxes etc and compile a contact list. Each actor will receive a call from the costume department to discuss costume and the primary actors will be invited back to check through all the costumes and have a fitting (even

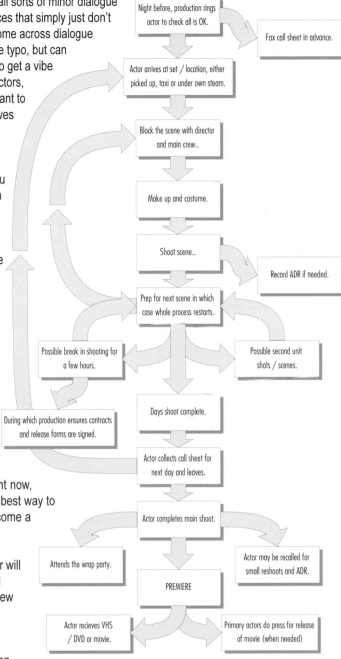

Casting and actors' flow chart Part 2

LIVING SPIRIT

● Living Spirit Pictures Limited, Ealing Film Studios, Ealing Green, Ealing, London, W5 5EP ●
● Tel 020 8758 8544 ● Fax/Messages 020 8758 8559 ● mail@livingspirit.com ● www.livingspirit.com ●

PERFORMERS RELEASE FORM

From: Andy Actor of *12 Any Street, Anywhere, London, UK*

To: Living Spirit Pictures Ltd *("the Company" which shall include it's successors, assigns and licensees)* of Ealing Film Studios, Ealing Green, London, W5 5EP

Dated: 01 February 2003

Dear Sirs

A Tale Of A Soldier (the "Film")

1. In consideration of the sum of £1 now paid by the Company to me (the receipt of which I acknowledge) I warrant, confirm and agree with the Company that the Company shall have the right to exploit any films, photographs and sound recordings made by the Company for the Film in which I feature, or any literary, dramatic, musical or artistic work or film or sound recording created by me or any performance by me of any literary, dramatic, musical or artistic work or film or sound recording included by the Company in the Film in any and all media by any and all means now known or invented in future throughout the world for the full period of copyright, including all renewals, revivals, reversions and extensions.

2. I irrevocably and unconditionally grant to you all consents required pursuant to the Copyright, Designs and Patents Act 1988 Part II * or otherwise under the laws in force in any part of the world to exploit such performances.

3. I irrevocably and unconditionally waive all rights which I may have in respect of the Film pursuant to the Copyright, Designs and Patents Act 1988 Sections 77, 80, 84 and 85**.

4. I consent to the use by the Company of my name, likeness, voice and biography in connection only with the Film.

5. The Company may assign or licence this agreement to any third party.

6. This letter shall be governed by and construed in accordance with the law of England and Wales and subject to the jurisdiction of the English Courts.

Yours faithfully

Andy Actor

* the "Performers Rights"
** the Moral Rights of an author

The release form is a legal document which gives you the right to use the performance of an actor or extra in your film. Most actors will already be covered in their main contract but it doesn't harm to have one of these sheets for each and every person who appears in front of the camera.

Legal notes

The release form covers any work created by the individual. Also, consideration must be given in any contract. A contract requires an offer, acceptance and consideration. It is a legal necessity. ('Consideration' does not have to be money, it can be provided by, for example, giving up a legal right).

though as it is a low budget film they'll probably be wearing their own clothes at least some of the time, if not all).

You are now rapidly approaching the first day of the shoot and a couple of days before, one of the production team will send out the first call sheet to the actors who are needed on day one, with a follow up call to make sure everything is OK.

The first day

It's the morning of the first day of the shoot. Nerves are running high. Tempers are frayed. But enthusiasm and optimism is at an all time peak. Production will have ensured that every actor needed on the first day will have received a call sheet outlining when they are needed, how long they expect they'll be needed for, what scenes will be shot and any other special considerations. They will also tackle the difficult problem of getting the actor to location or set. Will the actor get on a bus, train or drive themselves? Will you have to arrange for a cab or get a production assistant to pick them up? If you perceive that you will use a lot of cabs, then contact a mini cab firm and cut a deal in advance to cover the whole shoot.

So the actor arrives on set, and after being given a cup of tea and the usual pleasantries, they will be taken to set where the director and principle crew such as DOP, production design, sound, make-up, costume and script continuity block the scene. Blocking or a walk-through is kind of a physical rehearsal. The actors and the director will work through where each of the characters will be during a scene . . . perhaps Jane may start the scene sat on the sofa but walk to the window in the middle. This is a serious issue for the camera team, as they would have to deal with the interior and exterior lighting, the script continuity person may remind the director that Jane needs to be carrying the gun at this point, costume may realise that the actors feet won't be seen, which has an implication. Production design will see that an entire wall won't be in shot so they don't need to bother dressing it. Remember, this 'blocking' is not a rehearsal – you will be under pressure to shoot, shoot, shoot and not 'block' and you will be tempted to drop it. Do so at your peril as blocking almost always saves time in the long run.

Once the scene has been blocked, the crew will get on with their bit, whilst the actors are whisked off to make-up and costume, where they have make-up applied and change clothes. This should take around twenty minutes but more often takes thirty to forty.

So it's half an hour later and the actors have returned to find the set fully dressed and lit. The cameras are in position awaiting the first shot. Move the actors into position and run a rehearsal or two, mainly for camera so they know where actors are going to be for framing and focus. Often the camera department will mark the floor of the set with white sticky tape crosses so actors know exactly where they're meant to walk to and stop. It's called 'hitting their mark'. Inexperienced actors may screw this up or even resist it. What they don't know is that unless they hit their mark then they will probably be badly framed and out of focus.

The director will soon get a handle on how many rehearsals an actor needs and as a general rule, the sooner you get shooting the better. Only the most experienced and brilliant actors can maintain intensity and spontaneity on take seventeen. In fact, don't rule out the possibility of surreptitiously shooting rehearsals especially with young, inexperienced actors who tend to work best when the cameras are off.

Hopefully, you'll get the shot in two or three takes at the most and move onto the next shot. It will take the crew anywhere between ten and thirty minutes to reset for the next shot. If it is a complicated shot with track and dolly or a crane, that could go up to an hour or so.

Green room

Whenever you see the opportunity to get the actors off set and into a green room environment (be that a parked Ford Escort with a radio or a dedicated room with a TV), it will help. Actors hate sitting around. At least in a green room, they can read the script, rehearse with each other, watch TV or listen to the radio, make a phone call on their mobile and generally relax. They also need a space where they can emotionally prepare for the next shot or scene. Don't underestimate just how hard it is to act. The best make it look like falling off a log, but if that's what you think, then you try acting. You'll find it takes a special person to be able to scream, cry, undress, memorise lines, fake orgasms, emotionally expose themselves . . . all on cue and in front of twenty scruffily dressed crew members who can't stop talking about what is for lunch. Get into the habit of learning and remembering every actor's first name, it will help them feel more connected with you, and appreciated as a 'creative'. There's nothing worse than barking orders at an actor, especially when you start the sentence with *'YOU . . . ! could you just blah blah blah . . . '*

Second unit

There is also the possibility that if the actor has a break for a few hours, they

EXPERT OPINION

John Schwab
Actor

'My first experience of a no-budget film was called 'Nothing to Declare'. The film makers were short of funding so I ended up investing £100 and agreed to play a part. I was paid my expenses (ironically my own money!) and fed. I don't work on low-budget films for financial reasons, I do it because I like the work and I've yet to see an unhappy low-budget film set. I think this is because everyone wants to be there, you're not expecting big stuff like on some of the Hollywood sets I have worked. Working on these shoots gives an actor a chance to learn about the technicalities of film making, like cameras and lighting, things that on a normal shoot, the crew wouldn't take the time to speak to you about. As an actor I have to be proactive and I actually look for low-budget films. I want to get to know these film makers because they could be the next Sam Mendes and able to employ me in the future.

My main gripe though is that the film makers often over-hype their project without being able to deliver the goods. Sometimes film makers promise that your scenes will be shot in 3 days when, in fact it will take 3 weeks. Guerilla film making is brilliant, but you do need that devotion to professionalism.

Some actors think low budget films are below them, yet 90% of all actors are out of work! If I am not gainfully employed I use that time to try and work on low budget productions, to get more experience, work with new film makers and add to my CV. There's always something new to learn and I never know where the adventure will lead me . . . '

Christopher Villiers
twenty twenty casting

'Many low budget films take a lot of time and trouble to get the main roles right, but the smaller parts and especially the background artists, are often almost completely overlooked. If you can raise the profile of background artists and make them more integral to your film, the whole project will benefit.

If you cast background artists cleverly, it adds to the foreground, and can even save the production some money. A taxi driver who is really a driver, a ballet dancer who is really a dancer makes your production more authentic and creates a bubble of reality. You get through faster and save time and money. Low-budget films often cut down on the amount of background artist days and the film looks underpopulated, cheaper and less 'true' as a result. It doesn't have to break the bank.

Professional background artists cost money, and low budget film makers often don't consider or even budget for these performers, preferring to use cheap or free labour and friends. If you get people off the street you get people who turn up late, eat lunch, and then walk off halfway through, cold and bored – and that's the problem. But if you budget money for background artists, even though your budget is tight, you will get a pro who turns up on time and does their job.'

may be whisked away for a second unit shot or a pick-up shot. If you are going to do this then make sure your assistant director team know and are happy with it.

That's a wrap

At the end of the day when you call a wrap, get the actors off set and home as fast as possible. They should not be invited to carry lights! Give them a call sheet for tomorrow, check they are happy and send them on their way.

To view or not to view

Each day you'll see the material that you shot the day before. A thorny question is that of whether you should show the actors this footage or not. Your decision should be based on how it will affect their performance and not on your insecurity or precious nature as a film maker.

Some actors will benefit by seeing themselves and any doubts or reservations that they have about the production (remember you may have asked them to stand in front of a cardboard box which is supposed to be a spaceship) will be placated. Others will simply see that they are as fat, ugly, untalented etc. as they fear they are – even if the rushes are terrific and they look great. If you are editing during production, I have found it to be to everybody's advantage to show cast and crew some of these edited scenes (with some added sound effects and music). It is a confidence booster and a morale enhancer.

Say that again

If during a take there is a problem with the sound and you are unable to fix that problem, e.g. planes fly overhead, you cannot turn off the air conditioning, the location is next to the motorway etc, you will have to do a little ADR (automated dialogue replacement).

For example, you have shot a scene, but the sound is unusable. If it is at all possible, directly after you have completed the shot, take the actors to a quiet room, which has been deadened by draping the walls with duvets and ask them to re-perform the scene for the sound only. You may find some resistance to this as they will not believe that the sound can be re-edited to perfectly lip-sync the scene they just shot (and sometimes it cannot). However, nine out of ten lines will fit perfectly and you will enjoy the benefit of beautiful and clean dialogue recordings.

When a camera isn't in front of them, the performance an actor gives (for sound only) will often be subdued. Ask them to place themselves in the emotional space that they just occupied and re-perform the scene. Ask them to keep those all important energy levels up as this is the best way to get a performance that matches the pictures, both from a mechanical (it actually fits) and emotional (the performance is right) perspective. If you don't do this, you will have to do it later, either in your front room or a studio. Either way, it won't sound as good as months will have past, the actors will be in a different emotional place and the energy of the shoot will not be there. It might also cost you an arm and a leg to do.

Getting a great cast is pivotal to your movie, yet you don't have any money? Actors will work for very little, and you can also repay them in other ways too. Make sure they get a good copy of the film. If you really want to repay a debt, offer to edit them a showreel of their work. They will more than likely be delighted.

. . . **Curtain call**

This process of blocking, make-up, costume, setting the shot, rehearsals, shoot . . . then move on to the next shot or scene . . . will repeat until the end of the shoot, after which everyone will go away and you will edit the film.

During the edit you will isolate problem areas and more than likely, you will need to shoot some cutaways or additional sequences. You'll need to get your actor(s) back, so make damn sure you didn't fall out with them. You may also need to record some ADR to cover badly recorded lines or even put new lines into actor's mouths, generally added to the soundtrack whenever you cutaway from the actor's face.

After these re-shoots and ADR the next time you'll see the actors is probably at the premiere when everyone will be riding high and generally patting themselves on the back.

You will probably keep in touch with your actors by sending them a VHS and DVD of the completed movie. You may also chat to them about future projects. If the film is released you will meet again as they should be obligated to support the film by doing press. Agents may ask for payment for this but remind them that it is in the interest of the actors, as well as the film, to get good press. A half page photo and 600 word write up in a glossy Sunday magazine never hurt anyone's career!

Scheduling Blueprint

Sargent-Disc Ltd

Entertainment Partners'
Movie Magic® Scheduling™

Sargent/Disc, Pinewood Studios, Pinewood Road, Iver, Bucks, England, SL00NH
P:01753.630.300 F: 01753.655.881 www.sargent-disc.com

The schedule is the part of pre-production where you plan how, when and where you will shoot all the elements outlined in the screenplay. What do you prioritise? Actors? Locations? Stunts? It is all about finding the fastest, most productive and cost effective way of shooting your film with minimal creative constraints. In the making of your schedule you will be forced to deal with 'just how in the hell are we going to do scene 128?'

Schedule using cards . . .
cheap and easy, everyone can understand it and you can pin it up on a board. My personal favourite because it is fundamentally simple, no scary production board, no fiddly software, just a bunch of cards in order.

Schedule using a production board . . .
the way the industry likes to work is by using a series of colour coded strips that are sorted and ordered. It works brilliantly, but it is essentially a more complicated, colour coded version of the simple cards approach.

Schedule using software . . .
Movie Magic is the world leader, a computerised version of the production board. Sophisticated and powerful, but complicated for low budget film makers and expensive. Best avoided unless you have access to it for free or know the software intimately.

Location priority . . .
Where you will shoot will always form the starting point for any schedule. Moving a cast and crew is a waste of resources, and many locations can serve as multiple locations for your drama. Parking, facilities, permits and fees all impact your location choices.

Actor priority . . .
Some cast members may only be available for a day or two whilst others may have commitments such as a play or a properly paid job. You may need to adjust your schedule to accommodate this. Using kids can complicate things too.

Other Stuff . . .
There's a whole pile of other things that will greatly impact your schedule – stunts, night shoots, rain, special effects, events you need to shoot but can't move (carnival etc.), and all the other weird and wonderful things in your screenplay that seemed like a good idea at the time of writing.

Scheduling Blueprint

Most people understand that movies are rarely shot in sequence. That is, the shoot doesn't begin with page one of the script. There are 101 reasons why a film isn't shot in sequence, but the two primary reasons for low-budget film makers are locations and actors. The order in which the scenes are shot will be decided before the shoot and during the shoot when things invariably go wrong or re-writes need to be accommodated. This ordered list is called 'the production schedule'. In essence, it's a simple 'to do' list explaining the order of the scenes to be shot.

But really, why not in sequence? Ideally you would of course . . . But, for instance, if you have a star to play your villain who appears in six scenes (through the begining, middle and end of your story) but is only available for one day, it becomes apparent why a film cannot be shot in sequence. Now magnify that simple issue but add to it night or day, location availability, actor availability, special effects, etc. The schedule is a profoundly complex plan and must not be underestimated. A carefully considered and constructed schedule will produce more shots, and better shots.

There are a number of computer based programs that can help you produce your schedule, as well as more established techniques using strips of card (called a production board), but the simplest and most cost effective way to schedule your film is by using 4" x 3" address cards from your local stationery shop. In essence you'll summarise each scene, one to a card, then lay them out and shuffle them around until you find the most effective order. This extraordinarily low-tech approach can be understood by anyone in your production, unlike scary looking production boards or sophisticated software. Plus it will only cost you £4 as opposed to £400.

Who prepares the pudding?

Traditionally, doing the schedule is the job of the First assistant director (1st AD). Not wishing to belittle the enormous skill and patience of the 1st AD, I believe that for low-budget film making, the job of producing the schedule is that of the director and producer.

Failing to plan is planning to fail. This stage is where you map out where and how long it will take to shoot all the creative decisions you made in your screenplay . . .

Movie Magic is the most popular and common scheduling software program, but it is complicated and very expensive. It's great for bigger budgets, but for micro budgets, lower tech solutions such as stripboards or simple cards represent much better value for money.

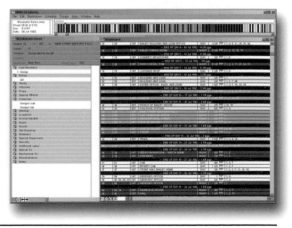

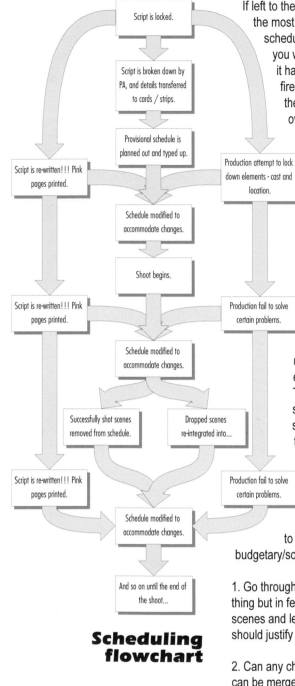

Scheduling flowchart

If left to the 1st AD, you are in essence bequeathing control over possibly the most important production aspect of your film. If they produce the schedule, you can look at it, comment on it and understand it . . . but you won't fully appreciate all of its complexity and the ramifications it has for your screenplay (and what do you do if they quit or you fire them half way through?) If the producer and director create the schedule together, then all of those scenes that have been over written will be re-written but more succinctly, and the scenes that have suffered the endless 'should we or should we not cut it out' debates will be abruptly answered.

The scheduling process will be so tortuous on the director that they will quickly abandon all ridiculous artistic notions in favour of pragmatic and practical solutions. When on-set and slipping behind schedule, the director will also have a profound understanding of how that 'slipping behind' is going to radically effect the quality and quantity of material that they are going to be able to shoot.

Working together on the schedule will give the producer a chance to fully understand and appreciate what the director is going to do in order to shoot any given scene. If unchecked, a director will always want too many shots – for example they will say 'I can only do the scene in five shots . . . ' The producer will then argue that it needs to do done in 'one shot . . . sorry'. An agreement will probably be found on three shots. Of course on the day you'll be so far behind schedule that you'll end up doing it in two shots, possibly one shot or you might bite the bullet and realize you didn't need the scene in the first place and hey presto, you're back on schedule!

Script prep

Aside from the question of whether your screenplay is ready to shoot (which it isn't, it never is!) there are a number of budgetary/scheduling issues to deal with.

1. Go through the screenplay and ask yourself 'can this scene say the same thing but in fewer words?' Not just dialogue, but character action too. Fewer scenes and less words on the page means less to shoot. Every syllable should justify its existence.

2. Can any characters be merged? Often secondary and tertiary characters can be merged so you may only have to accommodate one actor where previously there were two characters. Go through your script and be very hard on yourself. Play the 'what if' game and see what would happen if characters were entirely removed or merged with others.

Pink Pages . . .

During the shoot, dealing with schedule and script changes can be a production office nightmare. Once you do your first 'script lock down', make sure all scene numbers remain the same. Any new scenes will now be numbered alpha-numerically – Scene 22b, 106c etc. Re- writes during the shoot should be printed out on pink paper for all cast and crew. If yet more rewrites are done to the same scenes, then the next lot will be on yellow paper, then green and so on. Along with each new 'pink page' there should be explicit instructions . . . 'This new scene replaces scene 24. Please remove page 13 and replace with this new sheet'. The same process should be used for the schedule when new pages are created.

All this paperwork can cause a bit of a fuss in the production office, especially if the copier or printer unexpectedly runs out of paper / toner or worse still, it fails. Have a back-up at all times, you don't want to be forced to go down to the local copy shop and pay ten times the price.

3. Locations are a pain in the arse. Whenever you move a cast and crew, it takes hours, plus you have to get clearances, permits, recce for loos and catering etc. You need to strike a balance between enough locations to give your film visual diversity, but not so many that you spend more time sitting in the back of a truck going to your next location than actually shooting. Audiences are not impressed by locations so don't force the production to accommodate pet likes.

4. Costume. Get a grip on the visual appearance of your characters. If left alone, the cast and costume department may decide on numerous and complex costume changes, all of which will cost you time and money. If at all possible, get actors to wear generic clothing that they do not need to keep changing between scenes.

5. Plan those dialogue scenes. Within every movie, there will be peaks and troughs . . . moments where you can slow the pace down, or where you need to deliver more exciting coverage. Define these moments now and work out where you can shoot two pages of dialogue in one shot (and plan a really cunning and interesting way to shoot it), and where you will need fifteen shots to cover just half a page of action and dialogue.

6. The end. Always schedule slightly more than you need for the climactic scenes of your film. Audiences will forgive a myriad of sins if the end is really good. Schedule the most important scenes toward the middle of the shoot. At the start of the shoot the actors are not yet gelling, at the end, the crew are tired.

Drawing up your schedule is a bit of a head screw and one major problem is that the phone keeps ringing and people keep asking you questions - it is after all, a matter of days before you shoot.

7. Watch out for scenes within scenes . . . *Jane, whilst stood in the kitchen, looks through the window and out over the fields . . .* Will the kitchen location have fields

Hurry up and wait . . . Just how long will it take?

Simple dialogue scene

A couple of pages of two characters talking to each other is a scheduling godsend. Think of creative and interesting ways of covering this scene in a single shot. In my second film 'White Angel', the serial killer character occasionally recounts tales of his murderous activities. The dialogue and performance was captivating enough that we could stay on one shot , sometimes for up to four pages. This means four pages in one setup, for just an hour's work.

Simple dialogue scene version 2

Another simple way to get through pages quickly is to treat a dialogue scene as two simple reverse shots. Typically used for people talking to one another over a divide such as a coffee table, shop counter, bar etc. Shoot a mid-shot, then zoom in for a close-up. Then re-set the camera for a reverse mid-shot followed by a quick close-up. This will give you four shots from which to cut your scene. This will give you flexibility in the cutting room.

Complex dialogue scene

Scenes with several characters interacting can be difficult to cover as it becomes a bit of a head screw for the director to do multiple reverse shots, whilst under pressure. You maybe forced to shoot the scene like American TV shows such as 'Friends'. The camera /cameras are always on the same side of the line meaning that pretty much any shots should cut together without looking too unsightly. These kinds of scenes often take longer to shoot than you expect.

Action scene

Anything that involves a degree of action will take longer than you expect. This is mainly due to the fact that you need more shots as the pace of the editing will increase, and also that shots need to be meticulously choreographed. Stunt sequences are even slower to shoot due to the safety preparations. Wherever possible, get an active second unit to handle these kind of sequences.

Cut-aways and establishing shots

Wherever possible, break out of the main shoot and either pick-up after the shoot (during a minor crew re-shoot weekend) or pass it on to a dedicated second unit during the main shooting period. Shots would include establishing shot of building, close-up of newspaper headline, close-up of fish tank being hit by gun shots etc.

Nightmares

Add to any of the above the words 'night', or 'rain' and you are in for a glacial paced shooting nightmare. The rule of thumb is that it will take four times longer than you expect to shoot anything at night or with rain. Don't underestimate how long it takes to set up lights in the dark. Wherever possible in your screenplay make night into day and delete the word rain.

Track and cranes

Any time you use track and dolly or a crane, your shooting time will double. It just takes that long to set it all up. On the up side, a dull two-shot covering a page and a half of dialogue can be seriously spiced up by doing it with a track and dolly and keeping the actors moving. It will take longer to shoot than a simple locked-off shot, but the result will be much more attractive and energetic. Be pragmatic in your choice of track and dolly and crane shots.

Production

Always remember that the actors and cameras are only part of the equation. Crews need to get to and from locations, actors need to rehearse, actors need to change costumes and make-up, lines of dialogue may need to be wild tracked, locations and sets may need to be re-dressed etc. Factor these set-up, re-set and wrap times into your schedule.

Mixed bag

Other factors that will regularly drag you behind are . . . A camera team that is ponderous. Bad planning. Too many takes (usually fuelled by an inexperienced director). Actors consistently fluffing lines or not hitting their mark. Simple errors (such as costume continuity) which force a re-shoot. Exhausted crews slowing down as they don't have enough rest time. Too many location changes. Poor co-ordination between the set and the actors in their green room. Taking too long to get up to speed each morning as crew are late due to too little rest.

SCRIPT BREAKDOWN Page _112_ of _604_
PRODUCTION COMPANY - LIVING SPIRIT
PRODUCTION - ~~ROOFTHANN~~   DIR - CHRIS JONES

Scene Number 56+58	Length 1/8 PAGE	Story Day SD3
INT / EXT INT	DAY / NIGHT NIGHT	

Characters	Scene description
DAVEY (11) SARAH (12)	DAVEY AND SARAH PREP TO FOLLOW CONNOR TO HILL HOUSE

Story Location	Props
SARAHS BEDROOM	BINOCULARS, WATER PISTOLS, WALKIE TALKIES, KIDS TOYS * TV SHOWING VAMPIRE FILM!

Special Props / Special wardrobe	Atmospheric effects
TV SHOWING VAMPIRE FILM	N/A

Set construction / Location notes	Special Effects / Effects props (weapons)
COULD BE SHOT IN DAY WITH BLACKED WINDOWS	N/A

Additional Notes

KIDS IN SCENE SO NEED TO BE ON OUR TOES FROM A PRODUCTION PERSPECTIVE

*SCENE 58 LEADS DIRECTLY ON

You can download a free copy of this sheet from our website at www.guerillafilm.com

Breakdown sheet / cards

SC 56/58 (SD3) INT/NIGHT   1/8

DAVEY & SARAH PREP FOR GOING TO HOUSE WITH CONNOR

DAVEY SARAH	SARAHS BEDROOM	TV WITH VAMPIRE FILM

The script or scene breakdown sheet (left) is a tool used to help produce the schedule. On a micro-budget film, this stage can often be skipped and selective information transferred directly to either strips or simple cards (above right). The cards are put in order later, the schedule then typed up and later, a production assistant can fine toothcomb the screenplay for all the additional production information such as props, costume etc (although attention should be given to any element that would have a scheduling impact, perhaps a prop that you might only have for one day).

Notice how only information that would directly impact the schedule is written on the card, props listed are limited to things like the TV (as a special piece of camera equipment may be needed to film the TV). The top piece of information – INT / EXT – DAY / NIGHT etc. has been colour coded with a highlighter pen for quicker and easier sorting – blue for exterior night, yellow for exterior day, orange for interior night and white for interior day.

outside or will you shoot the POV of the fields in another place? Is this two locations but one scene?

Pacing the crew

If you split your shoot into thirds, the first third will be about the cast and crew getting to know about each other and the production and getting up to speed. The second third will be where everyone is at their most efficient; they're not yet jaded or too tired. The final third is where everyone starts to wind down a little; people are becoming a little blasé because they are more bored and efficient at what they do. They are also thinking about what's the next job for them. Understanding this arc will help you schedule. Scenes that are simple, *'Jack walks into the building etc'* should be scheduled at the beginning of the shoot (where possible). Scenes that are

Write a story that can be shot in a single location otherwise you will need to schedule for lengthy cast, crew and heavy duty equipment movement. Time spent moving between locations is time that you are paying for the whole production machine but not actually shooting.

Jonathan Newman
Filmmaker

'Scheduling a film can be a logistical nightmare, not just for the director, who typically shoots out of sequence due to the availability of actors, locations etc., but for the unlucky First AD and production manager who work out the fine details. If you're a multi-hyphenate film maker (ie, producer/director/writer/every-bloody-thing), it's most likely that you'll be arranging the schedule yourself, probably even First ADing the film as well. It's a lot of work but, frankly, if you're an organised person, with a bit of thought, you'll probably have the best idea of how the puzzle should fit together.

On my first feature film, 'Being Considered', I arranged the schedule and I First ADed the production. I arranged this shoot over a 4 week period. Over all, we shot for 21 days. There are over 30 different locations in the film, so it was logistically difficult to manage. In pre-production, it became apparent that some days had to be scheduled around certain locations, and their availability to us. If we were filming in an office in Soho, for example, I would group those days together consecutively. The next obstacle was the availability of certain actors. Saeed Jaffrey, for example, was only free on one or two specific days. This meant I then had to go back to our location (in this instance, a photocopy store) and plead with them to allow us to film.

A lot of scheduling is really about common sense. As a director, you should have a pretty good idea of how long a scene is going to take (this gets easier with experience). This is dictated by the camera and lighting set-ups, the choice of shots and coverage, and the varying complexity of the scene, which always takes much longer than you'd imagine.'

technically very difficult to achieve will fair best towards the end of the shoot and scenes that are going to be emotionally tough to perform for the actors, along with the major dramatic turning points of the story, should be scheduled towards the middle of your shoot.

Of course, you'll have to abandon this arc as your lead villain is available for three days only and those three days have to be in the first week of your shoot! Actor availability will always bugger you up.

Story days

Another issue you'll need to tackle before completing your schedule is that of 'story days'. Every story is set over a period of time. 'Die Hard' is set over a period of perhaps five hours – we, the audience get to see the edited highlights from those five hours which makes a two hour version of the story. On the other hand, 'Ghandi' may have been set over twenty five years and we get to see the highlights from these twenty-five years to make up a three-hour movie. With 'Ghandi' we only visit the story on selected days during those twenty-five years, perhaps fifteen days, which translates into fifteen story days for production to deal with. Whereas with 'Die Hard', which takes place entirely on a single day, there is only one story day.

Your story may be set over three months and in order to tell that story you may have to visit the characters on twelve separate days over that three month period. When you begin looking at your screenplay with a view to story days, the idea is always to minimize the amount of story days (which in turn should minimize production problems such as costume changes etc). Most often, a new story day will be dictated by either an obvious change of time in the plot of the story, or the passing of night and move to daytime. Take control of your story days and don't allow other departments such as production design, make-up, costume and continuity decide on the story days for you.

When you have 'locked' your screenplay, go through it and mark up the slug line for each scene with a story day code. For instance,

29 – INT. NIGHT – JACK'S FLAT (SD3)

This would be scene 29, set inside Jack's flat at night on story day three.

30 – EXT. DAY – JACK'S FLAT (SD4)

This would be scene 30, set outside Jack's flat during the following day, which would be story day four.

The simple organisation and inclusion of these story days abbreviated to numbers in brackets will help everyone understand whereabouts in time

Script preparation

Before starting your schedule you should go through your screenplay with a fine-tooth comb. Let's leave aside the issues of whether your screenplay is creatively ready or not, or if you will do lots of rewrites – let's assume it's perfect (oh boy!). Go through the screenplay and look for hidden scenes. These are scenes within a scene, typically someone looking out of a window – the shot of the person looking could be shot months and hundreds of miles apart from the reverse POV through the window. Of course, they may not, but at best it is a different lighting set-up and the exterior shot is subject to time of day and weather. Other things to look out for are scenes with a TV (you might need to make the TV program for this), scenes where you know you will shoot two reverses in different locations (must be listed as separate scenes for production to deal with them) etc.

```
INT. EVENING - SARAH'S BEDROOM

SARAH nervously watches the end of the movie - a
vampire blood bath. DAVEY rummages through a toy box
and pulls out a huge water rifle, considers it, then
dumps it. He retrieves two plastic walkie-talkies and
camouflaged plastic binoculars. There is a thump from
downstairs - DAVEY looks out to see CONNOR riding away
- DAVEY races for the door to exit.

                        DAVEY
        Come on!
```

This first script extract shows how the text appeared in the screenplay during the story development stages. As you move to production it will be modified . . .

This is the same scene but notice how it has been modified for the shooting script. First there are scene numbers. Second there are story days in the slug line (SD3 meaning Story Day 3 in this instance). Third, the scene has actually been broken into three parts, to accommodate the exterior night shot, contrasting with the interior night shots (which could be shot in the day with windows blacked out). Also consider the POV through the window. It might only show the actor in long shot, so could you get away with an actors double? Could this be a second unit shot?

```
56 INT. EVENING - SARAH'S BEDROOM (SD3)

SARAH nervously watches the end of the movie - a
vampire blood bath. DAVEY rummages through a toy box
and pulls out a huge water rifle, considers it, then
dumps it. He retrieves two plastic walkie-talkies and
camouflaged plastic binoculars. There is a thump from
downstairs - DAVEY looks out to see

57 EXT. EVENING - YARD POV FROM SARAH'S BEDROOM (SD3)

CONNOR riding away.

58 INT. EVENING - SARAH'S BEDROOM (SD3)

DAVEY races for the door to exit.
                        DAVEY
        Come on!
```

Optionally, in the screenplay you can also change to upper case all instances where a character(s) appears, major props and stunts, effects etc . . . Anything that the production department is going to need to arrange or consider. This will just make things easier to spot.

How the scene might play out

SC 86   SD3   SHOT 146
DAVEY looking toys in box.
SARAH sat in chair in
background watching TV . . .

SC 86   SD3   SHOT 147
DAVEY finds water pistol.
Puts it down and notices
through window . . .

SC 87   SD3   SHOT 147
CONNOR wheeling bike out
of yard . . .

SC 88   SD3   SHOT 148
DAVEY and SARAH exit.

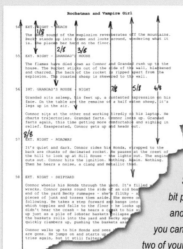

Length matters . . .

When breaking down the screenplay, the production assistant will give each scene a length or 'page count'. These figures are stated as fractions, yes I too feel the shudder of my primary school teachers cold clammy finger running down my spine . . . but fractions are the best way to do it, and it isn't that hard. All page lengths are calculated by the eighths . . . So a full page would be 8/8, a half page would be 4/8, a quarter would be 2/8, and one and a half pages would be 12/8 . . . ! Yes, a head screw. No matter how short the scene, the minimum length is 1/8, which reflects the fact that even the easiest of scenes to shoot will still take time to set-up, shoot, wrap and move on.

Shooting a ninety page script over twenty one days means you need to shoot about four and a bit pages a day – or does it? Well that is the average, but there will be days when you will do less, and hopefully the occasional day when you will do more (yeah right!) It's a useful equation so that you can keep your eye on how much you are slipping behind (and you will be behind schedule by day two of your shoot) but it's not to be taken as gospel. What counts is the overall shoot, not the daily count.

each scene takes place. You'll avoid those time wasting conversations about *'is this before or after the scene where Jane spilt the wine on her blouse, leaving a stain?'*

Lockdown

Let's make the assumption that you have completed your screenplay and that you have gone through it ruthlessly editing extraneous scenes, simplified locations, merged some characters and planned your story days . . . It's now time to produce your schedule.

This will probably be about a week to ten days before you start your shoot. You'll have already decided how many days you want to shoot (a decision based entirely on how much cash you have to spend and not on the artistic aspiration of the director or analysis of the screenplay). It will probably be three weeks, maybe a little more, maybe a little less. Much more than three weeks will stretch your goodwill and budget to snapping point, much less than three weeks will begin to impose intolerable creative restrictions upon the way you've chosen to make your film. Yes, there are always examples of people who have shot their movie in stupid amounts of time, Mike Figgis being the first to shoot a movie in real time. These are of course exceptions and not the rule.

Why leave it so close to when you're shooting you may ask? The schedule is a complicated document and it seems stupid to leave it so late to produce. Quite simply, you won't bite the bullet about your screenplay and it's bagginess until you have no choice. The production team will still be messing around finding locations and working out the peculiar impact these locations will have on your

There is never enough time, money or light. Make your compromises with the storyboard artists, months before the shoot. Compromises on set always lead to at best bad film making, at worst, disaster. If you resist that final script rewrite before the shoot, you'll be forced into it during the shoot when it becomes apparent something HAS to go.

Anatomy of a production board

After organising your strips and locking down your schedule, you should be left with a production board looking something like this. You could buy a professional board with strips, but to save cash you could also cut up strips of card. This image (below) taken from an Excel spreadsheet represents only three and a half days of the shoot. Remember, to modify the schedule using this type of production board. You can simply move around the vertical strips for each scene until you find a happy combination of cast / location / int-ext / day-night etc.

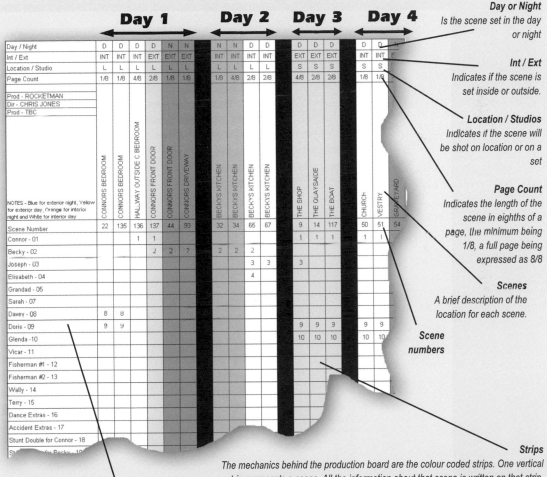

Day 1 **Day 2** **Day 3** **Day 4**

Day or Night
Is the scene set in the day or night

Int / Ext
Indicates if the scene is set inside or outside.

Location / Studios
Indicates if the scene will be shot on location or on a set

Page Count
Indicates the length of the scene in eighths of a page, the minimum being 1/8, a full page being expressed as 8/8

Scenes
A brief description of the location for each scene.

Scene numbers

Day / Night	D	D	D	D	N	N		N	N	D	D		D	D	D		D	D	N
Int / Ext	INT	INT	INT	EXT	EXT	EXT		INT	INT	INT	INT		EXT	EXT	EXT		INT	INT	E
Location / Studio	L	L	L	L	L	L		L	L	L	L		S	S	S		S	S	
Page Count	1/8	1/8	4/8	2/8	1/8	1/8		1/8	4/8	2/8	2/8		4/8	2/8	2/8		1/8	1/8	

Prod - ROCKETMAN
Dir - CHRIS JONES
Prod - TBC

NOTES - Blue for exterior night, Yellow for exterior day, Orange for interior night and White for interior day

	CONNORS BEDROOM	CONNORS BEDROOM	HALLWAY OUTSIDE C BEDROOM	CONNORS FRONT DOOR	CONNORS FRONT DOOR	CONNORS DRIVEWAY		BECKYS KITCHEN	BECKYS KITCHEN	BECKYS KITCHEN	BECKYS KITCHEN		THE SHOP	THE QUAYSIDE	THE BOAT		CHURCH	VESTRY	GRAVEYARD
Scene Number	22	135	136	137	44	93		32	34	65	67		9	14	117		50	51	54
Connor - 01			1	1									1	1	1		1	1	
Becky - 02				2	2	2		2	2	2									
Joseph - 03										3	3		3						
Elisabeth - 04										4									
Grandad - 05																			
Sarah - 07																			
Davey - 08	8	8																	
Doris - 09	9	9											9	9	9		9	9	
Glenda -10													10	10	10		10	10	
Vicar - 11																			
Fisherman #1 - 12																			
Fisherman #2 - 13																			
Wally - 14																			
Terry - 15																			
Dance Extras - 16																			
Accident Extras - 17																			
Stunt Double for Connor - 18																			

Characters
All the characters who appear in the entire project are listed, each with a unique number. Notice how their numbers appear in the individual scene strips to denote their presence in the scene. Also note how extras and stunt doubles are also listed as they are performers who will need to be scheduled and called to set.

Strips
The mechanics behind the production board are the colour coded strips. One vertical strip represents a scene. All the information about that scene is written on that strip, including characters, length, location etc. They are also colour coded so that it's easy to see day/night and int/ext, and schedule faster. Between each day there is a black bar to represent the rest break for cast and crew.

Overview
When looking at this schedule notice how, wherever possible, locations are blocked together (and day / night and int / ext are also arranged within each scene block). The actors are also blocked together, to minimise the days they will need to work. This way of working will also reduce the amount of time actors spend sitting around, waiting to complain about the awful conditions and terrible food.

schedule but most likely, is your cast. You simply won't be able to lock actors in until the last moment, which means you won't be able to check their availability until it feels like it's too late. This is especially relevant when you have managed to convince or cajole an established or famous actor to do a smaller part but have also agreed to squeeze them into a day or two. They won't agree to do the film (or even the dates of the days they will give you) until the eleventh hour. You can't force them to decide so you just have to play the waiting game.

Doing the schedule

Buy two packs of 3" x 4" index cards and ask a production assistant to produce a script breakdown using these cards. They will go through the whole screenplay writing out, one scene to a card, all the relevant information . . . such as scene number, interior / exterior, day / night, speaking characters, non-speaking characters, brief scene description, special props (carrying a gun may need the police to be informed for instance) etc. Take careful note to ensure the story continuity is taken care of. For instance, the script may not say that the character is carrying a gun, as the gun doesn't feature in what happens in the story. Nevertheless, the character is carrying a major prop in their left hand in the scene, and as such, everyone needs to know about it.

You'll need a big space for the next stage as you'll lay out all 200-300 cards on the floor and shuffle them around until you find the best order for the shoot. You will start by bunching locations together, then the day / night variants of each location, then you will re-order to accommodate other problems (actor availability, stunts, locations etc.)

Watch out for late nights followed by early mornings. Cast and crew will always need a good break between days so that they can rest, ideally at least 12 hours. This is particularly important for night shoots which run notoriously slowly and over scheduled. You may get away with shooting until 11pm with an 8am call the next morning once or twice, but this way leads to an exhausted, disgruntled crew who will make more mistakes and work slower.

While the casting for your main parts will remain in the air until the eleventh hour, your smaller parts will be cast. You will find yourself in the awful position of one agent screaming at you for confirmed dates, but you can't confirm the dates because another agent won't confirm the 'bigger' actor until the last minute. So they end up screaming at you! All you can do is juggle the phones, grin and bear it.

Order within the chaos

Eventually, patterns within your schedule will begin to appear as you find the best order in which to shoot. So far, it will have taken you a couple of days to get to this point and frustratingly, you will be unable to completely lock-down the schedule due to two reasons. Firstly, you will still be re-writing the script. Secondly, actors, especially the bigger names that you've attracted to smaller parts, won't commit until the eleventh hour. So you'll be forced to take your best guess about the schedule and simply crack on with it.

Once you feel you can go no further, pick up the cards and give them to your production assistant, asking them to type up all the information into an MS Word document. This will be your official Schedule and will be printed out onto white paper with one schedule day to a page. This means that if adjustments are made to any day, only that day in the schedule needs to be reprinted. Minor updates maybe added on different coloured paper and will be called Schedule Update 1 etc.

The director should know every word of the script intimately, almost to an evangelical level. Their knowledge is a powerful tool when creating the schedule, one of the reasons they should be involved. But the director of a low budget film MUST also have the most intimate understanding of the schedule too, something that won't happen if an AD creates the schedule.

Pin up

Take the 4" x 3" cards (on which your schedule was planned) and in chronological order, pin them up on the wall of the production office. As you go through scenes and they are shot, you can take their respective cards down. If a scene slips behind schedule, you can quickly look at the whole shoot and find a place where it can be re-scheduled. If you can't find a place to re-schedule a dropped scene, pin it to the bottom right of your pin board in a section called 'floating scenes'. If you ever get ahead of schedule on any given day (like that's going to happen!), then the first place to look for a scene to shoot is here.

During the shoot, the cards on the production office wall will disappear very quickly giving everyone an exciting visual reminder of just how far through the shoot they are and how quickly (or slowly) progress is being made.

Assistant Director
Blueprint

ovalpictures • ealing studios • ealing green • london • W5 5EP
t +44(0)20 8567 6655 t/f +44(0)20 8758 8427 e film@ovalpictures.tv

The assistant director, aka 'the first', aka '1st AD', or the assistant director team, is the primary interface between the idea factory of the director and the shop floor of that factory that is the cast and crew. In essence, the director explains what they want to do and the first assistant director will assemble and co-ordinate all the elements needed to realise that shot. This process of engineering ideas into practical realities is not as easy as it would first appear and there is a surprising degree of negotiation, compromise and sometimes even conflict between the director and assistant director in order to get the most out of the situation.

Asst. Director Blueprint

First find the first

Sometime before production is planned, the producer should start looking for a first assistant director. Depending on the size and scope of the production, there may also be a second AD, and perhaps even a third AD. But for now, you'll just be looking for your first. Ask film maker friends and advertise in all the usual places (www.shootingpeople.org for instance), shortlist the applicants and then meet up with the most experienced.

What you're looking for is someone who is happy for you to speak with previous producers and directors with whom they have worked. Someone who understands what you are trying to achieve and is comfortable with your financial and production restraints. Most of all, someone whose character complements the director – for instance, if the director is a little introverted and likes to 'hide' behind the camera, then look for a first AD who is flamboyant and will enjoy communicating with the actors.

If you have a little nagging voice warning you that this person may be a loose cannon or may exercise too iron a grip on the production, then perhaps you are best served by looking elsewhere. Above all, look for a realist with an optimistic streak. We all know that what we are doing is impossible, but we must believe it is achievable in order to get the very most out of every opportunity. If your starting point is always a conversation with your AD that goes *'that's impossible, we'll never do it, you're mad etc'*, then it's going to be tough. The conversation you want is *'okay, this is a tall order and I don't think we're going to do it, so we need a plan B and you need to trust me to tell you when we have to switch to plan B, but for now let's go for it and try and achieve plan A'.*

Script

The first thing your newly employed AD will do is, of course, read the script. They will come back to you with some comments about possible ways of reducing production stress. Often, this is things like merging characters, reducing extras, cutting down scenes, deleting scenes, merging locations, suggesting alternative and easier locations to achieve. Of course, the arrogant and insecure writer/director will no doubt reject these ideas straight away. But the smart film maker will listen as the AD suggests cuts

If the director is the accelerator of the production, then the assistant director should be the brakes. This creative and organisational tug of war is essential to get the most out of the limited resources. But keep cool and remember, it isn't personal. Everyone is on the same side.

The AD team, 1st AD, 2nd AD and 3rd AD, will run the set and make sure everyone is where they should be, when they should be there. The lower the budget, the fewer the ADs.

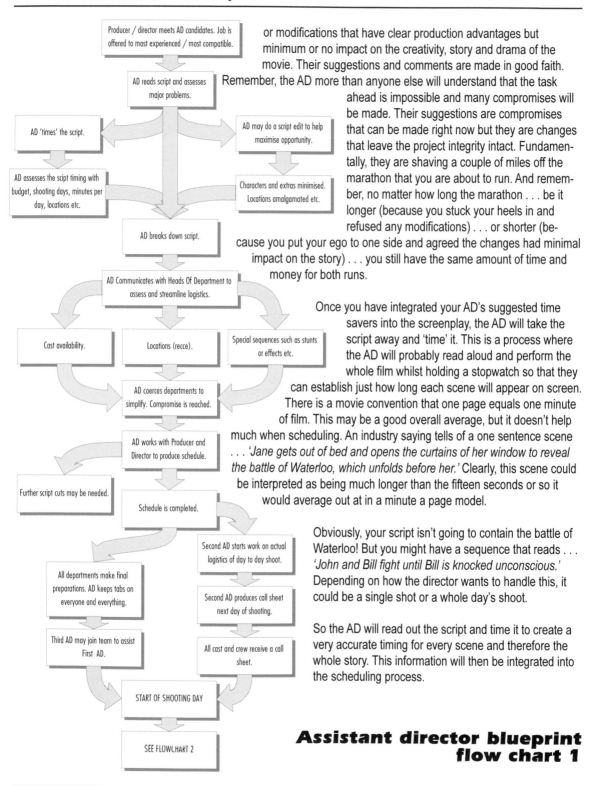

or modifications that have clear production advantages but minimum or no impact on the creativity, story and drama of the movie. Their suggestions and comments are made in good faith. Remember, the AD more than anyone else will understand that the task ahead is impossible and many compromises will be made. Their suggestions are compromises that can be made right now but they are changes that leave the project integrity intact. Fundamentally, they are shaving a couple of miles off the marathon that you are about to run. And remember, no matter how long the marathon . . . be it longer (because you stuck your heels in and refused any modifications) . . . or shorter (because you put your ego to one side and agreed the changes had minimal impact on the story) . . . you still have the same amount of time and money for both runs.

Once you have integrated your AD's suggested time savers into the screenplay, the AD will take the script away and 'time' it. This is a process where the AD will probably read aloud and perform the whole film whilst holding a stopwatch so that they can establish just how long each scene will appear on screen. There is a movie convention that one page equals one minute of film. This may be a good overall average, but it doesn't help much when scheduling. An industry saying tells of a one sentence scene . . . *'Jane gets out of bed and opens the curtains of her window to reveal the battle of Waterloo, which unfolds before her.'* Clearly, this scene could be interpreted as being much longer than the fifteen seconds or so it would average out at in a minute a page model.

Obviously, your script isn't going to contain the battle of Waterloo! But you might have a sequence that reads . . . *'John and Bill fight until Bill is knocked unconscious.'* Depending on how the director wants to handle this, it could be a single shot or a whole day's shoot.

So the AD will read out the script and time it to create a very accurate timing for every scene and therefore the whole story. This information will then be integrated into the scheduling process.

Assistant director blueprint flow chart 1

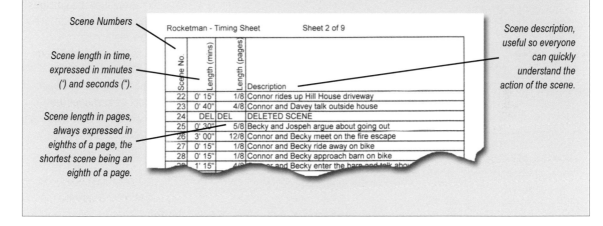

Page Count Timing Sheet

The old industry convention of a page of screenplay equals a minute of screen time does work as an average, but some pages can run to a couple of minutes on screen, where others can be very quick, well under a minute. When doing the schedule, the AD will have timed the script and created a report like this one, detailing the page lengths and associated estimated timings for each scene. This will help better estimate how long will be needed for each scene during the shoot.

Scene Numbers

Scene length in time, expressed in minutes (') and seconds (").

Scene length in pages, always expressed in eighths of a page, the shortest scene being an eighth of a page.

Scene description, useful so everyone can quickly understand the action of the scene.

Rocketman - Timing Sheet   Sheet 2 of 9

Scene No.	Length (mins)	Length (pages)	Description
22	0' 15"	1/8	Connor rides up Hill House driveway
23	0' 40"	4/8	Connor and Davey talk outside house
24	DEL	DEL	DELETED SCENE
25	0' 30"	5/8	Becky and Jospeh argue about going out
26	3' 00"	12/8	Connor and Becky meet on the fire escape
27	0' 15"	1/8	Connor and Becky ride away on bike
28	0' 15"	1/8	Connor and Becky approach barn on bike
29	1' 15"	4/8	...r and Becky enter the barn and talk abou...

Voice of concern

It's incumbent upon the AD to flag each and every potential problem and to quiz the producer and director on how they plan to approach it. Typically, a conversation will start with the AD saying *'it can't be done',* which will lead to discussion, argument and hopefully compromise and settlement. Understand one thing. The director will always want more than is actually possible. This is their baby and they are prepared to stay awake for three months whilst they prepare and shoot the film. But not everyone will share this level of enthusiasm, and the AD knows this. Usually, as long as this energetic and passionate debate doesn't get out of hand, it can be an extraordinarily liberating experience for both director and production. After all, the compromises suggested will almost always mean that the director will have more time and energy to work with the cast and crew in the making of the film.

Schedule

Traditionally, the AD will produce the schedule, but I would argue that the director and producer should have a controlling hand in this process. The schedule is a document that outlines when, where, how and for how long each and every scene in the film is shot. It is one of the most important documents to get right and will form the foundations for the whole production process (see scheduling section).

On lower budget films the director may well need to act as their own AD, shouting orders and taking charge of the set. Even so, they will always need a little help, so have a production assistant or runner close by for those occasional and awkward tasks.

Meet the crew

The AD will already have met the current crew members, production assistants, producer, director etc., but by now they will be taking

Helen Ostler
First Assistant Director

'The schedule is a very important document to get right, and it's no small task! Most experienced ADs will come with their own laptop and Movie Magic Scheduling software which will make life easier for everyone. When producing a schedule, an AD with experience will keep a close eye on potential problems, such as a photo prop of a character that needs to be shot before the scene in which it appears can be filmed.

During the shoot it's my job to keep the production moving and on schedule. It's not always possible and often compromises need to be made or scenes rescheduled. When this happens, it's vital that everyone knows about it or you could end up setting up a shot only to find out that an essential prop has not been prepared because no one told the production design team. No one likes to drop behind schedule, least of all the crew who find it demoralising, so try and keep on schedule. That doesn't mean shooting until four in the morning either, as that will lead to an exhausted and ineffective crew. Keep an eye on actors too, they have a habit of disappearing off-set without warning, which will of course slow things down. The 3rd AD should keep an eye on this.

The greatest sin an AD can do is allow a cast and crew to wait around when in actual fact, everything is ready and you are waiting for nothing. Of course no one in any individual department will notice this until the AD sees that everything is set and they are now waiting on the 1st! It's only happened to me once and it will never happen again!'

specific meetings with heads of departments to discuss how they plan to approach the film. Some of these meetings will simply be about getting onto first name basis, about procedures for communication and a safe opportunity for everyone to size each other up. The first AD is going to be looking for the heads of department (including the director) who are going to be a problem. Unfortunately, some people will behave as though their department is the most important and will refuse to budge on many issues. If there are problems already surfacing, you may be smart to replace the crew member now, no matter how good their CV and show reel.

The Holy Grail

All of these meetings, discussions, suggested compromises etc. are solely in the name of the Holy Grail for the first AD (and truth be known, it should be the Holy Grail for every cast and crew member) which is . . . *'how do we organise what we want to do to get the maximum value out of the time, money and human resources we have to hand?'* It's a simple concept, but one that is often forgotten in the heat of combative discussion. Everyone is on the same side.

Assistants to the assistant

In an ideal world, the first assistant director would also have a second assistant director and a third assistant director. This isn't always possible from a purely budgetary point of view and so the duties of the second and third ADs will be placed on the shoulders of production assistants, runners and, of course, the first assistant director.

But let's assume that there's going to be a second and third. What do they do? During the shoot, the first AD will almost always be on set, hands on and actually running the show. The second AD would be in the office co-ordinating future movements of cast and crew and organising and checking the next day of the shoot. They'll also produce a call sheet each day which will outline what is planned to be shot the next day. The third AD will also be on-set and they will be assisting the first AD in anything that they need. This can be anything from getting a cup of tea, to keeping a leash on an actor who will notoriously sneak off for a fag between takes and hold things up.

Countdown

In the final few days before the shoot, a number of things will begin to happen. The schedule should be completed by now and will have been passed around all the production staff and heads of department. The people looking after locations will now have specific dates to organise when and where they will shoot, so they can firm up on locations. The camera team will know when they need that special piece of equipment. Make-up, costume and production design will now know the order in which the stories will be shot, which will affect the order in which they choose to create or source their stuff.

AD Department Paperwork

The AD department generates a staggering amount of paperwork which is often printed, photocopied, faxed, e-mailed to all four corners of your production world. It makes sense then to invest in a good printer and don't use too small a font in the paperwork, especially for documents that will be faxed.

Timing sheet
A document that is used to list the estimated times each scene will run, alongside it's actual page length. This is used to get an accurate idea of how long each scene might take to shoot, rather than just relying on the old 'page a minute' equation.

Script
The First AD will have their own copy of the screenplay which they will constantly refer to, and make notes upon.

Contacts
A detailed list of cast and crew members with addresses, phone number, cell phones, fax numbers, e-mails etc.

Call sheets
Prepared by the AD team each day for the next day's shoot. It will outline what will be shot, when and where and for how long. It will also detail special equipment or shooting requirements as well as cast and crew call and wrap times.

Week at a glance
A kind of abbreviated schedule which shows an entire shooting week on a single, landscape printed page. Used to get information quickly and easily.

Schedule
The master document for the AD which details the order in which the production will be shot. This may be prepared by the AD, or the director / producer. Either way, it's an important document to get right, second only to the screenplay.

Movement orders
A detailed instruction set and map that is given to each crew member when there is a change of location. It is designed to get cast and crew between locations as quickly and efficiently as possible with minimum possibility of getting lost. (created by the Production Dept.)

Shooting order
An expanded and detailed version of the Schedule. This will be used only by the AD department and the heads of department such as make-up, camera, props etc. This document should contain information and contacts for all the production issues in each scene.

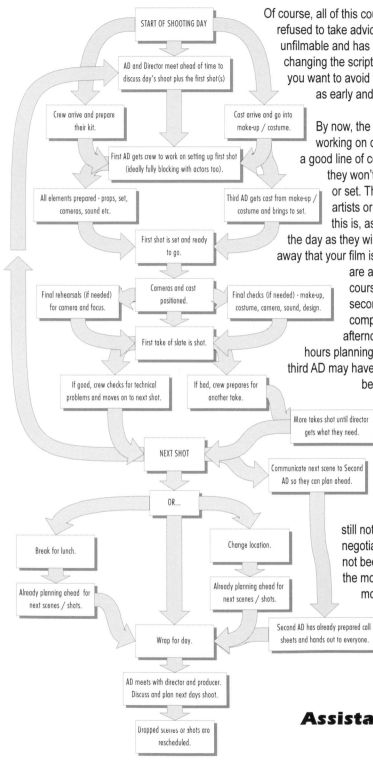

Of course, all of this could be screwed up because the director, who refused to take advice, has now realised that the script is unfilmable and has frantically re-written, thereby radically changing the script and forcing a re-scheduling. It's obvious that you want to avoid this, so make the changes to the screenplay as early and quickly as you can.

By now, the second AD will have turned up and will be working on contacting all the actors to make sure there is a good line of communication between everyone and that they won't have problems getting to and from locations or set. They will also be working on background artists or extras. Don't underestimate how much work this is, as you can't just ask your mates to turn up on the day as they will let you down. Extras are often a dead give-away that your film is low budget, the usual culprits being if they are all very young, inappropriately dressed and of course, if there are way too few of them. The second AD should also be given their own computer in the production office, as each afternoon of the shoot, they will spend several hours planning and refining the next day's call sheets. A third AD may have also been appointed, but their involvement before the shoot will be limited to just sitting in on meetings and perhaps helping make phone calls with the second AD.

The day before

Okay. This is a scary moment. You've planned your movie for perhaps years . . . and tomorrow you start to shoot it! Terrifyingly, so much is still up in the air. Actors are still not cast or confirmed, locations are still being negotiated and may fall through, costumes have not been checked etc . . . But it's impossible to stop the momentum and the whole team will simply move forward, using the production mechanisms, such as the AD team to ensure everything goes as smoothly as possible.

Assistant director blueprint flow chart 2

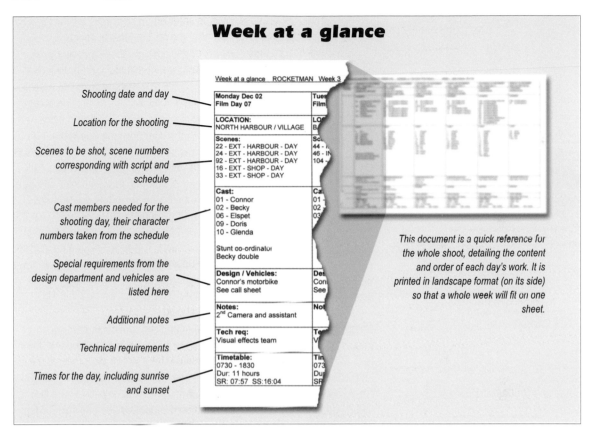

Week at a glance

Week at a glance   ROCKETMAN   Week 3

Shooting date and day —
Monday Dec 02
Film Day 07

Location for the shooting —
LOCATION:
NORTH HARBOUR / VILLAGE

Scenes to be shot, scene numbers corresponding with script and schedule —
Scenes:
22 - EXT - HARBOUR - DAY
24 - EXT - HARBOUR - DAY
92 - EXT - HARBOUR - DAY
16 - EXT - SHOP - DAY
33 - EXT - SHOP - DAY

Cast members needed for the shooting day, their character numbers taken from the schedule —
Cast:
01 - Connor
02 - Becky
06 - Elspet
09 - Doris
10 - Glenda

Stunt co-ordinator
Becky double

Special requirements from the design department and vehicles are listed here —
Design / Vehicles:
Connor's motorbike
See call sheet

Additional notes —
Notes:
2nd Camera and assistant

Technical requirements —
Tech req:
Visual effects team

Times for the day, including sunrise and sunset —
Timetable:
0730 - 1830
Dur: 11 hours
SR: 07:57 SS:16:04

This document is a quick reference for the whole shoot, detailing the content and order of each day's work. It is printed in landscape format (on its side) so that a whole week will fit on one sheet.

Sometime on the day before, the second AD will produce the first call sheet and pass it out to all cast and crew members who are present, and either call or fax those who are not.

D-day

On the first day of the shoot, everyone should turn up at the time that they were 'called' on the call sheet. For instance, if you plan to start shooting at 9am, you may have an 8.15 crew call and an 8am cast call for the actors in the first scene. The producer, director, other production staff and ADs may well turn up even earlier as so many problems are still unresolved. Typically, the AD and director will meet fifteen or twenty minutes before the main call time, have a cup of coffee and some toast and discuss the day's plans as well as the all important first shot.

Once done, the director may well go to the production office to help with production issues (such as yet unresolved cast) or to make-up and costume to meet the actors and chat about their characters. Meanwhile, the first will start the job for which they are known most – that is the drill sergeant on set. It's their job to tell everyone what to do, making sure it's done in the most efficient and time saving manner possible.

If you can't get Movie Magic Scheduler Software then you could always use the tried and tested age old route of using a production board. For more information on how to draw up a schedule, read the scheduling section in this book.

After a block through, their first job will be to tell the camera and lighting team what the first shot is. The teams will then set up the cameras (track and dolly if needed) and lights. This will take anywhere between fifteen and forty minutes (longer on the first few days as everyone is finding their feet). During this period, the AD will talk to all other heads of department including . . . the sound recordist so they will know where to position the sound assistant with the microphone, the production design so they know what part of the set or location is going to be filmed and what props will be used, make-up and costume to make sure everybody knows what they are doing etc. And as soon as everyone is ready, which ideally is approximately all at the same time (so that no one is waiting for anyone else and wasting time), the third AD will collect the actors from make-up and costume, bring them to set, there will probably be a couple of quick camera rehearsals, the first AD will ask make-up and costume to quickly check everything is in order, and you're ready to go for your first take.

Before you know it, it will have been shot and either accepted as a good take or rejected and re-shot. Eventually, and as quickly as possible, a good take will be shot, the first AD will make sure there are no technical problems and everyone will move on to the next shot. The director will quickly tell the first AD where they want the camera for this new shot, explain where the actors are going to stand and what the shot is actually going to do. The first AD will then relay this information to all cast and crew, who will then go off in their separate directions and quickly prepare for this shot.

Time after time

This procedure will repeat for every shot. The first AD should at all times know what is about to happen and what is planned in the very near future. Their skill lies in their ability to motivate and communicate without alienating. Some inexperienced ADs end up barking orders and pissing off crew members. The best ADs will always get the crew to be at their most efficient with a minimum of abrasion. But unfortunately, sometimes voices will be raised and arguments will flare up, and when they do, just remember it's not the first AD's job to be everybody's best friend, it's their job to keep the shoot on schedule and running smoothly.

Wrap

At the end of each day, the shoot will wrap and many of the crew will go home immediately. The second AD will now pass out the call sheets to all cast and crew members for the next day's shooting (they may already have done so). Following this, the director and AD (and often producer) will almost always hold a quick meeting to discuss the problems encountered during the shooting day, with suggested countermeasures so that

If you do not have any film insurance, always shoot two takes of every shot in case there is a problem at the lab or with the film stock and a shot is lost.

The daily call sheet

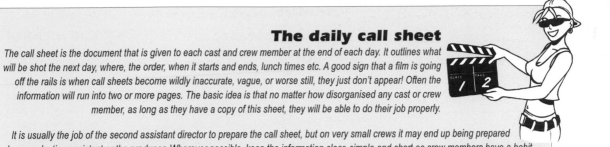

The call sheet is the document that is given to each cast and crew member at the end of each day. It outlines what will be shot the next day, where, the order, when it starts and ends, lunch times etc. A good sign that a film is going off the rails is when call sheets become wildly inaccurate, vague, or worse still, they just don't appear! Often the information will run into two or more pages. The basic idea is that no matter how disorganised any cast or crew member, as long as they have a copy of this sheet, they will be able to do their job properly.

It is usually the job of the second assistant director to prepare the call sheet, but on very small crews it may end up being prepared by a production assistant or the producer. Wherever possible, keep the information clear, simple and short as crew members have a habit of simply checking call times and wrap times before stuffing it into their back pocket never to be seen again. Call sheets can easily be drawn up in MS Word or Excel.

Shooting date.

ROCKETBOY CALL SHEET 22   **Date: Monday 21st March**

Production Office	Unit Office	UNIT CALL: 08.00
PM: Cara Williams	Loc Manager: Sarah Ewen	Breakfast on set at 07.30
LSP, Ealing Film Studios, Ealing Green,	Portacabin 3	Estimated Wrap 18.00
London, W5 5EP	Celador Estates	
Tel: 020 87588544	Cell: 555 5265 256	Weather - Fine and dry, clouds in afternoon
Fax: 020 8758 8559		

Director: Chris Jones   Producer: Kevin Thompson. Cell: 555 2325 2 1st AD: Jane Andrews. Cell: 555 255 2554

Production information, contacts and overall daily start and wrap times.

LOCATION 1: OLD TEMPLE MINES, off Junction road (see movement order)
LOCATION CONTACT: Mr Jim Jackson tel: 020 8555 2552552

Location information.

NO SMOKING ON OR AROUND SET

Scenes to shoot, in order with additional information.

Scene No.	Page	INT/EXT	Description	Story Day	Day / Night	Pages	Cast
22	15	EXT	THE MINE Connor and Becky arrive at mine entrance	2	DAY	4/8	1,2
24	15	EXT	THE MINE Connor and Becky leave the mine	2	DAY	2/8	1,2
35	22	EXT	THE MINE Connor and Becky sit at mine entrance, chatting	3	DAY	7/8	1,2
109	65	EXT	THE MINE SHACK Doris and Glenda plot outside mine shack	8	DAY	12/8	8,10
111	66	EXT	THE MINE SHACK Connor creeps into shack, unseen by Doris and Glenda	8	DAY	1/8	1, 8,10

Characters used, with call times, make-up and estimated shooting start (turnover). Each character has a number.

Actor No.	Artiste	Character	Pick Up Time	On-set to rehearse	M/UP Costume	Turnover
1	Jack Dawson	Connor	07.00	08.00	07.30	08.30
2	Jane Andrews	Becky	07.00	08.00	07.30	08.30
8	Patty Jones	Doris	13.00	14.00	13.45	14.30
10	Zoe Williams	Glenda	13.00	14.00	13.45	14.30

Additional information that may be needed.

REQUIREMENTS:
PROPS:	Love letters, mobile phone, rocket remote control
VEHICLES:	Motor bike
MAKE UP / COSTUME:	As per department
CAMERA DEPT:	High speed camera body, 200mm lens extra hire
CHAPERONE:	None
MEDICAL:	Nearest casualty, High Grove Hospital, High Street, Petersfield 555 125 1253
CATERING:	Breakfast on set at 07.30, lunch on set at 13.00, tea break at 16.30, no dinner
RUSHES:	To be given to Jane and driven to Soho Images
SPECIAL EFFECTS:	None
STUNTS:	None
FACILITIES:	Toilets are situated behind the Mine Shack

Advance schedule for next shooting day, to be confirmed in next call sheet.

ADVANCE SCHEDULE FOR TUESDAY MARCH 22nd (**NIGHT SHOOT****)**

Scene No.	Page	INT/EXT	Description	Story Day	Day / Night	Pages	Cast
130	88	EXT	THE CLIFF Becky argues and slips (STUNTS)	9	NIGHT	4/8	1,2
132	88	EXT	THE CLIFF Connor grabs Becky and tries to hold on (STUNTS)	9	NIGHT	1/8	1,2
133	89	EXT	THE CLIFF Becky falls, Connor leaps after her (STUNTS)	9	NIGHT	4/8	1,2
55	42	EXT	CLIFFTOP Connor shows Becky the sea gulls	5	NIGHT	16/8	1,2

Quiet please, we're going for a take!

The procedure running up to, and after a take, is designed to be efficient so that shots can be filmed as quickly as possible. This is how it works. Imagine that the camera has been positioned, the set dressed and the actors are ready. The director will have explained the shot to the actors and they will have been positioned in front of the camera. As a quick final check, make-up and costume will ensure there are no problems with the actors' 'look'. The camera team is in position, as is the sound team, with the assistant sound recordist positioning the microphone in the very best place (sometimes asking the camera operator to check the microphone is out of shot – 'edge of frame please!'). Everyone is now ready.

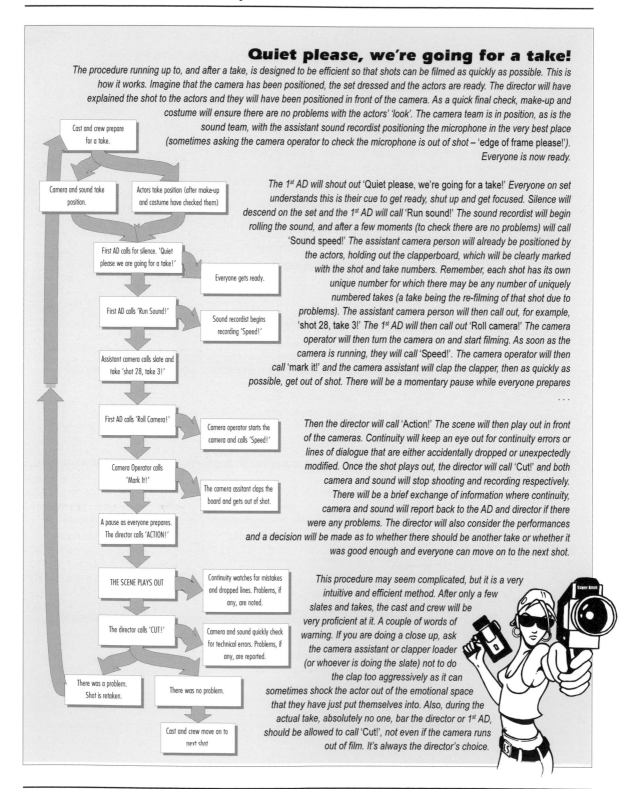

The 1st AD will shout out 'Quiet please, we're going for a take!' Everyone on set understands this is their cue to get ready, shut up and get focused. Silence will descend on the set and the 1st AD will call 'Run sound!' The sound recordist will begin rolling the sound, and after a few moments (to check there are no problems) will call 'Sound speed!' The assistant camera person will already be positioned by the actors, holding out the clapperboard, which will be clearly marked with the shot and take numbers. Remember, each shot has its own unique number for which there may be any number of uniquely numbered takes (a take being the re-filming of that shot due to problems). The assistant camera person will then call out, for example, 'shot 28, take 3!' The 1st AD will then call out 'Roll camera!' The camera operator will then turn the camera on and start filming. As soon as the camera is running, they will call 'Speed!'. The camera operator will then call 'mark it!' and the camera assistant will clap the clapper, then as quickly as possible, get out of shot. There will be a momentary pause while everyone prepares . . .

Then the director will call 'Action!' The scene will then play out in front of the cameras. Continuity will keep an eye out for continuity errors or lines of dialogue that are either accidentally dropped or unexpectedly modified. Once the shot plays out, the director will call 'Cut!' and both camera and sound will stop shooting and recording respectively. There will be a brief exchange of information where continuity, camera and sound will report back to the AD and director if there were any problems. The director will also consider the performances and a decision will be made as to whether there should be another take or whether it was good enough and everyone can move on to the next shot.

This procedure may seem complicated, but it is a very intuitive and efficient method. After only a few slates and takes, the cast and crew will be very proficient at it. A couple of words of warning. If you are doing a close up, ask the camera assistant or clapper loader (or whoever is doing the slate) not to do the clap too aggressively as it can sometimes shock the actor out of the emotional space that they have just put themselves into. Also, during the actual take, absolutely no one, bar the director or 1st AD, should be allowed to call 'Cut!', not even if the camera runs out of film. It's always the director's choice.

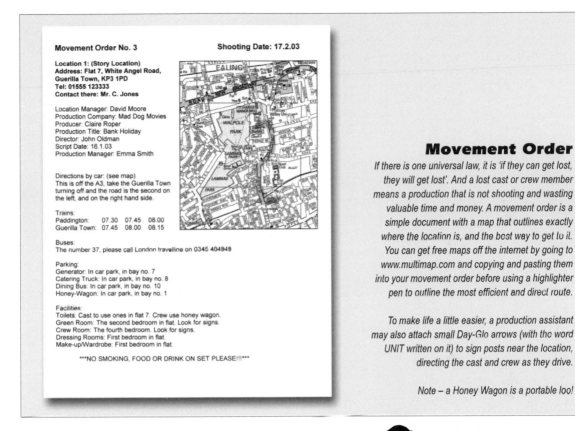

Movement Order No. 3　　　　**Shooting Date: 17.2.03**

Location 1: (Story Location)
Address: Flat 7, White Angel Road,
Guerilla Town, KP3 1PD
Tel: 01555 123333
Contact there: Mr. C. Jones

Location Manager: David Moore
Production Company: Mad Dog Movies
Producer: Claire Roper
Production Title: Bank Holiday
Director: John Oldman
Script Date: 16.1.03
Production Manager: Emma Smith

Directions by car: (see map)
This is off the A3, take the Guerilla Town
turning off and the road is the second on
the left, and on the right hand side.

Trains:
Paddington:　　07.30　07.45　08.00
Guerilla Town:　07.45　08.00　08.15

Buses:
The number 37, please call London travelline on 0345 404949

Parking:
Generator: In car park, in bay no. 7
Catering Truck: In car park, in bay no. 8
Dining Bus: In car park, in bay no. 10
Honey-Wagon: In car park, in bay no. 1

Facilities:
Toilets: Cast to use ones in flat 7. Crew use honey wagon.
Green Room: The second bedroom in flat. Look for signs.
Crew Room: The fourth bedroom in flat. Look for signs.
Dressing Rooms: First bedroom in flat.
Make-up/Wardrobe: First bedroom in flat.

NO SMOKING, FOOD OR DRINK ON SET PLEASE!!!

Movement Order

If there is one universal law, it is 'if they can get lost, they will get lost'. And a lost cast or crew member means a production that is not shooting and wasting valuable time and money. A movement order is a simple document with a map that outlines exactly where the location is, and the best way to get to it. You can get free maps off the internet by going to www.multimap.com and copying and pasting them into your movement order before using a highlighter pen to outline the most efficient and direct route.

To make life a little easier, a production assistant may also attach small Day-Glo arrows (with the word UNIT written on it) to sign posts near the location, directing the cast and crew as they drive.

Note – a Honey Wagon is a portable loo!

these problems do not recur. There will also be discussion about the next day's shooting and any other outstanding issues that affect the immediate shoot.

One of the last jobs for the AD will be any rescheduling required to accommodate the shots or sequences that were dropped during the day. Most day's shooting will result in some slippage behind schedule, even with the best intentions to stay on schedule.

As most people drift off home, the second AD may still be in the office calling and faxing cast members (who were not on set that day) with the call sheet for tomorrow.

Walkie talkies are the primary tool of the AD department. Not cheap plastic ones but high quality Motorolas which can be rented. They're not too expensive so it's worth getting several, at least one for each AD, production department, costume / make-up (beware, actors are in earshot in make-up and costume) and anyone else who would benefit from one. Don't let the director have one, they will only stress at the constant crisis conversations.

Production Team Blueprint

Practical Film Training

For further details e-mail us at
panico@panicofilms.com,
tel 020 7485 3533 or visit our website
www.panicofilms.com

The production team and the production office where they live is the central nervous system and control hub for the production. All other departments, such as camera, production design, casting, director etc., will be anchored to this epicentre. Some departments will work and liaise closely with production, while others will be more distant. All will maintain a strong link. The reason is simple. The production team are the mechanistic facilitators of ideas. Whenever someone comes up with that great idea, if they themselves or a member of their team cannot sort it out (for whatever reason, time, manpower or money etc.), it will filter its way through to the production team who will then sit in the production office and get on the phone, write an e-mail, fax or letter and endeavour to get the job done as quickly and with the least expense possible.

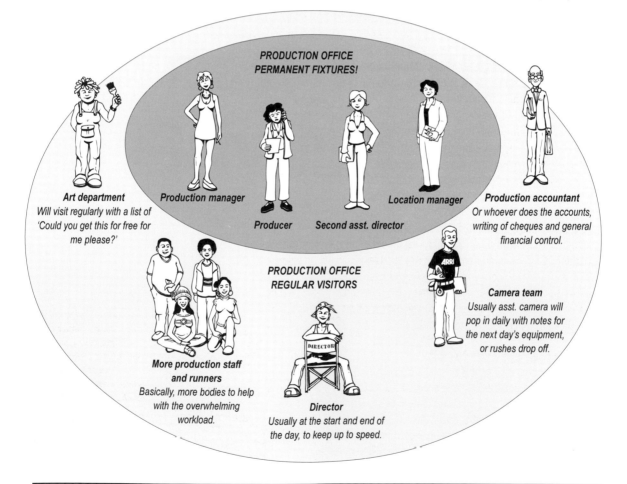

PRODUCTION OFFICE PERMANENT FIXTURES!

Art department
Will visit regularly with a list of 'Could you get this for free for me please?'

Production manager

Producer

Second asst. director

Location manager

Production accountant
Or whoever does the accounts, writing of cheques and general financial control.

More production staff and runners
Basically, more bodies to help with the overwhelming workload.

PRODUCTION OFFICE REGULAR VISITORS

Director
Usually at the start and end of the day, to keep up to speed.

Camera team
Usually asst. camera will pop in daily with notes for the next day's equipment, or rushes drop off.

Production Team Blueprint

The production team quickly get used to dealing with extraordinarily unreasonable and unachievable requests on a daily basis. And at the same time, they have to manage the daily running of the production, which can be anything from a quick phone call to check arrangements for the next day, to photocopying, buying the lead actors' special herbal tea, finding three elephants that were overlooked in the script breakdown and have now slipped into crisis etc . . . In short, they are the unsung heroes of your film.

The 'sort it out' end of the film making process. The production office is where the production team and producer will live. It's where problems will end up and ideally, where problems will get sorted.

The office

A film production office is not glamorous. There isn't much to it really, but what there is must work without failing. First there are phones, as many lines as you can afford as when the shit really hits the fan, so the production assistants hit the phones. Computers. Doesn't really matter whether it's Mac or PC, as long as it works and doesn't crash, and that there is a laser printer attached. An Internet connection, not a dial-up modem, as this will tie up your phone line, but a permanent, hard wired ADSL connection. A photo-copier. Nothing fancy, just for copying scripts, call sheets and other office paper work. A fax, even though this will be rarely used, as everyone is moving over to e-mail. Plenty of storage space for files, books, showreels etc. Try to keep the office as clean and organised as possible, as it will invariably be too small a space for too many people.

As production heats up, so will the noise level in the office. There will be constant complaints from people enduring a difficult phone call whilst having to put up with the ever present chatter and babble of other production people and the photocopier at full pelt. Don't underestimate how much of a problem excessive sound can be for the production team and wherever possible, use cordless phones so that conversations can be taken outside into the corridor or even onto the street.

Who's in the office?

There are a number of people who will populate the production office. Initially, it will be just the producer and director (maybe writer too), both of whom will be working on creative problems, such as script development and re-writes and casting, as well as straight production problems, such as locations and peculiar props. As the shooting date gets closer, other people will begin to appear.

Every director should, at some time in their life, act as a production manager. It will give them a profound insight into how much work needs to be done to accommodate a whim. It will also help them maximise the potential of their budget so that whatever finally makes it to the screen is the most important and best value stuff.

Production work is one of the least glamorous within the team. You are rarely on set, have no sexy kit such as cameras, don't hang out with the actors, and at least one poor bugger will have the thankless task of cleaning the loos. However, the production team are the true unsung troopers of your movie making experience. Buy them extra beer.

Production assistants

These are people who have the ability to organise chaos and to regularly and relentlessly pursue the impossible. A production assistant will join the producer and director a month or two before shooting and they will be adopted into the family. You'd better like this person because by the end of the film, they will truly feel like your brother or sister. Their job will be pretty much defined as this . . . *'sort out whatever needs to be sorted out'*. Yes I know it's broad, but it's kind of true. Of course, it all starts with the screenplay as this is the master document upon which all production problems flow, *'How are we going to achieve this?'*, *'How many of those do we need?'*, *'Do we really need that, can we cut it?'* etc.

The skilled production assistant is a combination of pushy and plucky, as well as pragmatic, courteous and above all efficient.

In the weeks leading to the shoot, there will be excruciating lows and exhilarating highs as precariously negotiated deals and requests either fall

The blag . . .

Getting stuff for free, or nearly for free, is the main job of the production manager, assistant, producer, line producer etc., on a low budget film. So what can you offer? First there is the obvious stuff, a ticket to the premiere and a credit on the film (make a list of people to whom you have made this promise NOW and update it constantly. Don't rely on your memory or scattered notes to put this list together later or you will forget someone important, who will subsequently get the hump and make your life a misery for some time.) Your cast will help too as everyone seems to want be associated with celebrity, no matter how minor.

Here's how the phone conversation might go . . . 'Hi, do you have a minute? Cool. My name is XXXX and I am from Acme Films . . . we are making this really exciting film called XXX about (very brief one liner here). We have a top actor (you add the name!) and we could really use your help in the making of this movie . . . We are a bunch of new and young film makers with a dream, and a fire in our bellies . . . Could you help us with (add here what you need for free) . . . You could even come down to the set sometime and see how it all happens, and come to the premiere too. We'll even give you a credit on the movie so you can see you name or company's name on the big screen . . . But, unfortunately, we just don't have any money . . . What do you say? Want to get on board?'

Be careful what you offer as you will need to live up to your promises. At all times be courteous and honest, it's simply the most effective way of getting the job done. Be brief too, no one wants their time wasted. Be enthusiastic and exciting. Be flirtatious if appropriate. A bored, male, middle aged businessman might get a rush if he gets a call from a bright, sparky flirtatious female PA . . . and that will get doors opened. Not very PC but this is Guerilla Film making! And if they can't help, thank them for their time and ask if there is anyone they might suggest who could help. More often than not they will give you a couple of leads. You may need to back up the phone call up with a fax, e-mail or letter, so keep a few stock letters on your computer desktop. Re-read every letter you send out and make sure there are no spelling mistakes or that no incorrect information has been hurriedly cut and pasted in by mistake (how many times have I sent the wrong letter to the wrong person and ended up pissing them off!)

When speaking to people in the film industry, remember, they have heard EVERY line before. So don't give them any lines, just appeal to their good natured self and ask for help. Sure you can brush their egos, but don't go over the top. You need to leave them with the feeling that they are doing some good and at no real expense to themselves. If you can offer any money, no matter how small an amount, it's real cash. You can offer to pay upfront or on delivery so they will not need to chase you later on, which can often work amazingly!

into place or fall through. At the end of each day, you'll probably hold a production meeting to discuss what went wrong, what went right, what needs to be done next, what needs to be done longer term and can you please pass me the beer and pizza? These production meetings will become kind of like social cathartic releases, where everyone can discuss the craziness of what is happening. Beer and wine, although not too much of it, is always welcome.

Runners

These are people who have very little experience, but loads of enthusiasm. As their job title suggests, their sole purpose is to run around picking stuff up, dropping stuff off and generally doing whatever they are told to do by the production staff. I would suggest you should try and find slightly older people with a car as their age will indicate a more serious desire to get into the film business (very young runners are often doing it on a whim and will drop out as soon as they realise that it is actually quite hard work).

AD team

At some point in the weeks approaching the shoot, the AD team will slip into the office, usually in the form of the second AD. It will be their job to organise paperwork such as call sheets and co-ordinate the next day's shoot. Of course, because your office is too small to start off with, adding this extra person into the mix can cause problems, especially if there are not enough computers or phones to go around. Sadly, many problems don't get sorted on low budget films simply because the relevant person cannot get to a telephone during working hours, at which point, the temptation to use over expensive mobile phones can often become too hard to resist.

Location manager

This person will look after the different locations chosen for the shoot. Initially, they will break down the screenplay, then start looking at locations (recce), weigh up all the production considerations for a given location, (such as any fees that may need to be paid, how far the location is from the unit base, facilities for catering, loos, parking etc.), present the options to the producer and director and then negotiate with the owners or managers of the location. They will pop in and out of the office during pre-production, often using production assistants as a secretarial service, as they may spend much of their time in a car and dashing around to find that perfect location. During the shoot, they will be on location with the crew making sure that everything goes smoothly.

And the rest

Then there are all the other people who will casually drift in and out of the production office as though it was a public urinal. This can be anyone from camera assistants, informing the production team that a new piece of equipment needs to be ordered for tomorrow, all the way through to

Claire Trevor-Roper
Production Manager

'The film will dominate your life for the foreseeable future so you must be enthusiastic about it 24/7 – whatever happens! Borrow office space and computer equipment if you do not have any of your own, with several very cheap phone lines. You, your assistant, the internet connection and fax can work simultaneously which is a very productive way to work. Give yourself lots of prep time with your team. Go through the script over and over and listen to their ideas, then debate with confidence.

Hire an enthusiastic assistant with a great telephone manner and precise office skills. Make sure that they know exactly who and where the crew are and what they are doing. As you approach the shoot, and during the shoot, maintain up-to-date cast and crew lists with all relevant contact information. The same is true with your suppliers, so always get to be on first name terms with them all, you never know when you will need to ask the impossible. And don't assume that because you don't have the ready cash that you will be turned down – it's always worth a second call back.

Attend crew interviews and make sure they take you seriously. Encourage respect. In initial conversations use terms like 'supporting', 'sponsoring' and 'nurturing' rather than promising money that you don't have. No one likes liars – and you want a relationship that works. Make sure during the shoot that everyone has somewhere where that they can be dry and comfortable. With regard to locations, the public will usually react generously to a film if they have not been badly treated before, so remember, you hold the reputation of future film makers in your hands when you are on location.'

stressed out caterers who have gone supernova because no one remembered to turn the fridge back on last night (it was switched off by the sound department as it was humming too loudly for sound) after the shoot and all the food has gone off.

Omnipotent production team

Here's the problem. If 'IT' goes wrong on the day, the production team will get the rap and be the people expected to fix the problem . . . *'Where are the goddamn elephants? I don't care who screwed up, just get me the goddamn elephants!'* Whether it's incorrect costumes, actors who are late, missing film stock etc., when the problem hits crisis, i.e. when the film grinds to a halt because the problem is so severe that shooting has had to stop, then the production team will be the people who will be expected to quickly and expertly fix the problem. With this in mind, the production team need to understand every aspect of every department, down to the tiniest detail. You will know a good production person by the way their mind thinks. Here's a typical conversation with a production assistant . . .

'So who's playing the character?'
'An actress called Jane Phillips.'
'And how close does she live to the location? Will she drive herself? Do we need to organise a cab? Can she drive because the character needs to? Is she wearing her own clothes or has costume design had a fitting? Is she vegetarian? What's her phone number? Has she been informed of the shooting dates and call times? Does she know this is low budget? Has she had a copy of the script yet? Is she confirmed with the director and producer? Has the deal been done with the agent? Has she signed the deal? When's her period? . . . okay, that about clears that up. Oh and one other thing, is she going to be a pain in the arse? OK next . . . ?'

Now I know most of those questions will already have been researched and answered by various other crew members such as the costume designer, producer, assistant director etc., but . . . if it goes wrong, the production assistants are going to have to fix it. Now extrapolate this thought process to every decision from areas as diverse as location management, film stock, equipment hire, costume, actors, catering, publicity, contracts, blah blah . . .

Not that I'm suggesting that just one person needs to ask ALL of the questions, but I am saying that collectively, the production team, be they a production assistant, a production manager or the producer has to have asked the questions and received appropriate answers. You cannot afford to leave any stone unturned.

Run up to production

In the months and weeks running up to production, the production

Keep a lever arch file for all letters and e-mails you write. Just print them out and file them one after another. This will create a perfect chronological record of all your correspondence should anyone ever question what you wrote and when.

Unit and location management

Taking on the job of location manager in low-budget film productions means that you are responsible for scouting for all the locations as well as taking on the job of the unit manager. You will need the patience of a saint and the easiest temperament in the crew. You are going to have to learn how to take your director's vision, theme and colour palette and match this with your producer's budget, the geography and the length of the shoot. You are the direct link from the public to the shoot. You must be a multi-tasker.

Make sure that the producer will cover your mobile phone bill and petrol. If possible, get space in the production office so that you have access to the internet and the fax, and see if they will hire you a car. However, if you have to use your own car, make sure that it is up to a lot of driving. Get a runner assigned to you as an assistant, and choose someone with lots of energy, an eye for detail and lots of charm. Work out how far, geographically, the shoot can afford to go. All unit moves take time and cost money in petrol, parking and drivers. The less moves there are, the smoother the shoot is. Remember that you or your assistant will have to be at the shoot as unit manager while prepping the next location as location manager.

Sit with the producer and work through your own budget, estimating where money is going to be most useful. See how many of the movie's locations can double (or even triple) up for each other. The producer / production manager will also know how many people will be required at each location, work those numbers into your plans. Go through the script. Work out each location mentioned, no matter how small. Sit with the director and the script and get as a clear an idea as possible of what the director needs and visualises for each location. Discuss your ideas of doubling up locations, or using the set should there be one built.

Source the locations. Charm the local councils. You will need to make friends with them as they supply permissions for filming and parking anywhere public. Remember that the councils do not know everyone in their borough. The council rules and regulations may be more stringent than the locals around you really require, sometimes they may not be stringent enough. Flirt and flatter everyone, people may have useful friends. Talk to other location managers that may have used something before that is perfect for you. Drive around the area that you want to film in. Always be brave enough to knock on doors. Always get the name of the person that you speak to. Remember that some places may well have had bad experiences with film productions, so always be polite and friendly.

Organise locations. Determine with the production manager what sort of unit vehicles you can have for the shoot, if any. Your cast and crew must always have somewhere warm and dry to rest, and access to decent toilets. Some of your locations will supply adequate facilities, make sure that expensive honey wagons (portable loos) are only hired for days that there are no alternatives. Discuss the catering requirements with the production manager. If this shoot cannot afford film catering, you may also take the responsibility of sourcing places for people to eat during the shoot. Once a location is settled on, pass the info of the café / pub to the production manager for them to work out the details.

Make sure your team of runners keep the place clean and it is left as neat and tidy as possible when the crew leaves. Ensure that the shoot interrupts the public as little as possible. When shooting in a residential area, send notes of introduction through every door with your mobile number as contact. Re-assure the locals that the council knows about the shoot and that you have all the permissions you need and that the police have been informed. If you are planning to make a lot of noise please also warn them of this. Remember that generator trucks are noisy and should not be parked near local homes if you can avoid it. Try to get them to complain to you first, rather than the council or the police.

Make sure the set is supplied with fire extinguishers and that you have a copy of the insurance document. Carry blank production office faxes with you. Carry the blank template of the productions location contract too. Take HODs (Heads of Department) to as many recces (pre-shoot visits to locations) as possible so that they do not turn up 'blind' to any location during the shoot. This is particularly important for the gaffer who may need to supply power to a location. Make sure that you talk to each of them in detail, show them where you envisage their own unit base to be and listen to their ideas. Always try to anticipate problems before they happen. Talk to the production manager about getting high visibility jackets for any crew, particularly runners, who will be out in the streets keeping everyone as quiet as politely as possible. Note that there are almost no occasions that crews are allowed to direct traffic in the street. You can ask someone to wait while sound is rolling, however, there are some drivers who will ignore this and drive on, within their rights!

Create location arrow signs if the shoot can afford them. Get them tied up the day before and remember to remove them. You will be supplying the production office with call sheet information regarding Health and Safety, parking and facilities as well as the location directions and maps for the movement orders.

Anonymous
Product Placement Agency

'We represent clients who manufacture a wide range of products. Many of them advertise their products in the usual ways – print, radio, TV – but product placement, where we can help, is the practice of supplying a producer with sample products which they will then feature in the production – be it TV or film.

The problem for us is that this kind of practice can be frowned upon by the broadcasters as it can technically be argued that it is an advertisement, clearly a problem for the BBC (where ads are not allowed) and ITV networks (who sell ad. time at a premium, which is why I have chosen to be anonymous here). So what we do has to be subtle. If a prop is featured, we try to supply that prop – for instance if a character makes a cup of instant coffee we could supply the production with that prop. It's common for us to supply an entire box of whatever is being featured, knowing that this will help the production in a small way. Unfortunately, unless you have Bruce Willis or another major star, no one is going to part with cash. Financial return for product placement is selective and exposure MUST be guaranteed, something low budget films cannot do.

Producers should contact us with the script when they know their dates and cast attached. We'll then supply them with whatever we feel is suitable, and probably other stuff too! It's free props and products for the producers and cost effective but low key product featuring for our clients. Everyone wins. There are a number of placement agencies all with their own clients, and products can range from toilet cleaner all the way to TVs and cars. With the expensive equipment, we just loan it to production.'

team will spend most of their life glued to a telephone and computer as they relentlessly search for the cheapest and most efficient way to achieve the impossible. The trick is to sort everything out now. That means going through the screenplay and writing down everything that needs to be organised and then finding a solution as quickly as possible. With months and weeks to spare, a hard working production assistant can get pretty much anything for free or for very little. And that's as good as money in the bank to a cash strapped producer – anything you do not have to buy is money saved from your precious and minuscule budget. Anything that isn't organised in advance will end up being paid for 'through the nose' on the day. I will say it again to be clear. If you want it cheap or for free, it's going to take time. If you want it immediately (because you didn't organise it in advance, you're now on set and everyone is waiting around for 'it'), then you're going to have to pay top dollar. Production assistants can work miracles if they have time.

Once a production manager has produced an amazing result (which they will), you will need to accommodate that result. This could mean a garage full of props and free booze. Never wait to get 'IT' (whatever 'IT' is) delivered next week or next month. Get it delivered today or tomorrow or as soon as possible. If you do not, you may find that amazing opportunity that has been negotiated disappears because the person you are getting it from has reconsidered and realised how stupid they are, their boss may have vetoed their decision (after returning from holiday), they may have moved jobs, god forbid, (and this has happened to me), they may have died and taken that amazing opportunity to the grave with them. *'If only I had asked for immediate delivery!'*

Placement

There are product placement companies, who will be happy to supply you with consumables and props for free in return for you featuring them in your film. Very rarely will they pay money, even though lucrative product placement deals are common myths in the film world. At this level, you have as much chance of finding hen's teeth as you have getting Coca-Cola to give you £100k to get your lead actor to drink coke in a scene. Let go of this idea and get working on finding investors instead.

The shoot

During the actual filming days, the production office will rollercoaster between pandemonium and dead silence. Often, it seems like all hell is breaking loose and there is a mountain of impossible problems to be solved. Other times, things will be running smoothly and there will be little more than happy chitter chatter between the production staff and the second assistant director as they prepare the call sheets for the next day's shoot. It's impossible to even begin to list the quantity and diversity of problems that will arise before, during and after the shoot. But no matter what they are, the production team will need to deal with them. The production team will often be the first to arrive to make sure that everything is under control, and the last to leave to make sure that the crew manage to *'get out'* without damaging anything and clearing up behind them.

Accounting during the shoot

Managing the money, writing cheques and generally keeping everyone on budget is a major task. On big films, you would have a *line producer* and *production accountant* to do this for you. Unless you can afford these people, you're probably going to have to do it yourself, or empower a production assistant to do the donkey work before you sign the cheques. As a general rule, if you don't have to pay during the shoot, don't pay! You can always write cheques after you wrap and this will give you the ability to reflect upon which are the more important bills to pay first. Someone within your team is also going to have to look after getting receipts from crew members and logging them into a computer. Petty cash is always a problem, as someone has to go to the bank and cash a cheque. Invariably, the producer or director won't have time to do this, so well in advance, set up a channel of communication between the bank manager and you (the producer/director) and explain that a specific production assistant will turn up every so often with a cheque and a letter asking for the cheque to be cashed.

Accounts. Phew! Don't underestimate this very important job. It's essential to know exactly where you financially stand at all times. Only through rigorous and accurate cash tracking will you know this. It's a dull job, it's also a bit of a head screw, especially when the phone is ringing and people are screaming about the disasters taking place on set. And hey, let's face it, who wants to do accounts when you could hang out on the set of your movie with actors, cameras and a crew? Keep on top of your accounts.

● Living Spirit Pictures Limited, Ealing Film Studios, Ealing Green, Ealing, London, W5 5EP ●
● Tel 020 8758 8544 ● Fax/Messages 020 8758 8559 ● mail@livingspirit.com ● www.livingspirit.com ●

From: Living Spirit Pictures
To: ████████████
Dated: 21/03/2004

Dear Sirs

ROCKET BOY (the "Film")

This letter is to confirm the agreement with us in which you have agreed to make available to us the following premises ████ ████ (the "Premises").

1. The premises shall be made available to us on a sole and exclusive basis in connection with the Film on 15/04/2004 to 17/04/2004 (the "Dates").

2. We shall be entitled to use the Premises as we may require on the days on giving you reasonable notice and as are negotiated in good faith between us but subject to the same terms as this agreement and on any additional days. You understand that we may need to return to the Premises at a later date if principal photography and recording is not completed on the Dates.

3. We have notified you of the scenes which are to be shot on or around the Premises and you consent to the filming of these scenes and you confirm that you will not make any objection in the future to the Premises being featured in the Film and you waive any and all right, claim and objection of whatever nature relating to the above.

4. We shall be entitled to represent the Premises under it's real name or under a fictional name or place according to the requirements of the Film.

5. We shall be entitled to incorporate all films, photographs and recordings, whether audio or audio-visual, made in or about the Premises in the Film as we may require in our sole discretion.

6. We shall not without your prior consent (not to be unreasonably withheld or delayed) make any structural or decorative alterations which we require to be made to the Premises. We shall at your request properly reinstate any part of the Premises to the condition they were in prior to any alterations.

7. We shall own the entire copyright and all other rights of every kind in and to all film and audio and audio-visual recordings and photographs made in or about the Premises and used in connection with the Film by any manner or means now known or in the future invented in any and all media throughout the world for the full period of copyright, including all renewals, reversions and extensions.

8. We shall have the right to assign, license and/or sub-license the whole and/or any part of our rights pursuant to this agreement to any company or individual.

9. We agree that we shall indemnify you up to a maximum of ████ against any liability, loss, claim or proceeding arising under statute or common law relating to the Film in respect of personal injury and/or death of any person and/or loss or damage to the Premises caused by negligence, omission or default by this company or any person for whom we are legally responsible. You shall notify us immediately in writing of any claim as soon as such claim comes to your attention and we shall assume the sole conduct of any proceedings arising from any such claim.

10. In consideration of the rights herein granted we will pay you the sum of ████ on 17/04/2004.

11. You undertake to indemnify us and to keep us fully indemnified from and against all actions, proceedings, costs, claims, damages and demands however arising in respect of any actual or alleged breach or non-performance by you of any or all of your undertakings, warranties and obligations under this agreement.

12. This agreement shall be governed by and construed in accordance with the law of England and Wales and subject to the jurisdiction of the English Courts.

Please signify your acceptance of the above terms by signing and returning to us the enclosed copy.

Signed...

NOTE – THIS CONTRACT IS PRINTED HERE AS A GUIDELINE ONLY AND SHOULD NOT BE RELIED UPON WITHOUT TAKING LEGAL ADVICE.

More contracts are supplied on the CD that accompanies 'The Guerilla Film Makers Handbook'.

The production office at Living Spirit, mid flow. It's a mess! Too much stuff, too little space, too many people – but what are you gonna do if you cannot afford any more!

Contracts

One of the duties of a production manager, or even the Producer, will be making sure all contracts get signed. Personally, I believe in keeping contracts as simple and clear as possible for everyone, which generally means a one pager for cast and crew, location releases etc. Just making sure everyone reads and signs their contract is a major undertaking (lord forbid if it were a twenty pager each and every time!), but it needs to be done. You can use the blank contracts printed in this book, the longer form contracts supplied on the CD with *'The Guerilla Film Makers Handbook'*, or you can go to a solicitor. I strongly advise having a solicitor look at whatever contracts you do choose to use, but as I stated earlier, my preference is for short and sweeter end of the paperwork. No one, not you, or crew members or actors and their agents, want to read protracted and litigious contracts for a project that essentially is going to pay nothing or very little. Make a space in the production office, usually a lever arch file, in which to store all the signed contracts. Remember, without contracts with your main crew and all actors, you cannot sell your film!

Office paperwork

One of the primary functions of the production office is to generate and duplicate all the production paperwork. The office photocopier will have a small rainforest worth of paper pass through its cogs by the end of the shoot. This will be stuff such as screenplays, call sheets, schedules, sound report sheets, camera report sheets, continuity report sheets, movement orders blah blah. As a guide, during the making of *'Urban Ghost Story'* we photocopied over 10,000 pages! This high volume is one of the reasons why you need a really good and robust photocopier. You cannot afford for it to break down. And like the laser printer in the office, make sure you order enough toner, paper and supplies to get you through to the end of the shoot. When script re-writes or schedule updates take place, these will be printed onto different coloured paper, so order in a few reams of coloured A4 paper in advance.

When you get a quote for something such as equipment hire, ask them to put it in writing on a fax. Ask them to include the dates, service, equipment or materials, and the exact agreed amount. This way you will avoid misunderstanding and people will find it much harder to retract an offer, especially relevant for when people are ill or move on and a new person takes over your job.

Sometimes, the production office may be closed by the time some crew members are able to pick up their call sheets for the next day. To avoid having to keep a production assistant in the office to wait for them (the production assistant needs to get to sleep remember), you can tape A4 card wallets to the production office door and store all the paperwork within them. No matter what time the crew member turns up, they will always be able to pick up the call sheet for tomorrow.

Them and us?

A common rift that divides the business people from the

creative people is that the creatives will often make unreasonable demands upon the business folk on what appears to be a whim, *'yesterday, they needed three elephants. Now they've changed their mind and want a giraffe instead! Who do they think we are? Don't they understand what we went through to get the three god damn elephants!'* It's important to remember that the creative team are just that, creative! They will constantly come up with crazier and crazier ideas in the name of telling the story in a more exciting, unique, effective and succinct way possible. It's up to the production team to facilitate these ideas and dreams, with as little self-righteous complaint as possible. But at the same time, it is incumbent upon the production team to let the creatives know when they have gone too far or when their new request may force a compromise in another area (time and money etc.) This is why it is important to have a healthy dialogue between the creatives on set and the production team in the office. When a conversation about a problem takes place, everyone needs to know that this is a conversation about a real problem and not a moan or a whinge.

Do it now! Make the call! Remember, most people work nine to five so you will need to call them in business hours. There is always a rush for the phone, especially in the mornings. Once you hit lunch, the people you call tend to disappear as they have long business meals and meetings, and sometimes don't get back to the office 'till late, at which point they don't want to talk to you, they have their own work to catch up on. Make the call NOW!

If it can go wrong . . .

. . . It will go wrong . . . twice! I've said it elsewhere in this book, but at the risk of being repetitious, the production team needs to be prepared for all and every imaginable eventualities. Plan 'A' should always have a plan 'B', plan 'C' . . . and so on. The truth is that until the shoot wraps, the production team will live in a constant state of crisis management, where everything conceivable is either going wrong or the production team is fighting like hell to keep it *from* going wrong. This is simply the way it is and the best way to cope with it is to accept that one can only do their best, and as long as they are doing their best, then the experience should be enjoyed for the roller coaster adrenaline rush that it is. Enjoy it, cos when it's over and you go back to your normal life, you will feel different and crave the crisis.

Costume
Blueprint

T : 020 8746 2020 F : 020 8735 2727
www.2020casting.com info@2020casting.com
2020 Hopgood St. Shepherds Bush W12 7JU

The role of the costume designer cannot be underestimated. Film making is a 'grande illusion' and inappropriate costumes, or simply badly realised wardrobe, will serve to fundamentally undermine the whole film. A sharp dressed lawyer who isn't quite sharp enough, a priest whose dog collar is clearly made of cardboard, a tramp whose clothes aren't quite broken down enough . . . all will flag your movie as being at best low budget, at worst, amateur.

Everyday contemporary

Clothes that are freely and cheaply available now, often in the high street or even in the actors' own wardrobe.

Special contemporary

Usually things like uniforms for police, nurses, traffic wardens, but also think about wedding gowns, ball gowns etc. All can be hired relatively cheaply but it all mounts up.

Everyday 'make'

Clothes that for one reason or another, need to be manufactured for an actor. Possible because they are very large or very small. Football teams and school uniforms will need to be fictional and therefore created or hired.

Fantasy and period

Clothes that aren't available in shops and must either be hired or made. Think medieval knights, science fiction etc.

Stunts, effects and doubles

Used when you need to double an actor or when the action requires duplicate costumes for possible multiple takes.

Mixed bag

All the other stuff such as jewellery, watches, boots, etc. All need to be planned and acquired.

Costume Blueprint

For low budget films, costume is mostly about dressing the actors appropriately and not trying too hard to impress the audience (as you simply don't have the budget to impress). At the same time as being appropriate and lower key than maybe you want to be, the clothes that the actors wear are the primary tools that they will use in the characterisation of the part they play. Actors take costume very seriously. Some simply want to look good, but the smart actors want to look *'right'*. Costume is a tool that will enable them to give 'more' when the camera rolls.

Inexperienced director

Outside of a few outrageous or dazzling examples (such as 'Priscilla Queen of the Desert', 'Moulin Rouge', most science fiction films and period dramas), audiences don't really notice costume. This doesn't mean that great thought and attention to detail hasn't taken place. Normally so much work has been done to make sure that the costumes seem utterly real to the characters in the story that they actually become invisible.

The inexperienced director therefore believes that costumes are simply the clothes the actor wears and 'anything' will do. Whilst in a worst case scenario this is true, it's no excuse to do a shoddy job. An inexperienced director under pressure, behind schedule and at the end of their tether can often be heard on set screaming 'I don't care what they wear, just get them in front of the camera'. Again, some truth to this statement in a worst case scenario. But beware, once a scene is shot the costume is inherently locked, at least for that scene, probably for that story day and perhaps even more. Don't rush into these decisions. As stated earlier, we all make judgements on how we look. An audience is no different.

Aside from putting actors in 'frocks' the costume department will also manage a tremendous amount of information and paperwork. Their planning will help ensure the actors turn up on set in the right costume, the right shoes, the watch on the correct wrist, the top two buttons of their shirt undone etc. The smallest of mistakes could completely blow a scene forcing it to be re-shot or even cut altogether. Recognise that the costume department is there to do a job.

When you meet someone, an instant impression is made based on the clothes they wear. It's no surprise then that when an audience meets a character in a film there will be an instant judgement based on their clothing. Enter the costume designer.

Early calls mean tired, bleary eyed actors. Tea, coffee and a toaster can soon become something to look forward to in the costume and make-up rooms.

Costume and make-up

For budgetary reasons, costume and make-up will almost always end up sharing resources such as transportation, rooms, wash basins etc. This fusion can create a 'warm and fluffy' environment where actors often hang out. It's a place away from the stress, strain and graft of the set, where things such as gossip, cigarettes and the occasional tipple, are tolerated. Consequently make-up and costume can often become spies for the production team, keeping an eye on the actors temperament.

Actors . . . bless them!

Most actors have egos that are somewhat large. It's a requirement really; it takes a certain type of person to want to be an actor . . . *and then to do it well!* Of course one wants to support actors in every way, but a sad truth is that all too often some actors don't know what they look good in, and more importantly may not know or care about what is appropriate to the character. There must be delicate and sensitive negotiation between producer, costume and actors about how the character should look. Occasionally the producer and director should sit in on fittings to check costumes are appropriate and wherever needed, lovingly and gently massage the ego. *'You look wonderful darling, just how I imagined him to look when I started writing three years ago . . . '*

Hiring the designer

After putting out your crew call you'll receive a pile of CVs, some of which will be from costume designers. As

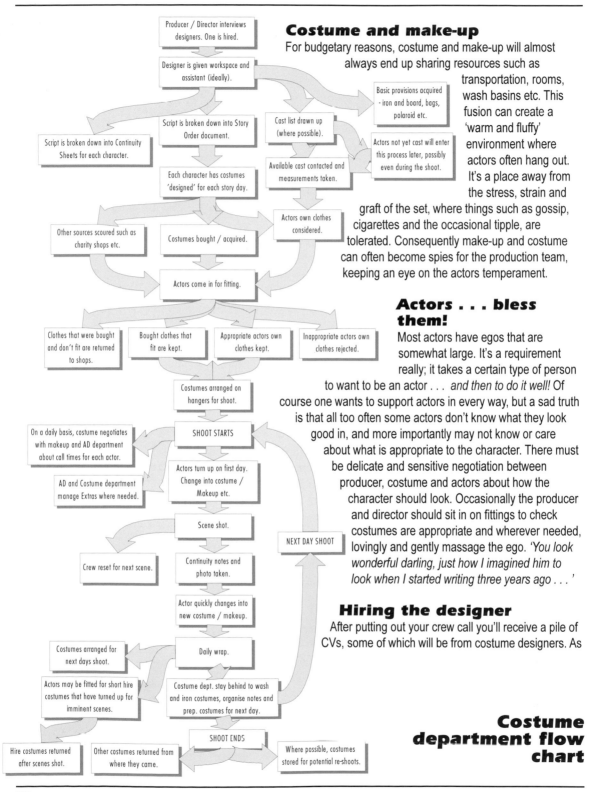

Costume department flow chart

- Producer / Director interviews designers. One is hired.
- Designer is given workspace and assistant (ideally).
- Script is broken down into Story Order document.
- Script is broken down into Continuity Sheets for each character.
- Cast list drawn up (where possible).
- Basic provisions acquired - iron and board, bags, polaroid etc.
- Actors not yet cast will enter this process later, possibly even during the shoot.
- Each character has costumes 'designed' for each story day.
- Available cast contacted and measurements taken.
- Actors own clothes considered.
- Other sources scoured such as charity shops etc.
- Costumes bought / acquired.
- Actors come in for fitting.
- Clothes that were bought and don't fit are returned to shops.
- Bought clothes that fit are kept.
- Appropriate actors own clothes kept.
- Inappropriate actors own clothes rejected.
- Costumes arranged on hangers for shoot.
- On a daily basis, costume negotiates with makeup and AD department about call times for each actor.
- SHOOT STARTS
- AD and Costume department manage Extras where needed.
- Actors turn up on first day. Change into costume / Makeup etc.
- Scene shot.
- Crew reset for next scene.
- Continuity notes and photo taken.
- NEXT DAY SHOOT
- Actor quickly changes into new costume / makeup.
- Costumes arranged for next days shoot.
- Daily wrap.
- Actors may be fitted for short hire costumes that have turned up for imminent scenes.
- Costume dept. stay behind to wash and iron costumes, organise notes and prep. costumes for next day.
- Hire costumes returned after scenes shot.
- Other costumes returned from where they came.
- SHOOT ENDS
- Where possible, costumes stored for potential re-shoots.

you're working on a tight budget with little pay you'll probably end up hiring a young and eager dresser or costume assistant. Meet up with each candidate, get a feel for how they will act under pressure, how tactful they are, and take a look at their portfolio – almost all designers will have a big black book filled with photos of their work. Follow your instincts and look for quiet determination, affability, tact, pragmatism, and not necessarily flamboyant ideas, years of experience or an impressive portfolio. This isn't great art, this is image crisis management with no budget.

Once you've met all your candidates and as the shoot approaches, you'll be forced to make a decision and hire the designer of your choice. As soon as that choice is made, you should give them a copy of the final locked shooting script with scene numbers and story days. You cannot keep changing scene numbers and story days as this screws up their notes and throws the management of their department into disarray.

Ideally, you'll also give the designer a space in which to work (this is often their front room until very close to the shoot) and an assistant.

Breakdown

The production team will be in full swing working on the schedule but costume need to prepare their own set of documents to help them plan and manage the shoot. First is the 'Story Order', a massively condensed version of the screenplay, summarising each scene and noting the characters therein. They will also create individual 'Continuity Notes' for each and every character in the film. This is a list of all the scenes in which a character appears plus a list of the costumes they wear. This is usually written in pencil until the actual shoot takes place and the actor stands in front of the camera – thereby finalising all costume decisions (you never know whether an actor or director may modify the costume just before shooting, 'I think you look better without the hat darling, lose the hat'.)

Production will also supply the costume department with a cast list and phone numbers. Costume will call actors and ask them for their physical dimensions so that they can begin looking for 'frocks'. When you make this call beware of calling too late at night or worse, early in the morning when the actor is treading the boards in the west end until late the previous night.

These documents along with several others that will be created during the process of the shoot will be meticulously filed and often referred to as the costume 'book' or 'bible'.

Kitting out the room

A costume room for the production should be fitted out as soon as possible. There is much more to this than you would first imagine as they will need storage rails, washing machines, dryers, ironing boards and iron etc.

Linda Haysman
Costume Designer

'Some directors and producers, inexperienced or not, think that costume designers have special trees in their back gardens that grow costumes overnight. We are unable to work real miracles without time and budget. Minor miracles we do as a matter of course, but even the simplest of costumes can take a great deal of time to prepare. It needs to be sourced or found, checked for size, purchased or rented, all before it even gets to the actor and then to the set. Perhaps it is because we all wear clothes that their design and management can become 'invisible' to the production team.

If you find yourself working with an awkward actor, and we all have, all you can really do is stand by your guns, be professional and get on with the job. It helps if you have done your homework, for instance, before you drag an actor around the shops or to a costumiers for a fitting, make sure you know exactly what you are looking for and have (ideally) arranged things in advance. Ask around about their reputation too, find out what films they have done recently or if they have just done a stint in the theatre, even if they are having a divorce! It will all help you connect. Don't let big actors intimidate you either, you are the designer and you should always try to be 'firm but tactful'.

The costume designer's job is really made up of three parts. 30% organisation, making sure everything is prepared and right, 20% design, actually creating the 'look' and frocks, and 50% psychology, getting the cast to feel right and comfortable in their costumes. The best actors always treat you as a good friend, they know you have their best interests at heart and if nothing else, it's your job to make them look good.'

Costume department workspace

The costume department is always in flux – washing, ironing, adjusting, fitting, prepping . . . They need space and the tools to do their job. The lack of simple things like a washing machine or ironing board and iron can cause the whole department to collapse. Just because their equipment is more 'domestic' and not cameras or lights, does not mean they are any less important.

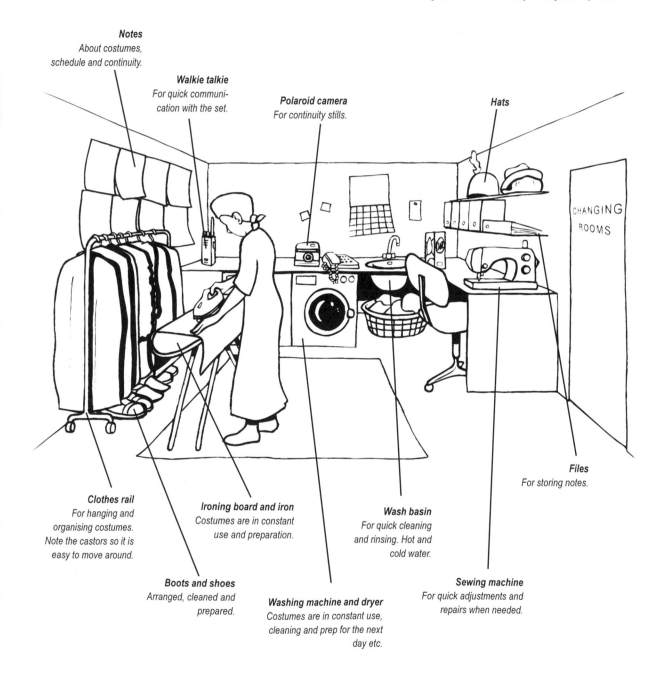

Notes
About costumes, schedule and continuity.

Walkie talkie
For quick communication with the set.

Polaroid camera
For continuity stills.

Hats

CHANGING ROOMS

Files
For storing notes.

Clothes rail
For hanging and organising costumes. Note the castors so it is easy to move around.

Ironing board and iron
Costumes are in constant use and preparation.

Wash basin
For quick cleaning and rinsing. Hot and cold water.

Boots and shoes
Arranged, cleaned and prepared.

Washing machine and dryer
Costumes are in constant use, cleaning and prep for the next day etc.

Sewing machine
For quick adjustments and repairs when needed.

Costume department paperwork

Like other departments on a film crew, organisation and paperwork form a central part of the job. Contacts, measurements, story days, continuity notes and photos all make the difference between decisive action and time wasting guesswork. Costume designers are often bonded to their note book which they often refer to as their 'bible'.

What the production dept needs to supply to the costume dept

Production will supply the costume department a number of documents as soon as they can. There can be considerable friction as actors are not confirmed and schedules remain unavailable until very late in the day (which means measurements can't be taken so little can be prepared). Worse still, there may be perpetual script rewrites that may force new story days and perhaps even new costumes . . .

Screenplay
Clearly needed as it is the blueprint for the story. Should be given to the designer as soon as they are hired.

Contact list
A list of actors' names, numbers, addresses, and agents' numbers. This will be updated almost daily in the run up to the shoot. It should also remain confidential as it contains sensitive information. We used Spotlight to add small thumbnail pics to put a face to the name.

Schedule
Unfortunately, it won't be available until just before the shoot. Whilst annoying, this shouldn't pose too great a problem for costume except when planning hire dates for some costumes.

Call sheets – Issued daily
A self contained plan for the next day's shoot. They'll have cast and crew call times, the cast call times usually negotiated between the AD and costume / make-up departments (as actors may need more or less time than expected to get their 'face and frocks' on.)

First fitting

As actors are hired, they will come in to meet the production team, but more importantly meet costume and have a 'fitting'. This is where actors will try the various costumes prepared by the designers. The lower the budget of your film, the more likely it is that the actors will supply their own wardrobe. There are a number of problems here.

Firstly, you need to convince the actor that they MUST leave all the clothes that the character will wear in the film with the costume design department. This means they may not have their favourite shirt for that party next Saturday night. And never rely on an actor to remember to bring their costume to set, let alone have prepared it and ironed it the night before. Secondly, actors may attempt to take too much control over the look of the character and may force the designer to let them wear clothes in which they feel they look good and are

In the haze of battle that is the film set, be aware that directors will often lose sight of the costumes, focusing on shots and the camera. They may only comment on costume when it is entirely inappropriate. The producer or writer are also good people to seek advice or approval from if the director has developed costume blindness.

The costume department's 'bible'

Somewhere in the costume department, and probably under the costume designers' arm, you will find a thick lever arch file which they will constantly refer to and update with notes and photos. So what exactly is in it?

Cast & crew contacts
A complete list of all contact details for all cast and crew members, including mobile numbers and agents where relevant.

Call sheets
Drawn up daily and outlines what will be shot the next shooting day. Will also include call times for actors with enough time for them to get into costume and make-up.

Screenplay
The actual shooting script which by now MUST have scene numbers and ideally story days marked in the slug lines for each scene.

Schedule
As created by the production team. Will often arrive late in the day.

Costume Continuity Sheets
Each character will have their own unique continuity sheets that will detail costume and modifications that might take place in the scene.

Story order
A document drawn up by costume / make-up / production which outlines the mechanics of the story. Scene numbers, description and characters. Designed to give people a quick snapshot of the who, where, what and when of any scene.

Polaroids
A visual reference for each character in each scene or story day.

Actor measurements
Names, contacts and all relevant measurements for actors, usually in inches.

comfortable (not that I'm saying actors should feel uncomfortable in their costume). Thirdly, many actors don't like to wear their own clothes as this somehow connects the person who they are with the character they play. This is a fairly nebulous concept but actors like to become new characters, not necessarily modify themselves to fit the character. Lastly, it sends a loud message to all actors that your movie is so low budget that you can't afford to buy or rent costumes.

Other sources

There are a number of other places you can go for costumes. Obviously, you can go down the high street and go crazy with your credit card. If you do this, keep an eye on your budget and only buy from shops that will do a full refund on items that you return (not that you will return them after shooting, but you will return them either because the actor is uncomfortable wearing them or they simply don't fit). Beware of unique items of clothing too. If that wonderful but one-off blouse is damaged irreparably, shrinks in the dryer or gets put into the washing machine with that red dress turning it pink, what are you going to do? Wherever possible, you need to consider seconds and even thirds of costumes. This is particularly pertinent when it comes to actors' doubles and stunt performers. Also consider scenes where blood may be splattered on clothing, or an actor gets drenched in water (how are you going to cope with take two if the clothes are wet?) etc.

Charity shops often appear like a wonderful source of eclectic clothing but the costume designer with only ten days to go before the shoot begins and thirty characters to dress, half of whom aren't even cast yet so their sizes are unknown, isn't going to enjoy dashing to all four corners of town just to peruse what might be a bargain on the top shelf of an Oxfam shop.

It's often possible to get clothes from designer labels too. It's a small investment on their side, they get their clothes on a famous 'artiste' and you get free costumes. The bigger the name of the actor the more likely this is.

Getting made

Some costumes are so unique that they will need to be made especially for the film. Clearly, you want to try and avoid this at the script stage as it will add significant cost to your production. Beware also of casting very large people in either height or width as finding costumes for them may become an impossible task with little or no money.

Colour

Many film makers have used costume to add value to their film. Think of film makers like Pedro Almodavar whose use of primary colours makes the characters almost explode onto the screen. Colour carries no inherent costs, so if your characters are flamboyant, allow them to dress accordingly. Think also about the rest of the scene, if the actress is supposed to look good

EXPERT OPINION

Peter Evans
The Costume Studio

'We get lots of calls from independent film makers, most of them with more enthusiasm than budget. What we try to get them to understand is that we are a commercial business, we must make profit if we are to stay in business. We will always help as much as we can, but there are limitations. We are an established company, and as such, must prioritise our business. Having said that, we have worked with some low-budget film makers and our efforts have been rewarded through very good word of mouth. Also, some people who we have helped have come back to us when they've had paid work, which is a nice reward for our initial investment.

I would always advise a new film maker to be realistic about their film. If you're going to make a low budget film and you have very little resources, don't set it in Italy in the 1500s or outer space, set it in Brixton today – aim realistically. We had one chap who wanted to do a WW2 picture and they came in with cast measurements and boot sizes etc., but from his budget it was clearly impossible – we wished him luck but had to decline to help. He was very depressed, but he had decided to do something particularly hard without sufficient resources.

Some film makers, especially students, have the arrogance of youth, and think they are going be the next Spielberg. Maybe they will but not everyone will be, so I would always advise a little humility, which will get you further with us. You must learn to walk before you can run. Aim realistically and look at your budget well before you get started.'

Actors' Contacts / Measurements

Rocketman - Female Characters

Character	Actor	Contact1	Contact2	Height	Chest / Bust	Waist	Hip	Inside Leg	Collar	Head	Shoe
BECKY	JANE WILLIS	020 8855 123	0797955512	52"	32"	23"	30"	—	—	—	S
SARAH	PETRA FRANKS	0208 55512	019775514	56"	34"	24"	34"	—	—	—	3
ELIZABETH	KATE ANDREW	?									

This first document, cast contact and measurements is in two sections – men and women. It is usually hand written as most of it is filled in quickly and on the fly, usually whilst on the phone or in first meetings and fittings. As the actors for some characters are not confirmed early enough, information may be entered in pencil and re-entered in pen when all is confirmed. Note that women do not need to have their inside leg taken, nor collar. Note also that men don't have their hip or bust taken! Sizes are usually still taken in inches and not centimeters. On the whole actors are very good at being honest about their dimensions as they know how stupid they will look if they turn up and don't fit clothes that have been made or bought for them. Beware of actresses who may have their ego wrapped up in their dress size. They may think they are a 12 but you may know they will look better in a 14. Take measurements, NOT dress sizes.

Story order

The story order is a kind of cross between screenplay and breakdown. It's essentially the screenplay broken down into its mechanical elements so that it is easy to get an overall view of the whole machine that is the story.

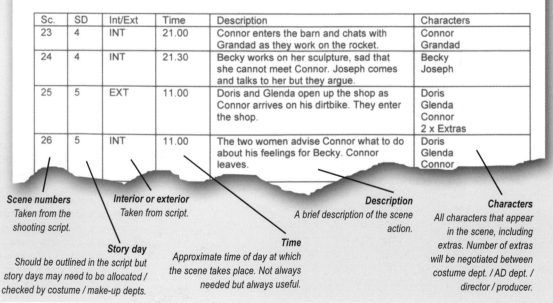

Rocketman Story Order - Page 4 of 22

Sc.	SD	Int/Ext	Time	Description	Characters
23	4	INT	21.00	Connor enters the barn and chats with Grandad as they work on the rocket.	Connor Grandad
24	4	INT	21.30	Becky works on her sculpture, sad that she cannot meet Connor. Joseph comes and talks to her but they argue.	Becky Joseph
25	5	EXT	11.00	Doris and Glenda open up the shop as Connor arrives on his dirtbike. They enter the shop.	Doris Glenda Connor 2 x Extras
26	5	INT	11.00	The two women advise Connor what to do about his feelings for Becky. Connor leaves.	Doris Glenda Connor

Scene numbers
Taken from the shooting script.

Interior or exterior
Taken from script.

Story day
Should be outlined in the script but story days may need to be allocated / checked by costume / make-up depts.

Time
Approximate time of day at which the scene takes place. Not always needed but always useful.

Description
A brief description of the scene action.

Characters
All characters that appear in the scene, including extras. Number of extras will be negotiated between costume dept. / AD dept. / director / producer.

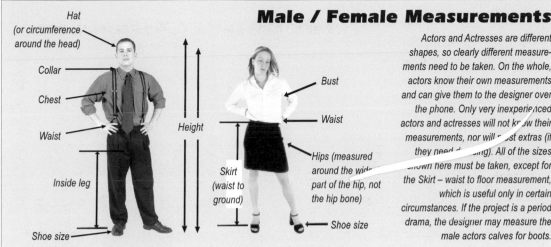

Male / Female Measurements

Hat (or circumference around the head)

Collar

Chest

Waist

Inside leg

Shoe size

Height

Skirt (waist to ground)

Bust

Waist

Hips (measured around the widest part of the hip, not the hip bone)

Shoe size

Actors and Actresses are different shapes, so clearly different measurements need to be taken. On the whole, actors know their own measurements and can give them to the designer over the phone. Only very inexperienced actors and actresses will not know their measurements, nor will most extras (if they need dressing). All of the sizes shown here must be taken, except for the Skirt – waist to floor measurement, which is useful only in certain circumstances. If the project is a period drama, the designer may measure the male actors calves for boots.

dancing, give her a dress that will look good on the floor. If it's a darkened dinner scene, do you want your 'dressed in black' actress to disappear into the shadows? If you can, get production design and costume to talk at length about colour and how each plan to use it so that actors and backgrounds don't clash – unless that is what you want.

Hire the frocks

There are many specialised costume hire companies who can supply anything from a medieval knight to a spacesuit. Even though your movie probably won't call for any unique or weird and wonderful costumes, there maybe a number of hidden horrors. Typically, things like police uniforms, traffic wardens, nurses, in fact anyone in uniform, can cost much more than you might expect, especially if they are dotted about the entire shoot. As a rough guide, one costume or uniform should cost anywhere between £50–75 a week to hire. So if your script reads *'six policemen burst through the door'* perhaps you should rewrite it to read either *'three policemen burst through the door'* or even *'six policemen burst through the door, three in uniform, three plain clothes.'*

Final few prep days

As the first day of shooting approaches, so the pressure will mount. Most frustratingly, the costume department will be at the mercy of casting. If they don't know who the actor is or what size they are, they can't prepare anything apart from brainstorming what the characters might wear. As time ticks down and the first day arrives, above all, the costume department must be sure that they can always cope with the next day's shoot. If they can do that, then the production will never be halted. It's a fairly terrifying concept, not knowing who or what the actors are going to wear in three days, but what are you going to do if you simply don't know who your actors are?

If a designer is not on set, it does not mean that they are idling the day away, chatting to actors and sipping coffee. More likely they are frantically running up and down the high street trying to find that elusive frock, or that they are fitting a costume for an actor who has just popped in. Extra costume design staff, or dressers, are a welcome help to a designer in overload.

Polaroid Moment

The Polaroid camera is one of the major hidden expenses for the Costume department. After each major scene, and at the very least each story day, a Polaroid photo of each character should be taken and notes quickly scribbled on it. Later it will be filed in the appropriate place in the Costume book that is steadily growing in size. It's important that this shot is taken after the scene has been filmed as often, subtle changes can be made to the costume during the shoot (for instance the director might want to lose the sunglasses as it makes the actor's eyes too dark). These Polaroid images will be examined regularly in order to check just how the actor should look in the scenes prior and post to the one just shot.

There is always pressure from actors, director and producer to minimise these shots . . . But do so at your peril. Major continuity errors can make a scene unusable, and how much time and money will that cost to re-shoot? And what if you lose your costume designer to a well paid job, whoever takes over can't just magically know what each character is dressed like, even with extensive notes – these images will save your life in that instance.

The bugbear with Polaroids is that whilst the camera is cheap, the film is very expensive, often around a quid a shot, but there are deals to be done. Get the production team working on this as early as possible. You'll need anywhere between 25 and 200 shots.

Why not go digital? The image is better, it's definitely cheaper to run and you could probably blag a camera and printer for free. The big disadvantage with digital cameras is that when the shots are taken they aren't printed there and then, which means the designer must remember exactly which photo is which when printed out later, unlike the instant note that can be scribble on a Polaroid. Plus (and never underestimate this) unlike the Polaroid, digital cameras and printers are high technology, which means people will get it wrong and it will fail.

As you move through the shoot, decisions are made by virtue of actors actually appearing in front of the camera in costume. From that point, the costume department's responsibility to that actor in that costume on that story day becomes a matter of continuity and management. In essence, this will free the designer to continue to work on actors who have not yet been cast or have just come on board and may be having their first fitting (even though you might be weeks into the shoot).

D-day

Sex scenes are always something that everyone gets a little nervous about. Flesh coloured underwear can help keep everything tucked in place if maximum flesh isn't on display . . . but if it is, Costume should be bonded to your actors side, just out of shot, ready with a bathrobe to fling over them as soon as cut is called.

What happens in the costume department on a typical day? First of all, the afternoon before, a member of the assistant director team will have come to talk to costume about call times for the actors. For instance, you may have a 9am call time for the crew but if the costumes and make-up are complicated, the actors may be called an hour earlier. The idea is that as soon as the lighting team and crew are ready, so the actors are in full make-up and costume and everybody is ready to rock'n'roll without a single lost moment.

Costume continuity sheets

The backbone of the Costume department are the continuity sheets for each and every character in the film. It outlines what each character is wearing, small modifications which might occur in the performance (loosening a tie for instance) and many other aspects. It will be planned out in pencil then overwritten in pen when it actually takes place. These notes will be cross referenced with the Polaroid shots that will also be filed in the costume department's 'bible'.

Character name
Each character in the story will have their own individual continuity sheets.

Drawings
Use quick sketches to help, such as this one which shows the way the actor has re-tied the scarf around their neck.

Story day
Should be outlined in the script but story days may need to be allocated by costume/make-up depts.

Scene numbers
Taken from the shooting script.

Set or location
Interior or exterior plus location, taken from shooting script.

Notes
Anything that is important to remember about the scene – 'removes glasses' or 'unbuttons shirt' for instance.

Costume
A complete list of all the clothing worn by the actor in the scene, which may also include the whole story day.

Scene break
A break in scenes, but not story day. When the character reappears in later scenes they may or may not be wearing the same costume.

Story day break
A hard story break which will almost certainly denote a costume change unless your character does not change clothes (uniforms for instance)

Note – These sheets will almost always be prepared by hand due to last minute changes on set.

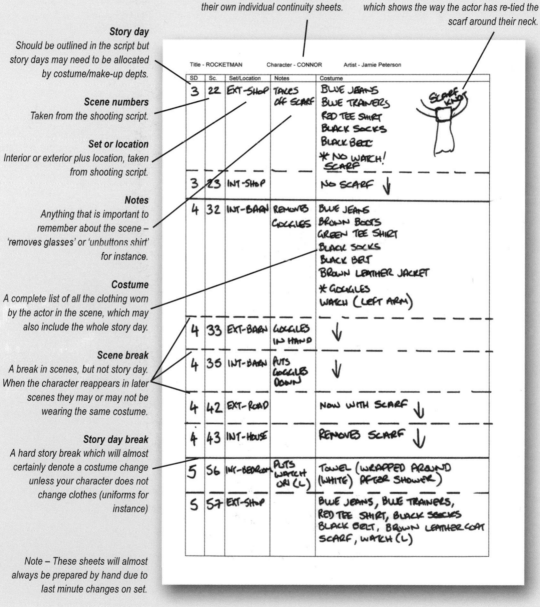

Title - ROCKETMAN   Character - CONNOR   Artist - Jamie Peterson

SD	Sc.	Set/Location	Notes	Costume
3	22	EXT-SHOP	TAKES OFF SCARF	BLUE JEANS / BLUE TRAINERS / RED TEE SHIRT / BLACK SOCKS / BLACK BELT / * NO WATCH! / SCARF
3	23	INT-SHOP		NO SCARF ↓
4	32	INT-BARN	REMOVES GOGGLES	BLUE JEANS / BROWN BOOTS / GREEN TEE SHIRT / BLACK SOCKS / BLACK BELT / BROWN LEATHER JACKET / * GOGGLES / WATCH (LEFT ARM)
4	33	EXT-BARN	GOGGLES IN HAND	↓
4	35	INT-BARN	PUTS GOGGLES DOWN	↓
4	42	EXT-ROAD		NOW WITH SCARF ↓
4	43	INT-HOUSE		REMOVES SCARF ↓
5	56	INT-BEDROOM	PUTS WATCH ON (L)	TOWEL (WRAPPED AROUND (WHITE) AFTER SHOWER)
5	57	EXT-SHOP		BLUE JEANS, BLUE TRAINERS, RED TEE SHIRT, BLACK SOCKS BLACK BELT, BROWN LEATHER COAT SCARF, WATCH (L)

SCARF KNOT

Wardrobe accessories box

The costume design department will carry around a 'toolbox' crammed with all sorts of quick fix goodies and emergency repair materials. Speed is always of the essence, especially when a quick modification is needed on set, so a portable kit like this should always be at hand.

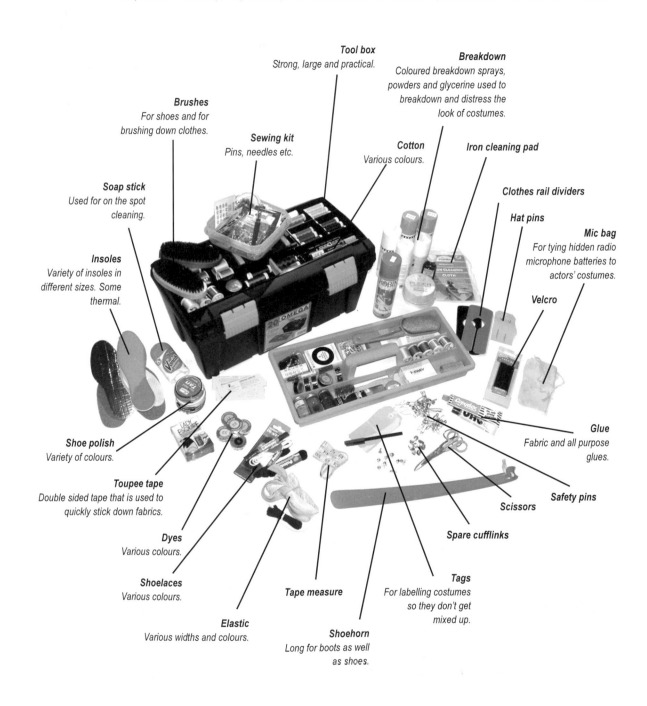

Tool box
Strong, large and practical.

Breakdown
Coloured breakdown sprays, powders and glycerine used to breakdown and distress the look of costumes.

Brushes
For shoes and for brushing down clothes.

Sewing kit
Pins, needles etc.

Cotton
Various colours.

Iron cleaning pad

Clothes rail dividers

Soap stick
Used for on the spot cleaning.

Hat pins

Mic bag
For tying hidden radio microphone batteries to actors' costumes.

Insoles
Variety of insoles in different sizes. Some thermal.

Velcro

Glue
Fabric and all purpose glues.

Shoe polish
Variety of colours.

Safety pins

Toupee tape
Double sided tape that is used to quickly stick down fabrics.

Scissors

Spare cufflinks

Dyes
Various colours.

Tags
For labelling costumes so they don't get mixed up.

Shoelaces
Various colours.

Tape measure

Elastic
Various widths and colours.

Shoehorn
Long for boots as well as shoes.

The night before, the costume department will organise all the costumes for the next day's shoot, making sure everything is washed and ironed and all costumes are complete.

On the morning of the shoot, the actors should arrive promptly for their call time. There will be a quick negotiation between make-up and costume as to which actor goes to which department first (assuming that didn't happen the night before) and then the actors will get changed and made-up. If you do not have proper changing rooms, then a washing line and sheet will do, especially for more professional and experienced actors who may be used to theatre. It's not ideal, but needs must. At first, actors and costume will take a while to get to know each other but after some time familiarity and confidence will mean that everyone gets on with their duties quickly and efficiently, and ideally in as high spirits as possible.

Actors can be forced to change very quickly, but usually it will take around fifteen minutes. If you rush them, they may be flustered, which you may pay for when they get in front of the camera. It's very important for the production and assistant director teams to listen to the costume (and make-up) department as this is about as direct a window into the actor's true feelings as you can get.

Once in costume and make-up, the actors will be ferried off to set and do their thing. During the shooting of the scene the costume designer will make extensive notes about the character's costume in the 'continuity sheets' (see box). These notes may have already been prepared in pencil but now as the costume has been shot, it will be overwritten in pen noting any modifications. Costume will also take a Polaroid photo at this point, quickly scrawling notes on the back about scene number, character and story day. These Polaroids will be stuck into the 'bible' later that day. Once the scene is complete, actors will be whisked off to make up and wardrobe as quickly as possible, then they will be prepared for the next scene as the main crew re-set and light. This process will repeat throughout the day and the entire shoot.

The sad truth is that whilst most crew go home as soon as a wrap is called, costume (who are usually first to arrive in the morning) are last to leave as clothes need to be washed, dried and ironed for the next day's shoot.

On location

Problems can occur when shooting on location without any proper provision for costume. At the very least, the costume and make-up departments should have their own vehicle, and frocks will be transported in large polythene bags, much like the ones you get from dry-cleaners, but tougher. If you can dress and make-up your actor

Special dividers that sit on the clothing rails can be labelled so that each characters costume has it's own 'place'. These dividers are invaluable in the often chaotic mess that is the too small, shared, overworked space costume department

One hidden expense is thermal underwear. Whatever costumes an actor is wearing, it is rarely appropriate for the weather, especially cold winter nights. The answer for your shivering actors is thermal underwear, worn beneath the costume. They may feel ridiculous and like a grandparent at first but, they'll thank you once they get outside in the cold.

before going to location, then that will help, but if there is a costume change at location, it's essential that production and the location manager fully appreciate that a suitable space will be needed. And that doesn't mean the public loos!

A little thinking ahead will keep actors very happy. You may be shooting on a rainy February night – the crew are wearing thermals and boots whilst the actors run around in very lightweight clothing. How much is an actor going to love their costume designer if the designer has made sure there are always warm blankets, towels to dry off, thermal underwear for cold nights, a huge umbrella for when it's drizzling, a jacket that is thrown over them as soon as 'cut' is called . . . And ohhh, clean, dry socks to keep tootsies warm? Think ahead.

That's a wrap

At the end of the shoot, clothes from the costume department will go in several directions. Actors will reclaim their beloved clobber, hired costumes will go back to hire shops (if they haven't already done so as you are paying by the week) and anything that has been bought by the production should be stored for future re-shoots.

Make-up
Blueprint

Make-up is often an invisible craft. When you watch a film, it's rare that you will notice the make-up, except when it's special make-up or really bad make-up. It can often be said of a film crew that they see make-up as unimportant and invisible too, which can of course cause friction. It's the primary job of the make-up artist to make sure everyone in front of the camera looks as good as possible, even when they are looking bad, and the production team MUST allow time for the make-up artist to do their job!

Normal make-up

Where an actor is supposed to look 'average' and appropriate to the character. Male characters generally take less time, female characters longer as often there is a degree of 'glam' to their look.

Special make-up

Cuts, bruises, gashes etc., not requiring any appliances or latex work. These can be a problem as they take time to get right, as well as being tough to do in the first place. Continuity is also important to get right with cuts and bruises.

SFX

Now we slip into special effects really, still make-up, but really the domain of specialised make-up artists who work with latex appliances etc. It's easy to get this horribly wrong on low budget films and all the cost and effort ends up on the cutting room floor.

Hair

If the hair job is complex or important to a character, make sure you have allotted enough time to get it right. Hair can take a very long time to do and actors may need a hair cut / colouring prior to the shoot. Beware of wigs as they are expensive, time consuming and easy to get horribly wrong.

The other stuff

Which can include tears with a tear stick, tattoos, blood and gore, body painting, simple ageing etc. Facial hair such as beards and moustaches need to be bought (expensive!) and applied with expertise or they will look terrible.

Work load

Can you do it fast enough? Multiple characters will mean multiple make-up artists, or at least a make-up artist with an assistant. Often there simply isn't enough people power to get the job done on time and crews can stand around waiting!

Make-up Blueprint

The make-up artist and make-up department on ultra micro budget films are, more often than not, forced to do little more than the very bare minimum required to get an actor or actress in front of the camera. Almost always, *'the look'* is going to be naturalistic and low-key. It simply takes less time to apply the make-up. But as the budget increases, along with the crew size, so the make-up department will do much more.

Many new film makers don't understand the value and importance of good make-up and hair. There's a reason actors look good in front of a camera, and when you meet them, your initial thought is, 'gosh, they aren't as good looking as I thought'. The reason is, of course, that the make-up artist and hair stylist has spent hours making them look beautiful for the shoot. Every bump and wrinkle expertly concealed. Every hair put in its place. In short, if you want your cast to look *'good'*, then you are going to have to invest time and money in the make-up and hair departments.

The Make-up artist is the person whose job it is to apply make-up to the actors, be it low-key contemporary, in-your-face drag-queens or complex Elizabethan drama . . . as well as looking after less obvious stuff, such as hair, beards, bruises, cuts, even tattoos.

Who to hire?

Like most crew members, you're going to be finding and interviewing people through places like Shooting People and, of course, through word of mouth. When interviewing candidates, you'll get a vibe for who will best fit into your team and who will complain about working conditions and lack of pay. The make-up artist will more than likely show you a fairly impressive CV and spend five minutes showing you their 'book' – aka their portfolio. Usually, this is ten or twenty pages of colour photographs from their previous jobs. This portfolio will give you a good idea of their artistic and technical expertise.

You also want to know that they have enough make-up and equipment for the shoot too. Most experienced make-up artists already own absolutely everything imaginable – lipsticks, foundations, eye-shadows of every conceivable colour, removal creams, the list goes on almost endlessly. The best deal you can cut is where they utilise all their own resources and you reimburse them for what they have used. This way, you do not need to buy large amounts of expensive make-up when you may only ever use a couple of brush

On ultra micro budget shoots, make-up is often little more than the bleeding obvious, foundation, blusher and lippy for the ladies, a powdering down for the chaps (sometimes even done by the actors themselves). But as you get more serious, so will the make-up department, at which point workload kicks in . How do you cope with multiple make-ups for a single scene? The answer is a second make-up artist or assistant, ideally a multi-talented person who can be shared with the costume department.

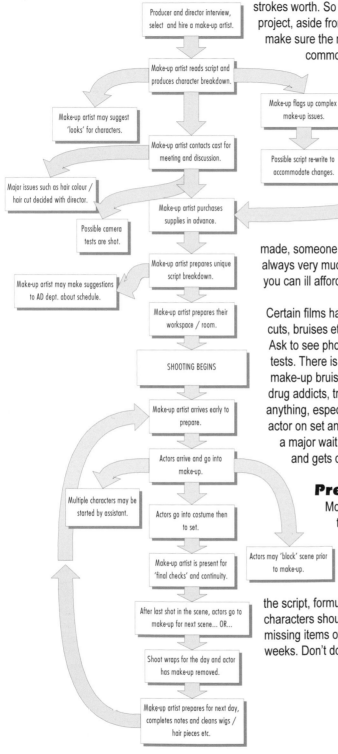

Producer and director interview, select and hire a make-up artist.

Make-up artist reads script and produces character breakdown.

Make-up artist may suggest 'looks' for characters.

Make-up flags up complex make-up issues.

Make-up artist contacts cast for meeting and discussion.

Possible script re-write to accommodate changes.

Make-up researches beards / tattoos / simple prosthetics etc.

Major issues such as hair colour / hair cut decided with director.

Make-up artist purchases supplies in advance.

Possible camera tests are shot.

Make-up artist prepares unique script breakdown.

Make-up artist may make suggestions to AD dept. about schedule.

Make-up artist prepares their workspace / room.

SHOOTING BEGINS

Make-up artist arrives early to prepare.

Actors arrive and go into make-up.

Multiple characters may be started by assistant.

Actors go into costume then to set.

Actors may 'block' scene prior to make-up.

Make-up artist is present for 'final checks' and continuity.

After last shot in the scene, actors go to make-up for next scene... OR...

Shoot wraps for the day and actor has make-up removed.

Make-up artist prepares for next day, completes notes and cleans wigs / hair pieces etc.

strokes worth. So fully consider what a make-up artist will bring to the project, aside from their talent and their enthusiasm. It's important to make sure the make-up artist is paid for their materials, as a common complaint I hear is that *'such and such a film maker never paid for my materials'*, which means that this make-up artist will never do another low budget film.

A production assistant should also be set the task of getting make-up for free. The Make-up artist should supply a list of all the common stuff and calls, letters, faxes and e-mails should be made. On every film I have made, someone has always managed to get something for free, not always very much, but every penny saved is money in the bank that you can ill afford to spend.

Certain films have special requirements, commonly things like blood, cuts, bruises etc. Do not assume your make-up artist can do this. Ask to see photos of previous work, or even ask them to produce tests. There is no bigger give-away of a cheap movie than a dodgy make-up bruise. This can extend to things like a 'hang-over look', drug addicts, tramps, even teary eyed moments! Don't assume anything, especially with newer make-up artists. When you get the actor on set and in front of the camera, if the make-up is not right, it's a major wait until it is corrected . . . or you shoot, it looks wrong and gets cut out! Either way, a waste.

Prep time

Most new film makers think that make-up is little more than a bit of lippy and a dabbing with a powder puff. It is so much more. Prep time is regularly ignored, almost always to the detriment of the project. At least one week, prior to the shoot, should be given to the make-up artist, so that they can properly read the script, formulate creative and interesting ideas about how the characters should look, take meetings with the director, shop for missing items of make-up etc. In an ideal world, this will be two weeks. Don't do the usual stupid mistake of hiring someone and

Make-up blueprint flow chart

asking them to turn up for the first time on the first day of the shoot. This will lead to mistakes, re-shoots and a generally stressful environment. You do not want this to be the first thing your actors experience about your shooting practices.

First things first

After hiring the artist, the first thing they will do is to read the script and then meet with the producer and director to discuss some of the more esoteric make-up issues raised. A good make-up artist (who understands they are working with a very tight budget) should make creative suggestions and at the very least should flag up expensive problems that may need to be re-thought. The most common discussions will centre around . . . an actor's hair, do they need a haircut or re-colouring or can it stay as it is? Do they need a wig because that's going to cost a lot of money and take time to get right? What about the cuts and bruises in the script? Can they be mini-mised? Can costume supply them with a bandage instead of a visual wound? Does there need to be so many significant make-up changes between the scenes? How glam is your version of glam? What about the tattoos? Who is going to do them and how close will they feature in camera? Can the schedule be arranged so the actor can grow stubble for the morning after scenes? Maybe you should re-think the actor wearing a beard in some scenes as this will need to be made and brought in, which is going to cost a lot of money and take a long time to apply? All these issues and many more should be discussed, and ideally, the script should be modified and re-written at as early a stage as possible, to accommodate any reasonable suggestions.

Once the script has been fully locked, the make-up artist will produce a script breakdown which will be very much like the one produced by the AD team and the costume department. Theirs will differ in so much as it will contain notes on various make-ups, looks and changes between scenes. This document may be stored in a file, along with other paperwork, or it may be stuck on the wall of the make-up room for quick and easy viewing. Wherever make-up changes to a character occur, the make-up artist will use a green highlighter to show this on the breakdown. Whenever there is blood, gore or special make-up, they will use a red highlighter.

First phone call

During their prep week, the make-up artist will call and meet all the major actors. Of course, this may be confounded by the fact that even though you are only a few days away from shooting, not every actor is signed! A meeting will be set up, often in conjunction with the costume department (so the actor needs only make one journey), and the make-up artist will discuss various issues with them. An actor knows their own face very well, a fact often overlooked, and will know how to make themselves look their best. Most often their ideas will be integrated into the overall scheme of things. At

Michele Baylis
Make-up Designer

'New film makers often make the mistake of under-budgeting for make-up, especially when it comes to things like wigs, beards, blood or gory effects. In some instances, new film makers think that you're just going to rub a little powder over the actor and that's it! Even that powder costs £25 a pop! Get your production team onto the problem of getting your make-up supplies if you cannot afford to buy it.

Not enough prep time is a common mistake too. For make-up artists, the idea of turning up on the morning and then wondering what you're supposed to be doing is just a nightmare. It's not uncommon for that approach to lead to serious creative mistakes where re-shoots may be needed. This could be avoided with camera and make-up tests, and adequate forethought. If you get respect from your director, you'll give so much back to them and work those long, hard and unsociable hours. As little as coming to the make-up room and thanking you for your work, or coming in first thing in the morning and saying hello can make all the difference.

If you're doing big make-up changes, try to group your scenes – it saves a lot of time and it's less exhausting for the actors. Give adequate time in the morning for make-up, I'd always prefer to come in early and get the work done properly rather then be called in later and rushed. I've also done make-up in the back of cars, buses, and rooms stuffed with camera equipment, but it isn't easy or fun! Give your make-up department adequate space to do their job, rooms with electricity and mirrors. Make-up is the first port of call for the cast and if they are made-up in a relaxed fashion, they will leave feeling good and ready for their shots.'

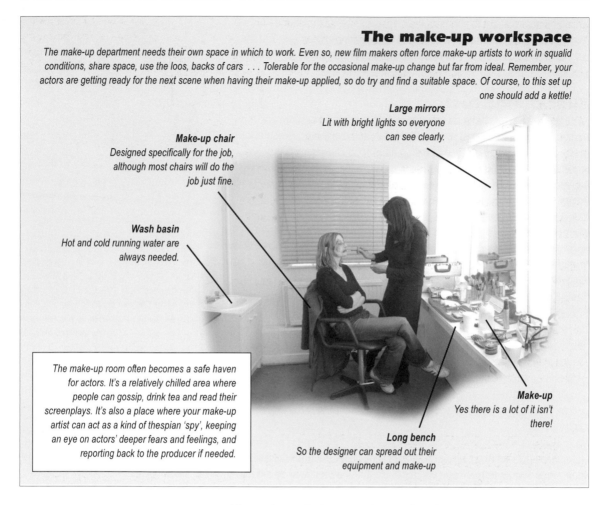

The make-up workspace

The make-up department needs their own space in which to work. Even so, new film makers often force make-up artists to work in squalid conditions, share space, use the loos, backs of cars ... Tolerable for the occasional make-up change but far from ideal. Remember, your actors are getting ready for the next scene when having their make-up applied, so do try and find a suitable space. Of course, to this set up one should add a kettle!

Large mirrors
Lit with bright lights so everyone can see clearly.

Make-up chair
Designed specifically for the job, although most chairs will do the job just fine.

Wash basin
Hot and cold running water are always needed.

The make-up room often becomes a safe haven for actors. It's a relatively chilled area where people can gossip, drink tea and read their screenplays. It's also a place where your make-up artist can act as a kind of thespian 'spy', keeping an eye on actors' deeper fears and feelings, and reporting back to the producer if needed.

Make-up
Yes there is a lot of it isn't there!

Long bench
So the designer can spread out their equipment and make-up

this meeting, major issues such as cutting of hair or re-colouring of hair, growing or shaving of beards etc., will be discussed. Actors are not props and a degree of sympathy and tact should always be used.

During this meeting, the make-up artist will be left with a clear indication of how difficult or fussy the actor is going to be. This information should be relayed to the production team and director if relevant.

Tests
If there are unusual or complicated make-up looks, or wigs and beards, you may want to shoot some tests. Not everything looks the way you think it will look on camera. This is most apparent with special make-up that can often look completely fake in the flesh, but utterly realistic on camera. These tests sound like a great idea, and they are, the only problem is that it's extraordinarily unlikely that you will get around to shooting them! There are so many other pressing problems to deal with. So when you talk with the make-up

artist and actors about the camera tests, keep in the back of your mind that you will probably run out of time and never get around to it. Accordingly, it's almost always better and less risky to opt for the simpler *'look'* than the *'exaggerated, complicated, untested look'*.

Space

More often than not, make-up will probably co-habit with the costume department. Nobody likes this, but it's a normal low budget cost saving reality. The make-up room should, at the very least, have very bright lighting (sometimes supplied by the camera department!), a chair for the actor to sit in, a large mirror, a long work surface and hot and cold running water. In fact, the make-up department can often feel a little like a hairdressers, with a radio quietly murmuring away in the background.

There will always be a temptation to ask make-up to utilise the back of a car, public loos, the back seat of a bus etc. in an attempt to speed up production or save money. Yes, this is possible on occasion, but new film makers have a tendency to try and make this the norm. Big mistake. Make-up can't do their job properly, actors get pissed off, stress levels rise and shooting slows down. Give them an appropriate space in which to professionally do their job. Anything less, even in the spirit of saving money, will probably cost you more money in lost time than you saved in the first place.

Production Title	ROCKETMAN
Artists name	MIKE HARRIS
Character name	JOE BROWN

Scene Number	14
Story Day	5
Date	14th MARCH 2004

Production Company	LIVINGSPIRIT
Makeup Artist	CARA

Base	Joe Blasco Olive, Beige
Highlight	Oyster (C.C)
Shading	Taupe
Powder	C.C. Gold
Pencil (EYES)	Mac Phone Number
Eye shadow	Soft Brown (C.C)
Eye lines	✓
Mascara	Lancôme Black
Moist rouge	
Dry rouge	Mac Prism
Lip colour	Bobbi Brown
Body make-up	Light Tan - legs only

Details of hair work

Hair in pleat at the back - wispy bits coming down around the face.

Prosthetics

Make-up continuity form

When there are multiple make-up changes for a character it can be easy to lose track of continuity, so this form is used to list the different products used on a character. There is a simple diagram which the make-up artist will actually apply the make-up to, as a final check for colours and placement.

Remember, characters may not always change their 'look' during a story day, but if they do, it's important to make notes. For instance, a character may go out to dinner in the evening which would mean a complete change of make-up and hair. This chart is most often used for female characters whose make-up may change subtly on different story days or different scenes.

Make-up scene breakdown

This document is much like the breakdown produced by the AD or the costume departments, but it differs in so much as it also carries notes on make-up. Where characters appear in a scene they will be highlighted in green, where there is a special make-up consideration, it will be highlighted in red. This document may live in a folder or may be stuck to the wall of the make-up department for quick access. If you have a colour printer then the text can be colour coded in the software, saving someone the job of going through it with highlighter pens.

ROCKETMAN SCENE BREAKDOWN WITH MAKEUP AND HAIR NOTES Page 2 of 14

Sc.	P	SD	WHERE	WHO & WHAT
17	10	D1	INT - BECKY HOUSE	BECKY and CONNOR chat.
18	10	D1	EXT - FERRY	Introduced – JOSEPH, 30s handsome, fit, small glasses. Arrives on ferry.
19	11	D1	EXT - HILL HOUSE	JOSEPH arrives at house and enters.
20	11	D1	INT - HILL HOUSE	BECKY and CONNOR stand over the CORPSE. BLOOD spattered on the wall. JOSEPH enters and sees body.
21	11	N1	EX - HILL HOUSE GARDEN	BECKY, JOSEPH and CONNOR digging in garden, covered in dirt and mud, and very sweaty. The blood drenched BODY is wrapped in clear plastic.
22	11	N1	EXT - TOWN HIGH ST.	CONNOR rides his bike through town.
23	12	N1	INT. BEDROOM	CONNOR arrives home to meet DAVEY who attacks him with a knife and grazes his face.
24		D2	EXT. GARDEN	BECKY an...

Scene number
As per the shooting script.

Page number
As per the shooting script.

Story day
Should be outlined in the script but story days may need to be allocated / checked by Costume / make-up depts.

Location
As per the shooting script.

Who and what?
Who is in the scene and what happens. Characters are highlighted in green, special make-up considerations are highlighted in red (such as blood, cuts, bruises, tattoos, sweat, tears, wigs, beards etc.)

Cast and character description

A fairly self explanatory document that lists characters, actors (and contact numbers if relevant), the description from the screenplay (with possible extra notes from the director) plus notes on the appearance of the character from a make-up perspective. All special make-up considerations will be listed here, such as wigs and beards, cuts, bruises, tattoos, sweat, special looks for scenes (such as a hangover) etc. Portions of this document may be left blank and filled in by hand during the production.

CAST LIST AND CHARACTER DESCRIPTION FOR 'ROCKET BOY'

Character	Actor	Description as per script	Notes
CONNOR	JOHN PETERS 020 8 XXX-XXXX 07977 XXX-XXXX	16, skinny and geeky, always a little unkempt and most comfortable in baggy T shirts.	Scruffy hair and pimples. Gaunt and pale. Bruising on face for last third of story.
BECKY	CARA WILLIAMS NUMBER TBC	15, skinny with cropped black hair and goth appearance.	Dyed black hair, needs cutting, almost white pallid skin, heavy black eye make-up (goth), ear rings, nose ring and green contact lenses. Long black nails for dream sequence.
JOSEPH	JOHN PETERS ...X-XXXX	42, athletic and good ...Small glasses and	Stubble and tired look for m... ...tory.

Polaroid moment . . . again!

As with the costume department, make-up will crunch their way through a terrifying number of Polaroid photos. Possibly even more than the Costume department, as continuity is so important, actresses playing with their hair being a prime example. These photos will also be very useful if you work your way through several make-up artists during your shoot (as is often the case) as many pros will give you a few days or even a week for free, but not six weeks! (see notes on Polaroid use in the costume department section too).

These Polaroids will be filed alongside the continuity notes on a folder, or sometimes they will be stuck into the screenplay on the blank side of the script page (the scene from which it is taken then faces the Polaroid). Notes will be made on the actual photo about scene numbers and characters as well as information that may not be clear on the picture (such as sweat etc.)The make-up artists may also take several shots, from the front, side and even back, as hair continuity is always a potential problem.

It may seem like a good idea to ask both make-up and costume departments to share a single Polaroid camera, but this regularly causes problems. Considering how cheap the cameras are (and you can always ask around and blag a second one too!), I would suggest getting a second one.

The first day

On the first day of the shoot, the make-up artist will arrive an hour before the cast so that they can prepare their room. They will lay out all their make-up and equipment, and ideally, the production team will have supplied them with a radio, kettle and toaster so that the cast always feel welcome.

When the first actor turns up, they will strip down to a T-shirt and the make-up artist will start their work. Depending on the condition of the actor (thespians being thespians, they may have spent the night on the tiles) a degree of puffy eyes and pallid complexion may need to be counteracted. First, the make-up artist will prep the skin with moisturisers, perhaps even cool eye pads, before applying foundation and then the make-up itself. Depending on the complexity, this can take anywhere between fifteen minutes to forty-five minutes, even longer for major glam looks with serious hair! This highlights a serious problem. What if there are four characters in the very first scene? The make-up artist can only do one at once, so it's wise to take a view before you shoot as to whether you will also hire a make-up assistant.

When producing the schedule, it's important to be realistic about

It's always worth checking make-up under the lights, as very often, what may look exaggerated or unrealistic in the real world and on set, will look entirely different once committed to film or tape. If you can, shoot tests.

The make-up department's 'bible'

Somewhere in the make-up department, and probably under the costume designers' arm, you will find a thick lever arch file which they will constantly refer to and update with notes and photos. So what exactly is in it?

Screenplay
The actual shooting script which by now MUST have scene numbers and ideally story days marked in the slug lines for each scene.

Cast & crew contacts
A complete list of all contact details for all cast and crew members, including mobile numbers and agents where relevant.

Call sheets
Drawn up daily and outlines what will be shot the next shooting day. Will also include call times for actors with enough time for them to get into costume and make-up.

Schedule
As created by the production team. Will often arrive late in the day.

Make-up story order
A document drawn up by the make-up department which outlines the mechanics of the story. Scene numbers, description and characters. Designed to give people a quick snapshot of the who, where, what and when of any scene. Characters are highlighted in green, major make-up considerations are highlighted in red.

Polaroids
A visual reference for each character in each scene or story day.

Character breakdown
A list of characters, actors, descriptions and make-up notes, detailing things like wigs, beards, cuts and bruises, tattoos etc.

Make-up continuity sheets
Each character will have their own unique continuity sheets that will detail make-up, possibly for each scene, and certainly for major changes.

how long make-up will take for each actor and build this in. It's also important that the director doesn't decide to have a character development meeting, take their cast on a guided tour of the set or even just meet for coffee and feel good hugs during the time when the actor should be sat in the make-up chair being prepared for the next scene. Everyone thinks that make-up can be done in minutes and that it is fundamentally unimportant in the grand scheme of things. Clearly, this is not the case.

Face on . . .

Once the actor has been fully made up, they will go to the costume department for a change of clothes. After that, they will be taken to set and rehearsed. Just before the first take, the first assistant director will call for final checks and make-up and costume will zoom in and touch up any imperfections. It's important to give make-up and costume this momentary breather, as there is nothing worse than an unsightly, rogue tuft of hair. Remember, it is their sole job to make everyone in front of the camera look as good as they can be and appropriate. Watch out for other crew members, including the cast themselves, the camera team and director moaning too much about final checks for make-up.

The scene will then be shot, at the end of which continuity notes will be made and Polaroid photographs of the actor from the front, side and sometimes even behind will be taken. Most of the time, the continuity concerns are going to centre around hair or special make-up, such as bruises etc.

During the shooting of this scene, the make-up department may have already begun preparing the actors for the next scene (if they are not already being utilised in the current scene). Again, this suggests that it is wise to employ an assistant who can take care of final checks and continuity on set while the make-up artist is working on another actor and saving time. Spend money to save money.

This process will repeat throughout the day, until the day's shoot wraps.

Face off . . .

A word of warning. Some actors will merrily traipse off home without having their make-up removed . . . *'but I have this party to get to, and I'm already late . . . I will take it off, I promise . . . '* This is acceptable every so often, but unless an actor can be trusted to thoroughly cleanse their face, it's better for everyone if the make-up artist does it. The reason is simple. After six weeks of skin abuse, an actor's complexion can be terrible, so that deep cleanse with a warm flannel, exfoliation, moisturiser and facial massage can be as important as labelling your film cans correctly! Remember, there is nothing worse than an actor with a whopping great spot on the end of their nose as it's virtually unconcealable. On the occasion that there is a blemish that is

Francesca Crowder
Hair Designer and Stylist

'A common mistake new film makers make is that they don't allow enough time to prepare hair or wigs. It always seems to be an afterthought. If you're working with wigs on a low-budget shoot then you'll have to get something from stock, opposed to making it from scratch as it would be too expensive. Like clothes, wigs need fitting, unless you want your actors to look like they are wearing a bad wig! If you want to use a wig you must commit to getting it right or it will look laughable, and that means time and money. People think that you can just stick on the wig and it will stay there all day without any attention. This is just not the case. The lighting needs to be very special too, and the hairdresser and lighting cameraperson may need to work together to ensure you can't see wig laces for example.

Some low budget film makers try to make too much of a statement with the hair and end up taking away from the focus of the performance. The character has to believable. To make it natural is better than to try to create something overly elaborate. Some film makers expect a lot out of hair changes and forget that these things take time. All the hair and make-up departments ever hear is 'how long is it going to take?' and then the AD pulling a face. It's deemed less important than the rest of the film making process when actually if you think about it, the first thing you see is the actor's face!

Wherever possible, use separate hair and make-up people – some people are good at hair and maybe adequate on make-up and vice versa. This will ultimately let your film down. Everyone has strong points and that's the only way you can get these things to work.'

Basic make-up kit

There is a lot more to make-up than most would ever consider. The kit here is very basic and when I took this photo, make-up artist Michele Baylis had actually brought her full kit, that was four, yes count 'em, four large cases worth! The problem for the make-up department is that they need a bit of everything, just in case of that very quick fix that is needed. And of course, if they do not have something, no one ever understands!

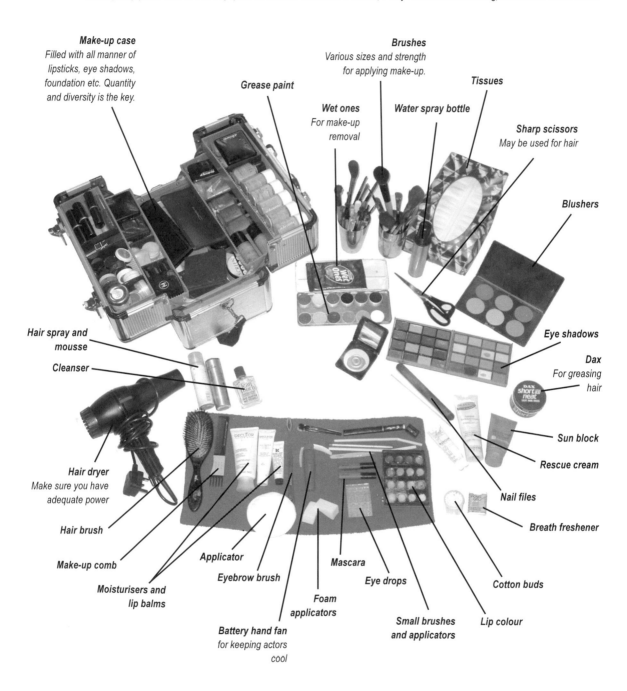

Make-up case
Filled with all manner of lipsticks, eye shadows, foundation etc. Quantity and diversity is the key.

Grease paint

Brushes
Various sizes and strength for applying make-up.

Wet ones
For make-up removal

Water spray bottle

Tissues

Sharp scissors
May be used for hair

Blushers

Eye shadows

Dax
For greasing hair

Sun block

Rescue cream

Nail files

Breath freshener

Hair spray and mousse

Cleanser

Hair dryer
Make sure you have adequate power

Hair brush

Make-up comb

Moisturisers and lip balms

Applicator

Eyebrow brush

Battery hand fan
for keeping actors cool

Foam applicators

Mascara

Eye drops

Small brushes and applicators

Lip colour

Cotton buds

Blood in a bucket

Every make-up artist has their favourite brand of blood, but the problem is, that pro blood is well, er, bloody expensive! Most special effects artists who need to supply blood by the bucket, rather than the dribble, use this recipe or a modification of it. Be mindful though, it's a messy business making blood.

Take a saucepan and add 500g of Lyle's Golden Syrup and heat gently so as to make it more fluid. To this add half a small bottle of cochineal food colouring. Depending on the brand, you may need to add more or less, so do it in dribs and drabs. Mix a heaped teaspoon of instant coffee in a quarter cup full of boiling water until it is entirely dissolved and add to the saucepan. Stir until everything is fully mixed. Now try it out by dripping into a sink. You may need to add or subtract amounts to this formula, depending on your personal views of how screen blood should look, and also on the cochineal colour and strength. Once this mixture cools off it will become more gooey again, so add 100ml of mouthwash. Mmmm. Because this is made of food products, actors can use it in their mouths. Tastes OK too! Beware though, cochineal can stain so be careful what you let it come into contact with. Once you have made enough you can bottle it up.

The big problem with blood is that it needs to be multipurpose, for which you will need different densities. Viscous blood for dribbling down faces or bodies, thinner for splattering on walls, and even thinner for pumping through pipes (to squirt or pour from wounds). Always, and I mean ALWAYS do blood tests as you can absolutely guarantee it won't go right in front of camera. Also, make much more than you think you need – and use it! Blood seems to disappear on camera. You might feel you have drenched you cast in the stuff, but when you get your rushes back you will be astonished and wonder where on earth it all went.

If you want some 'fresh scab', you can boil the blood down to a thick gluey substance which can be applied to actors skin for extremely convincing scabs. Be careful not to boil the mixture dry or it will solidify and burn, stinking out your kitchen!

difficult to conceal, be it a spot or a black eye for instance, the camera team and director should work hard to attempt to conceal the blemish through choice of camera angles. This doesn't always work, but it can help.

Plan for the next day

After the daily wrap and the actors have been cleaned and sent home, the make-up department will check the schedule for the next day and prepare their bits. If there have been wigs or facial hair, this will be cleaned and prepared for tomorrow. The make-up artist may also re-read the screenplay for the next day's scenes, just to make sure they are on top of all possible ramifications.

Battered and bruised!

Cuts and bruises are always a problem, for a number of obvious reasons. They take a long time to do and the make-up artist really needs experience of doing them (or they could end up looking rubbish and destroying the illusion of reality). Then there is continuity, not just in immediate scenes, but over time – what kind of bruises or scars will an injury leave, and on which story days will it be seen, and what stages will it be shown in?

This simple make-up took around 45 minutes and is for the look of a 'battered house wife'. As make-up artist Michele Baylis commented, 'many inexperienced make-up artists think they know just what a bruise and cut will look like. In fact they are extremely varied and random in appearance. If you have the stomach you should seek out some medical books of wounds and take a good hard look. This alone will greatly improve the quality of your work . . .' Very little make-up was actually used in this job and it cost pennies to produce. Inexperienced or over excited directors may suggest prosthetic appliances such as a heavily broken nose or extremely swollen eye. While possible, they cost a lot to produce, take an age to apply and can often end up looking rubbish too. Keep it simple!

Stage 1

This is the foundation of the injury. Decide the physical locale, in this case, the right eye, over the nose and right corner of the mouth. This foundation is a greasepaint, using reds, browns and purples, all blended together, and into with the actresses skin tones. An uneven, broken appearance works best as it will look more natural. Clearly, before work begins, a conversation with continuity, the director and maybe even the DP should take place, to make sure the make-up is being applied to the correct place!

Greasepaint in several colours, red, brown, purple etc.

Stage 2

The colours have been built up a little more to define the blackened eye and broken nose more, again using grease paint. 'Raw Flesh', a special make-up product that has a sticky gooey texture has been used to create scabs over the eye, cheekbone and corner of the mouth. You can make your own by boiling down home made blood (see recipe).

If you really must take the next step and get into heavy duty prosthetics and appliances, then there are couple of books written by the granddaddy of gore, Tom Savini, that are a must purchase. The first was released in the UK under the title 'Bizarro!', but they are more readily available in the US as 'Grande Illusions' and 'Grande Illusions Book II', Both are indispensable for new or aspiring make-up artists 'slash' special effects artist! Bring on the gore! www.savini.com/

Stage 3

The blood application stage is next. Not too much just yet, that will come later when the actress is on set, in front of the camera and in position (as the blood will quickly drip and smear and blood may need to run in a given direction, if she is lying down for instance). This is just to see how everything is working and get the blood application started. The make-up artist can also apply blood so that it will drip and run in selected areas (but it doesn't always behave on set remember!) Only the best quality blood should be used, and some blood looks different to others, so do tests. The cheapest way is to make your own (see recipe!).

'Raw Flesh' is a a deep red and gooey substance that is used for very real looking scabs.

Stage 4

The finishing touches start with a tear stick, a special make-up lipstick lookalike that is used to put a menthol like substance under the actresses eyes to make their eyes become a little bloodshot. Some cotton wool has been chewed and placed into the actresses mouth to swell out her top lip and distort the face. The hair and costume also play a huge part, in this case the hair was greased down a little to make it look more bedraggled. Actors often transform once they are in make-up. The new 'look' helps them connect with the emotion of the moment. As Michele says, 'it helps them so much because they can look in the mirror and they feel battered, bloody, greasy and tearful . . . '

A tear stick is used to create red rimmed eyes and tears.

Production Design Blueprint

Think of a movie like 'Alien' and you can see almost timeless production design at work. We know there are no spaceships with aliens on them and so therefore know that everything in front of the camera was created as an illusion. This is the job of the production designer. No matter the budget of your movie, the level of detail and love given to a movie like 'Alien' should be aspired to. Don't settle for what you've got, strive for excellence.

Action props

The stuff that characters handle, or are featured in the story, are the 'action props, the most important individual items to 'get right'. Some are simple and mundane, like a glass of water, others more revealing, such as an assassin's jewelled Samurai sword.

Dressing props

The stuff that is in the 'background' of the scene, including sofas, paintings (that are not featured), flowers, and all manner of general 'stuff'.

Locations dressing

Making a good location even better through the choice of dressing, possibly even re-decorating. Finding the best locations is a job for the location manager, but the production designer should be involved at all times.

Set building

With a set, the production designer can have complete control over the world they are creating, limited only by imagination and budget. Which pretty much screws most low budget film makers!

Weird stuff

Dogs, cats, police cars, fishtanks, dead bodies, breakaway glass bottles, computer monitors . . . a bit more than just a prop, something with special needs.

Atmospheres

Rain, wind, snow, even fire and water, all come under the auspices of production design, often hand in hand with special effects too, but must be considered at the very least. Beware, it's all pain and costly.

Production Design Blueprint

The job of a production designer is probably the broadest of all briefs. Their province is *'everything that appears in front of the camera!'* and often they will work in collaboration with make-up, costume and lighting departments. Unfortunately, by its very nature, the production design department is often the first to be compromised when budgeting for low budget films. Producers often naively believe that props, locations and dressings somehow magically appear, or they will be able to blag, borrow or steal from friends and relatives. This may be the case in some instances, but the production designer won't be happy with just any old prop or dressing. It's their job to find consistency, authenticity, thematic relevance and the aesthetic in everything that appears in front of the camera. Cutting the production design budget and being happy with pretty much anything that turns up in front of the camera is a lot like saying to the DP, *'just switch on that desk light and as long as we can see, that will do!'* Of course, that would never happen!

What lets most low budget films down from a production design perspective is a complete lack of forethought, which manifests itself in a haphazard and jumbled 'look'. Everything from clashing colours, very dodgy props, uninspired or just plain inappropriate locations, all serve to undermine the authenticity of a world that the film makers are striving to make real in the audiences mind. For instance, if your lead character were a racing car driver, he may drive an antique Merc around town and not the easy to get (because it's the directors mum's) Ford Escort. That's a simple and obvious production design choice, but a good production designer will apply that quizzical and illuminating thought process to every aspect of everything that will appear in front of the camera. There's a reason some movies look as good as they do, and that is, that a bunch of very smart people spent a long time thinking about how everything should look, and then turned those ideas into reality.

Clearly, on a low budget film, there are so many limitations from a financial point that not everything can be designed. But given time, a good production designer will come up with interesting and perhaps oblique ideas that will enhance and modify the world of the story in desirable ways. Whatever happens, don't just accept what is given to you on a plate. In my opinion, creating a tangible,

The all encompassing, sprawling, overworked, under appreciated production design team is responsible for creating the physical world for your story.

The production design team, starting with the designer, followed by the art director, props master, construction manager, painters, carpenters, decorators . . . It's a huge, sprawling department that has a wider brief than any of the others.

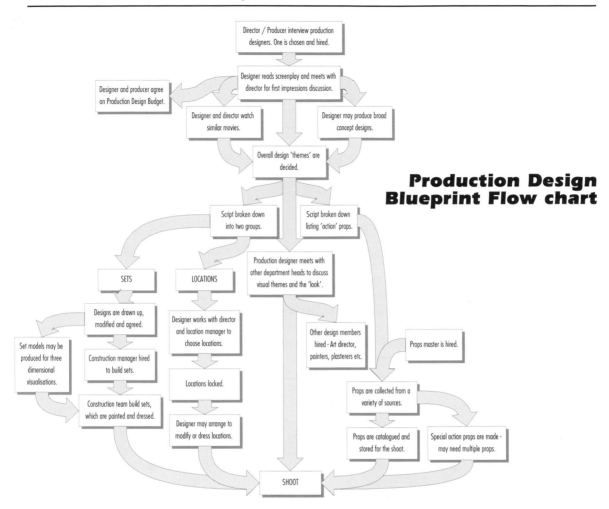

Production Design Blueprint Flow chart

(Flow chart boxes:)

Director / Producer interview production designers. One is chosen and hired.

Designer reads screenplay and meets with director for first impressions discussion.

Designer and producer agree on Production Design Budget.

Designer and director watch similar movies.

Designer may produce broad concept designs.

Overall design 'themes' are decided.

Script broken down into two groups.

Script broken down listing 'action' props.

Production designer meets with other department heads to discuss visual themes and the 'look'.

SETS

LOCATIONS

Designs are drawn up, modified and agreed.

Designer works with director and location manager to choose locations.

Other design members hired - Art director, painters, plasterers etc.

Props master is hired.

Set models may be produced for three dimensional visualisations.

Construction manager hired to build sets.

Locations locked.

Construction team build sets, which are painted and dressed.

Designer may arrange to modify or dress locations.

Props are collected from a variety of sources.

Props are catalogued and stored for the shoot.

Special action props are made - may need multiple props.

SHOOT

credible, detailed and interesting world for your characters to live in, and for the story to be told through, is more important than any other single department.

Hire the designer

Surprisingly, there appear to be quite a lot of good production designers who are willing to take a risk on a low budget film. Especially if they can see that the film makers understand the importance of their particular discipline. Most production designers on a low budget film will be doing it for the experience and credit. They may have been design assistants, art directors, even props masters, and this is their big break. Experienced designers are probably best avoided because they will find it hard to work within the almost suffocating environment of having no budget, time or resources to speak of. Depending on the size of your budget and scope of your project, you'll hire a number of people that will start off with the production designer. Personally, whilst you want to hire a pragmatist, I

When it comes to getting your props organised or the immediate shoot, double check everything. You never want to keep anyone waiting for a prop. The old carpet fitters' saying rings true . . . 'measure twice, cut once . . .'

would always look for an artist with passion. Someone who is going to strive to create a visually exciting and consistent world for the story. All too often, low budget production designers are relegated to simple quick fixers who plaster over cracks and fractures in the visual *'mise-en-scène'*.

You'll be building in quality, value for money, complexity and sophistication into your project if you find an enthusiastic and compatible designer as early on as possible on a project . At the script stage, the designer would be able to offer suggestions, not only on a budgetary level (i.e. merging locations, modifying props etc), but also enhancing story telling through creative and often inspired suggestions. Working these ideas into the screenplay, and therefore the fabric of your story, as early as possible will help everyone. If you think of your designer as a visual stylist and allow them as much creative scope as possible, practically and aesthetically, it can only improve your project.

Their mantra, and your mantra, should always be. . . IN FRONT OF THE CAMERA, NOTHING IS ACCIDENTAL.

Broad strokes

Early on in the project, the production designer(in their quest to find deeper meaning in everything than just functionality) may make suggestions . . .

Tonal palette – throughout the production, a colour scheme or a number of colour schemes within scenes may be suggested. On the surface, you might consider this to be impractical, perhaps even ridiculous. It may be so, but consider this. Ridley Scott shot *'Alien'* in rough chronological order. At the beginning of the film, the sets were light and clean. By the end of the film, they were dark and claustrophobic. Why? Because the production design team had subtly re-coloured and re-painted the entire set to get darker and more menacing as the story's tension heightened. Ridley Scott would actually carry a can of spray paint with him for on-the-spot touch-ups.

It will take some courage and commitment on behalf of the producer to agree to the production designer's requests that 'everything that appears in front of the camera should fit within a colour scheme', but it's worth it. Next time you watch a movie that you think of very highly, watch for the colours. Some film makers like Steven Soderbergh have taken this to extremes in movies like *'Traffic'*. Others such as Pedro Almodóvar embrace primary colours, whereas US director David Fincher goes for dark and menacing looks – *'Se7en'* is a kind of *'piss yellow'*, *'Panic Room'* a *'mouldy green and almost neutral'*. If you're unable to embrace a colour palette philosophy in its entirety – *'no we can't paint that wall green!'*- then at least exercise some damage control and attempt to remove unwanted colours where appropriate. The goal is to avoid a kind of *'colour mess'*, where all hues and tones on display serve to confuse the visual image rather than enhance or clarify.

Hauke Richter
Production Designer

'The essence of production design is to serve the story and it's important not to allow your own ego to get the better of you. You have to create a unique world, which is the world of your story. Everything within that world has to be real to that world, and that's not just the production design department, but all departments.

Art departments tend to be the busiest of all departments as there is so much to do. Everything in front of the camera needs to have been considered, found, agreed and prepared for the shoot, which also includes the choice of locations. The problem with low budget films is that the producer always under-budgets because it is not perceived to be as necessary as other items such as film stock. This is often a short sighted mistake, especially when you find the design budget is cut and the DP is being paid more than anyone else! When you think about it, whatever the DP lights, the design team has created or found! And at the end of the day, the story is still the most important aspect. On low budgets, almost all sets are locations and not built for the film as there is often not enough budget to build, or a build is not seen as a priority. Then the choice of location becomes more important and the designer should be involved in it. A common mistake is that low budget producers try and keep the designer out of that choice, and automatically the design and continuity of idea and concept can fall apart.

The director, producer and designer should collaborate, even before pre-production, and plan the best way to maximise their resources. With planning you can achieve amazing results, making the production look bigger, by creating a more interesting world.'

Concept art

Early on in pre-production, the director and production designer may work with a concept artist (who may also BE the production designer). The artist will create a series of images that capture the essence of what the film will 'look' like. As well as being a detailed visualisation of a moment from a scene or set piece, the artwork should also convey tone and feel, light and shade etc. These images will help the director stay focused, the crew know what they are fighting to achieve and the producer may well use them to help raise cash.

Pictured above is an image by Alex Fort for one of my current projects, 'Rocketman and Vampire Girl'. The brief was to capture the night-time feel of the movie, and of a fishing village in decay (hence this scene is set in the boat graveyard). The image also introduces Becky, the 'vampire girl' of the title

Think of the rose petals in *'American Beauty'* for instance. Then watch the movie to see where else the colour red appears. It's NEVER a mistake.

Visual motifs – the production designer will have hopefully come up with a theme for the film which can then be used to convey subtext within their design. This will be particularly relevant when looking for locations, props and set dressings. For instance, if the theme of the film were claustrophobia, then you may look for very tight spaces or large spaces to purposefully contrast the theme. In *'Resevoir Dogs'*, the warehouse where the bulk of the story takes place actually houses a hearse and casket draped in plastic. Why? Because there is a subtextural theme of death and decay. There is also a startling colour palette of black and white, decaying greens and an obvious spattering of blood red. Again, none of this is by chance.

First things first

The first job for the production designer will be to read the screenplay and break it down. If they have been brought on board well in advance, and before the script has been locked down into a shooting script, then the production designer can offer a number of practical suggestions about the merging of locations and minimisation of props etc. They can also spend this time looking for locations, researching themes and motifs, putting together concept artwork and maybe spending time designing the sets for the more important parts of the story. Working on these concepts this early on will help the film makers get 'real' about the story they're trying to tell.

Always shoot wide shots first, so that you can lock down the location. If you shoot the close up shots first then have a problem and need to leave the location (weather, light, time, money etc.) then you are screwed. If you shoot the wides first, you can always mock up for the close up shots with a micro set somewhere else.

Lockdown

Once the script has been completed and locked down as a shooting script, then the production designer can break it down into two main lists – location/sets and props.

First designs

After discussion with the producer about budget and the director about styles and themes, the production designer may (if building sets) draw some designs. These are not blueprints as such, more sketches of the impression that the sets will give to the untrained eye. If the designs are agreed, they will be drawn up as a large format A0 sized blueprints, and perhaps even modelled out of foam board too.

This sketch by Hauke Richter, for a film called 'Bloodline', shows the level of detail and thought that goes into the designs. To the right of the design is a large 'cyc', a painted cloth backdrop to give some texture and reality to the world beyond the walls of the set. This must be positioned some distance from the main set so that it can be lit evenly and also drop out of focus. A cyc can be custom painted, or rented from a back drop company such as Acton Backcloth. There would also be flying ceiling pieces, constructed from hessian stretched over a wooden frame (suspended from the studio roof and moveable that are).

This set was designed to be modified from the sets that we built for my last movie 'Urban Ghost Story'. In an attempt to share resources and minimise production costs, myself and film maker Simon Cox (director of 'Bloodline') agreed to build sets that could be modified, redecorated and redressed for both movies. Creating a new and original cyc would then be cost effective, building costs would be shared and rental times decreased. Also, sets would remain in place for longer, which could have been useful for potential re-shoots. Great plan except the money for 'Bloodline' never appeared and it folded in pre-production.

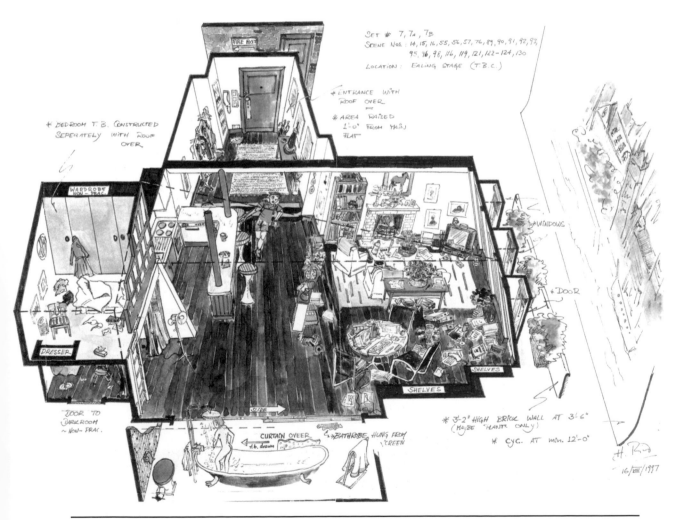

Set list and construction budget

Within this model there are two sets of documents. The first, the set list and construction estimate, is a simple list of ALL sets and locations within the story, plus script info such as page length etc. Each time the location is revisited within the story, it is given an alpha-numerical value. For instance, the first time we visit a location in the screenplay, it might be called 7a, the second time 7b and so on. The second, the construction budget detail, is a detailed document that lists EXACTLY what will be done at each location or set and how much it will cost etc. The two documents will be cross referenced regularly.

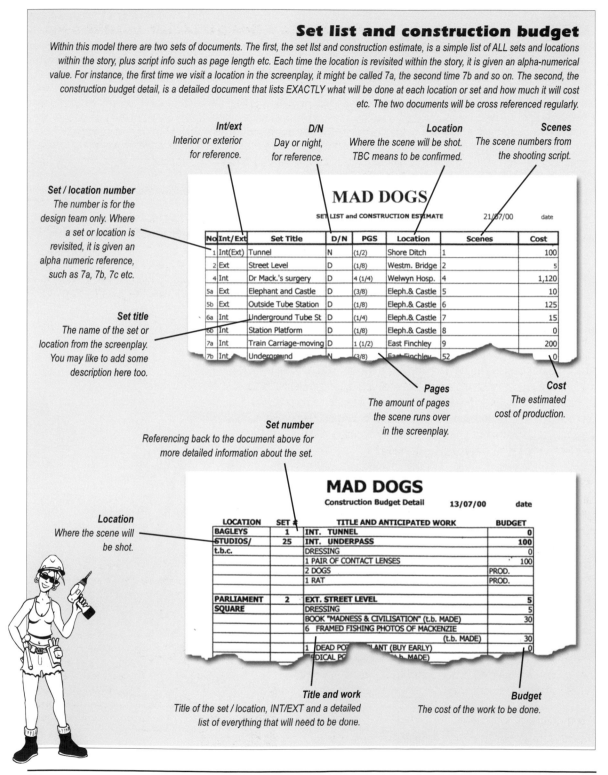

Int/ext
Interior or exterior for reference.

D/N
Day or night, for reference.

Location
Where the scene will be shot. TBC means to be confirmed.

Scenes
The scene numbers from the shooting script.

Set / location number
The number is for the design team only. Where a set or location is revisited, it is given an alpha numeric reference, such as 7a, 7b, 7c etc.

Set title
The name of the set or location from the screenplay. You may like to add some description here too.

MAD DOGS

SET LIST and CONSTRUCTION ESTIMATE   21/07/00   date

No	Int/Ext	Set Title	D/N	PGS	Location	Scenes	Cost
1	Int(Ext)	Tunnel	N	(1/2)	Shore Ditch	1	100
2	Ext	Street Level	D	(1/8)	Westm. Bridge	2	5
4	Int	Dr Mack.'s surgery	D	4 (1/4)	Welwyn Hosp.	4	1,120
5a	Ext	Elephant and Castle	D	(3/8)	Eleph.& Castle	5	10
5b	Ext	Outside Tube Station	D	(1/8)	Eleph.& Castle	6	125
6a	Int	Underground Tube St	D	(1/4)	Eleph.& Castle	7	15
6b	Int	Station Platform	D	(1/8)	Eleph.& Castle	8	0
7a	Int	Train Carriage-moving	D	1 (1/2)	East Finchley	9	200
7b	Int	Underground	N	(3/8)	East Finchley	52	0

Pages
The amount of pages the scene runs over in the screenplay.

Cost
The estimated cost of production.

Set number
Referencing back to the document above for more detailed information about the set.

Location
Where the scene will be shot.

MAD DOGS

Construction Budget Detail   13/07/00   date

LOCATION	SET #	TITLE AND ANTICIPATED WORK	BUDGET
BAGLEYS	1	INT. TUNNEL	0
STUDIOS/	25	INT. UNDERPASS	100
t.b.c.		DRESSING	0
		1 PAIR OF CONTACT LENSES	100
		2 DOGS	PROD.
		1 RAT	PROD.
PARLIAMENT	2	EXT. STREET LEVEL	5
SQUARE		DRESSING	5
		BOOK "MADNESS & CIVILISATION" (t.b. MADE)	30
		6 FRAMED FISHING PHOTOS OF MACKENZIE	
		(t.b. MADE)	30
		1 DEAD PO LANT (BUY EARLY)	0
		DICAL PO .b. MADE)	

Title and work
Title of the set / location, INT/EXT and a detailed list of everything that will need to be done.

Budget
The cost of the work to be done.

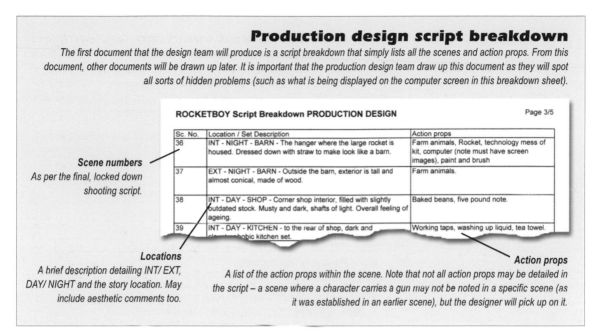

Production design script breakdown

The first document that the design team will produce is a script breakdown that simply lists all the scenes and action props. From this document, other documents will be drawn up later. It is important that the production design team draw up this document as they will spot all sorts of hidden problems (such as what is being displayed on the computer screen in this breakdown sheet).

ROCKETBOY Script Breakdown PRODUCTION DESIGN — Page 3/5

Sc. No.	Location / Set Description	Action props
36	INT - NIGHT - BARN - The hanger where the large rocket is housed. Dressed down with straw to make look like a barn.	Farm animals, Rocket, technology mess of kit, computer (note must have screen images), paint and brush
37	EXT - NIGHT - BARN - Outside the barn, exterior is tall and almost conical, made of wood.	Farm animals.
38	INT - DAY - SHOP - Corner shop interior, filled with slightly outdated stock. Musty and dark, shafts of light. Overall feeling of ageing.	Baked beans, five pound note.
39	INT - DAY - KITCHEN - to the rear of shop, dark and claustrophobic kitchen set.	Working taps, washing up liquid, tea towel.

Scene numbers
As per the final, locked down shooting script.

Locations
A brief description detailing INT/ EXT, DAY/ NIGHT and the story location. May include aesthetic comments too.

A list of the action props within the scene. Note that not all action props may be detailed in the script – a scene where a character carries a gun may not be noted in a specific scene (as it was established in an earlier scene), but the designer will pick up on it.

Action props

The locations and sets are effectively the settings for each and every scene. The list will contain scene numbers, rough descriptions, page lengths and other notes. Obviously, the shorter this list, the easier production will be. The production designer is fighting a constant battle of artistic excellence verses practical reality. This is no better expressed than in the dilemma of locations. Location 'A' is close to location 'B' which means moving between them is quick and easy. Location 'C' is much better than location 'A' but a long way from location 'B'. What are you going to chose?

Props fall into two basic categories – *'action props'* which are things that are handled by the characters or featured in the story, and all others, sometimes called *'dressing props'*, which are essentially dressings for sets and locations. Many props will be quite simple to find and a production assistant can be set the task of working their way through this long list.

From these two lists the production designer will draw up an estimated budget. More often than not, the budget is already fixed by the production, so the budget that the production designer draws up is really a list of things that they have to find at seriously discounted rates or for free. Again, a PA will be called in to help with this task. This lack of money is the genesis of the compromise at the heart of any failing micro budget movie's production design department. They simply have no cash and therefore no choice.

In most stories, there are lots of 'graphic' props - baked beans tins, newspaper headlines, posters etc. They are not hard to make, but it does take time to get them right. Get the computer whiz designer in your team onto the job now, it's amazing what they will be able to do with Photoshop, a colour printer . . . AND enough time!

The team
As production draws closer, other team members will start to

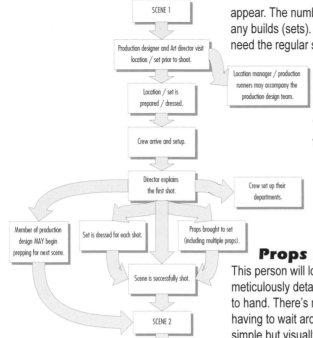

**Cont. . .
production design
blueprint
flow chart**

appear. The number is of course dependent on the budget and the scale of any builds (sets). In the first instance, the production designer will probably need the regular services of a production assistant to find stuff for free. This person won't be a permanent member of the production team, but pulled in on a daily basis.

Art director
This person is underneath the production designer, and their job will be to take care of making sure everything that is in front of the camera is in accordance with the production designer's wishes. Remember, the production designer may not always be on the set, as they could be working on other scenes in the film that will be shot in the very near future.

Props master
This person will look after all the *action props,* and ideally operate a meticulously detailed cataloguing system so that all props are always readily to hand. There's nothing worse than everyone being ready on set and then having to wait around ten minutes because the props master can't find a simple but visually important item. Sometimes you may need multiple props for multiple takes. An obvious example would be if a candle were to be lit in a scene. If the first take didn't work, you would need a new candle to light for each take. These props can trip up the inexperienced designer or props master. It always raises the question *'how many will I need?'* There is no straight answer. Just follow your intuition.

Construction manager
If you are going to build your sets, you're going to need an experienced construction manager who will know how to make them quickly and cost effectively. This is a very skilled job and you may do well to spend money in order to save money by hiring people with experience. If you are shooting in a studio, you may be able to plunder other sets that are being struck and skipped (keep an eye out). Remember, if you do build a set, you need to allow time to take it down and put it into hired skips.

Painters, decorators, carpenters etc.
Working beneath the construction manager in the building of sets will be a number of people who do all the miscellaneous tasks. One area of importance are the painters and decorators, as they add the final sheen of reality to what is clearly not reality. The painters and decorators are the people who will turn thin plywood into marble or tiled walls, Edwardian wallpaper, whatever is called for by the story and the production designer.

Your tools
Your construction team toolbox should include all the usual carpentry items,

Problem props

There are a number of recurrent props that appear in many stories that can often lead to headaches. Wherever possible, I would suggest cutting these props from your story, or replacing them with something more practical. You don't want to spend hours or days messing around with a trivial prop when you should be focusing on the major things like script and cast. Organisation is the key to success with props. Get your props sourced or built and stored as soon as possible.

Computers and TVs
Not only because you need to set them up so that they work on set, but also because you need to make sure that the camera team can photograph them properly (or they may flicker) and remember, someone needs to take care of what they are displaying.

Action vehicles
Whether it's the car driven by the hero, a police car or a van for the bank robbers, the production design team will need to find it, make sure it's insured and maybe even dress it. If you hire a white car, you can affix transfers to it to turn it into a makeshift police car.

Props from within the story
For instance, if a character takes a photograph which later features in the story, the later scenes cannot be shot without the photo as a prop. Check your screenplay for these hidden nightmares.

Animals
Whether it's fish, hamsters, cats or dogs, animals are a pain in the neck. Fish tanks go cloudy after they are set up, dogs need walking and crap, cats get timid, and hamsters are always asleep!

Water and fire
Any time you need to supply water to a bath tub or gas to a Bunsen burner, or even build a fire that can rage on cue, it is a problem to deal with.

Stunt props
Stuff that needs to be rigged (not exactly special effects) so it ends up in production design. Breakaway glass and bottles, or blood spattering on a wall for instance.

Magazines and newspapers
Anything in print will need to be custom designed and printed. Ensure that you have copyright clearance for all the images. Much of this can be done by a talented graphics artist with a colour printer.

Food
It needs to be edible and you need enough of it for multiple takes. You may also need to warm it up and make sure no one gets salmonella from it. Consult with the caterers.

Featured props
Where there may be copyright or branding implications, such as recognisable posters on a wall, recognisable cans of drink or burgers in a box etc. All need copyright clearing or disguising to the point of unrecognisability.

Guns
For very obvious reasons, guns are a problem. Depending on the scene and shots, you can often get away with using plastic guns and adding gun handling sound effects later, even gun shots. Whatever your needs, you'll be best served by asking for the involvement of an armourer.

Don't underestimate how much space storing and cataloguing your props will take. The props department may even need their own van, depending on how many location changes there are and the number of props.

including a large selection of screws, bolts and nails. You should also have electrical tools such as a jigsaw, circular saw, circular table saw, a cordless drill with re-chargeable batteries, an electric sander, rotary tools etc. This is all relatively expensive, but unavoidable unless you or your crew already own it. Otherwise hire some from HSS or buy from Screwfix for instance. For draughting, the designer will need a drawing board with T-squares and all the bits (which can be hired or blagged). Get a good selection of coloured and black pens, water colours, calligraphy nibs and pens, etc. You'll also need a 35mm camera to take location stills (don't go digital unless you have a printer). Always take 360 degree shots of locations as well as detailed close up shots, and mount them on large cards so everyone can easily and clearly see them. Every low-budget art director should have a full props tool box, including glass cleaner, silver polish, furniture cleaner, wax and dye for ageing, cleaning and polishing cloths, cotton wool, cotton buds, talcum powder, cobweb spray, brushes, a paint selection, food dyes, vaseline, etc.

Not only will this stuff help when dressing the set, but they'll also be vital during the filming. Normally, you have a props person on stand-by who has all this stuff, but you cannot rely on getting a props person on a low-budget film . . . It is mostly a one-man show, remember.

Props and organisation

Within your story, there will be a huge amount of *action props* (that's objects that are used by the characters in the film or feature in the story). Most of these props will be relatively simple, such as a toothbrush, wallet, remote control, or drinking glass etc. Others will be more difficult, such as guns, featured magazine covers and newspaper headlines (which may need to be created), breakaway bottles, dogs and cats, stickers to put on a white car to turn into a police car, food etc. All need to be thought about, prepared, checked, catalogued and stored for instant access when needed by the production team for shooting. Finding props, and more specifically the right props is often a grind. There are simply so many of them and so little time to

Design dynamics

When you consider how many creative people are involved in the making of a film, it's not surprising that there are regular and quite dynamic clashes. There are four main creative teams that impact the production design (remember, everyone, including the director, is here to serve the story . . .) The first is the director, whose choice of coverage and shots has a very clear and distinct impact. Next is the DP, whose lighting can significantly hide or reveal the set and its dressings. Sometimes the set will need hiding because it's rubbish, other times, the DP may choose to hide the set when the production designer wants it to be clearly visible. Make-up is the next department whose input can subtly impact the overall production design, but its rare that any conflicts develop here. Finally, it's the costume department where perhaps the greatest amount of collaboration is needed. This is especially relevant when it comes to the colour of clothing and even the costume designer's choice of clothes. No crew member should ever have the power to veto any other, at the end of the day this is a collaborative process, but in the event of conflict the director will no doubt choose.

The production design department paperwork

The production design department is somewhat sprawling and will need a big space from which to work. They often have large sheets of paper, books, drawings, and other bits of paper seemingly scattered about the place. It may look like a disorganised mess, but there is usually some semblance of order that may only be understood by the design team.

Script

The designer will have their own copy of the screenplay which they will constantly refer to, and make notes upon.

Call sheets

Prepared daily, this sheet will outline what will be shot, when and where and for how long. It will also detail special equipment or shooting requirements as well as cast and crew call and wrap times.

Schedule

The master document which details the order in which the production will be shot.

Script breakdown

Listing scenes and props in detail. Drawn from the shooting script.

Props list

A list of all the 'action props' in the film, listed by prop number and by scene number.

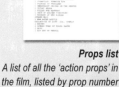
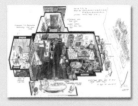
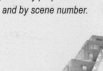

Budget breakdown

A scene breakdown with estimates for costing. Often two sets of cross referencing documents.

Models

Made from foam board and designed to give everyone a better appreciation of the three dimensional space the set will provide.

Schematics

Large, A0 sized plans for the budgeting and building of a set.

Designs

The master document which details the order in which the production will be shot.

Mike Power
Props Master

'As a propmaster I'm responsible for everything that is in front of the camera, with the exception of the actors. My main duties include overseeing the handling, use and authorisation of all props. I liase with the production designer, and crew up the props department, while compiling the props schedule and co-ordinating with other depart-ments. Props are split into two groups, 'action props' and 'dressing props'. The action props are things like cigarettes, glasses and newspapers. The dressing props are furniture and are generally everything that contributes to the ambience rather than the story itself.

These are managed by two types of props people, a dressing props man's job involves going into a room, removing whatever furniture is there, and placing the dressing props. After that, the standby prop man comes in. His job is to fill glasses, pass the cigarette to an actor and make sure that candles are lit. A good propmaster must have great organisation. We have a saying that 'with unprepared people the day never ends'.

The two essentials are that when the camera team are ready to shoot, everything has been done properly, and everything has been done safely. It costs a fortune if things are not ready or are incorrect. You also need to ensure that everything is properly maintained as props can cost £thousands and you may need insurance. If you want to become a propmaster, I would say that the most important thing you need is a love of films, especially their style. What makes it work is the detail you put in. If it looks comfortable, then you have done your job right, because the more realistic it looks, the better.'

do it. Compounding this problem is the fact that the Production Designer cannot just go down to the high street and buy a pile of props, nor can they wander round one of the Aladdin's cave like prop shops (where props can be hired by the week) as these facilities, whilst cheap for a major movie, are simply unaffordable for a low budget movie. So what do you do? Get on the phone and get busy.

Some props will need to be made specifically for the production. Where possible, these props should be flagged up early on and tackled before they turn into a minor crisis. Remember, if a prop is needed in a scene, no matter how insignificant or small it may be, the scene cannot be shot without it (unless the director is prepared to bluff it, that is, shoot without it and keep it either out of frame or substitute something similar in the hope no one will notice!) Some things that appear very simple in the screenplay can turn into a real nightmare on set, such as a computer web page – who is going to design and create it? And can you get computer monitors that will flicker at the right rate so as to look attractive when photographed? Newspaper headlines – who is going to design it and where is it going to be printed on newspaper stock? etc. No one is going to forget the *'shrunken head in a bottle of vinegar'* prop, and there will be many discussions about how it will be done, but what about that poster the heroine glances at? How will that be done? Insignificant prop maybe, but a pain in the butt!

Prop storage and movement

As props amass, you'll need to find a suitable space in which to store them. Don't underestimate how much *'stuff'* these props will represent, especially when you consider there may be multiples of some props. A rigorous and detailed cataloguing system should be developed by the props master, so that they can quickly access each and every prop when needed.

Crucial props

When making a film, you're going to be telling a story and building an incredible, perhaps even fantastical world in which your characters live. A major concern for any low budget filmmaker is that they do not pull off the illusion. Somehow the audience just doesn't *'buy it'* and they are left giggling at the ridiculousness of what they are watching. If this were the acting department, then a very bad actor could shatter the illusion that the audience has built. The production design equivalent could be an inappropriate or dodgy location, or more commonly (how should I put this?), a *'crap prop'*. Whether it's the obviously plastic gun, the ridiculously stupid bomb, the newspaper headline with typos, the rock that's clearly polystyrene, it doesn't matter, the illusion will still be shattered. Now here's the real problem. How do you know if it's a crap prop or not? Trust me, up close, many props on even the biggest films can seem questionable.

Actors are usually the first people to pipe up about something, because they

From idea, to sketch, to schematic, to model . . .

When designing a set, the designer will start off with an idea, then draw a detailed sketch. If approved, that design will then be converted into schematic diagrams, and perhaps even a model made of foam board. This process is crucial to help accurately budget the set, so that cost saving modifications can be implemented before getting to the build phase. It will also help the DP and director visualise the space so that they can better plan their shots and lighting set-up. With the model, it is possible to easily visualise and section off large parts of the set as unneeded (and therefore not be built, thus saving cash and time). The model is particularly useful for inexperienced directors who find it hard to place themselves (and the action) within a three dimensional space that does not yet exist.

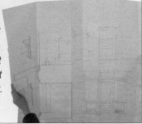

perceive that they will look stupid with the prop. For instance, firing what is obviously a plastic gun. This isn't necessarily the case and you could easily get away with the cheat, especially after it has been properly lit, sound effects have been added and the cast actively *'believe'* in the prop for the sake of the shot.

There are no hard and fast rules though. But if you do see that *'crap prop'*, and other people agree that you are not going to get away with it, then you may wish to reconsider its use. Often, important action props can be all but removed from the picture frame, and, through editing and sound, the story and illusion can be better pulled off.

Building a set

There are two distinct spaces in which you will shoot. Locations (which already exist and you may or may not dress) and custom built sets (which you will have to 100% dress).

On low budget films, shooting in a location offers a number of very obvious advantages. The sets are essentially already built and simply need modifying or dressing to accommodate the story and overall design themes. The downsides are that locations may be some distance apart (which will eat resources and time), there may be sound problems due to excessive noise, there may be large windows or low ceilings, there may be fees to pay, parking permits . . . blah blah. Look for locations that will need the minimum of dressing, that are already 'dressed' for your story. You can use lots of foreground dressing to create as much hustle and bustle as possible, as this can often fill large holes of empty screen real estate. Sometimes a designer's job is all about damage control, about covering up stuff. For instance, if you were shooting a period piece, you could use prominent foreground objects to cover modern stuff, such as a telephone box covered by an extreme foreground prop for instance. Camouflage nets, like the ones used by the army, are great for covering things like cars to make them blend into the landscape. In

When you build low budget sets, you will probably make them only eight feet high. If you have any tall actors you could end up being forced to keep the camera high and never shooting low angles as you may shoot off the top of the set!

Mark Sutherland
Construction Manager

'The construction manager's job is to realise the production designers ideas by translating them into a film set. Having a positive approach to the design that you are to build is of paramount importance. Ensure that the designer has finalised their ideas before beginning as any design changes will incur costs and take more time. It's you, not the designer, who will be remembered for going over budget or schedule, so you may need to sit on a procrastinating designer. It's imperative that you have regular meetings with the designer, just in case there are changes. If you are both building AND managing, make sure you can occasionally step back to review progress at least twice a day.

Check that you've sourced the best price for materials and be sure to order it yourself. Keep records in a planning book from day one. Make sure that materials are delivered on time as a construction crew standing around doing nothing is a frustrating waste. Companies, that will deliver screws and fittings (such as www.screwfix.com)to site the next day are invaluable.

People skills are important. Saying things such as please and thank you and making sure people are fed and are having adequate breaks is crucial, particularly when you want them to go the extra mile when you are up against it. To avoid dissent, lead from the front, be prepared to sweep up and make tea. Remember, most of the time, construction is hard manual labour. You will always be pressed to finish things as fast as you can, especially if the same set is to be dressed for a completely different look for different scenes. If you are tight for time be positive, and lets face it, you'll never be given all the time you need!
www.marksutherland.biz

reality, most low budget films will have the majority of their footage shot on location. Occasionally, they may dress an existing location to be another location, or they may build a micro set which is simply a couple of flats, or the corner of a room dressed to be something that it isn't. Micro sets are a very effective way of covering awkward but small scenes.

Full blown sets require detailed designs, followed by a model and schematic diagrams, rounded off by the actual build. If you are going to build sets, then logic dictates you will probably shoot in a film studio. The advantages of a studio based production are enormous. You will have production offices, space for make-up and costume, onsite catering, loos etc. You will also have a very large and silent space in which to build and shoot your sets. On the downside, studios are expensive and they can charge you premium for the power that you draw when lighting your film.

Many low budget film makers have blagged amazing deals with studios, or managed to find other suitable spaces, such as disused school gymnasiums and disused warehouses. Beware though, the alternative locations are not sound deadened and so you may end up with a bigger headache than you initially considered. Nor will they necessarily have facilities, even loos, or supply enough power (and so you end up hiring a generator).

The construction manager

This is the person who will oversee the building of your set, and to a large degree, how much money you spend or save will be determined by their experience and tenacity. The building trade is notoriously dodgy, and there is always a deal to be done. A good construction manager will know all the best places to buy the materials, AND how much it should cost. They will also know the quickest, cheapest and most efficient way to construct your sets. Tools are another issue, will they have their own or will you need to rent or buy some? Of course, health and safety is an issue too, so make sure they are qualified and that they run a *'tight ship'*. If there is an accident, YOU may find yourself personally liable.

Set aesthetics

Every set does two things. One is obviously to provide a practical backdrop to the scene. Second is to add another level of detail to the production design as a whole, building on themes already developed. The established themes will inform and embellish the set designer's choices, for instance if the theme is dark and scary, then that will guide the decisions of the designer in the planning of the set.

Every set is an opportunity to reinforce the themes of the film and thereby support and enhance the narrative. I believe that repetition of image develops a subliminal sense of the world for the viewer, which is a way a production designer can add depth to the story. Choice of colour and texture

Anatomy of a simple set 'build'

Most low budget sets are made up from 'flats' – eight foot by four foot wooden frames, clad with either plywood or sometimes even hessian (fabric). They are connected together to form realistic walls. A major advantage of a set is that the lighting team can position lights above, often fixing permanent 'star' lights in place to give an instant and even fill light.

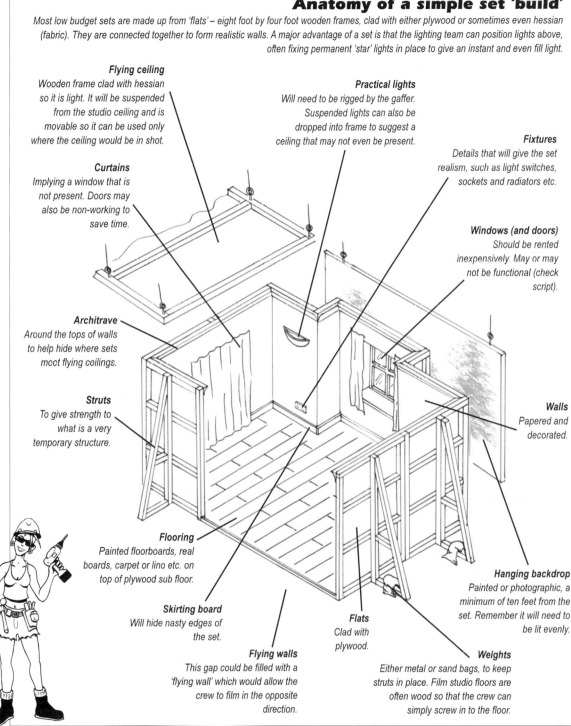

Flying ceiling
Wooden frame clad with hessian so it is light. It will be suspended from the studio ceiling and is movable so it can be used only where the ceiling would be in shot.

Practical lights
Will need to be rigged by the gaffer. Suspended lights can also be dropped into frame to suggest a ceiling that may not even be present.

Fixtures
Details that will give the set realism, such as light switches, sockets and radiators etc.

Curtains
Implying a window that is not present. Doors may also be non-working to save time.

Windows (and doors)
Should be rented inexpensively. May or may not be functional (check script).

Architrave
Around the tops of walls to help hide where sets meet flying ceilings.

Struts
To give strength to what is a very temporary structure.

Walls
Papered and decorated.

Flooring
Painted floorboards, real boards, carpet or lino etc. on top of plywood sub floor.

Hanging backdrop
Painted or photographic, a minimum of ten feet from the set. Remember it will need to be lit evenly.

Skirting board
Will hide nasty edges of the set.

Flats
Clad with plywood.

Flying walls
This gap could be filled with a 'flying wall' which would allow the crew to film in the opposite direction.

Weights
Either metal or sand bags, to keep struts in place. Film studio floors are often wood so that the crew can simply screw in to the floor.

If you build a set with windows or doors, you have to ask, 'what's on the other side?' Commonly this would be a painted 'cyc', or a rented hanging cloth with an image painted onto it. This painting isn't about detail, but about depth and atmosphere. To have a large one custom painted could cost something like £3k, so it makes sense to try and rent one. Painting one from scratch is a specialised job and if you try with your artist friends it may look unreal and ridiculous on film.

Film and TV studios are amazing places to shoot a movie. They have plentiful power, silent stages, loos, canteens, production offices, make-up and costume rooms, green rooms, skips to plunder, parking etc. Shooting on a stage also accommodates lighting that can be mounted higher than you would be able to achieve in conventional locations, which is a major advantage. The downside? You have to build EVERYTHING and studio rental space is never cheap.

may at first seem unimportant to a producer, but control of these things is what gives an image its purity. In many instances this is not expensive to do, it's more about the commitment of the designer, their team and indeed everyone else on the film.

To save money, you may need to do your own building. Professionals are never cheap, and as long as you keep your construction small and simple, anyone who can use a hammer is up to the job. Health and safety is of course an issue, and any major sets will more than likely need to have been constructed by professionals (or you could be liable if it collapsed for instance), so keep your sets simple and in the spirit of what you are trying to achieve. Work with imagination and not ego, this is not your big movie!

When building a set, there are three main considerations. First is the space itself, what is needed to accommodate the action. Second, the set is split into the background and the foreground – the background should be more generic and not interfere with the foreground (new film makers mistakenly spend too much time on the background, wasting resources and running the risk of overshadowing the foreground where the story actually takes place). The third consideration is the foreground. The designer should spend time working on key props or details that the audience will find striking and will be naturally prominent within the scene (without contrivance). For instance, if you are shooting a scene in a dining room around a table, the walls and background should be generic, whereas the contents on the table should be the focus of the design. You could say so much about the characters in this scene by observing *'how and what they eat'*.

If possible, I would suggest that the use of image and motif be woven into the world in two ways – *conscious and subconscious*. For instance, in *'Psycho'*, the stuffed birds are a motif that are consciously discussed by the characters (not only are there stuffed birds in the story but there is a stuffed Mother in the fruit cellar too!). Subconsciously though, the bird motif is ever present, even in the way Norman Bates moves, the way the knife in the shower scene echoes a birds beak, even Marion Crane is a bird name! Watch the movie, you will be surprised at how much and often the bird motif is present.

Your design mantra should be to say one thing effectively and not to get visually cluttered. Find the one key detail in a set or prop and focus on that.

The ten set building steps

The design process will begin with drawings and sketches, then that will be converted into a schematic drawing and perhaps even a model. Then the build will begin . . .

Atmospheric effects

Production design, and to some degree, the special effects department, will often merge to take care of atmospheric effects. These will include things like fog and mist (with smoke machines), wind (with large wind machines), rain (with a large rain rig), snow (goodness knows how they do that), fire etc. Here's the deal. You're a low budget film maker and you can't afford this stuff. Save it for your next movie which will be properly funded, and re-write your script now to remove these major production headaches. If you try and do it on the cheap – rain from a hose pipe etc. – you will fail miserably and produce a crap shot that you will cut and re-shoot without the rain (unless by fluke it happens to be raining when you shoot it). Yes I know some of you are dying to tell me that you have actually pulled it off and done this, there are exceptions of course, but on the whole, it will add virtually nothing to your story and significantly drain you of very precious resources.

1. Find out exactly how much set you need to build. Too often, new designers build a set when part of it will never be filmed. This of course assumes the director knows what they need, which they should do, but new directors are often bogged down and simply cannot make up their mind.

2. Determine any key structural requirements, for instance, is a character ever thrown against a wall, meaning extra reinforcements may be needed? Construct walls in as light a material as needed for the action of the scene. The two common solutions are to construct 'flats' (of various dimensions) that clip together quickly to form the overall walls. They are made out of 2"x 1" or 3" x 1" frames clad in either 1/8 " plywood OR medium grade hessian (which is a heavy, coarse cloth). Of course, plywood is stronger and more solid than hessian, but remember, we are not creating reality, just making something that looks real. All ceiling pieces should be made out of hessian as they may need to be suspended and moved regularly.

3. Doors and windows can be cheaply hired from companies (such as the Stockyard), however people often spend more money than needed. For instance, a hole in the wall covered by curtains may do the job adequately. Again, this will depend on the director knowing what they want to shoot.

4. The first stage of decorating is about defining the overall texture. Typically, this will involve either plain wallpaper to be painted (I recommend medium or heavy grade lining paper and not fine as it rips easily), or patterned wall paper, or finally paper which is then plastered over (plastering is not as expensive as you may think but it does take time and needs to dry too).

5. Occasionally, something more specialist is required. For example, brickwork or tiles, which can be bought in sheets that are roughly 3' 9" x 7' 9". It's called Vacuform and you can buy it from the Vacuform shop at Pinewood (costing roughly £8 a sheet). Of course this may need to be painted, which can seem off-putting to an inexperienced person,

Where possible, design and create sets that are quickly re-useable for multiple locations. It may need a quick redress or even overnight paint, but it's worth it as you will get to stay in a controlled environment and not waste time travelling.

Forced perspective miniatures

One of the really cool tricks available to low budget film makers (and not often used) is a forced perspective and miniature. Not that I am suggesting you build an alien city model, but it is possible to make very effective miniature models and hang them in shot when sets or locations need enhancing. Because the models are 'real' (opposed to painted or digital) the light will hit them appropriately and will look 'right', and as long as they are placed in the correct way, their perspective will work too. In the picture here, production designer Hauke Richter had suggested a quarter scale 'arch' that would be suspended in shot. The model would be very close to the camera and match the background, so that when you viewed the shot, the wall to the left would meet the arch above. As the audience would expect it to be real, they would simply 'buy' the effect. Forced perspective miniatures were extensively used in the 'good old days' of film making but as digital effects have become more common, so the simple

(above) A production design sketch of a location with a forced perspective archway above. The arch would be a small model, suspended a few feet from the camera, but in just the right position to seal the illusion.

(right) The forced perspective model from 'Urban Ghost Story', my hand holding it steady as it was suspended from fishing line and it was a windy day. Next time I would stick it to a sheet of glass!

solutions have been forgotten. We used a forced perspective model in our last film 'Urban Ghost Story', for a sign above a building. We couldn't afford a real twenty foot sign, so production designer Simon Pickup made a six inch sign which was suspended in front of the camera. And it worked a treat!

but it's not as hard as it sounds. For brick face for instance, paint all sheets a solid matte undercoat of the basic brown colour. Then with a slightly darker shade, dry brush rough textures on top. Then lightly dry brush lighter coloured highlights. Finally, wash over with a very thin basic coat of brown to soften the effects of the various layers. These Vacuform sheets can then be screwed or stapled to the set walls.

6. Decorating is the next stage. Painting and decorating involves selecting the colour palette, then determining the amount of contrast you want between the various background features – for example are the doors and the walls different colours or not?

7. Adding background detail involves the fixtures and fittings such as skirting board, architrave, light switches, radiators etc. This doesn't need to be perfect, you are not going to live here! Remember you may also need to pump water to any taps that need to work.

If you need a quickie set for a short amount of time, the cheapest way to do it is to hire some 'flattage'. If your set is going to stand for some time, it would be much cheaper to build from scratch than to hire flats.

8. Ageing is a process where the set is made to look 'older' and not newly decorated. Typically the walls and fixtures will be dirtied down to remove the sharpness. Use a bucket of water with a small amount of black paint that is sponged onto the wall (this slightly greys down the

The continuity report sheet

This sheet is filled out and used by the continuity person. There is one sheet for each and every shot in the film. It will be referred to when coming back to shoot additional work on a scene, or in the cutting room. Make-up and costume will have their own continuity sheets too, which may also be checked when doing re-takes or re-shoots some time later. Continuity is very important, BUT it is also important not to become a slave to it. All movies contain a huge amount of continuity errors, most of which are actually created in the edit. So the notion that continuity should always be perfect is a time and resource wasting mistake. Get it as close as possible whenever you can, but do not waste resources on re-shoots for purely simple or trivial continuity errors. A truth most people forget is that an audience will not notice ANY continuity mistakes IF they are engaged in what is happening. So get fixated on story and performance and not on continuity.

Slate
From the clapper board.

Lens
Indicates the focal length of the camera lens.

Distance
Indicates the approximate distance of the subject from the camera.

Stop
The lens 'F' stop on video, or 'T' stop on film.

Scene number
From the shooting script.

Filter
List of filters used, in this case a colour correcting 'wratten'.

Roll / tape
The camera roll number or videotape number.

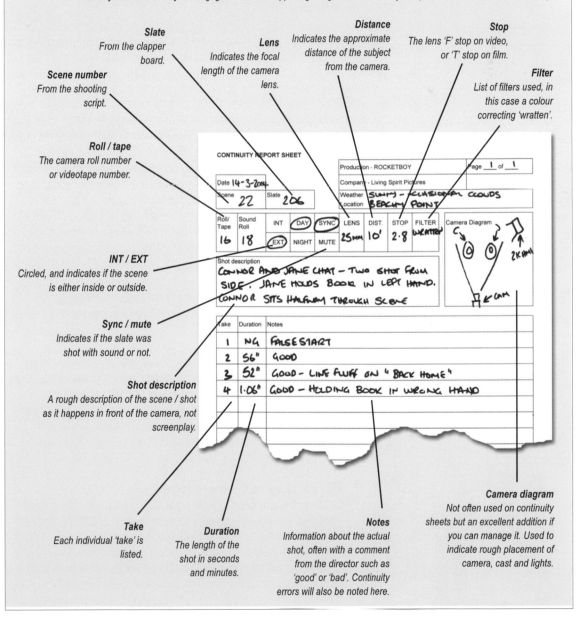

INT / EXT
Circled, and indicates if the scene is either inside or outside.

Sync / mute
Indicates if the slate was shot with sound or not.

Shot description
A rough description of the scene / shot as it happens in front of the camera, not screenplay.

Take
Each individual 'take' is listed.

Duration
The length of the shot in seconds and minutes.

Notes
Information about the actual shot, often with a comment from the director such as 'good' or 'bad'. Continuity errors will also be noted here.

Camera diagram
Not often used on continuity sheets but an excellent addition if you can manage it. Used to indicate rough placement of camera, cast and lights.

surfaces). A bucket of tea or coffee can also be used which can add a yellow smoke like tint to the surfaces. More specialist techniques can include dusting down surfaces with fullers earth, using Spray Mount (spray on glue) and dirt and grit to add rough and dirty textures, and also cobweb sprays and other specialist products (which can be pricey). Finally, there are a whole range of decorating techniques to create all manner of designs (for example marbling, and wood grain) which can be found in various interior design books, for instance *'Kevin McCloud's Complete Book of Paint and Decorative Techniques'*.

9. Practical lights (such as a desk lamp or hanging ceiling light) need to work, so the gaffer / DP will have to be consulted. The production design team will set out all the lights within the scene, again adhering to the same creative processes, but the cables will be connected and juiced up by an electrician, spark or the gaffer. Practical lights can be a great way of drawing the eye to, and alluding to, space that doesn't necessarily exist. For example, hanging an overhead lamp into the top of the frame creates the sense of a 'ceiling', even if one does not exist (if you can't afford a ceiling piece for instance). As another example, multiple corridor lamps on a single flat can create the sense of greater depth. Other tricks are the use of *Entrance* and *Exit* signs which create a sense of another world beyond the confines of a small set. One of the most common and best cheats is to fake an external streetlight streaming in through a set window – one lamp (with an atmos soundtrack added in post-production) can create the completely convincing illusion of an external world.

10. Once the space exists, you will need to put stuff in it. Namely props. There are two things to dress, the background and the foreground (or featured space).

The DP can help a cash strapped designer by placing light selectively. For instance, a cut out of a window silhouetted on a wall can imply a window that does not exist, or a small set shrouded in darkness with the occasional highlight can imply a huge and vast area. Encourage a healthy collaboration between the two.

For the background, it's really just a case of selecting props and furniture which have the right colour, texture and thematic relevance, and then placing them appropriately. Don't get fazed by furniture, it's still just a big prop and subject to the same creative processes. Some furniture can be fragile and expensive if damaged, so keep that in mind. For foreground and action props, now is the time to think carefully about the key image that you want to convey.

First day of the shoot

On the first day of the shoot, the production design team are normally exhausted already because they have been already building, finding and making stuff for the last few weeks (or even months). They will more than likely be way behind schedule, and most locations will not have been nailed down, nor will the sets be fully built. This will leave the production in a little chaos, but it's unavoidable and quite common, even on big films. If you are shooting on a set on the first day, you may find the construction team

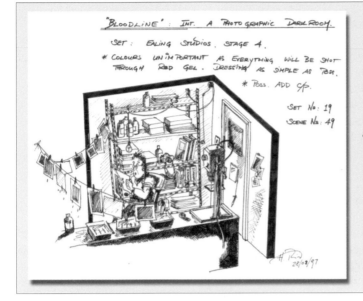

Micro sets

Small sets, that are usually nothing more than a corner of a room or a couple of flats that are then dressed appropriately, are a fantastic way to cost effectively shoot very short, but necessary scenes, that you don't really want to uproot your whole team to go and shoot. This design by Hauke Richter for 'Bloodline' is a classic microset design for a darkroom and was needed only for a very short scene. The door would probably not have been functional, and note how Hauke has kept the foreground busy with paper hanging up, all detail that keeps everything looking authentic and expensive. In post production, you can often invent completely new scenes to plug story holes, then get the cast back and shoot these scenes in a number of microsets over a pickup weekend. Doing this will also increase the location density within your story, therefore increasing eye candy and production value too.

hammering in the background between takes. This may go on for days! If you are shooting on location, you may find the production designer running off to check locations with the location manager while the art director or other production design team member oversees the shoot on set. Either way, the first day or two are normally quite chaotic. After some time, the pandemonium may die down, not least of all because as you move through the shoot, so the locations, props and sets decrease in number, simply because they have been shot! Back to the first day . . .

At the crew call time, the production design team will amass on set or location with the rest of the crew (it is not uncommon for them to have not slept the night before). The director and AD will block the scene with the actors before the actors go off to make-up and costume. Hopefully production design will have already begun dressing the set or location, but now the scene has been blocked, they will have a better understanding of exactly where the action will take place within the space that they have prepared.

As quickly as possible, they will dress the background with 'dressing' props and the props master will bring the relevant action props needed for the scene to the set. Once the actors return to set (in costume and make-up), which should now be lit and the cameras in place, the scene will be shot. A member of the production design team will keep a close eye on the shooting to make sure everything is as it should be and may make their own notes about background and foreground continuity. There will be a separate continuity person who will take care of overall continuity (see continuity box). During the filming of these first shots, the production designer may leave the

When writing, think about production design. You will have so little budget to spend on making your world that you should keep everything contained and easy to access. Look at what you have and draw from that. If your uncle owns a pub, then think about setting your film in a pub. You don't want to spend all your energy just sealing the visual illusion, you should be working on characters and story.

set to go to the next set or location to prepare it. The upshot is that the production designer is rarely on set.

Returning props

One major problem facing a low budget film maker is that of returning major props, such as furniture. If you've rented or borrowed it for a week in the middle of your shoot, then while you are shooting someone is going to have to take a van to collect it and later drop it off. With the best will in the world, this is a two person job and will take a couple of hours. Factoring in when this will happen and who will do it, or more to the point, who can you afford to lose for that amount of time, is always a production nightmare.

Get out!

At the end of shooting the scene, whether it's a location shoot or a set shoot, the production design team will probably be the last people to leave. If it's a major set, then 'striking' the set could be a big job (breaking down the set), taking a whole day for three or four people. Sadly, the broken down set will simply go in a skip and thrown away. If you're cunning, before you shoot you can arrange with other productions to acquire their set materials for a small fee or free, which will save building time and a wedge of dosh. The skip is your friend.

If you've been shooting on location, it's vital that you leave the location the way you found it. Unfortunately, film crews have a bad reputation, and rightly so! The truth is, that a crew of twentyfive-ish, dirty booted folk, carrying heavy mechanical equipment, spilling tea and dropping cigarette ash tend to leave a bit of a wake. You can nip this in the bud by asking people not to smoke or eat and drink inside, perhaps even to remove shoes and boots. Most crews who have any experience will understand this and will be sensitive about damaging other people's property. But it does happen, *'eek! You never told me the tripod scratched that 17th century wooden floor!'*

Store the stuff

When the film wraps it's a good idea to save and store as many props as possible, perhaps even a couple of flats from the main sets too. During post production, the director and editor will come up with a bunch of new shots and ideas for scenes and sequences that were either dropped during the shoot or have been invented to fill story holes. If you already have props, costumes and even a little set in waiting, then shooting this additional footage becomes much easier. Often, during the main shoot, lots of close-up shots will be dropped to save time. These close-up shots will be filmed in a pick-up shoot weekend sometime later and of course, the actual props will be needed for this. Typical examples will be a close-up of a newspaper headline, or the ingredients on the back of a bottle of poison.

Thanks to Simon Pickup and Hauke Richter for their help writing this section.

Sound
Blueprint

Edit at Ealing Studios.
Avid Media Composer Online + Offline.
Projections, Installations, Broadcast Documentaries + Features.
020 8758 8432
www.divapix.co.uk

Pictures LTD

The sound recordist is the person who is responsible for recording all the sound that happens during a take. Primarily, their job is to record the dialogue spoken by the actors and to record it as cleanly and 'flatly' as possible. The bottom line is always, 'is it clean?' (meaning are there any interfering sounds or background noises) and is it intelligible? (meaning can you understand what is being said?)

DAT

Digital audio tape, the most common and best recording format for sound. Record at either 44.1 kHz, 48 kHz, at 16 bit depth, and with or without time code. It's cheap, common and robust. The main choice for low budgeters.

Camera

If shooting on a video format, sound should be recorded directly onto the tape. Run tests with cheaper miniDV formats as the lack of control over levels would present a problem. The sound recordist will need to setup with the camera team to run a permanent umbilical cord from a portable mixer to the camera.

Others

Be they minidisk, older analogue formats such as a reel to reel Nagra, or even one of the new hard disk recorders – all should be avoided in favour of the awesomely cheap and reliable DAT recorder.

Shotgun mic

Such as a Sennheiser 416, mounted on a boom pole, will give excellent results. The best, most cost effective and versatile microphone you can get your hands on.

Tie clip

For those times you can't get a shotgun mic into position, tie clip or lavaliere mics are ideal. Usually they transmit via a radio signal, so you don't even need long cables. The sound they produce is unique though, often deep and nasal in quality.

Mixer

Depending on what format you shoot, you may or may not use a mixer. Micro budget films will probably not use a mixer, where shoots on any digital video format probably will, as there will be no extra recording device. Use an SQN mixer.

Sound Blueprint

Many new film makers make the mistake of either ignoring sound altogether or simply and naively believing that it will somehow take care of itself. After all, they could hear what the actors said, surely that *'came across on the sound recording thing?'* Recording sound is an exceptionally specialised discipline. More than any other department on a film shoot, sound cannot be botched. The sound is either clear and intelligible or not, either usable or unusable. Sure, there is a grey dividing line, but it isn't very wide and all too often, the sound recordist is vetoed on set as somehow, what they have to offer and the professionalism they should demand is somewhat of a nuisance and inconvenience to everyone else.

Understand fully the implications of ever uttering the dreaded words, *'we'll fix it in post'*. What could take five minutes to deal with on set or location could take five hours or even five days to deal with later. Listen to and trust your sound recordist.

The job of the production sound recordist is to record the sound of what happens in front of the camera. Most commonly, this is the actors' dialogue.

Finding a recordist

A good sound recordist is a tough person to find for a low or no pay indie flick (unlike camera people and composers who will be coming out of your ears!) If a sound recordist is any good, they will no doubt be in full-time, freelance employment and they'll need a lot of persuasion to get them to commit to your little production. Often your best bet is to approach an assistant sound recordist, aka boom swinger, and offer them a career break.

Most sound recordists own a well stacked arsenal of audio equipment, more than likely they'll already have everything you will need for the shoot. If there is anything extra needed, it will probably be an extra couple of mics, usually radio mics. You may want to consider whether you pay your sound recordist a little extra money for the wear and tear of their kit and in recognition of their saving you money (and think about insurance too, who pays if an actor accidentally flushes a radio mic down the loo?).

The sound team is lean and mean. Most commonly it is a sound recordist and a boom swinger (assistant). Their kit is minimal too, often no more than a DAT recorder, clip board, some mics, boom pole and baffle, cables and spare batteries and tapes.

Pre-production meeting

Before the shoot begins, you should hold at least one meeting with the sound recordist, editor, camera person, producer, director and

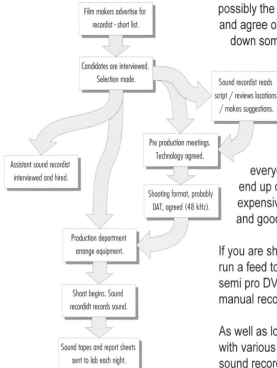

Film makers advertise for recordist - short list.

↓

Candidates are interviewed. Selection made.

↓

Sound recordist reads script / reviews locations / makes suggestions.

Pre production meetings. Technology agreed.

Assistant sound recordist interviewed and hired.

Shooting format, probably DAT, agreed (48 kHz).

Production department arrange equipment.

↓

Shoot begins. Sound recordidt records sound.

↓

Sound tapes and report sheets sent to lab each night.

Production sound flow chart

possibly the lab technicians. The purpose of this meeting is to hammer out and agree on the technology that will be used to shoot the film and to nail down some of the variables.

Almost certainly, you'll be recording sound on DAT (digital audio tape). DAT is a format that has been around for ages, it's cheap, everyone has it and it's relatively robust. Sound can be recorded at two sample rates on DAT, 44.1kHz and 48kHz. It doesn't really matter which you choose (as to hear the difference you'd have to be a dog!) just so long as everyone is in agreement. Time code is another variable, which could end up costing you money as time coded DAT machines are much more expensive than non-time coded DAT machines. Yes, time code is all well and good, but you simply don't need it. Save the money.

If you are shooting on tape, be it DV, DigiBeta, HiDef, then you will probably run a feed to the camera from a mixing desk (although most domestic and semi pro DV cameras are really not up to the job as most do not have manual recording levels).

As well as locking down the technology, the sound recordist will also meet with various production people, specifically the location manager. What the sound recordist will want to know is that everyone has considered the sound when looking at locations. It's obvious that shooting a period drama in a location right next to a motorway is going to lead to problems, but sometimes the acoustic implications are less obvious. . . *'Is there too much reverb or echo?' 'Is there air conditioning that cannot be turned off?' 'Is it on the flight path to the airport?' 'Are there main roads very close by?'* An experienced location's manager deals with all this stuff as second nature, but you probably don't have an experienced location manager (!), so just keep an eye on the ball. It's possible the sound recordist may want to visit locations too, but in practical terms, that rarely happens due to time and money constraints. The will may be there but the time and money will disallow it.

The assistant

The sound recordist will work with an assistant (aka boom swinger). In many ways, the calibre and excellence of the boom swinger will have a much greater impact on the quality of the sound than the sound recordist themselves! This is because the boom swinger is directly responsible for the placement and movement of the microphone in the shot. Placement is everything – this is why the sound recorded from the microphone on the front of a camcorder is rubbish. It's not that the microphone is that bad, its just that it's not in the right place, i.e. it's stuck on the front of a camera and not right next to the actors. The sound recordist and boom swinger will quickly develop a shorthand and bond that will allow them to communicate

While it's the job of the camera team to make sure that the clapper board is clearly labelled with the slate and take number, the sound recordist should also back up this procedure by checking the details on each and every slate. Getting it wrong will lead to confusion as the lab or editor will try and sync up the pictures from one slate or take with sound from another. Either way, valuable time and money will be wasted.

over a distance without having to shout. This is one of the reasons why a sound recordist will often suggest a boom swinger with whom they have previously worked and have a rapport with.

The kit

Whether the recordist owns all of their equipment or not, they will be responsible for its upkeep and transportation. Thankfully, this is rarely more than a couple of aluminium flight cases which are easily carried by a couple of people. If extra equipment is going to be hired, the production team should negotiate with the sound team what kit it will be and for how long it will be needed. The sound team will also need DAT tapes purchased well in advance and some petty cash to keep them in batteries.

The first shot

On the first day of the shoot, along with the whole cast and crew, the sound team will turn up and begin their daily routine of setting up and checking their equipment. Quick test recordings will be made and played back to check for problems. All batteries will be checked and if in doubt, replaced (there is nothing worse than losing signal during that important monologue, all because you are trying to save a couple of quid on batteries). A new DAT tape will be started and idented at the head with something like *'this is roll 14, and I am Joe Blogg's sound recordist for X movie recording on a Tascam DAT machine at 48kHz. The date is July 11th 2004, and here's some line-up tone'*. The sound recordist will then record some continuous tone which will be used later on to line up levels at the lab or in the cutting room (although line-up tone is not as important as it used to be now everything is switching to digital).

The first AD will then tell the crew what the first shot is and there may be a 'blocking' session (a kind of physical rehearsal without the passion of performance) with the director and actors. The sound team will watch this and plan the placement of the microphone. The cast will then go to make-up and costume, cameras will be set etc. and at the appropriate moment, the actors will return to set for a full rehearsal. The sound team will use the rehearsal to get used to the actors movements, where and when they will say lines and how loudly or softly they will deliver them etc.

On the whole, the sound team will work with just one mic that will be on the boom pole above the actors, or with a couple of radio mics that are hidden in the actors clothing. Obviously, there are infinite ways and combinations to mic-ing up the scenes, but these two will be the most commonly used.

Edge of frame

One major problem is keeping the microphone close enough to the actors to get a good, strong signal, but at the same time, keeping the microphone out of shot. We've all seen a mic bobbing into frame and sniggered at it. But

Jonathan Mitchell
Sound Recordist

'A common mistake is not considering your locations fully. You have to really think about access, noise control, light control and what effect you have on the community. Have a production meeting before hand and take the sound recordist to the location so you can access the situation. If you are renting equipment make sure it works as there's nothing worse than getting to location and finding you have a flat battery and pieces that don't fit. Talk through with the DP and find out how they are lighting the set as you may not be able to put a boom in.

As a director you need to know where and which sound you will use in the edit. For example if you are shooting a tight shot of two people walking and then you shoot the same sequence but in a wide, you should know that the sound from the tight shot will be used over the wide in the edit. This has to be communicated to the sound recordist so that they can accommodate it. As a sound recordist, it's quite normal to be hassled by the AD to shoot quicker and some people can get bullied. You have to stand your ground and explain what you're doing and they should be fine about it. After all, you are there to get the best possible sound.

Always get atmosphere tracks to cover what you are shooting so the editor has something to play with to make the shots work. It's easy to get rushed and then the atmos track gets dropped. Everyone says 'we'll fix it in post', but you've got to do it then and make everyone realise the importance of recording it then. You don't want to get into the edit and find you can't cut it because the sound recordist hasn't done their job.'

Balancing Act!

There are various flavours of sound signal and it's essential that you know which is which, or you could run into very serious problems.

First is signal strength – domestic level and professional level (aka +4dBV and -10dBV respectively). On the whole, domestic kit uses a voltage of about 0.3 volts, whereas professional kit uses a level of about 1.2 volts. The upshot is that if you stick domestic signal into pro kit, it's too quiet (not enough voltage), or pro signal into domestic kit, it's too loud and will distort (too much voltage). Camcorders that shoot miniDV and other bits of kit such as the cheaper DAT machines or minidisk recorders will almost always have domestic inputs, usually in the form of a minijack (3.5mm stereo jack plug). Pro kit such as DigiBeta cameras and higher end DAT recorders will have XLR connectors and will expect the higher voltage signal.

You can't just use an adapter to convert one plug to another type (3v to 1.2v), but you can pass the signals through converters to either boost domestic levels for pro-kit, or reduce pro levels for domestic kit. Often this is a small mixing desk or a converter box such as the DXA-4C (available from www.optexint.com). This cunning little box also deals with the other variable, balanced or unbalanced signals.

Most pro-kit uses balanced signals, whereas most domestic kit uses unbalanced signals. So what is balanced or unbalanced sound? It's a method of sending the sound signal (balanced) down a cable that makes it excellent at dealing with interference. But as usual, you just can't stick an unbalanced signal into a balanced input! So converters will be needed again.

So what's the best way to deal with your sound? If you are doing it properly you will have pro kit throughout, working at pro voltage levels and with a balanced signal. The only variables come into play when you decide that you want to record the sound onto a miniDV (which will probably use domestic levels and unbalanced signals). At that point, you'd be best to invest in a little box like the DXA-4C which would clip onto the camera body and convert all the sound. But before you even consider that, ask yourself, does the camcorder even have manual control over the levels? Because if it doesn't, it's verging on useless for recording sound. Thankfully the top end miniDV cameras do, such as the Canon XL1 and Sony PD150 (the Sony also accepts pro level signals and balanced sound). If shooting miniDV, be sure that the camera you choose to use does have manual recording levels before you commit years of your life to a piece of technology that could cost you an extra six months just unravelling.

consider this, the boom swinger cannot see what the camera operator can see and therefore has to use their skills and judgement to assess how close they can get the microphone. . . *And they always need to get the microphone closer!* During rehearsals, the boom swinger will ask the camera operator for *'edge of frame'*, meaning the point at which the microphone starts to creep into shot. During takes, it's not uncommon for the camera operator to occasionally give simple hand signals to the boom swinger to say that the mic is creeping dangerously close to the edge of frame (so ensure there is a dialogue between the sound recordist and the camera operator).

After the rehearsals, everyone will prepare for a full take. The first AD will call *'Roll sound!'* and the sound recordist will start recording. They will leave it anywhere between five and ten seconds for the equipment to get up to speed before shouting *'Speed!'* The clapper loader will then position the clapper board in front of the camera and read out the slate and take details, *'Slate thirty-two, take three!'* for instance. The AD will then call *'Roll camera!'* and the camera team will start the camera and call out *'Rolling!'* After a beat, the

Don't be an over excited or paranoid director who calls CUT! too early. Always wait at least a beat after the moment has passed.

Sound report sheet

The sound report sheet is the document used by the sound recordist team to tell the lab or editor what is recorded on which tapes, and other bits of information. It's printed on an A4 sheet of paper and filled out by hand. It will go to the labs with the negative, or the editing room with the videotapes later on.

Production info
All the usual and obvious stuff such as production, title etc.

Format
Referring to the format that the picture is shot on, just for reference.

Roll number
Each roll has a unique number.

Recording format
Almost certainly DAT.

Cam speed
If shot on film, the camera speed will be indicated here. You should be shooting at 25fps.

TC
Refers to time code. You will almost certainly use 25 base TC.

Speed
Not used unless you are recording on reel to reel machines such as a Nagra, which you probably won't.

Pilot Hz
Refers to the sync pulse within the power supply, UK is 50 Hz.

Sample rate
DAT uses 44.1kHz or 48kHz. Doesn't really matter which you use as long as everyone knows and agrees.

Transfer notes
Notes to the person who will transfer the sound from the master tapes to another format, usually at the lab.

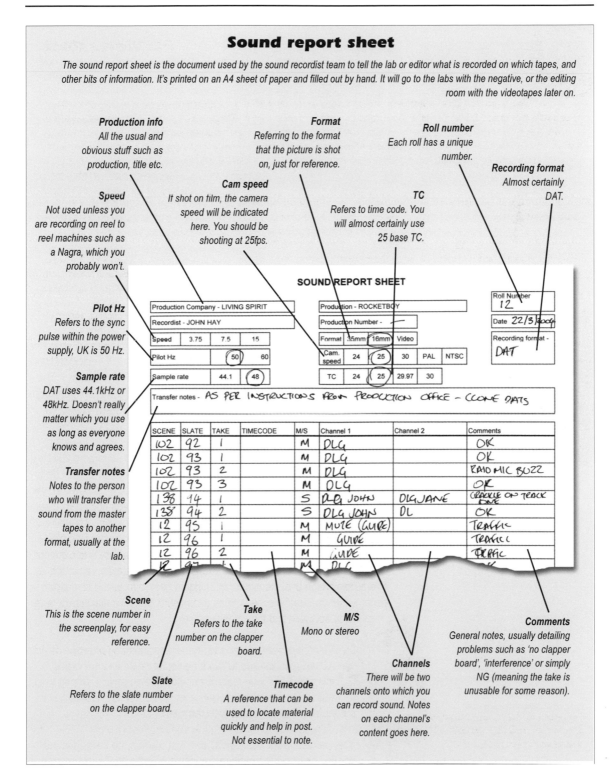

SOUND REPORT SHEET

Production Company - LIVING SPIRIT			Production - ROCKETBOY					Roll Number 12
Recordist - JOHN HAY			Production Number -					Date 22/3/2004
Speed	3.75	7.5	15		Format	35mm	16mm	Video		Recording format - DAT
Pilot Hz		(50)	60		Cam. speed	24	(25)	30	PAL	NTSC
Sample rate	44.1	(48)			TC	24	(25)	29.97	30

Transfer notes - AS PER INSTRUCTIONS FROM PRODUCTION OFFICE - CLONE DATS

SCENE	SLATE	TAKE	TIMECODE	M/S	Channel 1	Channel 2	Comments
102	92	1		M	DLG		OK
102	93	1		M	DLG		OK
102	93	2		M	DLG		RAD MIC BUZZ
102	93	3		M	DLG		OK
138	14	1		S	DLG JOHN	DLG JANE	CRACKLE ON TRACK ONE
138	94	2		S	DLG JOHN	DL	OK
12	95	1		M	MUTE (GUIDE)		TRAFFIC
12	96	1		M	GUIDE		TRAFFIC
12	96	2		M	GUIDE		TRAFFIC
12	97	1		M	DLG		

Scene
This is the scene number in the screenplay, for easy reference.

Take
Refers to the take number on the clapper board.

M/S
Mono or stereo

Comments
General notes, usually detailing problems such as 'no clapper board', 'interference' or simply NG (meaning the take is unusable for some reason).

Slate
Refers to the slate number on the clapper board.

Timecode
A reference that can be used to locate material quickly and help in post. Not essential to note.

Channels
There will be two channels onto which you can record sound. Notes on each channel's content goes here.

quiet set

noisy set

Dialogue recorded on a quiet set. Note how there is very little noise in quiet moments.

Dialogue recorded on a noisy set. Note how during quieter moments there is much more noise which will radically interfere with the editor's ability to edit the dialogue, and the mixer's ability to keep it clear in the final dub.

Noise floor

Wherever you choose to record sound, you will have a noise floor. This is the amount of noise present in the environment. For instance, in a recording studio, the noise floor would be very low and it would be easy to record good, clean dialogue. In a high street, the noise floor would be much higher, as people, cars and buses pass by and make noise. Recording dialogue in this environment would be much harder because the actor's words may be only slightly louder than the noise floor itself. The only answers are to either replace the dialogue with ADR, attempt to reduce the noise floor (for instance you might want to try and stop the traffic, and if you do, expect the police to turn up!), or (as is the most common solution), you get the microphone as close to the actor as possible.

AD will call *'Action!'* The shot will then play out. The boom swinger will watch the actors and attempt to keep the microphone pointed at the actor who is talking (often, they end up having to move around quite considerably). The sound recordist will keep an eye on the levels to make sure that an optimum recording level is always achieved, but that it never over loads or distorts.

Cut!

After the shot finishes, the director will call *'Cut!'* and the sound recordist will give it a beat or two before pressing either *'pause'* or *'stop'*. There will be a short debate as to whether another take is needed during which the AD will glance over to the sound recordist for a thumbs up or a thumbs down. There are so many potential sound problems, such as someone mowing their lawn, a dog barking, a plane flying overhead, an inexperienced PA who forgot to turn down their walkie talkie, extras chatting, camera noise, actors being too quiet or too loud (unexpectedly), microphone rustle, radio mic interference, blah blah, I could go on, but you get the picture. The good news is that on the whole, as long as everyone is professional, there are rarely problems with the sound.

Know your kit. Each morning, make sure you have had enough time to test and check all your equipment before turning over on the first shot. There's nothing worse than thinking everything is cool only to find out the batteries in the mic are flat!

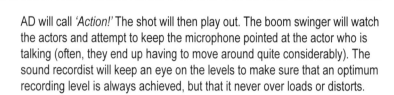

If there is a problem with the sound, then this could force a re-take. Beware, I said it earlier and I'll say it again, fix it now and not in post. Listen to your sound recordist and heed their advice. During this pause between takes or shots, the sound recordist will quickly fill out the sound report sheet (see diagram).

This procedure will continue all day. Upon wrap, the sound recordist will complete the report sheet and hand it over with the tape (that has

Mic patterns

Different microphones respond in different ways, and not all are suitable for recording actors' voices on set or location. Microphones that are used in film and TV tend to be very directional, or they can be hidden very close to the actor (radio tie clip mics for instance). Remember the golden rule though, if you heard a sound, the sound recordist probably did too.

The camera

Through the lens of a camera, there is a definite cut off at the edge of the frame. It's the nature of the medium. Therefore all manner of things can be happening just 'out of shot' and as long as it doesn't interfere with the actors' performance, there is no problem. Except of course, possibly for the sound . . . There is no definitive cut off with sound, so the acoustics of the entire environment will need to be considered closely when shooting.

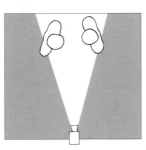

Omni-directional mic

These mics pick up sound equally in all directions. Because of this lack of directionality, they are not suited for film use (except as tie clip or lavaliere mics). They are most often seen in radio stations or board rooms for conference calls.

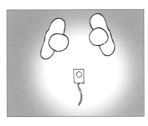

Uni-directional mic

Also known as a Cardoid mic, and are generally not suited for drama as it picks up so much sound around the set. These mics are often seen in the hands of TV reporters or rock singers, rarely on a film set.

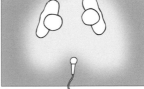

Shotgun mic

A directional mic that is the primary weapon of the sound recordist. Due to its directionality it is great for capturing dialogue when the mic needs to stay just out of shot. An older but still excellent mic to rent is a Sennheiser 416 (and 816 for ultra directionality). Most often seen on the end of the sound assistant's boom pole. Beware though, they can pick up sound from the sides and behind in unexpected ways.

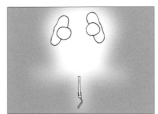

Tie clip or lavaliere mic

Tiny omni-directional mics that can be hidden on the actor or (very nearby), often attached to a transmitter and battery pack that is hidden in the actor's back pocket (watch out for actresses in skin tight dresses, where does the battery pack go?). Radio versions are most common as they need no direct cable connection to the recorder, but the cheaper ones can be subject to interference. An excellent choice but can produce bass heavy, even nasal sounding recordings.

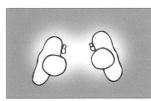

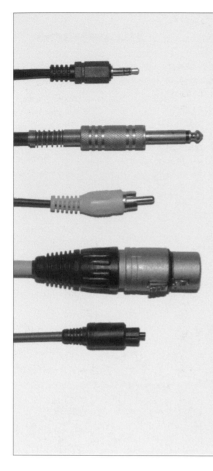

Connector cornucopia

3.5mm Minijack
Usually a stereo, domestic level signal carrier that is unbalanced. Often found on semi-pro mics, camcorders, minidisk recorders and cheap DAT machines.

¼" Jack
Can be stereo or mono, and is the physically bigger version of the 3.5mm minijack. More often found on cheaper mics and on musical instruments such as electric guitars. Not often used on a film set although very robust and common.

Phono
Most commonly found on semi-pro kit and hi-fi equipment. Not ideally suited for the film set.

XLR
The most common pro connector that can carry pro signals that are either balanced or unbalanced. This is the cable and connector you will see regularly. If shooting on miniDV you may also need a converter box to enable you to feed your camera (which is domestic level and unbalanced) with the signal it carries (pro level and balanced).

Digital signals
Digital sound can be carried in two main formats, SPDIF and AES/EBU. Both are excellent, SPDIF being the kid brother (and more common on cheaper kit). It usually connects using a phono plug, or an optical TOS link. AES/EBU is the more robust and professional connection, although there is no real technical advantage to it over SPDIF, as long as the SPDIF connection and cabling is up to scratch. At the end of the day, both simply allow the cloning of data, they do not process or convert, so go for convenience and cost. For instance, you may find your PC sound card already has an SPDIF input.

now been very carefully labelled) to a production assistant who will make sure that it gets either to the laboratory or the cutting room with either the exposed film stock or tapes.

Instant ADR
Sometimes there are unavoidable and unfixable problems with the sound on set or location. If this happens, you should strive to take your cast to a quiet place and ask them to re-perform the scene for the sound only. The sound recordist will then be able to get the microphone close to the actors, the new environment should be quiet (and can even be shrouded or covered with duvets to deaden the sound) and the result should be crystal clear and authentic dialogue. Because the actors have just been performing the scene, their motivations and timing are fresh in their mind and they will deliver a more accurate and dynamic perform-ance than if you asked them to re-create it six months later in a studio. I know you're saying to yourself, *'Hang on a minute, how can it possibly be in sync?'* Well it isn't, but on the whole, most of it will sync up and what doesn't can be edited or manipulated, and in a

You only do it once, but you will do it . . . The sound recordist yells, 'The fridge is making too much noise, turn it off!' . . . And then no one remembers to turn it on. Ooops! And you will need to pay to replace all the food that spoils.

Sound department minimum kit

The sound department can carry a surprisingly huge amount of kit, but for low budgets, it's better to keep everything lean, mean and simple.

DAT recorder
The actual machine that records the sound on to digital audio tape. Don't use any other format, unless recording directly onto videotape such as DV or DigiBeta via an SQN mixer.

Mixer
Small, battery powered professional mixer so the sound recordist can quickly change signals, mics or even mix signals.

Headphones
Always monitor sound through the best headphones you can get your hands on.

Kit bag
To carry everything around in, should be VERY sturdy.

Radio mic receiver
Permanently patched in and ready to record from radio mics placed on the actors.

Boom pole
For holding the microphone close to the actors without interfering with them, or the camera. Often used by the assistant sound recordist or boom swinger.

Magic arm
Quick release mechanical arm that can be used to mount a hidden microphone, either out of shot of behind a prop for instance.

Spare batteries
Both throw away and rechargeable batteries. Always make sure you have plenty and they are recharged (keep a charge in the car!)

Zeppelin
For placing over the microphone to help deaden wind sounds.

Wind jammer
For placing over the 'zeppelin' when it is windy.

Radio mic and transmitter
Battery powered microphones that do not need cables as they transmit over the radio waves. The lavaliere mic is hidden on the actors body.

Gaffer and camera tape

Sound report sheets

Stock
Always carry plenty of blank tapes.

Connectors
So that you can pretty much connect 'anything' to 'anything', no matter what the plugs are on the end of the cables.

Microphone
A high quality, powered microphone. The most important piece of kit. Start with a Sennheiser 416. It is often mounted on the end of the boom pole, in the zeppelin if outside

Dynamic microphone
Lower quality than powered mics but excellent for use in high volume environments, such as a shooting range or nightclub.

Cables
Loads of high quality cables, in different colours and lengths, with different plugs on the end.

Recording levels

Below are three waveforms from a track of dialogue that was under recorded, recorded correctly and over recorded.

Under-recorded	**Correct recording**	**Over recorded**
The problem here is that there is a low level of signal which means any inherent 'noise' could be increased when the signal is boosted. With digital equipment this is not as big a problem as it used to be with analogue formats, but it is still best avoided.	*The waveform peaks high but not over the limit, so there is good dynamic range (between the loud and softer moments). Ideal.*	*This is complete disaster as the signal will distort. Note how the waveforms hit the maximum levels and simply clip flat. This recording will more than likely be unusable.*

Sound is recorded between two extremes – if you like, a minimum level (being silence) and maximum level (which on tape is at the point of distortion). Unlike Spinal Tap, you just can't go to eleven! The sound recordist must constantly monitor the levels so that they never go into overload and distort, but are always way above absolute zero, or there would be no sound! In an ideal world, the sound levels would be surfing close up and personal like to the maximum level, but would NEVER hit it (commonly called clipping) where it would start to distort.

If you look at a DAT recorder, you will see two peak meters. These represent the sound levels that are being recorded onto the tape. The sound recordist will constantly turn the levels up and down to keep maximum signal but no distortion. There is a recording level dial on the DAT machine (or fader on a mixer if they are using one) which will be used to increase or decrease the recording level. That's kind of it! Technologically, it's quite easy to record sound, but experience will give you great sound almost every time, where the novice will hobble along and deliver only partially acceptable sound.

worse case scenario, abandoned. In my experience however, it almost always works. The actors won't like doing this ADR work because they will feel that it is unnecessary, and frankly they won't believe it will sync up. You need to encourage them and assure them that this will make the difference between a good moment and a great moment in the movie.

What to record?

A good sound recordist will want to record everything. Clearly this starts with the dialogue, but can end up with door creaks, cars passing, planes flying overhead, you name it. Whilst all this stuff is terrific, it will slow you down during the shoot. Guerilla Film making is all about *need* not *want*. Ask your sound recordist to concentrate on good, clean dialogue only and don't spend time recording anything else. Some recordists will want to record in stereo, one mic close-up to get good clean, thick dialogue, one further away to capture ambience and reverb for instance. Acoustically, this may be *prettier*, but again, you're just doubling the workload, not only during the shoot, but also in post production. I can't say it more simply, you just want good, clean, thick dialogue tracks.

Beware of mobile phones as they have a horrible tendency to ring at inopportune moments. Everyone on set must always turn off their phone. Even if they switch it to silent mode or vibrate, it can still interfere with the sound signal and completely ruin the take.

Buzz tracks

At the end of each scene, the sound recordist will want to record a buzz track. This is the sound that the 'world' makes during the scene. This is not an atmosphere track that will be added later in post production to create a more ambient world. The buzz track will be used by the editor to remove unwanted noises during a take. With digital technology and post production so common now, a long buzz track is not needed as the editor can cut and paste sections repeatedly. Thirty seconds will be more than adequate. Here's the killer though. To get an accurate buzz track for any scene, you need to record it at exactly the same time and in the same place as the slates and takes were filmed. That means the cast and crew will have to hang around whilst this buzz track is recorded (their physical presence impacts the acoustic world). You can guarantee that at least one time during your shoot, everyone will get the giggles during the recording of this buzz track and you will waste a considerable amount of time in the pursuit of accurately and clearly recording a lot of nothing! In a worst case scenario (and certainly in my experience) the editor won't even need a buzz track as

Mic Placement

There are several places where you can place or position a mic for maximum effectiveness. But remember, each location and set-up is unique . . . but here are a few examples of the most common places to position a mic.

Overhead on a boom

One of the most common positions, the mic on a long boom which allows the operator to move the microphone around easily and very quickly. One of the problems with this position is that actors feet and other motions, such as hands, might create unwanted noise that would pollute the sound. Actors can of course wear slippers, walk on a square of carpet and pretend to type on a keyboard (as long as it is out of shot).

Radio mics (Lavaliere mic)

Usually hidden in the actor's clothes. They are ideal for awkward locations and for when actors need to move around a great deal. However they can be a little nasal or bass heavy and can suffer from interference (radio versions).

Underneath hand held

Another common position (and can also be boomed from below too) which has the advantage of not being subject to foot steps and other noises. However, if the actors move around too much, the operator may not be able to follow as they are sprawled on the floor!

Edge of frame

Remember, the boom swing cannot see the edge of frame like the camera operator can. It is a fuzzy 'guess it's kind of there' area. This is why technical rehearsals are needed.

Hidden mic (plant mic)

A microphone which is fixed into position (behind this computer monitor for instance), either on the set and hidden, by, er, a plant (hence the name plant mic!) or other object or prop. This means you can potentially get the mic into a very good position, but if the actors move away from where they are supposed to be, there is nothing you can do and the sound may become too poor to use.

Adaptation

If there is one universal constant it's that one never seems to have the right cable! The answer to this dilemma is adapters – little clip on widgets that change male to female, XLR to phono, jack to jack . . . etc. You name it and an adapter will exist to convert it. Keep an eye on them as they tend to go walkies and they are not cheap to start off with. www.maplin.co.uk is a cost effective place to start shopping for them.

they will be able to take bits from quieter moments during the take and paste those over the unwanted sounds.

Trouble with the world

Most of the time, sound problems will be apparent, a car passing or plane overhead for instance. There are other, more peculiar problems to keep an eye out for though. Some film equipment, such as the transformers for large HMI lights can buzz loudly. When power cables are laid next to sound cables, a hum can be created on the soundtrack. The boom swinger will be constantly plagued by their microphone accidentally bobbing into shot or shadows from their boom appearing in the background. Generators make too much noise and have to be moved up the road, which means they need longer cables and more crew to handle the additional work. No matter what anyone tells you, film cameras make noise (which can sometimes be deadened with a 'barny' or even a heavy leather jacket). If you have a computer screen in shot, you may have to cope with the fact that the computer needs to be switched on, and that is going to make a lot of noise! All of these possibilities and a million others are why you hire the best sound recordist you can get and they spend their lives trying to get the microphone into the best position and as close to the cast as possible.

Trouble with actors

The sound department can often find itself a little maligned by the cast. Sound is one of those kind of invisible technologies. People assume that if the microphone is within ten feet, you will get perfect sound. Often you will hear complaints from actors that the sound recordist isn't very good because they keep asking for more takes. All too often, the reasons for needing more takes can be because of the actors! Common problems include things like . . . an actor who unexpectedly turns around in a scene (thereby masking their mouth), actors whose dialogue is delivered so fast that it overlaps with other characters (when the director needs extra space between the lines for editing), actors speaking too quietly, actors unexpectedly shouting, actors forgetting that they are wearing a radio mic and hitting it. This stuff happens and there's not a lot you can do aside from re-taking and asking the actor to modify their performance so that these problems are avoided. Somehow it still seems like it was the fault of the sound recordist!

When putting a radio mic on an actress or a child, it's often better to get the costume department involved as not too many actresses enjoy the thought of a sound recordist with his arm halfway up her blouse!

Actor's footsteps can be a problem. If their feet are not in shot you can place carpet on hard surfaces, or even ask them to wear loverly cosy house slippers!

In conclusion

It's simple really. Good clean, bright and crisp dialogue please. Nothing else.

Camera Department Blueprint

The camera department is where most people think movies are really 'made'. In truth, the camera is simply a recorder of how other artists, be they actors, director, production designer, costume and make-up, have chosen collectively to interpret the screenplay. Sure, it can often be a player too, through camera moves and re-framing, but it should always serve the story and not vice versa. A fact often lost on many new film makers who are obsessed by 'the image'. It's not how it looks, it's what it says. The camera department has three distinct divisions, really their own departments in their own rights, but so fused that they appear as one here — they are camera, lighting and grips.

Camera kit

This is the actual cameras, with additional lenses, stock, magazines, monitors etc. There are always add ons that surprise the production, such as filters, special lenses or unique bits of kit to do funky things. Of course, the camera department comes in two flavours, film and video.

Lighting kit

You can never have enough lighting, but more lights mean more crew and more power. Lighting is one of the areas that often betrays the budget of a film as it is simply under lit, not dark or underexposed, just unsophisti-cated, the results of an over-stretched department that is constantly hurried. Think about shooting abroad in amazing daylight!

Grips kit

This is the equipment upon which the camera is mounted. Be it a tripod with head, track and dolly or even crane. There are all manner of cheap and cheerful alternatives, such as wheelchairs, low cost DV designed tracks that run along ladders, even home made cranes, but if you can swing it, the pro kit will ALWAYS get better results.

Camera Dept. Blueprint

Most new film makers fixate on the camera . . . *'What camera should I hire?'*, *'What format should I shoot?'*, *'Should I shoot film or digital?'* Once they have procrastinated over these questions for some time, they then fixate on their DP, that is their director of photography, *'my DP is amazing! You should see their showreel, it's beautiful!'* Almost every director and producer seems to think that *their* DP is the best on the planet and that every shot they will compose, light and shoot will be a work of art. Not that I am saying that there is anything wrong with this, it's just usually at the cost of very important issues, such as script, casting, production design, make-up and costume for instance. For some reason, new film makers seem to forget that the camera department is just one of the tools that is used to tell their story. No matter how good your movie looks photographically, if the story doesn't connect with the audience, because the script isn't good enough, OR if the audience doesn't experience the emotion of the story because the casting wasn't good enough, OR if the audience doesn't believe the story because the production design didn't create a suitably convincing world, OR if there just weren't enough shots because the director compromised coverage in favour of *'stunning shots'* that took too long to set up, then frankly the *'amazing photography'* means diddly squat. A bad film told with pretty pictures is still a bad film. A good film with dodgy shots is still a good film.

To cap it all, film makers so often forget that audiences are just not interested in pretty pictures or production values. And even if they were, consider this. Your average slick TV commercial will have a budget of say $1m with which to create truly staggeringly beautiful images, which are then put in front of an audience, who lets face it, would rather make a cup of tea, chat to

The camera is the 'eye' of the film, it captures the events through which the film is told. Debates rage over formats but ultimately, it's all about story. A fact often forgotten by new film makers

The camera team, including assistants, grips, sparks and gaffers, can be huge! So much of film making can end up centred around acquisition of 'the image', and as the camera department is so large and dominant, it's very easy for other departments to suffer terribly.

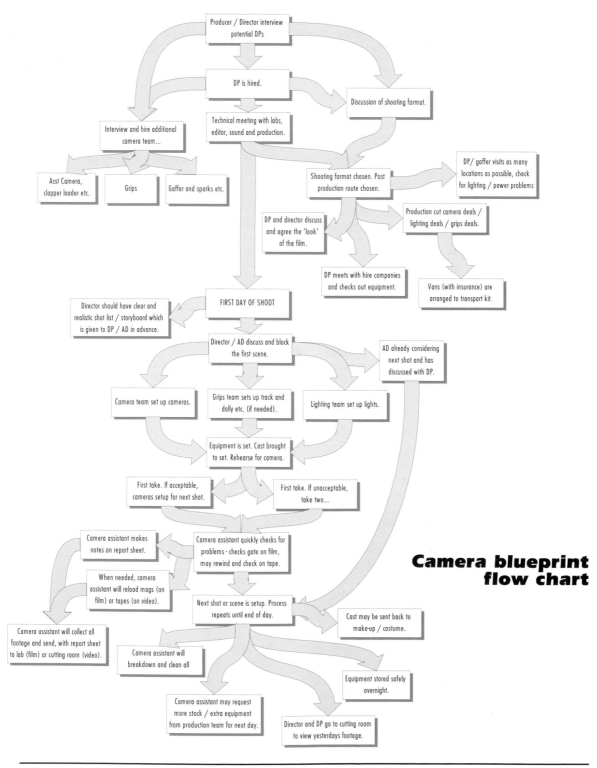

Camera blueprint flow chart

- Producer / Director interview potential DPs
- DP is hired.
- Discussion of shooting format.
- Interview and hire additional camera team...
- Technical meeting with labs, editor, sound and production.
- DP/ gaffer visits as many locations as possible, check for lighting / power problems
- Asst Camera, clapper loader etc.
- Grips
- Gaffer and sparks etc.
- Shooting format chosen. Post production route chosen.
- Production cut camera deals / lighting deals / grips deals.
- DP and director discuss and agree the 'look' of the film.
- DP meets with hire companies and checks out equipment.
- Vans (with insurance) are arranged to transport kit.
- Director should have clear and realistic shot list / storyboard which is given to DP / AD in advance.
- FIRST DAY OF SHOOT
- Director / AD discuss and block the first scene.
- AD already considering next shot and has discussed with DP.
- Camera team set up cameras.
- Grips team sets up track and dolly etc. (if needed).
- Lighting team set up lights.
- Equipment is set. Cast brought to set. Rehearse for camera.
- First take. If acceptable, cameras setup for next shot.
- First take. If unacceptable, take two...
- Camera assistant makes notes on report sheet.
- Camera assistant quickly checks for problems - checks gate on film, may rewind and check on tape.
- When needed, camera assistant will reload mags (on film) or tapes (on video).
- Next shot or scene is setup. Process repeats until end of day.
- Cast may be sent back to make-up / costume.
- Camera assistant will collect all footage and send, with report sheet to lab (film) or cutting room (video).
- Camera assistant will breakdown and clean all
- Equipment stored safely overnight.
- Camera assistant may request more stock / extra equipment from production team for next day.
- Director and DP go to cutting room to view yesterdays footage.

Formats

So many new film makers get stuck in the seemingly endless debates over which format to shoot. Film or video? DV or Hi Def? Super 16mm or 35mm? Here are a few simple answers as to when you should shoot which formats.

Video formats

DV (be it miniDV, DVcam, DVCPro etc.)
Shoot only when the story suits the format. These would be stories that are small, low key and intimate, where the insertion of a small, innocuous DV camera would not impact either the performances or the world. It may also be that the directorial style of shooting from the hip suits the story. Also, use DV when you have absolutely no budget. If you have some cash, strive for AND ACHIEVE a higher quality format such as DigiBeta. Many new film makers make the deeply regretted mistake of starting their project on miniDV only to realise the limitations of the format too late in the day.

DigiBeta
This is a fantastic, professional format that is ideal for shooting micro budget films, especially when the plan is to stay on videotape only (for sale to TV, DVD and video but NOT to play on a cinema screen). You can shoot in true 16:9 and the quality of images achievable is quite startling. You also have the benefit of cheap and reusable stock and a simple, tried and tested post production path. It is also possible to master your movie and blow up to 35mm and maintain visual excellence, which is much more questionable when having shot on DV.

Hi-Def
Essentially it's just high quality (definition) video, but it can be shot in progressive scan, which mimics the look of a film frame quite accurately. Hi-Def is probably the smartest option for the cash strapped film maker as you get the benefits of cheap and reusable stock, simple post production routes, and still maintain a very high resolution, future proof image. The downside is that there are few cameras out there and therefore getting a deal can be tough.

Film formats

Super 16mm
The lowest quality professional film format that you should consider is Super16mm. It has all the benefits of really looking like a movie because it is film, it's lightweight, robust and relatively cheap to shoot. Most importantly, it has that magic that you don't find on any video format, which is the 'f' word – film. All film formats create a sense of focus and urgency in everyone involved, which simply makes for better film making. On the downside, S16mm is not suited to post production special effects (because the image can weave from side to side slightly, although this is not noticeable to the viewer in normal shots) and in order to produce a 35mm blow up, you will need a 'fat cheque' at the very end of post production. The real strength of S16mm is that you do not need that 'fat cheque' in order to get the movie in-the-can and all the way through post production.

35mm
This is where you DO need that 'fat cheque' up front. The format is hellishly expensive to shoot, but it carries all the advantages of shooting on film and the images acquired are truly second to none. If you can afford to shoot on 35mm, then I would strongly recommend it. The cameras are bigger and heavier than S16mm and most often, have only small magazines, which carry around 2½ minutes of film at a time. Whatever film format you choose to shoot, I would recommend you always shoot it at 25fps.

their girlfriend on the sofa and fast forward through it. That's how interested audiences are in pretty pictures. Turn on MTV now and you will see what you are up against. You will not win. You won't match this. Let it go and work on telling the story in the best way that you can.

Now here's the rub. After saying all that, I'm now going to contradict myself and say that you should strive for the best images possible! But let me be clear, film making on a low budget is a juggling act and the savvy film maker will always know how much of their resources should be invested in

If shooting on film, a member of the production team should check with a member of the camera team how much film stock has been shot, so they can make sure you never run out of film stock and that your estimated stock budget is not unexpectedly being exceeded.

Definition

Much has been said about definition of various formats, that is, how much detail is actually contained in the image. These test images (all shot at the same time) on miniDV (Canon XL1), Digibeta, Super 16mm and 35mm, clearly illustrate just how little miniDV contains, when compared to 35mm for instance. These shots were correctly exposed and fully lit with key, fill and back lights. Sadly, these tests don't really show as much as I would like them to when sat on the paper of this page. On the screen, the differences are more marked, especially 35mm, which always gets a gasp!

MiniDV

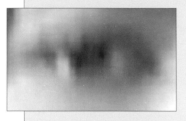

The image is by far the poorest in quality, and is also higher in contrast than any of the others. Still, it is surprisingly good.

Digital Betacam

We were surprised by just how good DigiBeta actually was, when compared to Super16mm, the image is different, but the resolution is comparable. Not as contrasty as miniDV.

Super 16mm

The lowest quality film format was surprisingly low resolution, although certainly more attractive to the eye than DigiBeta.

35mm

Significantly higher resolution than any of the other formats. At 300% zoom, 35mm contains about the same information as S16mm or DigiBeta. To the eye, the image is startlingly sharper and more attractive than any other format.

Hi Def v 35mm

There were enough rumours and myths flying around about HiDef and its similarities to 35mm to convince film maker Toby White to shoot the ultimate test. He and colleague Richard Hadley conceived a short film, called 'SNAP', to be half shot on 35mm and half shot on HiDef. They decided to assign each format to one of the two characters in the story so that, in the edit, the shots were continuously intercut and the footage could be directly compared, the actors serving as the reference for what was 35mm and what was HD.

35mm or HiDef . . . ? It's almost impossible to tell the difference on paper, but trust me, it's suprisingly tough to see the difference on the big screen or small screen.

Establishing wides were shot with both cameras and in post, the two halves of the frame from each format were then composited together to create a final shot that showed the two side-by-side. 'I'd seen a few comparative tests' said Toby, 'but none that demonstrated HD performing literally up against 35mm. The uniqueness of SNAP is that it makes a direct comparison across a variety of lighting scenarios.' Even respected industry experts had to agree that almost all the time, they could not see a significant difference between the two, 'people said that they stopped looking for the differences and just watched the action, the differences were so slight that even a discerning audience was more concerned with the storytelling.' In fact, often the only tell tale signs were the physical flaws in the 35mm such as slight scratches and dust! Toby noted that the HiDef performed very well under natural light and produced extremely clean and sharp images, something that occasionally gave the game away, some people suggesting that, in some cases, it looked a little like super hi res video. For SNAP, the HiDef was shot at 25p, (that is progressive scan to mimic the true 25 frames a second of film, and not the 50 fields of video).

Toby has also pointed out that 'the only real drawbacks with HiDef is that you cannot currently shoot slow motion, although you can mimic it in post production, and that whIle hire charges are currently similar to 35mm, HiDef is much more in demand so deals are harder to get . . . I was amazed at how well the HiDef performed!' The test proved that HiDef could mimic 35mm almost all the time, and actually improve on the format as the inherent photochemical flaws of 35mm were banished. Add to this the cost effectiveness of the stock, currently around £50 for a 40 minute reusable tape, compared to around £350 for 35mm stock, developing and telecine of around 10 minutes! A good rule of thumb is that overall HD production costs are about a third of those for film.

You can find out more by sending an e-mail to the terribly nice Toby White at toby@gangsterpictures.com

---

acquiring attractive images. For instance, check out some of the most successful, low budget features, such as Spike Lee's *'She's Got ta Have It'*, or Sam Raimi's *'The Evil Dead'*. There may be imaginative photography or bold images, but they are certainly not beautifully polished.

So why are new film makers so obsessed by amazing images? One possible reason, aside from a love affair with *'the image'* is that every new film maker began life as an amateur. Their prime concern is to fool the audience into believing that they are *'real'* film makers and not amateurs. How often have I heard some new film maker say something like, *'wow! It really looks like a movie . . . !'* This says more about the film maker's personal insecurities than it does about the audience's expectations, and I've got news for you, YOU *ARE* A FILM MAKER! AND YOU CANNOT FOOL

Aspect ratios

The shape of the frame in which your film is shot is called the aspect ratio. Most telly, like soap operas for instance, is shot in a 4:3 aspect ratio, kinda square. Most movies are shot in a 1.85:1 aspect ratio, which is close to the 16:9 of widescreen TVs. Then there are the super wide movies that are shot in 2.35:1, like 'Titanic' etc. Almost certainly, you will shoot in a 1.85:1 / 16:9 format, but it isn't that simple.

Film formats

4:3 Standard 16mm / 35mm frame

This is what standard 16mm shoots and 35mm too. In order to get a widescreen image from this frame, the tops and bottoms are cropped off. On 16mm this is not advisable (as the resolution is so low to start off with, by the time it's all blown up it could look horrendous). 35mm handles it beautifully though, AND 35mm has the advantage containing two aspect ratios on one negative, a full 4:3 framed image for TV versions of your movie, and a 1:185 cropped version (that is made in post production) for cinema and DVD. This cropping will take place in post production and the camera operator MUST be clear about what they are 'framing for' during the shoot.

1.85:1 Super 16mm

This is a great format for low budget film makers as it can be blown up to 35mm (optically or digitally) and 100% of the exposed image area is utilised. It's ideal for completing to a standard 35mm, 1.85:1 format for the cinema, and for DVD too.

2.35:1

This format, often called Cinemascope, is not ideal for low budgets as it has a few more expensive technical hoops to jump through to complete, and frankly, it's so wide, you may need bigger sets and therefore more lights blah blah . . . !
Leave this huge and glossy format for 'Gladiator' and 'Armageddon'.

Video formats

4:3 Standard Video Frame

This is the aspect ratio in which DV is most often shot. Most cameras come with an in-built 16:9 processor, but compared to the processors available in post production, you should avoid the in-camera ones like the plague. Unless you have a camera that has a true 16:9 chip, ALWAYS shoot in 4:3. (note – there are some 16:9 adaptors that screw on the front of the lens which can be used too).

True 16:9 (anamorphic)

This is still squeezed into a 4:3 'box' but, it contains the information to make a 16:9 image through processing at the viewing stage (on a video projector or widescreen TV for instance). This is the format that DigiBeta can shoot and is excellent. The squeeze is called 'anamorphic' and when unsqueezed the frame will be the same shape as the HiDef frame below.

HiDef 16:9 (non anamorphic)

This is an image that has no anamorphic squeeze and so is truly 16:9 widescreen all the way down the line.

THE AUDIENCE! You can impress your friends with pretty pictures, sure, but an audience will always judge a movie by a very simple benchmark, 'Was it any good and did I get bored?' Again, this has very little to do with beautiful images.

Beware of night shoots. When there ain't no sun, everything needs to be lit, which means you'll get half as many shots. It's also cold and no one can see anything. It's a god-damn nightmare on a micro budget!

The DP

The director of photography is one of the first people new film makers seek out. Who should you hire? Well this may seem a little contentious, but I think any DP who knows their craft should be able to deliver an attractive looking film. So given that, the qualities you should be looking for are . . .

Speed – they must be able to work quickly and efficiently and

Camera lenses on super 16mm

This series of images was shot on Super 16mm film and illustrates different lens focal lengths and their relationship to perspective. These were all shot on prime lenses from a distance of eight feet from the actress who, unless she had experience of photography, would not be able to tell which lens would give which shot. This is important to remember as most actors think that lenses are all kind of the same and shoot kind of mid-shots (a bit like the 25mm image).

If these shots were made using a 35mm camera, then the focal length would roughly double. For instance, if you shot on 35mm film, the 50mm lens would give you an image that looks roughly like the 25mm shot here. The same lenses are usually used on both 35mm and Super 16mm.

DV camera problems

The biggest and most frustrating problem with DV is that of lens width. Because the CCD inside the camera is so small, it's difficult to get a wide angle shot (without adding extra wide angle adapters and softening even more what is a very poor image to start off with). The shot below shows just how wide we were able to get using a DigiBeta camera, the inner box representing how wide we could get on the Canon XL1. Whilst this might not seem like a big problem, it can quickly turn into a nightmare if you are forced to shoot in confined spaces. Quite often, you will find that you just can't get everything in shot! Which then turns into a production problem 'We need a location with more space so we can get the camera further away.'

DV frame

DigiBeta frame

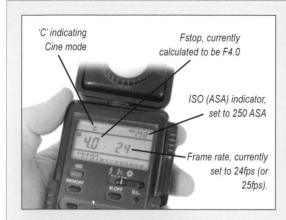

'C' indicating Cine mode

Fstop, currently calculated to be F4.0

ISO (ASA) indicator, set to 250 ASA

Frame rate, currently set to 24fps (or 25fps).

Using a Light Meter

To shoot a picture on film, means light must be focused through the lens and onto the camera gate. Too much light and the image will burn out, too little and it will be too dark or even completely black. Light can be measured with a light meter (all video cameras come with a built-in light meter). What the DP on a film will use is a hand held light meter, probably a Sekonic like the one pictured here. Most people are afraid of the light meter as it's often viewed as something similar to Harry Potter's wand! This is of course a mistake, it's a fairly simple tool that measures light and informs the DP what aperture the camera lens should be set to in order to expose correctly. Here's a rough guide . . .

Step 1 – Setting up the light meter

First set up the ASA (or ISO) of your film stock on your meter – it often goes from 12 ASA all the way up to 64000 ASA (!), but you will probably be shooting 200 ASA, 250 ASA or even 500 ASA for low light situations. It'll probably be a few button clicks to get to it. Next tell your light meter that you are shooting in Cine mode (not stills mode) and it will then offer a number of frame rates, from which you should select either 24fps or 25fps (it does not really matter which one as both are approximately the same). Now you are set!

Step 2 – Measuring the light

After setting up the lights, place the light meter close to the subject's face, point it toward the lens and press the button on the side. The white cone at the top of the meter will now register how much light is hitting the subject and calculate the aperture on the camera. You may want to tweak the lights at this point.

Step 3 – Setting the aperture

On the film camera lens there is a dial that has 'T' stops marked on it (on video it would be 'F' stops). If the light meter says 4.0, then set the camera aperture to T4. If you shoot now, the subject should be exposed correctly. Of course there is so much more to exposure and lighting than this, but this simple understanding is all you need in order to begin shooting film, even 35mm! It's not a dark art or rocket science.

As you experiment you'll learn how film responds to light, when you can open up the aperture more to make it brighter or close it down to make it darker. How much light you need to fill detail in shadow areas, how much light it will take to burn out to white and leave no detail, how far you can push underexposure until the image drops off to complete black . Now these questions DO start to push lighting into being a darker art, but the basics are easy peasy.

rarely make mistakes. I have worked with ponderous DPs, who frankly, dominate the whole experience in the naive belief that the only thing that really matters is a pretty picture. *'Coverage'* over *'Image'* any day in my book.

Temperament – they should be easy going, professional and hard working – AND pragmatic, understanding that sometimes they'll be forced to compromise for the greater glory of a good story well told. They should strive for the best images, BUT be content when forced to compromise.

Hard working – ironically, the DP is truly the only person on a film shoot (aside from the director) who never stops. The speed at which the DP works will dictate the speed at which the film is shot. A fast DP equals more coverage and coverage is your best friend in the cutting room. Don't forget, the camera team has the most physically arduous job on a film set. There is a huge amount of very heavy equipment that is constantly being moved. On big films, the DP would never touch the equipment. On your film, they will spend a great deal of time doing little more than physical labour.

Film maker – a DP who has either directed, produced, edited or written a screenplay, is a DP who will understand the greater glory of a good story well told. They will appreciate that theirs is a very important spoke in the wheel of the movie, but it is not THE most important.

Affability – given that the DP sits in front of the cast for such a huge amount of time, the DP who is a good *people person* will make your actors feel beautiful or handsome and keep their confidence boosted. Often, a secret dialogue will develop between the DP and the cast, where the actors will seek approval from the DP if for some reason they don't believe the director, *'Are they just saying it was really good, what do you think?'*

Technician – a DP has a huge amount of kit at their potential disposal. They should understand what it all does and the ramifications of using it. Such as, a savvy DP will understand that if shooting in a PAL country, they should shoot film at 25fps and digital at 25P (not 24fps or 24P) respectively. Beware of the inflexible technician DP who will insist on shooting at 24fps or the most expensive film stock (any film stock will do, as it's all excellent!).

Artist – the most difficult quality to find, as it needs to be reflected by the pragmatic technician. Very often, the artist DP is inflexible, aloof and down right infuriating. If you can find a truly creative and artistic DP who is a real pragmatist, then you are onto a winner, just like my DP Jon Walker. Hey did I mention that Jon is probably the best DP in the world? You should hire him!

What to avoid
Unfortunately, the job of being a DP seems to attract some people with

Claire Trevor-Roper
Production Manager

'Your camera/lighting team will respect your ability to negotiate their equipment lists, so get to know what everything is and what it's for. Accept that the lists may change if the schedule, weather or crew change, even if the director has a bright idea! Talk to your contacts at the camera, grip and lighting houses before the equipment lists are given to you and make friends. See what sort of deals could be offered, be honest, they will like you more. Hire companies won't let their equipment leave the building without insurance. Talk to the insurers of film productions, they will know the equipment, risks, language and may even know your DP and gaffer (which can work to your advantage).

When talking to the insurers you will need clear, concise equipment lists, the names of the drivers of the vans/trucks that hold the equipment and where it is all kept when not in use (weekends and overnights). They usually ask for the script and crew list too, so have those prepared. Get the DP and gaffer to check the lists (typed up neatly) before they go to the insurers.

Cut a deal with a secure parking company, one with 24hr manned security. Remember your drivers will also be members of crew and their day has to encompass collecting the truck (make sure you have requested free parking for their own vehicle during the working day) and then driving to location. At the end of the day, once the trucks are packed, they will have to drive them back. Think about how long the working day is and how many hours this is going to add. Involve the location manager so you can organise secure parking near the locations. This is obviously less of a problem if you are working from a studio.'

Jon Walker
Director of Photography

'Without doubt, the process of lighting is a scientific one; the physics of how light is transmitted, what colour it is and how bright it is, through to the chemistry of the way the film is processed and printed. You must understand this science. But this is only one side of the story. The other is the 'art', what look and style you want. There are different ways of approaching this. You can create a look and feel by working within a set of rules that you set for yourself. For example, a good principle in film lighting is to 'light from the back to the front'. That means exactly what it says – think about how light passes through things and try and define the foreground action by 'cutting it out' from the background. As soon as you put too much front light onto a subject it can spoil the mood. You could work to several different styles using each to subtly underpin different aspects of the story. Having a set of rules will help constrain you and in effect provide the starting point for each scene you shoot, rather than there be endless possibilities which won't tie together in the final film.

Each shot will have other shots either side of it, so it's not necessary for everything to be clearly visible. To clarify . . . if you were shooting a still photograph, then the whole picture must tell the story, but each shot in a film only tells a fragment of the story, so don't over-light to 'illuminate' the story, allow the camera and actors to 'illuminate' the story – don't be afraid of DARKNESS. Coverage is more important than that one perfect shot that took all day. There's only one master in a film . . . the story! I don't want to go to a film and just watch pretty pictures. Too many low budget films suffer because the DP is lighting their 'opus illuminatus' and when the editor gets to cut it up there's too few shots to tell the story. The rules you set at the start can help you make quick decisions on set.'

questionable or frustrating character traits. First is the inflexible artist, who holds holy all things framed in their viewfinder and sculpted out with their beautiful lighting. Boy oh boy, gimme a break!

Second, is the arrogant film school graduate who just thinks that light emanates from both their *'amazing and heart stopping'* lighting set-ups as well as their own arse (a trait often shared by directors who have also graduated from film schools). Avoid like the plague!

Crap DPs. Yes I know it's staggering, but some DPs simply cannot operate a camera or light a scene. Ask producers with whom they have worked for an honest and off the record appraisal. Take these comments onboard, irrespective of how good the DPs show reel actually looks (and always remember that every producer or director thinks that their DP is the best one on the planet! Did I mention my DP Jon Walker and how amazing he is?)

Choosing your DP

Once you've chosen your DP, you will have a number of discussions about the size of crew, shooting format, the overall look of the film etc. Most important to nail down as soon as possible is your choice of shooting format. I've been pretty vocal about this throughout the entire book, but I will state it again. Whatever format you think you can achieve, choose the one above. If you plan to shoot on miniDV, try and get DigiBeta. If you plan to shoot on DigiBeta, try and shoot Super16mm. If you plan to shoot Super16mm, try to get 35mm etc. Almost always, the inexperienced film maker goes with convenience when choosing a format, which is a mistake (especially when it comes to shooting on miniDV just because you already own a Canon XL-1S). DON'T DO IT UNLESS YOU HAVE TO!

The size of the camera team will be decided largely on a budgetary level. Will the DP operate camera or will there be a separate operator? Will there be an assistant? Will the assistant also act as the clapper loader? Will there be a second camera or second unit camera team? Will there be grips equipment and if so, how many grips? Who will be responsible for setting up the lighting and electrics? Does the gaffer have any sparks (assistants) and if so how many? How many trucks will be needed for all the equipment and who will drive the trucks and do they have insurance? It goes on . . .

Another very important meeting will take place between all the technological heads of department, such as editor, director, sound etc. at the laboratory, where every aspect of production and post production should be hammered out in meticulous detail. If you are shooting on tape, it's a good idea to go to a top online facility and ask one of their engineers to help you plan your post production route, they will more than likely be very happy to advise as long as you are not too arrogant. Everyone at this meeting, lab or online facility, should understand the impact of the choices on the production and post production route for their particular discipline or department.

Exposure

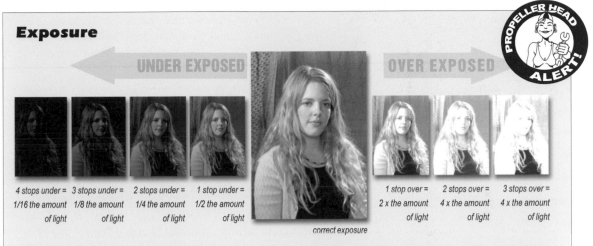

UNDER EXPOSED · OVER EXPOSED

PROPELLER HEAD ALERT!

4 stops under =
1/16 the amount
of light

3 stops under =
1/8 the amount
of light

2 stops under =
1/4 the amount
of light

1 stop under =
1/2 the amount
of light

correct exposure

1 stop over =
2 x the amount
of light

2 stops over =
4 x the amount
of light

3 stops over =
4 x the amount
of light

When you shoot a picture with a camera (digital or film) it is created by focusing an image through the camera lens onto an area within the camera where the image will be recorded – in the 'gate' and onto negative with film, or onto the CCD with digital. The trouble is, to get the image looking just right, there needs to be just the right amount of light. Too much light and the image will start to bleach out, too little light and the image will start to get dark and eventually turn black. The amount of light getting into the camera can be controlled by the aperture on the camera. Mechanically, the aperture is a lot like the iris in your eye. When it's dark, the iris opens up to let more light in, when it's bright, the iris closes down to restrict the light entering the eye. Same with a camera.

The aperture is a ring on the camera lens and is usually marked with numbers called 'F stops'. Photographically, light is measured in F stops – if you have ever been on a film set you might have heard the DP shout to the camera assistant 'two eight . . . !' This is short hand for the camera team. The DP has used their light meter to measure the amount of light on the set and knows that to expose it correctly (with the film stock in the camera) the aperture ring needs to be set to F2.8 (hence the comment 'two eight . . . !')

The upshot is that, if the camera team do their job well, all images should be correctly exposed. Occasionally mistakes do get made, or the light fades and the images are underexposed . . . And unlike our eyes, film and video do not deal at all well with too little light. As you can see from the images above, only a couple of stops either way can be disastrous. There is a little latitude at the labs to 'push' and 'pull' images back from the brink, but it can lead to unpleasant results such as excessive grain or milky grey blacks. It's essential to get the exposure spot on, perhaps even over exposing by half a stop on film (which will create more detail in the negative without losing the brighter areas).

A common mistake I have come across is when a new film maker has dived head long into their shoot, only to discover that a simple, ill informed choice has consigned them to an overly complicated and excessively expensive post production route. The most common mistake is a new film maker shooting at 24fps and not 25fps in the belief that 24fps is somehow 'the way its done', when in fact they have just made a technological choice that will cost them many thousands of pounds in post production and have no real-world impact whatsoever on the end result.

The look

In the weeks running up to the shoot, the DP and director should spend time discussing at length the visual style of the film. This is broken down into two parts – lighting and operating.

Simple lighting set-up

Even the simplest of shots needs to be lit properly, or it will look like your average home movie. This simple mid shot of an actress required four lights – key light, fill light, rim light and a background light. The overhead diagram to the right illustrates where each light was positioned.

Key light

The key light 'models' the subject and is often the most important light in the scene. It is often the foundation on which all other lights are based. In this case it is a light placed to the left of the actress, perhaps representing a window light source (in the story of the shot).

Fill light

This light is designed to 'fill' the harsh shadows created by the Key light, to create a more natural and rounded look. It will pick out detail and texture where otherwise there would be only dark shadows.

Back light

To add another dimension, a light source is mounted behind the subject. It hits the back of objects and the actress and gives a nice impression of three dimensionality.

Background light

This light has been positioned to illuminate the background of the scene to create a more natural look. Without it, there would be a fully lit actress sitting against a very dark background.

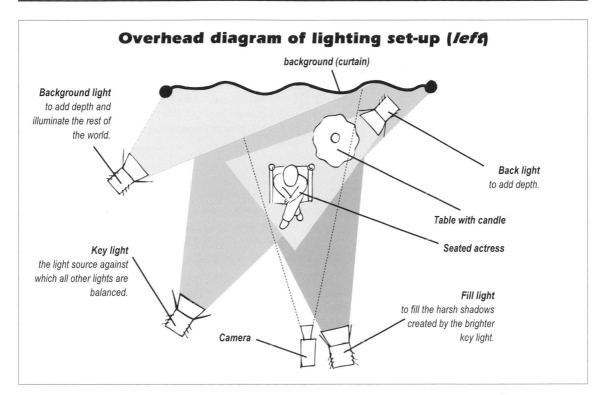

Overhead diagram of lighting set-up (*left*)

background (curtain)

Background light
to add depth and
illuminate the rest of
the world.

Back light
to add depth.

Table with candle

Seated actress

Key light
the light source against
which all other lights are
balanced.

Fill light
to fill the harsh shadows
created by the brighter
key light.

Camera

The choice of lighting style is one of the things that can significantly impact the speed at which you shoot. For instance, complicated, glossy lighting can take a great deal of time. Are you aiming for a film noir look, or social realism? Or Ridley Scott*'s'shafts of light'* look,or harsh and bright primary colours as used by Pedro Almodóvar, or the dark and moody look of 'Se7en'?

The choice of operating style will be the domain of the camera operator. It's essentially a discussion about framing and camera movement. Are you going to shoot images that are *'sat back'*, static and symmetrical in a Kubrick-esqe style, or are you going to go for a shoot-from-the-hip wobbly cam style like 'The Insider', or are there going to be lots of slick track and dolly camera movements like your average American action movie, or will there be super fast track and dolly Scorsese style, or even Steadicam overload, again, Kubrick inspired?

Of course, on a low budget movie, you're going to struggle to achieve any consistent look of excellence because there simply isn't time or re-sources, but as long as everyone is talking the same language, then the on-set short hand between DP, AD and director will speed things up.

Kit
Whatever format you have chosen, the producer or production manager will arrange a deal with the equipment houses based on an initial wish list supplied by the DP. In almost every instance, this wish list is

If you have been forced to shoot on DV, then the Canon XL1S is an excellent choice because of its lens interchangeability. The lens that comes with the camera is pretty good, but you can also hire superb television lenses, which will dramatically improve the quality of the image. Speak to the camera hire companies.

Colour chart and grey scales

If you are shooting on film, at the start of each day you should shoot a few feet of colour chart and grey scale. These will be used by the lab to get the correct density and colour balance changes that might occur due to slight changes in stocks, or the laboratory baths themselves. You can get these charts from the stock manufacturers (Fuji or Kodak), the labs or the camera hire companies. Some people choose to tape these charts to the clapper board, but that means that if it is to be useful, the clapper board should also be properly lit (which it rarely is!) and exposed accurately.

If you are shooting on video and plan to use a monitor to check your lighting, make sure you have a top notch monitor and that you use the colour bars from your camera to set it up properly.

unreasonable and unrealistic. The hire companies will know this and make suggestions that will modify the list, making the equipment cheaper to hire but stay in the spirit of the DP's aspiration. These lists can be encyclopaedic in detail, when you add up cameras, lighting and grip equipment.

Once a deal has been struck, the DP should visit the hire companies to check out and play with the equipment. Most important is the camera hire company, where the DP should familiarise themselves with the camera equipment. In a best case scenario, the DP will shoot a number of lens and exposure tests, so that they will better understand the limitation of the lenses and the exposure curve of the film stock they have chosen – some film stock handles more or less than the ideal amount of light better than other film stocks for instance. These same tests should also be carried out even if you are shooting on a video format, be it DV, DigiBeta or Hi-Def.

F/stops & T stops

The camera has a lens with an aperture, which has settings called 'T stops' or 'F/stops'. What's the difference? F/stops are a theoretical measurement of the amount of light that will pass through a lens and T stops are the actual amount of light passing through. The difference is due to factors like the thickness of the glass in the lens and internal reflection. There might be slight exposure differences between two lenses if you use F/stops for instance, but not if you use T stops. Video and stills lenses tend to be marked up in F/stops and film lenses with T Stops.

Location

The location manager will have been working their way through the screenplay and finding possible places to shoot scenes. Hopefully they will have been mindful of things like sound, but also of the 'look' and access to power. Once locations have been short listed, the director, DP, sound recordist and gaffer should visit them with the location manager. There will be an obvious discussion about the visual suitability of the location, but also there will be specific technical checks. How high are ceilings and can lights be mounted high enough? Are there strip lights and if so, can the unbalanced (colour temperature) tubes be removed and be replaced with special film strip lights? What power is available and can the gaffer tap into it? Will a generator be needed? If so, where will the generator be situated, so as not to interfere with sound? Is daylight going to be a problem as there may be large windows in a location where night time scenes will be set? . . . along with all the usual stuff that the location manager would take care of routinely, such as parking, loos, catering etc.

Transport

As production approaches, the production team will start working on hire vehicles. There will be a tremendous desire to force departments to share

The camera report sheet

This document is usually filled out by the assistant camera person. This one is for a movie shot on film, opposed to video (which would differ slightly), and is used by the laboratory and editor later on down the line. Each night, a copy of this document will be taped to the exposed film cans and sent to the lab (or if shooting on tape, a copy will be sent with the tapes to the cutting room). You will get a pad of these triplicate sheets from the hire company when you hire your cameras.

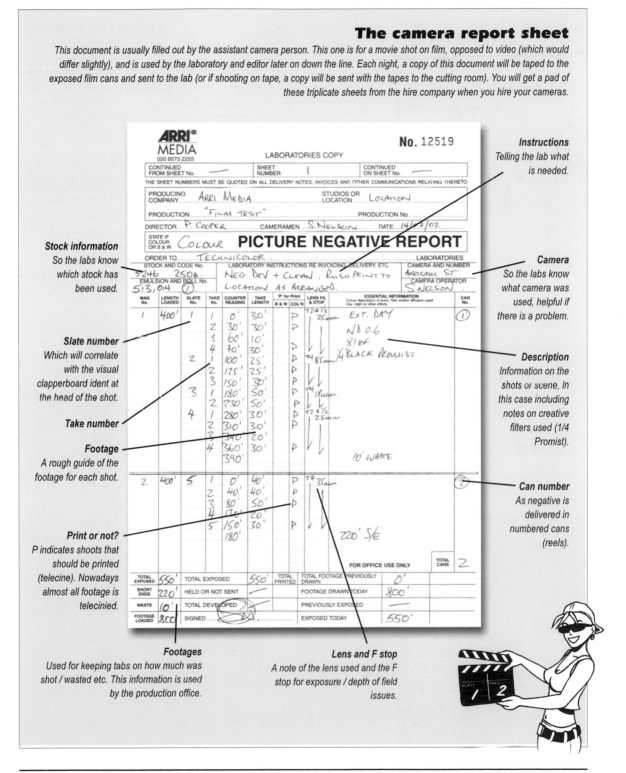

Instructions
Telling the lab what is needed.

Stock information
So the labs know which stock has been used.

Camera
So the labs know what camera was used, helpful if there is a problem.

Slate number
Which will correlate with the visual clapperboard ident at the head of the shot.

Description
Information on the shots or scene, In this case including notes on creative filters used (1/4 Promist).

Take number

Footage
A rough guide of the footage for each shot.

Print or not?
P indicates shoots that should be printed (telecine). Nowadays almost all footage is telecinied.

Can number
As negative is delivered in numbered cans (reels).

Footages
Used for keeping tabs on how much was shot / wasted etc. This information is used by the production office.

Lens and F stop
A note of the lens used and the F stop for exposure / depth of field issues.

A wider aperture and less light means that there is a narrower depth of field, which can help 'cut out' an actor against the background.

A tighter aperture with greater light means that there is a wider depth of field, which means the extreme foreground and background may be simultaneously in focus, creating a more 'cluttered' image.

Depth of field

When you photograph something you expect it to be sharp and in focus. Sometimes though, there are problems and an inexperienced director may complain that some of their shots are 'soft' or even out of focus, 'why can't they just focus the camera?' The problem is depth of field. When a subject is in focus, there is an area in front of the subject and behind the subject that is also in focus, but as you get further away from the focused subject, so it will start to go soft and eventually out of focus altogether. This is depth of field. That's OK, just focus the camera and it should be fine, yes? But . . . what if an actor needs to walk up closer to the camera? Walk out of the focused area? In that case, the focus puller will refocus the camera, live, so that the actor stays within the pin sharp part of the focus range. But consider this, the depth of field, that is the sharp area that is in focus, can sometimes be a matter of a couple of inches.

Depth of field is dictated by the type of lenses used and by the amount of light. The general rule is, the more light on the subject, the wider the depth of field, the less light, the narrower the depth of field. More light means that the camera aperture is closed down, less light means the aperture is wider (producing a narrower depth of field). The ASA of the film stock can also modify the depth of field (the higher the ASA the less light is needed, the narrower the aperture, the greater the depth of field), as can shutter speed on Video Cameras (the higher the shutter speed, the less light is hitting the CCD, so aperture must be set wider to expose correctly, producing a narrower depth of field).

The depth of field issue is an ongoing problem for low budget film makers as they never have enough lights and are constantly struggling to stay in focus. Creatively though, depth of field can also be used to 'cut out' actors against a background.

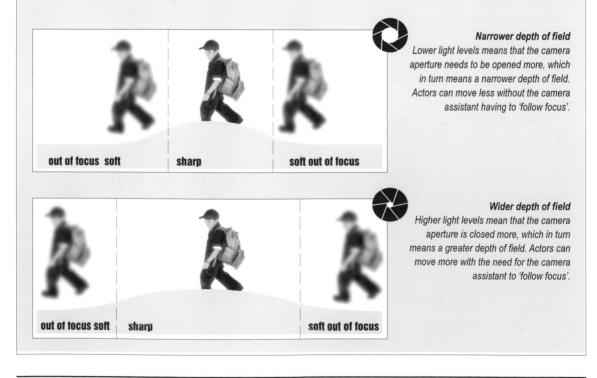

out of focus soft | sharp | soft out of focus

out of focus soft | sharp | soft out of focus

Narrower depth of field
Lower light levels means that the camera aperture needs to be opened more, which in turn means a narrower depth of field. Actors can move less without the camera assistant having to 'follow focus'.

Wider depth of field
Higher light levels mean that the camera aperture is closed more, which in turn means a greater depth of field. Actors can move more with the need for the camera assistant to 'follow focus'.

Your eye versus your camera

On set your eye will see lots of detail in both the highlights and shadows (middle).
On film however there is much less bandwidth and if exposed for detail in the highlights (right) the shadows will clamp right down, or if exposed for detail in the shadows the highlights will burn out (left).

Exposed for shadow detail | What YOUR eye will 'see' | Exposed for highlight detail

Your eye has tremendous bandwidth. You can look at something very bright and something very dark at the same time, and still perceive detail in both. A camera can not do this, it has much less latitude between darkness and light. This is one reason why inexperienced film makers are often surprised at how good their rushes look, 'it looked so flat on the day! It looks great here!' Essentially, shooting on film or video will increase the contrast so that shadows become much darker (or highlights could burn out although it is rare to make that creative choice). It's the job of the DP to measure all the light that is on the subject so that they control what is, and what is not 'illuminated'. This is one reason why it can take so long to light a scene. The DP is attempting to get the camera to record images that look like how we 'see'. Perversely, one of the easiest looks to achieve is a stylish film noir look because there is little attempt to fill shadows or create an image that looks 'real'. One simple trick to get closer to how the camera will 'see' is to wear sunglasses on set, even at night! The sunglasses will increase the contrast in your vision, leaving highlights where they are but clamping down the shadows and making them darker (but this is a rough guide). And you thought directors wear those shades to look cool! Actually, I think most do!

vehicles to save cash. Beware though, as this can be a false economy. You don't want the lighting team climbing all over unused grips equipment just to get to their lights for instance. It's usually best to hire a Luton sized van for the lighting equipment, a transit sized van for basic grips equipment and hopefully one of the camera team will own an estate car for the camera equipment. One discussion to have as early as possible is, *'Who will drive these vehicles?'* Are they comfortable with driving a truck, experienced, and what are the insurance implications? Do not leave this issue until the eleventh hour or I can promise you, the producer will end up driving the grips van, which is not a good use of the producer's time!

Alongside the question of who will drive the vans, is the obvious question, where will the vans be parked over night? Will hundreds of thousands of pounds of film equipment be in the back of those vans over night? If so, is it covered properly by insurance? If not, who unloads the vans every night to lock up the kit, where does the equipment go and who reloads it every morning? These simple practical issues can often

On an average day you will shoot around 20 different set-ups. It is hard to shoot more than that without compromising either the amount of takes, or the lighting. It can be very frustrating for a new film maker who is used to just grabbing a camera and shooting from the hip, but the images MUST be of a professional standard if the film is to be sold in the international marketplace.

DigiSlate

A DigiSlate is a clapperboard with the ingenious addition of a digital timecode display (hours : minutes : seconds : frames). You can either feed it with a SMPTE timecode signal, or ask it to count time through its own internal clock, and it will display the timecode whenever the clapper is open (it's blank when the clapper is shut to save battery power).

If used on a feature film shoot it can significantly speed up synching sound and picture either at the lab or in the Avid. If the timecode on the sound recordist's DAT machine is the same as the timecode displayed on the DigiSlate, it is a simple process to read the timecode as the slate claps shut and quickly find the corresponding audio clap at that point on the DAT tape, rather than listening manually for it.

The usual method is this: both the DAT recorder and the DigiSlate will be set to run in 'time-of-day' timecode – that is, they both count on their crystal-sync internal clocks. At the start of the shoot day the sound recordist will connect a cable from the timecode out of his DAT machine to the timecode in of the DigiSlate, thereby 'jamming' the timecodes together. The DAT recorder and DigiSlate will now be running in sync, displaying identical timecodes. However, after several hours they might drift off by a few frames, so at a convenient moment the sound recordist will 'jam' the slate again. The only problem with this method is that the DAT tape will have timecode breaks between every slate, which is fine if you are synching up at the lab (who use an edit controller and can jump past timecode breaks easily) but makes it very hard to load into an Avid (which prefers tapes with unbroken timecode).

One way round this problem is to run the DAT recorder in 'record-run' timecode, which means the timecode signal will run continuously down the entire tape, and transmit the SMPTE audio timecode via a radio signal to the DigiSlate. The added bonus of this solution is that you never have to 'jam' the DigiSlate, as it is always displaying whatever the DAT recorder is doing.

add two hours manual labour each and every day to an already over worked, over stressed camera team. Remember this, every time you say, 'of course we can shoot for twelve hours every day', are you actually asking some crew members to work a fourteen hour day, who then may have an additional hour of travelling either way?! Be considerate unless you want people to slow down through exhaustion, or worse, risk injury or accident.

First day

On the first day of the shoot, the camera, lighting and grips teams will turn up – along with everybody else. The director should have already planned out the shots for the day and communicated that to the AD, who will then instruct the DP to set up the first shot. Sometimes the director will bring the cast to set to do a 'block through' of a scene before it is lit. This is not a rehearsal, it's a kind of physical work through so that everyone knows the physical space in which the scene will be performed. The actors will then go to costume and make-up and the DP will tell his gaffer and sparks where to put the lights. If the shot requires any track and dolly, the grips will also be instructed to lay down some track and set up the dolly. Depending on the complexity of this first shot, it will usually take anywhere between 20-60 minutes to set up. When the crew is really rocking, it's on average around 20 minutes to set up, but this being the first day, you can bet it's going to be more like an hour.

Cameras, lights and grips all amount to a huge amount of VERY expensive equipment. You are going to need at least one and maybe two or three vans to drive the stuff around, so there is a hire charge there. But more importantly, who is going to drive? Do they have a licence? Are they comfortable? Are they trustworthy? Where will the equipment be stored overnight? What are the insurance demands for overnight storage?

Once the lights are roughly in place, the DP will start tweaking, often asking a runner or other unused crew member to stand-in, so the DP can see how the lighting will hit the cast. They will use their light meter to measure the quantity of light in any given space and generally and efficiently do their job, which is essentially to put light and shadow in the desired places.

At the same time . . . the camera operator will have been setting up the camera on a tripod (if it is a static shot) with the desired lens. They will frame the shot up and roughly focus the lens, sometimes using a tape measure to ensure that the shot is in focus (it is very hard to focus a film camera, especially under low lighting scenarios, such as night shoots).

At the same time . . . the clapper loader or camera assistant will have been in a different area or room that has been sectioned off for the camera team

Colour temperature

For the purposes of filming, light comes in two basic flavours, or should I say colours. Being a black and white book this is a pretty tough concept to get over, but let's give it a go. First off you have to understand that your brain is really good at making all light look kind of like daylight (that is white light), whatever its tinge or cast. Film stock is not so smart (or video cameras for that matter). For instance, some normal light bulbs burn with an orange glow, some fluorescent tubes give off purple or green light. Don't believe me? Take a look. Take a long hard look, especially at fluorescent tubes and you will see a difference. When driving at night, look through office windows and you will see all manner of different tinges to the 'white' glow.

The white flavour

The first flavour of light is called 'daylight'. Not surprisingly this comes from the sun in the first instance, but it can be mimicked with artificial film lights, usually HMI lighting (left). Daylight is kind of a white light, it's what we perceive as being most normal and flat, where colours are true.

The orange flavour

The second flavour of light is tungsten. This usually comes from a lamp that actually burns a filament, and it's really rather orange in colour (right). You may have noticed it momentarily when you turn on your lights at night and your eyes register the colours as being very warm and orangey, or perhaps when you shoot a photo and the flash didn't go off (the flash is white light by the way), then you get the picture back and it's all orange. That's the colour of tungsten light.

So how do we deal with this as we want everything to look 'normal', that is in a way that we perceive reality? Film stock, cunningly, comes in two flavours. Daylight and Tungsten. What a surprise! One for each flavour of light. 'Ah,' I hear you say, 'what if you have both types of light present in a scene?' Maybe a shot where there is a window with daylight coming through, but tungsten lamps in the room? Well you could shoot it with daylight film stock, meaning the light through the window would be the right colour, but you would then need to modify the lamps inside the room and cover them in a special clear blue sheet called gel. This would change the colour of the tungsten lamps to daylight (and also reduce the amount of light coming out of them too). The other thing you could do is put an orange gel on the window, turning the daylight into tungsten light and shoot the scene with tungsten film stock. Either way, what you must make certain of is that all sources of light are balanced the same – either daylight or tungsten, or you will be left with very weird lighting colours that will just look kind of crap and amateurish.

Video cameras, be it DV or HiDef, have their version of this which is called the White Balance, an electronic way of telling the camera what kind of lighting is being used. On the whole it's simpler, but the rule is the same. Always ensure all light sources are balanced the same, daylight OR tungsten.

Wide or long?

This close up was shot on a wide lens and on a long lens, on Super 16mm (Arriflex cameras).

The wide lens (above) is a 12mm lens which meant that the camera had to be positioned very close to the actress (about 18 inches) to accommodate the frame needed by the director. In the actual shot, you can sense her discomfort at having a camera 'right in her face!' The optics of the lens also mean that the shot is a little distorted and the actress is seen in a more unflattering way (as the lens distorts her features etc.) The background feels more cluttered too and overall it is, for my money, an uncomfortable shot. That's not to say it shouldn't be used, just that it is visually more uncomfortable. One upside is that you may be able to shoot in smaller locations as you can get 'more' with a wider lens.

Longer lens (above) is a 25mm lens and has a much more attractive 'look'. The actress is not distorted and as the camera is now some distance away (about eight feet) so she is no longer intimidated by its presence (and so her performance relaxed a little). The background is less messy too. Overall a more attractive shot. As a bonus, the further apart the actress and the camera, the less 'noise' from the camera could possibly pollute the sound recording. For my money, a creative improvement and a technical advantage too. Beware though, you need distance to shoot on longer lenses, so look for locations that are big.

There are two key stages for the DP - principal photography and the final print grading stage. The key thing to do in principal photography is to get the best negative you can (expose properly, don't under-light too much). You can do almost anything with a good negative, especially now with digital post-production). So when you're shooting night scenes, your rushes should be brighter than you know the final print will be (don't go mad - the mood should be there, but so should the details in the dark areas). The DP should be at the grade, they shot the film and their work isn't finished until the grade is finished! At the end of the day the grade is where the foundations the DP laid will finally show the 'glory' of their work.

and they will be loading a roll of film stock into the empty camera magazine. A film camera kit will probably come with three magazines, and it is the camera assistant or clapper loader's job to make sure that the magazines are always fully loaded. Once the film stock in a magazine has been shot (which will happen sporadically throughout the day), it is quickly and efficiently unloaded into an empty film can and re-loaded with a new roll of film stock. If shooting video, this job is a lot easier, as it's little more than labelling tapes, and sometimes striping tapes in advance (depending on the format and choice of post production route).

At the same time . . . the grips will be setting up the track and dolly (if needed). The director or AD will explain the shot to the grips, who'll then lay down metal track, which comes in 8ft lengths of 'straights' and 'curves'. Much of the grips time will be spent on levelling the tracks with a spirit level and using thin, wooden wedges to fractionally raise or lower the track where needed. This is because almost every surface is slightly uneven, which will create a bump or kick in the camera movement. Once the track is in place, they will carry the dolly, which is a kind of heavy metal camera platform, and place it on the tracks (this is usually a four person job). They will then run the dolly up and down the tracks, working on keeping everything smooth, sometimes using talcum

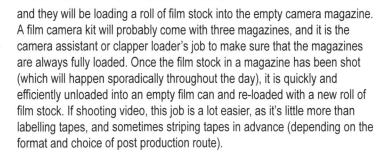

Cheap special effects filters

If you want a cheap way of doing a great 'in camera' effect, inexpensive plastic filters, like the ones made by Cokin (available from camera shops), are just the ticket. There are loads of weird and wonderful ones available and at an average of a tenner a pop, they're heaps cheaper than renting. Your DP may pass their spleen when you hand it over and ask 'em to stick it to the front of the lens with tape . . . but they do work, and work extremely well. I've used them to great effect in all the features I have made so far.

before   *after*

Polarising

Much like your polarising sunglasses, it you place the camera at a right angle, this filter can radically reduce reflections in a window. Obviously useful when shooting through glass on sunny days.

before   *after*

Close up filter

Most camera lenses do not get very close to a subject. So if you want that extreme close up of an eyeball or a phone book entry, you are going to need a close up filter. They look a bit like a large magnifying glass, and come in different strengths. I would buy the strongest.

before   *after*

Graduated filter

Used to create heavier skies for that Tony or Ridley Scott look. Many different colours are available, including a neutral grey which can be used simply to darken the sky so that it does not over expose and burn out, thereby losing the details in the clouds.

before   *after*

Split diopter

This is essentially half a close up lens. It allows the extreme foreground and backgrounds to be in focus at the same time. It's a weird effect, but very pleasing in the right circumstances. Often a vertical object such as a door, tree or wall is used to disguise the transition from one focus plane to the other.

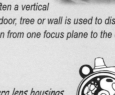

Annoyingly, some video camera lens housings rotate with the lens when focusing which can make using a filter almost impossible.

Martin Gooch
Camera Assistant

'Shooting on tape and film are different jobs. Assisting on tape is quite easy and anyone who has the desire and temperament will pick up the job quite quickly. Not so with film, it can be very complicated. You just can't blag your way when assisting on a film – you must know how all the bits fit together, how to load and unload film etc. One simple mistake could be disastrous. Film kit is much bulkier and heavier than video, especially with 35mm equipment. And there are so many aluminum flight cases that all look the same, so label each one for quick reference.

In between jobs, go to the camera rental companies and get to know all the kit. Being an assistant is always about professionalism and efficiency. You should always know how everything works and fits together (and there is always a new piece of kit) and be thinking ahead. For instance, if you are sitting around for 20 minutes, if you know the next scene is outside, you could start moving the equipment. Always be one step ahead. If there is a problem with any kit, deal with it immediately and demand excellence from the camera hire companies. If the camera fails or damages the film / tapes, it's YOUR fault. Test everything each morning, running it for a short time, making sure it works and isn't making any funny noises. No one will thank you when it goes well, but when there is a problem they will scream at you!

Make friends with the grips and lighting team as they will be your buddies and help you pack your kit late at night in the rain – there is no chance the make-up or wardrobe assistants will help you. Oh and buy a Leatherman and keep it clipped to your belt. It's one of the best investments you will ever make.'

powder on the tracks to help smooth out the shot. The last thing they will do is put the tripod head onto the dolly and then a member of the camera team will put the camera onto the dolly. Then the camera team and grips team will begin rehearsing the camera movement.

As you can see, the various members of the camera teams are pretty busy – before, during and after each and every shot.

Cast come to set

As everyone nears readiness, the AD will ask the cast to come to set and the first rehearsals will take place. During these rehearsals, a number of things will happen. The director will work with the actors, perhaps modifying the previous agreed movement in the blocking session, and a member of the camera team may mark the floor with white camera tape to give actors *'a spot to hit'* for focusing. The camera team will try out the camera movements and the focus changes that may be needed and the grips may rehearse the camera movements. After everyone feels confident that it's kind of getting there, the AD may call for a first take. Everyone will get ready, the AD will call for silence, and then the shot will be, er, shot! Almost certainly, the first take will not be quite right, so immediately everyone will re-set for a second take. It's often a good idea to do multiple takes of every shot for insurance purposes (the labs may have a problem or a tape may snag in a video player for instance). Once the director is happy, a member of the camera team will quickly check for technical faults. On video, they may re-play the tape to make sure it's okay, on film, they will take the lens off the camera and *'check the gate'*, that is look for dirt and fluff in the camera gate. If they find any, you may be forced to re-shoot. On the whole, most fluff and crap in the gate is unnoticeable once you get it into the cutting room.

This procedure will repeat throughout the day until wrap time.

Video assist and monitoring

If you are shooting on a video format, you can have a monitor on set, which will display what the camera sees. This should be an extremely high quality broadcast monitor that has been properly set up and calibrated by the DP. If it hasn't been properly set up, then what you are looking at is NOT what the camera is actually shooting and recording, so is misleading at best, downright wrong at worst.

If you are shooting on film, then there is no video image to view. To tackle this problem, video assist *aka* 'video tap' or 'video loop' was developed by the camera companies. It's a kind of tiny video camera that sits in the eye piece of the film camera and sends a video signal to a monitor. The problem with video assist is that it is very low quality and can really only be used as a rough guide for composition and framing. Very few crew members actually understand that the video assist image is nothing like what the film will

The camera assistant kit

The Camera Assistant will usually have a small black pouch that swings, bat belt style, from their hip. Inside is a well organised and tightly packed selection of peculiar tools and utilities. Aside from this bag they will also have a box with a bunch of other bits, which is where the clapperboard and aerosols (pictured here) would live.

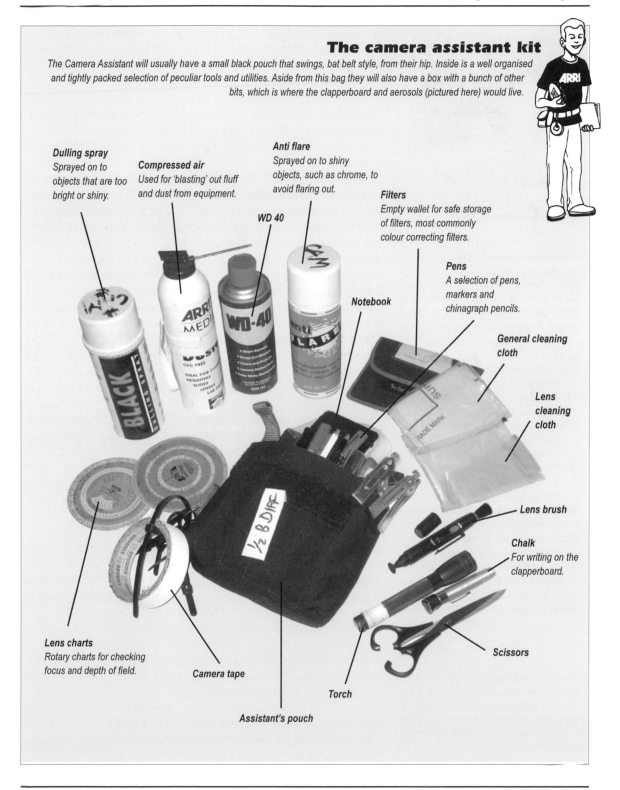

Dulling spray
Sprayed on to objects that are too bright or shiny.

Compressed air
Used for 'blasting' out fluff and dust from equipment.

Anti flare
Sprayed on to shiny objects, such as chrome, to avoid flaring out.

WD 40

Filters
Empty wallet for safe storage of filters, most commonly colour correcting filters.

Notebook

Pens
A selection of pens, markers and chinagraph pencils.

General cleaning cloth

Lens cleaning cloth

Lens brush

Chalk
For writing on the clapperboard.

Scissors

Lens charts
Rotary charts for checking focus and depth of field.

Camera tape

Assistant's pouch

Torch

Stuart Roweth
Gaffer

'the gaffer is responsible for putting the lighting design into action as they oversee the placement of the lighting, with guidance and instruction from the DP. The other main concern for the gaffer is for cast and crew safety. Often there are huge amounts of power surging through the cables that crisscross a film set or location and safety is paramount.

Shoots are divided into both night and day, and interior and exterior. A gaffer's job is about creating a natural and appropriate lighting set-up for a shot, when in fact the lighting is obviously artificial. It usually starts with a recce when I will look for common problem areas such as . . . Where can I get power from? Are the ceilings too low? How long will it take to rig? Are there any South facing windows where light may uncontrollably stream in (look for locations with North facing windows)? Are the walls white and therefore reflective? Is there a lift to the top floor, and how many journeys will that take to get the kit up, and how long will that take? What is the access to the locations? How much trouble will it be to set up a light outside the window to emulate daylight (a very common problem as locations may be on a third floor or there is no access for instance)?

When looking for a gaffer, find someone who is both trained and experienced, but also enthusiastic. Ideally, someone on the way up. It's often a shock to some new film makers that some gaffers and sparks do the job for the money alone and are in no way interested in the film making process! I, ike others, I started out as a spark, moved up through being a Gaffer and I am now a DP. It's how the business works.'

eventually look like and consequently, some people can get a bit stressed out. Personally, (and this is a very contentious point), I have always found video assist much more hassle than it's worth in the long run (on low budgets that is). After all, Spielberg didn't have it for 'Jaws' or Hitchcock for 'Psycho'. Here are my reasons. The image is rubbish. You don't get a sense of the actors real performance as you are sitting and looking at a fuzzy, black and white image instead of standing next to the camera and getting all the detail of the performance that the film will pick up. It takes more time to set up, which is a waste of resources. It encourages over fussiness, both in the director and the rest of the crew (. . . cut to a comment in the cutting room, *'Why on earth did we do seventeen takes of this shot when take two was fine?'*). Also, on a philosophical note, you have hired your camera team to do a job, and they should be capable of doing that without the director 'monitoring' their work. In summary, video assist may calm the paranoid little voice in your head, but it will cost you a lot of money in rental fees, slow down shooting, eat into VERY precious resources and more than likely, have absolutely zero impact on the quality of your film. If you feel the need to, please send hate mail to chris@livingspirit.com.

Cheap tricks

If you want to make a movie look more expensive than it actually is, there are a few cheap tricks you can employ. Of course, these 'looks' are not suitable for all genres, but they can be very effective.

Smoke machines – that layer of mist in the air will pick out shafts of light and also serve to 'mushy' up the image slightly so as to help disguise poor sets or lack of production design.

Keep it dark – if your sets are rubbish, keep the lighting dark, using a lot of backlight and rim light. Keep actors sweaty and glistening and use a smoke machine. Don't be afraid of a lot of 'darkness' in the frame, as long as it's attractive and the audience can actually see what they are supposed to see! *'If they can't see it they won't know it looks crap!'*

Filters – A *'black Promist'* (hired or bought), can add a very attractive 'sheen' to your movie. It's not to everyone's taste but some people like it. Do tests.

Long lenses – get the camera as far away as possible and shoot the action on the longer end of the lens. This will mean you need less 'background' (potentially saving production design and lighting resources), but it can also help 'cut out' the cast against the background. Most Hollywood movies shoot on longer lenses for a more attractive image.

Factors that affect the DP's job

There arc a number of common factors that can make the job of lighting and shooting harder . . .

Common mistakes & technical problems

Underexposed (film and video)

Caused when there is too little light hitting the film stock or CCD chip. Two common reasons are that there isn't enough light in the first place OR that the camera operator has set the wrong aperture and closed it up too much (the operator may have set it wrong or the DP may have given them the wrong T stop). It is possible to pull detail out of an underexposed shot (by grading), and on video images it is slightly easier, but on both film and video it will increase grain and noise and the results may not be attractive OR acceptable (right – note how the lamp cuts through but almost all other detail is lost).

Overexposed (film and video)

Caused when too much light hits the film stock or camera CCD chip. Caused by either the DP giving the wrong T stop or the camera operator setting the aperture incorrectly. The resulting images on video can be disastrous and un-saveable as there is no detail in whites. On film, there is more latitude to pull the image 'back down', but the results can be too poor to use (right – note how the whites have burnt out and NO detail is left).

Soft focus / out of focus (film and video)

Usually occurs when there is so little light that the camera operator has to work with a tiny depth of field. Any slight movement could make the shot go out of focus. Can also happen as a simple mistake. It's actually very hard to 'see' if a shot is in focus on a film camera, especially at night or when the aperture is closed down. Camera assistants will often consult a depth of field chart and actually measure the focus distance with a long tape measure. (right – note how the baby is in focus but actress is soft, due to a very narrow depth of field. This is a very common problem that needs constant attention from the assistant camera / focus puller).

Dust and sparkle (film only)

Caused when dust or fragments gets into the film magazines, or can happen at the lab too. It usually happens when the camera assistant loads the film, maybe they have had to work in a dusty environment etc. Due care and attention must always be taken when loading film stock (right – dust and sparkle can be painted out digitally in post porduction, but it can be time consuming and expensive).

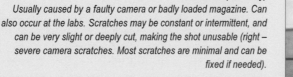

Scratches (film only)

Usually caused by a faulty camera or badly loaded magazine. Can also occur at the labs. Scratches may be constant or intermittent, and can be very slight or deeply cut, making the shot unusable (right – severe camera scratches. Most scratches are minimal and can be fixed if needed).

Common mistakes & technical problems . . . continued

Registration and weave (film only)

Film stock can gently weave from side to side, which is not too noticeable in most instances, but it can become a problem sometimes. Also, if the claws of the film camera are not correctly engaging with the film stock, all manner of weird flickering effects can occur. You might not know about this problem, unless the camera operator hears the magazine clattering, or until the next day when the viewing report turns up. (left – the film was not properly loaded and 'jittered' in the gate, causing a serious flicker and blurring of part of the image, making the shot unusable).

Fogging (film only)

Usually, this happens when the film stock is loaded or due to a faulty magazine. Light seeps in and damages the stock, most often it creates orangey glows or stripes to one side of the image (left – light somehow seeped in and has 'fogged' the film. Often fogging appears on one side only).

Hair in the gate (film only)

This is when a piece of fluff or a hair becomes lodged in the camera gate and is visible in the picture area. After major set-ups, the camera assistant will 'check the gate', that is, remove the lens and examine the gate for dirt and fluff. If they find anything they may request a re-shoot there and then (left – this is quite a huge hair, most often they are tiny bits of fluff that don't even show in the picture area).

Digital drop out (video only)

When a videotape is damaged, for instance it gets snagged on the camera heads, or it is affected by moisture or dust, drop out can occur and the image can be lost. Video is much more susceptible to problems with moisture and temperature changes than film (left – digital drop out can be brutal making shots or frames completely unusable).

Focus pulling – when a camera is focused on a subject, depending on the camera aperture, which in turn depends on the amount of light and the ASA of the film stock, there is an area in front of, and behind, the subject that is in focus. This is called depth of field. If the subject physically moves out of this area (that is in focus) then the camera will need to be re-focused live, and without error! This is the job of the focus puller. They must be 100% accurate, which is one reason why the camera department often ask for a number of camera rehearsals. The focus puller may mark up the focus ring of the lens (with a chinagraph pencil or camera tape) to correspond with white X's they have taped to the ground, where the actors stand at various points. This way, they are able to focus the camera without having to look through the lens (the camera being operated by the operator, whose job it is

Big light, little light . . . There's never enough

One of the problems with any film is that there is never enough light. This is a bigger problem for low budget films as the production cannot afford more and bigger lights, and even if they could, they would then need more crew, more power, bigger trucks, and so more catering and more blah blah . . . The trick is to balance production limitations with lighting needs.

Here's the problem with light – it's exponential. That is, as you double the distance from the light so you halve the intensity of the light. Looking at the example here . . . the top diagram has a smaller HMI light, say a 2.5k. Whatever light it puts out, there will be an area where it will eventually overexpose (as an actor gets too close to the light) or under expose (if they get too far away from the light). That means the actor CANNOT move past points 'a' or 'b' and must stay between them. The DP was also forced to put the light closer to the set just to get enough exposure at the window. The upshot is that only two thirds of the set are actually exposed correctly.

The lower diagram shows a light twice as bright, say a 5k HMI. The distance between point 'a' and 'b' is much wider and therefore the cast have much more room to move. The DP was also able to place the light further away from the window, giving a more even light throughout the set. This is one reason why movie studios are so large and why sets are never built up against the walls of the stage. The DP will always want to choose bigger lights to place further away, over smaller lights that are placed closer to the subject. The upshot is that the entire set is exposed correctly, wherever the actors move, they will be correctly exposed.

This was a very practical problem that was the source of much creative angst on my second film, 'White Angel' as we only had one large 2.5k HMI. Whenever we were shooting a daytime scene in a room, but it was actually dark outside (for unavoidable scheduling reasons we might shoot at night, or the daylight was so dull after 3pm for instance), the DP, Jon Walker, would have the nightmare of dealing with the fact that at one side of the room, the cast were burning out and over exposed, and on the other side of the room they were dropping into under exposure and getting dark. So scenes were forced to stay in a specific, rather narrow area. Any dynamism that the cast wanted to play with would simply get vetoed as impractical and impossible 'you will end up over exposed here, or too dark here . . . sorry!'

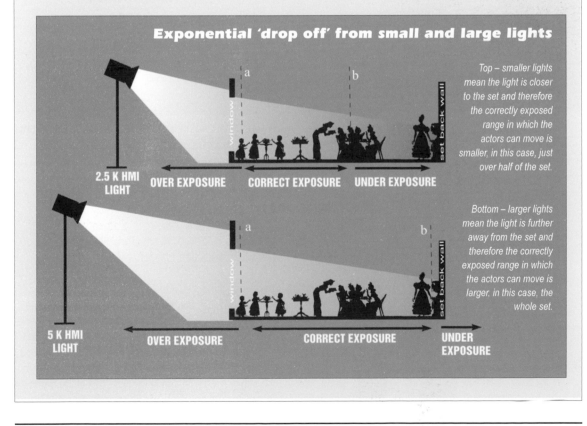

POWER

Electric power for your shoot is always an issue. You can't always just plug a light into the socket on the wall. On most film shoots the production will hire a generator that can supply power anywhere they can park the genny truck, but they are expensive 'cos you need to hire their operator too, old generators and ones not designed for film shoots can be noisy, and they are costly to run too. In a studio set, the production will probably buy the power they use from the studio owners, but check their prices before agreeing to hire a stage as they can be over priced.

For low budget films though, the obvious reality is that they are going to want to just draw power wherever they are. So how does that work? First, most pro lighting comes with a fitted 16 amp round, waterproof plug which can't be plugged into a domestic square 13 amp wall socket. You can hire or make jumpers that convert round to square though. Some low powered lighting, such as Kinoflo lights (like fluorescent tubes), are excellent for low budgets as they draw very little power and give off a lot of light. But if you are really going to 'go for it' in a location, you will need an experienced gaffer who can 'tie' into the house power supply, directly at the source (the power box under the stairs for instance). They will connect a box called an FDU (Final Distribution Unit) to the house power supply which will mean that up to 15kw of power is now available from one source. Without this box, the largest single light you could operate by plugging into the wall would be a Blonde or a 2k . And believe it or not, 15kw of power is not much, a couple of HMIs, some tungsten lamps and a few others will eat up most of the power. Then there is the rest of the house which needs power to operate. A crew member switching on a kettle or hairdryer at the wrong moment can often blow a fuse and bring the production to a halt! (keep spare fuses to hand 'cos this WILL happen). On locations, if the lighting in a given situation isn't good enough for a department such as make-up to do their job, the gaffer may also be responsible for getting light to them.

How much does the power cost then? Check with the electricity board, but it's currently around 8.5p per kilowatt hour. So to use 3k of lighting for an hour would cost 25.5p. Now do the maths, you will probably burn anywhere between 5k and 15k for twelve hours a day . . . that's probably about £1 an hour! Not too bad huh? If you are really organised in advance, you can ask the electricity board to uprate the supply so that you can draw more than 15Kw of power out of the house.

Remember, safety is always paramount. This amount of power can give you a fatal zap. The most hazardous situations are outside at night and in the rain, or in locations by a river or swimming pool. Don't even consider shooting near any water without a trained and experienced gaffer or spark who knows about power and safety.

to take care of camera movement and framing and not having to worry about focus). When crews are small, budgets tight and time scales even tighter, focus pulling becomes a very stressful job. Often the focus puller is asked to guarantee with 100% accuracy the focus of a shot without sufficient rehearsal. This is of course a mistake, as you end up burning film stock and wasting time both of which you can ill afford. If you are really pushed, keep actors in the same plane of focus, that is, if they move around, ask them to stay the same distance from the camera at all times and not walk toward or away from the camera. It's a far from ideal solution, but it works.

Anyone who doesn't fully understand how electricity works and who hasn't been professionally trained should stay well away. A zap from a 13 amp plug shouldn't kill, but a mistake when patching into the mains coming into the house will!

Tricky operating – there's an almost infinite amount of possible shots, each carrying their own unique operating problems, and some shots are very hard to operate. Simple shots like the camera creeping along the floor could take half a day to set up and shoot because you might need to dig a trench to accommodate the equipment! Most of the time, the biggest problem is getting *'the shot'* simply right. Panning and tilting, keeping the subject in frame and in the right part of the frame, ensuring focus is maintained, are all dead easy to do – *that is, if you*

Basic film camera kit

This is an Arriflex SRII, one of the standard Super 16mm workhorses. The camera department can become awash with kit, and often, many new film makers forget that it's what is in front of the camera that is important and not the 'toys' or 'shots' in of themselves. There isn't too much cosmetic difference between S16mm and 35mm cameras beyond the fact that the cameras and magazines are a little bigger. And the main difference between film kit and video kit is ruggedness and weight. Film kit is almost all metal, so it's damn tough and very heavy. The camera will be stored in a large aluminum flight case.

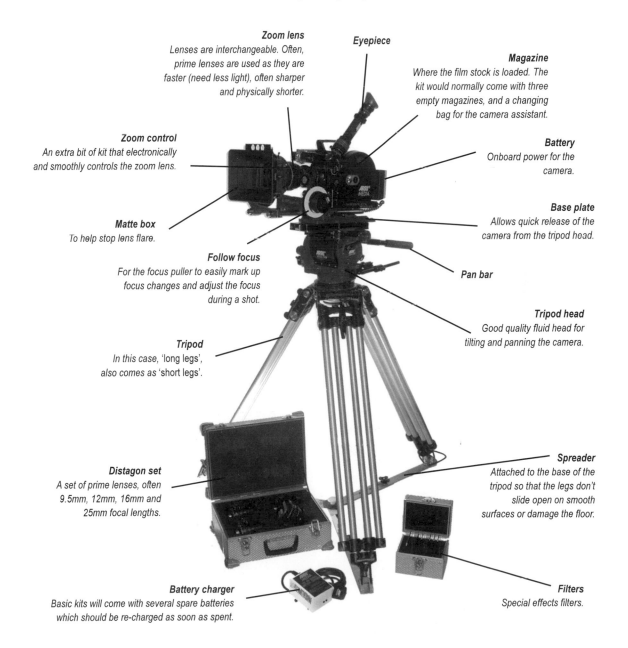

Zoom lens
Lenses are interchangeable. Often, prime lenses are used as they are faster (need less light), often sharper and physically shorter.

Eyepiece

Magazine
Where the film stock is loaded. The kit would normally come with three empty magazines, and a changing bag for the camera assistant.

Zoom control
An extra bit of kit that electronically and smoothly controls the zoom lens.

Battery
Onboard power for the camera.

Base plate
Allows quick release of the camera from the tripod head.

Matte box
To help stop lens flare.

Follow focus
For the focus puller to easily mark up focus changes and adjust the focus during a shot.

Pan bar

Tripod head
Good quality fluid head for tilting and panning the camera.

Tripod
In this case, 'long legs', also comes as 'short legs'.

Distagon set
A set of prime lenses, often 9.5mm, 12mm, 16mm and 25mm focal lengths.

Spreader
Attached to the base of the tripod so that the legs don't slide open on smooth surfaces or damage the floor.

Battery charger
Basic kits will come with several spare batteries which should be re-charged as soon as spent.

Filters
Special effects filters.

Basic DigiBeta camera kit

The Sony 7900 Digital Betacam camera is the workhorse of low budget work shot on the DigiBeta format. Unlike film, you can have a live preview of EXACTLY how your shot will look, so long as you have a good quality monitor that is set up correctly. Lenses tend not to be swapped, the camera and a single, motorised zoom lens being wedded for the whole shoot.

Zoom lens
Lenses are not usually changed.

Eyepiece

Battery
Onboard power for the camera.

Zoom control
Built in to the unit

Matte box
To help stop lens flare.

Base plate
Allows quick release of the camera from the tripod head.

Pan bar

Tripod head
Usually not as good quality as a film kit tripod head (due to the fact that the cameras are lighter).

Broadcast quality monitor
This must be high quality and set-up properly. It is used to preview the image, and EVERYONE wants to look at it!

Tripod
In this case, 'long legs', also comes as 'short legs'.

BNC reel
A long reel of video cable to feed a monitor further away than normal.

Battery
For the video monitor

Spreader
Attached to the base of the tripod so that the legs don't slide open on smooth surfaces or damage the floor.

Battery charger
Basic kits will come with several spare batteries which should be re-charged as soon as spent.

Filters
Basic kits will come with colour correction filters.

Cables
Additional cables for video and sound input / output / monitoring.

Wet weather hood
To protect the camera in poor weather conditions. Video cameras are less rugged than film cameras.

Steadicam

Steadicam is a device that's used to stabilise a camera when hand held would give too much vibration or shake, and where a track and dolly are impractical. It fills the gap between the two. It's a mechanical device consisting of a harness which the operator wears, which is attached to a flexible, sprung arm, onto which the camera is mounted. Effectively, the camera and operator are isolated, which means the operator can now move while the camera will remain steady. If you are going to use Steadicam on film you MUST have a video assist. It works by counterbalancing the camera with electronic parts (video monitor) through a gimble at the end of the isolation arm.

With Steadicam you can move the camera over rough ground, through doorways, up and down stairs, and along narrow corridors for instance, without the need for special rigs. It can go anywhere from ground level to about seven feet in the air, but it can only raise up and down around two feet at a time. Steadicam will never replace the dolly or hand held camera but it does enable film makers to get smooth, track like shots over difficult terrain. It is never 100% stable, and some people do expect it to be able to do anything, including flying! It is heavy and operators do get tired. With a heavy 35mm rig it's important to remember the operator will need to rest because the kit can weigh up to 40 kilos. Using Steadicam utilises all the same disciplines as any other department and, contrary to some inexperienced film makers' views, you can't just start shooting without the same planning and rehearsals.

A common mistake is that people think you can stick a Steadicam on any old operator, and it just isn't so – you'd be better off staying hand held in those instances. Steadicam operators are highly skilled in a very specialised job. If you need Steadicam for a shot, bring in a specialist for that shot, don't try and fudge it or it will probably fail and be a waste of time all round. Creatively, Steadicam comes into its own when the camera moves seamlessly with the actors and action and almost becomes another point of view within the scene. Many directors don't take advantage of the unique story telling capabilities that come from the natural fluid movements that the Steadicam can produce. Look at film makers like Alan Clark and Stanley Kubrick for innovative use of Steadicam.

For DV, there are a few camera stabilisers about. Steadicam JR and Steadicam Mini are both great for micro budget DV shoots. Of course, you will still need an operator with experience because, like driving a car, to do it well, you need plenty of experience. (left – John Ward, Steadicam operator) Check out www.steadicam.com'

don't have to do it and you just have to stand next to the camera criticising the operator! It's much harder to operate a camera than you would imagine and it takes extraordinary stamina, patience, a rock steady hand and an acute eye for framing and balance. Operating can get very difficult in some circumstances, for instance, when the camera is mounted in an awkward place, or at night (especially with a film camera) as so little is visible through the actual eye piece. During a night shoot, an operator may regularly work on instinct and not be able to actually see the subject and just trust their guts and experience! Holy cow batman!

Actors who can't hit their spot – inexperienced actors can cause problems for the production. Firstly, they often do not understand the importance of hitting their spot. In rehearsals, the camera team will mark the floor with little white Xs so the actors will know where to stand during the scene. This will allow the camera operator to know that they will be framed correctly, and for the focus puller to know that they will be in focus. The inexperienced actor, in the heat of the moment, may forget to hit their mark. Even if they put in the perform-

If you want an actor to look dead and they are having problems holding their breath, shoot them in slow motion. Any movements will be slowed down and any pauses will be elongated.

Lighting Kit

You can never have enough lights! Of course there are practical limits though, and this picture is a selection of some lights you could consider, with a few extras bits and bobs too. You will need a van to transport it all in, and if you had many more lights, you would also need a generator. You will also carry extras stands, cables and polyboards (for bouncing light) in the van. There is only one example of each lamp displayed here, but you may hire several of each.

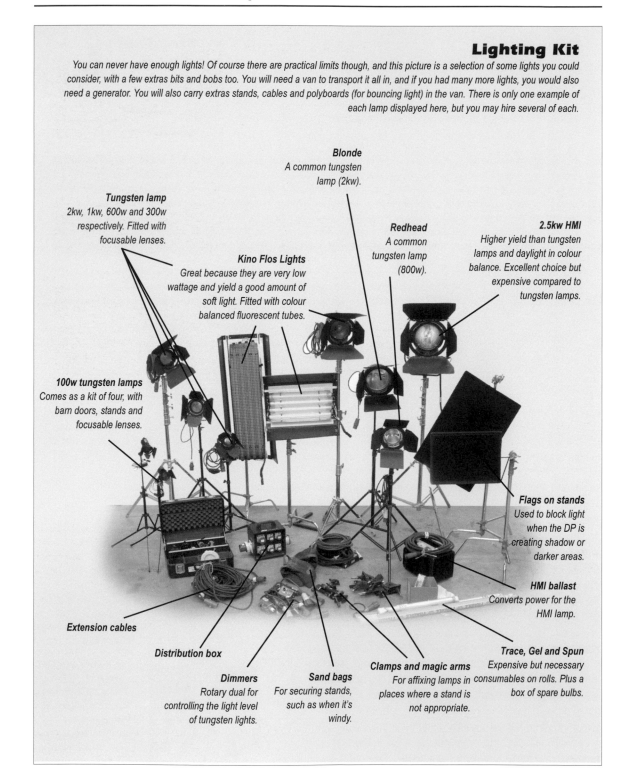

Blonde
A common tungsten lamp (2kw).

Tungsten lamp
2kw, 1kw, 600w and 300w respectively. Fitted with focusable lenses.

Redhead
A common tungsten lamp (800w).

2.5kw HMI
Higher yield than tungsten lamps and daylight in colour balance. Excellent choice but expensive compared to tungsten lamps.

Kino Flos Lights
Great because they are very low wattage and yield a good amount of soft light. Fitted with colour balanced fluorescent tubes.

100w tungsten lamps
Comes as a kit of four, with barn doors, stands and focusable lenses.

Flags on stands
Used to block light when the DP is creating shadow or darker areas.

HMI ballast
Converts power for the HMI lamp.

Extension cables

Distribution box

Dimmers
Rotary dual for controlling the light level of tungsten lights.

Sand bags
For securing stands, such as when it's windy.

Clamps and magic arms
For affixing lamps in places where a stand is not appropriate.

Trace, Gel and Spun
Expensive but necessary consumables on rolls. Plus a box of spare bulbs.

Bounce boards

One way of shooting very quickly is to shoot outside in bright sunlight. Of course in the UK you cannot guarantee endless blue skies, but in other countries you have a much better chance. If you are able to shoot in such an environment, or on a sunny day in the UK, the easiest lighting set-up is to stand the actor out in the sun, which will of course light them quite nicely. But there will be harsh shadows on their face.

You can then use a large sheet of white polystyrene as a 'bounce' board to reflect some of the sunlight back into the actors face. It's not in any way high tech, but it works and it's very fast. There are limitations, you have to get the bounce board kind of close if it is going to have an effect, which effectively rules out wide shots. Also, if you use a pro reflector made of material, if the wind blows and the reflector 'ripples' in the wind, so does the reflection in the actors face!

top right – the shot without a bounce board.
middle right – the shot with the bounce board in place.
bottom right – you can see how easily the bounce board is held in place by an operator.

ance of a lifetime, it may be useless because it's simply out of focus. Another simple problem is actors who will not do the same action repeatedly, in multiple takes. Not only does this create problems in the cutting room, but it can make life more difficult for the camera operator and the focus puller, as they are never quite sure what the actor is going to do. Of course, you don't want to pour cold water over spontaneity and creativity, but an experienced actor will know how to include spontaneous ideas into a performance that does not cause too many problems for the camera team.

Underpowered lighting – here's the deal. There's never enough light. So why not hire some more lights? Well for one, you can't afford it, nor can you afford the extra crew, power, trucks etc. So a trade off is made. However, there is one major problem with an underlit production. The lower the power of the light, the narrower the area of consistent exposure. A small light will only give a narrow band of area where the exposure is okay. If you move too close to the light, it will get too bright, if you move too far away from the light, it will get too dark. If you can afford very large, bright lights and set them up much further away, the band of consistent exposure expands dramatically, meaning actors can move around more freely without the DP having to worry about them underexposing or overexposing.

Anal directors – some directors are so physically bonded to the

If you want slow motion, shoot it in slow motion! No post production slow motion will look as good as in-camera, on-set slow motion. In fact, most post produced slow motion can look truly awful, and it can be VERY expensive as an optical effect. If you want that John Woo style slo-mo, the only way you can really do it is on the day, with the actors and a camera running in slow motion. DV cannot do slow motion, although you can fake it in post and it looks OK down to 50fps, but that ain't John 300fps Woo is it! Keerrrpooowww!

Basic track and dolly kit

Track and dolly is the simplest and most effective way to move the camera smoothly in a scene. There are several dollies but one of the most popular is the pneumatic Pee Wee dolly, pictured here. The dolly usually runs on metal track, but if the surface is REALLY even and smooth, it can run on rubber wheels too. The dolly is made of solid metal and is very heavy – great for shots as the inertia dampens movement, bad for crews backs, 'cos it's so damn heavy!

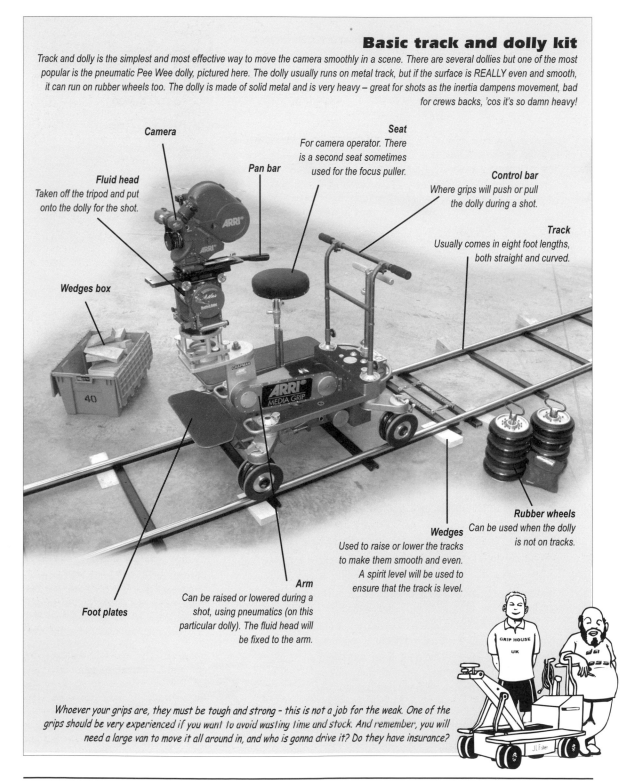

Camera

Seat
For camera operator. There is a second seat sometimes used for the focus puller.

Pan bar

Control bar
Where grips will push or pull the dolly during a shot.

Fluid head
Taken off the tripod and put onto the dolly for the shot.

Track
Usually comes in eight foot lengths, both straight and curved.

Wedges box

Rubber wheels
Can be used when the dolly is not on tracks.

Wedges
Used to raise or lower the tracks to make them smooth and even. A spirit level will be used to ensure that the track is level.

Arm
Can be raised or lowered during a shot, using pneumatics (on this particular dolly). The fluid head will be fixed to the arm.

Foot plates

Whoever your grips are, they must be tough and strong – this is not a job for the weak. One of the grips should be very experienced if you want to avoid wasting time and stock. And remember, you will need a large van to move it all around in, and who is gonna drive it? Do they have insurance?

camera eye piece that you wonder if they ought to have been a director of photography! It's the job of the DP and camera operator to shoot the movie in accordance with the explicit directions and collaboration of the director, and it can be extremely frustrating if the director keeps messing around with the camera. The director should check the frame and any camera moves, but their job should be taking care of the actors first and foremost. The real danger directors are ones who fixate and pore over their video assist, constantly complaining and moaning about minor changes in framing or camera movement during takes. Yes Kubrick was an amazing film maker (*'Take 56!'*), but he rarely had to get it in the can for $10k and in eleven days! If you want to behave this way, wait until you have a $50m movie!

Weather – It's obvious really, but less obvious is the sun. It is a whopping great ball of flire in the sky that can disappear behind clouds, or disappear altogether behind heavy, overcast skies! Hardly reliable in the UK! On super bright days, the sun can be so harsh, it creates heavy shadows so that you need to use extra lighting for actors' faces! (you can also use bounce boards, large pieces of reflective polystyrene). But it's the unpredictability of the weather that makes life difficult. You shoot one reverse of an actor in the morning in the sunshine, then the other reverse in the afternoon and the sun has disappeared behind dense overcast skies! And then the two shots are supposed to flow together in the edit. It's astonishing what grading at the lab can do to make shots look consistent, but there are limits. You can always ask the lab guys what they think. In the winter, daylight (or lack of) is always a real problem. There is just too little of it to start off with, and when it is around, it's often too dark to shoot anyway! The upshot is that on a grim, winter's day, you may only get a few hours between 10am and 3pm to shoot.

Night-shoot – the problem with shooting at night is that every single bit of lighting has been placed there. From a creative point of view, it's very rewarding to be entirely responsible for every aspect of the lighting, but it is also physically arduous. Add to this the fact that crews are physically out of step with their biological clock and really want to go to sleep, that it's probably cold, and if its winter, it's absolutely bloody freezing, no one can see anything, so it takes twice as long to do anything, blah blah. The upshot is that you will shoot roughly half to two thirds as many shots during a night shoot than you would during a day shoot. Avoid 'em!

Power – getting power is always a problem on location. This is partly because most film lights are not equipped to be simply plugged into the mains, and often, you need converters or junction boxes to do the job. Clearly, if you are shooting halfway up a mountain, you are going to need a generator, which is going to need a truck to pull it and it's going to be noisy. Or, you could hire a film generator which would come with an operator and a

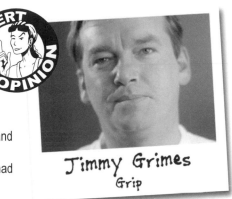

Jimmy Grimes
Grip

'Most experienced grips own their own equipment, with the exception of the dolly, which you will need to hire. It is also a good idea to own your own van. When you have a low budget, and less equipment, the grip equipment is often included on the camera truck.

An important point to remember is that grip equipment is always a lot heavier than you think it is going to be. A DV Camera, with monitors, and batteries is often about as heavy as a 35mm kit. With modern equipment, everyone has access to their own LCD monitor, the focus puller and the grip included.

An experienced grip won't need to use a monitor, although it obviously helps. With more experience, you find that you instinctively know what the parameters are by knowing what lens is being used. For example, you have more leeway with a wide angle lens than with a 50mm.

Health and safety is paramount! Never get bullied into doing a shot that you think is unsafe, always tell the DP or director, no matter how much pressure you are under. If you are setting up a tracking shot, make sure there are stops at the end of the track, and try, wherever possible to place an extra piece of track at the end to allow extra runoff.

When you are considering what van to hire, make sure that it is easy to load and unload, and remember that you are going to need to stand up when you are in the back. Transit vans are not high enough, and if you are trying to lift equipment in and out of them, before long you will get a bad back. The perfect van would have a tail lift, and I'd recommend a Renault Master.'

If you want a dolly shot but for some reason cannot use a track and dolly, use a zoom lens instead. As long as it is slow, a zoom can be VERY effective. Don't use it too often though as it can become tiresome, and NEVER operate the zoom manually, it will be wobbly and unusable! Hire a zoom control unit from the camera hire company.

whopping price tag. Even when you have power available, running power cables over long distances can have problems with power drop off, there are obvious health and safety issues (especially in wet weather) and the simple job of laying and then retrieving long cables is a quite enormous pain in the arse. Those of you used to just grabbing a DV camera and shooting from the hip will be seriously distressed by just how long it takes to do anything on a professional film set! Hire a gaffer who knows their job and you will save plenty of time messing around.

Flicker – all AC discharge lighting and arc lighting (fluorescent and HMI lights) flicker as the electric current 'pulses'. With fluorescent lights and older HMI lights this flicker is at mains frequency (50Hz in the). If your shutter speed is NOT divisible with this lighting figure then your rushes may flicker (i.e. 24fps does not fit into 50Hz, whereas 25fps does). This problem may not be noticeable in a film camera until you watch the rushes, but it will be noticeable in a video viewfinder. Modern HMIs are 'flicker free' and should give you no problems, but watch out for this in other situations, such as when you hire old and cheaper non flicker free lights, or when shooting with fluorescent tubes in a scene. The solutions are, shoot at 25fps, change the mirror angle (if you can) on the film camera, change the shutter speed on the video camera, or avoid lighting situations where there will be problems.

TV screens and computer monitors – if you want to film off a TV or computer screen, you may need to make some modifications or hire some extra equipment. If you are shooting at 25fps, which I hope you are, then shooting a TV screen isn't too big a deal as the camera shutter will match the refresh rate of the TV, although you may need to hire a piece of kit called a phase bar adjuster to 'tweak' it. If you are shooting at 24fps, you will need to shoot any shots with a TV screen in frame at 25fps or you will get a nasty black buzz bar rolling down the screen. A TV screen has a daylight colour balance, so all your lighting in that scene should be balanced for daylight (unless you want your TV screen to look blue). Exposure is more tricky, how much light is that TV actually pumping out? Even with a spot meter, the results can often be unexpectedly under or over exposed, so shoot some tests to be sure. If multiple TVs appear in a shot, then make sure they are all adjusted to be the same in brightness, colour and contrast. Computer screens are more problematic as they can have weird refresh rates. Ideally,

---

The ACM

Pretty much every member of the camera team will own their own version of the Bible, The American Cinematographers Manual – it even looks like a Bible! It's a small and dense pocket book that contains everything you ever wanted to know about all things cine-photographic. This is not a book for anyone who has a passing interest, it's a serious propeller head's manual, crammed with eye watering detail, charts and diagrams. It's essential if you are that way inclined, slightly more interesting than the Yellow Pages (and just as dense!) if you are not. It now comes in two distinct flavours – film and video. Both are available from amazon.com, but they are close to fifty quid a pop!

DIY SKATEBOARD DOLLY

I know, you must have that 'creeping dolly shot . . .' but you can't afford track and dolly from a hire company, or even if you get one for free then realise you'll need two strong people to handle it, insure it and find a van to move it around. There is a home made alternative. Many new film makers, especially those shooting on lightweight formats (primarily DV but also Super 16mm) have built their own – commonly referred to as a skateboard dolly. The following skateboard dolly was made by Steve-Marc Couchouron for his indie feature film 'Shadow Girl' (www.projectshadowgirl.com). Even though any skateboard dolly can look a little half baked, when set up carefully and with practice, the shots you can get are amazing, AND it shouldn't cost you too much to make!

Concept

The basic idea is that the wheels found on skateboards or rollerskates are secured to the bottom of a platform onto which the camera and operator sit or stand. The 'dolly' then runs on 'self aligning' track that is no more than PVC drainpiping, bought from your local DIY store. Ingenious huh?

Drawbacks

If the floor on which you wish to run your track is not even, then you will find it hard to get very smooth dolly shots. So look for locations with good, hard and level surfaces. Outside on the pavement is going to be tough, although if you had a large (eight foot) sheet of thick plywood, you could lay that down to give a smooth surface on which to operate the dolly. Of course then you would be limited to a maximum run of eight feet.

There are a few variations on this design, some with a larger or smaller platform, some with wheel sets doubled up (using sixteen instead of eight wheels), some with a seat . . . But they are all basically the same beast. The most important elements are, without doubt, the wheels themselves. They must be as high quality as possible, using bearings for maximum fluidity – and keep 'em oiled.

1. The platform

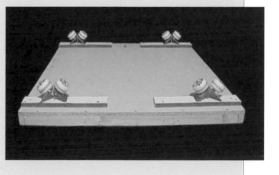

This should be made out of two 15mm (thick) sheets of plywood screwed together. By using two sheets, the platform will be strong and won't bow in the middle under the weight of the camera and operator. This dolly platform, which is 96cm x 82cm, was designed to be wide so that it could accommodate an operator more comfortably. If you want it to be able to pass through doorways then you will need to make it narrower, around 96cm x 60cm.

Securing the tripod to the dolly is always an issue. You could drill holes for the tripod feet, possibly even buy an additional 'spreader' or 'spider' which is permanently secured to the dolly, or construct a lip around the edge so the camera cannot slip.

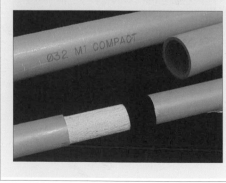

2. The handle

This is what is used by the dolly operator to move the camera and dolly back and forth on the track, although unless it is rigid, you may end up abandoning it and kneeling down to push it by hand, especially over short distances and for slow tracking shots. The handle featured here, in true guerilla film maker style, was fished out of a skip, but there are a hundred and one alternatives at any DIY store. If you do plan to utilise a handle, make sure that it is VERY rigid, which means permanently secured and made of metal or thick wood.

3. The Wheels

The hardest part to construct and one requiring spot on accuracy is the manufacture of the wheel assembly. You'll need to buy four sets of wheels (eight wheels in total). You can find these wheels in department stores, sports shops or dedicated skateboarding shops. If you double the amount of wheels, you will create a more stable dolly, but of course, as the wheels are the biggest expense, almost double the price of making the dolly.

Buy a length of 2" x 2" angle bracket and cut it up into four sections around two inches each. Drill holes on either side, and at the apex (where you will secure the assembly to the dolly), always carefully measuring and marking up before drilling – precision is key to the success of this piece of equipment.

Carefully attach the skateboard wheels, ensuring they are at exactly 90° (right angles). Failure here will result in a wobbly and unsteady dolly.

The assembly is then screwed firmly to a wooden bridging board, which in turn is screwed to the bottom of the dolly – again, making sure all dimensions and angles are correct or perfectly square.

4. The Track

Go to your local DIY shop and buy an even number of lengths of 32mm diameter PVC drain piping (run tests with other sizes if you like). They will probably come in eight foot lengths, and can be joined together using thick wooden stops cut into short lengths. You could also use narrower diameter piping for the joining stops. Beware, these joins in the pipe are always the weakest part of your shot as you will probably get a slight kick as you pass over it.

you should use computers whose monitors can be adjusted to either 50hertz, 75hertz or 100hertz (so it fits into the 25fps frame rate). A computer monitor is nowhere near as 'punchy' as a TV so you will need to do even more exposure tests. For 'Urban Ghost Story' we actually abandoned computer screens for wide shots and used 14" portable tellies being fed by a VHS loop of computer graphics. It worked extremely well and was a very practical solution to an exceptionally fiddly technological wiring nightmare.

End of the day
At the end of each day, the kit will be packed away for the next shooting day. After the daily wrap, the camera assistant will fill out any incomplete camera report sheets, put the exposed stock in cans and give them to a runner who will take it (along with the sound tapes) to the lab. If shooting digitally, the tapes will go straight to the cutting room. The camera assistant may also strip and clean the cameras at this time. A production assistant may also check on how much stock has been shot, and discuss if more needs to be ordered.

Return of kit
After the shoot wraps, getting the equipment back to the hire co. always leads to tears, mainly as you are always late and may incur extra hire charges or at least a stern look! Missing equipment is always a stinger too. That little camera widget that went down the drain was actually worth £300, and that tiny scratch on the lens is gonna cost you £450 to fix. Never mind breaking an HMI bulb which could set you back a grand (depending on the lamp)! Phew! During the shoot, a good habit to get into is to make sure the camera, lighting and grips teams can account for every single piece of kit. Experienced crew members will take care of this stuff as a matter of course. And remember, in order to return the kit at the end, someone will need to drive it to the hire companies (in a hired truck or van too), unload it and check it off the list. With a big lighting rig, this is a day's work for three burly sparks. Budget for this.

Re-shoots
Once the film is in the cutting room, the production team/director/editor will inevitably come up with a list of extra shots and scenes that need to be taken care of. There may well be several pickup shoots many months after the main shot has wrapped, initially focusing on close up shots of props (such as a newspaper or TV screen) and establishing wide shots, a building for instance. With additional re-cuts, new scenes, extra lines or close ups of an actor from an existing scene will have been invented to help tell the story. If care is taken to match eye lines and lighting, it is astonishing what you can get away with – huge continuity errors, mismatching hair cuts, different clothing etc., all can go unnoticed, just so long as it 'feels' right. The camera team for these re-shoots can be minimal, usually the DP and an assistant who will help with everything from changing mags / tapes, to adjusting lights. An enormous amount of shots can be

If you want a high angle shot or a crane shot but cannot afford the expensive grips cranes, you could hire a cheap 'cherry picker', the type of raised platforms used to change light bulbs in street lights. They are not ideal, a bit wobbly, but if you are prepared to compromise, you can pull off some amazing and very cheap shots.

The Mini35 adapter for miniDV

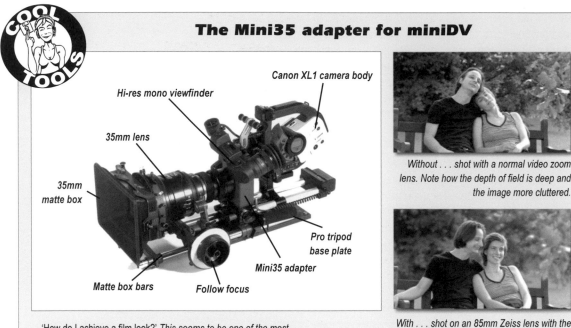

COOL TOOLS

- Canon XL1 camera body
- Hi-res mono viewfinder
- 35mm lens
- 35mm matte box
- Pro tripod base plate
- Mini35 adapter
- Matte box bars
- Follow focus

Without . . . shot with a normal video zoom lens. Note how the depth of field is deep and the image more cluttered.

With . . . shot on an 85mm Zeiss lens with the adapter. Note how the depth of field is narrower and so the couple are more attractively cut out from the background.

'How do I achieve a film look?' *This seems to be one of the most asked questions amongst the low and no budget film making community. The obvious answer is* 'shoot film!' *In my experience that has, more often than not, been impossible – I just haven't had the money to do it. At least for personal projects miniDV has been not just the format of choice, but the only option.*

This leads to question number two, 'So how do I make video look like film?' *There are many characteristics of 'film' that simply can not be replicated with video. The incredible exposure latitude of film remains out of reach for even the most expensive professional video formats, as does colour saturation and resolution. But aesthetically, one of the things that makes film look so much like, well er, film, is the ability to control the depth of field.*

Munich based P+S Technik's Mini35 works on the simple principle that video CCDs are very small and 35mm film negative is comparatively big – when it comes to getting that 'filmic' depth of field, size does count it seems. This is neither the time nor the place for a physics class, so I'll stick to the basics. If you use one of the many adapters available to mount a 35mm cine lens directly to your Canon XL1 you will find that you have converted even the widest of lenses into a virtual telescope! With the Mini35, however, you maintain all of the lens characteristics, as you would if you mounted it to an Arri 535. This is done by projecting the image created by the lens onto an intermediate screen the same size as a 35mm negative, then the image is projected to the cameras 3 CCDs – in effect this is like shooting 35mm and mastering your material onto miniDV. And it works! The images look much more like 35mm film, and the effect can be further enhanced by passing

the footage through a software tool like 'Magic Bullet' in post.

One issue to bear in mind, however, is that focus is much more critical when working with sharp 35mm lenses. Most miniDV cameras have viewfinders and screens that are not sufficiently resolved to judge critical focus, especially when pulling focus. It is recommended that you use a high-resolution field monitor, an LCD monitor, or, if you are working with the XL1, the Canon FU-1000 monochrome viewfinder.

The Mini35 is compatible with 35mm bridge plates, sliding plates, matte boxes and follow focus etc., a full range of film accessories, giving you unprecedented control of your miniDV image. And you aren't limited to expensive cine lenses either. Adapters are available for photo mount lenses such as Canon EF, Leica R and Nikon as well as Panavision anamorphics and other film lenses. The Mini35 is not exclusive to the Canon XL1 and XL1S; there are versions available for the Sony DSR PD150, VX1000 and VX2000 cameras, with an adapter for the Panasonic AG DVX100 in the pipeline for release sometime mid 2003.

For more information about the Mini35 check out their website at www.mini35.de and also www.pstechnik.de .

Jim Loomis, Film maker.

covered in just a few days in these re-shoot weekends, so they're good value. When hiring your DP, make sure that they know there will be re-shoots and that they are happy to come back. Practically, these shoots are like very small short film productions and generally run very smoothly. Everyone knows exactly what shots are needed, the props are to hand, actors are ready etc. It's usually one of the most fun shoots of the whole production.

Gels, trace, spun and the like is used to change the type of light coming from a lamp. It's hellishly expensive stuff too and most crews treat it like office paper, so make sure everyone knows that it needs to be saved and re-used.

Grading

When the movie enters the final stages, whether it was shot on film or digitally, or whether it is being post produced on film, tape or digitally, the DP should make themselves available for the grading process. Ironically many DPs don't get involved in this vital, creative stage of tweaking the image. In the first instance the grader will adjust the images to look consistent, then more work can be carried out to 'sweeten' the image. If you are post producing on film, then there are limitations to the grading process as you can really only mess around with colour balance and brightness (and even then, not too much). However, if you are post producing digitally, at either tape resolution or film resolution, then you can open 'Pandora's Box'. Oh my! Pretty much whatever look you can imagine, given time and money, is achievable. There is a lot of fun to be had here, BUT, these facilities are very expensive, so know what you want before you go in.

DV (miniDV, DVCam etc.)
Marcel Zyskind,
Director of Photography

'Ever since the DV format, be it miniDV or DVCam, came out, we have seen a boom in film making both professionally and non-professionally. This is the greatest advantage of DV. It has allowed you, me and everyone else who wants to make film, documentary, shorts, anything really, just to do it. Film schools use it, the police use it, I use it, your next-door neighbour uses it. Even my mother uses it! You don't have to sit around waiting for finance to show up, everyone with a computer can edit their own film, the same day they shot it. No need for laboratories and big bank accounts. It is a great opportunity for people to learn how to shoot. Make your own film school at home, why not?

I find that one of the things directors love the most about DV is that it gives them the freedom to let their actors improvise for as long as the tape is running in the camera, you can shoot up to an hour of footage on one tape. I think actors, after getting used to it, find DV quite challenging and interesting as well. Producers tend to like it too, since it is cheap. I like it because it has given me the opportunity to shoot films with very interesting directors. It's not all because of DV, but it certainly is one of the reasons. They wanted a young guy with some knowledge of this new format and you might find that many established Directors of Photography do not know the format or do not wish to work with the format. My luck.

I sometimes hear that DV is great because you don't need any lights to shoot. That's true. But you don't always need lights to shoot with film as well. It's all about the look you're trying to achieve. If you want a film shot only with available light, DV is great for that. DV is great to take that bit of 'holiness' that has always surrounded film making and bring it to a 'street level' where we all can have some fun with what we want to do. Shoot movies. In terms of camera selection, it has become somewhat of a jungle out there – there are countless semi-professional and consumer cameras available. If you are planning to buy, do some research and choose a camera with the features that you think suit your needs best. Is it the ability to change lenses, chip size, the size of the camera or what you have been recommended from other users?

Personally I find the Sony PD-150 and the Canon XL-1s to be great cameras. There are pros and cons to both, but the image quality and the cost of the cameras are great. They are easy to work with, they are lightweight, and you can get interesting set-ups that are very difficult to achieve with big film cameras. They can be less obtrusive in documentary film making because of their size and it's possible to be just a one-man camera, whatever the reasons might be. A good example of this might be 'In This World' which I shot for English director Michael Winterbottom. In the film we follow two Afghan refugees from Pakistan to London. We chose to shoot on DVCam on a Sony PD-150 with a 16-9 anamorphic lens on the camera. We were a very small crew and I alone was the camera team. I am not sure we could have made this film on any other format. One thing is certain, the DV format suited this film very well.

The greatest disadvantage of DV is that it is not film. You still do not have the same latitude and depth of field that the use of film stock and film lenses will give you. It is difficult, but not impossible, to fit some of the nice film accessories onto to your DV camera, which can improve the images you shoot. Pick it up, press the red button and you're off. It's never been this easy. The difficult part is getting together the $25 million you need to put your favourite actor in front of the camera . . .'

Super 16mm
Jon Walker,
Director of Photography

'When I began film making, the ideal format to shoot was 1.85:1 for that wider than a TV screen look, for feature films. However, to achieve this golden format without shooting on 35mm meant a sacrifice of quality; you had to 'letterbox' your print. When you're shooting on 16mm, which is a 1.33:1 (4:3) format, you literally chopped the top and bottom off each frame to change the aspect ratio, but you lose a good third of your negative at the same time. The result is rather grainy wide screen. The same letterboxing process is employed in producing 35mm 1.85:1 but the 35mm negative is much bigger and so the resolution loss is not a problem. Shooting Super 16 gives you nearly 50% more negative area in relation to the 1.85:1 format as opposed to shooting standard 16mm. So when there's no real prospect of shooting your masterpiece on 35mm, Super 16 is the obvious choice.

Not so long ago Super 16 was thought of as 'the outsider', there was no reason to shoot it for normal TV production (and some of those masterpieces of only 10 years ago would now look fantastic in 16:9) and only a very few 'low-budget' films stepped over the threshold of standard 16mm to the poor-man's 35mm. It couldn't be more different today. Anything shot on film for TV is now shot on Super 16, and all the broadcast video formats now echo this with 16:9. Certainly, in the UK Super 16 is the perfect film format for low budget film makers.

But enough about the cathode ray tube and more about the silver screen! Super 16 made the dream of 'getting it up there' possible. The results were amazing and the illusion of 35 certainly fooled everyone not 'in the know'! The prospect of post producing in High-Def also raises some very exciting prospects for the future.

So what's so great about Super 16mm? Well it is much cheaper than 35mm. The camera's are smaller and suit guerrilla film making. If shot with care, Super 16mm can produce the same feel and look as the larger 35mm format.

If you plan to blow up to 35mm then the key is to use good lenses and avoid faster stocks. The negative area is small compared to 35mm and therefore the graininess of faster stock can often show. Overexpose the film by a third to a half of a stop to give you a 'fatter' negative. A fatter negative will give you strong denser blacks, thus avoiding the 'milky' look that low-key scenes can sometimes be dogged by on Super 16mm. As for the cameras – they are all good; the Aaton wins on aesthetic grounds but the Arri SR is a tough piece of kit that does the business.

If you intend to blow up to 35mm then its worth testing the lens and filters you intend to use, as any defects will be more obvious on the final 35mm. Also, go easy on filters that modify the look of the image, such as pro-mist filters, because the blow-up process does produce some pro-mist like effects anyway.

35mm is obviously a superior format, but if you cannot afford it, Super 16mm will delight and surprise you. '

Camera 35mm
Gordon Hickie,
Director of Photography

"It still excites me when shooting on 35mm, to think that this small frame of film will fill the entire screen at the Odeon in Leicester Square. Although the actual 35mm frame is smaller than a 35mm stills camera frame due to the orientation of the film (vertical for motion picture film, opposed to horizontal for stills), the quality is still quite amazing. It has detail and a warmth and depth that 16mm and video still doesn't quite match. Although nowadays, with the advances in Hi Definition video technology and the quality of 16mm filmstocks, the gap has closed somewhat. Super 16mm is a great format but when you put 35mm side by side with it, the difference is very apparent. 35mm contains so much more detail, it's sharper, does not suffer from weave, and photographically it produces more attractive images. Also 35mm has a larger gate, so for example, you'll need a 50mm lens on a 35mm camera to achieve the same angle of view as a 25mm lens on a 16mm camera. It also produces a more pleasing image due to the narrower depth of field inherent in the size of the negative.

The question a film maker has to ask themselves is whether there is the budget for 35mm. A 1000' roll of 35mm film, which runs for approximately ten minutes, is much more expensive than a 400' roll of Super 16mm that runs for the same time – around three to four times as much. It's physically bigger and requires a larger camera, lenses and magazines. Although the camera crew stays the same size – a DP, camera operator, focus-puller and clapper / loader, moving the equipment from A to B takes more time and energy and requires real muscle power. So production set-up times tend to take longer. The advantage Super 16mm has over 35mm is that you can move around quicker and shoot more film without worrying as much about your budget. If, however, you are shooting on Super 16mm and plan to blow up your negative to 35mm, this can be expensive and may outweigh your shooting costs, so it's up to the producer to think this through carefully.

It doesn't really bother me what 35mm camera I use, as long as it's quiet (to keep the sound department happy!) and has a good range of lenses.

When it comes to grading, 35mm and 16mm are very similar, except for the noticeable grain difference and picture clarity. I recently saw some High Definition v 35mm comparison tests, which involved a short film shot on both formats. There were split screen sequences comparing the two and to be honest, the actual difference was extremely hard to distinguish, although it was only being viewed on a high quality broadcast monitor and not a cinema screen. I am usually able to spot the differences between most formats, but then I am an experienced technician who spends his life looking at camera images – I should be able to tell, it's my job! Often though, the public don't 'see' what the film is shot on. They are engaged in the story and characters. And remember, if the script and performances are bad, it doesn't matter what the film is shot on, it will still be a bad film.

I love American TV shows like 'The Sopranos' and 'The West Wing' as they are shot on 35mm, and the quality speaks for itself. If I were on a big budget film shoot tomorrow, I'd shoot on 35mm without question. But, for the new film maker, getting your film in the can is what's important, not the format it's shot on.'

Camera HiDef
John-Martin White,
Director of Photography

'As a DP, I am very experienced with all formats. A lot of people new to High Definition go in with the attitude that you don't need to light as extensively as with film. This is wrong. It needs a lot of work and skill. HD has a smaller contrast range and latitude than film. Latitude can be up to 11 stops with film, but with HD, its around 7-8 stops. Of course this depends on the set-up. A lot of film DPs are put off by electronic menus and high-tech gadgetry but nowadays, there is a selection of set-up cards available and when you know the look you want, you simply pop in the correct card and the camera is automatically set up for you. You can even create your own set-ups and incorporate them. However, the camera is still very sophisticated and has lots of technology that enables the DP to tweak each individual image.

Shooting HD is a bit like 400-500ASA film stock without the grain. Shooting outdoors is slightly trickier than with film, as highlights can look slightly electronic, but this can usually be treated in post. Scanning it out to film will also reduce any digital artefacts, neatly replacing them with grain. With film, you normally overexpose slightly for negative, but with HD you should slightly underexpose. If you over expose it, you'll burn out the image and lose the ability to bring it down in the grade. By underexposing you have the latitude to push the image, peak the whites and hold down the top end.

The camera works in a similar way to a digi-beta camera, except it has two modes – Interlaced (as per video which is very sharp and crisp) and Progressive scan which scans the image at 25fps (or 24fps) giving the image a near perfect film 'look'. The creators have done a lot of work to create this illusion. Even the camera viewfinder flickers in the same way as a 35mm camera, which can be a little off-putting when a DP new to HD picks it up. But I really believe HD is the way forward, especially with the fantastic HD projection systems now becoming available. The image quality is amazing and the Panavision and Fuji lenses are just breathtaking. I've also found that film tends to need more grading. You still need the same camera team with HD as with a film shoot. Obviously you don't get hairs in the gate and problems like that, but you can get 'head clog' which the loader needs to keep an eye out for. I lost an expensive crane shot once because we didn't check, and what was shot was unusable. I'd recommend that a HD broadcast monitor be used when shooting. This way you can see exactly what the camera is seeing. It's so much nicer than the crappy image you get from a video assist when shooting on film. It's also a good way to check the focus properly as the standard definition viewfinders aren't great. A HiDef camera can sit well on the shoulder and weighs in at approximately 8 kilos. The more modern cameras also have the ability to shoot slow motion, and when I saw the quality of this, I was completely blown away. It's amazing. The sound quality is also fantastic.

HD cameras are expensive to hire (but deals can always be done) but the tapes are cheap at around £40 (for 40 minutes). This has to be weighed up against stock, development, telecine, neg cutting and printing costs. I'm still excited by both film and HD and can't really express a preference. I do believe, however, that HiDef is an excellent medium for the new film maker. It gives just that bit more flexibility than film. And not having to wait to view rushes is a blessing. But the same disciplines are required, as it's easy to get carried away or play around with the menus during valuable shooting time.

I see HD as a new format rather than a successor to film. It's like we've been working with crayons for the last one hundred years. Now we have felt tips.'

Film stills

Shooting stills on a film can often feel like a chore and frequently gets left to one side as 'someone else's problem'. Delegate this vital job to someone with common sense and some experience, ideally a photographer who shoots film stills and knows what's required. Without lots of decent stills, you won't be able to sell your film, and extracting stills directly from the film itself won't provide the technical quality required.

While digital technology is sweeping the world, movie photos still tend to be shot on 35mm stills film stock. It also represents the best value for money when it comes to the cameras. You may be shooting your film on a domestic DV camera, but there is an expectation of extremely high quality where stills are concerned, and so the 'point and shoot' camera just isn't the tool of choice. However, any decent SLR with a good lens is up to the job, if it's in the right hands. When shooting stills on a film set, you won't use a flash and you will rely on the actual 'film lights', which surprisingly, are often NOT that bright. Fast lenses and higher ASA film stocks are the answer.

35mm equipment

There's no need buy the top Canon EOS camera, but the choice of lens is more important. Any good zoom lens could do the job, but remember that movies are often shot in lower lighting conditions, which might be impossible for a cheap zoom lens (as it needs a lot of light to expose properly). A zoom is fine for general stuff, but add to this some fixed focal length lenses (which tend to have wider apertures and therefore need less light). A standard 50mm lens is quite cheap AND has a large aperture of say F/1.7, which is a great all rounder. Probably the best lens to get if you can only afford a single one. A 28mm wide angle lens won't come cheap at F/1.7, but there are lots of good value F/2.8 lenses. If you can afford it,

you could also get a 100mm lens for portrait shots. Ideally, blag an old camera kit from a pro photographer. Although you may end up delivering your stills digitally, the quality and flexibility of film gives you more scope than shooting digital stills. The best combination is to shoot large numbers of 35mm stills on set with the action and possibly some medium format portraits of the main cast, and maybe some set-up action set pieces too.

Shooting on set

The point of a good film still is to capture the essence of the film – which means you will use the lighting and set-ups of the actual film. You won't have time to set up flashes either as the main cast and crew will just steamroller over your ideas. A stills photographer will only ever get a moment to snap off their shots. A good time to shoot stills is when rehearsals are taking place. The light and actors are set, but there's less danger of the stills camera causing a distraction. A good stills photographer should have an eye for a special moment and maybe take the opportunity to shoot extra stuff with the actors, where the photographer is 'calling the shots' for the best still picture. This usually takes place after a shot has taken place and the camera team are checking 'playback' or 'the gate'. Most scenes won't warrant stills being taken, but those that do, deserve extra effort. Often a pushed crew doesn't see the point of stills, but as a producer you can't make this mistake. A mixture of stills is good, some that directly reflect the shots in the film, and some that are posed. The stills photographer should try to capture what the film camera is filming, but there can be a problem as the actors are always 'in action' and therefore you may miss the moments captured so well by the movie camera. Still images have to tell the 'full story' whereas the moving image shows only parts of the story. That's why shooting some posed photos is a good idea, in order to capture the essence of a scene in a way suited to the still image. Avoid using flash photography as this will produce pictures radically different from the look of the film. Don't forget the odd shot of the crew too . . . if the film is a hit, the making of it might also be of interest to people. The director with the camera is an obvious shot that is essential for film festivals for instance.

Publicity

If time and money can stretch to it, shoot some specific images on a medium format. These shots may be used to create posters and other high profile images and they will need to be glossy and sharp. This is the 'fashion shoot' for the film and so it's worth getting an experienced photographer to do this.

above – three key photographic images used for my second feature film, the serial killer thriller 'White Angel'

Film to use

Traditionally one would shoot colour reversal (slides) but the world is changing . . . You could now just use shoot negatives and scan these at high resolution. These can also produce black and white images if required. Stick to the major brands, Kodak and Fuji, and as lighting can be minimal, you may need to shoot with a higher ASA to get good exposures . . . which means 400 ASA, and ideally 100 or 200 ASA in daylight. Avoid going over 400 ASA.

Catering Blueprint

Napoleon once said, 'an army marches on its stomach'. The same is true of a film crew. If you feed people with lots of good quality, high energy, healthy, and ideally hot food, you will get increased performance and decreased moaning. Many film makers make the simple mistake of under estimating how involving the job of the caterer can be, and end up producing very low quality food and spending more than they should. Plan, plan, plan.

Tea, coffee and water
The lubricant of a film crew, needing a kettle or water cooler, bins, cups, sugar and milk. You MUST supply this.

Snacks
If you can, snacks will always go down well, be they unhealthy freebie choccy bars or healthy fruit.

Breakfast
Up to you whether you supply this, but it's a major headache on top of all the major headaches involved in the making of your film!

Lunch
Sandwiches, baguettes and huge bread rolls are usually the best option, cheap, large, healthy and portable.

Dinner
Should be hot and in large quantities. Don't underestimate how important this is to a cold, tired crew on a winter's night shoot in the drizzle!

Elsewhere
If you can give your crew cash to buy lunch, or if you can do a deal with a local pub or café, that will save you a major logistical nightmare.

Catering Blueprint

The caterer is the person whose job it is to feed the cast and crew so that no time is wasted during the essential re-fuelling of everyone involved.

Catering for a large group of people is a much more involved task than most would initially think. It takes a lot of preparation and planning to get it right, and when you consider a film may shoot for four weeks without a real break, there really is no room to get it wrong. The secret to good film catering is to keep it simple. Don't attempt to provide exquisite and extraordinarily diverse dishes, just stick to a number of wholesome, easy to prepare (and serve), cost effective, healthy and hot meals. You are not preparing a four course meal for the Queen, you are re-fuelling a film crew. As long as the food is of an acceptable standard, and that there is enough of it, the crew will rarely complain.

Who to hire?

Professional film caterers are very good at what they do, but they are also expensive, often charging anywhere between £10-£15 per person, per day. So lets do the math, a twenty person crew with fifteen actors is going to cost anywhere between £350-£525 per day! And shooting for four weeks, that's £9,800-£12,600 in total. Clearly, out of our budget. Other professional caterers are a possibility, such as people who cater for weddings, but unless they have a fascination with movies or some other benevolent motive, they're going to end up doing it on the cheap. Most professional caterers will produce truly crap food if they are forced to do it on the cheap. They are a business and want to make money, and frankly, they will always place their profit margin above the crew's bellies. Another reason to hire a friend or family member who cares. Your best option is a friend or family member with catering experience and a desire to help and do the best job. It isn't rocket science, but you do have to love it or you will end up making cheap schlop. Asking around my film maker buddies, I consistently heard *'my mum did it'*, *'my sister-in-law did it'*, *'my ex-girlfriend did it'* . . . and all of them received glowing compliments.

What are you asking of a friend or family member when they get roped into feeding your cast and crew? First and most obvious, there's a lot of cooking to do. There's also a lot of running around buying stuff, taking stuff to set, setting up shop on set at regular meal breaks, clearing the mess, even managing tea and coffee. Make no mistake, this is as involved as the camera team or make-up and costume. It's not something for the weekend or *'I will knock it up after*

Script, cast and er, catering? Everyone asks. Sure they want to make a great movie, win awards, dazzle an audience, but . . . 'what about the food? Tell me the catering is gonna be good and I will do the movie!'

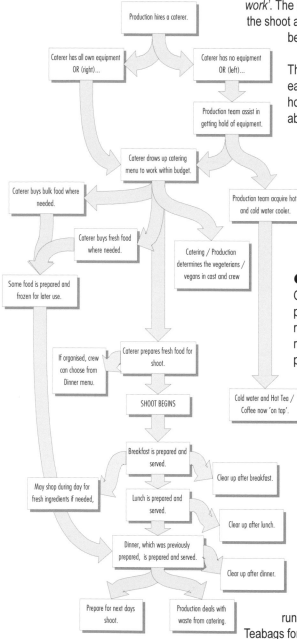

**Catering
Blueprint
Flow chart**

work'. The caterer should really be brought on board at least a week before the shoot and if you can afford it or persuade them, a couple of weeks before hand so that they have ample time to prepare better food.

The trick is planning. A cast and crew don't really care what they eat, as long as it provides them with sufficient energy, it is tasty and hot, it is healthy (ideally, but not essential) and most of all, there is absolutely loads of it.

I suggest drawing up a rotating six day menu. There will only ever be six main meals to conquer. Enough variety to get through a whole week, but not so much as to overwhelm the caterer with new culinary nightmares. At the end of this chapter, there are a number of simple main meal menus that will keep any cast and crew chugging along at an acceptable rate of knots.

Quality control

Good food always starts with good ingredients. Wherever possible, do not skimp on the ingredients to save a few pennies, rather find ingenious and new ways of acquiring the ingredients rather than just going to the local supermarket. Given time, a production assistant should be able to cut competitive deals with a few local suppliers who fancy their name on the credits of a movie and a ticket to the premiere. Local greengrocers, for instance, can be an extremely cheap and excellent source of top notch, fresh fruit and veg. Trade supply supermarkets like Makro are excellent for other ingredients, such as pasta and rice. Work hard enough and you will find a local bakers who will do an amazing deal for daily fresh bread. All of this pre-production work will take much longer than you think, but it will keep costs down and more importantly, provide the caterer with quality ingredients as and when needed.

Buy enough

Another common mistake made by new film makers is that they don't buy enough, choosing to *'economise'*. Of course what always happens is that whatever they have *'economised'* on runs out and has to be bought at top dollar from a supermarket. Teabags for instance. Do the maths. Twenty crew, fifteen actors, four weeks, three cups a day . . . equals, get this, nearly two and a half thousand teabags! That's also plastic cups, stirrers and spoons, sugar, milk, black bin bags to put the empty cups in too etc.

So in the week before the shoot begins, as you wander up and down the aisles of Makro wondering how much you should buy, don't skimp. Do the

Hot and cold water coolers

One of the most important issues for a crew is tea and coffee (and water as people can easily get dehydrated). If you have a sink nearby, you could use that with a couple of kettles, but the most elegant and cost effective solution is to get a hot and cold water cooler, the kind you see in offices with a large upturned bottle of water on the top. You will then have a constant supply of instant chilled and boiling water. The coolers can be rented for very little, although a good production manager should be able to blag one for free. Failing that, most companies offer a free two week trial, so take 'em up on it, then send it back and go to another company for another free trial! A crew will work their way through a staggering amount of water so either commit to buying it from the water company or figure out in advance how to refill the water bottles and give someone the job of dealing with it twice a day.

As for tea, coffee, plastic cups, sugar and milk . . . buy well in advance and buy in bulk. Always have a large bin next to the water cooler or run the risk of your set becoming littered with plastic cups and possible spillages.

maths and buy the stuff. You will need a large estate car for this visit, as you will be stocking up on stuff like plastic cutlery, plates, cups, napkins, cling film, greaseproof paper, tea, coffee, sugar, dried milk (for when you inevitably run out of fresh milk), blah blah. It's not a cheap business feeding a cast and crew.

The Plan

So here's what your caterer needs to commit to . . .

Breakfast – Are you going to supply it? Traditionally the film business supplies breakfast for its cast and crew as they start work so early. Personally, I think that as you are working on a low budget film, it's entirely appropriate to say *'breakfast is served ten minutes after you get out of bed in your kitchen! Please feed yourself'*. If you want to provide a token morning 'thank you' for your cast and crew, ask the caterer to supply a toaster and maybe even bake some muffins. If you really want to get serious, you could offer bacon butties, which always goes down a storm. But that will carry a cost and an additional amount of work to be done. So far, on the three feature films I have made, I have never had to provide breakfast and received only a few niggles (crew members, my e-mail is chris@livingspirit.com if you want to moan BTW).

Lunch – Served at midday, lunch should be large and portable. Huge baguettes filled with a variety of fillings, catering for both meaties and veggies, will always go down well. You can get away with this most days, but too much of it and a crew will start to moan. An occasional hot meal at lunchtime, be it baked potatoes or soup with bread, will always go down well.

Dinner – This is the main meal of the day (occasionally, you may not even need to cater for it, as you wrap before dinnertime), see the recipes. This meal is even more important when you are looking at a night shoot, and you may end up providing a dinner at

Make it the job of a PA or runner to make sure the director always gets lunch delivered to them. The director will rarely get a chance to make it to the dining area as they will always be dealing with other problems, viewing rushes, chatting to actors etc . . .

Sue Bamford
Caterer

'Food should be kept either cold or hot, but never warm – warm food is where bacteria grow. Invest in a food thermometer. The danger zone lies between 5°C and 63°C – within this range bacteria can multiply very quickly. So keep food above or below this range. Check your fridge temperature and make sure chilled food is kept below the legal maximum of 8°C, but ideally below 5°C. Hot food needs to be kept above 63°C, and when re-heating, make sure the centre of the food is piping hot, 70°C, for at least three minutes to be safe.

Food that is served at room temp, such as sandwiches, shouldn't be allowed to sit around before eating – especially true of anything containing meat, egg, or egg products such as mayo. Keep sarnies in the fridge until 20 mins before they are needed and do not keep them past two hours out of the fridge. Rice and pasta are also prime growing mediums for nasties, so make sure everything gets piping hot (if pre-cooked) and stays piping hot. After that it must be disposed of, and never, ever re-freeze food. Freshly made food for later use needs to be cooled fast and then either refrigerated or frozen.

The second basic rule is to avoid cross contamination. Keep raw and cooked foods separate, as well as any utensils or chopping boards. Raw meat should always go at the bottom of the fridge to avoid any possible drips. Your hands, tea towels, wiping cloths etc., will be the easiest source of cross contamination. Professional kitchens don't have tea towels as they're perfect breeding grounds for bugs. Use pull down roll from catering suppliers instead and remember to wash your hands thoroughly after handling raw foods, refuse (taking the bin bags out), blowing your nose or going to the loo!'

midnight instead of seven in the evening. The order of business is as usual, lots of it, hot, tasty and ideally good quality too.

Onset Extras – At all times, the cast and crew should have access to tea and coffee making facilities. This can be as simple as a kettle in the corner or a hot and cold water cooler. A large bowl of fruit constantly re-stocked with apples, oranges, and any other fruit that is in season and cost effective from the grocers (beware of bananas that bruise easily). For the sugar hit fiends, its a good idea to have cakes and muffins available and not chocolate bars. Rather than buy these, ask your caterer to bake them up. If you have a friend or relative who declined doing the catering but was kind of interested, ask them if they would undertake the job of making a shed load of cakes and muffins.

Head count – Central to the caterers equations will be the head count. How many people are they actually catering for? This may sound simple, as you could easily count your cast and crew. But here's the thing. There's always more people than you expect. Whether it's a visiting journalist, a couple of investors, an extra runner or an additional cast member, no one wants to go without their lunch! The upshot is that the caterer will always prepare a few extra meals.

Create the menu

Key to the caterer's job is the menu. This is the agreed list of meals that they will provide. As I said earlier, keep it simple. Wherever possible, the caterer should prepare meals in advance and either refrigerate or freeze for later consumption. For instance, the caterer could cook a meal that is three times more than they need, and from that one single 'cooking session' they could feed the crew on the day of cooking with the first third, then three days later with the refrigerated third, and ten days later with the final frozen third. One cooking session then provides for three major meals (remember to clearly label what you refrigerate and freeze, with what it is and when it should be used by). Create this menu as early as you can so that the production team have their say and the caterer can get on with sorting everything.

Catering for vegetarians and vegans is a major headache, well it is for me, as I am not a vegetarian! Just accept that a large portion of cast and crew will be vegetarian and you will have to cater for them. The upside of vegetarian food is that on the whole it is cheaper to make and healthier. Most of the recipes that we have suggested in this book are either vegetarian to start off with, or there is a vegetarian option that is easy to accommodate. Beware of vegans though, as they will make the caterer's life an absolute misery. Do not hire vegans. Sorry. You know my e-mail. Flame away.

Catering rough budget

This catering budget does not include food for meals, just basic supplies. It is split into two halves, supplies *and* equipment to blag. *The equipment, quite simply, should not be paid for. Ask around friends and family and you will get most of it without much effort. A production assistant should then be able to fill in the gaps. Of course, there may well be much more equipment needed too, not to mention a kitchen in which to put it all!*

Supplies	No.	Each	Total
Large roll of cling film (300 metres)	1	£3.35	£4.35
Large roll of tin foil (100 metres)	1	£12.75	£13.75
Large roll of grease proof paper (50 metres)	2	£4.15	£6.15
Plastic cups (2000 in packets of 200)	10	£1.69	£11.69
Foam cups (1000 in packets of 50)	10	£1.65	£11.65
Plates (1000 in packets of 100)	10	£3.99	£13.99
Dishes (1000 in packets of 50)	20	2.99	£22.99
Forks (1000 in packets of 200)	5	2.99	£7.99
Knives (1000 in packets of 200)	5	2.99	£7.99
Spoons (1000 in packets of 200)	5	2.99	£7.99
Stirrers (Box of 1000)	1	6.99	£7.99
Sanitiser (bacterial) 1 litre	5	£1.25	£6.25
100 bin bags	1	£9.99	£10.99
Salt and Pepper - shakers	1	£3.99	£4.99
Napkins (2000)	1	£7.99	£8.99
Kitchen roll	20	£0.75	£20.75
Large bottle of ketchup (1.3kg)	3	£1.99	£4.99
Tea bags (1000)	2	£15.79	£17.79
Coffee (1kg)	2	£11.90	£13.90
Coffee mate (1.5kg)	1	5	£6.00
Sugar (box of 600 sachets)	1	£3.69	£4.69
Wall paper table	1	9.99	£9.99

	TOTAL	£225.86

Equipment to blag
Serving spoons
Several large pans and pots
6 large bakers trays
Oven gloves
Cooler and cooler blocks
Apron
Hand whisk
Baking trays
Kettle (hot water)
Blender of some sort
Microwave ovens
Meat thermometer
A car to put it in!

As for the supplies (left), well it's pretty much basic requirements. The prices here are from the cash and carry superstore Makro and represent good value – but you should really try and get it all for free. Get a production assistant on the list now! You'll be surprised where a great PA can scrounge 2000 tea bags!

Get the kit

Assuming you haven't hired a professional caterer, whoever is going to do all the catering is going to need quite a lot of specialised equipment. First and most obvious, you're going to need a kitchen and a big one too! Ideally, the production manger may have found a local facility such as a closed down school or village hall with catering facilities, and that can be used as the catering base. Failing that, you will end up cooking from somebody's kitchen. The problem with your average run of the mill kitchen is that it's often too small and equipment such as the fridge, oven and hobs are hopelessly inadequate. However, as is so often with low budget film making, you are seldom left with a choice and you will have to make it work.

You're going to need some major pots and pans too! Usually, this kind of stuff can be borrowed from some other outfit that has to deal with catering, a job for a production assistant. There is more specialised equipment too, like blenders, food processors, large baking trays, large storage tubs for storing and freezing food etc.

If you have a young crew, you may get away with poor food as, after all, many of them will still enjoy junk and fast food. But on the whole, actors of any age are very conscious of what they eat and will demand a much higher standard of catering (as will older, more professional crew members).

EXPERT OPINION

Jill Irwin
Wild Cuisine

'On the low-budget films, a lot of people aren't being paid, so as long as they are kept going with food, everyone does a better job on the production. Because my partner is so skilled and all the food is homemade, we can produce something which looks high class but costs a little less. But in our business we need a minimum fee to supply catering, and the big problem is always low numbers. The more people there are, the more reasonable we can be. But the fewer the numbers so we are forced to charge more per head as we can't buy in bulk. There are minimum overheads. If a producer came to us and wanted to only pay for costs, we're not a charity, so we couldn't do that.

You should take into account how much there is to think about, such as licences on the street (council permissions usually involve money) and water and power. We can usually supply the power, which is a bonus, but many companies can't do this. But water and rubbish, for instance, can become major problems, especially if you are economising.

'We've done two or three low budget films where the producers were funding the whole thing themselves and the task of catering for everyone is daunting. We recently did a privately financed feature film where there was no dining bus and everyone sat outside with their meals. Luckily it never rained. Make sure you research all of your locations and figure out beforehand how the catering is going to be run.'

Food containers like the ones you get from a takeaway restaurant are ideal for storing ready made individual portions that just need re-heating. Transporting food to a cast and crew (if you're not going to deal with preparing and re-heating on location) can be a bigger problem than you might expect. The best way of dealing with this is to get hold of six or so bakers trays, the ones you often see outside a bakery and are used to transport loaves.

The caterer should also have a fully kitted estate car, possibly with a couple of microwave ovens in the back (that just need power from a socket someplace on set).

One major decision to make before the shoot begins is what kind of plates and cutlery are you going to use. Everyone likes to eat off a real crockery plates with metal knives and forks, but the problem is that the plates often break, they are heavy, and someone has to wash them. At the other extreme, there are paper plates with plastic cutlery, which the crew throw away after each meal. Neat and tidy but not very environmentally friendly, and no matter what anyone tells you, it's a real bugger to eat dinner off a flimsy paper plate, especially on a freezing night at 11pm, with inadequate lighting and a light drizzle! The half way house is toughened plastic crockery and cutlery, which won't break easily, is tough, durable and light. On the downside, it still needs to be washed, but that's not too much to ask, especially if you have access to a big dishwasher. The easiest option is still paper plates and plastic knives though.

The shoot – setting up shop

The caterer will go through a regular routine at mealtimes. It will start with preparing the food, either on location or elsewhere (with a plan to transporting the food to location). Just before mealtime, the caterer will set up a trestle table (that's a wallpaper table that should cost you £10 from your local DIY shop) with a paper table cloth for hygiene. The idea is to get a fast moving production line going, where cast and crew line up and are quickly and efficiently served their meal. At one end, they will have clean plates, cutlery and napkins. This will be followed by the actual food, served by the caterer and most likely a couple of production assistants that are roped in each and every meal time. Further on down the table, there will probably be a bowl of fruit, maybe some muffins, tea and coffee making facilities, cold water, and maybe some squash for those who need a little sugar with their water. Salt, pepper and sugar will always be to hand, as will ketchup – and don't buy the cheap ketchup as everyone will complain. At the end of this smorgasbord of culinary delights, there will be a large black bin bag stapled to the end to collect all the waste after feeding.

The crew will take about half an hour to actually eat and another half hour spread out before and after when they will have a rest, a chitter chatter, make that phone call, have a fag and make a cup of coffee before wandering back to set and their duties. Always allow adequate time for people to eat in comfort and do their stuff, but do keep the momentum up, as few of us relish the thought of getting back to hard and strenuous work after a large, lovely hot meal.

Once the crew have finished eating, the caterer will clear up the devastation and immediately begin work on the next meal. At some point, someone will have to deal with the rubbish, which might mean a trip to the local dump for a runner in a car. The caterer will also check that there is enough water, tea, coffee, squash, sugar, milk, fruit and muffins available to get through to the next major meal break.

An alternative to catering can be a well organised production team who cut a deal with a local pub or take-away close to where the production is shooting each day. The advantage of a pub is that it will have loos and a place, in from the cold, where everyone can sit and eat, but watch out for crew members drinking booze at lunch time!

Petty cash

However you plan to pay your caterer, make sure they always have a healthy cash float for unexpected necessities. Milk is one of the most common problems, as it quickly runs out or goes off. And no cast or crew member will ever understand why they can't have milk in their tea or coffee!

In summary

Remember, catering is mostly about delivering large amounts of good quality, hot and tasty food at regular intervals. It doesn't need to be great, but it does need to be good. Basic health and safety should always be adhered to unless you want half your cast and crew chucking up and losing a couple of days shooting. Hire someone who really wants to do the best job because they have an emotional investment in either you, the film maker, or the project, and not someone who can *'do it for the money'*.

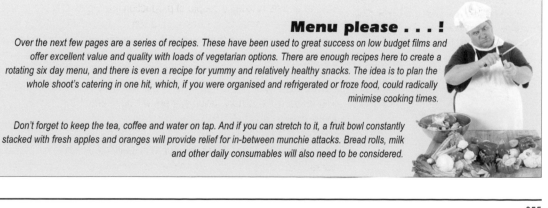

Menu please . . . !

Over the next few pages are a series of recipes. These have been used to great success on low budget films and offer excellent value and quality with loads of vegetarian options. There are enough recipes here to create a rotating six day menu, and there is even a recipe for yummy and relatively healthy snacks. The idea is to plan the whole shoot's catering in one hit, which, if you were organised and refrigerated or froze food, could radically minimise cooking times.

Don't forget to keep the tea, coffee and water on tap. And if you can stretch to it, a fruit bowl constantly stacked with fresh apples and oranges will provide relief for in-between munchie attacks. Bread rolls, milk and other daily consumables will also need to be considered.

Sandy Bamford's World Famous Passion Cake

Why? *It's a great mid morning or late afternoon snack, highly nutritious and healthy compared to a chocolate bar. Can also be used for making muffins for breakfast.*

Prep time – *20 minutes*
Cooking time – *45–50 minutes*
Approx cost per head – *£0.40*
Serves 24

Main cake
3 large carrots, 450g crushed pineapple, a cup and a half of light veg. oil, 4 eggs, 300g self-raising flour, 500g brown demerera sugar, 2 tsp baking powder, 1 tsp salt, 2 tsp ground cinnamon, 1½ cups of mixed, chopped nuts.

Icing (optional)
200g Philadelphia, 50g butter, 500g icing sugar, 1 tsp vanilla essence, a handful of chopped, mixed nuts.

Making the cake
Grate three large carrots and put into a large bowl. Open and drain the tin of crushed pineapple and add to the bowl of carrots. Add a cup and a half of light vegetable oil to the mixture. Add four eggs and mix the ingredients thoroughly.

Take a second bowl and add 283g of self-raising flour. Add 500g of brown demerera sugar and a teaspoon of salt and mix the ingredients. Add 2 teaspoons of ground cinnamon and a cup and a half of mixed, chopped nuts and again, mix the ingredients thoroughly. Add the dry ingredients to the wet ingredients and mix thoroughly. Yes, we know, it looks like sick, but it will make a gorgeous cake!

Pour the mix into a deep grease-proof pan and spread evenly. Put into a preheated oven for 45-50 mins (gas mark 4, 180° c)

Making the optional but very yummy icing
Add 200g of Philadelphia cream cheese to a bowl with 50g butter. Add 500g of icing sugar and stir. Add 1 teaspoon of vanilla essence (not just vanilla flavour) to the bowl and blend the ingredients until they are pulped. Once the cake has cooled, spread the icing evenly over the cake and sprinkle some mixed, chopped nuts over the icing if desired.

Don Corleone's Spaghetti Meat Balls

Why? *It's a tasty, cheap and nutritious dinner that can be prepared and stored in a fridge or even frozen. You can also use Quorn as a veggie alternative (add an extra egg to the mixture if you do this). This is a real crew winner.*

Prep time – *20 mins*
Cooking time
10 mins for meatballs
10-15 mins for sauce
3 mins for spaghetti
Approx cost per head – *£1.50*
Serves 10

Meatballs
1kg mince, a bunch of spring onions, 3 tbsp dried crushed chilli, 2 eggs, 2 handfuls of plain flour, a pinch of salt and pepper, 2 tbsp vegetable oil

Tomato Sauce
2 tbsp vegetable oil, 2 large Spanish onions, a head of celery, 3 mixed peppers, 1 fennel bulb, a handful of fresh parsley, 2 tbsp garlic puree, 28g butter, 227g chestnut mushrooms, 2 800g cans of chopped tomatos (with out herbs), 6 tbsp tomato puree, a handful of basil, 250g pasta/spaghetti

Making the meatballs
To a large bowl add the mince (whatever meat is desired, or Quorn). Finely chop a whole bunch of spring onion and add to mince. Add the eggs and dried, crushed chilli to the bowl and mix thoroughly. Take an empty bowl and line it with flour, then season it with salt and pepper. Take some of the meat mixture and roll into a squash ball sized ball. Roll it in the flour. Prepare a heavy bottomed frying pan with 2tbsp vegetable oil and heat. Add meatballs to the pan and batch fry them for 10 minutes, turning occasionally.

Making the sauce
Take a deep saucepan and add 2tbsp vegetable oil and heat. Roughly chop up two onions, chop the head of celery and add both to the saucepan. Roughly chop the peppers, (remove the pith and seeds) and add to the pan. Chop up the fennel bulb and 50g of parsley, (plus a few stalks) and add to the pan. Add 2tbsp of garlic puree and mix, then leave to simmer. Take the mushrooms and chop in half, then fry in 1oz butter until brown (in a separate pan). Once the sauce has cooked down for 5 minutes, add 800g of chopped tomatoes and 6 tbsp tomato puree (along with half a pint of cold water). Add the chopped basil and mix, then cook for a further 10 mins. Blend (with blender) the sauce so it is still slightly chunky and add the mushrooms. Add parsley to the sauce as garnish.

Making the spaghetti
Allow 50g weight of uncooked pasta per person (ideally quick cook spaghetti). Boil water in a pan, adding a pinch of salt and 1 tbsp olive oil then add spaghetti for three mins. Drain through a colander and serve.

Attack of the Killer Carrot and Coriander Soup

Why? *Cos it's just so damn yummy, and it's healthy too. It's filling and easy to prepare, best of all you can keep it simmering for hours, serving to cold and tired crew members in polystyrene cups. Can be prepared and frozen, then heated up later.*

Prep time – *15 mins*
Cooking time – *15 mins*
Approx cost per head – *£0.50*
Serves 5

Carrot and coriander soup
2 large Spanish onions
2 tbsp veg. oil
A large bunch of fresh Coriander
1 tbsp garlic puree
454g carrots
5 tbsp of Marigold Swiss vegetable stock
1 packet of pre-heated frankfurters (optional)

Making the soup

Add 2 tbsp of vegetable oil to a deep saucepan. Add the finely chopped onions to the pan and stir for four minutes. Wash the coriander and leave to drain. Add 1 tbsp of garlic puree to the pan. Grate 454g of carrots and add to the pan once the onions are browned off. Add 5 tbsp of vegetable stock to the ingredients. Add 4 pints water to the pan and leave to simmer for 10mins. Cut the stalks off the coriander and finely chop the remainder. Add half of the chopped coriander to the saucepan and blend (with hand blender) the soup mixture until it is slightly chunky.

Add a handful of fresh coriander to the pulped soup as garnish. Serve with loads of fresh and scrumptious bread.

For the non veggies

To give the soup a meaty, smoky flavour, add 6 frankfurters (whole) to the mixture and simmer for 6mins. Then remove them, blend the soup, and chop the frankfurters to add to the soup as a meaty crouton. Mmmmm.

The Tony Montana 'F**K YOU!' Burger

Why? *Burgers (for veggies and meaties) are always a favourite with the crew, and these veggie burgers are mouth watering. Even though they are made of lentils, I have found them not too windy too!*

Prep time – *20 mins*
Cooking time – *45 mins*
Approx cost per head – *£1.60*
Serves 5

The Tony Montana 'FK YOU!' Burger**
3 tbsp vegetable oil
1 clove of garlic
1 large Spanish onion
2 tbsp tomato puree
1 bunch watercress
1 tbsp fresh mint
2 tbsp plain flour
113g mixed, chopped nuts
1pint of Swiss vegetable stock
227g lentils
lettuce and tomato for garnish
5 burger buns

Making the burgers

Take a large frying pan, add some vegetable oil and heat. Crush the garlic clove and add along with the finely chopped onion. Cook for 2 minutes at a low heat. Add the lentils and stir. Add a pint of vegetable stock and leave to simmer for 40 mins (cover the pan). Once the stock has evaporated remove the pan from the heat and add a pinch of salt and pepper. Crush the lentils and add the 2 tbsp of tomato puree and stir. Add the mixed, chopped nuts, the chopped watercress and chopped mint.

Take a separate bowl and line with flour and season the bowl with salt and pepper and 1 tbsp olive oil. Take a tennis ball sized amount of the mixture and roll it in flour and add it to a frying pan of hot vegetable oil and fry for 5 mins each side. Garnish with fresh lettuce and put into burger bun.

For a meaty mix instead of veggie, simply use the meat balls recipe from Don Corleone's Spaghetti Meat Balls, and make burger sized patties instead of meat balls. Both veggie and non veggie can be prepared and stored in a freezer.

Maddame LuLu's Veggie Pasta

Why? *Because it's a firm favourite and drop dead easy to prepare, store and reheat. It's also vegetarian and so cheap to make, everyone can have as much as they like without busting the budget. Very easy to make absolutely LOADS of . . .*

Prep time – *15 mins*
Cooking time – *3 hours*
Approx cost per head – *£0.80*
Serves – *5*

Veggie Pasta
1kg of pasta
1 small cup of olive oil
3 tins of tomatoes (1.2kg)
100g grated cheddar cheese
1 large Spanish onion
10 leaves of fresh basil
300g frozen, mixed vegetables
7 garlic cloves

Making the sauce

Heat (moderately) the olive oil in a pan and cook the garlic until it is soft, taking care not to let the garlic burn (about two minutes). Add the tomatoes, basil and chopped onion and salt and pepper to taste. Simmer for two hours forty minutes over a low heat. It makes sense to make heaps of sauce and store it for later use as a super quick and easy dinner to prepare.

Making the pasta and serving

When the sauce is nearly cooked, boil the pasta until soft and drain. Boil the vegetables until tender then mix in with the pasta. Finally add the sauce and stir thoroughly.

To add a little flavour, when you serve you can sprinkle some grated cheese on top. Mmmm and dead easy to make too.

Moma Newman's Braised Brisket with Vegetables

Why?
Brisket is a delicious and inexpensive cut of beef. It is best prepared ahead of time as it is easier to cut when cold. It takes a long time to cook but is well worth it as it serves so many. It is also a very simple meal to prepare and it was a firm favourite with all the carnivores on Jonathan's film shoot.

Prep time – *10 minutes*
Cooking time – *4hours*
Approx cost – *£0.90*
Serves – *10*

Mama Newman's Braised Brisket with Vegetables
1 large rolled brisket (1.5kg)
3 bay leaves
3 400g tins of chopped tomatoes
6 large carrots
6 parsnips
A bunch of celery
Mixed seasoning

Prepare the brisket

Preheat the oven to 200c. Coat the meat with the mixed seasoning, add the bay leaves and place in a heavy cast iron pot. Pour the tomatoes over the meat, then cover with the lid and bake for forty minutes. Open and check that there is still liquid in the pot and add water if it is drying out (the liquid should fill the pot to the halfway mark). Turn the oven to 150c and cook slowly for three hours or until tender. Dice the vegetables and add to the pot one hour before the cooking cycle is complete.

Remove the brisket from the pot and allow to cool. Pour the sauce and veggies into a large container and allow to cool off too, and once cold, remove the excess fat.

Serving

Later you can thinly slice the meat, cover with gravy and re-heat through for about thirty minutes.

For the veggies?

Not much here to be honest as it's pretty much a slab of cow!

'Holy Macaroni' Batman!

Why? *It's cheap, nutritious, and easy to make, veggie or not. Always a popular favourite and easy to portion.*

Prep time – *20 mins*
Cooking time – *30 mins*
Approx cost per head – *£0.90*
Serves – *10*

For the macaroni
300g macaroni or short cut spaghetti, 50g butter, 150g button mushrooms (sliced), 3 large cans of drained tuna (or one large catering can about 600g), 400g good cheddar cheese, grated – chuck in some gruyere cheese if the budget stretches that far, 1 bunch of chopped spring onions, 75g fresh breadcrumbs.

For the sauce
900ml milk, or a mix of milk & stock, 75g butter, 7tbsp plain flour & 2 tbsps cornflower

Making the macaroni
Take a large saucepan of salted water and bring to the boil. Add 300g of short cut spaghetti or macaroni and cook until tender, about 8-12 mins. Drain well.

Making the white sauce
First we will make a basic white sauce by using 75g butter, 7 tbsps of plain flour and 2 tbsps of cornflower, 900ml (pint and a half) of milk, or a milk and stock mixture. Thoroughly blend the flour in a jug with about a third of the milk / stock mixture. Put the remaining milk and butter in a large saucepan and bring to a gentle simmer. When hot, briskly whisk in the flour/milk mix, and keep stirring until thickened to a coating consistency. In a separate pan melt the butter and sauté the mushrooms for a few mins.

Add in to the sauce the flaked tuna, pasta, mushrooms, chopped onions and two thirds of the cheese to the macaroni. Mix well, & turn out into a large roasting tin. Sprinkle with the remaining breadcrumbs & cheese and bake at 180° c for 30–40 mins. Serve.

If you are going to freeze, DO NOT freeze until the mixture is cold. To reheat from frozen, bake for 45-50mins.

Low Fat Vegetable Curry

Why? *Great vegetarian alternative, low in fat and terrific in flavour. Can be served with rice or chicken.*

Prep time – *25 mins*
Cooking time – *10 mins*
Approx cost per head – *£0.80*
Serves – *10*

Ingredients
2 large Spanish onions (sliced), 1 head of celery (washed & sliced), 6 large carrots (sliced), 6 small turnips (cubed), 2 bulbs fennel (sliced), 1 kilo courgettes (sliced), 2 heads cauliflower divided into florets, 3tsp cumin, ½tsp allspice, 1tsp ground ginger, 2 tsp turmeric, 3 tsp ground coriander, 2 tsp paprika, ½ tsp cayenne pepper, 4 pints vegetable stock, juice of 2 lemons, chopped bunch of fresh parsley, generous handful of fresh coriander (chopped).

Making the curry
In a large, deep, non stick saucepan, spread out the onions and fry. As there's no oil involved, they will sizzle and stick to the pan, but that's fine. Cook until they have browned but watch them as they can burn – keep on a medium heat. Stir in about ½ to 1 pint of the stock and stir well, scraping up any brown bits that have glued to the bottom of the pan – they're nice tasty caramelised onion bits.

Stir in the remaining vegetables, mix well and then add in the combined spices and stir. Bring to a simmer, so that the veggies are cooking in their own juices. The mix should get quite soupy and thick. Gradually, add in the rest of the stock and remaining ingredients, and simmer for a further 15 mins until tender and fragrant. Serve with rice.

Once cooked, the curry can be served with rice or cooled, portioned and frozen.

For the meat eaters, you could always offer some roast chicken pieces, one per person. The cheapest way is to joint whole chickens yourself – a whole chicken should supply about 6 pieces. Supermarket meat is often bland, it's produced so quickly these days that there is little time for flavour to develop. Use the Lemon and Garlic Roast Chicken recipe here for chicken pieces.

Lemon & Garlic Roast Chicken

Why? *It's stupidly simple to make and high in protein. Great with rice and bread, or the veggie curry.*

Prep time – *10 mins*
Cooking time – *2½ hours*
Approx cost per head – *£1.60*
Serves – *5*

Ingredients

1 whole chicken (cut up)
1 lemon
1 large onions
1 garlic clove
Olive oil
Fresh rosemary

Bake the bird!

Place the chicken pieces in a large roasting tin, chop up the onion roughly and add, then squeeze the lemon over the contents (you can chuck the squeezed lemon skins in the roasting pan as well!) Divide up a whole garlic head and add to the roasting tin along with a healthy glug of olive oil and some fresh rosemary. Give all this a good mix around with your hands, cover with foil and roast at 150°C for an hour and a half (turn up the heat to 180°c for a final half hour). That's it!

The raw ingredients – chickens, lemon, garlic, herbs and oil can be packaged up in advance and stored in the fridge for around three days, then just roasted on the day and can be served with plain boiled spuds, rice or pasta as well as the veggie curry.

Sue's Breakfast Tip!

One of the handiest gadgets to buy is an electric frying pan. These give a large surface area to cook on and can be used to do everything from stews to pancakes. They are especially handy for breakfast where you can prepare both eggs and sausages in the same pan. The secret to cooking breakfast is timing – sausages will take 20 mins or so to be thoroughly cooked, whereas eggs can be done in under three minutes.

Jacket of all trades – The Baked Spud

Why? *Soooooo easy to cook, easy to transport.*

How to do it . . .

Quantities are simple! One spud per person. Start your oven by pre heating to 180°c. While that's coming to temperature, rub each spud with crushed sea salt and oil (I like sesame oil, but basic veg or olive oil is fine) and microwave in batches of four for 15 mins. By this time the oven will be hot and you can move your spuds from the microwave to the conventional oven and bake for approx 40 mins, or until a skewer penetrates easily. This method cuts down on the usual cooking time for baked spuds but still gives a proper home-baked flavour. After the spuds are cooked they can be cooled and refrigerated for around three days, and can then be reheated in a microwave on site in about three minutes. You can do more than one at a time to speed up lunchtime through-put. Offer a variety of fillings – store them in stackable plastic tubs for transportation – such as tuna & sweetcorn mayonnaise, baked beans & cheese, cottage cheese and chives.

The Editor's Blueprint

The editor is, in many ways, the second director of the film. It's their job to take all the footage, both picture and sound, and cut it all together to tell the story in the best possible way. It's always a collaboration between writer, producer, director and editor, but the more experienced and bold the editor, the easier the whole post-production process will be.

Old Tools

The tools that are used by the oldest of old school editors. Steenbeck, Moviola, Pic-sync etc. Don't use them, even if you are offered them for free. It will take longer and cost more than non linear . . . unless an old school editor is doing you a major favour.

Avid Media Composer

The world leader in pro editing and has been around for years. Mature, stable, sophisticated and understood by any editor worth their salt. Find an old one and blag a deal. Even version 5 will do (circa 1993 technology!).

Avid Film Composer

Essentially the same as Media Composer except that it can handle movies shot at 24fps. But we always have shot at, and advise shooting at, 25fps which opens up the field for virtually any post production tool capable of putting one image next to another.

Avid XpressDV

The cheap, domestic little brother to Media and Film Composer. It's fast and stunningly versatile. A definite winner over any other semi pro system, as it integrates with other Avids (meaning you can edit on XpressDV but perhaps complete on top of the range Avid Syphony). Best choice for DV based projects and will even run on a laptop – Mac and PC.

Adobe Premiere

Once a contender, but has remained firmly at the lower corporate and wedding video end of the world. Cheap, versatile, quick and dirty. Play with it but don't cut your movie with it.

Final Cut Pro

A real contender to Avid XpressDV and has won many high profile converts. A fine tool but essentially, it isn't as widely understood and used as Avid. For my bucks, I would go with the pack leader.

Media 100

The Pepsi Cola of the pro editing world. Also a fine tool and very sophisticated, but at the end of the day if you can get a Media 100 you can probably get an Avid. Runs on two monitors.

Lightworks

Once head to head with Avid, was muscled out in the nineties, Lightworks is also a fine tool and loved by old school editors who migrated from cutting on film to cutting on a computer. Not as wIdely known or used as Avid but totally up for the job. Popular on Hollywood features.

The Editor's Blueprint

As a screenplay changes so much when you shoot it, so the editor should be free to rediscover the story. Many a day, week, even month, has been wasted trying to push and squeeze the footage that was shot on set so that it works in the way that the screenplay was planned. In essence, once footage is in the cutting room, the editor should be free to throw away the screenplay and find the best way to tell the story that has been captured in the individual shots. Often, this is quite different from the script, yet almost always an improvement

What are you looking for?

The editor should be many things. Firstly, they should be a consummate diplomat. They must be able to keep people calm, make everyone feel like their ideas are good, but at the same time filter everything so that the best creative decisions are made. This is no mean feat as almost everybody involved has an opinion and an ego.

Secondly, they should be a little bit of a propeller headed geek. Quite simply, much of editing is about managing the technology, which if they do well, will save the production heaps of time and money. For instance, if they don't know what frame overlaps on A and B roll Super 16mm neg cut means, then think twice before hiring them.

Thirdly, they should be courageous, lateral thinkers, unafraid of trying any idea no matter how crazy. The director will have shot the movie with particular editorial decisions in mind. The editor should re-envision these decisions and offer alternative and often oblique ways of telling the story through editorial changes. Above all, they should be in search of the best way to tell the story, not just technical excellence. For example, the editor should always favour better story telling even if it requires the use of uncomfortable or bad edits. There are no rules aside from 'tell the best story in the best way with the material that you have'.

Finally, you want to find someone with whom you will get on. The editing of your movie should be one of the most fun and exciting stages of your film and you don't want to be embattled through the whole process. Before hiring, always have that chat about favourite movies just to make sure everyone is

The editor will take the shots and sticth them together to tell the story. The hard thing about editing is getting beyond the mechanics of whether shots, cuts or scenes work, and reaching the story and asking if THAT is the best it can be.

If you want real power in the cutting room, learn how to edit with Avid. Now that Avid XpressDV is so widely available, there's no excuse for not learning the tools of the trade. Nor is it as hard or scary as it looks, so roll up your sleeves and get learning. A director who can also edit is an empowered director.

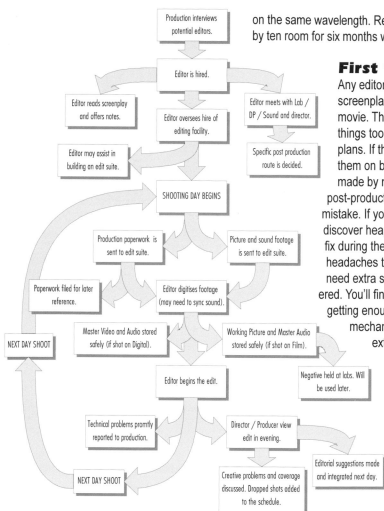

Production interviews potential editors.

Editor is hired.

Editor reads screenplay and offers notes.

Editor meets with Lab / DP / Sound and director.

Editor oversees hire of editing facility.

Specific post production route is decided.

Editor may assist in building an edit suite.

SHOOTING DAY BEGINS

Production paperwork is sent to edit suite.

Picture and sound footage is sent to edit suite.

Paperwork filed for later reference.

Editor digitises footage (may need to sync sound).

NEXT DAY SHOOT

Master Video and Audio stored safely (if shot on Digital).

Working Picture and Master Audio stored safely (if shot on Film).

Editor begins the edit.

Negative held at labs. Will be used later.

Technical problems promtly reported to production.

Director / Producer view edit in evening.

Editorial suggestions made and integrated next day.

NEXT DAY SHOOT

Creative problems and coverage discussed. Dropped shots added to the schedule.

Editing Stage 1
The Shoot

on the same wavelength. Remember, you may be in a darkened eight by ten room for six months with this person. You want to get on.

First things first

Any editor worth their salt is going to ask to read the screenplay before they accept the job of cutting your movie. They are going to want to know a few other things too, such as budget, cast and your distribution plans. If they decide to do the job, you want to get them on board before you shoot. A common mistake made by many new film makers is that they put off post-production until after the shoot. This is a critical mistake. If you edit your film alongside shooting, you will discover heaps of small problems that are very simple to fix during the shoot, problems that would be major headaches to correct after the shoot. You'll discover you need extra shots to bridge edits that you never considered. You'll find out about coverage, in essence are you getting enough shots to make it work, even just on a mechanical level? A good editor will also suggest extra shots or 'cutaways' that will help in the storytelling. During the post-production of the three features I have made, the first two were cut after the shoot (which was a nightmare) and the third was cut during the shoot – allowing us to make bold, creative decisions that massively helped the storytelling.

One of the major reasons new film makers don't tackle post-production until they've shot the film is that they simply can't cope with what they perceive will be yet more production problems . . . *'I don't want to hear about it unless it will shut down the shoot . . . editing? Shit we will do that later . . . What do you mean the lead actor has just dropped out . . . etc....'*

Try and overcome this psychological overload. Explain to the editor what kind of mixed up and scary place you are in and encourage them to 'manage' themselves. More than likely, if you are very cash strapped, you will have either blagged a very old off-line Avid or have acquired a domestic Avid Xpress DV system. With the right preparations, both systems are more than adequate for the editing of your film. Ask the editor to take charge of the organisation and setting up of this edit suite. Obviously, the production team will be involved In finding the equipment in the first place, but once the deals have been struck, the editor should take over and set up.

Proposed Routes

Brief descriptions of routes proposed for the shoot and edit (which is by no means ALL of post production) of three projects, shot on miniDV, DigiBeta and Film (super16mm).

Micro digital – miniDV shoot

1. Shoot on a Canon XL1 in the 'frame' mode.
2. Shoot in 4:3 aspect ratio but frame for 1.85:1 (do not use internal 16:9 function).
3. Hire in or get hold of a better lens, ideally a broadcast lens.
4. Record sound on DAT at 16bit and 48 kHz.
5. Feed DAT output directly into Cannon and record at 16bit 48 kHz.
6. Picture will run at 25fps (50 fields).
7. Edit on Avid XpressDV.
8. Final edit could be completed on Avid XpressDV and dumped up onto DigiBeta later . . . or it could be re-mastered at a top facility who will handle colour grading and make legal all video and audio levels.
9. Top facility can take the 4:3 video edit and pass it through a box (such as a S&W Arc) to make a best quality 16:9 version.

Midlevel digital – DigiBeta

1. Shoot on a DigiBeta camera, ideally one with true Progressive scan, if not in normal interlaced mode.
2. Shoot in 16:9 if camera supports true 16:9.
3. The lens will probably be fine.
4. Mix sound with an SQN external mixer.
5. Feed sound directly into DigiBeta camera and record at 16bit 48 kHz.
6. Picture will run at 25fps if shooting in true progressive scan, or 50 fields if interlaced.
7. Edit on Avid Media Composer (ideally) or Avid XpressDV. Master tapes will need to be copied, with time code, onto DV for XpressDV or Beta SP for Media Composer (if a DigiBeta is not available in the suite, which it almost certainly won't be).
8. Off-line edit will be re-captured from master DigiBeta camera tapes at a top facility. The picture will be 'graded' and a 'film look' added if needed.
9. The image was almost certainly shot in 16:9 so no conversion is needed.

Low level film – S16mm Film

1. Shot on S16mm film. Film should be shot at 25fps and NOT at 24fps.
2. Record sound on DAT at 44.1khz.
3. Film processed and telecinied onto BetaSP (or DV). Sound is transferred and laid back onto both BetaSP and new clone DAT (with audio that perfectly matches picture and timecodes). This is your new master sound.
4. Edit using Avid Media Composer (ideally) or Avid XpressDV (ensure timecodes are accurately transferred).
5. Avid generated EDL which is sent to neg cutters.
6. Film enters labs post production stages and will finally be telecinied onto DigiBeta or HiDef.

Before you go

Prior to the shoot, it's essential to have a production meeting with the director, cameraman (DP) producer, sound recordist and editor. If you are shooting on film, this meeting should take place at the lab with the lab guys. Its purpose is to iron out and quantify the entire post-production process so that decisions that are made during the shoot don't cause problems later on down the line (that might cost a fortune to fix). For example, shooting at 25fps (frames per second) on film as opposed to 24fps (which many people think is standard) will cost a lot less to deal with in post-production (in PAL countries such as here in the UK).

After this meeting, type up an explicit list and description of the whole post production process and give a copy to every technical crew member – director, producer, DP, editor, sound recordist and most importantly, laboratory (if shooting on film).

Room setup

Wherever you decide to put your edit suite – the attic

The space in which you choose to cut your film is very important. You are going to be in it for many months so it should be as big as possible. Access to a microwave oven and tea and coffee is essential, as is enough floor space to stretch out and have a snooze. If the room is too small, cabin fever will set in.

Pro edit suite

The pro edit suite will offer a more professional editing solution, complete with extra hardware such as PPM meters, BetaSP deck etc., but if you get one cheap or for free, it will probably come in a very very small room, or you will need to find a room. Either way, this is the rough guide to an Avid Edit Suite…

Shelves
Used for storing master tapes, but always there for access when needed.

Client monitor
Big monitor so that people at the back of the room can watch the edited video without cramping the editor.

Avid breakout box
This is the main hardware for the Avid, where video and audio are digitised and played back. It is connected up to the patching bay.

VHS deck
Used for making quick play out tapes so people can watch the work at home.

Monitors
Two monitors to spread out the visual workspace.

Edit monitor
A small high quality monitor used by the editor to watch the video.

Speakers
High quality sounds can be heard in full depth and fidelity.

DAT
Digital audio tape player recorder for digitising sound at top quality.

Mixing desk
Not really for mixing sound, more for ease of monitoring the various audio sources used in the cutting room.

PPM
Audio meters to help ensure sound is not over or under recorded. Edit suite may also come with a Waveform and Vectorscope used to monitor video signals (not really needed for offline editing).

Extra storage
External hard drives used to store video and audio footage. In this case it is SCSI, but cheaper firewire is becoming more common.

Keyboard and mouse
Avid has a special colour coded keyboard. Don't fear it, it's pretty simple once you get a good look at it.

BetaSP deck
Used to capture and playback video and sound.

Avid computer
The computer used to drive the Avid software and Hardware.

Good chair
Essential, you are going to spend a lot of time sat in it.

Extras
There's probably going to be a bunch of other things too . . . A Zip drive for backup of your project, a patching bay so that you can easily change the set-up without having to climb behind all the equipment, a CD player for digitising music and sound effects, a sound effects library (if you are lucky) so that you could easily add effects, and of course a kettle, small fridge and microwave oven.

in a big post-production facility that you have blagged for free, or your mum's spare bedroom with your own Avid Xpress DV system – it should be set up and fully functioning before you start shooting.

Sound advice

Everyone knows just how important the 'picture' is, but for some reason, people rarely consider what will happen to their sound. Picture and sound are usually shot / recorded seperately (picture on film or digital videotape and sound on digital audio tape). It's always advisable to get the picture and sound married as soon as possible, whether you're shooting digitally or on film.

More than likely, sound will be recorded on digital audio tape (DAT) at 48khz. Ideally, if you have shot digitally, you should set up your camera to accept a direct feed from the DAT machine and record the sound onto the digital tape alongside the picture (whether it's DV, DigiBeta, Hi Def etc.) This will mean that on your master camera tapes, you will also have the master sound already perfectly sunk up. The DAT that you also recorded on set will then become an audio backup. On film, as long as you have shot at 25FPS, you can ask the lab to synch the DAT audio to the camera negative (see technical post-production section). Either way, this means that on day two of principal photography, the editor will have tapes with both picture and sound in synchronisation and can immediately begin editing. If you do not sort out synchronisation of your sound beforehand, the editor will have to spend three or four hours each day synching the sound on the Avid (note also that there is no direct backup for sound sunk this way, if you lose this Avid or suffer a major hard disk crash, you will probably have to manually re-synch all the sound again. If you had sorted out synch-sound on your tapes, it would be a simple case of batch re-digitising the tapes, which would be an automated process and take only a few hours).

First day

On the first day, the editor won't have much to do because there is no footage to cut yet. Their job will begin on the second day. Each day of the shoot will be similar and this daily procedure will simply repeat.

On the morning of the second day of the shoot, a number of things should have landed on the editor's desk. There will be quite a lot of paperwork, including continuity sheets, camera report sheets, sound report sheets, lab report sheets (if you shot on film). All of which will be meticulously organised and filed for later use. The most important things to arrive will be the tapes of the footage shot *yesterday*.

They will of course be the rushes, sound and picture. Remember, this part of the editing process is only about making editorial decisions and not about the final version of your film. You will probably go somewhere else to

Eddie Hamilton
Editor

Editing is about instinct, gut-reaction, does it feel right? There are grammatical rules of film – crossing the line is 'wrong' for example, but you learn to forget those and concentrate on how to tell the best story. 'Moulin Rouge' for example, crosses the line continuously and I for one loved it. The Editor is independent of the high emotions on set, 'that crane shot took 4 hours to set up, we must use it', or 'I didn't get on with that actor'. You see the footage for what it is and can edit accordingly. Keep a clear memory of how you reacted the first time you watched the rushes, you will rely on this to guide you as you become closer to and over-familiar with the film.

When cutting a scene the editor should imagine what's going through the audiences' mind. What do they need to see next to understand the story? Whose point of view is the story told from? What's happened previously? When reading a script I write detailed notes for each scene to remind me where each character is in their journey. Because films are usually shot out of sequence (and therefore cut out of sequence) it ensures I can quickly find where I am in the story and won't forget an underlying subplot carried from a previous scene, for example.

Pacing a movie is one of the hardest skills for an editor to learn. Knowing when to keep the pace brisk or to let the film breathe is tricky, but your audience will feel uncomfortable if it isn't right. Try to avoid editing by committee. You will dilute the artistic and creative thrust of the film, usually taking the edge off the piece. Following the director's vision through the whole process is the only way of creating a memorable piece of cinema.

Format and kit?

The route you choose for post production will depend on what format you shoot and the tools available to you. Broadly, there are two routes – domestic and semi-pro kit for which we would recommend Avid XpressDV or full pro kit for which we would recommend Avid Media Composer. Each have their foibles and here is a summary of how each would impact your choices.

Editing on a DV system such as Avid Xpress DV

1. Shot on DV with sound transferred onto DV tape live on set – in this case, the tapes that you will edit will be the master tapes. You may wish to make cloned back ups of these tapes each day for insurance purposes.

2. Shot on another digital format such as DigiBeta or High Def and transferred to DV – in this instance, the camera tapes will have been transferred along with the live sound onto DV tapes (it's essential that all time codes are accurately copied too). Editing these tapes will mean that you are editing a copy of the masters and when you finish editing, you will take your edit decisions (EDL) on a floppy disk to another facility who will take your master camera tapes (DigiBeta, High Def etc.) and recreate your edits at top quality, mastering onto something like either DigiBeta or High Def.

3. Shot on film and transferred with sound onto DV – in this instance, the labs will have processed your camera negatives overnight and transferred it onto DV, then they will add the sound using the clapperboard and create new clone DAT tapes with the same time code as the DV (which in turn relates 100% accurately to the frames of the master camera negative). You must ensure that the DV editing system you are using accurately uses the time codes on the DV tape.

Editing on a Pro system such as Avid Media Composer

(Most Avid Media Composers come with a Beta SP deck and no DV deck, nor does it have firewire input, output or control).

1. Shot on any digital tape format and transferred to Beta SP – in this instance, all the camera tapes and sound in sync will be transferred with time code to Beta SP. This is not a clone, this is a copy, but that's ok because you're only going to use it to make your editorial decisions. Later, your digital tapes will be recaptured on a high resolution system.

2. Shot on any digital tape format and a digital deck hired in – instead of the Beta SP machine that came with the suite, you will acquire a DV deck, or DigiBeta deck, which will be used to playback tapes and digitise into the Avid. Later, you will recapture your shots on a high resolution system.

3. Shot on film and transferred to Beta SP – in this instance, the labs will have processed your camera negatives overnight and transferred it onto DV, then they will add the sound using the clapperboard and create new clone DAT tapes with the same time code as the DV (which in turn relates 100% accurately to the frames of the master camera negative). You must ensure that the DV editing system you are using accurately uses timecode.

complete it, a facility that can master to DigiBeta and do you a proper and very attractive grade for the image (grading is where the image is adjusted to look more consistent and often can be radically improved from a creative viewpoint).

The first job for the editor will be to transfer the video and audio onto the Avid. Labelling tapes is very important as the numbers given to each tape form a direct link between the decisions you make on the Avid and your final mastering from either videotapes or film. As a general rule, keep the naming and numbering of tapes very simple. Ideally, just numbers. Always convert these numbers into a three digit number. For example, 1 would become 001, 36 would become 036 etc. (this is to help the computer keep everything in order).

If using Avid Xpress DV, the information from the DV tapes is cloned onto the computer hard drive at 5:1 compression. This means that the picture and sound are exactly the same as what is on the videotape. You will need approximately 10gb of storage for every hour of material. If you are using an Avid Media Composer, you can choose either higher or lower compression ratios but usually you will work at something like either 20.1 or 10.1 compression. You will need much less storage space to handle this.

Understand, or at least make sure your editor understands, all the technological hoops you will have to jump through. Most important is the link between timecodes, batch capturing and negative cutting. Send a test EDL to the neg cutter, making sure all timecodes match. If you get it wrong, you may need to completely re-cut the entire movie!

During the process of cloning (XpressDV) or copying (Media Composer) the footage onto the computer, the editor will break it down into shots and takes which will be listed in the bins. It's important to label these shots clearly and accurately and wherever you use abbreviations (as you inevitably will), make sure that they are easy to understand (the editor may also use FLeX files on a floppy disk from the lab).

Once the tapes have been digitised, they should be stored safely for future use, which usually means on the top shelf on the edit suite. If you shot on film, then your master negative will still be stored at the laboratory and will stay there until you come to the neg cut later on down the line.

Editor's paperwork

In the cutting room the editor will have a large lever arch file for paperwork. On top of the paperwork below, they will also receive a daily call sheet (which will also be filed). On the whole, these documents will rarely be referenced, although initially the lined script from continuity will be used quite a lot.

Screenplay (lined)
The editor will already have their own screenplay. Each day, continuity will draw up a 'lined script' visually showing where shots started and ended. The editor will replace pages in their screenplay with the 'lined' version from continuity as and when they arrive in the cutting room.

Camera Report Sheets
From the camera team, explaining which shots are where and on which tapes / rolls, highlighting any technical issues (such as day for night, under exposure, slow motion etc.)

Sound Report Sheets
From the sound team, explaining which sound is for which shot. Will also highlight technical issues (such as traffic noise, boilers etc.) Will also detail wild-tracks of effects, any ADR (actors re-acting without the camera) and room tone 'buzz tracks'.

Lab Report Sheets
From the lab and only used if the production was shot on film. These will note which shots and slates are on each lab roll and detail any technical issues. If sound was also sunk at the lab (which we recommend) then there may be a second report sheet for the sound (although not always).

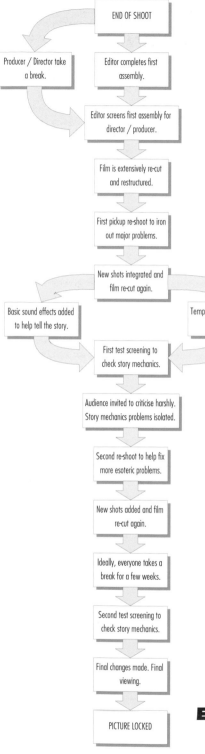

END OF SHOOT

Producer / Director take a break.

Editor completes first assembly.

Editor screens first assembly for director / producer.

Film is extensively re-cut and restructured.

First pickup re-shoot to iron out major problems.

New shots integrated and film re-cut again.

Basic sound effects added to help tell the story.

Temp music added to help tell the story.

First test screening to check story mechanics.

Audience invited to criticise harshly. Story mechanics problems isolated.

Second re-shoot to help fix more esoteric problems.

New shots added and film re-cut again.

Ideally, everyone takes a break for a few weeks.

Second test screening to check story mechanics.

Final changes made. Final viewing.

PICTURE LOCKED

First cut

It's time to start editing. The editor will check the scenes that have been shot with the script to get an idea of the story being told. Then, using the best takes, they will put the scene together. Some scenes will come together very easily, others will be difficult, possibly even impossible to make work effectively (which normally means the scene needs extra shots, to be re-shot or possibly even ditching altogether). Over the course of the day, the editor should be able to cut most or all of the scenes that were shot the previous day. In the evening when the crew wrap, the director and producer will probably visit the cutting room to look at these scenes. Some scenes will look great, others will look terrible. There should then be an open discussion about what to do with the problem scenes (re-shoot, extra shots etc.) before everyone leaves for the day.

The next day . . . and the next . . .

The next day, the whole process will start again . . . the editor receives the rushes, logs and digitises onto the Avid before assembling the scenes and screening in the evening.

One very exciting aspect of editing as you shoot is that you will get a very good feeling for how your movie is coming together. What was once a nebulous idea was first turned into a specific instruction set on paper, has now been expressed by actors, captured on film, edited and exists as a piece of real bona fide CINEMA! It's heady stuff.

End of shoot

As the film wraps, the editor will continue editing whilst the director and producer mop up the immediate mess and then run to the hills for a short break. It's not essential to take this break and every atom in your body will want to get into the cutting room to start work with the editor, but a short breather will allow you to recharge and reflect, but most of all you will get some perspective on what has happened.

I thought the shoot was over?

Remember, a movie is made in three distinct stages. The script, where anything goes, imagination and perceived budget the only limitations. Then the shoot, where all the ideas in the script were acted out and filmed, sometimes improving the material, more often modifying it and occasionally jettisoning because it doesn't work or isn't needed. Now you're about to enter the final creative third of your project and it's time to rediscover the story – *based on what was actually captured on set*. However…a bitter pill needs to be swallowed – *you have yet to finish writing and shooting*.

Editing stage 2
The edit

Inexperienced and insecure film makers often rigidly dig their heels in saying that *'the shoot is over, my work is brilliant'* and they just want to get it completed. I say *edit your film, look at it, write some new scenes, shoot those new scenes, edit them in, drop older scenes that don't work … re-evaluate, re-shoot, re-cut …* in essence, you're going to continue script development in post-production.

When you think about it, this an obvious and logical thing to do. If you are a new film maker, it is unlikely your script was brilliant or your direction inspired … you are learning your job, not yet a master craftsperson. So like all great art, go back and improve it. How many times you go back will depend on how serious your problems are, how much in denial you are, how much patience you have, how much time you can buy. Just remember, there is always room for improvement and as James Camcron says, *'movies aren't completed, they're abandoned'*. It's time to brace yourself yet again, it's going to be a rocky ride.

. . . Tumbleweeds blow across the street

As you enter this final stage, a couple of things will have happened that will make life slightly more uncomfortable. You'll be down 'cos you'll have probably realised that your script wasn't as good as you thought it was and that you should have continued script development, nor was the coverage in the shoot good enough *'there's never enough time, money or light to get the shots'* (this never changes, regardless of the budget). The actors weren't as good as hoped, the sets poor, costumes dodgy…etc. In short, it isn't the movie that you had imagined. Not by a long shot.

To add insult to injury, you've run out of cash because you went over schedule. The phone is ringing with companies to whom you owe money and they are making unpleasant demands. Worse still, all the energy and enthusiasm that you fed off during the shoot, all that good will and experience that you drew from your crew, it's all gone. It's just you and the editor now. Overnight you have gone from thirty people saying *'Yes we can do it!'* to two in a dark room, ignoring the ringing phone and saying *'Gosh, I'd hoped that shot was better'* and *'Oh dear, that's not going to work . . . what are we going to do?'* There is a silver lining though – you have actually made a feature film! It's now just a matter of putting the pieces together in the best possible way and keeping the wolves at bay until you have done so. The eternal optimist in you will be screaming *'Yeah but think about the possibilities!'* And so with dread in your step, but hope in your heart, you start the final creative lap.

First assembly

Regardless of whether you took a break or not, within a day or two of completing the shoot, the editor should have cut together the first assembly. This will be all the scenes, usually cut in the clear and obvious way that they

Jonathan Newman
Director and Editor

'Had I known how to edit when I shot my feature 'Being Considered', I certainly wouldn't have hesitated to cut my feature film myself. As luck had it, I was taught how to use an Avid about 2 years ago, and I now have one installed on my home computer. Every director/film maker should learn how to edit. Apart from learning an extra trade (hey, if you can't find work as a director…!), it also teaches you valuable filmic lessons relating to timing, types of shots, framing etc. As a result, I've been able to cut every project I've directed since – no need to find, rely on or pay, (if money is an issue) an editor.

Most directors, and humans, for that matter, would probably be put off by the site of an Avid console and keyboard. But let me tell you right here, it's not as complicated as it looks. Once you learn to master your basic elements, i.e., splicing in picture and sound at a designated point, it won't take long to pick up the more advanced features. Editing, as well as directing, gives you far more control over your material. After all, you shot it, so you have the best overall knowledge and memory of what you have and where it's supposed to go.

As directors, we are always editing in our head when we decide what shots we want to use to cover a scene, so it's logical to take the process to the next step. Now, with mini DV, and bigger and faster computers, home editing is accessible to all. Anything you shoot can be transferred to mini DV and digitised into your computer. There's no excuse NOT to go out and make a feature film.'

Who is in the Re-shoot crew?

This will depend very much on what you plan to re-shoot, but even major scenes can be handled with minimum fuss and a micro crew if you are organised. It will take place from Friday night to Sunday night. Cameras will be collected as early as possible on the Friday for the weekend hire. Some hire companies are great, understand the pressures you are under and will let you take the kit at lunch time on Friday, effectively giving you an extra half day.

Clearly the crew will include the director and producer, and possibly the writer (who may well help out in production now). If not, then you will need an extra production person to help with 'stuff' before and over the weekend. The DP will probably need an assistant, although if the director is camera orientated, they may help out instead. Ideally though, an extra set of hands here will make a big difference. If there are any actors, you will need a make-up / costume person (so make sure you keep hold of all continuity notes). Sound should be taken care of by either the director or producer and only recorded where absolutely needed – that means dialogue and nothing else. Production design may be prepared in advance by the producer and director, a huge pile of props in a box waiting to be shot 'conveyor belt' style. Anything more ambitious and a person looking after what is in front of the camera and props will be a great help.

Above all, keep it small and organised.

were shot (as directed), the scenes will be ordered in the same way as the screenplay had planned and an occasional title card will pop up to say 'missing shot' or' scene' (where things for one reason or another didn't get shot). The editor won't yet have brought their true creative flair to the film, they will have simply have assembled the framework.

Viewing this first assembly is usually a very depressing experience. It's over long, baggy, badly paced, bad performances, bad edits, bad shots, bad sound…in fact it's quite simply rubbish. It's time to unleash the eternal optimist. Roll up your sleeves and get stuck into clearing away the crap to reveal the diamond that is your movie. This process is not exclusive to low budget or first time film makers. The first assembly on almost every film is more about what's wrong with the film than what's right. You have many months ahead of you to meticulously hone and re-envisage your movie, so don't panic or get too depressed.

First re-cut

After the screening of the first assembly, there should be a free form discussion between editor, director and producer to try and come to some broad agreement about what action should be taken. There will be a huge amount of obvious editorial changes and over the next week or so, the editor and director will probably fix hundreds of small problems. They'll drop lines of dialogue, move scenes around to restructure the story, trim out pauses and gaps thereby increasing the pace of story, and they may even add a few sound effects and temporary music just to get an impression of what the movie will be like.

Then there will be a second screening which will be much more positive and exciting. Large chunks of the movie should now feel like they are kind of working. But still, there are major problems and in an ideal world, there would be another period of re-cutting.

Re-shoot

Eventually, you'll get to the point where you need to do your first (and probably minor) re-shoot. The producer will get a small team of camera, camera assistant and maybe a production assistant and you'll shoot for a long weekend. Because everyone is rested, the crew is small, the shots specific and contained, this re-shoot weekend represents extraordinary value for money. During the main shoot, you may have only got twenty shots a day. On this weekend re-shoot, you'll probably get one hundred shots. These two days could add 10-20% more shots to your movie. As micro-budget film making is always a *war of coverage*, this little skirmish will take you one big step closer to victory.

The kinds of shots you will be getting are close-ups of newspaper headlines or books, a dramatic shot of a match igniting, a POV shot looking out of a window, an establishing shot of a building, an establishing shot for a scene where the actors are walking in the distance (these will probably be doubles wearing the same or similar costume), shots of hands picking things up or putting things down, fingers pointing to phone numbers etc. You could probably get away without many of these shots, but their inclusion will radically improve your final movie, so resist your urge to say *'Hell, I can't be bothered'*. It is incumbent upon YOU to make the most of this opportunity. You have a couple of years of your own investment. You have your investor's money. You have the cast and crew whose involvement was based on your enthusiasm for your dream. Hold steady and go the distance.

Unlike short films, it takes a couple of hours to watch your film, then hours to discuss it . . . It's the best part of a day to have a screening with a full discussion!

Once you have these new shots on tape, the editor will cut them into the movie, probably perform another nip and tuck on the story, will add some sound effects and a bit of temporary music from other movies before having yet another screening. This third screening will be the first time your movie starts to feel like a real movie. You'll be quite excited about it and now is the time to put it in front of a test audience.

Test screening

Many film makers resist test screenings as they fear that somehow their creative vision is going to be dumbed down or they are being forced to feed the appetite of the public at large, whom they do not trust. Whilst I sympathise with these views, I have personally found test screenings to be revelatory. Let's be clear. Some people just aren't going to like your film. Others are. Neither matter because what you're looking for is information

We are all experts

A fact often overlooked by film makers is that everyone is an expert. Not necessarily an expert in film making but an expert in film and story consumption. We've all got years of expereince consuming stories told through sound and picture – be it in the cinema, video or TV.

And here lies the magic. It's very easy to watch a film and be clear about what is wrong with it. Anyone can do it, and we do it all the time. Why then is it so stupefyingly difficult to envision a screenplay, or even watch an edit, and be clear about what is, or is not, wrong with it? Mainly, it's perspective. In essence, you can only ever see or experience a story once for the first time. A luxury that we film makers never have. The point of test screenings is to find out if the mechanics of your story work, not necessarily 'like it' or 'don't like it'. If you think of your story as a road map, you the film maker are the cartographer and architect. You take your audience on a journey along the roads you have planned, hopefully at the right speed and with enough twists and turns so that they can never second guess what is around the next corner. Sure, they'll probably know the destination, but getting there isn't as important as the journey they took on the way.

Disaster for you the film maker, is when you think the audience is driving along the road that is your story only to discover that they took a turn a while back and are completely lost. There is nothing more frustrating than watching a film and not understanding what is going on. If that happens, your audience will get bored, switch off and then you are lost too. And here lies the magic formula. You need to give them enough to know where they are going but never so much that they can guess the route beforehand. They should be kept in a state of semi confusion, wondering how on earth it's all going to work out. Never so confused they give up, and never so informed they figure it out in advance.

(above) The real location hallway from White Angel.
(below) The set built in the garage, complete with front door that lead nowhere and stairs that you couldn't climb. But it enabled us to re-shoot the whole end of the film and cost just over £100 to make.

Case Study – White Angel

Sometime after completing my second feature, White Angel, a serial killer thriller, I sat down with pen, paper and stopwatch. I discovered that 37% of the movie was actually made up from re-shoots! That means that over a third of the film was shot with a crew of two, and at the most three! Much of this re-shoot footage was purposefully dropped from the main shoot to speed things up. It was the usual stuff such as close up shots of news paper headline, hands picking stuff up etc. But there was also a large amount of major re-shoots, including a completely new ending. During tests we had found that the end we had shot just didn't fit with the rest of the movie, and so we had to re-shoot it all! Very quickly we discovered we were not going to get back into the house where we had originally shot, so we set about rebuilding large parts of the house as sets inside our own home and garage. The building task was mainly undertaken by DP Jon Walker and production designer Mark Sutherland.

The most impressive 'build' was the garage which was converted into the hallway of the house in the story . . . This was going to form the main location for the entirely new ending, a deadly fight between the two lead characters. It must have been a strange sight for cars driving past – a garage that looked like a hallway, complete with front door and stairs, with two people attempting to kill each other!

Thankfully the illusion worked and the new footage cut seamlessly into the movie. I can see the difference between real and fake, but no one else seems to see it – movie fixed!

about how to better tell your story, not *'I like'* or *'I don't like'*.

For this screening, the editor will copy the whole movie with all the sound, sound effects and temporary music onto a VHS or DV videotape (you might even add temporary titles to help the audience get the feel for it). You need to arrange a convenient venue with a good sound system and bright and clear video projector. Find twenty people who you don't know (that usually means friends of friends) and invite them to come and see your movie. There's no point asking friends as they will be astonished that you even made the film . . . *'My god it wasn't what I expected. It was in colour and had sound for a start!'*

Explain to your guinea pigs that the film isn't complete, the picture isn't colour balanced, the sound is unmixed and the music isn't the final score. Ask them to turn off their mobiles as you'll need their undivided attention. Finally, before screening the film, notch up the heating and give them all

For perhaps the only time in your film career you won't be rushed by the powers that be. So take your time. You are baking a very big cake and it's your first go. Don't mess it up by rushing it. Watch, contemplate, reflect, modify, improve . . . Then watch, contemplate, reflect . . .

pizza. Invite them to fall asleep in your film, there's no better way of finding out where they are losing interest.

Screen the movie and watch them as they go through the journey that is your story. You'll quickly get an idea where they are getting bored. After the screening, ask them specific questions about where you feel you may have particular story problems *'Did you understand Bill was married to Jane?'*, *'Did*

Case Study – Mrs Miller in Urban Ghost Story

During test screenings on my third film, Urban Ghost Story, it became obvious that the audience had forgotten a few things . . . A major character had remained underdeveloped in the screenplay (isn't hindsight great huh?) We discovered that in the various cuts of the film that we showed to small gatherings, many forgot who this character was and how they impacted on the story. Their presence was vital to the story and if people weren't 'getting it', we had a serious problem. So we devised some new scenes and shots. OK here's the deal. The story is about a 13 year old girl, Lizzie, who is killed in a joy riding accident – but after being dead for 184 seconds she's brought back to life by paramedics. The story follows what she feels came back with her from 'the other side...' Guilt or ghosts? In the crash there was also a boy, Kevin, who was killed outright. Kevin was Lizzie's best friend. And his mother, Mrs Miller, was the character that the audience kept forgetting about.

First changes

In the original screenplay, Jason Connery's character, a journalist sniffing for a story, knocked on Mrs Miller's door and asked her a few questions. She was so enraged by this that she just slammed the door in his face. What we planned to re-shoot was a close up of the scene but now give her some new dialogue. We knew the reverse shot of Jason reacting would work fine (Jason was now in LA too!), so in essence, as long as we could make the cut work, we could put whatever dialogue we needed into the scene. The dialogue we put in Mrs Miller's mouth was pretty much all plot, but a good actor like Carolyn Bonnyman (who played Mrs Miller) could work wonders with our wooden words. She did a splendid job.

The wide shot from the main shoot.

The trick to making the shot work would be to get the eyelines right, the camera angle the same as if we had just zoomed in for a close up, and the lighting and set dressing similar. We shot the new close up in the doorway to the edit suite and the keen eyed ones amongst you will notice that in the close up, the light switch in the background disappears and the coat hanger is replaced by my jacket on a broom pole! But we get away with it because it 'cuts', it looks similar and the actor is convincing.

The close up reverse of Jason Connery from the main shoot. Notice how it cuts with the close up of Mrs Miller (below) even though they are months apart and even in a completely new location.

Double jeopardy

We also inserted a shot of Mrs Miller near the very start of the movie. We opened up an important courtroom scene on a new re-shoot close up of her in tears (shot against a piece of wood in the production office, nowhere near the courtroom location that was shot three months earlier). We hoped that this close up would emphasise her presence.

Finally, we created an entirely new scene where Mrs Miller meets Lizzie at the graveside of Kevin, her dead son. Clearly Lizzie feels guilty and sad that her friend was killed. When Mrs Miller turns up they just look at each other. Nothing is said but you know that Mrs Miller is deeply wounded and there is very serious resentment. Lizzie leaves.

Mrs Miller re-shoot. New location, new lines, the illusion sealed with the eyelines, angle and good acting. The cut between the wide (above) and this close up was made on the action as she steps into shot, helping hide the cheat.

We shot this without sound or lights, just a camera and actors. We dashed into the graveyard, shot it early on a Sunday morning (thereby not having to deal with the council who wanted £1000 a day to shoot there!) and were out before anyone knew what was happening. This scene reinforced the character interrelationships and established the sense of distance between Mrs Miller and Lizzie. Crucially though, we the audience got to meet Mrs Miller twice in a matter of minutes, sending a loud signal – this character is important, remember her! If you want your audience to remember something, show them to it twice within a few moments, then it has a better chance of sitting in their memory, or even subconscious.

Mrs Miller in the courtroom scene, shot three months after the main shoot, a sheet of plywood in the background.

The upshot of these very minimal re-shoots is that we managed to fix a major breakdown in our story mechanics.

Common editorial mistakes

Getting to see your film again for the first time is always going to be impossible. So you never really know if it is working or not. This can lead to fixation on detail, 'Does that cut work . . . ?' rather than looking at the overall, 'Does the movie work?'

Common mistake number one . . .
It doesn't make sense

Everyone who read the script, then saw the actors perform it, and finally viewed the edit, will have no problem understanding the story. But they know the story, unlike the audience who get to experience it for the first time when they see the movie. Subtleties of performance or lines of dialogue that mean one thing to the film makers can mean something almost diametrically opposed to the audience. During your discussion after the film it's a good idea to check that all your plot mechanics are working, that all your character inter-relationships are understood correctly. Otherwise, you could end up with one audience member thinking Bob and Jane are brother and sister, whilst another audience member may think they are husband and wife. Clearly, this presents two very different stories. Confusion will mean your story breaks down, makes no sense and is therefore boring.

Common mistake number two . . .
It's slow

All those times in the cutting room when the director was saying 'no, no, no. Its a beautiful shot, let it breathe...' will now haunt you. You will sit through this screening wishing every single edit to come earlier. In your head, you will be screaming 'No, no, no, stay awake because the next scene is really good...oh dear god, hurry up, hurry, hurry, hurry'. If the director is present at this screening, it maybe a wake up call but beware, it may lead to further denial – 'They just don't understand my art...they are plebs'.

Common mistake number three . . .
Too Heavy handed

Being expert consumers, audiences are extraordinarily adept at extracting information from subtlety. Usually, this comes from an actor's performance, where lines in the script can often be dropped because the actor is saying so much more with their eyes. For instance, an actor filling up with tears may not need to say 'I love you', their performance says it with greater profundity and subtlety, the words end up telling the audience how to feel instead of allowing them to find out for themselves. In the same ballpark, you may find that you can drop large chunks of dialogue that seemed to be important in the script, but somehow have become repetitious or overstated in the final movie. In all instances, these are very tough edits to make for inexperienced film makers and ultimately, the only way to be sure that the choices you have made are right is to put it in front of an audience.

Common mistake number four . . .
Bad, bad film making

Let's rule out that your whole movie is awful. Lets assume that there are just a few trouble spots. There is no magic formula here, aside from a re-write or re-shoot (which still may not fix it), but if your movie has a moment that is truly awful, cut it out. If you can't, reduce it to the very least it can be: it's barest essence. Don't ever linger when you know the scene is soooo bad that you are going to shatter the illusion for the audience.

Fake mistakes

Ironically, much of the stuff you thought of as a problem, such as dodgy edits, shaky camera work, soft shots, poorly executed scenes, slightly unconvincing sets or locations etc., just aren't a problem. Whilst you were in the cutting room you would say 'No, no we can't do that. We'll never get away with it...will we?' It turns out that nine out of ten of these things will go completely unnoticed by the audience. They won't notice slightly poor technical film making, nor will they be impressed by what you think of as great moments and flashy sequences. They just want a good story told well.

If only we could turn back time

During cutting, alarm bells will occasionally begin to ring and you will remember all those times in script development when someone would say . . . 'You know you have a problem here...' and you'd reply, 'Oh we will get away with it...', 'No one will notice that' or 'We don't have time to improve the script, we have a movie to shoot!' All the problems with your screenplay will now stand out ten feet tall. You'll spend a large amount of time working your way out of corners that you could have avoided with more script and story development. But it's a double edged sword, sometimes you just have to go shoot your movie, even if the script isn't ready, or momentum may be lost. But as a rule, the old saying is soooooo true . . . 'If it ain't on the page, It ain't on the stage...'

you remember the gun was left on the back seat of the car?', 'Did you understand why Jack kissed Jane?' etc. For the first ten minutes of this discussion everyone will be polite and generally positive. No one wants to hurt your feelings. But then someone will crack and say something bothered them and the floodgates will open. Keep asking questions to get an open discussion going about how they felt during the film. This can be brutal, but if you don't do it now, you run the risk of it happening behind your back at the premiere, or worse, in the press when the film is released (if it is released). You'll probably find you have fallen foul of a number of common mistakes.

True horrors

We've all been in a cinema and turned to a friend...*'This is really boring...'* Oh the sin of all sins for a film maker. Audiences won't forgive you for being too slow or laborious. Nor will they forgive a story that doesn't connect with them, or actors for whom they feel no empathy, or a plot with no momentum etc. These are the areas that you must focus on and whenever called to do so, you should be happy to sacrifice to the *god of storytelling* all those shots and moments that you thought were either beautiful or profound but actually have reluctantly come to understand that they are kind of boring. Pace, pace, pace.

Re-cut number four

Directly after the test screening, the editor, director and producer will collaborate on yet another major re-cut and re-shuffle, integrating the valuable information gathered from the test audience. It's now time to bite the bullet on some of the more serious issues of the film, such as plot not working or character relations not working. Ideally, it's time for yet another re-shoot. This one will be a bit bigger and you may need to bring back costume or make-up as well as camera, sound and maybe even production design. Again, you may be able to squeeze it all in over a single weekend, but aside from shooting more establishing shots, hand shots, close-ups etc, you'll be grabbing close-ups of actors to augment or clarify scenes or even shoot completely new scenes that will have been written to help with failing story mechanics. Obviously, getting your actors back is paramount and one hopes that you didn't fall out because you abused them during the main shoot.

Wherever you plan to insert a close-up of an actor into a scene, you will need to study the make-up, costume, geometry and eye lines so that the new shot will slip into place effortlessly. On the whole, it's amazing what you can cheat and get away with. As stated earlier, the audience is only interested in a good story well told and are rarely bothered by dodgy shots or edits. Story, characters, plot.

Time for a break

It's not always possible, but it's helpful if everyone could take a month off to get perspective. When you return to the film, you will see it with fresh eyes, much more in line with an audience's first

Resist listening to compliments from friends and family who come to your test screeninegs, they are just amazed that got off you arse and did anything. It's nice to hear but remember, they will have no objectivity . . . and worse, they may lull you into a false sense of security . . .

Final cut . . . Again?

Here's a sad truth. I have never met a new film maker who was happy with the final cut of their first movie. There are a number of obvious causes – poor acting and coverage, rushed sound mixing, duff script to start off with . . . it may be that they could spend a decade re-cutting, never getting what they want, where the prudent course would be to move on. The material just wasn't good enough.

But often there is another reason. They fought long and hard in the cutting room but eventually locked picture, not because they had the best cut, but because they were financially, emotionally and spiritually spent. A year intensively making a movie for no money is a tough place to be creative. They could no longer see their film, they could only see shots and hear sounds. It's a bit like a relationship breaking up. They know it's wrong but don't know what to do to fix it. They know they are in love but the spark has gone and it's time to move on. Then sometime later, often a year or so, they catch their movie unexpectedly and see it with truly fresh eyes. This is often a revelation as they can now see just how much baggage was left lying around on the screen. The urge to re-cut can then become insatiable and real improvement can be made in a very short time.

Now let's be brutal here. How many times have you sat through a directors re-cut of a Hollywood movie and thought 'Gee I see why they left those scenes on the cutting room floor – I wish they had stayed there!' Currently, I personally believe that most movies are too long, and no I am not talking about 'Lord of the Rings'. Hands up if you have ever seen a movie that is too slow? OK, a few then. Oh, a lot? And how many times have you seen a movie that was too fast . . . Anyone? Anyone? Hmmm. This pacing problem is the issue that these new film makers will often come back and address (probably at video resolution only) for their video and DVD release. Take that 94 minute movie down to an 86 minute movie without really losing anything. I know we did it on both 'White Angel' and 'Urban Ghost Story' (although thankfully on UGS we managed to buy enough time in post to make these radical cuts before we actually committed to 35mm). In both cases the results were astonishing and the movies were transformed.

reaction. You will have let go of all the petty *'I love'* and *'I hate'* scenes / shots etc. and see them for what they truly are. Directors often loosen their grip on what they perceived to be pivotal character moments or beats that were *'beautiful'*. Everyone will favour telling the best story in the shortest possible time. Final cuts will be made, perhaps even more test screenings. You may choose to show the film 'off-the-record' to some industry people to get their informal opinion. But eventually, the picture edit is completed and the movie is 'locked'.

The movie will now pass into a much less creative stage, where the picture is conformed to a very high technical standard, titles and effects are added and the soundtrack is filled out and mixed.

At some point you are going to need a trailer cutting, so why not now with an editor who knows the material? The editor will resist this suggestion explaining that they cannot see the wood for trees, that they are exhausted, that they just DON'T WANT TO DO IT!!!!! But if you persist, they will relent and do a great job because they really care.

The main creative part of the editor's job is now over and they may well leave the project for other people to oversee track laying and sound mixing, onlining pictures (if the project was shot on video) or neg cutting and printing (if the project was shot on film), telecine, grading etc. If you can convince them to hang around, it will make your life much easier, unless you are adept at post production yourself. Otherwise you may end up needing, or even acting yourself, as a post production supervisor, which in truth is the job that remains. Editors love to cut images and sound and dealing with the myriad of headaches thrown up in this final technical stage of post production isn't too enticing.

Post

Traditional Lab

Blueprint

SOHO IMAGES
FILM LABORATORY
DIGITAL POST

This section deals with a project that is shot on film (not digital), specifically Super 16mm which will be blown up to 35mm so that it can be shown in cinemas. Without getting drawn into the film v digital debate, for my money, shooting on film is going to produce a more attractive image and attract a more professional and experienced cast and crew.

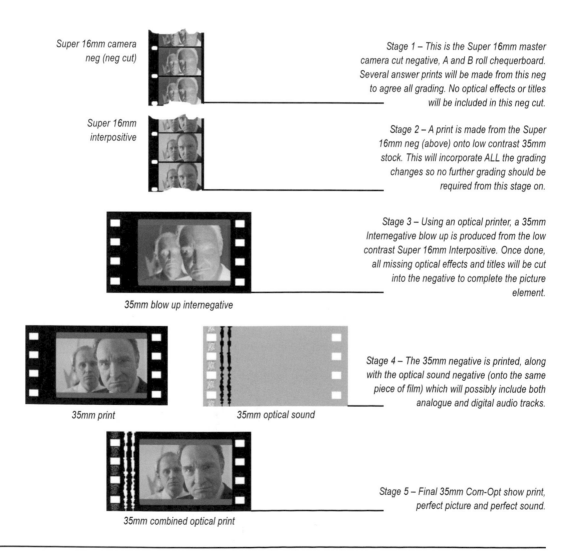

Super 16mm camera neg (neg cut)

Stage 1 – This is the Super 16mm master camera cut negative, A and B roll chequerboard. Several answer prints will be made from this neg to agree all grading. No optical effects or titles will be included in this neg cut.

Super 16mm interpositive

Stage 2 – A print is made from the Super 16mm neg (above) onto low contrast 35mm stock. This will incorporate ALL the grading changes so no further grading should be required from this stage on.

35mm blow up internegative

Stage 3 – Using an optical printer, a 35mm Internegative blow up is produced from the low contrast Super 16mm Interpositive. Once done, all missing optical effects and titles will be cut into the negative to complete the picture element.

35mm print   *35mm optical sound*

Stage 4 – The 35mm negative is printed, along with the optical sound negative (onto the same piece of film) which will possibly include both analogue and digital audio tracks.

35mm combined optical print

Stage 5 – Final 35mm Com-Opt show print, perfect picture and perfect sound.

Post Traditional Lab Blueprint

If you plan to shoot on S16mm to blow up to 35mm, we suggest the following route . . . Shoot S16mm film (any stock), at a frame rate of 25fps (not 24fps as you may be advised by others). Record the sound on DAT at either 44.1kHz or 48 kHz (it doesn't matter too much which you choose as long as everybody knows which one it is). You should try to cut on an Avid Media Composer or other Avid-editing platform that you can get your hands on (you can do it on XpressDV if you are careful). You will A&B roll neg. cut before making a S16mm inter positive followed by a 35mm inter negative blow-up. The sound will be mixed in either analogue Dolby (SR) or Dolby Digital and an optical soundtrack will be shot and married to the 35mm internegative. The propeller heads amongst you will be saying, *'I see, that's the way we should do it.'* The non-propeller heads will be saying, *'Dear God, what on earth are you talking about?'* Don't worry if you don't understand. Just make sure that whoever you are working with understands (entirely) the procedures and ramifications outlined in this paragraph above.

Cutting the deal

There are only a few laboratories in the UK that will process S16mm. They will all compete for your business and if you are a good producer, you should end up with quotes from all of them that are roughly in the same ballpark. On the three features that I have made, I have used three different labs. All of them have had their problems, but personally I would recommend going with either SoHo Images or Technicolor. How much should you pay? It's difficult to say because everybody has their own unique deal, but overleaf there is an example laboratory budget that you can use as a (very) rough guide.

Wherever possible, keep everything under one roof. You may find that you get a great quote for the first part of post production from one lab, but that you could get a cheaper negative cut if you move the film out of the lab for that middle stage before taking it back for the later stages. If you do this, and then discover there is a problem, no matter what the problem, the two companies will blame each other and you'll be piggy in the

Post production on film, opposed to digital, has been around for a hundred years and works extremely well. It is the stage where your film rushes are edited into a final version that can be projected.

Before production begins, it's essential that the director, cameraperson, editor, sound recordist and producer all attend a meeting at the laboratory so that the whole post production process can be outlined and hammered out. If you skip this meeting, you increase the probability of a technological screw-up, which could cost you a huge amount of money to fix later on in post.

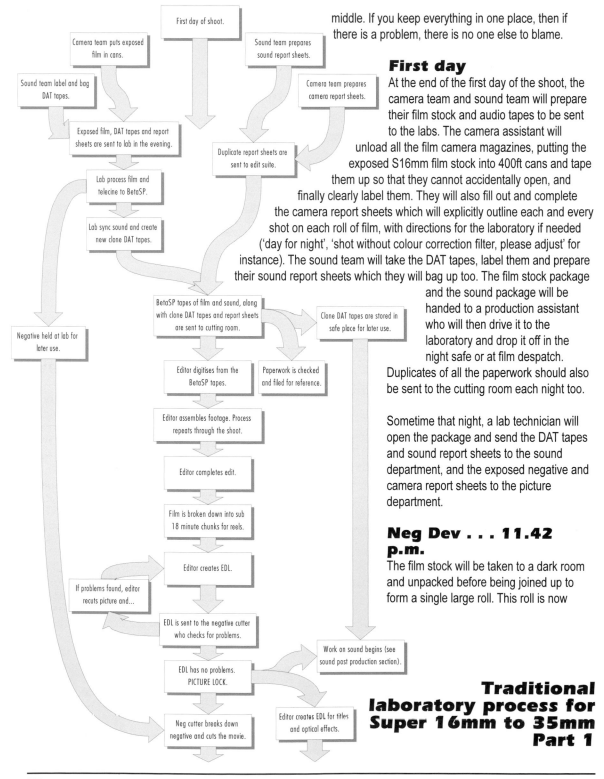

First day of shoot.

Camera team puts exposed film in cans.

Sound team prepares sound report sheets.

Sound team label and bag DAT tapes.

Camera team prepares camera report sheets.

Exposed film, DAT tapes and report sheets are sent to lab in the evening.

Duplicate report sheets are sent to edit suite.

Lab process film and telecine to BetaSP.

Lab sync sound and create new clone DAT tapes.

BetaSP tapes of film and sound, along with clone DAT tapes and report sheets are sent to cutting room.

Clone DAT tapes are stored in safe place for later use.

Negative held at lab for later use.

Editor digitises from the BetaSP tapes.

Paperwork is checked and filed for reference.

Editor assembles footage. Process repeats through the shoot.

Editor completes edit.

Film is broken down into sub 18 minute chunks for reels.

Editor creates EDL.

If problems found, editor recuts picture and...

EDL is sent to the negative cutter who checks for problems.

Work on sound begins (see sound post production section).

EDL has no problems. PICTURE LOCK.

Neg cutter breaks down negative and cuts the movie.

Editor creates EDL for titles and optical effects.

middle. If you keep everything in one place, then if there is a problem, there is no one else to blame.

First day

At the end of the first day of the shoot, the camera team and sound team will prepare their film stock and audio tapes to be sent to the labs. The camera assistant will unload all the film camera magazines, putting the exposed S16mm film stock into 400ft cans and tape them up so that they cannot accidentally open, and finally clearly label them. They will also fill out and complete the camera report sheets which will explicitly outline each and every shot on each roll of film, with directions for the laboratory if needed ('day for night', 'shot without colour correction filter, please adjust' for instance). The sound team will take the DAT tapes, label them and prepare their sound report sheets which they will bag up too. The film stock package and the sound package will be handed to a production assistant who will then drive it to the laboratory and drop it off in the night safe or at film despatch. Duplicates of all the paperwork should also be sent to the cutting room each night too.

Sometime that night, a lab technician will open the package and send the DAT tapes and sound report sheets to the sound department, and the exposed negative and camera report sheets to the picture department.

Neg Dev . . . 11.42 p.m.

The film stock will be taken to a dark room and unpacked before being joined up to form a single large roll. This roll is now

Traditional laboratory process for Super 16mm to 35mm Part 1

called lab roll 1 and will be 2000ft long or less (that is four and a half camera rolls). If you have over 2000ft to process in one night, they will start a second lab roll. The first lab roll will be called, spookily enough, lab roll 1, the second being lab roll 2 and so on. At the head of each lab roll, a technician will take a hole punch and physically punch a hole in the film stock. This is a very important marker which we will get to later. Each lab roll will then be passed through the negative developing baths, much like huge industrial sized versions of what you find in your local one-hour photo shop.

At the end of this, the lab should have a developed lab roll which will then be sent to the telecine department. Remember these guys work over night so it's probably something like 3 a.m. right now!

Telecine...03.01 a.m.

Telecine is the process where the film stock is electronically copied on to a videotape. At this point of post-production, the telecine is purely for reference purposes. Later on, the labs will come back to your master camera negative to make much higher quality copies and versions. Because film is physical and mechanical and videotape and non-linear editing is electronic,

Negative Processing and Tape Tansfer inc Betas, sync, clone dats and delivery	£0.25	40000	foot	£10,000.00
Negative Cutting (cost per cut or per reel)	£3.25	800	cuts	£2,600.00
S16 grading copy	£0.25	3600	foot	£900.00
Super 16mm IP	£0.70	3600	foot	£2,520.00
35mm blow up IN	£0.85	9000	foot	£7,650.00
Optical Sountrack Transfer	£0.30	9000	foot	£2,700.00
35mm Check print	£0.18	9600	foot	£1,728.00
Low Contrast Print for Telecine	£1,100.00	1	each	£1,100.00
Optical Effects (If cannot be done at Lab)	£750.00	1	each	£750.00
Titles	£1,250.00	1	each	£1,250.00

£21,198.00

Tradtitional Post Budget

Shooting on film is expensive. This budget doesn't even include the cost of the stock, just the processing, so brace yourself . . . The route here is for shooting on S16mm film with a plan to blow up to 35mm for cinema projection. There are alternative digital processes now which are competitive, and you could also shoot on film but master to tape only (either DigiBeta or one of the emerging HiDef formats) which would mean you don't need several of these stages, but until digital projection is truly here, you would not be able to screen it in a cinema.

The first line is the negative processing, transfer to BetaSP, sound sync and generation of clone DATs. There is 40,000 foot of stock, which equates to around 100 camera rolls. Of course you could do it for much less, we managed to shoot our second feature 'White Angel' on 54 rolls! If you sync the sound yourself (and I would not recommend you do) you could shave a couple of pence per foot off the bill. The next line is for the negative cutting. There are various possibilities here, charging per cut, per reel or an overall deal for the whole job. The Super16mm grading copy is the first print, minus optical effects and titles, and will be viewed to discuss the colour grading of the image. There may be several passes at this, but you should only pay for one. The Super 16mm IP (inter-positive) is the first stage in the blow up process, the 3600 feet referring to an estimated running time of 90 minutes at 25fps. The 35mm blow up IN (inter-negative) is now printed on 35mm film stock so it is physically bigger, 9000 feet to be precise! Ouch, that one hurts the purse too! The optical soundtrack is the cost to transfer the final sound mix onto film so that it will work on a 35mm print. The 35mm check print, a final screening print, is slightly longer to accommodate the fact that there are leaders on the film, which will add to it's length. Subsequent prints should cost you anywhere between £700-£1000. The Low Contrast Telecine print is a special print that is used for putting onto videotape (you cannot use a normal projection print as it is too contrasty). Optical effects are all those special mixes or dissolves, slow downs or speed ups, re-frames etc. Best avoided of course. The titles are the front credits and end roller. Simple black on white. Anything fancy and you can add another couple of grand.

Paul Collard
Soho Images

'While there is a lot of excitement about digital post production, traditional post production for simple films where there are no major effects above the occasional dissolve and title, is still a very good option. Many new film makers get seduced into shooting digitally because of the clear cost saving up front, but they fail to consider post production and often get stuck there. There have been incredible developments in new film stocks, offering reduced grain and filming in lower light conditions, making traditional film making, both shooting and post production on film just as viable as ever. Most films are still post produced this way (circa 2003).

As a way to save a little money, many film makers choose not to have the sound synchronised by the lab. But this means the editor needs to spend time each day synching the sound and the film makers are forced to wait to see their rushes with sound. Eventually, most change their minds and ask us to synch the sound for them, so I would suggest doing this in the first place.

Digital film making is a very exciting option. We have seen projects shot on many different formats, DV, DigigBeta, 35mm, S16mm, HiDef etc., which can often be inter-cut quite success-fully. Editing with Final Cut Pro and Avid XpressDV is also common now, although telecine of film must go onto DVCam and not miniDV (which does not carry timecode). From your home edit system you can then edit your film, generate a cutting list for the neg cutter, or even master a version which could be screened for distributors and sales agents as a 'nearly complete' project. This means you don't need to produce the extremely costly 35mm blow up until you know you have a buyer for your film.'

there needs to be a bridge between the two technologies – mechanical and electronic. This bridge is timecode – every frame of film has a unique time code which will be generated when the film is transferred to videotape. Remember that punch hole? That will be used as an absolute physical reference for the timecode. For instance, this is lab roll 1, so the time code (which is expressed in hours, minutes, seconds and frames e.g. 01:22:11:24, which means, one hour, twenty-two minutes, eleven seconds and twenty four frames) would begin at the punch hole and would start at 01:00:00:00. If you advanced by one physical frame of film, the time code reference would then change to 01:00:00:01. Using this process, there is a rock solid relationship between the physical and electronic worlds.

Later, when you have edited your movie on an Avid, the computer can create an EDL, (an Edit Decision List) which will contain a long list of timecodes. These timecodes will allow the neg. cutter to absolutely reference each and every frame of film and cut up your negative to match the decisions you made in the Avid edit suite.

Back to that first night at the labs. The neg has been developed and is now sitting in the telecine department waiting for a bleary eyed operator to come in at 3 a.m. and transfer your rushes. The operator will line up the punch hole at the head of the reel and tell the equipment that because this is lab roll 1, the time code will start at this frame at 01:00:00:00 (if it were lab roll eleven, the time code would start at 11:00:00:00 for example). The operator will then transfer the film with very little modification to brightness and colour balances. This is commonly referred to as a 'one light transfer'. During the telecine, the operator will make notes about potential problems and generate a document called 'the lab report sheet'. Generally this will flag up any technological problems, such as excessive dust or sparkle on the picture, camera scratches, unexpected under exposure or over exposure, incorrect colour balance, even microphones popping into frame. Later, this report sheet will be sent to the cutting room with the BetaSP rushes and a second copy may be faxed to the production team so that the camera team can examine it to see if there are any technical problems they need to deal with (such as camera scratches).

After the telecine is completed, the operator will then re-can the lab roll and it will be sent down to the vaults for use later in the process. The Beta SP tape, along with the lab report sheet will then be sent down to the sound department.

Sound sync . . . 05.24 a.m.

The synchronisation of the sound at the laboratory is always a thorny issue, for two simple reasons. First, the production could save money by asking the editor to synchronise the sound in the Avid edit suite, but this will mean

The lab report sheet

This is the piece of paper you will get back from the lab when they have processed your negative. With this one from Soho Images, it can also be delivered digitally. It will often be faxed to the production office before the rushes are delivered so the DP can check for problems such as excessive dust and sparkle, negative scratches and that the printer lights are all as expected (implying that the exposure has been correct).

Lab roll no.
All the camera rolls are spliced together by the lab into larger rolls. These rolls replace camera rolls for identification purposes during postproduction, now there is one videotape for each roll for example.

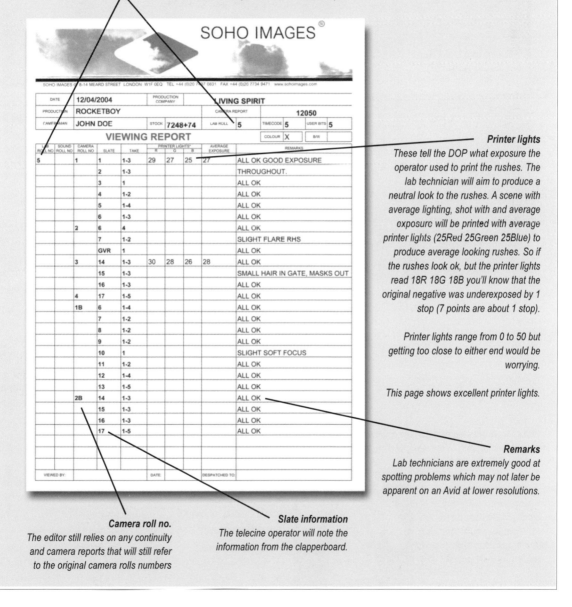

Printer lights
These tell the DOP what exposure the operator used to print the rushes. The lab technician will aim to produce a neutral look to the rushes. A scene with average lighting, shot with and average exposure will be printed with average printer lights (25Red 25Green 25Blue) to produce average looking rushes. So if the rushes look ok, but the printer lights read 18R 18G 18B you'll know that the original negative was underexposed by 1 stop (7 points are about 1 stop).

Printer lights range from 0 to 50 but getting too close to either end would be worrying.

This page shows excellent printer lights.

Remarks
Lab technicians are extremely good at spotting problems which may not later be apparent on an Avid at lower resolutions.

Camera roll no.
The editor still relies on any continuity and camera reports that will still refer to the original camera rolls numbers

Slate information
The telecine operator will note the information from the clapperboard.

Punch hole

At the head of each lab roll (which can be up to 2000 feet in length – 45 minutes ish) there is a physical punch hole. This represents the first frame on the reel. As you advance a frame of film, so you advance a frame on the electronic time code. The top left number on this frame is the lab roll number, in this case, lab roll 53. The bottom left is the film Key Kode which is generally unused. The lower right number is the timecode, 06:00:00:00. There are only 24 hours in a time code cycle so after 24 hours it simply recycles over and over.

When doing your rushes telecine, ask the operator to transfer the material in a letterboxed 1.85:1 mask with lab roll number, Key Kode and timecodes burnt into the black areas at the top and bottom of the frame. Do not get a 16:9 telecine or a 4:3 telecine, and as you shot at 25fps, so you will transfer at 25fps. Simple!

Burnt in information

This is a frame from the BetaSP rushes, from lab roll 52 (top left) and time code 06:05:58:24 (bottom right). The electronic timecode means that the neg cutter can go to lab roll 52, then spool forward XXXX frames to the exact frame. Cool huh? Don't worry, the neg cutter isn't some nerdy guy who can figure out hours, minutes, seconds and frames in decimal world, they have software that does it for them.

that they don't have the luxury of time coded clone DATs for later audio auto conform (and you really want this), plus they will have to spend several hours every day synching the sound and not actually getting on with cutting the picture and drama to see if there are any problems that can be quickly sorted on set. Secondly, if the production shoots at 24fps (against the better advice of this book!) then the laboratory will not be able to sync the sound and it will have to be done manually by the editor anyway.

Don't choose the cheapest lab just because they are the cheapest. Often saving a little money but going with a cheaper labscan end up costing MUCH more. All labs make mistakes, but some more than others. Ask around before you choose the lab to whom you will commit your entire project and always see if you can get a competitive deal out of the top ones.

Lets assume that you have decided to have the labs sync the sound. First, the sound department will take the DATs of the live sound recorded and digitise them into a computer work station. The original DAT will now be stored and more than likely, never used again. Because sound is handled digitally there is no quality loss – cloning is the key word here.

The sound operator will then run the Bela SP tape and start synching the sound from set with the pictures on the BetaSP using the clapper board as a visual and audio reference. One of the reasons why it's essential to get a good, clear and clean 'clap' at the head or tail of every shot is that without it, the labs will not attempt to sync the sound and the editor will be forced to eye match it later. This is a waste of time all round and there really is no excuse for failing to get a good 'clap' for every shot.

By the end of this process, there will be perfectly synchronised picture and sound and the sound operator will copy this sound onto the analogue audio tracks of the BetaSP. They will also, and this is the cunning bit, lay off the sound on to a time coded DAT that has exactly the same time code as the BetaSP. So this lab roll 1 will start at 01:00:00:00 on both the Beta SP and the cloned DAT and can be tracked back accurately to the master camera negative. This also means that later on in the sound process, all the edited sound can be auto con-formed in a sound editing facility using the edit decision list from the Avid.

Occasionally, wild tracks or atmospheres will have been recorded on set, which will have no corresponding picture. These additional sounds will be recorded at the end of the BetaSP and the cloned DAT (again with matching timecode).

When you strike a deal with the lab, you will be assigned a laboratory contact. This is the person who you will call when you need to discuss anything with the laboratory and it helps avoid getting lost in the process of speaking to six different people, all of who will pass the buck. Beware though, lab contacts tend to start work in the early hours and have often gone home by mid afternoon, so if you need a conversation to take place, make sure it happens in the morning.

Delivery . . . 08.14 a.m.
The clone DAT, the Beta SP and the lab report sheets will then be sent as quickly as possible to the cutting room so that the editor can begin work.

FLEx file
A FLEx file is a simple text file listing the timecodes and key numbers associated with the slates in a particular roll of film (usually supplied on a floppy disk from the lab). This speeds the process of importing and digitising the material into the Avid and eliminates a layer of human error which could have costly consequences.

When the roll of negative is loaded into the telecine machine, the punch hole will be lined up with the corresponding hour timecode on the videotape (e.g. neg roll 3's punch hole would be at 03:00:00:00). The film key number (a machine readable bar code and human readable number running down the side of the negative) is read by a computer at this point and (should be) checked by the telecine operator to check it's correct.

The telecine session starts, and the computer keeps track of the film key numbers and correspond-ing video timecodes. The telecine operator will hit a key whenever a new slate is spotted running through on the negative, and make a note of the slate number. The computer will automatically make a note of the key numbers and video timecodes at this point. The computer will also spot if a new camera roll runs through the telecine, because at this point the key numbers will change radically.

When the telecine session is over, the computer will create a text file listing all the slates in that roll of neg with their corresponding key numbers and video timecodes. This is called a FLEx file (e.g. UGS003.FLE). You can then convert this into Avid readable form using a program called "Avid Log Exchange" which creates ALE files to be imported into Avid bins. Sometimes the telecine house will create an ALE file for you as well. You can then digitise your slates into the Avid automatically with all the correct key numbers ready to go!

Sometimes the production will request VHS tapes of the rushes too, but if you are going to pay for these, I would suggest saving the money as realistically, no one will ever have time to look at them.

To the cutting room

On the morning of the second day of the shoot, the editor will excitedly unpack the BetaSP, clone DAT and report sheets for lab roll 1, that's yesterday's footage. The clone DATs should be stored in a box, high up on a shelf and out of the way for now (they will be used in the sound editing process later). The editor will then take the BetaSP and digitise it on to the Avid. Remember this is only a working copy and will only ever be used for decision making. This is not the quality of the finished film.

During digitisation the editor will check with the report sheets to make sure there are no unexpected errors or missing material. The producer may also sit in on this digitisation to watch the rushes as they play for the first time.

Once the footage has been digitised, the editor will break it down, labelling each shot and take with a brief description and quality comment. The editor will then edit the shots, usually a scene at a time. This process will repeat itself every day of the shoot until the film wraps and the editor finally completes the edit.

Picture lock

Before locking picture, there are a number of creative editing stages that you should have passed through. As we're dealing only with the technical issues in this chapter, we'll assume that you have passed through these stages (see The Editor's Blueprint).

Reels

When a film is screened in a cinema or at a film festival, it is delivered in 2000ft rolls. These cans are about 18 inches across and an inch and a half deep. Each reel will last for around eighteen minutes (ish) each and they will be cut together at the cinema before being projected. Here's the problem. Wherever those reels are joined, there will be an unpleasant jump in the picture and thump in the sound where the projectionist has taped the reels together (yes taped!). Depending on how many venues the print has visited previously

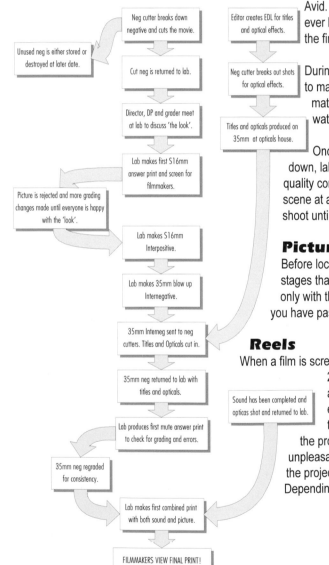

Neg cutter breaks down negative and cuts the movie.

Unused neg is either stored or destroyed at later date.

Cut neg is returned to lab.

Director, DP and grader meet at lab to discuss 'the look'.

Lab makes first S16mm answer print and screen for filmmakers.

Picture is rejected and more grading changes made until everyone is happy with the 'look'.

Lab makes S16mm Interpositive.

Lab makes 35mm blow up Internegative.

35mm Interneg sent to neg cutters. Titles and Opticals cut in.

35mm neg returned to lab with titles and opticals.

Lab produces first mute answer print to check for grading and errors.

35mm neg regraded for consistency.

Lab makes first combined print with both sound and picture.

FILMMAKERS VIEW FINAL PRINT!

Editor creates EDL for titles and optical effects.

Neg cutter breaks out shots for optical effects.

Titles and opticals produced on 35mm at opticals house.

Sound has been completed and opticas shot and returned to lab.

Traditional laboratory Process for Super 16mm to 35mm print. Part 2

and how carefully the projectionist has taken the print apart after screenings, you may find that around the reel changes, the film is damaged. It's not unheard of for a projectionist to carelessly lop out a chunk of your movie! With this in mind, you should engineer that your reel changes happen at the ends of scenes where as little as possible is going on in the drama. Never put important dialogue or action around a reel change (ideally, these would be establishing shots). Also avoid any music over a reel change as this will sound terrible in the cinema. At some point after the picture is locked, the editor and director should go through the movie and make up the reels. Check with the lab about exact footages that they can handle and remember if it is 2000ft that may include leaders.

Neg cut

Assuming you have arrived at the best possible cut of your movie, it's time to move on to the negative cutting process. You have creatively edited your film and it's now time to take all those editorial decisions and have them applied to your master camera negative. The way this works is that you export a cutting list (EDL) from the Avid and send it to the neg cutters. This list is simply a document that explains where each and every shot comes from and where it fits into the final movie. The neg cutter will look at this list, chop up the master camera negative and stick it all together to exactly match the edits that you made in the Avid. This is a scary time because sharp blades are about to come into contact with your master camera negative. If any mistakes are made, they are very difficult and expensive to put right.

Neg cut considerations

There are a couple of things you need to consider if you're going to neg cut your film. First because you are working in a real and physical world you cannot re-use shots as you would if you were cutting on video. Every frame of film is unique and if you want to re-use it, you will have to create an optical copy which will be expensive and poorer in quality than the rest of the movie. So here's the deal. If you know that you are going to want to re-use shots, for instance maybe there is a flashback sequence that recurs several times in your story, then shoot it several times so that you have a piece of original camera negative for each recurrence in the story.

The second thing to keep in mind is that because S16mm film is so physically small, there is no space between the frames to make a cut (unlike 35mm where there is plenty of space to make a cut). The upshot is that to join two pieces of S16mm film together, you would have to destroy a frame of film at the beginning and end of each shot. This is why S16mm is A&B roll checkerboard neg cut. Essentially, this means that on one roll of film (the 'A' roll), all the even numbered shots are assembled, and on the other roll (the 'B' roll), all the odd numbered shots are assembled. The labs would then make a print, first of all printing roll A, then roll B on to the same roll of stock.

J ason Wheeler
Negative Cutter

'In the cutting room, too many directors create 'effects' such as a speed-up or re-frame without understanding the consequences of that choice – it could be a complicated optical effect that may protract post production and cost a lot of money. Too many new film makers don't understand what neg cutting is and therefore have unrealistic or naive expectations of the process. Another common problem is that the neg cut is THE final stage for picture, you can't put off any decisions now, and that final step is fraught with a myriad of little problems and issues which need to be addressed. You just can't put it off anymore.

I'd love a producer and editor to come to me before they make any post production decisions, so that we can iron out the whole process. It makes my life easier and saves them money. During the shoot, stay with the laboratory to do your rushes telecine as this is the link between your picture cut and the negative. You may get better deals with other telecine outfits but if they make a simple mistake, you may not discover it until it's too late, and then YOU may be forced to spend weeks unravelling it.

Producers should understand all aspects of post production so that silly or short sighted mistakes are avoided. Saving money 'now' may cost much more later. Get it right first time by planning in meticulous detail. If you shoot Super16mm I would suggest doing a digital blow up to 35mm and not a traditional optical blow up. The costs are similar and a digital blow up will give you much greater creative freedom with grading, re-using shots, re-frames, motion effects etc.'

EDL – Edit Decision List

CMX 3600 is the most common and robust cross platform EDL that we have come across. Make sure that when you supply your EDL it is on the correct format disk, most cutters use DOS format. Note also that a CMX 3600 can only handle 999 cuts. You will probably never see your EDL in this format, printed out that is, as it's almost always electronic . . . But then if it can go wrong . . . Better to at least understand the process when you consider that sharp blades are about to come into contact with your master negative!

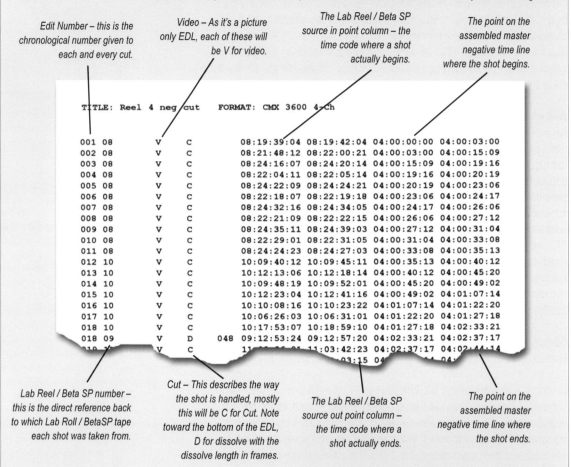

Edit Number – this is the chronological number given to each and every cut.

Video – As it's a picture only EDL, each of these will be V for video.

The Lab Reel / Beta SP source in point column – the time code where a shot actually begins.

The point on the assembled master negative time line where the shot begins.

Lab Reel / Beta SP number – this is the direct reference back to which Lab Roll / BetaSP tape each shot was taken from.

Cut – This describes the way the shot is handled, mostly this will be C for Cut. Note toward the bottom of the EDL, D for dissolve with the dissolve length in frames.

The Lab Reel / Beta SP source out point column – the time code where a shot actually ends.

The point on the assembled master negative time line where the shot ends.

Get it? Hmm, I understand, it's a bit of head screw. Just check out the diagram and I think you'll understand . . . eventually! Again, don't worry if you don't, just make sure your editor does. It's important to remember that you will lose a frame directly preceding and post every shot.

Some versions of Avid have dupe detection which you can use to check for frame overlaps, or you can send a copy of your EDL to the neg cutter and ask them to check for frame overlaps and duplicate material. If any problems are found, then you will have to go back to the cutting room and re-cut around these issues. Most of the time, this means little more than trimming out one or two frames, but it MUST be done. This is one reason why you cannot move on to other stages of post production, such as sound and music, until you have absolutely locked picture.

The neg cutter will take a few weeks to assemble the picture. If you had any optical effects such as slowing down a shot or speeding up a shot, then there will be holes left in the neg cut for these to be inserted at the 35mm stage later on. Wherever possible, try and avoid optical effects as they are messy and expensive. If you want a slow motion shot, you should have shot it on set in slow motion! Titles are the same as opticals in so much as they will be created on 35mm and cut in to the final 35mm negative blow-up later on down the line.

Back to the lab

After the negative has been cut, the reels will be sent back to the lab and a S16mm answer print will be made. Prior to making this print, the cameraperson and director should have met with the colour timer or grader (this is the person who's job it is to take care of the colour balances within the film) and have discussed the overall look and feel they are trying to achieve. The first job of the grader will be to make the film look consistent, as though it were all shot in order and in moments that follow one another. They will also darken shots that need to look more like night and correct shots that may have been incorrectly exposed for instance. Within fairly narrow parameters, it is astonishing what they can achieve. But, they are not miracle workers and the tools that they have at their disposal are nothing like the kind of tools that you may be used to on a computer, such as the colour grading in Avid or Adobe PhotoShop. For instance, simple things such as making a colour shot into a black and white shot are simply not possible within the traditional methods of colour grading.

Once this first answer print has been made, the film makers would come to a special private screening at the laboratory where the film will be projected and viewed for the very first time. It will have black holes where the optical effects and titles are going to go and it will not have any sound, but that's OK because right now, it's all about getting the picture right. There will be lots of tweaking, *'that scene was too purple, the last shot was greenish, the whole of the bedroom scene was too bright'* etc. It's important to completely communicate everything you want to change with the grader. It's also important to listen to their experience, especially when they are reaching the limits of their technological capability. This is not a time to procrastinate, nor is it appropriate to request one thing and then later on down the line, completely change your mind.

After this screening, the grader will go back and re-grade the whole film and make another print. Once again, the film makers will be invited to come and view the re-graded movie and request any changes that are needed. This process will usually

Ask around other producers and find out what kind of deals they got with the labs as deals can vary radically. This is especially relevant when it comes to final prints as labs often charge film makers more than they charge distributors.

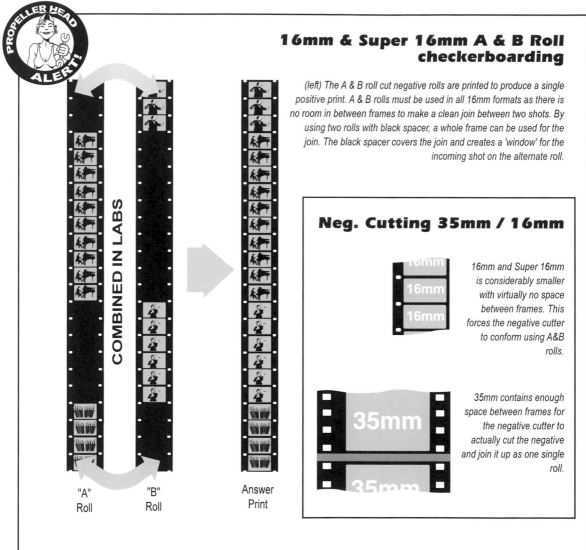

16mm & Super 16mm A & B Roll checkerboarding

(left) The A & B roll cut negative rolls are printed to produce a single positive print. A & B rolls must be used in all 16mm formats as there is no room in between frames to make a clean join between two shots. By using two rolls with black spacer, a whole frame can be used for the join. The black spacer covers the join and creates a 'window' for the incoming shot on the alternate roll.

COMBINED IN LABS

"A" Roll

"B" Roll

Answer Print

Neg. Cutting 35mm / 16mm

16mm

16mm

16mm and Super 16mm is considerably smaller with virtually no space between frames. This forces the negative cutter to conform using A&B rolls.

35mm

35mm

35mm contains enough space between frames for the negative cutter to actually cut the negative and join it up as one single roll.

16mm negative join in detail

Exposed negative frames – the frame directly before and after a shot is used to join the negative to the black spacer.

Overlap frame – used to join onto black spacer and effectively destroys the frame.

Black spacer – used to create unexposed windows for printing A & B roll checkerboard negative.

be completed within three or four passes at the most. You don't pay for each pass (of course this depends on the deal you have cut with the laboratory), but it is understood that you will try your level best to get it right in as few passes as possible. Never ever go to the next stage unless you are completely and 100% happy with the grading of your film. There is tremendous temptation to skip a final grading session because you are under time pressures and the grader will say something like, *'Don't worry, we'll integrate those last few changes in the blow-up'.* If you do this, you can bet your bottom dollar that when you see your final blow-up, you will be unhappy with these final tweaks, but it's too late then as you've just spent £10k doing it. Get it right at the S16mm grading stage and no later.

S16mm IP – (Interpositive)

Now that the picture has been fully graded, it's time to begin the lengthy and expensive blow-up stages, the first of which is the S16mm interpositive. Currently, your film is broken down into five reels (that is if your movie is around ninety minutes), each reel having an A roll and a B roll of negative. These reels will then be printed on to a single piece of S16mm low contrast, positive film (which will include ALL the grading choices you have made) for each reel. At the end of this process, you will be left with five reels, all printed on positive stock and no longer an A and B roll cut. There will still be black holes where titles and opticals will be inserted later and you won't ever view this print as it is used only in the manufacture of the blow-up.

35mm IN – (Internegative)

Each of the new low contrast, S16mm reels will now be passed through an optical printer which will blow them up to 35mm film. This is a very slow and expensive process. While you will feel the need to pick up the phone and hassle the lab, it is perhaps prudent to let them know that you are on their case but never push them too hard. You don't want them to make mistakes under pressure. It may take anywhere between a week and a month to make this 35mm internegative. Once it has been produced, the lab will immediately make a 35mm print and screen it for the film makers. Often there are still problems and the lab may go back and re-print a reel for instance. Again the titles and opticals will still be missing.

Titles and Opticals

The title and optical elements should have been produced by now and will exist on 35mm film stock. You may need to have done a telecine of these elements so that the editor can create a new EDL for these new clips (the opticals and titles roll, on 35mm, will be yet another lab roll). The lab will send the five 35mm blow-up negative reels, the titles and opticals negative and the EDL to the neg cutters, who will then cut the titles and opticals into the 35mm negative. The neg will then be returned to the lab who will make yet another print, checking the grading of these new titles and opticals (so that the colour balance matches that of the rest of the film). The film makers

Steve Boag
Titles – Cineimage

Titles and opticals on film

Film opticals are notoriously hard to get right – that means that any special effect that isn't a straightforward dissolve (these can be achieved by A&B roll neg cutting) should be avoided if at all possible. Audiences are impressed by a good story well told, not by Star Wars style wipes! Effects achieved at the press of a button on an Avid have to be painstakingly recreated from the original negative by a lab technician. This can take weeks to get right and cost a fortune.

The main problem is because opticals are a photochemical process and simply can't see the results until they're printed at the lab – you are relying on the expertise of the optical technician and are basically `flying blind'. Film opticals will soon be a thing of the past, but for the next few years they will remain cheaper than their digital equivalents.The best option is to plan ahead and shoot everything. Shoot slow motion by overcranking the camera, shoot speed up footage by undercranking the camera, shoot your opening credit sequence by getting the art department to lay out the text, even shoot your end title cards the same way (you don't have to have a credit roller).

However, sometimes a step printed slomo – printing the same frame more than once (e.g. twice for half speed) – can provide a dramatically different effect to an in-camera slomo. Or if you are not A&B roll neg cutting, any dissolves or fades to black will need to be achieved optically. Or you may want your opening title cards running over moving footage (very expensive – £thousands). Or you may want to flop a shot so it appears that an actor is looking in the opposite direction. These effects and more will take you into the realm of the film optical.

Before you can do anything you must lock your edit so that nothing will change picturewise. Go through the reels and note down any effect that isn't a cut (or simple dissolve if you're A&B roll neg cutting). Now work out all the source material you need to achieve these effects. You have to make a list of all the slates needed, with neg roll number, key numbers and video timecodes. This is called an Optical pull list. The Avid can do this automatically, sorting all the shots in neg roll order, although it's a good idea to double check the Avid's numbers from the burned in key numbers to check they're correct.

Reel TC	Duration	First/Last Key	Neg Roll	Cam Roll	Clip Name
02:08:13:10 02:08:25:13	18+03	KI 28 1620-4124+13 4142+15	045	A61	49/04
02:08:28:11 02:08:35:28	11+06	KI 28 1620-4219+01 4230+06	045	A61	49/05
02:08:44:20 02:08:50:23	9+03	KI 28 1620-4691+12 4700+14	045	A61	52/03
02:09:41:05 02:09:45:18	6+11	KI 28 1620-4826+06 4833+00	045	A61	52/03

Sample optical pull list

The neg cutter will pull these slates in their entirety so that the whole shot is preserved (flash frame to flash frame, or from the moment the camera turned over until the camera cut). This process should happen before the main neg cut. These new rolls of neg will be sent to the opticals house.

You now have to instruct the optical technician exactly what effects need achieving, again with key numbers, feet & frame counts, neg rolls, video timecodes etc. This is called an optical list, and again the Avid can make this list for you, but double check it against the burned in key numbers to make sure.

For your opening and closing credits you'll need to supply a carefully spell-checked Word document of cast and crew names (and a font) so that artwork can be created, and supply exact timings (in feet & frames) for how long each card should remain on the screen, and how many frames to fade them on and off. This can easily turn into an extremely long and dense document (sometimes hundreds of pages for effects heavy films), another reason to simplify your edit and remove as many opticals as you can. Play out the entire film from the Avid onto BetaSP in reels and send this along to the opticals house. The optical technician will take the raw negative and make 35mm interpositive duplicates of the sections needed (blowing up from S16mm if required as opticals are always created on 35mm).

The opticals will then be painstakingly created according to your lists (get them right!), and using the Avid video playouts as a guide. The interpositive elements will be re-photographed on an optical printer, creating new master negative elements. The next morning the technician will view a print of this neg at the lab to see if it looks satisfactory.

Cont . . .

cont . . . Titles and film opticals

When the process is complete (weeks later) the whole new roll of opticals will be telecined onto a tape and redigitised into the Avid. You can then check them frame by frame against the Avid sequence and ask the opticals house to re-do any that aren't exactly correct (usually about 15% of them).

Once satisfied, you can note the key numbers of where the opticals cut in and out, and inform the neg cutter where to insert them into your master neg reels (or 35mm internegative if you're working from 16mm).

```
==============================================================
OPTICAL #2.3            Assemble Event #128      total length:   11+05
     02:09:41:05
                        Camera      Reel
                        Count       Count
--------------------------------------------------------------
| KI 28 1620-4826+06   [1] |   0+00    071+12
| Neg Roll: 045            |
| Cam Roll: A61            |
| Clip: 52/03              |
|                          |
|--------------------------|
| KI 28 1620-4830+01       |   3+11    875+07  | KI 02 1710-4483+15    [2] |
|                          |                   |                           |
| Dissolve     3+00        |                   | Dissolve     3+00         |
|                          |                   |---------------------------|
| KI 28 1620-4833+00  6+11 |   6+10    878+06  | KI 02 1710-4486+14        |
                                               |---------------------------|
                                               | Neg Roll: 046             |
                                               | Cam Roll: A62             |
                                               | Clip: 53/02               |
                                               |                           |
                              11+04    883+00  | KI 02 1710-4491+08    7+10 |
==============================================================
```

Sample optical list for a 72 frame dissolve

One problem you always come up against doing film opticals from 16mm negative is that the grading will come out wrong. The rest of the 16mm neg will be graded, but the 35mm opticals will not have had the same grading look applied, so when they're cut into your final 35mm internegative they can look out of place.

One solution to this is to grade the sections of neg around the opticals beforehand and pass this grading information onto the optical technician who will incorporate this grading while he's creating the opticals.

The other solution is to adjust the grading slightly for these optical shots when the release prints are made. But this is a last resort, as the lab will often forget to incorporate these grading changes.

will of course come and view this print and if all has gone well, this should represent the end of the picture process at the laboratory.

Sound

As you have been going through this laboratory process, you should have also been working on the sound. Ideally, you will have completed your final sound mix and sent it to the lab to *'shoot an optical sound neg'* as early as possible. This is a piece of 35mm film with the sound printed on it. There are several sound formats you can use, but it's most likely you will use the twin track analogue (Dolby SR encoded) tracks and possibly Dolby Digital or DTS tracks too (see sound editing section). At some point after the 35mm blow-up, the sound will be married with the picture and from that point on, every 35mm print that you view, whether it's one to check the grading or a show print, will have sound. Once the sound and picture are married, the 35mm print will be referred to as a Com-Opt (Combined Optical) print.

And that's it . . . Phew.

Keep your titles simple. No one is impressed or fooled by a flashy and expensive title sequence. White titles on a black background will do nicely, and it's the cheapest way of doing it too!

Post Production Sound Blueprint

Most new film makers think that the sound for their film is limited to dialogue, obvious effects such as gun shots or wind, and the occasional spattering of music. But it is so much more, and one area where for little more than a few weeks, extra hard work, YOU can massively improve the production value of your movie. The sound is one of the last stages where you can add a new layer of direction, through subtle acoustic design. The hardware is cheap, the software tools almost always free, so what's the problem? Go create!

Dialogue

The sound of the actors' voices that was recorded on set. Should be clear and crisp. Don't worry about getting other sounds off set, just the dialogue.

ADR

Re-performance of the lines, sometime later, often in a home made studio. Can suffer from being dull and flat, requiring audio sweetening in the final mix to match the set dialogue.

Sound effects

Mono and stereo sound effects. Most are obvious, car doors and gunshots etc., but you should build up a rich and interesting soundscape using your sound effects.

Atmospheres

Continuous 'sound' that appears throughout a scene. Not usually what was recorded on set, but pulled off sound effects CDs and in stereo. Keep 'em as thick and rich as possible.

Foley

Performed by a foley, or footsteps artist. A recreation of all the actors' movements within the film to add audio sweetness and fill out the M&E mix for foreign territories.

Music

Both background and foreground music, usually specially composed but could come from a library or other musical sources. Beware of overuse.

Post Prod. Sound Blueprint

New film makers regularly make the common mistake of thinking that the sound is little more than dialogue, a few sound effects and music. This lack of appreciation is enhanced by the very real lack of cash that the production is suffering from after going over budget in the shoot, and months of editing. Understand that if you compromise too much in your final sound stages, later on during sales and distribution you will be forced to return to it and re-do it properly.

The job of sound

The soundtrack of your film is a powerful story telling, and story enhancement tool.

First of all, and quite obviously, it should relay the dialogue that the actors speak. If you are going to have a character say something, it must be clear and understandable to the audience. In the cutting room, you may understand what a mumbled line is all about (as you wrote the script and stood next to the actor when they said it) but a virgin audience may not. So make sure that all your dialogue can be understood.

Secondly, sound is used to help seal the illusion that what is on the screen is *real*. Therefore, everything in the picture (and world of the story) that could make, or appears to make a sound needs an accompanying sound effect – car doors, ticking clocks, cats purring, gunshots etc. Most of it is pretty obvious. Peculiarly, the real sound made by something often doesn't fit and a new, manufactured sound is put in its place. For instance, anyone who has fired a gun knows that it sounds nothing like the guns in movies such as *'Die Hard'*. The deal is not *'is it real'* but *'does it sound real?'*

On a similar note, as long as a sound effect is present to annotate something on screen (that the audience expects to be accompanied by a sound) even the most ridiculous or even entirely inappropriate sounds will sometimes fit. For instance, why does Harry Potter's broomstick sound like a fighter jet? Clearly, there is a link in the audience's mind and they feel comfortable marrying this sound and picture. In essence, like editing, sound editing relies a great deal on

The movie soundtrack should be a rich blend of dialogue, sound effects, atmospheres and music, expertly mixed and balanced by a dubbing mixer.

Cool Edit Pro, a shareware sound editing program, is just one of the superb and cheap tools in your audio track laying arsenal. Available from www.syntrillium.com.

399

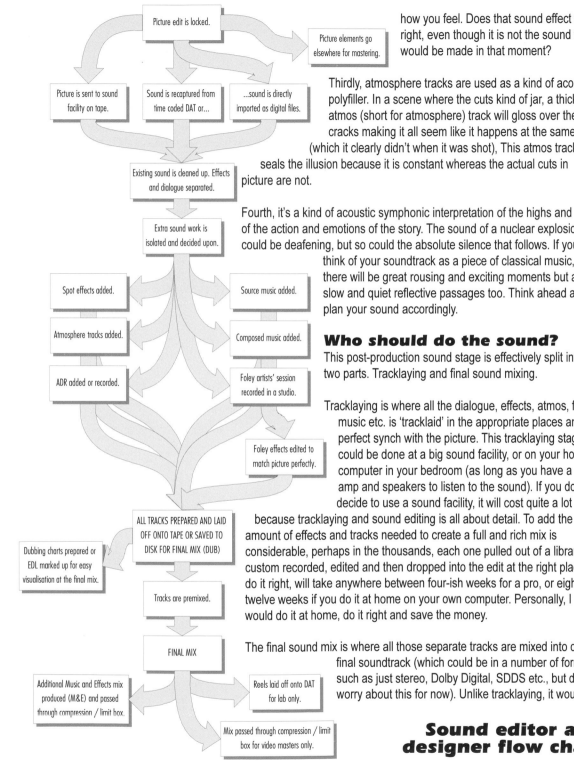

Picture edit is locked.

Picture elements go elsewhere for mastering.

Picture is sent to sound facility on tape.

Sound is recaptured from time coded DAT or...

...sound is directly imported as digital files.

Existing sound is cleaned up. Effects and dialogue separated.

Extra sound work is isolated and decided upon.

Spot effects added.

Source music added.

Atmosphere tracks added.

Composed music added.

ADR added or recorded.

Foley artists' session recorded in a studio.

Foley effects edited to match picture perfectly.

ALL TRACKS PREPARED AND LAID OFF ONTO TAPE OR SAVED TO DISK FOR FINAL MIX (DUB)

Dubbing charts prepared or EDL marked up for easy visualisation at the final mix.

Tracks are premixed.

FINAL MIX

Additional Music and Effects mix produced (M&E) and passed through compression / limit box.

Reels laid off onto DAT for lab only.

Mix passed through compression / limit box for video masters only.

how you feel. Does that sound effect feel right, even though it is not the sound that would be made in that moment?

Thirdly, atmosphere tracks are used as a kind of acoustic polyfiller. In a scene where the cuts kind of jar, a thick atmos (short for atmosphere) track will gloss over these cracks making it all seem like it happens at the same time (which it clearly didn't when it was shot), This atmos track seals the illusion because it is constant whereas the actual cuts in picture are not.

Fourth, it's a kind of acoustic symphonic interpretation of the highs and lows of the action and emotions of the story. The sound of a nuclear explosion could be deafening, but so could the absolute silence that follows. If you think of your soundtrack as a piece of classical music, there will be great rousing and exciting moments but also slow and quiet reflective passages too. Think ahead and plan your sound accordingly.

Who should do the sound?

This post-production sound stage is effectively split into two parts. Tracklaying and final sound mixing.

Tracklaying is where all the dialogue, effects, atmos, foley, music etc. is 'tracklaid' in the appropriate places and in perfect synch with the picture. This tracklaying stage could be done at a big sound facility, or on your home computer in your bedroom (as long as you have a good amp and speakers to listen to the sound). If you do decide to use a sound facility, it will cost quite a lot because tracklaying and sound editing is all about detail. To add the amount of effects and tracks needed to create a full and rich mix is considerable, perhaps in the thousands, each one pulled out of a library or custom recorded, edited and then dropped into the edit at the right place. To do it right, will take anywhere between four-ish weeks for a pro, or eight to twelve weeks if you do it at home on your own computer. Personally, I would do it at home, do it right and save the money.

The final sound mix is where all those separate tracks are mixed into one final soundtrack (which could be in a number of formats, such as just stereo, Dolby Digital, SDDS etc., but don't worry about this for now). Unlike tracklaying, it would be

Sound editor and designer flow chart

foolish to do this final mix at home, as perhaps more than any other stage, getting the right balance for all your dialogue, effects and music is a dark art. More likely, you'll do your final mix in a film dubbing theatre, which is rather terrifyingly one of the most expensive environments on the planet. Still, you will get a deal so do not worry about it for now. For a film that will be released in a cinema it's essential to do your final mix in a Dolby equipped theatre. If you don't, you could end up with an awful sounding movie. Of course, if you are going for TV/video/DVD only then you could mix in your bedroom (I would still recommend a dubbing theatre though).

Picture lock

Let's assume that you've locked picture, which means you can no longer go back and modify any of the picture edits. Locked means locked! An EDL has been sent to the neg cutter and they have verified that everything is OK (this EDL check only takes place if you have shot on film and are going to perform a neg cut. It does not apply if you are finishing the picture digitally, either in a full Digital Film facility or on tape such as DV or DigiBeta). The picture should have been broken down into sub eighteen-ish minute chunks for each projection reel at the lab (or 2000'). A VHS of each of these reels with burnt in timecode in the picture area and SMPTE timecode on track two of the VHS audio has been sent to the composer (see Chapter 21).

Preparations

Let's assume you aren't going to hand a tape to a top sound facility and pay them lots of money to do the work for you – you've run out of dosh and have accepted that if the job is going to be done with the right amount of detail, and love, then you (or the propeller head in your team) is going to do the job.

A very hard lesson I have learnt on every film that I have made, (and you'd think I'd have learnt it by now), is that you never have enough time to do it all properly. I don't know why this is the case but I do know that it happens on almost all films, be they micro-budget or mega-budget. So it's likely you are going to do the same. The last few days of tracklaying and preparation before the final sound mix will almost certainly be the hardest days of the entire production. This is the only time, in my entire life, that I have experienced the *'I worked for 72 hours without stopping'* myth, and it's actually true. So be warned and buy some caffeine pills.

Plan, plan, plan

Like all the stages in your film manufacturing process, planning is the key to doing it cheaply, effectively and as quickly as possible. Work out a schedule with a very healthy over-run, find and choose a space to work in, and talk through all the technological steps – for instance, how are you going to get the sound in and out of your computer? Speak to mixers, even if you do not know where you are going to mix, most mixers will be happy to give you ten

Danny Sheehan
Sound Designer

'Most film makers think of sound design as kind of painting by numbers, just a matter of filing out the obvious blanks. Whereas I would suggest that, unlike with the picture which is locked as soon as you shoot it, when it comes to the sound you can paint and extraordinary acoustic world for your film as long as you are creative and take the time to do it properly.

It always begins with the original dialogue tracks. Ideally they should be as clean as possible and you should spend a great deal of time getting them right, both on set and in the editing when preparing for the sound track laying and final mix. If the dialogue tracks are good you can add whatever you like, but if they are a mess, you can often loose detail in other effects easily because there is so much noise.

I think of the soundtrack as a piece of music with highs and lows – one could use atmospheric drones for moodier moments or loud effects for punctuated stings. Think of yourself as a composer, but using sound effects instead of musical notes and instruments.

People tend to always want more effects, and often bigger ones. But sometimes the absence of sound, or a carefully chosen and subtle effect can tell the story in a more effective way. Again, be creative. Sound effects don't always need to be real, it's about what sounds right and is most effective. For instance, you could use a gunshot for a car door. Of course, this will be dependent on the movie, and its style and tone of course.'

48 kHz or 44.1 kHz?

Digital sound can be recorded at two different (and of course incompatible sampling rates). These are 48kHz and 44.1kHz. You can use either for your film as there is very little difference in quality between the two. Theoretically, 48kHz is slightly better, but I would argue that few set ups would ever reproduce an appreciable difference, and even your average labrador would struggle to differentiate between the two. This choice of sampling rate will almost certainly be decided and chiselled in stone on the day you start shooting, as the sound recordist will take the first step. Don't let them decide for you, choose yourself, based on the reasons below.

The elements that you will use in your soundtrack will have a specific sample rate, so no matter which route you choose, there will be some conversions required. Personally, I would work at 48kHz now, but that is merely a personal choice. But then, I might do it 44.1kHz . . . (how helpful is that!) In truth, it doesn't really matter as both are equally flawed. Just so long as you appreciate the differences and don't expect everything to play without some conversion or tweaking at some point.

Kit and what it can do

DAT – *Works at 44.1kHz and 48kHz. Digital Audio Tape. Used to record onset dialogue and effects.*

DV – *Works at 32kHz (which you don't want to use) and 48kHz. All DV formats can record and play sound at both sample rates.*

CD – *Works at 44.1kHz. Will be used for some music tracks and for sound effects.*

Minidisk – *Works at 44.1kHz Can be used for recording simple spot effects and is a cheap and robust format.*

Computer – *Works at 44.1kHz and 48kHz. Whatever computer and software system you use to edit and tracklay sound, it can handle both sample rates.*

Digital Betacam – *Works at 48kHz This professional mastering format can only work at the higher sample rate.*

DA88 – *Works at 44.1kHz and 48kHz Used to transport large amounts of audio data as it can hold nearly 1000 minutes of digital audio. Also used for mastering.*

35mm print – *Works at 48kHz (and analogue). The various audio encoding formats for 35mm are diverse and robust.*

DVD – *Works at 48kHz. This domestic format works only at the higher sampling rate.*

The question is, 'how do I convert one sample rate to another?' There are software tools that can do this, but I find them to be slow and can add curious digital artefacts which are unpleasant to the ear. The quickest and easiest solution is to digitize from an analogue source. For instance, if your project is at 48kHz and you want to add some sound effects from CD (which is 44.1kHz), just plug the analogue out of the CD into the analogue in of your computer, press play on the CD and record on the computer and the computer will record sound at 48kHz. There is a great deal of audio snobbery about how good your digital to analogue converters are, as well as various other serious propeller head geeko-speak. Don't worry about this stuff, as long as what you hear sounds good, it will sound good to the audience.

minutes to help you figure out how you are going to overcome the hurdles you face.

The workshop

Sound editing and manipulation on a computer is a mature technology. Many people have their own recording studios in the basement, attic, spare bedroom etc., and if you can get full access to one of these little gems, it could make life very pleasant. More than likely though, you'll set up your own little facility. It doesn't need to be much, just a PC or Mac with software, a good sound card for digitising audio and playing it back, an amp and speakers, a small mixing desk, a microphone with long cables, and the appropriate tape deck (probably DAT or DA88 for the final layoff).

The track laying set-up is pretty much the same as that of the music composer's home studio, minus the keyboard of course. See Chapter 21.

The space in which you put all this kit is important too. Find somewhere that is very quiet as you may need to record lots of sound effects, and you can't do that if the number 57 bus rumbles past every four minutes. This alone means that most of greater London isn't going to work out unless you live in a particularly quiet back street and don't mind recording your effects at 3am. You also need to consider who else is sharing that space as you will make an almighty din all day and all night for the month or three that you spend designing and creating your movie's acoustic soundscape.

Depending on how cluttered the room is, you may need to add some sound deadening. This is not sound proofing, so it won't stop sound leaking in and out of the space, but it will help deaden sound (both listening and recording). as hard surfaces are covered and therefore sound will bounce around less (reducing natural reverb and leaving clean and crisp sound). Duvets and blankets make an excellent choice for sound deadening and should be hung on walls and draped on hard surfaces.

The tools

44.1kHz or 48kHz – Simple post production routes

So you have shot your movie. Here are two models based on what sample rate you shot your movie at.

44.1kHz route
On set sound is recorded at 44.1kHz, and all stages until final master will remain at 44.1kHz.
Avid project is set up to work at 44.1kHz.
CD sound effects can be directly imported without conversion.
CD music can be directly imported without conversion.
Composer will master music at 44.1kHz before it is digitally imported into project.
Final mix will pass through an analogue desk and be converted up to 48kHz. Final mix will be used for 35mm print (probably Dolby digital), DVD (Dolby digital) and DigiBeta (stereo mix at 48kHz).

48kHz route
On set sound is recorded at 48kHz, and all stages until final master will remain at 48kHz.
Avid project is set up to work at 48kHz.
CD sound effects are recorded into project via analogue inputs.
CD music is recorded into project via analogue inputs.
Composer will master music at 48kHz before it is digitally imported into project.
Final mix will be performed at 48kHz (no conversion needed). Final mix will be used for 35mm print (probably Dolby digital), DVD (Dolby digital) and DigiBeta (stereo mix at 48kHz).

There are heaps of software programs that could do the job, but ironically, you probably already have one of the best tools for the job. This is the non-linear editing system you have used for the cutting of your film so far – it could be Final Cut Pro, Media 100, Adobe Premiere, but the best option for a number of very boring technological reasons is Avid XpressDV (another good reason to have chosen Avid as your preferred post-production tool).

The process

Later, we'll go through a step-by-step of how to record, edit and tracklay sound, but for now, let's just look at the overall process.

So you've set up your own little tracklaying facility using Avid Xpress DV as the core tool. You may need some extra hard drive space, but it's unlikely as audio files are much smaller than video files. The sound for your whole movie will probably be only a few gigabytes in size and certainly nothing like the tens or even hundreds of gigabytes required by video files. The editor should have already broken the movie down into reels and the first job is to go through the existing dialogue and organise it for the sound process (the final mix stages need to be meticulously organised).

The dubbing mixer may need to adjust the levels in a dialogue scene where one character was close to the microphone and therefore louder, the other character further away and therefore quieter. They could do this by moving their faders up and down throughout the scene, but this will take many, many attempts to get right. However, if you cut the dialogue up so that one character's voice is on one track and the other character is on an entirely separate track, the mixer can simply adjust the levels for each track and then play the scene, getting it right in almost the first pass.

So the first job is to go through the whole movie and break down the dialogue so that where necessary (and it isn't always necessary) characters' voices appear on separate tracks. Any 'live' sound effects that are not overlapped by dialogue (perhaps a character walking down a corridor and their footsteps are very distinct and there is no dialogue) should now be dropped down onto a sound effects only track. You should strip out any temp music, as you won't be able to use this (remember, your composer should be scoring and recording a new soundtrack right now).

Once you have done this, you will probably be left with four tracks of mono dialogue, chequer boarded and clearly labelled. You'll also have a couple of mono sound effects tracks (the live sound that was recorded on the day) plus any additional sound effects that you added during the picture editing process (to help tell the story). Make sure the sound effects you are using are in no way in breach of copyright, which means if you just pull them out of your favourite movie, you can't use them. This organisation and housekeep-

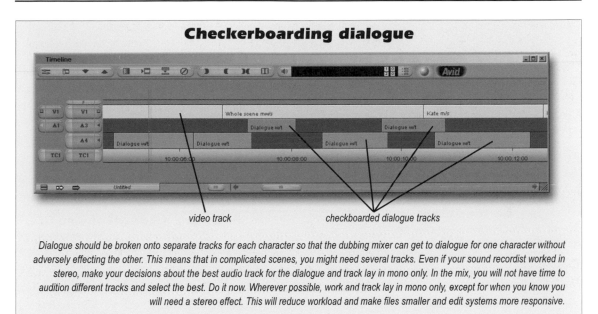

Checkerboarding dialogue

video track   checkboarded dialogue tracks

Dialogue should be broken onto separate tracks for each character so that the dubbing mixer can get to dialogue for one character without adversely effecting the other. This means that in complicated scenes, you might need several tracks. Even if your sound recordist worked in stereo, make your decisions about the best audio track for the dialogue and track lay in mono only. In the mix, you will not have time to audition different tracks and select the best. Do it now. Wherever possible, work and track lay in mono only, except for when you know you will need a stereo effect. This will reduce workload and make files smaller and edit systems more responsive.

In this example, it is a scene between two characters and it is all ADR, the live onset dialogue was abandoned because it was unusable.

ing should take a couple of days.

Organisatlon and limitation
Avid XpressDV will only play back eight simultaneous tracks of audio. This is not a problem because almost always, you will be working on tracks individually.

For each reel of your film, create three additional copies. The first copy will be for dialogue and live sound effects. The second copy will be for sound effects (some in stereo). The third copy will be for atmosphere tracks. The fourth and final reel will be for Foley tracks (footsteps and clothes rustles) and music. Of course, you may combine some of these tracks and may even condense them down to three or even two copies.

Track laying
Starting at the beginning, you will go through the movie and start adding sound effects and atmospheres. You can get these atmos and effects off sound effects CDs from a library. It used to be pretty tough to find sound libraries but if you ask around in all the usual places, such as Shooting People, you'll probably find someone who will either rent a library to you cheaply or lend it to you. As long as they own the library, then you, as their client, have the right to use all the effects in your movie. Cool!

When going through your movie, look at every single action and

Play a movie on DVD and turn off the picture, listening to the soundtrack only. Soak up the rich detail that has been crafted for you ... That is your aim. If you want to hear a direct comparison, listen an episode of ER, which will have a full soundtrack that is lovingly crafted, and then watch any UK hospital drama and listen to that sound, which is far from lovingly crafted! The difference is staggering.

Track laying example

This is a screengrab from the software used to track lay my last film, Urban Ghost Story. It represents about two and a half minutes of screentime and contains thirty two channels of audio (twelve tracks in mono and ten tracks in stereo). Urban Ghost Story was not terribly effects heavy, but it was very atmospheric, so there was a lot of attention paid to the atmos tracks.

Dialogue tracks (mono)
There are three dialogue tracks, broken up so that one character appears on each track. If you zoomed in on this time line and looked at only twenty seconds, you would see that each line has been labelled. In-between lines there are sometimes a little room atmos inserted to cover up any unwanted noise or sound from set.

Set FX (mono)
These are sounds that were recorded live on set, broken apart from the dialogue so that they can be used in the M&E mix. This is usually stuff like footsteps or the sound of washing up etc.

Panic (mono)
Nothing on this track for now but it was used for audio that we were almost certain we wouldn't use, but kept . . . just in case!

ADR (mono)
There are two tracks of ADR for where actor's dialogue has been replaced.

Foley (mono)
There are two tracks of Foley, one for footsteps, the other for everything else, including the rustling noises of clothing.

Spot effects (mono)
Two tracks of spot effects, mainly used for stuff like doors closing, and other character driven sounds. In this instance it also contains a baby crying and some rummaging sounds.

Spot effects (stereo)
Four tracks of stereo effects, including a police siren. At around 05.45.00 you will see there are a number of effects in a row. This was a lift door that we wanted to use for an audience 'shock', so a number of very over-the-top effects were laid next to each other (including a large steel door, a sword being sheathed and a gunshot . . . oh and an elevator door to seal the audio illusion).

Atmos (stereo)
Four layers of atmos . . . phew! Well the movie was supposed to be very atmospheric! The first scene was set in a loo, so you can see there was a room noise called corr-l2, a toilet cistern, and water drips. When combined they made the sound of a spooky loo!

Music (stereo)
There wasn't too much music in this reel so there was only one track used.

Screengrab showing track laying software with tracks: REEL5.EDL; timeline markers 5:00:00, 05:00:30, 05:01:00, 05:01:30, 05:02:00, 05:02:30; tracks labelled Dialog 1, Dialog 2, Dialog 3, Set FX 1, Set FX 2, Panic, ADR 1, ADR 2, Foley 1, Foley 2, SpotFX 1, SpotFX 2, SpotFX 3, SpotFX 4, SpotFX 5, SpotFX 6, Atmos 1, Atmos 2, Atmos 3, Atmos 4, Music 1. Clip labels include "Ho, w", "Cor", "ADI", "Roll 5 footsteps", "Roll 5 clothes", "Baby c", "Rummaging", "Police siren", "Jabba'", "Lift r", "cor-l2", "cistern", "cor-l", "drips(s)", "windy", "winc", "wind", "western", "office", "wind-b", "THE MUSIC". Timecode 05:04:19.21.00.

movement and ask yourself *'does that need a sound effect?'* Think about the world in which this scene is set. Is there anything off screen that would either help the story or fill an acoustic gap? Think police sirens in American movies, the dog barking in the distance as the hero creeps up the night time garden path, the cry of a hawk in that high altitude shot, the helicopter passing overhead as the hero hides. There are infinite ways to add production value and enhance your story through the use of sound. Unlike other stages of the film making process, this is cheap to do as it requires nothing more than a microphone, sound effects library, computer and you or your propeller head to drive it for a couple of months).

Perhaps one of the best investments you can make is that of an excellent micro-phone. You'll be surprised just how much and how often you will end up relying upon it.

Be creative. Be oblique in your choice of effects. Go for rich, thick, dynamic sounds. Don't be happy with just one effect or atmos – you may have a simple room tone inside a room, but is it raining outside? (that would be two atmospheres). You can re-use effects occasionally, but if you repeatedly use the same creaky door, the audience will soon pick up on it, so modify or change effects.

What you can't find on a sound effects CD, you're going to have to manufacture. There are two ways to do this. Either go out into the real world with a portable recording device such as a DAT or Minidisc and record effects, or, record them directly in your home made suite. Recording in your suite means that you can digitise directly onto the computer's hard drive, trim and clean up an effect and drop it into place very quickly. On all my films I have found it possible to record an incredible spectrum of effects just using the 'stuff' in my house as props. One of the best props I ever owned was an old, wooden, squeaky chair with which I could create specific creaks and groans that almost followed actors' movements.

Working through your movie and annotating everything with its own effect can take an absolute age. I would bank on six to eight weeks of solid work.

Music, maestro!

During this process, you'll occasionally pop over to the composer's recording studio and listen to what they've done. Aside from the custom written score that the composer is working on, you're going to also need to find some of that background music for the scenes in places like nightclubs, elevators, shopping malls, teenage bedrooms etc. Anywhere that music plays in the fabric of the world and could actually be heard by the characters in the story. This is usually called source music. Once all this music has been found or recorded, it will come to you on either CD or DAT and you can tracklay it into Avid XpressDV.

One minor problem that you might want to consider is that of acoustic overload. If your scene has a lot of dynamic action with big sound effects

Music editing

Occasionally, you will be forced to edit a music track, perhaps to fit more comfortably in the allotted space, or for other reasons. Either way, music editing is fiendishly difficult at first, mainly because unless the editor knows what they are doing, the edits can sound awful. This is because we are all creatures of rhythm and can instantly sense when that rhythm has been interrupted. Thankfully, it's quite easy to learn the tricks. Essentially it's all about tapping your feet and counting. If you count on the beat of a piece of music, you will find a pattern in the rhythm. In the track below it's in four four time for example.

Music is broken into chunks called bars, and within each bar there are a number of beats. Try it out on a piece of pop music. On the major beat start counting and I bet it will go ONE . . . two . . . three . . . four . . . FIVE . . . six . . . seven.... eight.... NINE . . . and so on. You can make an edit on most beats, but it's always better to make the cut on the end / start of a bar. If you mark the start of a bar and the end of a bar and remove the whole bar, then apply a very short one frame audio dissolve to the edit, the likelihood is that it will sound fine. Just shorter. And that's the essence of music editing. Try it out, digitise some music and cut it around in your sound editing software.

More atmospheric music is even easier, often you can just cut it to the right length and apply a long dissolve, perhaps two seconds, to the edit. If it works great! Beware though, composers and musicians will hate you for this sacrilege.

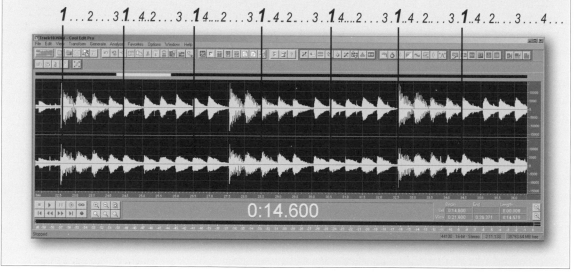

and big music, there is only so much headroom to accommodate it. If you don't pay attention, your sound can become a kind of mushy noise, so if you know you want a big musical stab, leave the sound effects out (or minimal) and vice versa. In essence, you don't want your sound effects and music to fight for acoustic dominance. One must always be symbiotically dominant over the other, and this should always be a creative choice rather than a rushed result in the final mixing session.

Foley

Also known as 'footsteps', this is produced in a separate recording session where a Foley artist watches the film and then physically re-performs the actions of the actors (to picture). Most obviously, this is things like footsteps, but it also includes clothes rustles, bag rummaging, coins in pockets, in fact anything that the actor does in front of the camera. Foley artists are expert at this physical recreation and can work very quickly,

If you cannot afford a Foley artist, you can do it yourself. It will take you a long time as you will be slow, and everything will need to be edited, but it can be done. If you choose to do this, call a few Foley studios and ask if you could sit in and watch for a hour or two so that you can see how it all works.

The Foley studio

This studio is much like a full blown dubbing theatre, but usually much smaller, with a simpler desk and not too many bells and whistles. The studio is often used to record ADR too. The floors can be pulled up to reveal several different surfaces (for the foley artist to do footsteps) and the walls are lined with different doors for opening and closing sounds.

During a Foley session, the artist will watch the footage projected on the screen and then re-create the performers movements and actions in sync with the picture. This is a very specialised job and a good artist should be able to do a whole feature film in a day as long as you go at rocket pace.

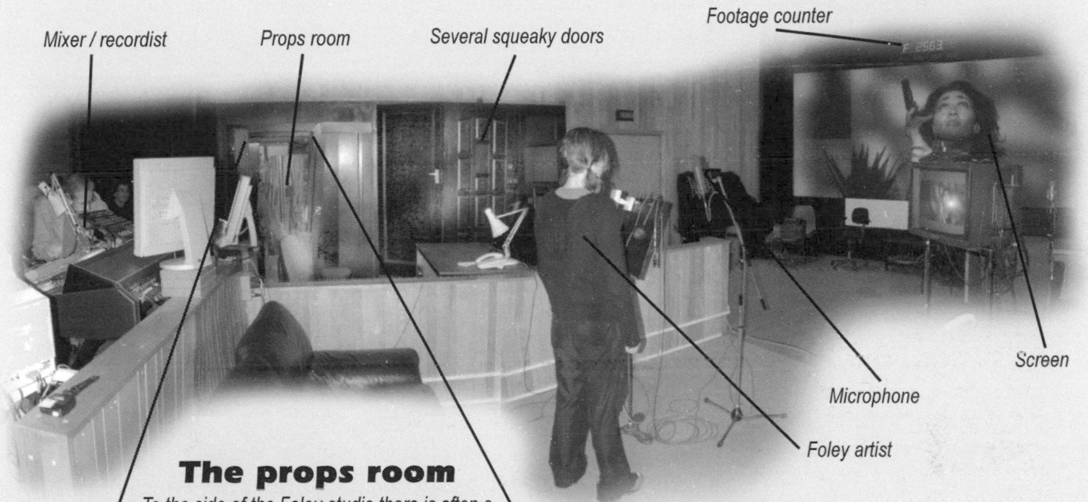

Mixer / recordist   Props room   Several squeaky doors   Footage counter

Screen

Microphone

Foley artist

The props room

To the side of the Foley studio there is often a room that is filled with all manner of props. A great Foley artist will take items and use them to recreate sounds – and not just the sounds appropriate to the item. There is a famous story about 'The Exorcist' and a Foley artist who recreated the famous head turn scene sound effect using a leather wallet filled with credit cards. Remember, it doesn't need to be real, just sound real.

Foley artists are so good at re-creating sound effects that if you actually took your time and went through recreating everything, you may find that the investment in an extra day for Foley and studio hire could save you much more in both time and money for track laying. First and foremost, the Foley artist will take care of the obvious 'human' sounds, but they can also do pretty much anything else out side of obvious stuff like police sirens etc. In your Foley session, keep an eye on time, and if you find yourself dropping behind, start omitting stuff so that you can keep on schedule. As long as you get the clothes rustles and footsteps, you could easily fill in the blanks during additional tracklaying.

Felicity Cottrell
Foley Artist

'One film I worked on was the most appalling pile of poo. The director was so enthusiastic and we couldn't tell him how bad it was. If you want to make a film you have to set your sights higher than that and credit your audience with a little common sense. The biggest mistake young film makers make with Foley is that they think we don't know how to do our job. If people want to give us input we do like it, but I really loathe it when they tell us how to do things. That is a common mistake and they assume we know nothing, which can be very irritating. They bring things in that they think we can use for a certain prop which are ludicrous.

Sometimes we can use something completely bizarre that makes a really great sound to accompany the images on the screen. For example, we went to Greece to do a film and we brought a 'dinky car' and we have used that to make the sounds of a gun being handled. It works really well! You can use a lock for a gun too! It doesn't have to be the correct thing at all! In fact, often the real thing doesn't actually sound right! For example, you can use quarter inch audio tape wrapped and a table leg and make that sound like a creaky door opening.

If a producer is restricted by budget you can go to the theatre with the absolute minimum list of noises you need, record those, then spend a lot of time in the editing room cutting new effects (off CD) into place. That said, under-booking the time can be awful as you look at the list and the amount of studio time and it's never enough! Concentrate on the foreground action more than the background and you'll save loads of time and money. A Foley artist can work very fast but you do need to be clear about what you need or want and not procrastinate.'

sometimes even doing footsteps for two characters at the same time! (with a different shoe on each foot). You will need to record this session in a dedicated recording studio that's decked out with all the bits – the floor can be pulled up to reveal gravel, salt bags for snow, wooden floors etc., the walls might be lined with ten different doors and there'll be a storeroom adjacent that will be filled with an Aladdin's cave of junk (that has been amassed over years of foley sessions).

After the Foley session, you will need to transfer these recordings to your Avid XpressDV, edit out the gaps and adjust the timings of many of the foley effects. If you are working quickly (as you probably will be because you have no money) many of the Foley effects will be out of sync by a few frames and you will need to manually pull everything back into sync. Ideally, you should also label each little chunk of Foley. This will take a couple of days to break down, organise and clean up.

You may be tempted to skip this Foley stage, but beware, you will also need to produce a separate soundtrack of your film called an M&E (music and effects mix) for foreign territories. This mix includes all sound *except the dialogue*. If you pull the dialogue out of your movie, you are often left with nothing more than a few sound effects, some atmos and music. The actors will be silent, even in their movement and it will sound empty. All of which means foreign buyers will reject your film and you will be forced to go back, record a Foley session, re-mix your sound, re-master your movie etc., so get it right in the first place.

ADR – automated dialogue replacement

Or to you and me, re-recording voices to dub over the original actor's performance. Buy why would you do this? Several reasons. During the shoot, there may have been scenes where the dialogue that you recorded was so polluted by external sound (traffic, planes etc.) that it was unusable, except as a guide. Also, you may want to replace an actor's voice (as we did in *Urban Ghost Story*, to turn an Englishman into a Scotsman). Lastly, script changes may require that you put new dialogue into a character's mouth (we call this plot dialogue, where for some reason, the audience doesn't 'get' something in the story, so we have to spell it out – *'we have to get out of the building in the next thirty seconds or the building will explode and we will all die'*). Normally, this new dialogue is inserted into a character's mouth whilst they are out of shot, or we are looking over their shoulder. Clearly we must not be able to see their face as there will be a lip sync problem.

Whatever the reason, if you need to replace dialogue, you will need to get the actors back. Most people go to a dedicated ADR studio for this, but I have found this to be overkill. I ask actors back to my bedroom tracklaying suite to re-record their lines. In the business, actors usually watch their performance and say the line in sync, attempting to get it to match. We have found that if you just show the actor their performance of the line of dialogue that needs to be replaced and then ask them to re-perform it without looking at the screen, their eyes closed, putting themselves emotionally back in the same space as the character, that they will provide a much better performance. Nine times out of ten, these lines will perfectly fit over the old lines. And where they don't, they can be re-performed, or even edited.

To record these lines, we set up a small 'duvet tent' inside which the actors would stand, a small desk in front of them with a cup of water, microphone and lamp. Nothing fancy. But it works a treat. Most actors don't believe that their dialogue will fit because you are recording it 'wild', but as you are recording straight onto the computer, you can edit it and drop it into place within a moment to be sure that it is exactly what you want. Voilá.

Final prep – transport and charts

As you complete your tracklaying, and prepare for the final mix, there are two major factors that need to be considered. These are *'how am I going to get the sound to the dubbing theatre?'* and *'do they need the dubbing charts to be on paper or electronic?'* You should already have the answer through detailed conversation and tests with the dubbing facility that you have chosen. You have . . . haven't you?

Getting your sound to the mix

Currently, the sound for your movie exists as digital data on your computer hard drive. Depending on compatibility, it is conceivable that you could take your hard disk to the dubbing theatre, plug it in and they can directly import it into their software. To non-propeller heads, this sounds like a simple and logical solution. But to the propeller-heads amongst us, it sounds (quite rightly) like an incompatibility nightmare waiting to happen. So run tests before you go to the final mix.

The other way to get the sound to the mix is by laying it all off onto a number of time coded DA88 tapes. A DA88 tape is a Hi8 tape that has been formatted for digital sound, and can hold eight tracks of sound, up to one hundred and twenty minutes in length. This is a superbly compact and lightweight solution, but you need to make sure that the dubbing facility can handle DA88 and also factor into your schedule the fact that you will need around two days to lay off the sound from your Avid XpressDV onto the tapes (as you can only lay off two tracks every time and you may have up to thirty two tracks! That's sixteen passes of a ninety minute movie broken into five reels!)

ADR is a great secret weapon in helping the plot of your film if it is failing. Don't be afraid of adding the most outrageously obvious lines to clarify the plot. If the audience doesn't 'get it', ADR can be your last and very blunt instrument to be used to fix the problem.

If you can get the technology to talk to each other, taking your hard drive with the audio data stored on it is the simplest way to do it.

Mixing formats you should consider . . .

Simple stereo (cheapest choice)

No licensing is needed and the mix will be in simple left and right stereo.

Dolby (second best choice)

This is used for video, DVD and TV only. It is a simple left and right mix. It can be played back through cinema Dolby equipment but all sorts of weird effects could occur.

D I G I T A L

Dolby Digital (best choice)

A digital format that encodes left, centre, right, left surround, right surround and sub woofer channels into a single file. Free to use on DVD and other mediums (although a licence is still needed from Dolby). If the film is to be screened in cinemas you will need to pay Dolby. DTS is a similar competitor.

SDDS (expensive and over kill for low budgets)

The SDDS tracks are optically printed on both sides of a 35mm print. SDDS provides 6 channels (left, centre, right, left surround, right surround and sub) or 8 channels (left, centre left, centre, centre right, right, left surround, right surround and sub) of high quality digital audio. The worldwide licence fee is $5k.

DTS

dts

DTS offer competitive mixing formats, such as DTS (analogue) which is a kind of clone of straight Dolby, and DTS Digital which is similar to Dolby Digital but not as widely used (so DTS Digital is best avoided for low budget films).

Dubbing charts

The person who is going to mix your film has, obviously, never seen it before. They don't know what it's about, what sound effects and dialogue is in it or where the music is supposed to fade up or down. At the same time as not knowing anything, they are expected to take lots of separate audio tracks, EQ those tracks, balance them, send them off into different speakers, and all in a few stressful days. The answer to this nightmare are the dubbing charts (see example). These are like a road map for the soundtrack and detail exactly where every piece of audio begins and ends. Traditionally, these were hand written on paper as large charts and whilst many dubbing mixers, especially the experienced old school mixers, prefer paper charts, there is a definite move towards digital charts that appear on a computer monitor and scroll along with the picture. Avid XpressDV can print out it's timeline, in effect, creating a dubbing chart.

If you are going to take your hard drive to the dub, make sure all your sound and files are stored on an external drive, and that drive is compatible with the kit at the the theatre – SCSI or Firewire? Mac or PC? Or are you going to take your sound on tapes and disk such as DA88 or Jaz disks? All are possible. Make calls and run tests first.

The electronic dubbing chart can be created from an EDL or even by importing the Avid project from a floppy or Zip disk. However you do this, it's imperative to run test EDL's well in advance of the final mix or you could find yourself grinding to a halt because you have no dubbing charts to show the mixer. If it turns out that you are going to have to manually draw up the charts by hand, don't underestimate how long it will take and schedule two or three days to do this as painlessly as possible.

Understand that sloppy, badly labelled and inaccurate dubbing charts will cost you lots of money. The dubbing theatre is a very expensive place per minute and the last thing you want to do is slow the whole proceedings because the mixer isn't psychic and doesn't know what is coming next.

Day of the dub

For the purposes of this model, we're going to work on a three day mix. This is an insanely short period of time for so much work, and you may be forced to seriously compromise, but at the end of the day, it is all you can afford.

The final mix is one of the most exciting stages during the making of the film (just topped by the premiere). You will need to take with you a BetaSP or DV tape of each reel (with the correct time code), your sound either on tape or hard drive and your dubbing charts either as an EDL or on paper. If you've never been in a dubbing theatre, prepare to have some fun. It's dark, with heaps of flashing lights and a mixing desk with silver faders – to the uneducated it looks a little like the flight deck of the space shuttle. Coooool!

At one end, there is a large cinema screen. At the other, there is a large video projector, mixing desk and banks of sound processing equipment. Around the room are the speakers – the left, centre, and right speakers are usually situated behind the screen, with surround sound speakers mounted on the side and back walls. In front of the mixing desk there are normally a couple of fiendishly comfortable and immensely large leather sofas. Within fifteen paces, there is always a fully charged coffee machine.

Leader of the pack

It's important not to lounge on the sofa – which you will want to do 'cos you might not have slept for days – but to grab a chair and sit next to the dubbing mixer, so that you can quickly chat over decisions about what's coming next. This means that you stay in control and can keep up the pace. If the director or editor is left to do this alone, you'll only get half your movie mixed in the allotted time, which is of course no use to anyone. You need a full movie!

Defer to the expert

Neither you, the editor, the director or any other member of your team is likely to have spent much time mixing movies. So when a creative discussion occurs (which should be as infrequently as possible), always listen to the mixer. They do this day in and day out. For instance, one of the common mistakes that directors make is that they think that the music is being mixed too low. Dubbing mixers are familiar with creative types who stomp their feet and moan and whine. On the whole, mixers are extremely good diplomats. But time wasted over whether the door creak needed to be louder or quieter is not money well spent.

Tim Cavagin
Dubbing Mixer

'Low budget films never have enough time. A major feature could mix for weeks, a low budget feature could be forced to do it in three days. Ironically, the low budgeters are the ones who need to be most organised, but they always seem to be the least organised! It's perhaps inexperience, which is why I always suggest that at least one member of their team has mixing experience, or at worst, they spend time getting advice from a mixer. Getting the most out of your final mix is all about preparation. You don't want your mixer to spend half of your precious and expensive time fixing simple problems that could have been fixed outside of the dubbing theatre.

In terms of importance from an audio point, dialogue is top, followed by music, then sound effects, then Foley. I spend a great deal of time on the dialogue tracks. There is nothing worse than really badly mixed dialogue that is hard to understand because the mix was rushed. It's always a dead giveaway of a low budget.

During the mix, don't get bogged down in trivial detail. This 'dog bark' or that 'dog bark' doesn't really matter. Sure on a $100m film you can argue over it, but for low budgets, you just have to get on with it. Often it is better to just get through to the end as quickly as possible, being guided by the mixer, and stopping only when major creative decisions need to be made. If there are a few 'big' moments in the film, we can always spend a little extra time on them, as long as you have paced yourself and stick to the schedule.'

Anatomy of a dubbing chart

Most dubbing charts are still written out by hand, a laborious job at the best of times, but absolutely essential. Avid can print out a timeline (which can sometimes be used) and many dubbing theatres can interrogate your EDL / Avid project and build an electronic dubbing chart from that information, but it depends on what software you used, what software they use and of course, if they can handle it in the first place. It's odd but the bigger and more prestigious the dubbing theatre, the more likely it is that they are going to insist on paper dubbing charts. These sheets should be big, at least A3 (ideally bigger). You can buy blank charts which are huge (speak to the theatre about where to get them from). Highlighter pens are used to mark up effects to help make quick visual references easier when under pressure.

Production information
The head of each chart should carry basic information about the movie.

Effect label
Clear and concise description of specific effects.

Track headings

Reel number

Sheet number
In case the sheets get mixed up.

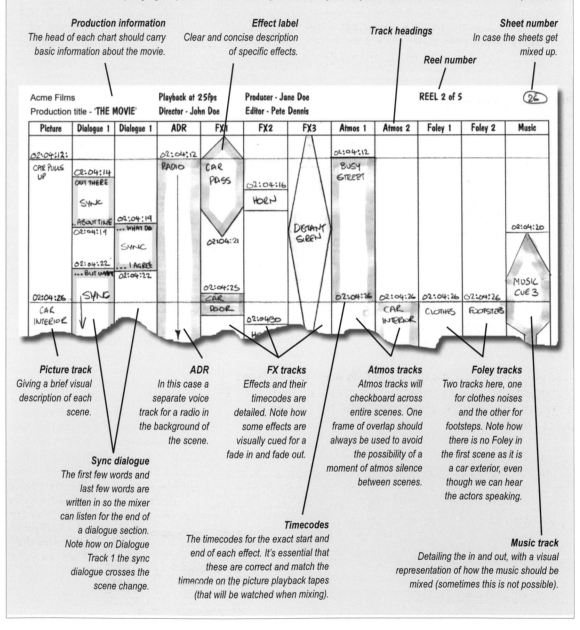

Picture track
Giving a brief visual description of each scene.

Sync dialogue
The first few words and last few words are written in so the mixer can listen for the end of a dialogue section. Note how on Dialogue Track 1 the sync dialogue crosses the scene change.

ADR
In this case a separate voice track for a radio in the background of the scene.

FX tracks
Effects and their timecodes are detailed. Note how some effects are visually cued for a fade in and fade out.

Timecodes
The timecodes for the exact start and end of each effect. It's essential that these are correct and match the timecode on the picture playback tapes (that will be watched when mixing).

Atmos tracks
Atmos tracks will checkboard across entire scenes. One frame of overlap should always be used to avoid the possibility of a moment of atmos silence between scenes.

Foley tracks
Two tracks here, one for clothes noises and the other for footsteps. Note how there is no Foley in the first scene as it is a car exterior, even though we can hear the actors speaking.

Music track
Detailing the in and out, with a visual representation of how the music should be mixed (sometimes this is not possible).

The three day dub

When you speak to a dubbing facility, they will tell you that you need a month in which to mix your film. Of course, that's not going to be possible and you're going to attempt to do it in three days. This chart assumes that you are very organised, everything has been properly tracklaid, you have excellent dubbing charts, that creative discussions in the mix will be almost non-existent, and ideally, your film is no longer than ninety minutes. You'll try very hard to make it in these three days, but...you will fall behind schedule and just about finish the final mix by the end of day three, which will force you to come back another day to do the M&E mix. Every final mix I have ever done has started well, but as the end approaches, it inevitably turns into 'push the faders up and CHARGE!'

DAY 1	DAY 2	DAY 3
		foley premix
dilaogue premix	atmos / FX premix	Final mix begins
lunch	lunch	lunch
dialogue premix	atmos / FX premix	Final mix
atmos / FX premix	foley premix	
go home!	go home!	go home!
track lay missing effects		AND CELEBRATE! Plan to return for M&E mix

Picture playback

In the good old days (yawn) films used to be mixed whilst viewing the film cutting copy – the movie was actually projected in the dubbing theatre! Nowadays it's almost always done from videotape. BetaSP is the universally preferred format (and as long as you shot at 25fps you don't need to fiddle around with anything here).

You will probably have five (twenty minute) BetaSP tapes, one for each reel. There will be time code on each tape. For instance, reel one, on tape one will start at timecode 01:00:00:00, and reel two, on tape two, will start at time code 02:00:00:00, and so on (you'll make these tapes from your Avid). If you have cut on DV, you need to check with the dubbing facility that they can handle DV, but however you make up these tapes, it's essential that you burn visual time code into the image so that even if there is a nightmarish time code screw up, there is always a 100% accurate visual reference that the mixer can use to sync up picture and sound.

Be warned, during the mix, this tape is repeatedly wound backwards and forwards and pretty much hammered. DV tapes are not as robust as BetaSP so if you must use DV, make sure you have backup tapes for each reel in case of a snag or snap.

Pre-mixes

The first job will be to pre-mix some of the tracks. As you may have as many as thirty two tracks to mix into as few as two tracks (for a simple stereo mix) you can see why this would be an overwhelming task. Pre-mixes are a way of grouping chunks of sound and, well er, pre-mixing them. For instance, taking four tracks of dialogue, one track of ADR and creating a single track of dialogue pre-mix, where all the levels have been balanced and EQed (equalised).

Surround sound is very exciting the first time you can actually use it and there will be a great temptation to overuse it. Defer to the experience of the dubbing mixer and keep the effect for when you need it.

Dialogue pre-mix

The first pre-mix to be done will be a dialogue pre-mix. This is the

During the mix, keep an eye on the time and stay on schedule. If you don't, the end of your mix will turn into a nightmare with no time to do anything other than push the faders up and hope it all sounds OK! And of course, the part of your movie that will be most rushed will be the end, precisely the part you want to sound best!

hardest part and will require the most work. The dialogue tracks will go through a number of processes in order to create the pre-mix. These include…

Levelling the dialogue – this is where the mixer will adjust the relative levels of the dialogue so that they all sound about the same. In reality, an actor whispering will be very quiet, and an actor screaming will be very loud. After levelling, the whispers will be a little bit quieter than normal conversation and the screams will be a little bit louder than normal conversation. The idea is that you don't have to be constantly turning the volume up and down on your TV when dialogue gets too loud or quiet.

Compressor – this is a digital tool that takes any sound, in this case the dialogue, and compresses it where needed. For instance, it's used when an actor goes from talking normally to shouting in the same sentence. The mixer could just pull the levels down, but the compressor dynamically keeps the signal down without too harshly impacting the performance. It does a better job.

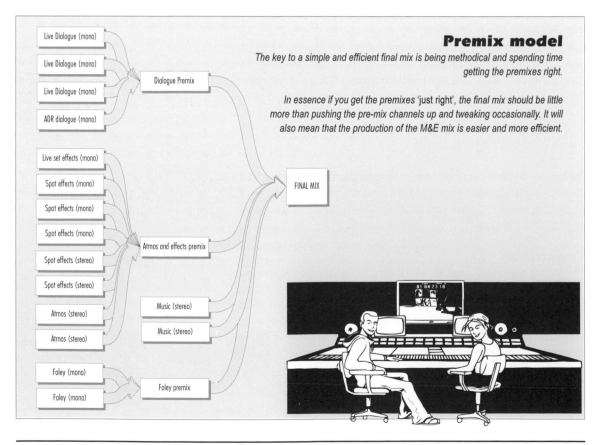

Premix model

The key to a simple and efficient final mix is being methodical and spending time getting the premixes right.

In essence if you get the premixes 'just right', the final mix should be little more than pushing the pre-mix channels up and tweaking occasionally. It will also mean that the production of the M&E mix is easier and more efficient.

Live Dialogue (mono)
Live Dialogue (mono)
Live Dialogue (mono)
ADR dialogue (mono)
→ Dialogue Premix

Live set effects (mono)
Spot effects (mono)
Spot effects (mono)
Spot effects (mono)
Spot effects (stereo)
Spot effects (stereo)
Atmos (stereo)
Atmos (stereo)
→ Atmos and effects premix

Music (stereo)
Music (stereo)

Foley (mono)
Foley (mono)
→ Foley premix

FINAL MIX

Reverb – sometimes referred to as *'putting a bit of room around it'*. This is a digital process that many people think of as *'echo'*, but is in fact a reverberation that will mimic the acoustic environments in which the scene is set. Obvious examples are things like cathedrals and caves, but even a small room has some reverb, and applying this effect to all the dialogue in a scene will help give it consistency and reality.

Gates – a noise gate is another digital tool which can cunningly remove all the sound below an adjustable level. For instance, if you have a scene that had a background rumble, you could apply a noise gate that would allow anything as loud as the actor talking to pass through, but when the actor is not talking, it would cut the sound. The upshot is that it can remove un-wanted background noise during the gaps, but it won't remove that back-ground noise whilst the actors are talking. However, with a carefully chosen and slightly louder than normal atmos track, this background noise appear-ing whilst the actors are talking can be disguised and hidden.

De-esser – this very specialised box of tricks targets the unpleasant and aggressive sibilance that you sometimes get when actors say words that include an 's'. This 's' can sometimes seem unnaturally loud, even painful to the ear. The de-esser will deal with this and dynamically correct it.

Exciter – if an actor's performance is slightly flatter than you would like, (which is common with ADR) you could pass it through an exciter, which will make it more dynamic, giving it greater punctuation.

Other bits – of course, there are any number of other audio effects that you could apply, but generally, these are only used in instances where you need effects such as spooky voices from the dead or alien conversation etc. If you have a lot of this in your movie, you would probably have already applied an effect before going to the final mix.

The dialogue pre-mix is probably the most important stage of your final mix because it's essential that everything that is said by the actors sounds appropriate, is clear and distinct. Fundamentally, if the audience cannot hear or understand the characters in the film, it just isn't going to work as well. The dialogue pre-mix will also take longer to do than any other stage.

In our three day dub model, it will take most of (if not all of) day one to do the dialogue pre-mixes.

Effects and atmos pre-mix

If you had enough time and a big enough budget, you would probably pre-mix the effects and atmospheres separately. But you don't have that luxury so your effects and atmos will be pre-mixed together. It's much the same process as the dialogue pre-mix except there will be less messing around

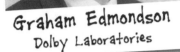

Graham Edmondson
Dolby Laboratories

'Whatever the budget, you simply can't afford bad sound. A quality film soundtrack to complement your picture is the only way to successfully tell your story in a believable, emotional, and exciting way. Too many new film makers come unstuck by not thinking about sound until the very last minute, when the budget is depleted.

While shooting on location, special attention should be paid to recording high-quality dialogue tracks. Always ensure that the microphone can 'see' the lips and check that your recordings are not distorting or picking up unwanted noises. However well-equipped your dubbing studio is at a later stage, you can never truly fix bad dialogue recordings. Make sure you record plenty of 'wild track' on location (recordings of location atmospheres and sounds made when the camera shoot has finished), you may find this invaluable at a later stage to ensure a scene's realism.

Take time to learn about the cinema sound format options available to you for your film and don't fall into the trap of thinking that two-channel stereo mixed in your bedroom will suffice. Use of an approved film dubbing studio is the only way to go. They are aligned to exact cinema standards and will produce your master mix to the correct technical requirements ready for the lab, thereby guaranteeing that what you heard in the studio will be what you hear in any correctly aligned cinema. Approaching a major film dubbing facility may seem daunting, but they are generally a very charitable lot and you may be amazed at the deal they can offer you. And trust us here – you won't regret a penny of what you spend when you wow your audiences with fantastic sound.'

Before the mix, have a meeting, or at least a long phone conversation, with the mixer. Explain what your movie is about, how you have approached the sound, both technically and creatively, and plan out your schedule for the days you have booked. You only have so much time and need to make sure it all gets done. Then stick to that schedule!

with tools such as reverb, compressors and EQing etc. But because the atmospheres and effects create the ambient world, you will spend more time sending effects to various speakers. This depends on how you plan to mix your film, but we'll assume that you are mixing in either Dolby Digital or one of the other multiple speaker surround sound systems.

The dialogue pre-mixes will have almost all been mixed for the centre speaker, with the occasional line being mixed to the left or right. The effects and atmos' will be mixed to come from almost every other speaker, but on the whole, they will conform to these rough mixing guidelines.

Specific spot effects – things like car doors, gunshots, keyboard typing etc. Anything that is directly linked to the action of the actors. On the whole,

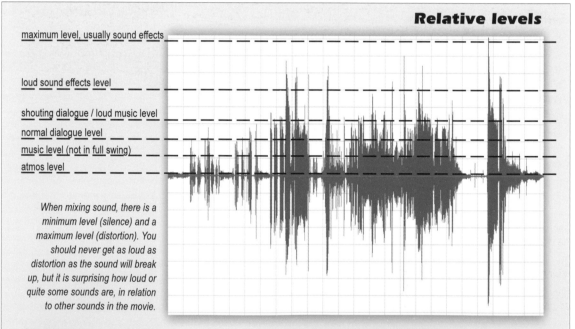

Relative levels

maximum level, usually sound effects

loud sound effects level

shouting dialogue / loud music level

normal dialogue level

music level (not in full swing)

atmos level

When mixing sound, there is a minimum level (silence) and a maximum level (distortion). You should never get as loud as distortion as the sound will break up, but it is surprising how loud or quite some sounds are, in relation to other sounds in the movie.

Atmospheres, unless a loud wind or rain etc., tend to be the quietest effect, followed by music, which is often a surprise to many people. Of course music can rise up to be very loud, but on the whole, it is often similar to atmos, but more empathic – think of it as dynamic emotional atmospheres. Louder still is normal conversational dialogue. You might have thought that this would be louder, but you can't go too loud for this or where are you going to go when you need to get REALLY loud, for a bomb exploding for instance. Dialogue tends to be about halfway up the scale. That's followed by shouting dialogue, raised voices and music that rises for the moment. Louder still are sound effects that need some punch, beaten to the loudest effect position only by the occasional effect that is designed to be extremely loud to the audience (easy to spot these moments in cheesy horror movies).

Your sound must always live between these two extremes, and on the whole, burble around the middle, dropping very low or rising very high only for acoustic effect.

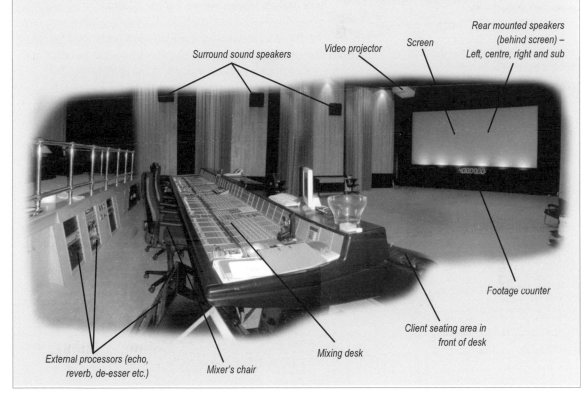

The dubbing theatre

One of the most expensive environments on the planet, the film dubbing theatre. It's essentially a cinema with the chairs removed and mixing desk and other audio processing and recording equipment installed. It's often dark and subdued, but at the same time, can be extraordinarily tense if you are up against it, and you will be! Most major feature films will take anywhere between four and six weeks to mix their film. You will take anywhere between two or three days to do the same.

Surround sound speakers

Video projector

Screen

Rear mounted speakers (behind screen) – Left, centre, right and sub

Footage counter

Client seating area in front of desk

Mixing desk

External processors (echo, reverb, de-esser etc.)

Mixer's chair

these will be mixed to come out of the centre speaker, so that they match the dialogue.

Wider spot effects – things like a car passing, a hail of bullets, an explosion etc. On the whole, these effects will be stereo and mixed to come out of the left and right speakers, creating an attractive and wider sounding effect.

Ambient spot effects – things like specific thunderclaps, police walkie-talkies in the background, helicopters and planes passing over etc. On the whole, these effects will be mixed in stereo and also sent to the surround sound speakers. They are specific sound effects, designed to help build the acoustic world and plug holes in the mix.

Atmos – things like wind, room tone, rain, interior car sounds. On the whole, they will be mixed in stereo and pushed out to the surrounds, to create an all encompassing acoustic world. Almost without exception, they will be a continuous sound that will last for the entire scene.

If push comes to shove, you can always use a little extra music to help in a scene that is in a real mess, especially from a pacing point of view. Wall to wall music propping up a dodgy scene is always a dead give away of a production in real trouble, but it will work and most people won't notice why the scene is poor, but they will probably feel that it is sub standard.

During this pre-mix, you may find that some spot effects are missing. Either you forgot to tracklay them or it has become apparent that something more is needed. Rather than messing around in the final mix, auditioning CDs and attempting to fill these gaps, just make a note of where and what they are and that evening, tracklay these new effects and bring them to the mix the next day. You may have to bring them as individual effects, but the mixer will quickly drop into the right place, or you may have laid them off onto tape which the mixer can sync up. It's unlikely that you will go back and pre-mix these effects and they'll be mixed into the final mix on the last day.

Ideally, you'll have started the atmos/effects pre-mix in the late afternoon of day one and be completing it around lunch to mid-afternoon of day two.

Foley premix

If time permits, you will do a Foley pre-mix, but on such a tight schedule it's probable that you will run out of time. If you do squeeze it in, it will make the final mix quicker and easier to do. It's not too hard, as essentially, it's all about throwing all the foley tracks together, getting the right levels, and ditching the effects that don't work or are superfluous. The Foley will be pre-mixed in mono to come out of the centre speaker as the sounds are directly linked to the actor's actions. Occasionally, some Foley may be mixed to the left and right speakers or even the surrounds if a particular effect is required (for instance, the character is listening to footsteps 'out of shot' and so they may be mixed in the surrounds).

The Foley pre-mix should take around three or four hours in our model and will likely take you to the close of play on the second day.

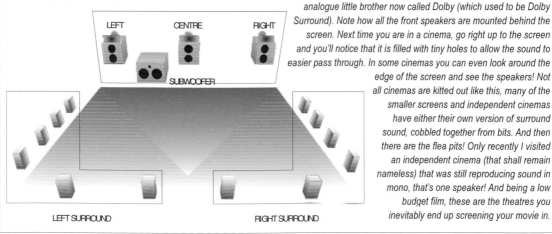

Cinema surround layout

This is a pretty average 'small theatre' that will playback surround sound encoded soundtracks. Usually this means Dolby Digital, or its analogue little brother now called Dolby (which used to be Dolby Surround). Note how all the front speakers are mounted behind the screen. Next time you are in a cinema, go right up to the screen and you'll notice that it is filled with tiny holes to allow the sound to easier pass through. In some cinemas you can even look around the edge of the screen and see the speakers! Not all cinemas are kitted out like this, many of the smaller screens and independent cinemas have either their own version of surround sound, cobbled together from bits. And then there are the flea pits! Only recently I visited an independent cinema (that shall remain nameless) that was still reproducing sound in mono, that's one speaker! And being a low budget film, these are the theatres you inevitably end up screening your movie in.

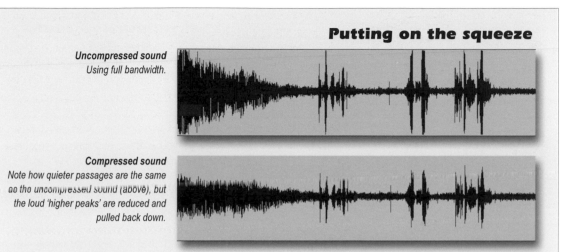

Putting on the squeeze

Uncompressed sound
Using full bandwidth.

Compressed sound
Note how quieter passages are the same
as the uncompressed sound (above), but
the loud 'higher peaks' are reduced and
pulled back down.

When you mix your movie in a film dubbing theatre, it will sound terrific. It should do, it's about the best environment on the planet in which to listen to the soundtrack for your movie. It will be very dynamic – quiet bits will be quiet, loud bits will be VERY loud. That's cool, 'cos it's supposed to be listened to in a cinema. But what happens when it comes to TV? Your average TV has a crappy speaker that would struggle to reproduce such a dynamic mix. So you will need to process your soundtrack through a box called a 'compressor'. This cunning little box takes the sound and leaves the middle ranged sounds (such as conversation) where they are (or sometimes will be boosted and made louder) but will pull all the louder sounds down. The upshot is that voices remain the same and loud sounds, whilst still present and 'loud sounding' are actually significantly reduced in level. This means viewers watching your movie off broadcast TV or video will not be constantly turning the volume up and down.

And for those of you who have wondered when watching commercial TV – 'are the ads louder than the movies and programmes?' Technically no, but they are put through a similar process where ALL the sound is boosted up (expanded rather than compressed) to be as loud as possible, even the normal voices. Which means all the audio is always at the loudest end of the scale, even if the actual effects are soft and quiet (such as a thunderous whisper!).

When you are doing this mix you will be hooked up to a little box called a PPM meter. The mixer should know all about this, but you should keep an eye on the PPM to make sure that the sound levels NEVER peaks over six on the dial. Anything over six will be considered an illegal audio track and rejected by the broadcasters. This is a historical point really as in the days gone by, anything peaking over six could in effect blow the transmitters for the TV stations. The BBC were so worried about this that mixing desks were redesigned so that the faders worked the opposite way around (pushing the fader up would actually reduce the signal). This was to counter the possibility that a presenter could have a heart attack, slump forward, push the faders up and blow the transmitter! How considerate.

Final mix

This is it. The moment of truth. The dubbing mixer will take the dialogue pre-mix, the spot effects and atmos pre-mix, the foley pre-mix and the music (which has not been pre-mixed) and do the final mix. You'll find it hard to contain your excitement, as you hear dialogue, sound effects, atmospheres, foley and music all expertly combined and for the first time you will see your film in its almost completed state. Boy does it really come to life! Because you have spent time doing the pre-mixes, this final mix should run quite smoothly. The only major work will be to accommodate music, which the mixer has not heard yet, and any new spot effects that you have tracklaid in the last forty eight hours (to plug holes).

Item	Amount
Microphone	£150
Cables	£20
Computer and software (should already have)	£0
External drive	£150
Sound effects hire	£100
Dubbing charts	£5
Blank stock (DA88)	£40
One day in foley studio	£500
Foley artist	£200
Three Days in a dubbing theatre	£3,000
Extra M&E halfday	£500
Dolby Licence (may not need)	£3,200
Possible total	£7,865

Post production sound budget

This budget is a bit of an all rounder and assumes one or two things. First off you are going to track lay yourself with your own existing hardware / software (that probably means Avid XpressDV or Pro Tools that you have blagged for free). Second, and I would recommend this, you buy a decent microphone and very long cable (you will end up running all over your home with the mic when recording your own effects, and it will always be connected to your computer). I have assumed that you are going to get your sound to the dub on your external hard drive, and that you will mix and master to DA88. If you are going to take your sound to the dub on DA88 tapes and not a hard drive, you will need to hire a DA88 deck which will cost about £150 for a weekend hire. There's some photocopying onto big sheets for the dubbing charts and somehow you will need to find or blag a sound effects library for next to nothing.

For the mix there is a day in a foley studio with a Foley artist, then three days final mix and a half day(ish) for an M&E. These are all great deals. You might not get them this cheap, but then again, you could also improve on it.

As for the Dolby licence, you may find ways around this and may not even need to pay for it if you do not release in a cinema.

It will take the best part of a day to do this mix and at the end, the dubbing mixer will probably lay the final mix down onto a time coded DA88. This tape will contain six separate audio channels, left channel, centre channel, right channel, left surround channel, right surround channel and sub-woofer. The remaining two audio tracks should be used for a stereo mix of all the other tracks (left speaker will go left, right speaker will go right, the centre speaker will be split left and right, left surround will go left, right surround will go right and the sub-woofer will be split left and right) and it may also be passed through a Dolby SVA box to create an analogue Dolby mix. This is not the standard way of doing things, but it does work for DVD mixes and TV. For a cinema mix, Dolby Digital is mastered to an MO disk (a high capacity disk) before being converted at the lab to an version which is printed onto the film.

Use sound effects to bridge scenes, a plane flying over, a police siren, etc. Or bring a scene in gently running the sound, such as a line of dialogue, momentarily over the preceding scene. This can be a simple way to help pace too.

At the end of each reel, the dubbing mixer will quickly deal with 'overlaps'. Because sound and picture are not encoded in the same place on a piece of film, you always need an extra bit of sound at the beginning of each reel. So the dubbing mixer will take the last second or so of the previous reel and add that sound to the start of the next reel (before the start of picture). Don't worry if you don't understand this, just make sure that your dubbing mixer does it.

M&E mix

Now I know that you've done the final mix and you've popped a bottle of champagne, but you now have to do the M&E mix. This is a special mix for foreign territories and is simply the movie minus the dialogue. There is always a tremendous temptation to say *'oh we'll do the M&E later'*, but if you do choose to do it later, it will take you much longer than if you just roll up your sleeves and get on with it now. It's not a big job, just a morning or afternoon, and as you've already done the final mix, the dubbing mixer will know the movie and can do the M&E quickly and efficiently.

Dosh

Paying for the final mix is always a bit of a problem for two simple reasons. First off, it's expensive. Even if you've cut a great deal it's still going to be a hefty wodge of dosh. Secondly, you've run out of cash so you can't pay. This

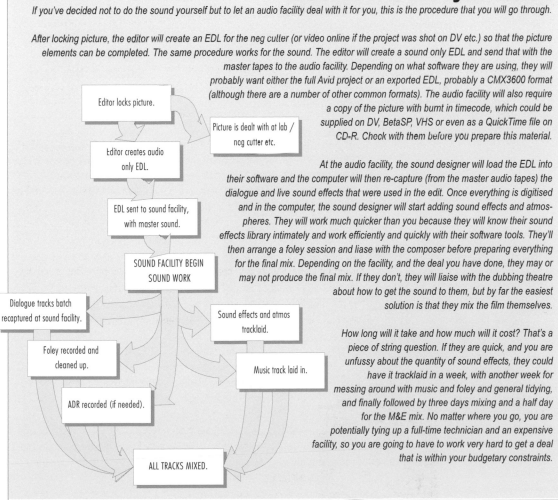

Someone else does your sound

If you've decided not to do the sound yourself but to let an audio facility deal with it for you, this is the procedure that you will go through.

After locking picture, the editor will create an EDL for the neg cutter (or video online if the project was shot on DV etc.) so that the picture elements can be completed. The same procedure works for the sound. The editor will create a sound only EDL and send that with the master tapes to the audio facility. Depending on what software they are using, they will probably want either the full Avid project or an exported EDL, probably a CMX3600 format (although there are a number of other common formats). The audio facility will also require a copy of the picture with burnt in timecode, which could be supplied on DV, BetaSP, VHS or even as a QuickTime file on CD-R. Check with them before you prepare this material.

At the audio facility, the sound designer will load the EDL into their software and the computer will then re-capture (from the master audio tapes) the dialogue and live sound effects that were used in the edit. Once everything is digitised and in the computer, the sound designer will start adding sound effects and atmospheres. They will work much quicker than you because they will know their sound effects library intimately and work efficiently and quickly with their software tools. They'll then arrange a foley session and liase with the composer before preparing everything for the final mix. Depending on the facility, and the deal you have done, they may or may not produce the final mix. If they don't, they will liaise with the dubbing theatre about how to get the sound to them, but by far the easiest solution is that they mix the film themselves.

How long will it take and how much will it cost? That's a piece of string question. If they are quick, and you are unfussy about the quantity of sound effects, they could have it tracklaid in a week, with another week for messing around with music and foley and general tidying, and finally followed by three days mixing and a half day for the M&E mix. No matter where you go, you are potentially tying up a full-time technician and an expensive facility, so you are going to have to work very hard to get a deal that is within your budgetary constraints.

Editor locks picture.

Picture is dealt with at lab / neg cutter etc.

Editor creates audio only EDL.

EDL sent to sound facility, with master sound.

SOUND FACILITY BEGIN SOUND WORK

Dialogue tracks batch recaptured at sound facility.

Sound effects and atmos tracklaid.

Foley recorded and cleaned up.

Music track laid in.

ADR recorded (if needed).

ALL TRACKS MIXED.

usually means that the dubbing theatre will hold onto your tapes until you pay. Of course, you can't finish your film without the tapes, so somehow you have to overcome this problem.

My approach has always been to make sure I save enough money in the budget for the final mix, and cut the best deal I can, offering to pay on the day. If you are working in downtime, this small job for a big dubbing theatre is just a little cash bonus. They will do it because they like you or the project, and because they are not doing anything else. And any cash is better than no cash, they just want to make sure that you don't rip them off and they don't have to chase you for payment.

How much should it cost? As little as you can get away with. I've heard of people getting completely free dubs but I suspect you'd be hard pushed to find somewhere to mix your film (who is used to mixing films) for under £500 a day, and more likely £1000 a day.

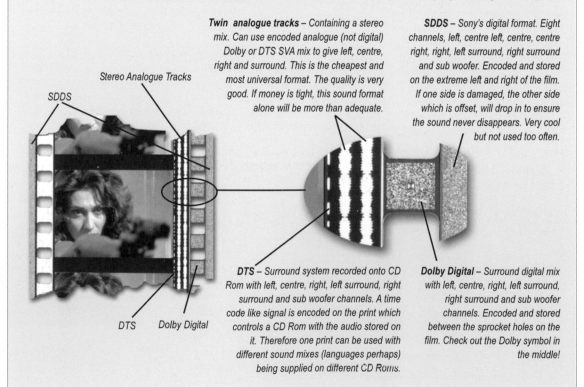

Sound on film

When your film is screened in a cinema, the projector can read sound information in several different ways. Not all systems are compatible with all projectors but the Stereo Analogue Tracks should playback on any projector, Dolby Digital coming in second place.

Twin analogue tracks – *Containing a stereo mix. Can use encoded analogue (not digital) Dolby or DTS SVA mix to give left, centre, right and surround. This is the cheapest and most universal format. The quality is very good. If money is tight, this sound format alone will be more than adequate.*

SDDS – *Sony's digital format. Eight channels, left, centre left, centre, centre right, right, left surround, right surround and sub woofer. Encoded and stored on the extreme left and right of the film. If one side is damaged, the other side which is offset, will drop in to ensure the sound never disappears. Very cool but not used too often.*

SDDS

Stereo Analogue Tracks

DTS   Dolby Digital

DTS – *Surround system recorded onto CD Rom with left, centre, right, left surround, right surround and sub woofer channels. A time code like signal is encoded on the print which controls a CD Rom with the audio stored on it. Therefore one print can be used with different sound mixes (languages perhaps) being supplied on different CD Roms.*

Dolby Digital – *Surround digital mix with left, centre, right, left surround, right surround and sub woofer channels. Encoded and stored between the sprocket holes on the film. Check out the Dolby symbol in the middle!*

Academy / SMPTE leader and sync plop

Academy or SMPTE leader is the numbered clock countdown that runs before every reel of your finished film. Academy leader counts in feet from 12 to 3, SMPTE leader counts in seconds from 8 to 2 (the same duration for both as 3 feet of 35mm film equals two seconds of screen time), followed by black.

When running this through a projector, you will hear an audible single frame of 1kHz tone – called a plop – that will sound at 3 feet, or 2 seconds, or 48 frames before the first frame of picture on the reel. There are then 47 frames of black before the picture starts.

When creating your final reels in the Avid you should digitise some Academy or SMPTE leader and place it before the head of each reel. Because it is eight seconds long, your timelines will start eight seconds before the hour (e.g. 00:59:52:00 for Reel 1 to 04:59:52:00 for Reel 5). Ensure that one frame of tone is placed on the audio tracks exactly on the last number of the leader (48 frames before picture starts). This is a good check for the sound editors and dubbing mixers to ensure their equipment is running in sync.

When the optical soundtrack is married to your final print, the sound actually runs 20 frames ahead of the picture. This is because on a film projector you cannot have the sound head adjacent to the bright projection lamp – it would melt! The sound head is below the projector lamp and consequently the sound needs to run ahead of the picture by the corresponding amount – 20 frames. You don't need to worry about this, but a cinema projectionist does!

The one frame sync plop is visible to the human eye as a series of sine waves down the optical track. When marrying the optical track to the film print you can check the sound is then running correctly 20 frames ahead of the picture.

Where next?

So you've paid your bills and have your final mix on a single DA88 in your hand (or an MO disk if you mised in Dolby Digital for cinema release). If you have completed your movie for the cinema, this MO disk (for Dolby digital) or DA88 tape (for analogue Dolby) will now go to the lab, who will convert it to an optical sound negative. This is a piece of film with the sound encoded optically onto the edge so that when you play it on a projector in a cinema, the projector can read these tracks and provide a soundtrack (between the sprocket holes with Dolby Digital).

If you are finishing to video and DVD, then there are a couple of other technical hoops that you will have to jump through (covered in Chapter 22).

If money is REALLY non existent, you could do you own mix at home, although it will never sound as good as if it were done in a studio. On the upside, you can then spend as long as you like tweaking the sound. If you can, go to a dubbing theatre and spend just one day premixing the dialogue tracks, then you can mix in all the effects, atmos, Foley and music at home. Mixing voices is fiendishly difficult and one of the big red flags with low budget films is bad sound, especially unintelligible dialogue. This is only suitable for films that go straight to video and TV, not the cinema.

How to track lay your film with Avid XpressDV on a PC

Adding sound effects is very easy using Avid XpressDV. Best of all though, Avid XpressDV has tight integration with some of the top end software tools you will end up using for your final mix.

How it works is this. Existing sound, such as dialogue etc., is tidied up during the edit. ADR (actors re-voicing) is recorded and dropped into place. New sound effects are recorded, tidied up and dropped into place. New sound effects and atmospheres are pulled off CD (effects library) and dropped into place. The music is recorded and dropped into place. Foley is recorded, edited and dropped into place. Then the whole lot is exported and saved on a disk, taken to the final dub and mixed. That's it! Sounds easy, and it kind of is, except it's a lot of work and can be fraught with technical problems. So do tests. Then test the tests!

What will you need?

Assuming you haven't already got a set-up which you used to edit the picture element of your movie (and are now going to slightly modify for sound use) you are going to need a computer, ideally with a big monitor and an excellent amplifier with top notch speakers. Don't use the free pokey little ones that came with your set-up, invest, or better still, blag from your brother in law (who is a HiFi enthusiast), a couple of excellent speakers and an amp. You'll also need a lot of free hard disk space, so you might want to buy an extra drive.

Getting sound in and out of your computer is also an issue as most sound cards that are already part of your computer are good, but not THAT good. Check out a dedicated sound technology store and buy the cheapest audio card that is up to the job. Shouldn't be much more than £100. You'll also need all the cables to connect it all up, perhaps even a small mixing desk to make life a little easier (I bought the Spirit Folio Notepad which did a fine job).

Next there's the microphone. A good one please. It doesn't need to be directional, or even THAT good. Sennheiser do a range of cheap but excellent mics. Don't use a dynamic mic (unpowered). You should be spending at least £100, and more like over double or triple that really (the Sennheiser K6 body and add on modules range being a great choice).

Last but not least, an exceptionally long microphone cable, ideally 20m! This is because you will wander all over your flat or home with the mic while the computer records as you scrape, creak, rattle and roll all manner of curious objects to create that weird sound that you just can't find anywhere else.

Lets assume that you have already watched your movie and made a long (and I mean really long!) list of sound effects you need. They will come from two separate places – libraries, either online or CD, or custom recorded (probably by you).

Custom recording effects using Cool Edit Pro

1. Setup

Go to www.syntrillium.com and download Cool Edit Pro, a commercial program for sound editing on a PC. You can use this version for 21 days before you have to register and buy, so there you go, you have a deadline! Once installed, run it and it will ask you a bunch of questions about things like scratch disks (where you want temporary files saved etc.) after which it will start up properly.

2. First run

OK, I know the first screen looks pretty scary! There's lots of screen stuff going on. You don't need to worry about most of this for now as this is the multi track mode. We are going to be using Cool Edit Pro for recording, editing and preparing individual effects, not for multi-track work. In the top right of the screen there is a button that looks like a waveform – click this to take you to the individual track view (this button just switches you between the two modes).

On the right hand side of the screen is a track view which shows the waveforms of the sounds. On the left there is a kind of bin, much like the bins in Avid XpressDV. There will be a bunch of 'instrument' sounds in this default bin which you can delete by selecting them and hitting the delete key.

3. Set-up to record (Windows audio set-up)

Depending on which version of Windows you are using, this process can differ. Windows has it's own audio input / output interface which Cool Edit Pro uses and you must set this up before you can playback and record effects. Most of the time this will work by default, but you may need to mess around with the Sounds and Multimedia applet in the Control Panel. See also the setup instructions with your soundcard. Also, make sure that you switch off ALL recording inputs except the microphone so that there is no additional noise or interference (you do this in Volume Control applet, then the Recording option). Hook up your mic and you should be ready to rock!

4. Recording new stuff

Start up CEP (Cool Edit Pro) and make sure you are in edit view (single track) and not multi-track view and Go to the File Menu and select New. A dialogue box will pop up asking you what sample rate you want. You will almost certainly be working at 48 kHz (although you could be working at 44.1kHz so make sure) so select that and click OK. You will record almost all sound effects in mono, so select mono, and the resolution you will be using is 16 bit. After selecting these options click the OK button. You are now ready to start recording. Notice how a file has appeared in the bin to the left, currently called 'Untitled' – this is the empty file you have just created.

5. Start recording

First make sure you are viewing the recording levels, go to the View menu, then Show Level Meters. The levels, a kind of long horizontal bar, will appear at the bottom of the screen. Set up your mic and props to record an effect, turn down the volume on the amplifier to avoid feedback (or better still, wear headphones), rehearse a few times, then press the record button on the transport at the bottom left of the screen. You will now be recording and the sounds you make should be digitised to the hard drive. Remember you want to get as strong a signal as possible, without distorting, so keep an eye on those levels as they dip up and down. Don't worry about performing the effect quickly, just get it right and do a few variations. Then click the stop button on the transport at the bottom left of the screen.

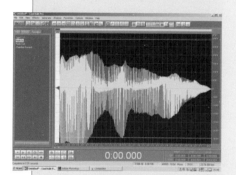

6. Edit the effect down

Now you will need to trim out the unwanted parts of the effect, leaving only the actual sound you want with no extra baggage around it. Cool Edit Pro is extremely easy to use for editing sound, just select what you don't want with the cursor and hit the delete button. Cool Edit will then delete that part of the sound. And er, well, Cool! That's simple. You may need to zoom in and out of the entire recording so that you can clearly see it all, which you can do using the various Magnifying buttons on the panel to the bottom left of the screen. You can also drag along the effect by grabbing the green bar just above the waveforms windows. Delete the audio before and after the portion of the recording you want. Remember, you want nothing but the actual sound effect.

7. Prep for export

To make life a little easier later on you can now add very small fades at the start and end of the effect. This can help if the effect abruptly starts or ends unattractively (these fades are only to help the mixer). Select a small portion at the head of the effect then in the left hand pane, click on the favourites button and a short list of processes will be shown. Double click on Fade In and the effect will be processed, creating a lovely fade in. Now do the same with Fade Out for the end of the effect. Obviously, at any time you can listen to the effect and hit Undo if you are not happy (ctrl+z).

8. Export

You now have a short, tidied up sound effect that is ready to be exported. Go to the File Menu, then Save As..., the Save Waveform As dialogue box will appear. From here you can save an individual file that Avid XpressDV can import. Organisation is key, so setup an empty folder into which you will save all your effects, and remember to give each clip a descriptive and unique name – you'll be surprised how quickly you will build up a library of custom effects, and their names have a habit of blurring into one mental mish mash. Name the clip (Door Crash.wav for instance) and the file will be saved. You can now carry on creating new effects or import the effect into Avid XpressDV for track laying.

9. Importing the effect in XpressDV

I will assume you know how to edit in Avid XpressDV, so actually dropping the effects in place shouldn't be a problem. You should have already broken your movie up into reels, and made duplicate time lines for sound effects only. Where possible, effects should be checkboarded and grouped together. Effects should be track laid in mono, unless you specifically want an effect in stereo (to save space as you can only have eight tracks running on any one time line copy). Effects will come from two sources, the effects you custom recorded, but also from sound effects libraries.

10. Importing a custom recorded effect

It's a good idea to create a bin in Avid XpressDV for each type of sound effect (eg. CD Spot FX, CD Atmos FX, Custom Spot FX, Custom Atmos FX etc.) There will be hundreds of individual sounds and this will help you find them as you tracklay. Click on the bin you wish to import to and select File, Import. The dialogue box will open. Under Files of type select Audio Files. Now find your sound effects folder and press Ctrl-A to select all the WAVs, or select them individually. Video Resolution doesn't apply, but do select the Audio Drive you want to import to. Then click Open. All your sound effects will now be imported into your Avid project and the WAVs copied to your selected media drive. If the sample rate of the WAV is different to the project (it shouldn't be if you've followed these instructions) Avid will ask if you wish to convert it, click Yes. Keep importing until all your sound effects are in the desired bins. When you're finished it's a good idea to sort them alphabetically by clicking on the Name column heading and pressing Ctrl-E.

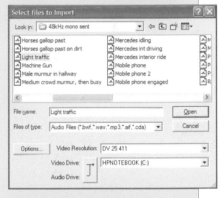

11. Importing a sound effect from CD

Avid XpressDV can directly import a track from a CD. Sound on a CD is recorded at 44.1kHz which will not play if you have been working at 48kHz (which you probably have). The solution is to either import the track and allow Avid to sample rate convert it in the process (it can be slow, a couple of minutes for a 30 second clip for instance), or you can digitise it from an analogue source such as a CD player (which will do it in real time). Digitising from a CD player is the same process as recording from a microphone, but using a CD instead.

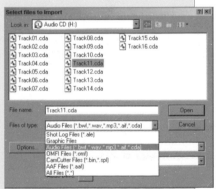

To directly import into Avid XpressDV and sample rate convert, go to the sound effects bin you created earlier, right click in the bin and select Import from the menu. The Import dialogue box will pop up. By default, Avid will assume you are importing a graphic file, so go to the File Types drop down box and select Audio Files. Then select the CD Drive. A number of files should appear starting at Track01.cda. These are the raw CD files and need to be converted before then can be used. Select the one you want, and remember that they are always named as tracks and numbers, never with the names of what is actually on the CD (such as 'door creak' for instance). Select the one you want and click on Open. Avid will bring up a warning box asking if you would like to perform a sample rate conversion from 44.1kHz to 48kHz. Click on Yes, or Yes To All if there are multiple tracks. A status bar will pop up telling you how much has been imported, followed by another status bar telling you how long it will take to convert to 48kHz. This is entirely dependent on the speed of your CD drive and computer processor. After it's done, it will appear in the bin (named Track020.cda) for instance. Rename it straight away so that you know what it actually is. Double clicking will now launch the file and it will appear in a source window. Hit play and you should hear it. You are now ready to edit it into the timeline.

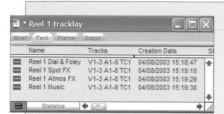

12. Duplicating your master sequences

You can only listen to 8 channels at once on XpressDV so I would recommend making a bin for each Reel of your film and duplicating your master sequences four times in each bin (click on the filmstrip icon and press **Ctrl-D***), one for each type of sound effect . . .*

1 – Dialogue and Foley (6 mono channels dialogue and on-set FX, 2 mono channels footsteps & clothes foley),
2 – Spot FX (4 mono channels, 2 stereo channels),
3 – Atmos FX (4 stereo channels),
4 – Music (4 stereo channels).

Now is the time to clean up your edited sound and make sure it ends up in the correct sequence. Then edit in your imported effects accordingly. Remember you don't need to adjust the gain on each clip – this will be done at the final mix. Leave everything at 0dB.

13. Consolidating your media after the track lay

Track laying your entire film will literally take weeks of solid work (suddenly you'll understand why there's an Acadamy Award for sound editing!), and when it's all done you have to export your timelines so they can be loaded into Pro Tools (the most popular professional sound editing system) for the dub. First you must consolidate each sequence. The reason you do this is so that you only export the sound you've actually used (for example, ten seconds of birds tweeting instead of the two minutes you originally imported). If you don't consolidate, your export file will be many gigabytes larger than it needs to be. So highlight the sequence to consolidate, click on the burger button in the bottom left corner of the bin and select Consolidate. *I would suggest 200 frame handles (extra sound exported in case you need it – it doesn't show up on the sequence, it's just there in case you need to extend a sound effect during the dub). DESELECT* Delete original media files when done *– this is crucial otherwise your original master clips will be deleted, and you don't want that to happen. DESELECT* Skip media files already on the target drive *– you'll probably be consolidating to the same drive that the media is already on and you actually want the files to consolidate. Then select the* Target Drive, *click* OK *and away you go. The process will take some time and your bin will be full of new master clips when it's finished. Check on the timeline that all the labels now have .new after them – this means the consolidation has been successful. Make sure you consolidate all four sequences for each Reel before you continue.*

14. Exporting to Pro Tools

Exporting to a Pro Tools compatible OMF is actually the easiest part of the process. Highlight the sequence to export, select File *from the menu, then* AvidLinks . . . *then* Digidesign Pro Tools. *Make a new folder on your hard disk in which to put all the OMFs. The file name will be the name of the sequence so that's OK, then all you need to do is ensure* Embed Audio in OMF file *is checked,* Save as type *is* OMFI Files (*.omf) *and click* Save. *The PC will chug away merrily for a while and you'll have a brand spanking new OMF on your hard disk – this effectively contains your timeline and all the sound media associated with it in one clever file. It's a good idea to burn this onto a CD and take it to the dubbing theatre to check it will actually load in before making the other OMFs for the other sequences.*

15. Printing the timeline as a dubbing chart

Finally load your printer full of paper and ink and print out the XpressDV timeline – this is to use as paper dubbing charts. (They're not up to professional standards because each dialogue clip won't be named and you'll have to read the timecode from the bottom of the printout, but they will do in emergency. It's very common to use the Pro Tools scrolling screen as a digital dubbing chart anyway, but ask the dubbing mixer if these printouts are OK in case). Back to Avid XpressDV . . . firstly I would reset the Timeline to it's default look – click on the burger button in the bottom left corner of the Timeline window and select **Default Setup**. *Now select* **File** *on the menu, and* **Page Setup** . . . *ensure* **Orientation** *is set to* **Landscape**, *then click* **OK**. *Now select* **File, Print Timeline** . . . *and click OK. Note that the*

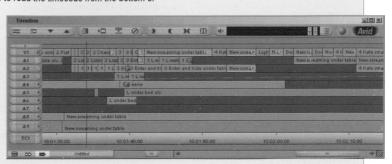

Timeline prints out at the same zoom level as you are currently working at. If you zoom all the way out the Timeline will print out far too cramped to read. Experiment with zooming in slightly until all the clips, labels and associated timecodes can be read easily on the printout.

17. Exporting your picture as a DV stream

One way of getting the pictures of your movie to the final mix is by exporting a DV stream of each reel. With suitable hardware on the Pro Tools sound editing system, you can attach this file to the timeline and Pro Tools will display the picture on a TV monitor accordingly. Avid XpressDV does not have a feature (at the time of writing) of burning in the timecode of the edited sequence (Avid Film Composer version 11 does). One way around this is to create a title in the title tool that shows the timecode at a useful point in the sequence. For example, on the first frame of Reel 4, create a title that says 04:00:00:00 and display this for one frame. Do this every five minutes down the sequence, and on the last frame too (which would be 04:19:24:18 for example). (Alternatively you could use the free Timecode plugin which will burn timecode into your picture, BUT, you will have to render it before laying off to tape).

So now you should have a timeline with a single frame title every five minutes displaying the timecode at that point in the sequence. This will allow the sound editor to check that your sequence is running in sync with Pro Tools. Now export the sequence by highlighting it in the bin, select File, *then* Export . . . *Now click* Options . . . , *then click* Export As *and select* DV stream. *Now click* Format Options . . . *and select* PAL *under* Video Format *and select* 44.1kHz *(or 48kHz if that's what you're using) under* Audio Format. *Click* OK, *click* Save, *enter a filename for this sequence, and click* Save. *It will take a while to export each 20 minute reel (a few hours). The files will be a few gigabytes in size but the quality will be lovely. You'll have to burn a DVD-R of each file, or put it on an external Firewire hard drive to deliver to the sound editors. They'll load it onto their system and you should have picture running in sync with your sound!*

Music
Blueprint

Music is the final creative stage where you can radically alter the feel, tone and pace of your movie. Think what John Williams did for Star Wars and Jaws, what John Carpenter did for Halloween, what Strauss did for 2001 . . . Most new film makers are happy with what they are given resulting in an uninspired score. Seek out the best and most appropriate music for your film and work as hard with your composer as you would with any other creative on your team — camera, actor, editor, screenwriter . . .

Composer – electronic

A creative who chooses to compose and perform their music electronically, using MIDI instruments and samplers. Often they have no choice but to use digital equipment as they have no performance skills or contacts and may not be properly trained. Remember, many memorable scores are electronic, such as horror guru John Carpenter's stuff.

Composer – analogue

A creative who will probably use computers but may not be a master of the technology. They will lean toward samplers and 'real' instruments, perform some tracks themselves (as they are probably skilled musicians too) and ultimately compose for 'real world' instruments. Remember, a string quartet can be effective and is only four players, but you can't afford the London Phil!

Computer composed

A new breed of computer program that puts the power to compose firmly in the hands of anyone with a good ear but no musical ability. Neither the Holy Grail for cash strapped producers or the tools of the antichrist to evangelic composers. If used sparingly and with sensitivity, you can plug some holes in your score for free, and get to collect royalties too!

New bands

Don't pursue major acts for that great track. Any band who has made it to the top, or even half way there, is not going to let you use their music unless you pay thousands of pounds. Seek out an unsigned band with a cool demo CD and use their music. They get good coverage, and you get free music. Good all round.

Library classical

Music libraries are a great place to get relatively cheap classical music. Anyone dead for over 75 years is public domain (composition NOT performance), so you can have a blast of Beethoven or Wagner without having to worry about acquiring the compositional rights. Music libraries have hundreds of hours of top performances and recordings to plunder.

Library contemporary

Whilst libraries do the classical music thing very well, the other stuff they offer can be a little dull. It's often cheaper and gives better results if you can get a composer to write original music for you. Some libraries do have music from major contemporary artists, but on the whole, it doesn't represent good value for money when it comes to micro budget films.

Music Blueprint

It's almost a certainty that you won't consider who will compose the music for your film until you get into the cutting room. The selection of a composer is one of the final 'creative collaboration' decisions that you will make, yet in consideration of just how important music will be to your film, it's staggering just how late people leave this. The common complaint I hear from composers is that they get hired too late in the process and are expected to perform miracles in a matter of days, working with little or no budget.

Often over used, music is the final creative veneer you can add to your story. It may seem a simple process but it can easily turn into a legal minefield.

Temp-tastic

Through editing, you'll have used music from other movies, referred to as 'temp' music. Clearly you can't use this music for a number of copyright infringement reasons, but if you have been selective with your music choices and sensitive in its placement, this temp music score can act as a good indicator of what you want and need from your composer.

Please apply here

When you reach the first fine cut of your film, you should have started looking for a composer. You can place ads on Shooting People, contact music supervisors, ask around other film making colleagues, and invite composers to send to you a CV, showreel and CD of their music. It used to be hard to find a composer, now everyone seems to have their own bedroom studio! Don't be too impressed by a studio with its thundering demo music, flashy lights and racks of sleek black boxes interconnected by a seemingly impossible jumble of cables – remember, you are hiring the artist and not the tools.

95% of the applicants will be rejected pretty much straight away as they will be over-qualified and want paying too much, under qualified and compose dreadful music, or simply inappropriate and their music really does not fit with the style of your film (although you should try to avoid falling into the trap that creatives are merely defined by their last few jobs). As soon as you want to pass on a composer, send them a polite rejection letter and return their CD and show reel so they do not clutter up your in-tray. Composers tend to get on the phone and pester you to make a decision, so let them know asap so that they don't tie up your phone and your time. Get into the habit of listening to their demo CDs on your way to and from the cutting room, whilst in the loo, during your lunch break, anytime you can spare without being forced to listen to 20 disks at once.

Beware of actors bursting into song, or even humming in front of the camera as this is a performance with performers' rights and compositional rights attached. Many songs thought to be in the public domain are not – 'Happy Birthday' for one! If you use it and don't buy the rights, you could be sued and someone else might end up owning your movie!

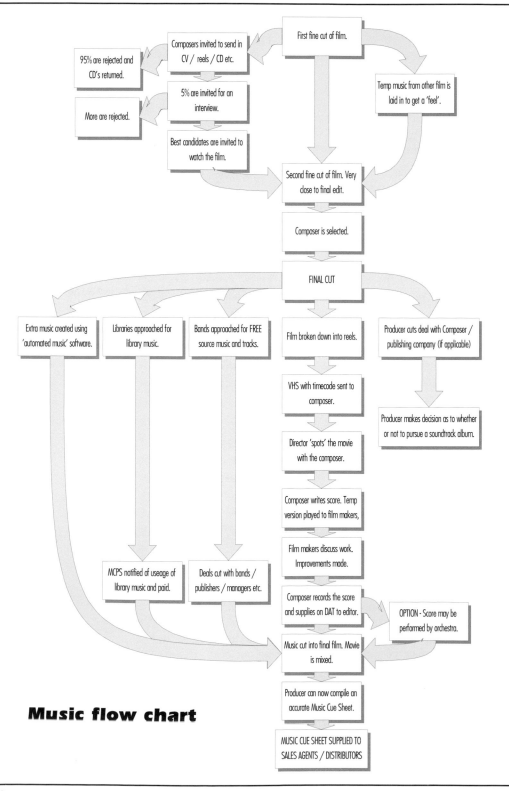

Music flow chart

First fine cut of film.

Composers invited to send in CV / reels / CD etc.

95% are rejected and CD's returned.

5% are invited for an interview.

More are rejected.

Best candidates are invited to watch the film.

Temp music from other film is laid in to get a 'feel'.

Second fine cut of film. Very close to final edit.

Composer is selected.

FINAL CUT

Extra music created using 'automated music' software.

Libraries approached for library music.

Bands approached for FREE source music and tracks.

Film broken down into reels.

Producer cuts deal with Composer / publishing company (if applicable)

VHS with timecode sent to composer.

Producer makes decision as to whether or not to pursue a soundtrack album.

Director 'spots' the movie with the composer.

Composer writes score. Temp version played to film makers,

Film makers discuss work. Improvements made.

MCPS notified of useage of library music and paid.

Deals cut with bands / publishers / managers etc.

Composer records the score and supplies on DAT to editor.

OPTION - Score may be performed by orchestra.

Music cut into final film. Movie is mixed.

Producer can now compile an accurate Music Cue Sheet.

MUSIC CUE SHEET SUPPLIED TO SALES AGENTS / DISTRIBUTORS

The right rights . . .

Compositional rights
This is the composer, the person who actually wrote the notes on the paper, or in their software. These rights will be assigned to your production company (in the form of mechanical rights) so that you can add the music to your film. So you will need a contract between your composer and your production company.

Performance rights
This is the performer, be they a cellist, singer, bongo drummer, or sixty piece orchestra. If your composer is the sole performer then things stay simple, but if your performers come from a series of different sources you could find yourself chasing signatures on lots of pieces of paper. You will need a contract between all performers, probably including the composer, and your production company.

Contracts?
Where to get your contracts? 'The Guerilla Film Makers Handbook' has composer and performers contracts on the free CD that comes with the book. If you use an orchestra then your music 'fixer' should take care of all the performers contracts for you. You can also download from our website at www.guerillafilm.com.

First meeting

The few that are suitable should be invited in for an interview for you to see if they will fit within your team (composers are artists and you want to know if there will be creative clashes). They are master craftspeople and most will have the ability to play several instruments. They may also know many performers and musicians and will almost certainly own a home recording studio. These are all assets that you will plunder.

After meeting a few composers, there will be one or two who stand out as favourites and you can invite them to watch the film. By now, you should have a second fine cut of your film that will be very close to the final edit. Eventually, you will decide on a single composer and they will be hired for the job.

Do the deal

It's time to cut the deal. You will agree to pay them an amount of money and give them a full screen credit as composer. They will agree to compose, perform, arrange or hire performers, record, master and deliver the musical score of the film on a format such as DAT, CD or even data (within the agreed time frame).

There are several negotiable elements that will spring up at this point. First is that of the movie soundtrack which you

Don't allow your composer to come to your final mix - they will complain if you have made any necessary and brutal music edits, and they will always feel that their music has been mixed too low.

The publishing company

The publishing company represents the interests of your composer. Whenever the composer's work is screened commercially, there is the possibility that certain rights kick in and royalties become due. For instance, in many European countries, if a film is screened on TV, royalties should be paid. This is why the music cue sheet is so important . . . and if there's one group of people on the planet who have their business sewn up, it's the musicians.

Here's how it works. You make a film and sell it to German TV (for instance) who then screen it and by law, pay certain royalties (these royalties are very complex and differ widely, but you don't pay so you don't need to worry about it for now). This money is paid to the German version of the Performing Rights Society (PRS) who then check the Music Cue Sheet and forward the money to the PRS here in the UK . . .

who then distribute the cash to the publishing companies of the various composers listed on that document (remember there may be several – your composer, the band you used for several tracks, library music etc.). As an example, when White Angel *(my second feature film) was screened on German TV, the composer Harry Gregson-Williams received £700 via his publishing company.*

So how can you get a slice of that pie? For beginners, 50% of the royalties (by law) MUST be paid to the composer. So that's half gone. The other half is up for grabs and you could get all of it or a part of it. The composer / agent / publishing company will argue that they should get it all as they weren't paid very well in the first place. If you do manage to get them to agree to letting you have all or part of this remaining 50%, you will then need to cut a deal with a publishing company to pay you your split (in practice this will probably end up being the same publishing company as the composer's).

The reality of this situation is far from ideal. You are under pressure, broke, late for your deadlines, over-budget, stressed out . . . and the composer already assumes that they will get ALL of the royalties…! So you will end up giving it all away. Try not to do this, hold onto your fair share (which I would argue should be the remaining 50%, but no one else will see it that way!) as it may represent the only real revenue you will get from your film!

Contractual issues . . .
Contractually you want to look out for a clause that refers to a 'mechanical synchronisation levy' or 'mechanical royalties'. This is a payment that a UK distributor would be forced to pay, per VHS or DVD, to the publishing Company upon release (and it can be a significant payment too). If you let the composer keep this in the contract then you will find it hard to attract a distributor as before they even get the film on the shelves they will have to pay the publishing company a sizeable chunk of dosh. The phrase you want to see inserted into the clause is that you, the producer 'would use reasonable endeavours to ensure that mechanical royalties are paid for the use of the music in videogrammes of the film. The composer will have no claim against the Company for such royalties if such payment is not secured.' The upshot is that you ask the distributor for it, they then say 'Get out of here!' and will refuse to release your film if you insist on it, so you agree with them and drop it.

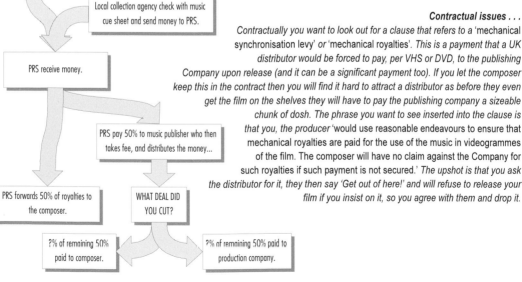

may perceive will be a great hit on CD. It's very unlikely that this CD will generate anything more than a bloody great headache and it's up to you whether you want to chase this for little or no reward. On the other hand, by law, there are a number of rights associated with the music which you can access. The composer will want to hold onto these rights and you maybe forced to let them do so, but if you can hold onto any of them, this will probably mean money that will come back to you in a couple of years via the PRS.

Composition begins

Back to your movie . . . The composer has been hired. The movie has been cut and the picture has been locked. The editor will now break the movie down into reels (probably five) and lay off each of these reels onto a VHS videotape with burnt in time code in picture, and audio time code on track two of the VHS. This time code is absolutely essential to the composer, as they will use it to synchronise their home recording studio equipment to the movie. Without it, they cannot guarantee synch and therefore cannot compose music to the picture. Some composers may prefer to use a quicktime or AVI movie from your non-linear editing suite.

If you are using a professional editing system it's easy to switch visual time code on and off from the Beta SP deck (there's a switch on the front of the machine). The audio time code can also be taken from the Beta SP by connecting the time code out (on the back of the Beta) and connecting it to track two of the audio VHS. When you play the Beta you should hear the high pitched noise of audible time code.

If you have cut on Avid XpressDV, things become slightly more complicated as there is no way to generate audio timecode from within AvidXpressDV so you can't easily lay down timecode. In this instance you will have lay down 'wild' time code (timecode that has no direct correlation between the pictures and sound) so that the composer can sync their equipment to the tape. There will be no direct way of laying the music into your film automatically so most composers will record a bit of the sync dialogue a few seconds before the music cue begins so that the editor can use this to sync the music to the picture. You may need to buy or hire a piece of equipment that can generate SMPTE timecode for this purpose . . . . Or you could just beg your composer to work with a Quicktime or AVI movie on their computer . . .

Spotting the movie

Once the composer has the picture element in their studio (whether that picture comes off tape or disk) they will be able to go through the movie with the director and 'spot' the music cues. This process of 'spotting' is where both the director and the composer will instinctively want to put more music into the movie than the movie actually needs, so try and hold back.

Dominic Beeton
Composer

'My studio is based at home and is mainly software based, reflecting the trend amongst composers. Music software is a mature technology and it's amazing what can be done with a relatively modest cash outlay on the tools. The composer who writes with pencil and manuscript is a dying breed, usurped by a generation of composers who are able to produce full orchestral scores in their home studios, even down to producing a surround sound mix.

I can now produce a fully orchestrated score synched to picture so that a film maker can hear what the score will sound like. Changes can often be made on the spot, before a single penny is spent on the most expensive part, the recording of the live instruments. What happens next depends on the budget of the production. For cash strapped productions the sampled orchestration might be 'enhanced' by bringing in live musicians such as a violinist, saxophonist or trumpeter, all of which are fiendishly difficult to emulate convincingly. The downside of this is that a lot of time is spent on orchestrating the score and producing cues which at the end of the day the director may reject, whereas if the idea had been played on a piano the director may have turned it down straight away. Some cues may also be turned down because the samples aren't convincing whereas if they were actually played by a real orchestra they would sound fine.

Despite the technological advances of sampled orchestration and the excellent quality of samples, I can't see that there will ever be a substitute in terms of richness and emotional impact for a full orchestra.'

Exporting your movie for your composer

By now you should have cut your movie up into sub 20 minute chunks, to match the reels that your movie will eventually be made up into when on 35mm film for cinema projection (incidentally, these size chunks also make the work more manageable too, so even if you are not planning on a 35mm print and intend to stay on video only, you might want to still work this way). Each reel should have it's own time code, reel one picture starting at 01:00:00:00, reel two starting at 02:00:00:00 etc.

To add burnt in timecode, and assuming you are using AvidXpressDV, go to your Avid installation disk and under the folder Goodies, you will see a sub folder called TimcodeAVX in which there is a file called timecode.avx. Copy this file into the Avid AVX Plugins folder on your hard drive and restart Avid XpressDV. You will see there is now a new effect called Timecode which can drag and drop onto your movie like any other effect. It will need to be rendered before you can export it as a quicktime file.

If the composer is using Pro Tools, or a similar program, they will probably want a Quicktime file to sync the music to. This file needs to be high enough quality for them to see detail yet small enough to keep the data transfer rates down. Each reel will need to be exported separately and encoded using Quicktime or AVI formats (do not use MPEG for this!). Most will probably want Quicktime . . .

You will need to turn off any tracks with temp music (as the composer won't want to hear that when they are composing). Select the clip for reel one and from the File Menu select Export. This will bring a Save As Box up. In the bottom click on the Options button and the Export Setting dialogue box will pop up. Make sure Video and Audio are selected (so it will export both Video and Audio and not just the video or the audio on its own).

At the top select Quicktime Movie from the drop down box, then select the Custom check box to bring up the Advanced Video Format options which will appear below.

In the middle section select Quarter Size in the WIDTH x HEIGHT

section (click on the burger bar). In the COLOR LEVELS section select RGB, in the FILE FIELD ORDER select Single Field and then from the PIXEL ASPECT RATIO select Square if your project is 4:3, and 16:9 Non-square if your project is in 16:9.

Finally, click on the Format Options button (at the top of the dialogue box) which will bring up the Movie Settings dialogue box. Click the Video Settings Button and select Sorenson Video 3 and Millions of Colours from the Compressor drop down boxes. Slide the Quality slider all the way to best. In the Motion settings it should be 25 frames per second, and limit the data rate to 90 Kbytes/sec. Hit the OK button to close the Compression Settings window.

Click the Audio Settings button and select IMA 4:1 from the Compressor drop down box (this will compress the audio with no real loss of quality), 48 khz from Rate, 16bit in Size, and Mono from Use. Hit OK to close the Audio Settings dialogue box.

Now hit OK to close the Movie Settings dialogue box and hit Save to close the Export Settings box. Finally, name the file and hit the Save button. The AvidXpressDV will now compress and create a new Quicktime file.

With these settings, each reel will be an excellent balance of quality / compression for the composer and will end up at about 150mb in size. Depending on your computer each reel could take several hours to create, so factor this into your schedule. You will probably give these files to your composer on a CDR so make sure there is a CD Recorder on the system you are using.

Each reel will have a number of music cues which will be numbered 1M1 (reel one music cue one), 1M4 (reel one, music cue four), 3M2 (reel three, music cue two) and so on. This method of spotting and numbering is industry practice and simply a way of compartmentalising and managing the creation and production of musical elements.

Once the spotting session is completed, the composer will be left to work their magic and write the music. At various points, the producer and director will visit the composer so they can listen to and comment on their work. If you have made the right choice of composer then this should be a joyous process. The composer will have written their music using synthesisers and if time and money allow, it's usually desirable to replace the electronic version with real world instruments and voices.

Sometimes a composer is multi-talented and will be able to play various instruments or may have friends who are talented musicians. More often, budget and time get the better of the process and the score remains electronic, which ultimately means blander and a sometimes a little soulless music (of course some scores are designed to be electronic and these can work very well). As a rule, don't ask your composer to try and make their synthesisers and samplers sound like a big orchestra as they won't (even though the tests they do will sound terrific).

Featured or background?

Music in your film will fall into two categories. Music that is heard by characters in the film, such as music on a radio or an opera singer (commonly called source music or featured music), and music that is not heard by characters in the film, the musical composition (commonly called background music – although the front and end credits music is called featured music, whilst the rest of the score is called background music – go figure!). Make a list of all the source music (heard by the characters) and get to work on getting it for free or as little money as possible.

Not all the music in your movie needs to be custom composed – that night club track, elevator music, occasional music stab, track on the radio – there are several other places you can go to get music for these kind of sequences.

Ditch the headline acts

Firstly, it isn't worth pursuing tracks written and performed by top bands (you won't get far without a serious wedge of dosh), so pursue new bands who will be delighted to give you tracks for free in return for the publicity. As long as they have a publishing company, they should also

Howard Price
EMI Music Publishing

'Many new film makers ignore publishing rights for the music because they don't appreciate their value, especially in the long term. When a film is broadcast or shown publicly, certain rights are used and royalties paid. The composer (who has cut a deal with a music publisher) will see a large slice of those rights. If the film maker is smart they will have cut a deal with the composer in advance for a share of those royalties. It's a good idea to cut your deal with the composer BEFORE any music is written, then place those rights with a reputable publisher who can then administer, collect and seek further usage for those rights.

As a rough guide, if a new film maker made a low budget film that had the success of a film like 'Lock Stock . . . ', they could be looking at a return of tens of thousands. However most low budget films do only a fraction of that business, but even so, they will do some business which will generate royalties. As a rule of thumb 1% of UK box office will go to the PRS which will then be split between the different rights holders on a pro rata basis – for instance you might have 20 minutes of score and 10 minutes of songs making 30 minutes in total. Usually, video and DVD use is fully bought out when the deal is cut, but TV broadcast is not and can generate further revenues. Broadly speaking, ITV will pay £75 per minute of music, BBC £50, Ch4 £25 and Ch5 £10. Then there are overseas performances, all generating even more royalties. When you consider you might make many films in your lifetime, these royalties could represent a nice little retirement bonus.

We often get offered low budget films but have to pass on many as we don't feel they will be sufficiently successful or the music isn't particularly strong.'

The home recording studio

This is without doubt, the nicest, most compact and organised home studio I have ever seen! More often they are a jumble of cables, with old and new kit balanced precariously, last night's take out still lingering and empty beer cans on the sofa . . . But essentially, here's what's in the home studio.

Microphone
Used to record live musical instruments, voices and sounds. A good mic. can make an enormous difference and remains one of the most comparatively expensive bits of kit in the home studio.

Keyboard
A midi keyboard is the primary input tool of the composer. They can assign any synthesized voice or sampled sound to trigger when notes are played.

Speakers
The bigger and better the more accurate the sound. One of the best investments you can make and you won't need to upgrade in 18 months, unlike your computer and software.

Mixing desk
The desk is used to help mix the music, that is, set each track's dynamic level in relation to the other tracks. Much will be done using the mouse but some composers will use a mixing desk. The better desks come with 'flying faders' that will move up and down on their own, in accordance with previous mixing sessions. This makes tweaking much easier.

DAT
Final mastering to DAT (Digital Audio Tape) at 48khz. The DAT will also be hooked up to an amplifier and speakers, the bigger the better. You could also master to CDR for speed and simplicity (CDR 'audio' works only at 44.1khz but CDR data can work at both 44.1khz, 48khz or even higher). You could also export a digital file such as a WAV and burn that to a CDR as data.

Breakout Box
External input / output of audio is better than internally fitted cards as computers can generate interference. Check how many I/O (in and out) the breakout box / hardware can handle. Eight in / eight out is ideal.

Extras
You'll need heaps and heaps of power sockets and a room where you can turn the music up loud. You'll work late, so find a place with deaf neighbours! Cables are also essential, don't invest in cheap ones, buy the best you can afford. If your composer does not want to work with digital video Quicktime files you will also need a HiFi stereo video recorder which will be used to playback to the movie. The timecode recorded on track 2 of the HiFi sound tracks of the VHS is used to lock the computer to the tape. Wherever the tape goes, so the computer (and sequencer software) will chase.

Computer
The heart of the system. You'll need a fast processor, lots of hard disk space and a CDR. The program that will bind everything together is the sequencer. This can play heaps of MIDI tracks (for snythesisers and samplers) and also record numerous tracks from the 'real' world via the microphone. The number of recorded tracks that the software can simultaneously playback will depend on processing power, RAM and storage. So the bigger and faster your computer, the better. You will need some software synths and samplers, usually 'plug-ins' that simply reside inside your sequencer (see box to the right) Top rate soft synths and samplers are now VERY cheap as the computer based music industry is very mature.

Synthesiser or sampler?

Electronic music uses two very distinct technologies to make the sounds that we interpret as music – synthesised sounds and sampled sounds. Both are edited in, and controlled by, music software that uses the MIDI interface.

Synthesised sounds . . .

or notes, are an electronic sound that has been engineered to sound like something real (such as a violin, choir or paving slab being dragged!) or something entirely new (such as a deep droning electronic synth sound).

Samples . . .

on the other hand, are short recordings of an instrument or voice. Samples usually sound better as they are 'real' recordings as opposed to the computer generated sounds of synthesised music. Samples are often looped and re-engineered to do more than the 'naked' sound. Established composers usually have access to large sample libraries performed by excellent musicians.

On the whole, less connected and inexperienced composers will use more synthesised sounds, where experienced composers will draw more on samples and even record new tracks and samples. Low budget movie music is almost always a combination of the two, often with samples leading the piece (voices, violins etc.) and synths providing oomph or atmosphere in the background.

Don't believe any composer who tells you that they can make their set-up sound like the London Symphony Orchestra. It may sound impressive, but it won't sound like the LSO. Ask them to play you something that was created using their kit, then play a CD of some 'real world' performance and compare the two. The technology is getting better so do tests, listen and be critical.

Sequencer

The software used to stitch all of these sounds together is called a sequencer. On the computer screen it is usually arranged as a 'time line' with multiple tracks, some samples (either performed and recorded or pulled out of a library) and some synthesised 'voices' and 'instruments' backing the more attractive samples. You don't need to know how this software works, but a basic understanding will help you get more out of

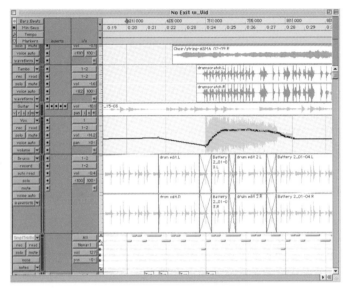

your composer. There can be any number of tracks, often ten, twenty, thirty tracks of instruments, all lovingly equalised, balanced and mixed. Most new sequencing programs are extremely good, easy to use and cheap (hence everyone has their own home recording studio). What lets down many home set-ups is the peripheral stuff – sound cards for digitising, microphones, poor monitoring setup etc.

ProToolsFREE!

One of the best programs you want to look out for is Pro Tools, a firm favourite with composers, and wouldn't you know, there is even a fully featured free version called Pro Tools Free available from www.protools.com. Download it now as you don't know when Digidesign may change their minds and withdraw it!

Right – ProTools LE running on an i-Mac with the external MBox – ideal cheap, industry standard digital input / output box.

Encourage your composer to be thematic. They won't want to keep repeating the same theme as they will see that as not stretching their creativity, but often, the best musical scores are repetitive, certainly thematically repetitive. Ideally, the audience should be humming the music when they leave the theatre.

collect royalties a few years down the line so they will make some cash too (this does not come from you or your sales agent, but directly from broadcasters etc. by legislation). You can find bands on the Internet or by placing ads in the back of magazines (such as NME) that are read by bands. You may need to cut a deal with these bands, their publishers and managers, but stand firm on the zero payment policy as talented bands with a CD full of cool and original music come ten a penny.

Music libraries

Maybe you want a blast of Wagnerian Ride of the Valkyries? You can buy this, at a non-negotiable fixed rate, from one of the many music libraries. When it comes to classical music written by composers who died over 75 years ago, music libraries are absolutely fantastic and their recordings are often superb.

This is how it works…you know you will need around two minutes of classical music and you know where it will go in the movie. Contact the libraries (a list is available from the MCPS at www.mcps.co.uk) and they will send you a number of CDs. Listen to the discs, make your choice and cut the music into the film. Then time how much you have used and contact the MCPS who will send you a usage form (or you can fill out the online one) which you accurately fill out, return and pay the bill.

On the surface, you might think it expensive – 30 seconds costs £410 for feature films and £250 for TV and video (remember your film may not go theatrical). When you consider you may only use 60 seconds, that it was written by a world famous composer, is performed by someone like Pavarotti, you may reconsider as it could radically improve the drama of your film and production values.

In the UK, the MCPS handles all library music usage. You can get a list of all the UK based music libraries from their website and you can even fill out the usage forms online.
www.mcps.co.uk

Music libraries will also offer you hundreds of hours of dodgy, contemporary and specially composed music which on the whole you want to avoid like the plague as it is all too often generic, soulless and ultimately very expensive to use (as it's charged at the same rate as the LSO playing Wagner).

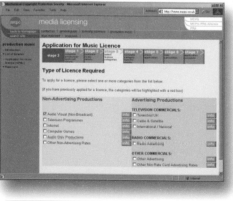

A.I. Music

Another peculiar source of music is from a new breed of music creation software that can be used by people who have no musical abilities. This software uses pre-recorded samples and loops which you string together on a time line, and on the whole, is surprisingly good. Whilst I wouldn't recommend you think about producing an entire score using this type of music, if used selectively, (occasional music stab, elevator music, non-specific source music in the background, nightclub music etc) it can be a fantastic way of producing high quality, free music. As a further inducement to use this kind of music, if you, the film maker, use

Music common mistakes

Too much music

When you have a poor scene and you add music, it somehow glosses over the problems . . . But the big problem you can't avoid is that your whole movie needs music to gloss over the problems.. and you end up with wall to wall music which the audience ceases to hear as music and it simply becomes part of the noisy background. Hold your music back for when you really need it. E.g. in Aliens, during the climactic fight between Ripley and the Queen Alien, there is no music – a less experienced director might have insisted on music to manipulate the audience's emotions. Having too much music in your film also stretches the composer. It's common sense that if they are going to write thirty minutes of music in three weeks they are going to do a better job than if they have to write sixty minutes in the same amount of time.

Fixation on big bands

Outside of a few instances, the use of popular music from an established artist adds very little to your film. Absolutely forget The Stones, Beatles, Elvis...and forget almost every other band you've ever heard of. You just can't afford them. Yes, some film makers on very low budgets have managed to convince established bands and their record companies to put their music into the movie, but its taken an enormous amount of time and energy to arrange – considering the pay off, it's simply not worth it. Approach unsigned or signed bands with a smaller label and invite them to send you some CDs.

Dreadful music

(enhanced by the former, too much music) Low budget film makers often seem astonished that the music that has been composed for them actually holds a melody! And they fail to notice that the music is awful. The primary culprit here is the inexperienced composer trying very hard to make their synthesiser or sampler sound like an orchestra. If you can't fake an orchestra, don't try. Simply go for an electronic style score. That doesn't mean it has to sound synthesised. Often, the best mix comes from a combination of synthesisers and one or two live instruments often played by the composer or the composer's mates.

Fighting effects

When tracklaying your film with sound effects, there is usually no co-ordination between the sound effects editor and the composer, so when "the car explodes" there is a loud explosion at the same time as a music crescendo. In the final mix, you'll realise that you can't have both, so you'll have to sacrifice one, probably the music. If you had been more co-ordinated (and if your composer is experienced) you would have placed the music crescendo a moment after the explosion so that it doesn't fight with the effect.

Loud music

Inexperienced film makers often push the level of the music in the final mix. Be guided by the dubbing mixer when they say 'I think the music's too loud.' The reason you want the music to be louder is that to your eyes and ears, its very fresh (you've probably only heard it once and never with the film). In the final mix, you sit there thinking 'this wonderful new, fresh and vibrant music is making my old, tawdry and sluggish movie come to life'. Only later will you realise that the music is probably dreadful. There's too much of it and you've mixed it too loud! So you failed on the first three points here! This is a very seductive issue and the final creative element to deal with. You don't want to be having an angry conversation about it in one of the most expensive environments on the planet – the dubbing theatre!.

Amateur composers

Much the same as using amateur actors. Start at the top and work down, inviting established composers to write for your film. Most composers will consider a low-budget film if they have no other work, or if they like the film makers and project (even if the money is poor). Composers receive royalties that bypass you the film maker. When the film is screened in various territories they will receive significant money which may still be being paid to them in 50 years! (assuming the film is still being shown). They will often take your music, modify it slightly, and put it into a music library where it can earn them even more royalties.

Virtual composers

Sonic Fire Pro is one of a new generation of music tools which can be used by people with no classical training in music, but with an ear for what does and does not work. Sonic Fire Pro works by importing your video clip, then allowing you to cut and paste clips of music onto the time line, thereby building up the music soundtrack. All the music is properly recorded, often with big orchestras, and best of all, the synchronization rights have been cleared for you so you can use as much of it as you like in your film without having to pay any more. Many of you, certainly the composers out there, will be cringing at this 'virtual composer concept...' but trust me, the results are much better than you would ever think. Where Sonic Fire has got it right is that it doesn't rely on computers to synthesize sound, it simply takes properly recorded music, breaks it down into generic clips and bars, then allows you to put them in an order to match your movie. The sound quality meanders between pretty awful for the cheesier corporate style themes, to breath taking, and I mean BIG Hollywood feature film sounding, for the more movie style music . . .

Aside from the software engine, you will also need to buy the sound palettes, these are CDs of music clips that are arranged in themes. Most are just not right for your film, unless you need fairly cheesy music for elevators musak, news stings, TV clips, radio clips, nightclub beats etc. etc. (all of which are frankly production nightmares to acquire and clear cheaply, so it answers this problem too!). But some, such as Cinematic Excellence and Suspense Action really are the biz.

The screen grab above shows you how it all works. There's a video screen on the bottom left, a palette of different music clips to the lower right, and a timeline at the top. Just drag and drop the clips where you want and Sonic Fire will make it all work seamlessly. You can order a free demo CD from their website at www.smartsound.com.

this software to make music, you are theoretically the composer and performer and therefore if you get representation from a music publisher you could collect royalties as a composer (this depends on the individual package you use).

A real orchestra

If you decide that you must have that authentic orchestra feel, there is no reason why you shouldn't hire an orchestra, but there are a few low-budget myths to dispel beforehand. Firstly, it may not be as expensive as you think, possibly coming in as low as £7-15k. Second, don't hire your old school orchestra, as they will sound rubbish, not only because they are inexperienced and sub-standard players but also because you will need to properly mic up and engineer the recording.

Composers dead for over 75 years are copyright free. That means you can use their music, be it Beethoven, Mozart or Wagner for instance, for free. But you will need to either buy a recording of it, or arrange for someone to record it for you. Search for some classical piano music, find a talented pianist and record your own music!

So where do you get an orchestra? UK players aren't cheap (though there's an argument that by the time you've messed around with say an Eastern European orchestra, it would have cost the same and been a lot less hassle – hmmm, not sure about that but I have heard it a lot. Maybe people are looking after their own well paid jobs?). However, there are other international

Orchestra budget

	Each	Number of	Cost Per Session	No. of sessions	Total
String Players	£37.50	25	£937.50	2	£1,875.00
Wind players	£37.50	6	£225.00	2	£450.00
Brass Players	£37.50	6	£225.00	2	£450.00
Piano	£37.50	1	£37.50	2	£75.00
Percussion	£37.50	2	£75.00	2	£150.00
Translator	£37.50	1	£37.50	2	£75.00
Manager (Prague)	£60.00	1	£60.00	2	£120.00
Studio Hire (Prague)	£350.00	1	£350.00	2	£700.00
Engineer (Czech)	£125.00	1	£125.00	2	£250.00
Conductor	£200.00	1	£200.00	2	£400.00
Orchestrator (22 mins music)	£100.00	22	£2,200.00	N/A	£2,200.00
Fixer	£500.00	1	£500.00	1	£500.00
Flights/accom/food etc.	£500.00	1	£500.00	1	£500.00
Total					£7,745.00

This budget is for a 40 piece orchestra in Prague, Czechoslovakia. The players are excellent but there is much snobbery in the business and many composers will want to work with British musicians (Brit players however are significantly more expensive).

The recording sessions last for four hours, with two fifteen minute breaks. You can record as much music as possible during the session (unlike the UK where your sessions last three hours and a max of 20 mins can be recorded) but on average you will probably get down 12-18 minutes. That means you'll need a minimum of two sessions, maybe even three. The Prague players cost £37.50 per session for a world buy-out, as opposed to £144.00 per session for UK players for a world buy-out (and you need a world buyout or you could be paying extra fees for years to come).

Clearly there is a major saving there. However, there are extra expenses such as a translator, hotel and accomodation etc. If you want a choir, they can also be hired for £37.50 per singer per session.

In the UK, you will also have to pay 'porterage'. This is a fee charged to move large instruments such as percussion or a double bass. UK restrictions also apply to 'doubling', the practice of recording a piece twice and mixing them together to create a 60 piece string section where you actually only had a 30 piece section. Cunning!

A criticism I have heard, although this may be sour grapes from people being 'done out of a job', is that the Czech engineers and recording equipment isn't as good as the UK counterpart. I would suggest getting hold of a CD of music (from your fixer) recorded by the engineers and performed by the players so that you can listen to what it actually sounds like. I believe you will be very happy. If you are not you can hire UK engineers at around £250 per session and fly them over instead. On the whole, these people do not do deals as they are working very cheap to start with.

The orchestrator is the person who converts the composer's computer MIDI files into sheet music for the musicians. They will charge by the minute of music composed. Quotes range from £100-£150 per minute and deals can be done, especially when not confined by the UK Musicians Union. The software they will use for this process will probably be either Sibelius or Encore, both mature professional products.

If your composer is VERY brave and well trained, you could get hold of this software and do it yourself. But beware, if you screw it up, you could spend a great deal of time trying to figure it when you have a very expensive orchestra sitting around and waiting for you to make up your mind. You can download a free demo of Sibelius (see pic) from www.sibelius.com.

Tadlow music are a good company to contact for music fixing (hiring and arranging an orchestra / studio etc.) and they can be contacted via www.tadlowmusic.com

MUSIC CUE SHEET		Sheet No...1	Of...5

Film Title - **MY MOVIE**	Director - **JANE DOE**	Film Duration - **92'35"**
Prod. Company - **MY COMPANY**	Producer - **JOHN DOE**	Music Duration (total) - **28'12"**
Alternative Title -	Production Year – **2003**	Trailer / Promo / Programme - (T/P/F) - **F**
Country of Origin – **UK**		

Music cue title and ISWC no.
This is the name of the track. You will also use the codes that you created in your spotting session with the composer to list the tracks – so 1M1 refers to the first music cue in reel 1, where 2M4 refers to the fourth music cue in reel 2. The ISWC is like the ISBN number used for books and you'll find one on most commercial recordings (usually on the spine of the CD for instance). If your music has been written specially, you obviously won't have an ISWC number. If you can't find the ISWC number, leave it blank.

Performer(s)
Simply a list of the various performers who actually performed / sang the music. On a low budget film, this will most often be the composer.

Publisher / CAE no.
The publishing company that represents the composer / arranger / author and its respective CAE number. If you have used music that comes from a source that doesn't have a publishing company (such as an actor singing or unsigned band) then you should list it as Unpublished.

ISRC
ISRC is not yet used in the industry so you can ignore it for now.

Catalogue number
This is the number you will find on commercial recordings so that it becomes easier to track down the specific recording. Often found on the spine of a CD for instance.

Video clip duration
This won't really factor into your work so ignore it for now.

Music cue duration
This lists the length of each cue in minutes and seconds.

Cue No.	Music Cue Title and ISWC No. (if known)	Composer / Author / Arranger / CAE No.	Publisher / CAE No.	Performer(s) Video / Record title	Catalogue Number	ISRC No.	Music Orig. Code	Music Use Code	Music Cue Dur.	Video Clip Dur.
01	1M1 - Opening titles	Jeff Davies (C) CAE: 555 121 335	Acme Music Publisher Ltd. CAE: 555 289 895	Jeff Davies	-	-	X	F	1"12'	-
02	"Running on empty"	Pete Stevens / Dave Jones (C) CAE – None	Unpublished	Thundercracker	-	-	C	F	0"22'	-
03	1M2 - The Chase (Incidental Music)	Jeff Davies (C) CAE: 555 121 335	Acme Music Publisher Ltd. CAE: 555 289 895	Jeff Davies	-	-	X	B	2"39'	-
04	Water Music	Handel CAE - N/A (Public domain)	Public domain	London Symphony Orchestra	AcmeLibray 22512	-	L	F	0' 6"	-
05	"Here Comes The Drizzle"	Jane Aston (C) CAE: 555 125 245	EMZ Music Ltd. CAE: 555 552 378	Monotones, The	AcmeDisc 2135431	-	C	F	0' 22"	-
06	Nightclub Beat	John Dingle (C) CAE - 555 112 489	Computer Music Ltd CAE - 555 569 872	Boston Orchestra	-	-	L	B	1'56"	-
07	1M3 - Say Goodbye (Incidental Music)	Jeff Davies (C) CAE: 555 121 335	Acme Music Publisher Ltd. CAE: 555 289 895	Jeff Davies	-	-	X	B	3' 36"	-
08	Beethovens Fifth	Beethoven CAE - N/A (Public domain)	Public domain	Steven Sanderson	-	-	P	F	1'36"	-
09	1M3 - Say Goodbye	Jeff Davies (C) CAE: 555 121 335	Acme Music Publisher Ltd. CAE: 555 289 895	Jeff Davies	-	-	X	B	3' 36"	-

Composer / author / arranger / CAE no.
The name of the composer and their CAE number. The CAE number is a unique code used in the music business which helps collection agencies around the world identify individuals and companies. The Composer writes the music, the Author writes the lyrics and the Arranger is a composer who adapts an existing work (only required if the music being reworked is in copyright). Composers dead for over 75 years are out of copyright and should be listed as Public Domain.

(C) = Composer (Music)
(A) = Author (Lyrics)
(C/A) = Composer/Author (music & lyrics)
(AR) – Arranger

Music origin code
Where the music came from.

L = Live performance (maybe your characters are watching a band, listening to the opera. Remember an actor singing a song in your film is a performance and you will need both performers and compositional rights cleared before using).
C = Commercially recorded music, such as a band.
L = Library music, which in some instances may include music that you have used software like Sonic Edit Pro to create (check the install disks).
X = Specially commissioned music, essentially the music that has been written for your film by the composer.

Music use code
The music use code can be either F for featured music, or B for background music.

F = Featured music, music that the characters can hear. A jukebox, the opera, a nightclub, the radio, a group of friends singing a greeting for instance. It also includes the composers opening and closing tracks.
B = Background music, the music that the characters do not hear. Essentially the composer's music and any other tracks you have used to accompany the drama.

Anatomy of a music cue sheet (left)

The music cue sheet is the document used by collection agencies around the world, to collect and distribute royalties when they are generated. For instance, in some countries, when a film is screened on TV, royalties should be paid to the composer as well as (possibly) YOU via the publishing company (although you will need to have cut a deal for this to happen – see earlier in this chapter). This cue sheet is a very important document and you will not be able to sell your film to anyone without it being completed accurately.

The top of the sheet includes information that is all pretty obvious, but it's the lower portion that starts to get a little cryptic. Note that minutes and seconds are described using ' and ". For instance ten minutes twelve seconds would be 10'12".

standard orchestras you could hire. Prague, for instance, is a common place to record low budget film scores and the results can be outstanding.

Hiring a fixer

The music fixer is a person who is a cross between a production manager and a casting director, but works with musicians instead of actors. In essence, they will arrange the orchestral players, the recording venue, the contracts etc. (for which they will take either a flat fee, or percentage of the job, usually 10-15%). Below the fixer there is often a 'contractor', a person with unique knowledge of the individual players. You don't want to hire a classical performer if the score is supposed to have a jazzy feel do you? The contractor will know who the best people for the job are. It is possible you could bypass the Fixer and go straight to the contractor, although the fixer does offer more of a *one-stop-shop* for an area of film making that is notoriously difficult to navigate, even for experienced producers.

You won't be able to afford a full orchestra but a happy middle ground is hiring a small orchestra of say 40 players then augmenting that recording with additional electronic work using samplers and synthesisers (or doubling). A typical 40-piece orchestra might compose of something like 25 strings, 6 wind, 6 brass, 2 percussion and perhaps others such as piano or harp (depending on the type of music).

Musicians are hired in blocks of 4 hour sessions. In a 4 hour session you should be able to record about 15 – 20 minutes of finished music, and no, the orchestra doesn't need to rehearse in advance of the recording session as they are that good. Each player will cost you £37.50 per session (in Prague and it's non-negotiable) and this will buy all world rights for you. The music fixer will take care of finding all these musicians for you. Be cautious though as you may plan for two sessions but find that you are inexorably slipping into a third session, increasing the cost of

Nothing will get you that big movie sound like an orchestra. Whilst using orchestras, such as this one in Prague, may be cheaper than here in the UK, there are a lot of extras you need to factor in.

James Fitzpatrick
Music Fixer - Tadlow Music

'Producers rarely allow enough budget for the music, plus they have often overspent in production and look for places to cut back in post, music being an obvious choice. This, combined with the natural urge to 'over-score' a movie, that is, write too much music, can often over stretch the process and result in the score being either rushed, or worse, lowered into the realm of synthesisers. Not that I have anything against synths, when used appropriately, they can be wonderful. My problem is when they are asked to imitate an orchestra. Live instruments carry much more 'humanity' than their electronic equivalents and it's often a shock for the first time composer and director when they hear the score played by real instruments. I would recommend any new film maker to go to listen to a real orchestra before they produce their score, so that they can experience its' dynamism and flexibility.

The Hollywood trend is to over-score. Too much music ends up with the audience 'not hearing' the music, diminishing its impact. Zulu by John Barry is often cited as a great score, but few know that there is around 15 minutes of music in a 140 minute movie.

I'd advise inexperienced composers to allow a professional to conduct, resisting the urge to do it themselves. This will save a lot of time and allow the composer to sit in the control room and 'hear' what it will actually sound like off tape. They'll learn more this way. Big scores are recorded in up to 32 tracks, but for low budget productions, it's more cost effective to record in stereo, much like the majority of television scores are produced.'

hiring the orchestra and studio. And no, you can't hire the players for an extra half hour if you overrun, you can only hire them for 4 hours at a time.

Value for money

Getting the most out of your time with an orchestra is dependent on two major factors. Firstly the complexity of the music itself. The more complex, the more time it takes to record. Secondly is organisation. If you don't have clear and accurate score print outs, usually via an orchestrator, then things get VERY slow and you can find yourself sitting around for hours as musicians, composer and translator frantically attempt to make sense of it all.

The orchestrator

Most composers will say, 'sure, I can print out a score, my software supports that…', but unless they have done it before, or REALLY know what they are doing, you'd be better served by hiring an orchestrator, or make sure the composer really can do the Orchestrating. The orchestrator (and below them there might be a 'copyist' who will do the donkey work) is a person who will take the composers' computer MIDI files and convert them into the sheet music that the players will read when they play their instruments. It's a very specialised job and you can't afford to get it wrong. You could hire a UK orchestrator, or one based in Prague (if you are recording your score there.) Your music fixer will be able to advise you who to hire, and it will cost you somewhere in the region of £100-£150 per minute of music scored. So there's another reason to keep the quantity of music down!

The final thing that will need to be prepared is a 'click' track. You will probably take with you to the studio, a tape of the movie onto which the click track will be recorded. The click track is like a metronome, except in this instance, it can speed up or slow down dynamically with the action of the film. The conductor will use this click track to keep the music in sync with the picture, as it was originally intended by the composer. If the click track goes wrong, you may find that the music quickly drops out of sync and you may be forced to butcher the music in the cutting room in order to make it fit.

Studio space

The music fixer will also take care of hiring the studio and venue which will come with all its' own microphones, music stands and seats, as well as the recording technology and engineers. The composer might act as the conductor (or you might hire someone to conduct) and you will also need a copy of the movie on video (with burnt in time code in the picture) so that the conductor can watch the movie and conduct it so that the music 'hits' the various visual cues (if you have a good click track you might not need to run the picture whilst some composers opt to record the score in freetime, that is without any visual guide or click track, which often gives a better performance).

Remember also that you will need to leave time and a little budget for the composer to print out the musical score for each of the players. Once you've recorded your music, the composer may take it away, digitise it into their music software and begin augmenting it by adding samples and synthesised tracks.

Mastering

Ultimately, the score will be completed, performed and recorded to DAT or DA88 at 48khz (probably not at 44.1khz). This master will then be sent back to the cutting room or sound editing facility and will be cut into the movie before going to the final mix or dub.

Music cue sheet

The producer can now fill out an accurate and detailed music cue sheet. This document is essential for sales as it is used by music royalty collection companies in each country to collect royalties and pass them on to their members (i.e. your composer and even you if you have managed to cut an appropriate deal with the publishers). The music cue sheet is simply a list of composer, publisher, duration and other information about the music you use in your film. It will take a few hours to fill out, will be 3-7 pages long and you can do it in MS Excel or another suitable spreadsheet programme. Once you have completed it, make sure you get all the Music Publishing Companies to sign off on it to avoid you ever being accused of trying to pull a fast one.

Mastering
Blueprint

MIDNIGHT
TRANSFER
179 WARDOUR STREET
LONDON W1F 8WY
TEL 020 7534 3400
FAX 020 7534 3401
www.midnight-transfer.co.uk

A long time ago in a galaxy far, far away (it certainly feels that way!), you had this bright idea to make a movie. And you've done it. It's been a hard slog. You've teetered on the edge of bankruptcy and endured such horrific, creative compromise that you've regularly asked yourself why on earth you did it. However, you HAVE done it, and creatively, your movie is pretty much finished. You are about to enter the final manufacturing stage for your film, which is the process of mastering it. You're going to bring all the picture and sound elements together and create a final, single master of your movie. When I say mastering, what I'm really referring to is a videotape version of your film that will be used for sales to video, TV, DVD etc. This also includes potential HiDef mastering and digital mastering to film and video at the same time. If you shot on film and completed on film, you have already finished a version which is ready for final mastering.

Mastering Blueprint

There are 1001 ways to deal with the final mastering of your film, and no matter what I write here, you will be offered all manner of different routes that may well offer creative, technical or financial advantages over my suggestions. The routes that I am going to suggest in the next few pages are representative of what I feel are the cheapest and most efficient ways to end up with a master that you need or want.

Mastering is the very last stage in the making of your movie. All of those problems that you have brushed under the carpet for the last eighteen months now need to be dealt with. You can no longer procrastinate.

Get it right

So far, in your film making adventures, you've probably run a gauntlet of compromise and cheeky tricks that have enabled you to save money. In essence, you've been getting away with it. But now, you can no longer get away with it. There are no cheats or cheap tricks when it comes to final mastering. If the final master that you deliver to sales agents or distributors does not meet rigid, exacting and extremely high technical standards, then the film will be rejected. You will then be asked to correct all the problems, and if you cannot correct them, then you will be in breach of contract. Remember that phrase you used to say on set, *'We'll fix it in post?'* Well get ready to pay for that big time.

If that wasn't bad enough, there are several different master versions you need to create, not just one, and the facilities that you will use to do this are hellishly expensive. It's very difficult to get deals in these places because they have heavily invested in all the cool toys and need to re-coup their outlay. Just make sure you're sitting down when you talk to these people on the phone and asking for a quote.

What are you going to do?

The process of mastering is primarily about gathering all the images and sound (be they on a 35mm print, bits of S16mm camera negative, DigitBeta tapes, HiDef tapes, DV tapes etc.), putting all the shots or clips in order, modifying the images to be as attractive and consistent as possible, ensuring that they will meet rigid, technical broadcasting standards and to lay it all back down onto a high quality videotape.

Mastering your film is both exhilarating and stressful. The possibilities are endless, regarding, tweaking, cleaning up dirt, adding titles, re-framing etc . . . But it is so VERY expensive that you are limited. The sheer length of your film, ninety minutes, means that going can seem very slow too.

Sometimes the material may need a lot of additional work to either 'sweeten' it or to clean up and fix technical errors, such as

Eddie Hamilton
Editor

'Finalising the opticals, designing the opening and closing credits, grading the picture and finally producing a show print is more detailed and time-consuming than you can imagine. The scope for mistakes is vast because of the number of people involved in the process. When you're editing, it's just you and the Avid, but as soon as you have to achieve anything on film it becomes a massive undertaking, with various people in different departments at the lab all doing their little bit. You have to communicate your ideas in absolute detail (which is surprisingly hard) – something that might seem obvious to you will take ages to explain before other people understand clearly.

The other problem is that there are no short cuts, in time or money. It takes weeks to grade your film and get the opticals made, and it will cost a lot of money. Any time you do film opticals, you will be staggered by the bill. The best thing to do is plan ahead and shoot any effect in camera on set before you get into the edit suite. But there's always ideas you come up with during cutting so be prepared to face the nightmare of film opticals.

You mustn't skimp when preparing the video master tapes either. You have to pay someone a decent sum who knows what they're doing. If you don't get your telecine done properly, it will fail a quality check and your sales agent will ask you to do it again, at YOUR expense. The same applies to your TV sound mix and M&E. Spend the money and get them done well. On a low budget feature it will feel as if the task of delivering your film will never end. Some technical niggle always crops up that needs sorting out, and the contractual paperwork alone would drive most people round the bend! But you will get there eventually . . .'

dust and sparkle, camera scratches or even remove an unwanted microphone boom. If you have shot on videotape, this is the point at which you will probably add titles and any special effects that you may have custom created or produced yourself. You may also add a 'film look' too.

The process is similar (but still different) for the distinct disciplines of having originated your material on either a video format or film.

The sound should have already been completed at a mix and it should really be a simple matter of transferring it from one medium (probably DAT or DA88) onto your master tape (while double checking it technically).

The bare minimum

At the very least, you should be preparing a PAL, DigiBeta tape with line up tone, bars and a clock, followed by the movie, mastered in 16:9 anamorphic, fully graded and sweetened, with titles (ideally black on white, not over picture or you will need to create a second master without titles for foreign territories), and sound – the full mix in stereo on tracks one and two, the music and effects mix on tracks three and four (this may be split music on one channel and effects on the other channel, or as I prefer, a stereo mix on tracks three and four). You may be offered one of several tape formats onto which to master – DigiBeta is the one to choose though. Other formats, such as D1 for instance, are great, but they are sooooo expensive and offer no real advantage for a low budget film. Wait till you are hired to make a Bond movie, then you can use the most expensive formats. At the other end of the scale are the DV formats, but you don't want to go there either as the quality just isn't good enough (although you could run off a miniDV copy of the master tape, recorded in long play so it fits on one tape, and then you can use it to make your own VHS dupes at home).

Why use the professionals?

You need to get this stage right. That's why. Putting it simply, if you don't meet the rigid technical standards required by the business, your film will fail and you will need to re-master at great expense. The professionals do this day in, day out. They have the kit to do it quickly and efficiently, they have the experience to know what you can and cannot get away with (and what you may need to do to fix it), and from a creative point of view, they will squeeze more attractive images out of your material (be it negative or videotape). Top companies who specialise in mastering, pride themselves on technical excellence, and if there is a problem with the masters that they have produced, they will very likely correct them for free. You will not get this level of professionalism and service from a small company or one man band with a Mac and the latest cool software.

A word of warning about doing it on your desktop. Everyone gets very excited about the prospect of mastering their movie on a PC or Mac. Sure,

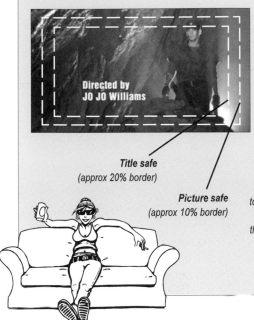

Title and TV safe

When your film is presented, be it on TV, cinema or DVD, there is a good chance you will lose some information around the edges. This is especially true for television, but it is also common with theatrical projection too. You want to avoid putting important picture information too far to the edges of frame, or it may be lost when viewed out in the real world. In the diagram this is called 'picture safe'. Inside that box there is another box called 'title safe' which are the boundaries for placing your titles. This example is for a 185:1 aspect ratio image for DVD and cinema, but it's likely you would also produce a 4:3 aspect ratio version for TV as well. In this instance you would be forced to crop off the left and right of the image, so make sure that when shooting, your camera operator bears this in mind (unless you want to do a lot of work in telecine). Title placement is especially important, as you can see from the example. On a domestic TV (right) you can see just how much can be lost. That's why picture framing and title placement is so important.

Title safe
(approx 20% border)

Picture safe
(approx 10% border)

it's possible and the software tools available are very sophisticated and god damn cool. But . . . you need to ask yourself, do you really know what you are doing? Can you guarantee video levels are legal? Do you have a broadcast monitor with which you can view the images (so that you know what you're actually doing to your pictures)? Have you considered rendering overhead (for instance, for a ninety minute feature, applying a film look with Magic Bullet could take something like two weeks!)? The professionals have the kit to do it in real time, the equipment to monitor everything properly, and most importantly, the expertise to know that it is being done correctly.

Aspect ratios – the choices

Almost certainly, you will have shot your movie in a 185:1 aspect ratio (which is about the same as 16:9 on tape). You should master your film in 16:9 anamorphic to DigiBeta, and from that tape you will be able to make ALL other versions of the film, such as a 4:3 master for broadcast television and domestic video (VHS rental). Thankfully, most of Europe has gone 16:9 including UK terrestrial channels, which means it's likely that your film will be presented in widescreen when broadcast. However, VHS rental in the UK and US television/video rental still requires 4:3 video masters. Annoying isn't it! Most of the time, you can create this 4:3 master by passing your 16:9 master through a box, something like a Snell and Wilcox Arc. But beware, you must make sure your titles and action stay within the middle portion of the screen and never drop out of shot to the left or right where the image is cropped.

Making a movie creates a mountain of 'stuff'. Negative, master tapes, sound tapes, NTSC and PAL versions, DA88 audio tapes, Dolby Digital MO disks, dubbing charts . . . . The problem is, what do you do with it all? You don't want to ditch it, nor do you really want to keep it. Some stuff can be stored at the labs (Soho Images do not charge to store your neg for instance) but most of it is best kept in your brother-in-law's attic!

Aspect ratios

The best format in which to master your movie is now 16:9. This is a widescreen image that is usually mastered in an anamorphic format (squeezed) so that it can be delivered in a 4:3 box (if you are mastering to DigiBeta). This means that the signal is backwards compatible with the video delivery systems currently in place (such as broadcast TV networks). From this 16:9 master you can make all the other tapes you need. Spend your money on getting this one thing right, and all other derived masters should be excellent.

16:9 anamorpic master (left)

This is how it actually looks on the tape. A widescreen image that is squeezed into a backwards compatible 4:3 box.

True 16:9 (as viewed)

When the 16:9 image is played on a widescreen TV, the TV will stretch it out horizontally to fit in a wider box. This format is ideal for European broadcast TV, DVD etc.

Letterboxed master

You can make a letterboxed master from the 16:9. It's used for some TV stations and also letterboxed VHS, although this is very rare now.

4:3 TV / VHS rental master

You can make a 'zoomed in' 4:3 master for some TV stations, such as ones in the USA, and also for rental video. Make sure no important picture information or titles disappear to the left or right of the image.

All these versions can be derived from the master by making a copy, and passing the video signal through a box such as a Snell and Wilcox Arc. It will perform the picture changes in real time and the quality is excellent. Beware though, the Arc does cause a one or two frame picture delay, so sound can drop out of sync. Make sure whoever is doing these conversions knows this and has a setup that will also delay the sound too.

If you shot on a DV format that did not have a true 16:9 chip, or you didn't use an anamorphic lens converter, you will already have a true 4:3 master. Now the opposite of what you have just done will take place. The image will be passed through the Arc and stretched to create a 16:9 anamorphic master. This time, you will lose picture at the top and bottom, so again, make sure no important action or titles fall into this area.

If you manage to shoot 35mm and shot it 'open gate', then you will be able to pull both the 4:3 and the 185:1 aspect ratio masters off the negative (again, subject to framing and action not causing any problems).

Telecine

If you shot on film, then at some point, the film will be passed through a telecine machine. TK as it's known in the business, is a process where the film is photographed frame by

Your sales agent will demand a HUGE list of items to be delivered for your film. You won't have the budget to do this (it will run into the tens of thousands), so get the most important thing right, a PAL, 16:9 fully graded Digibeta (or even HiDef). From that tape you can make pretty much every other master you will need. Just make sure you do this one tape RIGHT! Oh, and NEVER give your sales agent a master, as they will lose it. Make a clone for them!

Telecine

The TK suite is run by a colourist, or TK operator. It's a darkened environment full of high tech kit and large leather sofas. The main room (below) consists of a long desk, with monitors and controls. There is usually a smaller, side room where the actual telecine machine is contained. To one side there will be a pile of your film stock and tapes.

Speakers
To monitor the sound.

PPM Meters
To monitor audio levels.

TK computer control
A computer controls the more sophisticated elements of the TK suite, such as aspect ratio and zoom etc.

Monitor
Displaying the pictures.

Grading controls
To modify colours and density etc.

Audio playback
DAT and ¼" tape playback for sound.

Level Meters
Waveform and Vectorscope monitors which keep track of legal colours and video levels.

Telecine controls
Machine control for the TK apparatus (fast forward, rewind, play etc.)

TK Machine

(left) This is the actual machine that plays the film and re-photographs it, turning it into an electronic image that can be recorded onto videotape. There are different heads for different scenarios, the most common for mastering being a 'wet gate' which submerges the film in a liquid to reduce the effect of scratches.

Telecine head
Where the film is transferred.

Film reels

Glass door
TO seal the machine into its own room to reduce audible noise and dust.

Grading Controls

(below)The heart of the system are these three trackballs with an outer rotary ring on each. Each ball can be rolled towards a different part of the colour spectrum (ie: Red, Green, Blue etc.) and the rotation of the outer rings either lifts or drops the video level (blackness or brightness) within each contol eg: to get more contast, you would rotate the lift ('black level') outer-ring down and rotate the gain ('highlights level') outer-ring up. These three controls are VERY powerful, but they need to be in the hands of an experienced pro, or you could spend forever messing around.

Rotary wheel **Lift** **Gain** **Gamma**
Increases or decreases effect.

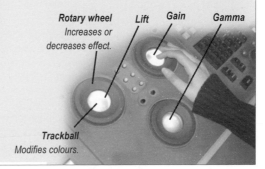

Trackball
Modifies colours.

There is no difference between blank NTSC and PAL tapes. They are the same. However, a 90 minute BetaSP tape will record 90 minutes of NTSC, but because the tape runs slower for PAL it will record nearly 110mins of a PAL signal. DigiBeta however will always do what it says on the box. A 124 minute tape will give you 124 minutes in both PAL And NTSC.

frame (in real time) and transferred onto a broadcast quality videotape. It's kind of like a film projector with a video camera built in. These are extremely sophisticated and highly maintained bits of machinery. It's essentially the point at which the analogue world of film enters the digital world of tape (of course, you can telecine onto analogue formats such as BetaSP as well).

Telecine will normally take place in two ways. Ungraded or graded. Ungraded telecine, sometimes referred to as a 'one light transfer' is a process where the operator sets up a general setting for the film and transfers it in one pass, often without stopping except for reel changes (or major grading problems). Graded telecine, is where every shot is scrutinised and potentially modified. This is why a final grading session can take so

Bars and clock

When you master your film, you will put colour bars, tone and a clock on the tape before the film begins. This information is used by video duplication facilities and television stations when broadcasting your film. The colour bars should match the video levels of the final movie and will be used to line up video levels when broadcasting for instance. The tone is the audio equivalent, and is used for lining up the audio levels when being broadcast. The clock is a countdown to the beginning of your movie. Of course, the tape must also have accurate timecode too. Here's how it should all appear on your tape (some TV stations require slight modifications to this generic line up).

BARS

TONE: 1000 Hz @ -14.0 dB.1

TONE: 1000 Hz @ -14.0 dB.1

00:00   09:58:00:00   09:59:00:00   10:00:00:0

09:57:00:00	09:58:00:00	09:59:00:00	09:59:30:00	10:00:00:00
1 minute of	1 minute of bars	30 seconds of	30 second	Movie starts.
black.	and tone.	black.	countdown.	
			Fade out at	
			09:59:57:00	

Black the tape to prepare it. Starting at time code 09:57:00:00, lay down 'black' until time code 10:00:10:00. Insert edit in at 09:58:00:00 and lay down 1 minute of colour bars and audio tone. The tone should peak at 4 on a PPM. The video levels of the colour bars should be at 0.3v for black and 1v for white on the wave form monitor. This will take you to time code 09:59:00:00. Go back to 'black' for 30 seconds from 09:59:00:00 to 09:59:30:00.

Then lay down a clock from 09:59:30:00 to start of picture at 10:00:00:00. The clock should cut out at 09:59:57:00. The clock should also include information about the contents of the tape, including title, production company, mastering company, date, audio information, running time in minutes and seconds and anything else relevant. The movie should start at 10:00:00:00 and run, uninterrupted, until the end. After the movie finishes, you should run a further 5 minutes of 'black'. The audio levels should never peak over 6 on a PPM and should burble comfortably around 4 during average dialogue scenes. The video levels should never peak over 1v, or drop under 0.3v.

If you deviate from any of these points in any way, unless specifically instructed to do so, you can be assured that your tape will fail quality control checks. The videotape format you will almost certainly deliver will be a 16:9, PAL DigiBeta. It's extremely unlikely that you will be able to deliver or master onto a DV format.

Legal signals

When you master a film to videotape (be it DigiBeta or HiDef etc.), there are a number of very simple but exacting standards that you must meet. This applies to both sound and picture. Top facilities may pass the signal through a 'legaliser' box which will guarantee a legal signal.

Picture

When the final video signal is laid down to tape, it should be monitored on an external box called a vectorscope. It's essentially an oscilloscope that measures the voltage of the video signal. This signal should never peak over 1 volt or drop below 0.3 volts (the 1 volt representing absolute white, the 0.3 volt representing black). As long as your engineer knows what they're doing, this should never be a problem.

(right) The Vectorscope is monitoring the voltage levels of the colour bars (twice because a single frame of video is made of two fields). The white bar on the left is peaking at just under 1volt, the black bar on the right is peaking at just over 0.3volts.

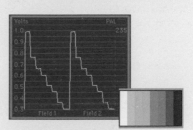

Sound

A similar process happens with sound, whereby the engineer will monitor the audio levels through a PPM box. This has a scale of 0 to 7 on it, and the audio signal should never peak over 6. At the beginning of the tape, the engineer will lay down some audio line up tone and which should peak at 4 on the PPM.

(right) the PPM is monitoring line up tone, which is peaking at 4. This example is slightly high on one channel, which the engineer would fix.

long. Hours can turn into days, days can turn into weeks . . . But not for you! The hourly rate for a good telecine will run into the £hundreds, so sit back and let them do their wizardry with the minimum of fuss and ego – you just don't have £20k available to do what they would do on a Harry Potter movie for instance.

Tools

When grading pictures, the telecine operators have access to some very powerful image tools. Of course they can modify obvious stuff like brightness and contrast, colour balance and colour correction, colour density etc . . . But they can also mess around with more sophisticated and esoteric tools too. If you want to see what cutting edge of grading is like, watch MTV for a couple of hours. Most promos for bands are shot very quickly and their incredible 'look' is created more in post production than on set. At a recent telecine I attended, a grader commented to me that the trend is moving toward a DP shooting 'flat' images, where there emphasis is on capturing detail, then creating the look they want in 'the box'. This is even more relevant now films may be shot on 35mm, graded in a tape/ digital environment, then put back to 35mm film for theatrical presentation (but get 'yer chequebook out for that one!) There are of course limitations, but it is amazing what can be done. If you intend to do a lot of work in this environment, be prepared to work in down time,

Many new film makers regret shooting on miniDV because by the time they have shot their movie and gone through that hell, then spent an age and fortune on trying to make their DV footage look like film, and then do a digital transfer to 35mm, they may as well have shot on film in the first place!

The recording report

Whenever you produce a tape at a professional facility, they will create a recording report, a piece of A4 paper which will live in the box with the tape. This is a log of everything on the tape, where it came from, what was done to it, who did it, when it was done, even the machinery used. This is an essential piece of paperwork that is invaluable when attempting to track down faults that happened some time in the past.

Tape number
Facilities will sell you a tape at a massive mark up, so take your own stock. But if there is a problem with the tape they will say, 'well you didn't use our tapes, so it's not our problem . . .'

Sub title
A brief description of what it actually is, in this case a telecine of a 35mm print.

Format
The type of tape used.

Standard
The TV standard, essentially PAL, NTSC or SCEAM.

Audio layout
DigiBeta has four audio tracks. In this case the stereo mix has been recorded to tracks one and two (left on track one and right on track two) and the Music and Effects Mix has been recorded to tracks three and four (music on track three and effects on track four).

Picture source
Where did the pictures actually come from? In this case a low contrast 35mm print, but it could also be another source, such as DigiBeta camera tapes for instance.

Audio source
Where did the sound actually come from? In this case a time coded DAT tape.

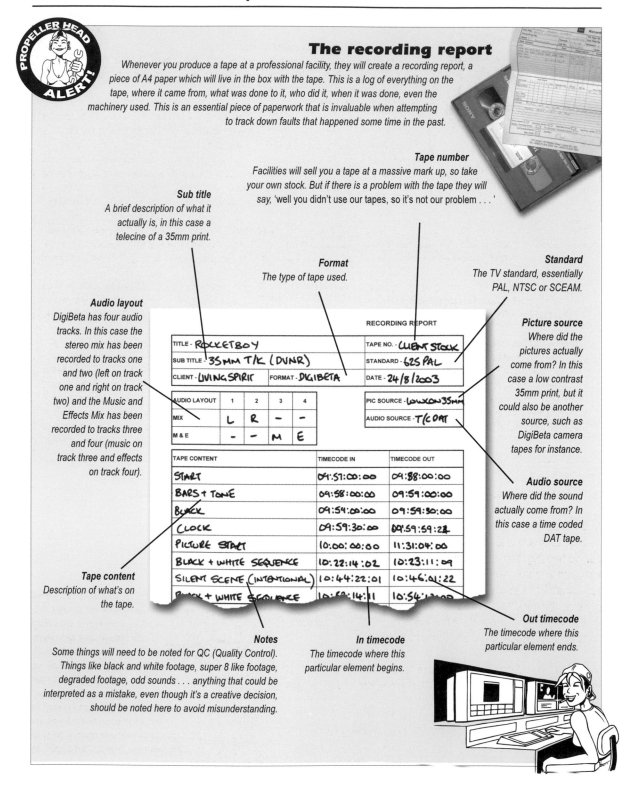

Tape content
Description of what's on the tape.

Notes
Some things will need to be noted for QC (Quality Control). Things like black and white footage, super 8 like footage, degraded footage, odd sounds . . . anything that could be interpreted as a mistake, even though it's a creative decision, should be noted here to avoid misunderstanding.

In timecode
The timecode where this particular element begins.

Out timecode
The timecode where this particular element ends.

The recording report form reads:

RECORDING REPORT

TITLE - ROCKETBOY
SUB TITLE - 35MM T/K (DVNR)
CLIENT - LIVING SPIRIT
FORMAT - DIGIBETA

TAPE NO. - CLIENT STOCK
STANDARD - 625 PAL
DATE - 24/8/2003

PIC SOURCE - LOWCON 35MM
AUDIO SOURCE - T/C DAT

AUDIO LAYOUT	1	2	3	4
MIX	L	R	–	–
M & E	–	–	M	E

TAPE CONTENT	TIMECODE IN	TIMECODE OUT
START	09:57:00:00	09:58:00:00
BARS + TONE	09:58:00:00	09:59:00:00
BLACK	09:59:00:00	09:59:30:00
CLOCK	09:59:30:00	09:59:59:21
PICTURE START	10:00:00:00	11:31:04:00
BLACK + WHITE SEQUENCE	10:22:14:02	10:23:11:09
SILENT SCENE (INTENTIONAL)	10:44:22:01	10:46:01:22
BLACK + WHITE SEQUENCE	10:52:14:11	10:54:12:05

Simon Cox
Director and Editor

Know what your delivery master is going to be! An obvious point, but the amount of new film makers who trip up here is frightening. I would create a DigiBeta master for yourself and make subsequent clones from that. It's digital and the quality's fantastic. To do this you'll need to go to a professional post production facility. But beware, these places can sting you for a fortune, so forward planning and preparation are crucial. Whatever format you decide to shoot on, ensure your chosen post production facility has the player to suit – rushes are on DVcam, not mini DV for instance, watch out for this one! What is your sound on? DAT, CD, Mini Disk, DA88? Has it been mixed yet? Or are you expecting the online editor to do that? It can really cost you if you thought they will just 'knock up a quick mix' for you. Go to your post production facility before hand and really hammer out what you need to take along, and what you expect to leave with. What do I need – the rushes? The telecine master? The neg? The DAT tapes? An EDL? What format?

Credits. Do you expect them to create an end roller for you? Can they import a word processor file from you, or will they be expected to type it in? Remember they charge by the hour and it won't cost you very much to type it all up before hand. Keep an eye on them when they do your titles, they can make fundamental cock-ups too. Remember, the make-up artist will never forgive you if she's spelt wrong!

Grading. Don't get too arty. A good grader should help you find the look for your film quickly. But beware, tweaking the greens and blues on every shot can take hours, if not days. If your want a certain look for your film, take in some examples before hand and get them to show you that they can achieve it. A good facility house will have no problem doing this on some of your rushes before hand. Don't be afraid to ask.

Mistakes in a post production facility can cost a fortune. Write a comprehensive list and tick off each job as it's done. If you are delivering for TV, will you need a clock at the front? What information needs to go on the clock? What type of delivery tape will your client require? Digibeta? HiDef? D1, D2, D3? What country is it going to? What format will it need to be? NTSC? PAL? SECAM? Make sure you know. All this stuff takes time, make sure you've planned for everything, they're charging you by the hour remember. Don't be led into a false sense of importance just because of the fancy leather sofa and the attractive runner bringing you drinks, you're paying their wages. And never pay the list price. If you're doing your telecine and sound dubbing at the same place, push hard for a superb deal. Shop around and play one off against the other. You'll be surprised what you'll get! This is the point where there's no turning back, no final tweaking. It's finished and it will be judged, for better or worse.

unsociable hours, buy lots of lunches and shower gifts. With good will and perseverance, it is possible.

When it comes to costing for the telecine (and final mastering), I have found the best approach is to fix an amount of money that you can afford and then go begging. You also need to be clear about exactly WHAT you want, and when you want it by (if you can fit in down time you will always get a deal). You can save a bit of money by taking your own blank tapes, as the ones the facilities will sell you will be four times the street price (check they are cool about this beforehand). But start at the top. Go to the best people and work your way down.

For *Urban Ghost Story*, the first telecine cost £600 and the eventual master was rejected by the German distributors. We had to go back and do it again, and because it had failed, the company re-did it for us but insisted it was my mistake and charged £400 to do it. It was re-submitted to Germany and it failed again. I couldn't mess around any longer, so I went to a company called 4MC (now Ascent Media) and hired one of their top telecine / grader operators and spent a whole

Before going to any facility to do some work, give them a phone call to make sure that they can handle everything that you are taking to them. Typically, this would be stuff like, can they handle all the tape formats that you have, that your EDL is in the right format, that your digital files will be readable etc? If you don't make this call, you can guarantee that whatever format you take with you, they will not be able to read.

The dreaded fax! QC Failure!

Any experienced low budget film maker will know how it feels when that awful fax comes through – 'QC Report – FAILED'. QC, or quality control, is an independent check on your tape and run by a top facility (someone like Ascent Media), where an engineer watches, listens and scrutinises your film. They will monitor specific technical things like audio levels and video levels, as well as make more subjective comments about the amount of dirt, sparkle and scratches, even how 'dark' the film may be. Intentional black and white footage has been known to fail QC (so mark up your VT report sheets with your master tapes as having black and white footage, and that it's a creative choice and not an error!). In fact, anywhere that could be considered a technical mistake (where you have made a creative decision – video footage that is grainy, low audio levels, Super 8mm like footage, very dark scenes etc.) you should mark it up on the 'VT record report sheet' that will live in the box with the master tape. I know it's staggering, why would they not understand that this is a creative choice? But sometimes they don't, so why take the risk?

You can't get around a failed QC report. All you can do is fix all the problems, resubmit and hope they are truly fixed and that no other errors will be spotted. This is why I always pay top dollar for my final mastering, and I use a company who also does QC themselves. If it fails, I say 'fix it, I paid top dollar and it should not have failed . . . ' And they do. When you get to this end of the business, companies are VERY professional and pride themselves on technical and artistic excellence. Unlike the small facilities who will do it on the cheap. The QC sheet will always refer to a specific tape, and the problems detailed will always be accompanied by timecodes detailing where they occur (or an example if there are too many to log). It is rare for problems to be consistently present throughout the entire film.

Continued over . . .

day working on the film. It was passed through DVNR (a grain and dust reduction process), then it was passed through a 'spotting' process (where an operator manually paints out dust, sparkle and fluff) and mastered to DigiBeta in 16:9. 4MC guaranteed that it would pass Germany's exacting tests. And it did. Of course, the whole process cost the extremely cut down rate of £2k!

Grading

If you shot on tape (as opposed to film), and are mastering your picture, you will still go through a grading process. It's almost exactly the same as the telecine process, except you obviously don't use a telecine machine. The tools such as colour balance, density, brightness contrast, gamma etc., remain the same. Given time, a grading session can produce staggering results that will greatly enhance the visual impact of your work. Of course, this is all time that you want to spend in one of the most expensive environments on the planet, working on cutting edge technology with highly skilled artists and technicians.

Cleaning up

If you skimp on the final mastering, there is a good chance that you will fail the stringent QC (quality control) checks that will be performed on your tapes. If you do fail, you will have to pay to fix the work or re-master. And you will probably pay for the QC in the first place!

Film can be a slightly messy shooting format. Sometimes the shots can be very dirty and contain dust, sparkle, camera scratches and drying marks etc. All these imperfections and blemishes could cause your film to fail when it passes through Quality Control, so it's best to correct them now. Telecineing through a process such as DVNR will take out some of the dust

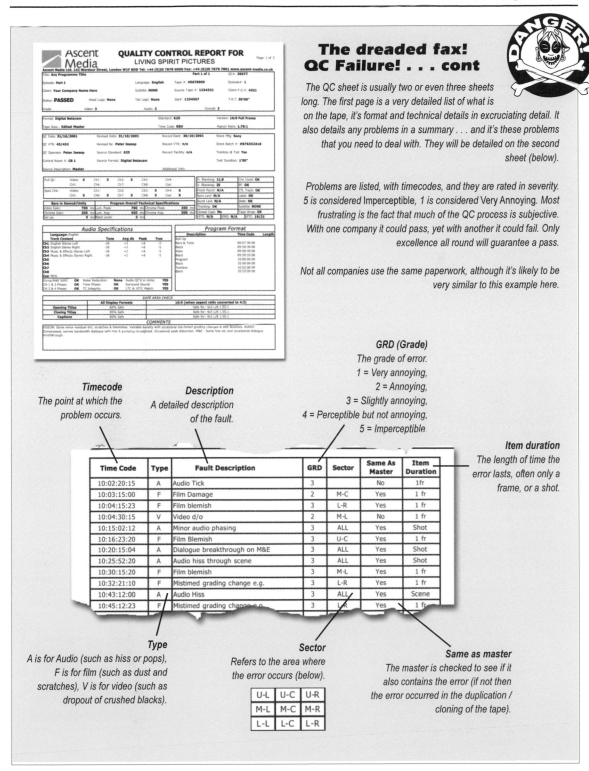

The dreaded fax!
QC Failure! . . . cont

The QC sheet is usually two or even three sheets long. The first page is a very detailed list of what is on the tape, it's format and technical details in excruciating detail. It also details any problems in a summary . . . and it's these problems that you need to deal with. They will be detailed on the second sheet (below).

Problems are listed, with timecodes, and they are rated in severity. 5 is considered Imperceptible, 1 is considered Very Annoying. Most frustrating is the fact that much of the QC process is subjective. With one company it could pass, yet with another it could fail. Only excellence all round will guarantee a pass.

Not all companies use the same paperwork, although it's likely to be very similar to this example here.

GRD (Grade)
The grade of error.
1 = Very annoying,
2 = Annoying,
3 = Slightly annoying,
4 = Perceptible but not annoying,
5 = Imperceptible.

Timecode
The point at which the problem occurs.

Description
A detailed description of the fault.

Item duration
The length of time the error lasts, often only a frame, or a shot.

Time Code	Type	Fault Description	GRD	Sector	Same As Master	Item Duration
10:02:20:15	A	Audio Tick	3		No	1fr
10:03:15:00	F	Film Damage	2	M-C	Yes	1 fr
10:04:15:23	F	Film blemish	3	L-R	Yes	1 fr
10:04:30:15	V	Video d/o	2	M-L	No	1 fr
10:15:02:12	A	Minor audio phasing	3	ALL	Yes	Shot
10:16:23:20	F	Film Blemish	3	U-C	Yes	1 fr
10:20:15:04	A	Dialogue breakthrough on M&E	3	ALL	Yes	Shot
10:25:52:20	A	Audio hiss through scene	3	ALL	Yes	Shot
10:30:15:20	F	Film blemish	3	M-L	Yes	1 fr
10:32:21:10	F	Mistimed grading change e.g.	3	L-R	Yes	1 fr
10:43:12:00	A	Audio Hiss	3	ALL	Yes	Scene
10:45:12:23	F	Mistimed grading change e.g.	3	L-R	Yes	1 fr

Type
A is for Audio (such as hiss or pops), F is for film (such as dust and scratches), V is for video (such as dropout of crushed blacks).

Sector
Refers to the area where the error occurs (below).

U-L	U-C	U-R
M-L	M-C	M-R
L-L	L-C	L-R

Same as master
The master is checked to see if it also contains the error (if not then the error occurred in the duplication / cloning of the tape).

The dreaded fax! QC failure! . . . cont

Video blanking (rare)
Problem – this is where a border has been put on the master, either at the top and bottom or on the sides. If it extends too far into the picture area it will fail.
Solution – don't put any video bars on your master.

Crushed blacks (common)
Problem – the video levels drop below 0.3v and picture information. is lost.
Solution – the video signal can be boosted, but this should never have happened if you had kept an eye on the waveform monitor.

Crushed whites (common)
Problem – the video signal has peaked over 1v and so picture information in the whites is lost.
Solution – the video signal can be clamped down, but this should never have happened if you'd kept an eye on the waveform monitor.

High error rates (rare)
Problem – the DigiBeta machine used to master the tape produced too many digital errors for it to play back on other machines, although it would play back the tape itself.
Solution – either clone onto a new tape from the original machine or completely re-master!

Picture drop-out (medium)
Problem – distortion & errors, caused by dust or tape problems.
Solution – most commonly this will mean transferring to a new tape and cleaning up the errors, either in a paint program or by going back to the source material for the problem shots.

Audio dropout / spikes etc. (common)
Problem – there can be errors on the sound which means it may spike or pop, or disappear all together.
Solution – go to the original mix and check it. If it's OK then re-lay onto master. If not, you may need to re-mix the audio for that part.

Audio peaking (medium)
Problem – the audio peaks over PPM 6 and potentially distorts on transmission or duplication.
Solution – re-lay the sound pulling the levels down at that point, or pass the sound through a compressor / limitor box.

Weave (rare)
Problem – the image gently weaves from side to side. Only a problem on film, usually Super 16mm, and most noticeable on titles or static shots. Rare to be a real problem.
Solution – not much can be done, short of major digital stabilisation. Get your chequebook out!

Joins kick in gate (rare)
Problem – the physical edit on film actually jumps on screen. Caused by a cheap neg cut and most common on S16mm.
Solution – do your neg cut with a good company in the first place!

Audio too low (medium)
Problem – the audio is too low. As well as a technical problem, this may also be because you have a very dynamic mix, or it may be a creative choice.
Solution – remix and re-dub onto master tape, or pass the mix through a compressor limitor to make the quieter bits louder.

Too dark (subjective)
Problem – the picture is deemed consistently too dark. Even if you have made a 'dark' film, this can be a problem.
Solution – re-grade, making the picture brighter.

Too grainy (common for S16mm without DVNR)
Problem – the picture contains too much grain, usually a problem from Super 16mm only.
Solution – re-telecine, passing the image through a DVNR box, which will dynamically process the image and reduce the effects of grain (as well as dust and sparkle).

Dust and sparkle (common)
Problem – Image contains dust & sparkle. Only a problem for film.
Solution – passing the telecine through DVNR may help, but most likely you will need a de-spotting session where a technician manually 'paints out' the blemishes.

Hairs in gate (medium)
Problem – a hair was trapped in the camera gate when shooting. Only a problem with film.
Solution – either replace the shot OR manually paint it out. Any foreign object can cause a similar problem (such as a boom in shot etc.)

Audio hiss (common)
Problem – the audio is poorly mixed and has a lot of hiss.
Solution – possible to filter some, but you may need to re-mix properly.

GO TO THE TOP PEOPLE! GET IT RIGHT! ...OR YOU WILL GO BACK TO FIX IT

and sparkle, but some problems will need to be manually painted out. This can be done in a spotting session where a technician manually paints out the belmishes. It's a slow and painstaking job, but if you get a fussy international buyer, you could be repeatedly rejected until you do it properly.

Laying back the sound

No matter what format you have mixed your film in, be it Dolby Digital, DTS or just simple stereo, you will need to produce a stereo version for television and video. This simple stereo mix should have been prepared at the final mix, or a subsequent audio facility, and it should be put onto tracks one and two of your DigiBeta master (with the music and effects mix on tracks three and four). Make sure that the sound mix is not Dolby SR encoded or this will bugger up your ability to keep your master multi purpose (Dolby SR is not a surround sound system, it is a noise reduction system). The sound, in this case, will more than likely come to the final mastering session on either a time coded DAT or a DA88, and its just a matter of transferring one to the other.

If you produced a Dolby Digital mix, then this will not be integrated into your DigiBeta master tape, but will be supplied as a separate element on either DA88 or more commonly, MO disk.

If you mixed in Dolby Digital and you worked in film reels, be aware that your sound will be in chunks of around 18 minutes. You may need to do a new 'conform' where you stitch all the audio reels together into one long chunk for DVD mastering.

Textless backgrounds

When you sell a film to a foreign territory, they may want to replace your titles. If your film contains white titles on a black background only, they can simply drop new titles on top of your old titles. If you have titles over any picture elements, you will need to supply the buyers with textless backgrounds, that is, the footage on which the titles normally sit, but obviously without the titles. They can then add their titles. It's common practice to put any textless backgrounds at the end of the master tape, after the film, marking it up clearly on the record report sheet that accompanies the master tape.

Keep you masters safe

It's astonishing to think that anyone would be in any way lackadaisical about their masters, especially when you consider how much time, energy and money has been spent in their manufacture. Taking this one step further, you could argue that this master tape represents the entire investment, both emotional and financial, in the project. So keep your masters safe!

John B Claude
Colourist

'A telecine operator, sometimes called a colourist, works with the production at two main points. First is during the shoot when the rushes are transferred to tape for editing, and second is when mastering the film at the end, for release on TV and video or DVD. During the shoot, when I transfer the rushes, I always tend to slightly 'lift' the image so that the editor can see the details in the darker areas. I'll also flag neg defects so that the production can deal with them. An important aspect is to make sure all the 'numbers' (keycodes / timecodes etc.) are rigidly accurate. These numbers represent the only link between editorial decisions made on a computer and the physical film. This is paramount.

The second time I work with the production is during a final grading session. I would suggest the film maker should have a clear idea of exactly what they want each scene or segment to look like. We have tremendously powerful grading tools and it's easy to become overwhelmed by the possibilities and waste time, which of course costs you money. I extensively use match frames, that is, a screen grab of a shot so that I can compare it to other shots in the film without having to rewind the tape. This is a very useful tool to help you keep the 'look' consistent.

In the final mastering session there are a huge number of ways to get onto tape the 'image' that you want – but key to this is starting with good material, for instance negative has much more detail available than a normal print. So I'd always telecine from neg, interpos or a low contrast print, never a projection print. If you shot on tape (DV, DigigBeta, HiDef etc.) then of course you would not telecine, although similar grading tools would be used for the final mastering.'
john@midnight-transfer.co.uk

DV post to look like film

The most common indie production shooting format is currently DV, be it miniDV, DVCam, DVCPro (all are flavours of the same beast). There are a number of inherent problems with DV though, which may not be apparent at first glance. Without wishing to engage my very large and currently rotating propeller on my head, DV uses a pretty poor way of encoding colours into the signal. It just isn't very robust, which means it doesn't really handle things like 'bluescreen' for special effects very well at all. In fact the colour component of the DV signal is very fragile. Plus, the whole image is highly compressed at 5:1.

It's almost always shot in a 4:3 aspect ratio, which means that in order to make a cinema version (or DVD) of that tiny DV frame, you will need to crop off a chunk from the top and bottom of the screen too (do not use the internal camera 16:9 processor unless it is a true 16:9 CCD chip!) The BIG problem with video though, is that it is interlaced. Each single frame contains information for two sub frames, called fields. Effectively, video shoots at 50 half resolution frames a second, opposed to film which could be shot at 25 full frames a second (HiDef can shoot full frames too). This interlacing is one of the things that helps give video that 'look' that makes most of us cringe.

One of the major areas of software and hardware video development in is in de-interlacers and 'video to film filters'. If you look at some action on a full video frame, you will see the interlacing (Avid only previews single filed so you will never see it on a computer monitor in an Avid suite). If you pass the video frame through a de-interlacing process, the interlacing 'look' can be reduced and even removed. Not all tools are the same, and undoubtedly, you would be best served by going to a top post production facility and try to blag the deal of the century. One of the best tools is called 'Magic Bullet' and is made by The Orphanage (founded by a group of ILM rebels).

Tom Bridges from Split Image adds . . .
We all know that film doesn't look like video, but why? Two main reasons. As we know, in contrast to the interlacing of video signals, film records full frames, which gives us a subtle but substantially different feel to moving images. Next, there is the response of film to light, the

chemistry involved in exposing and developing film. This is clearly a world away from the electronic signals in video cameras and leads to a very different response, and a very different image.

Magic Bullet, a software plug-in for After Effects, redresses the balance. The first part of the process is related to de-interlacing the footage and de-artefacting it, essentially getting rid of any digital nasties. This gives you the motion qualities associated with film, and it does it better than any other system I know of. If you want, you can output a digital answer print from Magic Bullet, which can be transferred frame-for-frame onto film for distribution. Next, extremely sophisticated grading tools are used to emulate the photochemistry of film. From different film stocks to different processing – you want a bleach-bypass look? No problem. Colour reversal film stock? Filmic cross-dissolves? It's all there.

A word of warning though. Magic Bullet will not make substandard footage look like it was shot by Janusz Kaminski. Although it can make mediocre footage look substantially better, it really shines when fed high-quality images. With well-shot DigiBeta, for example, the differences between treated video and film really can be indistinguishable. In my experience, video often looks like video because it has been treated like video. Because the format is so forgiving of mistakes, video is often poorly lit and shot. This doesn't need to be the case!

Tom's tips for Magic Bullet

If you're thinking about shooting video with an eye to making it look like film, there are a few simple guidelines to follow.

1. Never, ever, overexpose your footage. Once it's gone, it's gone forever. There is simply no way to restore the lost information, and it's a classic symptom of the dreaded video look. Don't underexpose either. It'll just look awful when you try and correct it.

2. Shoot with a shutter speed of 1/50th. This closely approximates the standard 1/48th of film, enabling you to get filmic motion-blur.

3. Turn off any sharpening controls. Most video cameras electronically sharpen their images, which can lead to some nasty artefacts. Decent cameras will allow you to reduce this.

4. Filters are your friends! Use neutral density, especially, and open up the iris. It'll allow you to reduce the depth of field, making your images much more filmic. Problems with overexposure in the sky, underexposure of your subject? Use a graduated neutral density filter. You'll need a matte-box attachment for your camera. These can be expensive, but they're worth it.

5. Use the best format you can afford. DV is great, but it's not a patch on formats such as DVCPRO50, DigiBeta, and HD. Magic Bullet like to have as much information as possible to work with, and part of DVs efficiency means that a lot of information gets discarded.

6. Get some advice. If you're really serious about getting the best possible images from video, I recommend you talk to a specialist before shooting. 'We'll fix it in post' is not something you can always do, especially on a limited budget, and it's much better to identify any potential issues before you've spent all of your money. Similarly, you'll have the benefit of people who really understand the software and can leverage all of its power to your advantage.

Magic Bullet and other digital post-production techniques are immensely powerful tools. In experienced hands, almost anything can be improved. You can now shoot digitally, get more of your budget up on the screen, treat it in post, and still get fantastic results. It requires a lot of care and attention to detail, but it's possible and it'll start to happen more and more.

For anyone tired of the soulless, sterile imagery you so often get with video, it's the only way forward.

Tom Bridges
tom@split-image.co.uk
www.split-image.co.uk

Never give your master tapes out. Instead, make clones and allow those out. Carefully and clearly label all your master tapes, and if you can, write descriptive notes and stick them to the case – if you're ever wondering what exactly is on that DigiBeta tape, you cant just pop it in your video recorder to have a look! Don't underestimate how much you will forget over time. You might have gone through hell creating your various master tapes and may think you will never forget what's on them, but trust me, three years down the line, you will have no clue unless you made extensive and accurate notes, and kept the recording report sheets safely in the case with the tape.

Making your DVD

It's tough to get into a cinema, and when you do, you don't last long! Most people will not see your movie in a theatre, so DVD is as close to a cinematic experience as you can hope to offer most people. So you are undoubtedly going to want a great disk!

Why you shouldn't master your own DVD for release . . .

Almost every piece of domestic post production software under the sun now claims to be able to make DVDs. Most of the time, what it really means is that it can export an MPEG2 stream, which can be turned into a DVD. However, there are a lot of reasons why you shouldn't master your own DVD at home.

Quality

Unless you are prepared to spend an absolute age rendering and creating your MPEG files, you'd be better served by going to a professional facility, set up to master movies on DVD. Most cheap or free software Mpeg encoders are okay, but not great. You've spent years making your movie and DVD is where most people will see it, so do the best you can.

Testing

You need to be sure that the DVD you create will play back on every DVD machine. Companies that make DVDs professionally, can make this guarantee. You, with a PC or Mac running a £30 piece of software cannot.

Copy protection

You cannot use professional copy protection systems on your domestic DVD mastering software. If you want to stop low tech piracy, then you will need to use a system like Macrovision.

Delivery

Most DVD duplication facilities, where they actually press thousands of disks at a time, require your DVD master to be delivered on a DLT tape. DLT drives are not very common, although you can buy them very cheaply on E-bay (often as little as £25 'cos they are kind of old technology and low capacity by today's standards). Your DVD mastering software MUST be able to master the movie to DLT, you cannot just copy from one to the other.

Sound

If you have mixed in Dolby Digital 5.1, how are you going to get that mix into your DVD mastering software? You cannot just bring in a bunch of audio files.

Farting around

You will spend so much time trying to make it work that you will more than likely abandon it and end up blagging a deal with a top facility anyway!

What you can do to make a better disk . . .

However, there are a number of things that you can definitely do to make your DVD mastering process easier, cheaper and improve the content radically. Most distributors don't care about DVD content (although they will tell you that they do!) so if you want a cool disk of your movie, it's up to you to make it happen. The idea is that you create all the elements for the DVD, take them to a mastering facility, with an explanatory flow chart as to 'what does what' when the buttons are clicked. This is pretty much what I did for my third movie, Urban Ghost Story, all the way down to 3D animated menus. The whole lot was bolted together and mastered by a top company for around £500! Here's a list of what I would suggest is appropriate.

The movie

Delivered on DigiBeta in 16:9. It should be fully graded and have all the titles. If you mixed in stereo only, then the audio will almost certainly be taken in at the same time as the picture, off the DigiBeta tape.

Menus

You should create all your menus and buttons in Photoshop. All the elements in the menus, such as pictures and text should be kept as separate layers, so that the mastering company can access these and create the animated buttons (the files will be saved as native PhotoShop files, such as menu003.psd). These images should be formatted in 16:9, the frame size being 1024 by 576 pixels, and in RGB colour (although they will be re-sized and squeezed to be 720 by 576 by the mastering company)

Animated menus

If you plan to do any funky animated menus, for instance, using After Effects or 3-D Studio Max, I would suggest rendering them at 1024 by 576 (full frames and not interlaced) and saved as Quicktime files (uncompressed). They will be pretty huge!

Sound

If you mixed in 5.1, then the sound will be delivered on a separate tape or disk, possibly a DA88 or an MO disk (check that the mastering facility can handle this).

Documentaries

You should have plenty of behind-the-scenes footage, which you can edit together with clips from the movie and custom shot interviews with the film makers (and cast) to make a 20 minute doco. This can be edited and mastered on your home editing system, such as Premiere, Final Cut Pro or Avid XpressDV. Remember to put a clock at the head of this documentary. This should be in 16:9.

Deleted scenes

If you have any particularly good or interesting scenes that you cut, then edit them together, add some sound effects and music and shoot some interview introductions with the film makers putting the deleted scenes in context. Again, this can be done on a home system and delivered on DV. This should be in 16:9.

Music

If you have the rights to do it, you can also put the music on the DVD (remember to produce a menu for these audio clips). The music should be supplied in either AIFF (Mac) or WAV (PC) formats, stereo and at 48kHz.

Photo gallery

If you want to show some photos from behind-the-scenes, or stills from the movie, they should be supplied as a series of numbered TIFF files in RGB colour and 16:9 aspect ratio, which means a 1024 by 576 image size.

Commentaries

If you want to put any commentaries on the film, then you will need to record them. Don't go to an expensive facility, just set up in a relatively quiet space and record it yourself. You'll need a VHS and TV to watch the movie, and rather cunningly, you can record the audio onto DV. Set the camera up to film the TV screen (this will only be used as a visual sync guide when you master the commentary later) and plug a microphone into the mic socket of the camera. Put on headphones so you can hear the movie soundtrack (without interfering with the commentary). Start recording on the DV camera and play back the VHS tape, then begin your narration. You will stop and start at regular intervals, and rewind the VHS where needed to re-do bits. At the end, you can re-edit this on your home editing system and lay it off back onto a DV tape with the sound recorded at 48kHz (you'd be advised to put a huge title over all of the picture saying 'guide only' so that no one can accidentally use your DV version to master the final movie). Or you may be able to deliver the audio as a separate WAV or AIFF in stereo and at 48kHZ. If you do, make sure the file begins at the very first frame of picture (which will correspond to 10:00:00:00 TC on the DigiBeta tape).

Trailers and promos

If you have them and want to put them on, then just send them to the mastering facility. Often promos may be delivered on a low quality format such as BetaSP, which is fine. Just make sure that if your whole DVD has been mastered in 16:9, then your trailers and promos are also mastered in 16:9.

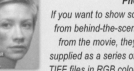

Chapters

A list of timecodes where you would like each chapter selection to begin would make life easier too. If you have done chapter selection menu screens then this is essential.

Note – All your elements will need to be either re-sized or re-rendered for NTSC. Animations for NTSC should run at 30 fps (progressive scan/full frames) and the frame size is 853 by 480 (this is a true 16:9, un-squeezed image for NTSC that will be resized by the mastering company). Don't put off making them now, do it ALL at the same time 'cos it's a real pain in the butt six months later!

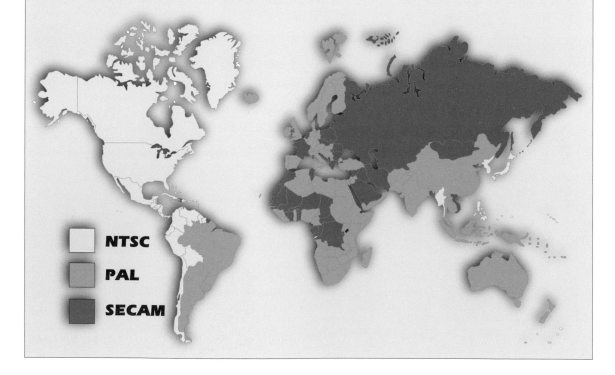

PAL and NTSC

There are a number of TV formats around the world, but the two most common are PAL and NTSC. PAL is used in the UK, Australia, Germany and South Africa for instance, and NTSC is used in the USA, Canada, Japan and Korea for instance. There is another format, SECAM (used in France for instance), but that is less of a headache as it's really very similar to PAL. The problem with PAL and NTSC is that they run at different rates. PAL runs at 25 fps (50 fields a second) and NTSC runs at 30fps (60 fields a second).

To sell your film you will need two masters, one in PAL and one in NTSC. Let's assume that you have made a PAL, 16:9 master, fully graded with sound etc. and recorded to DigiBeta. There are a number of ways you could make an NTSC tape from this master. The first and simplest method is to take it to a facilities house who can then make a 'systems transfer dub'. That is, play back the PAL tape, pass it through a box, which turns it into NTSC, and then record it onto another tape . . . all in real time. It's quick and dirty, the quality is OK, but not great. A much better and less used route is actually available on many newer Online Avids as standard. You will need an Online Avid suite, with DigiBeta (capable of playing and recording in both NTSC and PAL), and it should have the 'Universal Mastering' option.

Create a new project, setting it up as a 24P project. Digitise your material, ideally through SDI, and at a compression of 2:1. In real time, the Avid will take the PAL interlaced fields and create true progressive frames (this process will work REALLY well for film, less well for video treated to look like film and dreadfully for video material). It then slows the 25fps footage down to 24fps. You can then do a digital cut back to tape in NTSC and the Avid will sort out all technical stuff. The picture quality is nearly as good as if you had done this as a telecine as there are virtually no motion artefacts and all the usual naff stuff you get with PAL to NTSC systems transfers. Wherever you plan to do this, remember it will take a couple of hours to digitise in, some time to mess around, then a couple of hours to put it back down to tape.

NTSC

PAL

SECAM

Mastering Models

The following pages outline a number of mastering models that will all end up with a 16:9, PAL DigBeta with sound master (and some times other masters too!) The proposed models all differ in many stages, but there are a number of common issues to deal with.

First is having the initial conversation with the facility who will do your work, and running some simple tests. Get them to check your material before you commit to doing the job. You need to be sure that they can actually deliver what you want. Take some of your rushes in and ask them to have a quick look, maybe even play around with a shot or two and show you what they can do. You may be surprised at what they can or cannot do, especially if this is your first time grading and mastering. You are about to enter a very expensive environment, you should know what you are getting into.

Second, get your materials to them as early as possible. All too often, new film makers turn up to the final telecine or mastering session with elements completely forgotten, *'What do you mean you need the master sound?'* There also tends to be a lot of 'stuff' (tapes, tapes and more damn tapes!) which quite frankly isn't a whole heap of fun to carry about on the tube – it's very heavy and cumbersome! Now I always get a cab there and back so that I am relaxed, focussed and ready to work. And as for the myth that taking your master tapes on the tube will somehow mysteriously erase them, I have yet to come across someone who that has happened to, and neither has it happened to any of my tapes – and they have all been on the tube at some time!

Third, try and do an all in deal. That is, they agree to do everything that is needed to make the master tape for a fixed price. You will not be on an hourly rate and therefore everyone can relax – you and the technicians too. At the same time, you must understand that this doesn't mean you can be overly fussy or disrespectful of the good will that is being extended to you. Don't take the piss. Know what you want and don't mess around. Now is not the time to discover the artist in you.

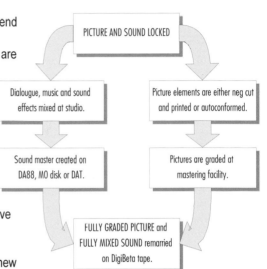

As soon as you have a master completed, run off a couple of clones for safety. Remember, they are not copies, they are clones, so exactly the same as the original.

Over the next pages there are four mastering models.

Shoot film, master to 35mm and TK

This is for productions that shoot film, post produce traditionally at the lab, then take a 35mm fully graded print to the telecine and master to DigiBeta.

Shoot film, TK rushes and tape grade

This is for productions that shoot on film, then telecine and post produced to tape resolution only, onto DigiBeta. This is ideal for TV, video and DVD. It can also be transferred to 35mm with surprisingly good results.

Shoot tape, offline and master to DigiBeta

This is for productions that shoot on tape, either DV or DigiBeta, and post produced to tape resolution only, onto DigiBeta. This is ideal for TV, video and DVD. The video image will probably be processed to look more like film. It can also be transferred to 35mm with surprisingly good results.

Shoot film, digital post, transfer back to film

This is for productions that shoot film, then scan the film into a powerful post production suite at film resolution, grade, then archive to a data tape. All masters, both tape and film, can be created from this digital master. This is a great process BUT expensive.

Finally, agree to supply your own blank tape stock. It will cost you a third of the price that the facility will charge you. In an emergency, you can zap over to Wardour Street and buy your stock at a pretty good price from Stanley Productions.

At all stages you should invite your DP to come along as they will have insight into the image that you may not. And after all, the grading could profoundly effect their work, so it's only courteous.

No matter how organised you are, how clear you are about what you want and need, this final mastering stage always takes longer to do than you expect – creative choices, funky cool software, toys that fix all manner of problems, technical screw ups, crashing computers . . . But more than anything, this is because this IS the final stage and nothing can be put off anymore. So you tend to procrastinate that bit more. You want to be sure.

Wherever possible, try and keep all the work in one facility. If you have a problem at any point, and you have taken your work between several different facilities, odds are, everyone will blame each other and your movie will go unfixed leaving YOU to foot a bill for the work to fix the mistakes.

If you go to one of the major facilities, you could even pay them to do a quality control check after they have done all the work. It will cost a little money, but at least you'll know that if they find any problems, they'll be obliged to fix them (probably for free too!) A passed QC from a major company such as Ascent Media is probably going to be good enough for any sales agent or distributor of your film. It's a smart move that few of us rarely do, mainly because we think that we will getaway with it. Still got that low budget mentality.

All of these proposed models (over the next few pages) deal with sound and picture separately, and assume that sound has already have been mastered and mixed, and all that is left is for it to be married up to the final graded picture and laid down onto the master tape.

MODEL ONE
Shoot film, master to 35mm & TK

This proposed mastering model is for a production that's shot on either S16mm or 35mm and has gone through the traditional post production routes of internegative, interpositive, optical sound etc. Much of the final grading and construction work will have already been done by virtue of making a final theatrical print version (35mm print).

To make a television master, you should telecine either a low contrast 35mm print that has never been projected and has been specially made for the purpose of telecine, or you could make your master from one of the intermediate stages, such as the interpositive. But from my experience, that just leads to more headaches, as some elements, such as titles and opticals may not be integrated into that interpositive.

If the film was shot on S16mm and has been blown up to 35mm, then the image will probably be quite grainy and may be a little contrasty. The telecine operator should be asked to pass it through a process such as DVNR to reduce the grain. The telecine operator will line up a DigiBeta tape (probably a 124 minute tape) with bars, tone and clock. They will then begin the telecine of reel one. Some time will be spent getting the density and colour balance right, and agreeing an overall 'look'. As the whole movie has already been graded on film at the lab, the telecine process for this print should be quite quick. The grader will probably only stop occasionally for shots that are too dark or too bright. The transfer should be in 16:9 anamorphic. More than likely, the grader will watch the whole of reel one, stopping and starting to tweak when necessary, and logging all the changes into the computer. At the end of reel one, they will rewind and actually record the telecine to tape, the computer making all the adjustments that were previously logged (in real time). Depending on the complexity of the reels and the fussiness of the film makers, it should take around an hour per reel. Plus a couple of hours for messing around. So as you can see, it's a day long job. The telecine operator will transfer all five reels and then the picture element is done. Next, the DigiBeta tape will go to the sound department, or a separate sound facility where the sound will be transferred onto the audio tracks of the master.

FULLY GRADED 35mm PRINT WITH TITLES AND OPTICAL SOUND.

Picture is telecinied, graded and processed through 'noise reduction system' and recorded onto DigiBeta tape.

Sound is transferred onto tape (previously mixed).

Fully graded 16:9 DigiBeta used to make subsequent clones and alternative versions.

MODEL TWO
Shoot film, TK rushes & tape grade

This model is for productions that will end up on videotape only, for sale to video, TV, DVD etc. (although there is a new digital process that can take this type of master tape and blow up to 35mm film with astonishing results). The production will have shot film, probably S16mm (at 25fps) and during the shoot, the rushes will have been transferred, in 16:9 and with a very 'flat' grade, to DigiBeta. For the purposes of the creative editing, the lab would also run off either BetaSP's or DVCam tapes, which would be used for the off-line edit (on Avid for instance).

The production would then edit the film and eventually lock picture. They will then take the master DigiBeta tapes, along with an EDL (or an Avid project, assuming you have cut on Avid and the mastering facility are also going to use an Avid to grade and master) to an online facility. The facility will then auto-conform your pictures at a very high resolution (essentially, they will rebuild your edit from the master DigiBeta tapes, and NOT the off-line BetaSP or DVCam tapes). Once the material is in the computer, the grader will start work. They will make all shots look consistent, and probably apply an overall 'look' to the production. Because you are working in a digital environment, all sorts of very funky toys become available. Title sequences, simple visual effects, cool colour balancing etc., are all pretty quick and easy to do for an operator who knows their kit. The flat telecine grade that was done during the shoot means that the operator will have a great deal of latitude to play around with – the rushes tapes, which have probably never looked very inspiring, will contain a great deal of detail in the common problematic areas, highlight and shadow for instance. This is very important, because unlike film, (even though you shot film, your master is now a digital videotape), video has a sharp cut off point. When it goes to black, it's black forever, and when it goes to white, it's white forever.

S16mm Film is Telecinied to 16:9 DigiBeta with a flat grade.

Offline tapes edited. Picture locked.

Pictures recaptured at 'online facility'. Pictures are graded. Effects and titles added.

Pictures laid back onto DigiBeta, with previously mixed audio.

It will take about three to four hours to batch digitise all the material into the online machine, and then I would suggest at least a day to grade it (and it could be considerably more, it all depends on the material, the film makers, the grader and overall fussiness). If you want titles, then have them already typed up on a floppy disk (that you know they can read). Once the movie has been fully graded and you're happy, it will be laid back to a new 124 DigiBeta tape with the relevant bars, tone and clock. After you have completed the job, ask the operator if you can take a copy of the project on a Zip disk – so take a blank disk with you (this is not the actual film media, just all the information needed to re-build the project at a later stage or perhaps somewhere else, with all grading information intact). Depending on the hardware and the facility, you may also be able to directly output an NTSC master at the same time. If this is possible, do it, as it will save you a lot of headache later on. It's likely that this type of facility will also digitise your sound for you, and also lay that onto the DigiBeta master.

An alternative route for this process is to do an overlength neg cut which is telecinied instead of the DigiBeta tapes being graded. This is similar to the final model here (digital film) except everything is done at PAL TV resolution instead of film resolution.

MODEL THREE
Shoot tape, offline & master to DigiBeta

This model is for productions that have shot on either a DV format or Digital BetaCam (although you may have also shot on BetaSP, which in my opinion is preferable to MiniDV, if you can get the cameras).

Movie shot on miniDV. Tapes are cloned to DVcam each night, producing backup and unbroken timecode.

Pictures are locked.

EDL and tapes taken to online facility where tapes are redigitised, graded and titles and effects are added.

Pictures are laid back onto a DigiBeta with sync sound (which has been previously mixed).

For the sake of clarity with this model, we will assume that this shoot is on miniDV. At the end of each shooting day, the camera tapes would be sent to the cutting room. I would suggest that it is a good idea to transfer all camera tapes to a new tape (onto DVCam as this format has professional and robust time code) to guarantee unbroken time code, and to create a safety back up (DV tapes are small and fragile. If it snags, that is your only copy unless you made a back up!) Remember, DV is digital, so cloning from one tape to another is lossless.

Once new tapes have been created, the editor will digitise it into the Avid and the production will edit the movie. Once everything has been creatively locked, you will go through the fairly normal debate with yourself about whether you need a professional online or whether you can do it at home on your own system . . . 'its digital innit? So there ain't no loss of quality . . . ' I would always recommend doing your final mastering and grading at a professional facility. They will get it right and produce a much more attractive end product.

When finding an online facility, make sure that they have had experience of DV and know how best to handle its limitations. They will recapture your footage from an EDL, or the Avid project (if you and they worked on Avid). During the online, the footage could be taken in through firewire, which would clone the material onto the computer hard drives, or you could take it in through SDI and capture it at a much higher resolution so that any further work that is done to the footage is created at this higher, less lossy resolution (any format that uses compression is lossy – in essence, information is thrown away to keep the data bandwidth lower). As with the other models, the grader will now work their wizardry and add titles etc. One major visual issue that film makers spend an awful lot of time and energy attempting to get right is 'the film look'. I've said it before in this book and I'll say it again. The best way to get the film look is to shoot film! There's no point in going into a detailed explanation of how best to make your video look like film, because no doubt there will be some new tools on the street that didn't exist when I wrote this text, a new one seems to appear every month! (see Magic Bullet in this section).

Once the image has been completely processed and looks just how you want it, it will be laid down to a DigiBeta master, with the relevant bars, tone and clock and the sound which has been previously mixed will be added. Unlike the other mastering models, you will walk away with a 4:3 version, and not a 16:9 version. This is because you will not have shot your material in 16:9 (unless you had a DV camera with a 16:9 chip or you shot DigiBeta in true 16:9, or even Hi-Def). From your 4:3 master, you will be able to make a 16:9 anamorphic master, by passing it through a box like a Snell and Wilcox Arc (which will do it in real time) or by using the 'Pan ans Scan' motion effect in Avid.

MODEL FOUR
Shoot film, digital post, transfer back to film

This mastering model uses cutting edge technology that is currently in flux. New companies offering various flavours of this technique have sprung up and other new companies have folded in a very short space of time. It is truly an emerging industry. In essence, it works fine with both film and HiDef, but there is no advantage to this route if you shot on DigiBeta or DV.

If you shot film, you would do your off-line cut as normal, and then there would be an over length neg cut. This neg cut differs to the usual A & B roll neg cut, or single roll neg cut, that you would have if you were making a print directly from the negative, in so much as it has 'handles'. Essentially, it isn't really a neg cut, but more of a way to organise all the shots that are used in your movie, into a number of manageable reels, as opposed to the tens of thousands of camera feet that maybe available.

This over length neg cut will be taken to a digital film facility, along with a compatible EDL, and the shots that make up your movie will be scanned into the computer at very high resolutions. Once in the computer, the grader will pretty much do the same as they would in any of the other processes. However, the quality can be quite staggering as you are working at very high resolutions, and the pictures are taken directly from the camera negative. The film will be graded and tweaked, probably much more so than in the other models, because to post produce in this environment is going to cost you the same amount of money as you might spend on a small London flat! Once the grading has been done and the picture has had all the extra bells and whistles (visual effects, titles etc.) added, the picture information will be archived to a data tape as a back up.

The pictures will then be scanned onto 35mm negative which will be used to make 35mm cinema prints. The sound should also have been dealt with by now and there should be an optical negative to marry up to the 35mm negative, so that all prints have synchronised sound.

The main advantage of this process is that you have all the bells and whistles available in the digital domain, but you get to shoot film and end up on film. You can also make every conceivable master from this very high resolution version of your film. The quality will be consistently impeccable. Of course, the down side to this process is the price tag. Ouch!

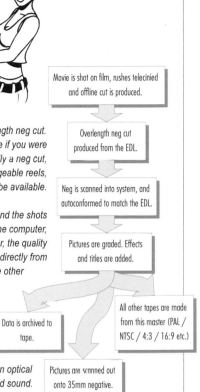

Movie is shot on film, rushes telecinied and offline cut is produced.

Overlength neg cut produced from the EDL.

Neg is scanned into system, and autoconformed to match the EDL.

Pictures are graded. Effects and titles are added.

Data is archived to tape.

All other tapes are made from this master (PAL / NTSC / 4:3 / 16:9 etc.)

Pictures are scanned out onto 35mm negative.

Film Festivals
Blueprint

BRITISH
COUNCIL

Creating opportunity for people worldwide.

Film Festivals and Film Markets are often confused by new film makers. Markets are where films are traded. Festivals are venues where films are screened for pleasure to the general public, and hopefully one or two media types such as distributors. Festivals are often set-up and run by film lovers who want to meet film makers and screen new and interesting films. They are an essential part of the marketing for new film maker's movies, are a lot of fun and you can even win awards.

Reasons to go to a film festival . . .

Because it will platform your film . . .
Being selected for a prestigious festival, or better still winning awards, will give you something to put on your press pack and posters. Those little fig leaf thingies with *Winner of* . . . and *Official Selection* . . . we have all seen them. You will also get press reviews, hopefully good ones, all of which will help with international sales and platforming YOU as a film maker.

Because they will love your movie . . .
It's a bitter pill but your movie is probably at best a pale imitation of your aspirations at the onset of production. The great thing about festivals is that the audiences are very forgiving of the weaknesses in your film, especially if you have tried to do something original or brave. Festival audiences are especially pleased when you have travelled half way round the planet to introduce the film. Soak up that applause baby!

Because you might win . . .
Everyone loves a winner. Not only might you get a small golden statuette on a lump of onyx, but you might even win some cash. Cash prizes are often attached to some kind of theatrical deal on which you must spend the money.

Because you might meet a distributor . . .
Major festivals are often attended by local distributors on the look out for new product. There's no better place for a distributor to see your film than in an enthusiastic, packed, festival screening.

Because you need a break . . .
It's true, you need a holiday. Choose festivals in places that you want to visit and not places that simply invite you. If you are a Brit, the British Council may cover some expenses, the festival covering the remainder.

Because you will make new friends . . .
You will meet and bond with other film makers who share the common experience of surviving a low budget film. You might also meet and make friends with more established film makers. These friendships often flourish and friends can become allies. Oh and you might even watch some movies too!

Reasons not to go to a festival . . .

Because you need to write that new script . . .
Most new film makers are broke. It's quite a novelty then, to be whisked around the world on other people's expense accounts, to venues where people tell you just how amazing you are as a film maker. Rather than receiving a year long ego brush (as you become a festival junkie), you should be targeting a major festival where you will do well, using that to platform you as *'talent'*, then set up meetings to get a deal for your next film. It's a year between *'new and hot'* and *'so last year . . . '* There's always someone *'newer'* and *'hotter'* behind you.

Because you can't show it . . .
Most festivals only accept films on 35mm. If you shot on another format (DV, S16mm etc) you will need to make a costly blow up (which you might need to do anyway). Some festivals now project video, but not all. The tide is turning and in time, digital video projection will replace 35mm but for now (2002), festivals still want a 35mm print.

Because you are busy . . .
It's all happened for you and you are on your next film. Movies are like love affairs, as soon as you have a new one, the last one seems like an albatross around your neck. Remember a lot of people helped you get to where you are at and part of your deal was to platform the film for them, as well as you. If you can't attend, ask others (DoP, writer, editor, cast) to go in your place.

Film Festivals Blueprint

Film festivals are one of the major perks of being an independent film maker. They generally run from anywhere between a few days and a couple of weeks and are located in major towns and cities around the world. They are often run by people who love movies, are attended by people who love movies, and also attended by distributors, sales agents and talent agents. Film festivals are about the best audiences you could ever wish for your film and accordingly, provide you with the best screenings.

Most festivals require your film to be supplied on a 35mm print, virtually none accepting 16mm prints. Digital film makers who don't have 35mm prints face the problem that some festivals won't accept their film, but with every day the tide is turning and by the time you read this it is quite possible that all film festivals will be screening digital content through a digital projector off DVD, MiniDV, Digibeta or a new HD format.

So how do you get to film festivals and which ones should you attend as it often seems that every large town on the planet has a film festival?

Simple plan

Firstly, you need a plan. What do you want to get out of your festival experiences and exposure? In no particular order, here are a few things . . .

An ego brush, it's great to screen your film to an audience who is simply dying to love it. *Great press*, unless your film is totally incompetent, someone somewhere will recognise the rough diamond and write really nice things about it. *Distribution*, many of the major festivals double up as mini markets and venues for talent scouts. *A holiday*, yes you need it, you want it, enjoy it. *New pals*, festivals are a magnet for other film makers with whom you can share war stories and get drunk with in the wee hours. *Awards*, many festivals carry awards, some of which have cash attached (everyone loves an award winning film and film maker).

Festivals fall into two rough categories. Primary 'A' list festivals, such as Sundance, Berlin, Cannes (festival, not market) and Toronto. These festivals are tough to get into and can directly lead to film makers careers being launched and

Film Festivals are where you get to show your film to audiences around the world, maybe win prizes, get press, travel, and generally enjoy the creative fruits of your labour.

Knowing the where, when and the theme of film festivals used to be half the battle. Now all you need to do is go to the British Council's website at www.britfilms.com/festivals for perhaps the most comprehensive, up to date and detailed listing on the planet.

Film Festival flow chart

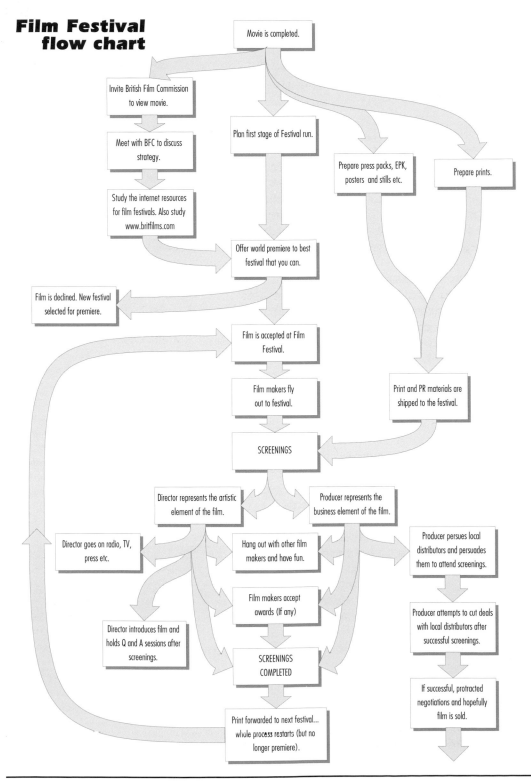

Movie is completed.

Invite British Film Commission to view movie.

Meet with BFC to discuss strategy.

Study the internet resources for film festivals. Also study www.britfilms.com

Plan first stage of Festival run.

Prepare press packs, EPK, posters and stills etc.

Prepare prints.

Offer world premiere to best festival that you can.

Film is declined. New festival selected for premiere.

Film is accepted at Film Festival.

Film makers fly out to festival.

Print and PR materials are shipped to the festival.

SCREENINGS

Director represents the artistic element of the film.

Producer represents the business element of the film.

Director goes on radio, TV, press etc.

Hang out with other film makers and have fun.

Producer persues local distributors and persuades them to attend screenings.

Film makers accept awards (If any)

Producer attempts to cut deals with local distributors after successful screenings.

Director introduces film and holds Q and A sessions after screenings.

SCREENINGS COMPLETED

If successful, protracted negotiations and hopefully film is sold.

Print forwarded to next festival... whole process restarts (but no longer premiere).

their films securing distribution. You need to apply to all these festivals and you will do well to get into any.

The second category works on a kind of sliding scale of importance based on your needs. For example, on my third movie Urban Ghost Story (UGS), the Edinburgh International Film Festival was important. UGS was shot in London but set in Glasgow and premiering at Edinburgh helped seal the illusion that it was a Scottish film. It was also pivotal in securing a respectable talent agent for my business partner and director of UGS, Genevieve Jolliffe. Ask yourself . . . do you want to visit the place? . . . do they have awards? . . . is it a genre festival or specialised group festival (for example Horror festival or Gay and Lesbian festival). These 'B' list festivals rarely lead directly to a career launch or a distribution deal but they often help. Never discount the possibility that even the most obscure, far flung festival might lead to that chance encounter with a person who may well be pivotal in the launch of your career or movie.

The web is a terrific resource here, not only at the British Council website, but every festival worth attending now has it's own site, often with maps, hotel guides etc. Do your research!

Rule Brittania!

If you are a British film maker, you will be in the enviable position of being able to work with the British Council. The British Council is Government funded and its sole purpose is to promote British culture abroad. The upshot is that if you make a film, the British Council will work with you to place that film at foreign festivals, often covering much of the expenses of attending, organising it, and even taking care of print shipping. If you are not a British film maker, then you will have to do much of the legwork yourself or do as many American film makers do and hire a Producer's rep or PR company (although because of the British Council we have yet to do this).

So the movie's completed. First off, contact the British Council and invite them to a screening or send them a VHS of your movie. Follow up with phone calls or a meeting to discuss a strategy for your film's festival run.

Based on which month you are currently in, you can draw up a plan of attack of the festivals you want to attend, targeting the 'A' list festivals first. You only have one world premiere to give away, so choose carefully. Once your film is on the festival circuit, and if it is at the very least an interesting film, you'll find that programmers from one festival will attend another festival to find films for their own festival. This way, you will start to receive invitations to many festivals you may not have even considered.

A word of warning . . .

You may find yourself turning into a festival junkie and attending festivals

Paul Howson
British Council

'What do festival programmers look for? A good story well told, certainly, (which doesn't always mean straightforward narrative), but above all originality, cinematic virtue, something that makes them suddenly sit up and take notice. Programmers are like talent spotters. They just love it when they're digging through a pile of submission tapes and come across buried treasure: Christopher Nolan's ultra-low budget 'Following', or Pawel Pawlikowski's 'Last Resort': unheralded and highly original films that got programmers excited.

Because it's so difficult for independent features to get a theatrical release, for many film makers the festival circuit really is an alternative form of distribution. This way you can get your film seen by audiences around the world (and bask in applause in many languages) and, occasionally, distributors who watch it with a large and enthusiastic local audience may pick it up.

If you're making a feature and don't yet have a sales agent on board, we'll be happy to advise you on a festival strategy: which ones to target, which to avoid, when and how to submit your film. For some festivals such as Berlin and Toronto we will organise preview screenings in London, twenty or so titles over a couple of days, and if you want to be part of this we need to know you're out there. And for some festivals we can help you get there for your international premiere, to enjoy that moment when the opening credits roll.'

Taking a few friends to a festival means you can have bodies handing out fliers with times and venues of your screenings, all of these people wearing T shirts for your movie of course. They can also handle fly postering freeing you to do the schmoozing with the important folk.

simply because you're invited – travelling and attending festivals takes a physical, emotional and financial toll when you should be spending your time working on your career options and planning the next film. The other problem, which is less apparent, is that of print availability. Each and every 35mm print of your film costs about £1k. Clearly, you're not going to have a shed load of them.

A print can only ever be in one physical place at a time and often will need a week to get to a festival and a week to get to the next festival (assuming the print doesn't get stuck in customs as it often can). The upshot is that you can't just attend any festival, as you have to check print availability. If you have two or three prints knocking around the film festival circuit, just monitoring checking and chasing these prints can turn into a full-time job (especially when you consider you may well have to send press materials, EPKs, etc as well as organise your own travelling, and sometimes, accommodation).

To add to your headaches, a print has a certain life and often starts to fall apart after going to ten or more festivals. Who knows how the projectionist will treat your print at the Outer Mongolian Festival? Occasionally I have been to a festival where the print is quite old and been horrified to discover that the film had been re-perforated! On the whole though, the audiences will tolerate this as they are getting to see a unique film that they would never see if it were not showing in the festival.

Applications

Depending on the festivals that you approach, some will require you to fill out a form and send it along with a VHS tape and sometimes an application fee, usually $30-50, but it can be more. If the British Council has been involved in negotiating the festival attendance, they will often take care of this for you. If a festival accepts your film, the first thing to do is check your print availability and ensure that the print will get to the festival in plenty of time.

Shipping a print to a festival costs around $100, but there is an unwritten rule which stipulates that a festival will pay for the shipping one way. If you can get your print to a festival, the festival should pay for it to go to the next festival, who will then pay for it to go to the next festival and so on.

Separately from the print, you should send copies of your paper press pack, your EPK (Electronic Press Kit), a couple of VHS screening tapes and DVDs if available, posters and any other promotional material you feel is relevant.

Managing a successful festival run with two or three prints can be a full time job. The application forms alone are enough to send a shiver down the spine of most creatives.

Who is going to go?

OK, assuming it isn't impounded in customs, your print arrives at the festival on time, your publicity material has arrived a week earlier and everything is set. The final variable is who, if anyone, is going to attend and represent the film makers. Festivals love Directors. It's sad but true that festivals perceive directors as creative gods and producers as glorified tea-makers. The upshot is that the festival will often fly and accommodate the director aka film-god but decline travelling expenses for the producer aka tea-maker (although they will almost always accommodate anyone from a film who manages to make it to the festival, even if that ends up being at the foot of the director's bed).

Let's assume the director is going, all expenses paid by the festival and the British Council, and the Producer is also attending paying their own way to get there but being accommodated by the festival. (You may ask how the festival can afford to do this. Firstly, they will sell tickets for your film of which you will get zero. Secondly, they will have corporate sponsors that will often include airlines and hotel chains who donate a number of flights and rooms.)

Don't forget your toothbrush!

Before you leave there are a number of things to check. Obviously your passport, but also whether you need any jabs (especially for far-flung equatorial festivals), fill your bags with as many posters and flyers as you can carry plus ten VHS or DVDs. You may also have produced some unique and tricksy publicity materials to help your film stand out from the crowd. As ever, you will have announced this *'exciting breakthrough'* on your website which you will keep updated whenever possible.

Even though you have dressed like a slob for the last two years whilst making the movie, now is the time to replace your wardrobe. You are what you wear. Most of the time you can wear casual clothing but you will need some smart clobber for those fancy parties and premieres. For your Q&A wear something that stands out, not the usual posh black that most media types gravitate too. I have a number of offensive Hawaiian shirts that certainly raise an eyebrow!

Your limo awaits

When your plane touches down you will be greeted by a representative of the festival who will take you to either the festival HQ or your hotel. You'll be given a festival pass to identify you, some local maps and a festival booklet outlining all the films screening and where and when they can be seen.

Depending on the festival, you will then either be left to your own devices or be introduced to a festival rep who will act as a kind of assistant, letting you know of special events

When it comes to books on festivals there is really only one – Chris Gore's 'The Ultimate Film Festival Survival Guide', currently in its second edition. Most useful is its detailed info on each festival, including info on hotels, maps, even profiles. Gore is a self confessed festival veteran who has first hand experience so you know you aren't reading what the tourist information kiosk would give you. Detailed. Authoritative. Humorous.

Occasionally you will get a festival that REALLY wants your movie but frankly, you just can't be bothered (maybe you are maxed out on credit cards, moved on to better things or are working on your next script). Don't decline the invitation, charge them $400 as a fee, and they pay all expenses. It's free money and you might win an award!

Film Festival budget for 1 print and 6 Festivals

Film Festival Budget	Festival 1	Festival 2	Festival 3	Festival 4	Festival 5	Festival 6
Print	£800	£0	£0	£0	£0	£0
EPK (Beta dupe)	£10	£10	£10	£10	£10	£10
Paper press pack x 10	£10	£10	£10	£10	£10	£10
Shipping of print	£100	£0	£0	£0	£0	£0
Accomodation	£0	£0	£0	£0	£0	£0
Food	£50	£0	£50	£0	£50	£0
Fun	£50	£50	£50	£50	£50	£50
Taxi / Train to and from UK airport	£50	£50	£50	£50	£50	£50
New clothes	£150	£0	£0	£0	£0	£0
Application fee	£25	£15	£40	£0	£0	£15
10 VHS screeners	£10	£10	£10	£10	£10	£10
3000 Flyers	£500	£0	£0	£0	£0	£0
3000 Post cards	£200	£0	£0	£0	£0	£0
1000 Posters	£1,500	£0	£0	£0	£0	£0
5 x Radio CDR EPK	£5	£5	£5	£5	£5	£5
	£3,460	£150	£225	£135	£185	£150

	Total	£4,305

This budget assumes a number of things and is only for the attendance of six festivals, roughly six months to a year's worth of festival circuit. It is for one print only, should you need to attend more consecutive festivals you may need to produce more prints, each of which will cost anywhere between £700-£1k. The majority of the spend is up front as once you have your materials and a print and the first shipping bill paid, it all becomes very cost effective. Clearly if you are submitting to a video festival with a tape (DV, DigiBeta or DVD) you can deduct the costs of making a print.

Many of the publicity materials such as flyers, posters, and post cards will also be used in other areas such as the domestic theatrical and video release and international sales. Remember prints, especially festival circuit prints, have a shelf life. After five or ten festivals your print could easily be worn out and a new one may need to be struck.

and screenings. Most of the time you will be given an itinerary which will include evening parties, screenings of your film, (which you will be expected to attend), Q&A sessions and more often than not at least one formal sit-down dinner with the festival organisers, local dignitaries and one or two other film makers or attending actors. Depending on the festival, there will be anywhere between a handful and a roomful of film makers in attendance with whom you may well form allegiances, make friends and get drunk.

Prints moving around the festival circuit are subject to enormous wear and tear. You have no idea how a projectionist will treat it and more often than not your print will return a few frames shorter than when you sent it out. This is because prints are shipped in rolls, usually five, joined together into one roll for projection, then cut up back into five at the end. How sure are you that the underpaid and overworked projectionist is going to lovingly disassemble your print - or are they going to just hack it apart?

Make first contact

As soon as you arrive at the festival, it's a good idea to track down the press department where you can let them know of your complete availability for all forms of press, you can quiz them about the possibilities of fly-postering for your film and also leave them with additional press packs and posters. Some festivals will look down on vandalistic style fly postering, whereas others will encourage it as it simply serves their end (to get as many paying bums on seats as possible). You'll probably spend one or two evenings with smaller posters and flyers, a staple gun and car, driving around the town . . .

On a technical note, it is always worth dropping by the projectionist and checking that they know in which aspect ratio your film is to be presented. Also ask them to turn up the volume, I have never been to a screening where the sound is too loud, but I have been to plenty where it's been too quiet.

Why am I REALLY here?

Whilst attending the festival, aside from having lots of fun, there are two basic agendas. One is to artistically support the film, the other to pursue the commercial potential of your film and yourselves as valuable talent.

Artistically supporting the film will generally be the job of the director, and will entail doing newspaper, magazines, TV, radio interviews etc, introducing each and every screening of the film and doing a Q&A session at the end. Your introduction can set the tone and your nervousness on stage with the spotlight on you will endear the audience to you, so camp it up *'Yeah baby!'* The Q&A is an opportunity to perform and be seen by the talent spotters in the audience.

Think of your Q&A as something akin to stand up comedy and not film school lectures. This is a business of entertainment. Following the Q&A, audience members sometimes like to come up to you, congratulate you and offer you their comments as to what they liked or disliked about the film.

At the same time as the director prancing about on stage and generally camping it up, the producer should be working hard with the festival to target potential distributors, TV reps and agents etc, who are in attendance and to convince these people to go and watch your film. In advance you might want to have called the major players (assuming this is a major festival) such as Miramax etc., to see who, if anyone, is attending, and get their cell phone number.

If you are lucky enough to convince a distributor to attend a screening, you have a golden opportunity to go out for dinner after it and attempt to cut a deal whilst the movie is still fresh in their minds and goodwill is at it's highest. This doesn't happen too often but it can happen. Only once have I managed to cut a deal directly following a screening at a festival (and then no middleman could take an unwelcome cut).

There will be a number of screenings, usually between two and five, starting anywhere between 8 am and midnight. Often the festival organisers will schedule these screenings over three to five days so that you, the film

Kelly Clement
Taos Talking Picture Festival

'As the director of programming at the Taos Talking Picture Festival (New Mexico, USA) I am looking for many things in a film, but most important, be it documentary, animation, experimental or drama is good storytelling. The festival is basically non competitive, but we do offer one prize which is quite unique – five acres of land here in Taos! The philosophy behind this idea was to give film makers land so they would always have a place where they could come to be creative. In essence to nurture a creative community of film makers.

Most of the films we present are on 35mm, and while we have always screened video, there is a very definite trend toward digital movies. The number of DV submissions is skyrocketing. This is a very exciting democratisation of film making, but while everyone thinks they can make 'Citizen Kane' on their G4, the reality is often a long way from that. When film makers shoot film they only have one or two shots at getting it right, so thought and preparation goes into it. When shooting video you can shoot almost infinitely, so while the technology empowers almost anyone who wants to try to make a film, it can also foster lazier film making – a fact that is reflected in many of the submissions that I look at.

My advice to the DV film maker is to pay attention to their craft. So much of what I see just isn't filmic in any way. Don't rush it. Film makers should give their projects the time that they need, and it will show in the work. www.ttpix.org

One off poster!

If you are attending a festival for the first time and you don't yet have any kind of distribution deal, nor do you have funds to print up loads of cool posters, you could make up one or two using your computer printer and a shareware program called Poster (www.postersw.com).

You'll still need to design your artwork in something like Photoshop and then bring it into Poster which will print it out onto loads of A4 sheets (the bigger the poster, the more sheets it will print onto). You'll then need to cut them up and stick them all together (ideally using Spraymount, not tape – see left) and voilà

, a poster for next to nothing! These posters don't look good in light boxes (the kind you find outside cinemas) as they are stuck together and the light shines through making it look a mess. You can also use your colour printer but don't use a high res dpi, just use the low res 300dpi to save print time. Remember, inkjets are more susceptible to water and splashes than laser printers (in black and white). If you are forced to use black and white, got for a stark and bold image that looks like it was designed for black and white and isn't just printed that way to save cash.

It's far from ideal but it might only need to be in prime position for a couple of days before you can take it down, bin it and print another!

maker, will be able to attend all of the screenings without having to give up two weeks of your life. They always think you are busy on your next project and don't realise that the festival is an opportunity to leave the country and the debt collectors behind.

Your presence, no matter how small or large the festival, should always be felt and your movie should always feel like a *MUST SEE*. You might want to consider hiring a professional publicist who will work aggressively on your behalf to place your movie at the top of the media coverage pile. It's a good idea if you manage to get into a festival such as Sundance, or Toronto (the 'A' list festivals) but for smaller ones you might well save the couple of grand it will cost you to hire such a pro. You can do much of it yourself, assuming you have the energy.

Spending your time zipping around the globe on someone else's account, attending festivals where you are worshipped as a talent to be reckoned with, and generally having a good time may sound like time well spent . . . But maybe you should be developing that new unputdownable screenplay and taking those meetings with the people with power whilst you are still a hot and relatively unknown property.

You might want to throw a party to introduce your film, but that is also expensive. You'll need to hire a venue, organise tickets and invites (and you only landed yesterday!) and worse still you'll need to pay for the booze (unless you get a sponsor) as you just can't ask people to buy their own drinks, especially the journalists.

Final thoughts on your way home

After all the screenings are completed you'll be whisked off to the airport and flown home and the print will stay put awaiting shipment to the next

Q & A session tips

When your film is screened at the festival, it's expected that you'll introduce it and hold a Q&A session after. These sessions are important as distributors and agents (who may be in the audience) can gauge your enthusiasm, talent and performance abilities.

1. Be nervous. You may naturally be on the edge of your seat, but if you are not, fake it. Audiences will warm to you if they feel you are terrified.

2. Thank the audience for coming and see your movie, and remind them that this a very special screening for you as it is . . . the premiere, this country's premiere, the first time you've seen it with such a big audience, etc.

3. Camp it up! Not that I'm saying that you should say 'fiddlesticks' every third word, but your cultural heritage is part of what makes you and your film interesting.

4. If you are really bold, as you climb onto the stage to introduce the film, trip up and stumble.

5. When doing the Q&A session, kick off as soon as you can. Ask the organisers to start as soon as the credits roll by dipping the music and bringing the house lights up. You don't want to let any of the audience leave as the credits are rolling.

6. Don't be an artist. There's no greater way to bore an audience stupid than to reflect on the navel-staring you performed during the 'conceptualisation of your allegorical story of the inner child's journey from the womb to the grave . . . blah blah blah', BORING! Tell them a funny story.

7. If an audience doesn't start asking questions, launch yourself into some entertaining anecdotal but relevant story.

8. Have a list of questions and give it to the organisers who can sit in the audience. They can then ask questions to which you have amazingly good and amusing answers.

9. Keep answers short and sweet. If you have inexperienced actors with you, beware, they may ramble.

10. Ask audiences to tell their friends about the next screening, remembering to give them times, dates and venues. Also, tell them you'll be in the bar outside should anyone want to chat. It's a good way to get free drinks and sometimes a free dinner.

Dealing with the press

1. Every festival will have a press secretary whose job it is to market the festival. Marketing your film is a bonus by-product of marketing the festival. As soon as you get to the festival, make yourself known to the press officer and enthuse about any marketing opportunities.

2. Understand that it is your job to market both the festival and your film.

3. When doing any TV or Radio, repeatedly mention the name of the festival, the name of your film and try to mention screening times, dates and venues.

4. When doing TV and Radio, try and keep your answers and comments short, to the point and sweet. They are looking for soundbites.

5. Arm yourself with press packs, CDs with photos, EPKs, CDs with music and sound clips (for radio), posters etc. Have these to hand at all times as you never know when the next marketing opportunity will arise.

6. When doing interviews for print, the atmosphere can be very laid back and often takes place over drinks. Remember, there is no such thing as 'off the record' so if you don't want it to go in print then don't say it.

7. Ask for copies of all press and chase people as they probably won't send it without being reminded . . . get their business card so you can send them that e-mail when you get home next week. Give them your business card too.

8. Finally, and most importantly, always be complimentary about other films and film makers and be consummately enthusiastic about your movie and film making in general.

REMEMBER – At all costs, always say what you want to say, no matter the question!

Checklist – Don't forget your toothbrush!

What you'll need to take with you to a festival . . . The usual stuff . . .

☐ Clothes, suitable for the climate.
☐ Toothbrush and toiletries (although you'll probably come home with more than you took, care of your hotel).
☐ Passport – check one month before going, it might have run out.
☐ Local cash and credit cards.
☐ Local translation book.
☐ All the other stuff you take on a normal holiday.

The not so usual stuff . . .

☐ Backpack – you spend a lot of time walking around with 'stuff'.
☐ Tux or posh frock and shoes for that gala premiere.
☐ Flyers, as many as you can carry.
☐ Medipack with aspirin etc. – party, party, party!
☐ Laptop – keep working on that new project whilst looking out at the inspiring mountains / sea / ghetto etc.
☐ Mobile phone for emergencies. Call your provider to switch on international roaming before you go. Leave switched off and check once a day.
☐ Posters – ideally ten in a cardboard roll to keep them in good condition.
☐ EPK – on Beta, may need NTSC depending on where you are going.
☐ Press packs – the festival can copy them so make sure you have at least one excellent quality copy.
☐ Camera – so someone can click away when you go up to collect an award (hopefully!)
☐ CDR – with PDF of press pack and hi res. stills, ideally ten.
☐ VHS / DVD – to can give to journalists / distributors who didn't make the screening.
☐ Business cards.

festival. Hopefully, the experience will have left you wiser, with greater insight into the strengths and failings of your film. You might have some good reviews and press quotes, plus an address book full of phone numbers of new pals (who you will inevitably bump into at a festival on the other side of the planet six months later). You'll also have greater confidence in your public speaking abilities, oh and a whopper of a hangover.

Upon reflection . . . Prior to completing your film, you will have started thinking about film festivals and perhaps may have even applied to some. Some people may advise you that this is a good plan. I do not. Complete your film in as much time as it takes, never rush to make it to a festival, there is always next year. The only important thing is to make the best film possible with the limited resources that you have. One cheap resource you will have in abundance is your own time. Hopefully this extra time will give you the chance to reflect upon your film and make changes in the edit so that you maximise the potential of the story you conceived, the rushes you shot and your initial aspirations when you decided to make the film in the first place. You can't rush genius, doubly true when you ain't even a genius!

It's been mentioned several times in this book . . . but hey, let's drum it home. Always be prepared to answer that simple yet defining question *'so what do you want to make next?',* especially when asked by a rep from some company like Miramax. The process of making your film will have left you close to being comatose, but aside from finishing your film (a feat in itself), you need to have developed your next film! Should you then meet that all important person at a festival who asks you *THE* question, not only do you have an answer, you have a script in your backpack.

Press
and Publicity
Blueprint

Press equals success. It doesn't really, but to most people, if you are getting press then you are a success. The problem facing new film makers is that they have run out of money, energy and perhaps even karma! Add the fact that they don't like their movie as it's not what they set out to make, they have seen it countless times, and you have a recipe for complacency. Put all these feelings behind you and remember why you decided to make your film in the first place. Your time in the spotlight is fast approaching . . .

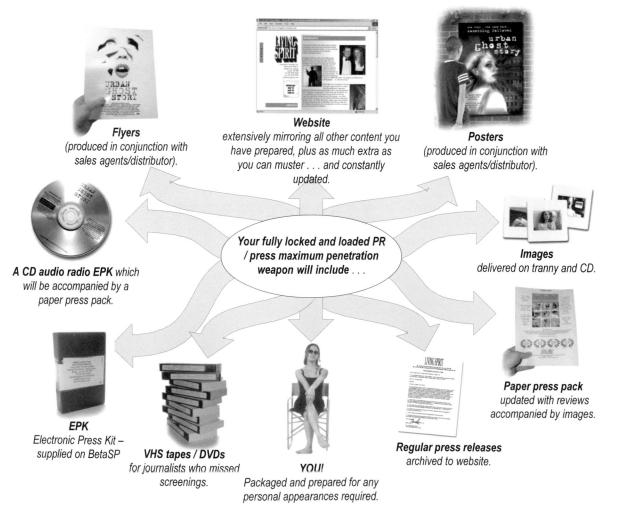

Flyers
(produced in conjunction with sales agents/distributor).

Website
extensively mirroring all other content you have prepared, plus as much extra as you can muster . . . and constantly updated.

Posters
(produced in conjunction with sales agents/distributor).

A CD audio radio EPK which will be accompanied by a paper press pack.

Your fully locked and loaded PR / press maximum penetration weapon will include . . .

Images
delivered on tranny and CD.

EPK
Electronic Press Kit – supplied on BetaSP

VHS tapes / DVDs
for journalists who missed screenings.

YOU!
Packaged and prepared for any personal appearances required.

Regular press releases
archived to website.

Paper press pack
updated with reviews accompanied by images.

Press and Publicity

People won't go and see your movie if they don't know it exists. The two primary ways of reaching your audience are through advertisements (which you can't afford) and through the media such as print reviews, radio features, magazine interviews etc, all of which are free! Managing a successful press campaign is all about planning, being fully prepared, persistence, and more often than not, performance.

When you conceive of your project, you need to start thinking . . . straight away . . . about the press. Most new film makers make the understandable mistake of believing that all press is good. Whilst true to some extent, you have to temper the statement by adding . . . *as long as you control when it appears.* If you are going to get a full page feature in a national newspaper, you want that to happen in the week that your film is released so that if anyone reads about it, they can actually put some money in your pocket by either going to the cinema or renting it on video etc.

Your press story(s), whatever you have concocted to get that one page in the national newspaper, will only be reported once. You cannot go back and give them the same story and expect the same kind of coverage a year later (when your movie is in theatres), so don't blow your opportunities too early.

If you have one mantra for your press and publicity, it should be . . .

'I WILL BE PREPARED AND REHEARSED AND WILL STRIKE ONLY AT THE CRITICAL MOMENT.'

Anchor

Central to the publicity for your film will be your website. It's not that your website is an amazing PR tool, it's just that it is an excellent delivery mechanism for both the press and media, and also interested parties such as cast, crew, investors and the general public. Over time your website will

'There's an old saying that money teaches the price of everything and the value of nothing. It is a maxim that's particularly apt when it comes to buying advertising: you know which spots are the most expensive but the real skill lies in finding the most effective.'
FT 24 July 2001

Press flow chart

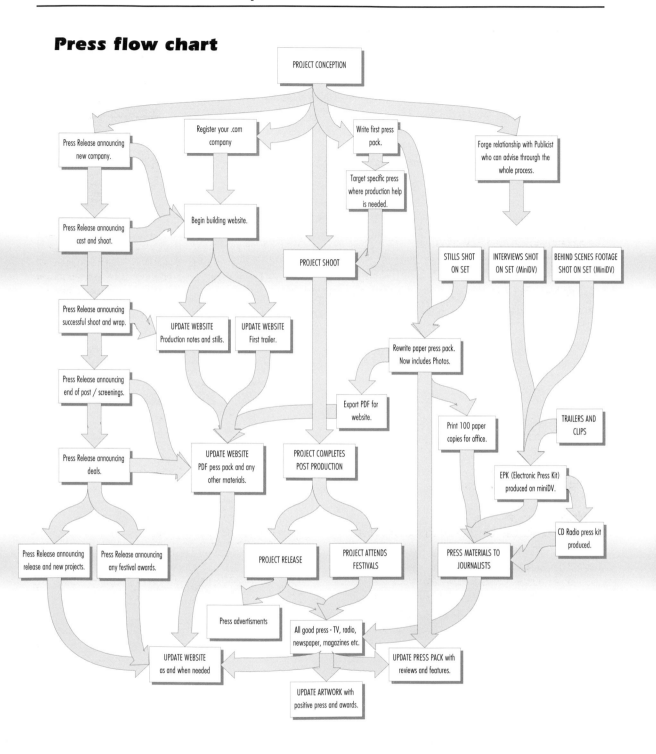

form a kind of anchor for your press. Whatever happens in the real world will be duplicated, promoted and archived on your site.

Rather than going into a huge tutorial of how to build a website and mindful of the fact that technology is ever changing, we will skip much of it here. Go and buy the best and simplest book about building websites and registering domains etc.

Register your *.com* or *.co.uk.* Now you are the proud owner of a slice of cyber space real estate. It will take you some time to get your website up and running, so for now you might want to put a simple *'about my company'* page up with details of the project and contact information.

Bring in the big guns

The professionals in the PR world are *publicists*. These are people who spend all day on the phone, taking meetings, sending out press materials and forging relationships with members of the media so that they can get the highest possible profile for their clients. Normally you would be their client but you don't have a budget, so you can't afford them. Develop a relationship with an established PR agency who is willing to take you under their wing because they like you or your film, and ask if they might help you with a strategy and possible contacts. You will do all the donkey work and they will act as an occasional advisor/mentor.

Ideally, find a junior publicist who needs to cut their teeth on a project whose success or failure will not reflect upon the company for which they work. Ask them to act as your publicist. Whatever money you can afford to spend on a publicist will be money well spent.

Value for money

Without doubt, the best and cheapest asset that your press campaign can offer is you YOU, yes YOU! An intelligent, well rehearsed, clear and concise, witty yet insightful, enthusiastic and positive film maker makes for compelling interviews. Of course, you may not believe you have all, or any (!) of these qualities. If not, you need to work on it. No one on the planet will sell your film with as much passion and energy as you will.

The Writers' and Artists' Yearbook is a cheap and essential source of contacts within the media. It covers newspapers, magazines, radio, TV, plus much more. All with names, addresses, e-mails and contact numbers.

LIVING SPIRIT   PRESS RELEASE

● Living Spirit Pictures Limited, Ealing Film Studios, Ealing Green, Ealing, London, W5 5EP ●
● Tel 020 8758 8544 ● Fax/Messages 020 8758 8559 ● mail@livingspirit.com ● www.livingspirit.com ●

FOR IMMEDIATE RELEASE

THE GUERILLA FILM MAKERS HANDBOOK TOPS 1000 COPIES A MONTH

Date 19/02/97

Ealing Film Studios, West London... 'the ultimate guide to UK film production...' is exceeding both the publishers and authors expectations. Sales are running at over 1000 copies per month - 'It's an astonishing figure, considering it's essentially a text book' commented Jane Greenwood of Cassell Plc, the book's publishers.

'I always knew it would do well', comments Chris Jones, co-author 'because it's the kind of book you can pick up, open at any page and start reading - I haven't yet met a film maker who can put the book down without wanting to buy a copy!'

The Guerilla Film Makers Handbook is an easy to access book about making films in the UK. It contains three major sections, The Anthology of a Movie where the whole production process is broken down and demystified, Case Studies where producers tell the sordid and often hilarious truth about how they got their movie made, and the Toolkit, a collection of documents needed to make a film (plus a directory of contacts).

Comments co-author Genevieve Jolliffe - 'Having made two low budget feature films, we felt we understood the whole process pretty well, certainly better than most producers, both new and veteran. We decided the best approach would be to ask experts in all areas of film production the ten questions to which every producer ought to know the answers. We discovered very quickly that not only did most producers not know the answers, but they didn't know the questions in the first place. That's why they can't put the book down!'

'The approach was important too, with every page containing pictures and diagrams, without a descent into the mindless techy type approach that bores most creative people to tears' remarks Chris Jones, 'we've even seen a massive increase in traffic on our Internet web site. It's gone up from 100 visitors a week to over 4000! There's an awful lot of interested people out there'
The Guerilla Film Makers Handbook also contains the legal contracts required to make a film and has an optional software toolkit.

Chris Jones and Genevieve Jolliffe are the co-directors of independent feature film company Living Spirit Pictures. If you would like any more information, please call Chris Jones on 0181 567 5295

Contact
Living Spirit Pictures, Ealing Film Studios, Ealing Green, London, W5 5EP
Tel 020 87588544 Fax 020 8758 8559
mail@livingspirit.com www.livingspirit.com

END OF RELEASE

Get into the habit of writing great press releases and send them out via mail, fax and e-mail.

A 12-year-old on drugs is far from fiction

TRUTH ... Heather believes the film is based on fact Picture: BRIAN LOGUE

By BRIAN BEACOM
Showbiz Writer

TEEN actress Heather Ann Foster has landed a major role in a new movie playing a TWELVE-year-old who regularly pops ecstasy.

But the Lenzie-born schoolgirl reckons producers of the new film, *Urban Ghost Story*, weren't being sensationalist in portraying the lead character as a juvenile druggie.

Heather, now fourteen, is cast in the lead role as Lizzie in the new movie alongside Jason Connery and James Cosmo. Her ...

TEEN ACTRESS HEATHER KNOWS NEW MOVIE IS CLOSE TO TRUTH

there are other reasons.
There's no doubt the screenplay will be accusing the ecstasy epidemic sweeping the country ...

But Heather believes based on fact. She points countless numbers of that age taking the d...

"A 12 year old taki... uncommon, there isn't a ...

"It's not ... goes on in ... more hidde... But it ...

she had a part in *Taggart* ...

Local press played key roles in the success of Urban Ghost Story *at the UK box office. My home town of Wigan was targeted for the 'local boy does good' angle. Lead actress 13 year old Heather Ann Foster, who was from Glasgow (where the film is set) also helped by stirring up the controversial theme of young people and drugs, a theme touched on in the film. This helped in achieving tremendous box office in Glasgow.*

At all times attempt to control the media. Easiest to control is the 'when it is said . . .', less easy to control is the 'what is said . . .' Maximise your press by co-inciding it, wherever possible, with the release or particular event you want to publicise. There is no point getting great reviews for a film to be released in three months time, or worse, last month and now it is gone! Most publications have 'lead time', which may mean magazines work three months in advance where some papers may work three days in advance.

LEAD TIMES
MAGAZINE FEATURES
3 MONTHS
MAGAZINE REVIEWS
2 MONTHS
NEWSPAPER SUPPLEMENT
1 MONTH
NEWSPAPERS
1 WEEK

You also have greater access than anyone to the *how, why, where* and *how much* of your project. Plus you know all the good *behind the scenes* stories. In short, YOU are the headline act! (along with the film of course).

First things first

You've bought your .com. You've bought your limited company. You've decided on your project. It's about time the world knew about it! It's time to write your first press release.

Press releases are the most common and simple delivery mechanisms used by the media business. Generally, a press release is a single side of paper announcing a story . . . *'Company A employs twelve new staff in major expansion . . .', 'Company B secures movie rights to exciting novel . . .'*, or in your case it will probably read *'MyNewCompany announces director and writer hired for exciting new British movie . . .'* and the release will go on to dangle some carrots in front of the press.

Who do you send it to?

Targeting your press release(s) is very important as there is no point sending a release to *Electronics Weekly*. In the first instance, you are going to look for the trade press such as *Screen International, Moving Pictures, Variety* etc. Then you might widen your releases to reach the consumer magazines such as *Empire, Total Film* and *Film Review*. Finally and close to the release of your film you will widen yet further seeking more personal stories about you or the film and hit anything from *Woman's Own* (as your film is about a young single mum), *UFO Magazine* (as your film is about UFOs) or mags like *Elle, Cosmo, GQ* and *Loaded* where you will be the story.

Of course, being a start up company and having no established talent attached, no one is going to write anything based on your initial press release. That's OK because this first release is all about getting out there, learning how to write a release and letting the editors know that you exist. For now, send it out and archive the release on your website. Who knows, it may get reported anyway!

Local boy does good

One area where you will get a lot of positive press coverage is in local newspapers. The local press is excellent for boosting morale or getting press which you can show to investors (which in turn excites them). Most of it though will help with production problems. This isn't so relevant if you are shooting in major cities such as London (as local press is kind of ignored), but if you are shooting in a smaller town, anyone who is interested in film making will get wind of your project through the local press and contact you. Whether you need a hundred teenage extras or a bakery to supply you with bread for the crew, the local press can help.

So press release number two might be *'Fledgling film company strikes deal with bakery . . . '* Attached to this release will be a glossy 10x8 photo of you stood outside the bakery, shaking hands with the owner.

If a local newspaper photographer comes to take a picture, you need to understand that they are not looking for a sophisticated film maker, all intellectual and thought provoking. No, they want film cans, baseball caps and clapper boards, so keep a few props to hand.

Approaching D-Day

As you get closer to the first day of the shoot your interest in the press will dwindle as more serious and compelling issues such as cast, location and script will be playing on your mind. Even so, send out a press release once you have locked your cast and started shooting. Again, it's unlikely this will be reported, but your existence will have begun to filter into the system. Archive your press release to your website (which by now should be fully up and running) and get on with making the best movie you can.

During the shoot, there are a number of press related things that you must shoot and record.

A picture says a thousand words

Most new film makers don't understand how important still photographs are to the success of their film. If there is one complaint I regularly hear from the press, sales and distribution, it's that the film makers don't have ANY good photographs.

Whether you hire a photographer, or you, or a member of your crew shoot them, you must take as many 35mm colour transparencies as you can. No one during the shoot will see the value in shooting these pictures. At best, taking pics will be considered a necessary evil, at worst, they will be refused and forgotten about.

The kind of pictures you are looking to get are shots of the actors on set, in costume, properly lit (no flash) and acting out a scene. Some will be group shots, others individual portraits. All are important. Ideally, you are looking for images that in some way capture the essence of your story. Later on down the line, when your film is reported upon, you will select one or two primary stills that will come to visually represent your film, so you want them to be good.

Occasionally, you may want to shoot one or two crew shots for more

Lisa Richards
The Associates PR

'There's a positive media bias towards cinema releases but with a low budget independent movie your options can be limited. With so many press screenings each week, getting your film seen can be difficult. Reviews are really important, particularly when there's no money to spend on a marketing campaign, so don't be too precious about only showing your film on the big screen and have tapes available. Even if you've got a 'great angle' you're unlikely to persuade magazines to write features about your film without seeing it.

It's disheartening if press screenings are poorly attended but on the positive side, a reviewer who spends hours in a screening room watching formulaic Hollywood blockbusters and then sees an entertaining, low-budget, inventive Brit film, even if it is on video, may be more inclined to write something positive. You can maximise this effect by having lots of information about the production available. Good stills are essential, and often overlooked when the budget is tight. If a picture editor has a great image from your film you could take precedence over a far bigger release.

When it comes to interviews, put yourself forward as well as your actors. You may not have made the greatest film ever but an in-depth conversation with a new film maker could be far more appealing than an utterly unrevealing Q&A with a famous Hollywood star. With this in mind, if you're working with a publicist make sure you sell yourself to them as well. They will have to persuade magazines to write about you and your film and need to be confident that you can shine in an interview.'

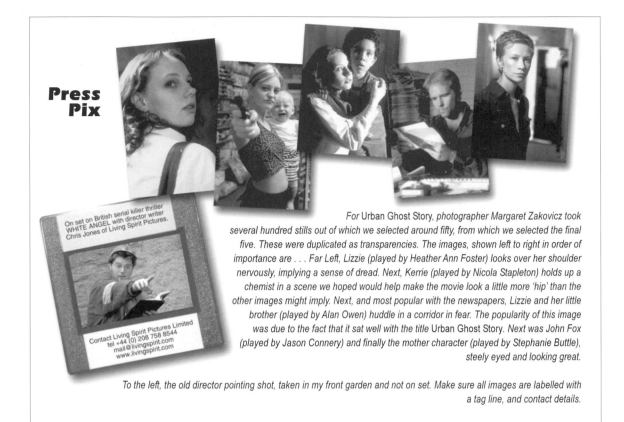

Press Pix

On set on British serial killer thriller WHITE ANGEL with director writer Chris Jones of Living Spirit Pictures.

Contact Living Spirit Pictures Limited
tel +44 (0) 208 758 8544
mail@livingspirit.com
www.livingspirit.com

For Urban Ghost Story, *photographer Margaret Zakovicz took several hundred stills out of which we selected around fifty, from which we selected the final five. These were duplicated as transparencies. The images, shown left to right in order of importance are . . . Far Left, Lizzie (played by Heather Ann Foster) looks over her shoulder nervously, implying a sense of dread. Next, Kerrie (played by Nicola Stapleton) holds up a chemist in a scene we hoped would help make the movie look a little more 'hip' than the other images might imply. Next, and most popular with the newspapers, Lizzie and her little brother (played by Alan Owen) huddle in a corridor in fear. The popularity of this image was due to the fact that it sat well with the title* Urban Ghost Story. *Next was John Fox (played by Jason Connery) and finally the mother character (played by Stephanie Buttle), steely eyed and looking great.*

To the left, the old director pointing shot, taken in my front garden and not on set. Make sure all images are labelled with a tag line, and contact details.

technical journals and publications. You'll also want the old *director directing* photograph too. This image is yet another one that somehow eludes most productions and is essential, especially for international film festivals. Considering the director is directing ten hours a day, probably for three or four weeks, it's astonishing that a production team couldn't get it together to capture just one moment. If you miss it, fake it. YOU ARE THE STORY!

Taking photos on a film set is like breaking up with your girlfriend/boyfriend. It's never a good time, so shut up and get on with it.

Handling your own marketing campaign is a graft but at the end of the day it's little more than researching who you should contact, making those calls, supplying the materials, chasing the article / feature, doing the interviews and buying the copy at the shop / videoing the programme off the telly.

Behind the scenes

Alongside the photographs, you're going to need some video footage for your EPK (Electronic Press Kit – see later). This footage can be shot on miniDV, using a good camcorder like the Canon XL-1 or the Sony VX 2000.

You're looking for several things . . . First, simple and steady shots of the cast and crew at work. Old favourites include the director shouting and pointing, the clapper-board

When being interviewed

1. Have a list of questions prepared which you can offer to the interviewer (who probably isn't prepared).

2. Most of the time you will be asked very similar questions. Be rehearsed with answers that are poignant, concise, profound, amusing etc. Ask to see the questions in advance, ideally faxed the night before.

3. If you are being recorded (opposed to live), pause before answering. This will give the editor a clear editing point.

4. Say the name of your movie and not simply refer to it as 'the film' or 'the movie'. If people don't know what the film is called, they won't go to see it.

5. Wear something interesting so that you will at the very least, stand out.

6. Some interviewers may have an axe to grind. If you don't want to answer, politely decline. Or you can simply launch into something that you want to talk about, namely, your movie. Watch politicians who are expert at not answering but sounding kind of like they did! Always stay cool and if caught off guard, pause and think before you answer.

7. Always have your stuff with you – press pack, stills, EPK, poster etc. You never know when they will come in useful.

8. If at all possible, be amusing. Anecdotal yet relevant stories are always a winner.

9. Ask the interviewer how long they want you to speak for. There is a world of difference between a fifteen-second soundbite and a five-minute interview, especially when you have to get the name of your movie across.

10. Prepare a business card with your name, how you would like to be credited and phone number. This way you can rightly complain if they spell your name wrong.

11. Don't be afraid of having words put into your mouth by the interviewer . . . Can you say it like this? . . . Use your brain though and don't say anything you feel uncomfortable with.

12. If you want it to stay out of the press . . . I slept with my lead actor . . . etc. then don't say it. Nothing is off the record.

13. Always be complimentary about other film makers and their films, and about the people you have worked with.

Perfect website

1. Register an easy to remember .com or .co.uk name.

2. Keep your website simple and fast loading. Resist the urge to use extensive flash content as this impresses no one. People are looking for a well designed, fast loading, intuitive site.

3. Don't use streaming video, or at the very least offer streaming video with the option to download entire movie files. If you only have streaming video, most users who have only a modem connection will watch your video at one frame every five seconds, which let's face it is not video! People will happily download 10mb if they get a higher resolution, very watchable clip or trailer.

4. Research and test extensively the best video compression technologies for your clips. Whether you choose Windows Media, Real Video, Quick time etc. Your goal is the largest frame size, with the highest frame rate, but . . . with the smallest file size! Not an easy task.

5. For your website pages, don't use black backgrounds with white text. Users who print out your pages will get blank sheets (white text doesn't print well on white paper!)

6. Think forward. Your website will grow quickly and in many directions. Be prepared for this growth.

7. Hire your brother-in-law's kid to do your site. You should be spending your time making your film, not managing your website. A techie teenager will probably do a better job too.

8. Check out the competition. Look at other websites and copy what you like.

9. Start a newsgroup. This is simply the best way to get information about your company and movie to anyone who is interested.

10. Remember you are marketing your company to consumers, but also to a few very important film people. Executives in Hollywood will research you and your company via the internet before taking a meeting.

Alan Morrison
Reviews Editor - Empire

'Don't think that magazines are there to serve film makers. Readers and sales figures always come first. If an editor thinks they'll shift more copies covering the new Tom Cruise film, you're going to be well down the pecking order. But staff on these titles are also film fans, so they'll have an interest in your work if you can find the right angle to pitch to them. Define that angle: the cast, a story quirk, production trivia, anything that sets your film apart.

You'd rather have your work seen on the big screen but with six or seven films released weekly, journalists have most evenings booked for screenings and commercial releases will take priority. Lunchtime slots might be better. Send in a tape/DVD and follow up with a call to check it was received. Don't be too pushy at this stage, but throw in some of your unusual facts. Call again in a few days to ask if it's likely to be covered and if any materials or info is needed. If an editor has a tape to hand it's amazing how much more likely it is to get in. A full press pack with stills and, vitally, sleeve artwork (for a video / DVD) will make life simpler from the magazine's point of view as it means fewer follow-up calls. If a published review is a no-no, ask if the journalist is willing to watch the film and send you some informal comments. If a slot comes up and they've already seen your film, then it's got a better chance of slipping in through the back door.

Be prepared to take it on the chin as you'll likely be judged on the same level as the blockbusters. Most reviewers do make allowances but if they're doing their job properly, their concern is whether or not the reader is getting their money's worth.'

clapping, the camera dollying etc. Shoot these sequences on a tripod making sure you hold the shot a few seconds longer than you think you need. Also turn off any image stabilisation that the camera may have, as this reduces picture quality. Do not use the 16:9 feature on your camera, shoot everything in 4:3. If you are clear and determined you can get all of these shots in a few hours. Don't shoot too much or you will end up with hours of rubbish. Select your shot and get it, then move on.

The final thing you need to acquire for your marketing arsenal are interviews with the primary cast and crew. Don't make the mistake of saying *'We don't have time to do the interviews now, so we will get the actors back after the shoot'* because you probably won't (they may have moved onto other projects, be unavailable, or worse still, you may have fallen out with them).

Again, these sequences can be shot on miniDV, but it is essential that you use a pro or semi-pro tie-clip microphone and don't rely on the mic attached to the camera. Shoot your interviews in a nice quiet place and wear headphones to make sure the sound is clear and bright. Interview the actors who play your primary characters and any famous actors who play any characters. Finally, interview the director.

Sorting the pieces

Once the shoot has finished and you have begun true post-production, you'll need to spend some time organising the press elements that you acquired during the shoot. First off, send out the obligatory press release announcing the successful completion of your shoot and archive to the website.

By now your stills photographer will have passed on several hundred transparencies. Go through these shots and select 50 of the best, including one or two of the crew and the obligatory directors shot. Put the rest in a folder and forget about them for now (you may never go back to them).

The 50 you have selected will form the movie image library for your PR campaign and will also be passed onto your sales agent to support international sales. Take these stills to a bureau and have all fifty scanned at a very high resolution and burned onto a CD-ROM. You can then view these 50 images on your computer and select the very best five images that represent your movie. Along with the *'director directing'* shot and one *'behind the scenes'* shot, take these seven slides to a bureau service and have them duplicated 100 times. This is expensive but unfortunately many magazines and newspapers still do not trust or understand digital content and you will need to supply them with slides. Put these 100 sets of 7 slides in a box and forget about them for now.

Go back to your CD-ROM with the 50 images and select 20 of the best, which will be uploaded to your website.

What is in the press pack?

1. Front cover

It should feature the title, tag line (in the case of White Angel that was . . . 'He Kills . . . She Kills . . . Together They're MURDER'), and a strong bold image, ideally the poster. Also, all the main credits as you would get on a movie poster, plus explicit contact details (inc phone, fax, mob, e-mail, website). If you have won any awards put them here, alongside any good quotes from other journalists.

2. Synopsis

You'll need two, the first about half a page, the second a couple of pages long. The first is more of teaser, much like the back of a video box, the second more in-depth and will be used by journalists who want to write about the film but maybe haven't seen it. Don't give away the end! You might ask a film maker friend to write these synopsis for you, as often you don't go for it, saying . . . 'I can't write that, it's too cheesy'. Cheese is your friend.

3. Cast and crew

Biographies and short quotes with the primary cast and crew. Quotes are needed so that journalists can pull them out of the press pack and add them to their text, thereby giving the impression that they actually asked the question. So keep the quotes juicy (you will probably write them, not the actors). Each person should get about half a page (All the main characters, any cameo stars, director, producer and writer at the least).

4. Prod. notes

This is kind of the story behind the making of the film. Remember you are writing this for the press so talk it up. This should be three or four pages long. You can add shots from your stills CD to break it up if you like. Again, add quotes . . . the director said 'I felt the theme of the movie was blah blah blah . . . '

5. Credits

You will also need to add a complete cast, crew and technical credits list here. You should already have this prepared from when you typed them out for the end roller in post production.

6. Additional notes

Not absolutely needed but anything that will help you get more coverage is good. The main theme of Urban Ghost Story was the question of whether poltergeists exist. So we wrote a couple of pages about famous cases and the theories for and against. This was picked up several times and used in features.

What is in the press pack?

7. Thumbnails

If you are supplying a CD with stills, you should print out a page of 'thumbnails' of the images. Some software like Thumbs Plus does this automatically. Explain exactly what is on the disk and in what format your photos are saved. The best formats are lightly compressed JPG (Jpeg) files and compressed TIFF files.

8. Reviews

If you have had any good reviews you can add them at the end. Make sure you get good clean scans of all the reviews and articles. Don't put reviews in that flag any serious weak points with your movie. Over time you will be able to add to these reviews as your movie attracts more and more press.

9. Accompanying CD

Along with your press pack you should supply a CD with images, Quicktime trailers, music and perhaps even combined with the radio EPK as a single disk. (in time this may all be combined as a DVD which will include everything. Clearly mark the CD, don't send it out blank or scrawled on with a black marker.

Online delivery

Paper press pack

This should be delivered as a PDF file. You can use Abobe tools to do this but they are expensive. PDF995 (free from www.pdf995.com) does the job very well. It acts like a printer, except instead of printing out pages, it saves a PDF file on your hard drive. It's simple, free and fast. You will need Acrobat Reader (The PDF reader free from Adobe) to read it.

Make free PDF's with pdf995, free from www.pdf995.com

Radio press pack

The audio files you created for you radio press pack can be converted into MP3 files and saved to your website. There are heaps of MP3 encoders for free download and you probably have one already! The movie clips, trailers and music should be encoded in stereo at 44.1khz, 16bit and at a 256kbps data rate. The interviews are the same except in mono. These files will be very big, maybe up to 50mb, but you can store them on the free webspace you got for free with your ISP package.

Musicmatch , free from www.musicmatch.com

Images

Each photo image to be included on your site should be saved as a very large JPEG. Typically, a file which is 1500x1000 pixels and 72dpi will create a 100k file (with medium compression). You'll also need a tiny 150x100 pixel thumbnail for viewing on your page. If bandwidth isn't too important to you, increase the physical dimensions of the image and not the compression quality. A bigger file with more (medium) compression is better than a smaller file with less (low) compression.

JPG compression settings in Photoshop. If you don't have photoshop, try Paint Shop Pro evaluation from www.jasc.com

EPK

Whilst it isn't possible to really deliver your EPK via your website just yet, in time it will happen. Prepare for this in your website design strategy.

PR and Publicity Budget

Publicity Budget	each	number of	total
Transparency scanning (50)	£2.00	50	£100.00
Transparency dupes (100 copies of 5 images at £1 each)	£5.00	100	£500.00
Press pack dupes (toner costs)	£0.50	100	£50.00
Sending 100 press packages (P&P)	£1.00	100	£100.00
VHS dupes	£3.00	20	£60.00
Flyers - hopefully paid for by Int Sales Agent	£0.00	0	£0.00
Posters - hopefully paid for by Int Sales Agent	£0.00	0	£0.00
CD Duplication (stock and labels only)	£0.50	100	£50.00
Transport for interviews	£100.00	1	£100.00
EPK Dupes from MiniDV to BetaSP	£20.00	5	£100.00
Website hosting and domain registration	£200.00	1	£200.00
Magazines in which you are featured (archive)	£2.50	30	£75.00
Phone	£150.00	1	£150.00
Total			£1,485.00
Publicist (optional) for one main event	£2,000.00	1	£2,000.00

The most expensive and annoying costs are the duplication of photos for stupid journalists who still don't understand the fact that you can send them a digital image. In time this is bound to change so you may well be able to simply drop that cost altogether. One area where you can save is by sending an SAE with all your releases and chasing them up. This is unusual but it is acceptable to request expensive photos to be returned. Forget about the paper press packs. The publicist is the only floating cost as it really is up to you whether you hire one or not. If you do, and £2k is a great deal, you will get amazing coverage. But you can do SO much on your own too, and maybe £2k is better spent elsewhere.

For Trannie dupes and scanning contact Joe's Basement Ltd, 113 Wardour St, London W1F 0UN. Tel: 020 7439 3210
For your video dupes contact Stanley Productions Ltd, 147 Wardour St, London, W1F 8WA. Tel: 020 7439 0311

Website overhaul

Now you need to embark upon a major website update. It's up to you how in depth you want to make your site, but if anyone is interested enough to come to your site to find out about you or your film it makes sense to give them something worth their trouble. We have worked very hard on our website at www.livingspirit.com to supply as much information as possible about our movies.

Big tease

During post-production, the thorny issue of the trailer will arise, primarily because people will keep asking you to see some of the movie. Rightly, you will resist the urge to show them the movie (you will won't you!) but you can satiate your urge to show off by cutting one or two promos and showing them instead.

The first promo you will edit will be three or four minutes long, an international sales promo, that will be pretty much a condensed version of the

Be prepared! Simple questions the press may ask . . .

Q – Why did you choose to make this film / story?

A – Try and find a human or intellectual answer to this. Don't just admit you wanted to make a film with fast women and fast cars . . . Surely you were trying to take the urban thriller genre into new territory by blah blah blah . . .

Q – What was the budget?

A – This one is tricky as distributors and audiences are fickle. A movie that didn't cost very much is a cheap movie, and who wants to buy or watch a cheap movie? Not that you can talk up the budget too much either. If you have made a commercial style movie, the question is best avoided, and at worst answered with the phrase 'It's low budget, and I can't say how much because of our investors . . . ' If you have made a more personal film that might find a discerning audience, don't be bashful and sing about how low your budget was. The discerning audience won't go away . . . (you hope).

Q – How did you get X in your film?

A – X being your biggest name. Be honest and sincere and attribute much of the success of your film to this person and their immense skills as an actor. It was a privilege.

Q – Is it hard to make a film in the British Film Industry / Can you comment on the current state of the film industry?

A – You have made your film outside of the industry as you have been proving yourself, now the phone is ringing off the hook! You are excited by the recent success of (insert brit movie here) as it shows that audiences want to see good quality, entertaining British films. It's an exciting time and you aim to be part of it.

Q – Where and how was it shot?

A – This is your cue to launch into . . . 'Well funny you should ask because . . . ' and recount some amusing and anecdotal story.

Q – Who are your influences?

A – Your cue to talk passionately about your lifelong love of movies, your first movie experiences (both making and watching) and how Jaws / Star Wars / Raging Bull / 8½ etc. changed your life forever.

Q – Isn't it hard for British films to get distribution?

A – Not that you have found, but then that may be reflected in the type of film you have made and just how much audiences in test screenings have loved it. So did the distributors and the cinema owners . . . In fact, everyone loves it!

Q – What is next?

A – You have several projects at the moment and Hollywood is seriously considering one, but you can't say any more as agents are involved and it is potentially a delicate time. But the apparent interest in your next film is a reflection of the success of your current film. Remember you are here to promote your current film, not wax lyrical about how you have this Oscar winning project for the future . . .

Q – Where is it playing? When is it out?

A – Even if they don't ask this, you give 'em the answer. The readers / viewers / listeners need to know the name of the movie, and where they can buy a ticket / rent it / buy it to keep etc. 'Oh and did I mention our website at www . . . !'

movie. This promo will never be seen by the general public and used exclusively for international sales.

The second promo should be a short and sweet 60-second teaser that you can compress and upload to your website. In due course, and closer to the completion of your film, you will also cut a new and fuller trailer which will also find its way to the website and hopefully cinema screens.

Paper press pack

You can use Microsoft Word to write your paper press pack, which can include images and funky layout if you wish. Once your first draft is completed, checked and double checked, you can save it, print out 100 copies, and export a PDF (Adobe Portable Document Format – see boxout) to include on your website. The 100 copies you've printed out will be given to journalists and interested parties whenever requested.

Occasionally you can update your press pack to include good reviews, good quotes, additional production notes etc. At the same time, get into the habit of updating your website too.

EPK

The electronic press kit is a videotape with shots from behind the scenes whilst making your film, loosely edited interviews with your primary cast and

Get into the habit of collating and archiving all your press coverage. That means buying copies of all your reviews and features in magazines and news papers. Cut them out, label them and stick them in your clippings book (ideally A3 in size) and stick them on your shelf. With TV features, ideally tape them onto MiniDV then edit them down and put back onto MiniDV. Always edit and archive as soon as you can. If you don't, you could end up with a huge pile of material and no real idea of when and where it all comes from. Don't underestimate how important this is, our press materials were recently pivotal in getting a USA permit to work, as it supported our claims that we were serious film makers.

So you want to place an Ad?

Paper Press	¼ b&w	¼ Col	½ b&w	½ Col
The Sun (National paper 1 day)	£10,020	£12,480	£19,873	£24,752
Daily Mail (National Paper 1 day)	£8,040	£11,580	£16,080	£23,160
Ealing Lader (Free weekly paper)	£7,541	£939	£1,503	£1,879
Gazette (Local paper, 35p weekly)	£785	£982	£1,571	£1,964
Empire Magazine (Monthly)	£1,050	£1,050	£2,000	£2,000
Time Out (London / weekly)	£940	£1,313	£1,769	£2,573
Radio	Number	Av.£ (each)	Spend	Listeners
LBC (London radio) (30 sec)	25	£50	£1,250	0.75m
Classic FM (national radio) (30 sec)	34	£1,132	£38,500	6.5m
Radio Clyde (local radio in Scotland)	40	£40	£1,600	1m
TV	Peak	Off Peak	Viewers (Peak)	Viewers (Off)
Carlton London (30 secs)	£30,000	£15,000	12m	0.5m

Anorexic budget – Most advertisement is out of your budget. However, radio ads do seem to be reasonable value for money. If you are going to do an ad, be bold and smack them in the face!

Next time you have the radio on and are doing something else, take note of how many ads you actually 'hear' and how many are filtered out by your brain. It is amazing just how few get through!

Radio delivery – You can produce your own 30 second commercial on your PC, with music, voice over and clips. This can be delivered to the station on CD and they will load it into their system . If there is any music included they are going to ask you for the paperwork to ensure that you have the right to use the composition and performance of musicians and composers. Speak to the in house producers at radio stations about the best way to make your commercial. The station is also going to check for what they call 'claims' . . . So you can't say 'the scariest movie ever' although you could say John Doe at the Evening Standard said 'the scariest movie ever'. **All prices are approx. and negotiable.**

Putting on the squeeze . . .

Putting video on the net requires a little technical knowledge, and to get the best results, a lot of trial and error. Video files, at full size and res, are HUGE. So you can't just put it on the internet as it would take days to download! Whatever clips you are putting on your website, you will need to compress them (a process where the video is examined by your computer and it removes, in varying degrees, information from the image to reduce size). The deal is simple, the more (higher) the compression, the smaller the file size, AND the poorer the image quality. Even the best compression techniques for say 'broadband' connections are still (circa 2002) poor and not suitable for watching a whole movie. But it is ideal for short clips such as your trailer . . .

Currently I would use Real Video as to my eye, it gives the best trade off between file size and image quality. To create your Real Video clips you can use free tools from Real (www.real.com), tools bundled with Premiere, or the best tool for the job (though it aint cheap) Media Cleaner Pro. It isn't just a matter of conversion though, you will need to experiment with frame rates (although I would always suggest keeping it at 25fps), file sizes, noise reduction etc, to get the best results from the smallest possible file.

If you have shot in 16:9 or 1.85:1 aspect ratio, make sure you crop out the black bars at the top and bottom of your screen. Retaining these bars simply adds about 30% more redundant image area, which means your files could be 30% bigger for no real reason!

Things to consider when compressing your video . . .

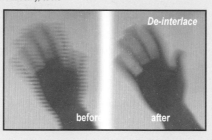

Pretty much every good editing package comes with a cool, wizard driven Real Media export facility, but for ultimate control, you should upgrade to the full Media Cleaner Pro.

Type of media – *Are you going to use Quicktime, Real Media, Windows Media, MPEG1 . . . ? Do tests to see which is best.*

Frames per second – *I wouldn't drop frames (to say 12 for instance), stay at 25fps.*

Noise reduction (NR) – *This is a cunning filter that will take your video and remove noise and grain whilst leaving the details. It doesn't always work and sometimes can lead to smudgy looking images, but when done right, it radically improves quality. Do tests.*

De-interlace – *You need to use this, especially if you have shot on video, or you will get weird jaggy artefacts. It will make your clip clearer and smoother (see left).*

Audio data rate – *How much of your file are you going to give over to the audio content? You can drop it from stereo to mono to save a little bandwidth here. Do tests but on the whole I would favour a slightly higher rate than suggested so that you have clean, clear dialogue and music.*

Video data rate – *This is the big one, where most of your bandwidth will be eaten up. Do tests to see what the results look like, then check the file sizes. You'll be amazed at the differences in file sizes. 10mb can often be reduced to 3mb with just a few tweaks. I find Real Media files encoded at around 300kbps and at 25fps to be very watchable.*

Image size – *Just how big will the dimensions of your frame be? The smaller the frame, the smaller the file. You can resize the clip on playback so people can watch it full screen even if the frame is only 320x240 pixels for instance. Test test test!*

Meta data – *This is a bit of text that is encoded into the file that will display in the playback window (usually the clip name and copyright owner).*

Codec – *This is the type of compression algorithm (rocket science alert!) that is used to compress your video. Do tests, research on the web. Look at other files you download and see what they used.*

Easy video streaming with Real Media

DIY Streaming

Streaming is the current buzzword, the ability to watch clips in real time as they download . . . But it assumes your viewers have a fast enough connection (broadband at least). So offer both, Broadband and download for watching later.

On your website you might have a directory called clips in which a number of clips reside. Lets say you have a real media file called TRAILER.RM which is your movie trailer. You can have a hyperlink to this file so that if anyone clicks on it, it will download to their hard drive and they can watch it when it has downloaded later.

You could then have a second hyperlink which links to a simple text file called TRAILER.RAM. This file tells the clip to play as it is downloading so that folk who have a fast enough connection can watch it straight away.

To write your own RAM file open Notepad (or another text editor) and type (all on one line) . . .

```
http://www.mywebsite.com/clips/TRAILER.RM?
                            mode="compact"
```

(where you insert your own website name etc.) Save this file as TRAILER.RAM into the clips directory of your website and set up a hyperlink to it. If anyone clicks on this second hyperlink it will start to play the clip immediately.

Urban Ghost Story Trailer
(Download 1.7mb)
(Broadband Streaming)
What did Lizzie Fisher bring back from the other side when she was revived at the scene of her accident?

---

crew, clips from the movie and any trailers you have. The whole tape should run for anywhere between 20–30 minutes and each section and clip should be clearly identified, labelled and have a timing in minutes and seconds.

The *behind the scenes* shots and interviews can contain normal audio but the clips and trailers should be included twice, the first pass with stereo sound, the second pass with split audio (mono effects on one track and mono dialogue on the other track – this is a music and effects mix (M&E) for broadcasters, especially in foreign territories, so that they can add their own dialogue). You will not be able to produce your full EPK until you have completed post-production as you simply won't have all the elements ready.

The best way to deliver your EPK is on BetaSP videotape, although in time we will see a convergence of a single press kit on DVD including the full video EPK, the radio EPK (see later), the paper press kit, stills and perhaps even the music score. If you are going to use the music score you must ensure that you have acquired the relevant rights from the composer and the performers.

The beauty of an EPK is that broadcasters get to use FREE material from which they can edit a short feature, and you get your film publicised on TV for FREE. No one pays, you just have to get them the tape at the right time. Anyone who has a cable or satellite movie channel will be used to these little production featurettes that tend to appear between movies.

Remember to consider that your EPK may well make it to foreign shores such as the USA, where the TV standard is NTSC. You may need to do a systems transfer version for this. Your paper press pack should be written and formatted for printing on Letter sized paper for America (8.5 inch by 11 inch) which will also print out conformably on UK A4 paper (8.27 inch by 11.69 inch). Remember this especially when making your PDF file or the Americans will get press packs where the last two lines will drop off the end of the paper!

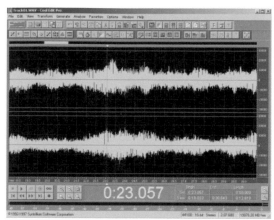

Don't forget about the radio. It's often listened to passively – you don't need to switch it on and concentrate (like TV) or pick it up and flick (like magazines). It's also listened to whilst travelling or in the work place. Use your sound editing software on your computer to record, edit, and then burn to CDR an extensive radio press pack and you will have something that not even the biggest promotional campaigns usually have! Local radio can be especially cost effective.

Occasionally a radio station may request support material but there is no time to send a CD. MP3 files encoded at 128kbps, 441.khz and 16bit stereo are ideal. You can e-mail them or having them ready and waiting on your ever useful website. Remember, if you don't have any good interviews on tape, interview yourself and tell those great stories!

It's on the wireless

Alongside the EPK, you should create a CD audio radio press kit. Most people don't bother with this, which is the primary reason why you should! Using software like Cool Edit Pro (PC) create a number of audio files . . . These should include . . .

1. The audio to the trailer(s)
2. The audio for three movie clips
3. The audio for the interviews with primary cast and crew.
4. One or two music tracks which have been composed for the film (check with composer).

You might want to augment these interviews with a much longer interview with the director as this will give the radio broadcasters much more to play with. You can record these interviews at home as long as you have a good microphone and sound card in your computer, and a quiet sound deadened space in which to record it (use duvets draped on walls and furniture to deaden sound).

Once you have edited all the tracks, remembering to keep everything loose so that they can tighten and re-edit wherever they want to do so, you can use your CD burner to make 100 copies. These will be sent out, along with an explicit and detailed track list explaining what is on the CD and a copy of the paper press pack, to radio stations when the film is released.

Persistence pay off

Upon completing post-production, it's time to send yet another press release announcing the *successful completion of post-production*. By now you should have had at least one or two phone calls from journalists who want to know more about this persistent little company that keeps sending press releases to them. As usual, archive your press release to your website.

Now that the movie is completed you'll be attempting to attract distributors, sales agents and be courting and courted by film festivals. Hopefully you will attend a few festivals and start to get good reviews which you will build into your website and press pack. If you're lucky enough to win an award then of course send out a press release and add the little fig leaf clip art with *'winner of . . . '* to the cover of your press pack. You may also add any good press quotes and fig leaf 'awards' to your poster artwork if timing works out.

Sending out

After speaking to editors, researchers and journalists, make sure you always do what you say you will. Always send out press packs and materials by first class mail. Sometimes journalists will come to you, but more often you will go to them. Before meetings listen to their show or read their magazine so you have a full appreciation of where they will be coming from.

Buy a copy of the *Writers' And Artists' Yearbook* and start approaching magazines and publications. And be creative! For *Urban Ghost Story* we came up with the the idea that Genevieve (the director) was 'psychic', which managed to pull several features in!

Not everyone understands computers. Leave a copy of your press pack on your computer desktop. You never know who you will need to ask to print out a copy whilst you are at a film festival or away and remember, it can't wait till you get back!

Think big and approach everyone*. Spend time in a big newsagents and draw up a long list of magazines and newspapers (writing down their phone numbers from the inside cover so you don't need to buy the magazine). Look through the radio listings and find specific shows that cover film. Failing that, blindly approach every radio station in the country offering an interview / feature / review. Do the same with TV, you'll be amazed how many late night shows will cover a film release.

*Please read the section on releasing your film for information about co-ordinating with the SFD and setting up screenings for journalists.

Don't underestimate the cost of sending out press packs and always chase editors and journalists to return those expensive trannies. Always send press materials out promptly, use new padded envelopes, clearly and well labelled. Check you have spelt the person's name correctly. This is the first impression you are giving.

Sales and Distribution Blueprint

Shooting People

The fastest growing UK online film makers' community
www.shootingpeople.org

Sales & Distribution

Sales and distribution encompass a huge area of the film making process. Often misunderstood or simply ignored by new film makers, it's the area in which it is hardest to succeed. Anyone can make a movie, but can you sell it? Or more to the point, is it sellable? The sales business is split into two rough areas, domestic (that's your home country, but many US companies think you mean America when you say domestic) and International (the rest of the world). Within these two distinct areas there are a number of rights available.

Theatrical release
Your movie is screened in cinemas, typically indie theatres and smaller chains, although multiplexes do take low budget indie pics. Expensive and most often loses money.

VHS and DVD rental
The first line of real revenue if you can get your movie into the video shops. Video rental is split between majors such as Blockbuster, and minor chains and individual independent shops. Typically happens six months after the theatrical release (if one took place).

Non theatrical
The peculiar market of oil rigs, airlines and ferries. Who'd have thought it but these markets can generate significant revenue streams. Typically happens at the same time as, or before, the video rental release.

VHS and DVD retail
Your movie goes on sale in high street shops, video shops and online stores. Typically takes place six months after the video rental release.

Video on demand
Currently delivered by services such as Sky TV, along with a series of test companies. Inevitably, video on demand will replace video rental entirely. It's just when and who will be the market leaders. Typically takes place around the video retail release.

Pay TV
Services such as Sky or the FilmFour channel who offer subscription movie services. Typically happens some time after the video retail release and represents a good sale if you can get it as there are no revenues, just a one off payment.

Free TV
All the terrestrial TV channels and many of the cheap or free satellite / cable / digital channels. Typically takes place six months after the pay TV release. Again, no royalties, just one payment.

Future formats
Impossible to predict with accuracy but there is a feeling that theatrical release will go digital, opening up possibilities for micro budget movies that couldn't previously afford a 35mm transfer, video on demand will replace all video rentals and retail will be dominated by DVD.

Distribution Sales

The Deal Maker

The sales agent is the company or person who will sell your film abroad. It's much like any other agent – they put the product out in the market place, hype it up, market it, field offers and hopefully close deals. They should then manage the distribution of all the film elements to the people who are buying the film, and distribute any remaining revenues to the film maker. It sounds easy, but in practice, a plethora of problems often occur leading to the film maker becoming disheartened and the film generally remaining fully unexploited.

In the real world of fully funded film making, a sales agent will be attached to a film before it is even shot. Unfortunately, they're not interested in you because you are unproven, working with what will probably be a sub-standard screenplay, at the best featuring actors who are vaguely recognisable, with a director who is not only unheard of, but inexperienced too.

So don't be surprised if every sales agent you approach before the film is made doesn't even return your call. To them, you are small fry and they just don't want to waste time with what is probably going to be another low-budget, independent, unwatchable film. That's *their* perception. Your perception is going to be almost diametrically opposed and undoubtedly, you'll already have booked your tux for the Oscars.

A word of caution

By all means, believe whole-heartedly that your film will be the exception to the rule that all first films are rubbish. It is this self-belief that will propel you through the hard times of the film making process and provide you with the metal to contemplate your second film. However, no matter how optimistic you are, do not under any circumstance bank on any kind of financial success from this, your first film. Even if your film is a masterpiece, you will almost certainly lose money. In the long run, you'll come out smelling of roses, as your second film will probably deliver on the promise of your first, and you will receive a fat pay-cheque, personal assistant, and a driver, all to do day-in and day-out what you love. Think Chris Nolan, who made an exceptional debut film *'Following'*, which was followed by *'Memento'*, and the rest is history. This is the arc one would

The sales agent is the person who will try and sell your movie across the globe.

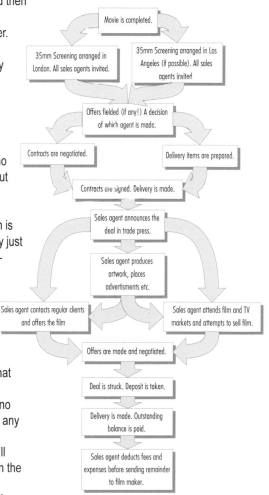

Lise Romanoff
Vision Films

'It's a sad fact that most films, deservedly or not, fail to get a major theatrical release. It's hard for new film makers to accept that their film, for a number of reasons, will be better suited to TV, video, pay per view markets. In fact, a smart producer might bypass the whole theatrical release issue and master to tape for TV and video sales only. Sure your movie will still be a feature film and look like a feature film, but it will be sold immediately and directly into the TV / video market.

There are a number of traps to avoid. If your film includes extreme sex or violence, make two versions, one more sanitised for the TV market, the other for pay per view and DVD / video. Be clear about the film you are making, it's genre and therefore your audience. Films are sold and labelled according to genre and you should avoid crossing genres – a romantic horror film is going to be a tough sell no matter how good the agent. Get the best cast you can afford, a recognisable name will always significantly help, no matter the genre. Check with your international sales agent before casting though as a UK name may not have any value internationally.

Movies sold for TV don't have the same luxury as theatrical or video releases. The audience will give you only a few minutes to hook them before they switch. You don't have a captive audience so it's essential to get on with the story and drama. A buyer for a major UK broadcaster looked at the first 15 minutes of all my films and bought only the ones that hooked him, rejecting the rest. It was a bit of a wake up call for some film makers!'

ideally follow, make a great first film, make an even better second film, then kick back and enjoy the opportunity to make almost whatever you want, and get paid handsomely.

Hope for the best . . .

But expect the worst . . . In a nutshell, you the film maker need to take a reality check about your film and accept that it may be unsellable(!). You must also be professional and realistic about fulfilling your obligations with regard to the delivery list (see chart); they can't sell your movie if they don't have a professional package. Communication is the key to a successful and stress-free marriage between film maker and sales agent. If they can't sell your movie, then you have to accept that, you just need to know the facts.

Self sales?

After months, no . . . years, of blood, sweat and tears, your movie is completed. Now you need somebody to sell it for you. It is possible for you to sell your film internationally, however, a number of factors will probably suggest to you that this is not a good idea. Firstly, by now you probably hate your movie. Secondly, you know that it cost next to nothing and you'll be painfully aware of all its weaknesses, so that when you come to cutting a deal, you'll probably just be so amazed that somebody is even interested that you'll accept the first offer on the table. Thirdly, and perhaps most importantly, you'll probably meet a sales agent who will seduce you with a sales report suggesting your film's value is in the £millions. High on the apparent belief the sales agent has placed in both you and your film and intoxicated by the silly figures on the sales report (which would mean you can pay off all your debts and perhaps even have some money left over), you will probably sign the deal.

Meet and greet

So let's assume you are going to do a deal with a sales agent, this is how to get one and how to deal with what happens.

Firstly, arrange a screening at a preview theatre in London, such as Mr Young's in D'Arblay Street (ideally, you should mirror this entire process with sales agents and a venue in Los Angeles). Get hold of a copy of the last product guide from Screen International for one of the major markets, (the markets are Cannes, MIFED and the AFM). Within this booklet you will find a list of all the active sales agents in both LA and London as well as other places around the world. Contact them all and invite them to a screening. You'll need to give them some warning, ideally around four weeks, and there is some argument to avoid Fridays, lunchtimes and early evenings as nominated screening times.

Keep calling the sales agents to ensure they will turn up, send them faxes and paperwork and get the name of the person who will attend. You're going

International Sales – Common Problems

Film makers' problems

1. Unrealistic view of their film. It simply isn't as good as, or as valuable as they believe.
2. Inability to make full delivery of items needed to sell the film. (See delivery list)
3. Poor casting
4. Difficulties arising from the fact that the film was not made with a specific audience in mind.
5. Poor stills (although this is usually overcome).

Sales agents' problems

1. Sales agent is either dishonest or too optimistic and supplies film maker with unrealistic sales projections
2. Sales agent is disorganised and disorganisation leads to inaccurate reporting.
3. Sales agent is dishonest.
4. Sales agent has poor reputation and contacts, often born out of poor business practices or dishonesty.
5. Inability to close deals.
6. Lack of communication between sales agent and film maker leading to film maker becoming disillusioned.
7. Agent doesn't accurately or regularly account to film maker.

to be looking for the senior person from the company to come and see the movie, but often they will send one of their minions. If the decision-making party does not attend then it's unlikely they will take the film, certainly they will either want another screening or a VHS tape, both of which are far from an ideal situation.

On the day of the screening, have somebody with a clipboard and pad on the door taking names and business cards. Have press packs ready and hand them out to your guests. After allowing five or ten minutes for late guests, start the movie (you don't need to introduce it) and wait.

Running the gauntlet

Brace yourself. This screening is not for the faint-hearted. Within ten minutes, a good third of your audience will probably be on their way out. If you're lucky, they'll smile at you politely as they hurriedly scurry away. These people just don't want your film. It may not be their type of product, or size of budget, or they just might not like it. Within forty minutes and in dribs and drabs, another third will leave, and possibly one or two new ones will turn up late to watch twenty minutes from the middle of your movie.

Over the remaining duration, you'll probably fixate on all those scenes that you felt you should have cut out but were left in. You'll become acutely aware of the slower moments of your film and wish to God that you had heeded advice and tightened your movie. The remaining audience, bar a handful, will slip away and when the credits roll, the die-hard sales agents who endured your movie will dash out with little more than a nod. You'll probably be feeling a little down in the mouth, when hopefully your mobile phone will ring . . . *and it's a sales agent expressing interest in your project!*

You want to look eager and confident about your film but don't agree to anything, sign any papers or look too excited about any interest. Be professional. Be cool!

Playing the field

In an ideal world, there'll be more than one sales agent interested.

What a sales agent needs to successfully sell a film

Checklist . . . and it isn't rocket science!

1. A good movie – Obvious I know, but you'd be surprised how few people realise this, or perhaps more truthfully, are in denial about their movie.

2. Cast – Who are the actors in your movie? The cast is one of the most important elements the sales agent has to sell your film. This doesn't mean an ex-soap star.

3. Title – The title of your movie is one of the only direct points of sale that you have. Make sure it's a good one that accurately encompasses the concept and theme of your movie.

4. Genre – Make sure your film exists within an understood genre. A sales agent shouldn't have much problem shifting a thriller with a strong 'thrilling' title and recognisable 'thrillery' actors. Ask how well they would do with a comedy about child abuse!

5. Poster – Or as the sales agent calls it, the key art. It should be bold and simple, in portrait aspect ratio, and like the title of the film, should accurately conjure the theme and feel of the movie. If you have a good cast, no doubt their face will appear on the poster, alongside their name at the top.

6. All the elements described in the delivery list.

Get all of these elements right and you're onto a sure-fire winner when it comes to the commerce of film making, not necessarily a success when it comes to the artistic side of film making.

You will go and meet with each and they'll probably schmooze you. If they *really* want your film, they should offer an advance. In our experience and at this level, an advance from a sales agent is virtually unheard of, and the mere offer of an advance is a sure indicator that the agent is super keen. If offers are made you will be able to weigh up each deal and play off the agents against one another, hopefully improving your deal. This kind of deal making isn't for the faint hearted and it's important to follow your instincts.

The most important factors to look for are . . . *Personal relationships* – do you believe they will always take your call? *Integrity* – are they going to tell you the truth? *Professionalism* – are they going to do the job and close deals? On the whole, we have found UK sales agents for independent films to be less professional and higher charging than American equivalents. The only problem with the LA based agents is that if you need to go and bang on their door, and you live in Milton Keynes, there's a very clear problem.

Doing the deal

Let's assume that you've met with a number of agents and have a good vibe about one. You decide to go with them and they produce a contract for you to sign. It's likely this contract will be a hefty tome, and you need a media lawyer to take a look at it. More than likely you are too broke to afford a media lawyer, so you will have to read it to yourself. If this is the case, go over our checklist which lists most of the common things they will try to get, and what they mean.

Making delivery

At the same time as dealing with the contracts, they will also supply you with a terrifying list of delivery items. These are the physical items that the sales agent requires in order to sell your film to foreign territories (see chart). You cannot get around the delivery list, although you can deliver the barest minimum in almost all cases. Depending on how *complete* your *completed* film is, just to make full delivery could cost you £50k. So don't believe the myth that you can complete your movie on an iMac, there is a world of difference between creative completion and distribution completion.

Once you make delivery and the deal is signed, the sales agent will probably announce the deal in the trade press such as in Screen International, and they will contact all the buyers in foreign territories with whom they have an existing relationship. They may send them a flyer and an invite to a screening at the next market, or they may send them a VHS and try and cut a deal as soon as possible.

Minimum guarantees . . . or so they say

In order for the sales agent to move quickly, they will have supplied you with a list of territories with minimum guarantees. This means that in any given territory, you and they will have agreed an absolute minimum figure that you

International sales minimum delivery

Not all of these items will be needed by a sales agent, but most will. Some items, like the E&O policy can be negotiated around as it is usually only needed for the USA. The cost of making up this extensive list of items could feasibly cost more than the production costs of an ultra low budget film. Speak to your sales agent and negotiate an exact list, with a budget for making up that list, BEFORE you sign any sales agreement.

Release print – *35mm com/opt print (combined optical print). Used to screen the film at markets in a cinema environment.*

35mm lab elements – *including 35mm Interpos / Interneg, made from the original negative. 35mm optical sound neg, made from master sound mix. You have already made this in order to produce your final print, and it will be held at the lab.*

Sound master mix – *on either DA88 or DAT. Some agents may request a 35mm sound master which you should avoid. This sound mix will also be on the DigiBeta on tracks 1 and 2.*

Music & effect mix (M&E) – *used for foreign territories to re-voice the film. Supplied on DA88 or DAT. Some agents may request a 35mm sound master which you should avoid. This sound mix will also be on the DigiBeta on tracks 3 and 4.*

Textless title background – *35mm Interneg / Interpos / print of sequences without title elements. Used by territories to re-title in their native language. Video versions of the textless backgrounds will also be needed.*

35mm trailer – *including access to interneg, interpos, optical sound, magnetic sound master and M&E mix. It is common now to produce the trailer on DigiBeta and digitally copy the video onto film. The quality isn't as good but it may be adequate and certainly cheaper and easier to produce.*

Videotape – *full screen 4:3 and Widescreen 16:9 versions on Digital Betacam, including stereo sound (on tracks 1&2) and M&E (on tracks 3&4). Also textless background versions if you have titles over picture. Quality must be impeccable.*

Videotape trailer – *full screen 4:3 and Widescreen 16:9 versions on DigiBeta, including stereo sound (on tracks 1&2) and M&E (on tracks 3&4). You will also need a trailer with textless backgrounds.*

Stills set – *100 full colour transparencies will be requested but you can get away with 20 as long as they are good.*

Screenplay – *transcript of final cut including all music cues. This isn't your shooting script, but an accurate and detailed transcription of all the dialogue and action. You will need to sit down with your PC and a VHS and do it from scratch.*

Distribution restrictions – *statement of any restrictions or obligations (e.g. the order in which the cast are credited).*

Music cue sheet – *an accurate list of all the music cues, rights etc. See the music cue sheet later in the book. Used by collection agencies to distribute music royalties.*

US copyright notice – *available from The Registrar of Copyright, Library of Congress, Washington DC, 20559, USA. Download Form PA from the internet (www.copyright.gov).*

Chain of title – *contracts with everyone involved in the production and distribution of the film. Needed to prove that you have the right to sell the film to another party. Usually the writer, director, producer, musician, cast and release forms from all other parties involved.*

Certificate of origin and certificate of authorship – *available from solicitor. You go in, pay a small fee, swear that the information is correct, they witness it and you have your certificates.*

Certificate of nationality – *available from the Department of Culture Media and Sport, Dept., of National Heritage, Media Division (Film), 2/4 Cockspur Street, London, SW1Y 5DH.*

Credit list – *complete cast and crew list, plus any other credits.*

Errors and omissions insurance policy (E&O) – *a policy that indemnifies distributors and sales agents. Available from specialised Insurers (approx. cost £4-10k). You may be able to negotiate around this, agreeing to supply it if and when it is needed by any specific distributor.*

Lab access letter – *a letter to the sales agent giving them access to materials held at the lab. Remember, if you haven't paid your lab bill yet, they may not give you this letter.*

Press and reviews – *copies of all press and reviews. Don't give them the bad reviews.*

EPK – Electronic Press Kit – *BetaSP of interviews with actors and principal crew. Shots of crew at work, plus clips from film and trailer. You will also need a split M&E version so that interviewees voices can be dipped down allowing a translation to be spoken over the top.*

Mini documentary – *more common now and seen as a sweetener. Essential if you want a successful DVD release. Ensure someone shoots some DV footage on set.*

DISTRIBUTION LICENSE AGREEMENT

THIS AGREEMENT is entered into as of April 19ᵗʰ 2001 by and between: ▓▓▓▓▓ whose address is ▓▓▓▓▓ Contact: ▓▓▓▓▓ ("Licensor") of the first part

and ▓▓▓▓▓ ("Distributor").

Subject to timely payment of all moneys due Licensor and Distributor's due performance of all other terms of this Agreement, Licensor licenses exclusively to Distributor, and Distributor accepts from Licensor, the following Pictures in the following Territories on all the terms and conditions of this Agreement.

This Agreement consists of the following parts: Deal Terms being (the Basic License Deal Terms, Financial Deal Terms and Delivery Deal Terms), the AFMA International Multiple Rights License Standard Distribution Terms and Conditions, and the AFMA Standard International Schedule of Definitions (draft V.022294). All parts of the Agreement will be interpreted together to form one Agreement. Where not defined where they first appear, words used in this Agreement are otherwise defined in the Standard Terms and Conditions under the Schedule of Definitions (draft V.022294) or in accordance with industry customs.

Where either party is an agent for a principal, that party represents and warrants to the other that it has full authority to execute this Agreement on behalf of its principal and that its principal will be bound by its term.

License Fee Allocation

DEAL TERMS:
PICTURE (S): 1) ▓▓▓▓▓ $4,500.00

GRAND TOTAL LICENSE FEE: $4,500.00 Net US Dollars
MATERIAL COSTS: $150.00
GRAND TOTAL DUE: $26,400.00
RIGHTS GRANTED: All Forms of Television Rights: Pay, Cable, Satellite, FTV (including Orbit, Star, and MBC)

Reserved rights including but not limited to Theatrical, Internet, Video/DVD, Soundtrack CD/Merchandising and any others not specifically outlined herein are EXCLUDED from this contract and are therefore not granted.

TERRITORY: All Arabic speaking Middle East and North Africa
AUTHORIZED LANGUAGE(S): English with Arabic subtitles
TERM: 5 Years, Unlimited Runs Start: June 1ˢᵗ, 2001, End: December 31st, 2006.
PAYMENT SCHEDULE: 100% by May 20ᵗʰ, 2001
DELIVERY MATERIALS: BetaSP Pal Masters, English Scripts, 3-6 35mm publicity slides for each picture, Music cues, Trailers
DELIVERY SCHEDULE: Distributor shall be responsible for shipping costs. Delivery of materials shall be made 14 days from payment.

TECHNICAL ACCEPTANCE OF DELIVERY MATERIALS: No Censorship clause applies. Distributor shall check the materials for technical acceptance within 30 days from delivery. If master is found to be technically faulty, Distributor shall return master along with lab report to Licensor and Licensor shall have 30 days in which to replace master. If no notice of faulty master is given to Licensor within 30 days, then master shall be deemed technically accepted. If Licensor cannot deliver a technically acceptable master then Licensor may replace Picture, with the approval of Distributor, or must refund the allocated License fee.

DISTRIBUTOR CREATED MATERIALS: Distributor shall provide Licensor access to the Foreign Language Tracks, Masters, advertising and promotional materials, artwork and other materials created by Distributor or its Sub-licensees pursuant to this Agreement.

APPLICABLE LAW: The parties nominate California law to govern their relationship and nominate Los Angeles as the venue for arbitration. In the event of any dispute hereunder the prevailing party shall be entitled to recover its reasonable attorneys' fees. Save as provided for herein, all other terms and conditions so far as may be relevant shall be governed by the provisions of the AFMA Standard Terms and Conditions.

ARBITRATION: Any dispute under this Agreement will be resolved by final and binding arbitration under the Rules of International Arbitration of the American Film Marketing Association in effect when the arbitration is filed (the "AFMA rules"). Each Party waives any right to adjudicate any dispute in any other court or forum, except that a Party may seek interim relief before the start of arbitration as allowed by the AFMA Rules. The arbitration will be held in Los Angeles, California. The Parties will abide by any decision in the arbitration and any court having jurisdiction may enforce it. The Parties submit to the jurisdiction of the courts in the Forum to compel arbitration or to confirm an arbitration award. The Parties agree to accept service of process in accordance with the AFMA Rules.

NOTICES: All notices required or desired to be given hereunder shall be in writing (unless otherwise herein specified) and shall be transmitted by personal delivery or by prepaid fax, telegram, cable, telex or prepaid air mail. Licensor's and Distributor's respective addresses for notices shall be as set forth above. Either party may change its address for notices by so advising the other party in writing. All notices given by mail shall be deemed given when received but in any event not later than fourteen (14) days from the date of deposit in the mail. All notices sent by telegram or cable shall be deemed given when received but in any event not later than two (2) days from the date of deposit in the telegraph or cable office or with respect to a fax or telex from the date of transmission of such. All notices given by personal delivery shall be deemed given when received.

ADDITIONAL TERMS & CONDITIONS: Failure to pay, or report, in accordance with this Agreement shall be deemed a Material Breach and that if Distributor fails to make timely payment, or report in accordance with the terms and provisions of this Agreement within 14 days following Licensor's notice of said Breach, Licensor shall have the right to terminate this agreement and the rights licensed thereunder without prejudicing any of Licensor's rights at law, in equity or otherwise.

AGREED TO: FOR & ON BEHALF OF ▓▓▓▓▓ FOR & ON BEHALF OF ▓▓▓▓▓

_____ _____
Distributor Licensor
Its: Its:

The AFM Agreement forms the central hub of most international sales – that is, between the sales agent who represents your film, and a company who will buy your film for a specific territory. It's good for all parties as it is clear, concise and most of all, recognised by almost everyone.

would accept for your film. This gives the sales agent a minimum that they need to hit in order to cut a deal without prior consultation with the film maker. They may get offers below the minimum guarantee and you may choose to accept these deals, but the agent will not be able to close the deal without your prior consent.

Wheeler dealer

A major part of the sales agents' job is that of attending markets. There are a number of feature film markets and a plethora of TV and Video markets each year. Big agencies will probably attend all, but the smaller agents with whom you are probably dealing will only attend the important ones. This isn't a problem because if they don't attend, you don't have to pay for their attendance out of your returns. Often deals lost through not attending smaller markets can be compensated for with greater sales at the larger markets (see chart).

In attending a major market, the sales agent will do a number of things. Firstly, they will contact the market organisers in advance, and book a stand or hotel suite where they can set up and sell their 'wares'. There's probably a fee involved and of course the rental of the space. The agent will contact all the industry publications, such as Screen International and Variety, and they and their 'product' will be listed in the product guide for that market. They will book theatres during the market in which to show your film. There'll probably be somewhere between three and five screenings over the duration of the market and hopefully, your agent will place ads in trade magazines to publicise the event (screening time, venue, movie poster, etc). Whilst at the market, the sales agent will set up a stand with posters, a big TV and a showreel of the trailers for the movies that they're selling. They will use this stand to attract passing custom and also to hold meetings with buyers who they either previously knew or have responded to the advertising and have gone to see the film.

Plain and simple contracts

Most agents now use a standardised contract for their deals, known as the AFM contract. This takes the legal check aspect out of deal making and allows agents and buyers to sign deals with confidence. You want to make sure your agent is happy using these contracts

Attending a market isn't cheap, and alongside all the expenses such as poster printing, flyers and running off VHS 'screener tapes', the agent will claim expenses such as airflight, accommodation, catering etc. Check with film makers whose films have previously been handled by the sales agent and ask if these guys are the kind of people who like to fly first class and eat out in expensive restaurants every night. Remember whatever they spend, you pay for, or at least a share of.

The Screen International Product Guides, published around each major market (Cannes, MIFED and AFM) are a great place to get information about active sales agents – who they are, where they are and what they are selling.

Should you go to the markets?

Yes. It's essential to go to at least one film market (probably Cannes for we Brits), in order to soak up the atmosphere of a sales market. It will probably be a shock to the system to see just how down market the whole process is, and you'll probably come to the realisation that its somewhat like a glamorous version of a second hand car dealership.

One of the things that will happen at the first market you attend is that the trade press will review your film. If you get a good review in *Variety* for instance, this becomes currency that you can use in order to persuade buyers to attend screenings of your film. Sales agents are phenomenally busy during the market, and accordingly, there are a number of ways in which you can help them. A simple one is fly-postering (which is illegal of course!). Every morning fly-post the Croisette in Cannes (sticking to walls,

The future – high definition video?

As if life wasn't hard enough, the word on the street is that mastering your movie to a higher quality format than Digital Betacam is the way of the future. Already major players in the States are mastering to HiDef video (and as usual there are a number of formats here). The obvious advantage is that of resolution, as HiDef formats contain images significantly larger and therefore sharper and more detailed. The other advantage is that it can be used to make all manner of different format videotapes (16:9, 4:3, 1:185 letterbox etc.) with little or no perceptible loss of quality. The downside is obviously the cost. Whatever format you shoot – film or tape – consider a HiDef format for final mastering as you may well be forced to re-master in a few years time anyway. The telecine machines are essentially the same, although some older kit is not suitable. The facility where you would normally do a telecine to DigiBeta will just plug a HiDef recorder in where a DigiBeta used to live. In terms of costs, it will probably set you back anywhere between two and three times as much as a conventional telecine to DigiBeta. There are inherent costs when duplicating from the HiDef formats too . . . tapes and machine time are considerably more expensive, but in the long run you have one master that is future proof AND you can make all other masters, PAL and NTSC, 4:3, 16:9 etc., from this one tape.

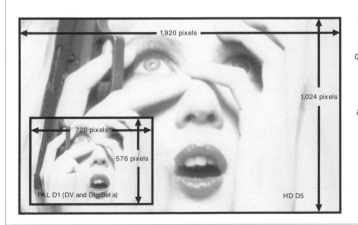

1,920 pixels

1,024 pixels

720 pixels

576 pixels

PAL D1 (DV and DigiBeta)

HD D5

International sales – typical balance sheet

TOTAL MONEY IN

Territory	Deal worth	Y1 Q1	Y1 Q2	Y1 Q3	Y1 Q4	Y2 Q1	Y2 Q2	Y2 Q3	Y2 Q4	Y3 Q1
Sale 1	£45,000	£0	£4,500	£0	£0	£20,250	£0	£0	£20,250	£0
Sale 2	£3,000	£0	£300	£0	£2,700	£0	£0	£0	£0	£0
Sale 3	£20,000	£0	£2,000	£0	£0	£0	£9,000	£0	£0	£9,000
Sale 4	£10,000	£0	£500	£0	£9,500	£0	£0	£0	£0	£0
Sale 5	£1,000	£0	£0	£0	£0	£0	£500	£0	£0	£500
Sale 6	£1,000	£0	£500	£500	£0	£0	£0	£0	£0	£0
Sale 7	£500	£0	£0	£0	£0	£500	£0	£0	£0	£0
Totals	£80,500	£0	£7,800	£500	£12,200	£20,750	£9,500	£0	£20,250	£9,500

TOTAL MONEY OUT

Sales Expenses	Y1 Q1	Y1 Q2	Y1 Q3	Y1 Q4	Y2 Q1	Y2 Q2	Y2 Q3	Y2 Q4	Y3 Q5
Commission 20%	£0	£1,560	£100	£2,440	£4,150	£1,900	£0	£4,050	£1,900
FedEx (Average)	£65	£65	£65	£65	£65	£65	£65	£65	£65
Flyers	£1,000	£0	£0	£0	£0	£0	£0	£0	£0
Advertisments	£0	£1,500	£0	£1,000	£0	£1,500	£0	£1,000	£0
VHS Dupes	£0	£100	£0	£0	£0	£100	£0	£0	£0
Digi System Xfer.	£0	£800	£0	£0	£0	£0	£0	£0	£0
Hotel and Flights	£0	£4,000	£0	£1,500	£0	£4,000	£0	£1,500	£0
Quality Control	£0	£0	£400	£0	£400	£0	£400	£0	£400
Remastering	£0	£0	£0	£0	£0	£0	£3,000	£0	£0
Misc Delivery Items	£2,500	£0	£2,500	£0	£0	£0	£0	£0	£0
Trannies	£0	£500	£0	£0	£0	£0	£0	£0	£0
Photocopier	£25	£25	£25	£25	£25	£25	£25	£25	£25
Totals	3,590	8,550	12,140	5,030	4,640	9,670	3,490	6,640	10,130

	Y1 Q1	Y1 Q2	Y1 Q3	Y1 Q4	Y2 Q1	Y2 Q2	Y2 Q3	Y2 Q4	Y3 Q1
TOTAL MONEY IN	£0	£7,800	£500	£12,200	£20,750	£9,500	£0	£20,250	£9,500
TOTAL MONEY OUT	£3,590	£8,550	£12,140	£5,030	£4,640	£9,670	£3,490	£6,640	£10,130
BALANCE	-£3,590	-£4,340	-£15,980	-£8,810	£7,300	£7,130	£3,640	£17,250	£16,620

GRAND TOTAL IN	**£80,500**
GRAND TOTAL OUT	**£63,880**
BALANCE TO YOU	**£16,620**

This balance sheet is fairly typical and illustrates the kind of problems faced by an independent film maker when dealing with International Sales. In this example the film has performed moderately well making seven International sales, some of which are for small amounts such as £500-£1k, some for bigger amounts such as £20k or £45k (note – sales agents almost always trade in US$. We have used £GBP simply for clarity). Of course a film may sell to more territories, although if you do, you will be doing extremely well and will be bucking the trend.

*The example shows two halves – **total money in** and **total money out**.*

First lets look at the total money in, the upper portion. On the left, there is a list of seven sales with the total deal values. The first shocker is that you don't get all your money at once. So for sale one, worth £45k, the deal is struck in year one, quarter two (this could well be the Cannes film market and the deal could be for a territory such as Germany). The sales agents take 10% deposit

cont . . .

International Sales – Typical Balance Sheet (cont)

worth £4,500 and then it takes nearly a year to get the second payment £20,250 and yet another nine months to get the remaining £20,250. Why does it take this long? Distributors like to stagger payment to help their cash flow, but mostly it's because you screwed around and didn't manage to fulfil the full delivery requirements for the sales agent (typically, your master telecine will repeatedly fail quality control – so get it right first time!)

So the sales agent has made seven sales, collecting revenues in just over a two year period. These sales total £80,500. Remember you're on an 80/20 split in your favour, which sounds pretty good. Why on earth then are you only getting £16,620?

Let's now look at the second section, total money out.

First of all, the agent will take 20% commission straight off the top. This is their fee and they are going to get paid come hell or high water. There are a number of regular overheads that they will deduct. These include Fed-Exing packages, producing flyers, running advertisements in trade magazines at the markets, making VHS dupes to send to potential buyers, producing a DigiBeta PAL to NTSC transfer (because you didn't supply them with one), hotel and flights and other market attendance costs. There is also quality control (where you pay a third party company to check your delivery materials for technical quality. If they fail, you have to make a new master and pay for quality control again.) Re-mastering because your master failed QC (quality control) and you now have to do it properly. Miscellaneous delivery items, which you didn't sort out properly and the sales agent is now forced to sort out on your behalf, duplication of transparencies and finally some photocopying.

So let's just re-think this. Money comes in, the sales agent takes their 20% commission then they start to pay off the bills incurred in the sale of your film. The upshot is that they make £16,100 profit, plus cover ALL of their expenses, leaving only £16,620 for you at the end. If you feel that's fair enough, then let me hit you with this one. They probably won't pay you for six months which means it could well be years before you start to get any revenues, and then only in dribs and drabs.

on car windscreens, lamp posts etc.). You can guarantee the posters will only stay up for a couple of hours at the most, but doing this will mean that every single person attending the market will see your poster, know the title of your movie and hopefully this will pique their interest. Remember you are marketing both the movie to the industry, and YOU as a film maker – *'Oh you're the guys with that movie I keep seeing the poster for – so what are you doing next?'*

Support your local sales agent

Another thing you can do is chase the journalists from the trade magazines to run features about your film. Don't rely on the sales agent to be organised or clear-headed enough to organise press-clippings as and when they happen, so you should take this task upon your shoulders and get down to a copy shop and make 100 copies of that great review for the sales agent to hand to a buyer when the meet. Think of yourselves as a support network for the sales agents, after all you are business partners now. Don't get all egotistic and self important, *'I'm not doing that darling, I am the director!'*, the whole purpose of a market is to sell your film and make new contacts.

It's all soooo exciting!

One of the more exciting aspects of attending a market for the first

Sales agents will seduce you into doing the deal, giving you reports and buying you expensive lunches . . . But after you sign they won't return your calls and you will be left feeling 'humped and dumped!' Don't accept this. Get on the phone and make yourself a polite but ever present voice in their daily life.

Don't be convinced by the sales agents estimates – they probably won't make all the sales on the list (maybe only a few) and they almost certainly won't get close to the asking prices. A closed deal with money on the table (and in your pocket) is always better than the promise of a bigger deal that might not happen. Always take the money!

time is the moment when you realise somebody is going to make an offer on your film, and that offer could potentially be in the tens of thousands of pounds.

The first thing to realise is that no matter how much the deal is worth, the sales agent will only collect at most 25% as a deposit, perhaps as little as 10%. The balance will only be paid after full delivery, and is often split 50% on delivery and 50% on release within the given territory. The sales agent will deduct their commission, then their expenses before giving you your slice, sometimes keeping hold of it for three to six months first (by which time yet more expenses may appear). The upshot is that you never seem to catch up to the agent's commission/expenses and rarely receive a cheque of any consequence. This goes on for years and very quickly one can become jaded. It's a terrible thing to know that somebody else's business is profiting from your hard work and initiative whilst you are struggling to feed yourself.

Can you please tell me how much . . . !

One of the most common and frustrating problems is that of reporting. Agents will be obliged to account to the film maker on a regular basis, usually every three months for the first two years, then every six months thereafter. In reality, they don't report on time, often months and even years late. It's extraordinarily frustrating when you can't get a piece of paper out of an agent, even if it's to only say no sales have been achieved, which you can pass on to your investors. The only way to deal with this is to become a thorn in the side of your agent and relentlessly call, write and annoy them – all of which distracts them from selling films!

That was last years film . . .

Your movie will remain on the sales agents A list for the first year or so, after which it will slip into their back catalogue, and they will acquire new A list titles. Once it slips into that back catalogue, its potential value is greatly reduced. So its important to try and maximise that first year when the movie is new and hopefully perceived as a hot property. If sales go exceptionally well, then it is likely that you will indeed make money from your movie. However, after studying many low-budget British pictures, there are only one or two instances where films have done well internationally, and very rarely have they broken even.

Market research

After looking at the movies that have been successes, two trends appear.

Firstly, there is the exceptional and quirky low-budget film – think *'Clerks'*. This is often a comedy or comedy-drama and its low-budget status afforded the film makers the opportunity to do things in ways that are unusual. These

International sales estimates

This chart is to be taken with the BIGGEST pinch of salt. First off, there are NO tables from which you can draw sales estimates. Every film is different, every agent is different, every market and year in which sales are made is different, it is constantly changing – VHS, satellite, DVD, pay per view, the internet – all have historically shaken up the market and redefined the way it works. Who knows where the internet will really lead us, or globalisation, HiDefDVD, digital film making, digital cinemas . . .

The chart is printed simply to give guidance. It is drawn up in part by a sales agent and in part by myself. It represents the possible prospects of an independent genre film with a good strong plot and NO name cast. It would have been completed on 35mm and would be excellent in every technical respect. This is NOT a DV feature film, there are simply not enough DV films out there to make any kind of chart of any real use.

Oceania	Rights	Low	High	Guess/Buyout
Australia	Vid	$2,500	$7,500	
	PTV	$9,000	$15,000	
	FTV	$20,000	$30,000	
New Zealand	PTV	$3,000	$7,500	
	CTV	$500	$550	
	FTV	$7,000	$12,000	$20,000
West Europe	Rights	Low	High	Guess/Buyout
Dutch Belgium	FTV	$4,500	$9,000	
Netherlands	CTV	$7,500	$12,000	
	FTV	$9,000	$12,000	
Benelux	PTV	$15,000	$20,000	
	Vid	$2,500	$7,500	$15,000
France	PTV	$50,000	$80,000	
	CTV/Sat TV	$10,000	$24,000	$25,000
German speaking	PTV	$10,000	$50,000	
	All TV	$25,000	$85,000	
	Vid	$10,000	$50,000	$65,000
Italy	TV	$25,000	$80,000	$20,000
Portugal	All rights	$3,000	$10,000	$3,000
Spain	PTV	$10,000	$20,000	
	SatTV	$7,000	$10,000	
	FTV	$10,000	$60,000	
	Vid	$7,500	$30,000	$1,000
UK	PPV	$5,000	$30,000	
	PTV	$25,000	$75,000	
	Dig. SatTV	$15,000	$20,000	
	FTV	$10,000	$50,000	$40,000
Denmark	TV	$6,000	$8,000	
Finland	TV	$6,000	$8,000	
Iceland	TV	$2,500	$4,000	
Norway	TV	$5,000	$6,000	
Sweden	TV	$6,000	$10,000	$1,000
Israel	All rights	$2,000	$6,000	$1,000
Greece	All rights	$2,500	$7,500	$1,500
Cyprus	TV	$500	$1,000	$500
Turkey	All rights	$1,000	$10,000	$500
Middle East	Rights	Low	High	Guess/Buyout
Middle East	PTV/Sat	$2,000	$8,000	
	TV/Vid	$4,000	$10,000	$1,000
Africa	Rights	Low	High	Guess/Buyout
Total Africa		$4,000	$20,000	$2,000

The real use of this chart is to lie to yourself, to look at the best case scenario, focus on that and build your plans accordingly. Hey I have done it, we all have. There simply are no precedents worth building your business upon. This is high risk, high adventure kind of stuff. You can help yourself with things like genre, cast, plot strength, acting, awards . . . But it might not help either. Just remember, sales could, and have been for reasonable films in the past, a big fat ZERO! All you can really do is make the best possible film and trust that if you have done your job properly other people will like it and want to watch it and buy it.

The chart does not include America as it is very hard to get a deal in the USA and figures can swing so outrageously that it makes it impossible to make even the wildest guess. But if you must . . . think of it on a par with the UK. Nor does the chart deal with any theatrical distribution. On the whole that won't happen, and if it does, the cinema

Cont . . .

cont . . . International sales estimates

release will lose money and be reclaimed from video / DVD / TV etc., meaning you get less money. Besides, it most likely you will do a complete buyout and whoever buys it for a given territory will have the right to do almost anything they like – cinema, TV, DVD, video . . . who knows, they may even give it away free with corn flakes!

Asia	Rights	Low	High	Guess/Buyout
China	CTV	$2,500	$5,000	
	TV/Vid	$2,500	$10,000	$2,000
Hong Kong	PPV	$2,000	$2,500	
	FTV	$5,000	$7,000	
	TV/Vid	$5,000	$10,000	$5,000
India		$1,000	$5,000	$1,000
Indonesia		$1,500	$7,500	$1,000
Macau	TV		$500	$500
Malaysia	TV/Vid	$2,000	$5,000	$1,000
Philippines	All rights	$1,500	$7,000	$2,000
Singapore	TV	$1,500	$3,000	$1,000
Sri Lanka	TV	$700	$1,200	$500
South Korea	Vid	$10,000	$15,000	$10,000
Taiwan	Vid	$2,500	$5,000	
	TV	$3,500	$7,000	$1,000
Thailand	TV/Vid	$1,000	$3,500	$500
Pan Asia Satelitte TV	PTV	$7,500	$17,500	$5,000
Japan	Rights	Low	High	Guess/Buyout
	All rights	$20,000	$60,000	$1,000
S. America	Rights	Low	High	Guess/Buyout
Arg, Para, Urg, Chile	Sat TV	$1,500	$2,000	
Colombia	TV	$2,000	$4,000	
Ecuador	TV	$800	$2,000	
Mexico	CTV	$1,500	$10,000	
	FTV	$10,000	$25,000	
	Vid	$5,000	$10,000	
Peru	TV	$2,000	$4,000	
Puerto Rico	TV	$3,000	$5,000	
Venezuela	TV	$2,000	$9,000	
	Vid	$1,000	$5,000	
Brazil	PTV	$7,500	$20,000	
	FTV	$7,500	$15,000	
	HV	$5,000	$10,000	
Pan Latin American TV	PTV	$4,500	$25,000	$15,000
East Europe	Rights	Low	High	Guess/Buyout
Baltics	TV	$400	$750	
Bulgaria	TV/Vid	$500	$1,500	
CIS	TV	$2,500	$7,500	
	Vid	$2,500	$7,500	
Czech	TV/Vid	$2,000	$4,000	
Croatia	TV/Vid	$1,000	$2,500	
Former Yugoslavia	HV	$1,000	$3,000	
Hungary	TV	$2,000	$5,000	
Poland	PTV	$4,000	$5,000	
	FTV	$5,000	$12,500	
Romania	TV	$1,000	$2,000	
Slovakia	TV/Vid	$1,000	$3,000	$1,000
Totals		$490,400	$1,277,500	$244,000

It's all pretty obvious what the chart means. The first column is the territories, the second column the rights (broken down), the third column is 'low sales' (the film performs badly), the fourth column is 'high sales' (the film performs well) and the final column is based on a 'what if . . . ' and 'what has happened . . . ' with other film makers. Part guess and partly based on real sales for a number of films, it represents the kind of wholesale buyout you might get offered.

Timescales? Jeepers. Think years not months.

Truthfully, closing ANY deal and getting a cheque is nothing short of a miracle. So as said earlier, break out the salt cellars.

films often do well, but more importantly, launch the careers of film makers who are perceived as being unique voices and talent. They often get swallowed up by Hollywood, and in most instances only make a couple of movies before disappearing into B grade movies.

The second and considerably more bankable option is to make a straight genre film – typically horror or thriller – check out the Screen International product guide from any of the three main markets and you will see page and after page of thriller posters that you have never heard of nor will ever see. These movies tend to be simplistic but well plotted, with low-budget movie stars (if you can afford them), strong titles and artwork. Often the films look slick but the movie itself is pretty brain-dead. However, these are the easiest films to sell internationally and a well-plotted, slick-looking thriller with notable cast made for £100k, if placed with a reputable and aggressive agent, should net the film makers a very healthy profit.

The only problem is that one doesn't fall in love with these projects and you don't find yourself jumping out of bed in the morning, excited by the prospect of making the film. In short, motivation to make these films is difficult to muster, even on a healthy budget, let alone on a micro-budget.

Disappointed!

So far in over ten years of independent film making, I have yet to come across a film maker who is happy with their sales agent. They often have feelings of somehow being cheated, that the sales agent has given up on their film, that the sales agent never understood what the film was in the first place, and they want to move to a new agent. This throws up a number of issues.

Firstly, a sales agent won't want to let you have the film back unless they are contractually forced to. This usually means a clause where they have failed to *'deliver'*. In our experience it's best to put a clause in the contract stating that if they do not achieve a given amount of sales after one year, then the rights revert to the producer. This means that if they do not sell the film, then you can move on, and if they do sell the film, then hey, what do you care? They're doing a good job.

Biting the bullet

Secondly, it is hard to admit, but maybe our films aren't as good or as internationally attractive as we would like. In fact, in many instances, for whatever reason, the films are genuinely either very difficult to sell or impossible. Nobody wants to hear this but it must be said and it would account for a sales agent who is unable to sell your film. Common reasons that a film is difficult to sell are (and in order of horror) . . . your film is crap . . . your film is dull in concept . . . your film is glacial in pace (this can be corrected) . . . your film is introverted and quirky to the point that it defaults to

Lise Romanoff
Vision Films

'Imagine yourself in a video shop looking at all those titles on the shelf. Ask yourself what jumps off the shelf and why? Will your film do the same? Assuming you can give your sales agent full delivery (see list) and a half decent film, then there are a number of things you need to ask – ideally before you make the film!

What is it? What's it called? Does it fit in a genre? Who's in it? What's the tag line? You should be able to pitch the film, based on genre, cast, title and plot in thirty seconds. You should have a key image that represents the movie, maybe a single shot or a photomontage with a logo. If a good sales agent has all of these things, then they should have a much better chance of making great sales.

The kind of agent you are looking for is one who will turn every stone in an attempt to get the deal, who won't tie you into a long term contracft if they're not making sales, who will share agreements and show all expenses receipts. Not all agents are the same. Ask previous clients if they are happy with the agent's work, you'll get an honest and clear answer. At the end of the day you want someone who will work very hard for you, never give up, but at the same time, it is important to understand that your film may be at best a hard sell, at worst unsellable . . . but a strong story, clear genre, good cast, good execution, and complete delivery package, will all certainly make your chances of success considerably greater. If you have realistic financial expectations and understand the time frame that it takes a distributor to make a dent in your deficit (it takes 10 times longer than you wish), you will be a happier producer!

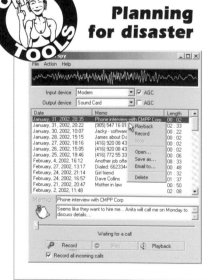

the earlier points . . . your film is too colloquial . . . Bad script . . . Bad actors . . . The list can go on.

If this is your first film, and you are reading this after you have completed it, you'll probably be nodding your head when I say *'if only I knew what I know now before I had started'*. Making your first low-budget feature is often a gruelling assault course on the creativity of any film maker. It's a statistical fact that your first film will probably be at the very best barely passable and at the worst unwatchably awful. For those of you who think I'm talking out of my arse* it's worth asking yourself *'how much actual market research have I done?'* and *'Is the choice of movie I am making based on what I want to make or what I know from research I can sell?'* There's nothing wrong with making a movie that you want to make, and in fact, it's probably the best thing to do, just don't be surprised if nobody wants to buy it. Neither am I saying *don't make your film.* You need to make it in order to make your next. What I am saying is don't *expect* success.

(remember if you have got this far in the film making process you probably have an ego the size of a planet – an important factor in getting your film made, but please put that ego in a bottle for just a few moments and try to take on board these last few paragraphs. Once done, file in your subconscious and re-release the ego.)

Each market will also print a book or list of buyers, like this one from Cannes '98. This is not a list of sales agents, but a list of companies and executives attending the market who have the power to buy a film for any given territory. The lists often contain corporate info including contact info and photos (sometimes also containing information on where these people will be staying during the market). These are the people you need to target if you have decided to sell the film yourself.

A final thought

No matter the subject of your film, and even if you feel its story is obscure to the point of being ridiculous, if YOU are into it, then someone somewhere

---

Planning for disaster

Of all the people who you will work with, sales agents and distributors will probably cause you the most problems. For whatever reason, your film is rubbish, the agent is dishonest etc., you will probably cross swords at some point. It's therefore a good idea to keep a complete record of all your contact with them. After meetings send a fax, letter or e-mail to set out what was discussed and agreed. Keep a special file on your shelf for this correspondence.

When it comes to phone calls you can hook your phone up to a tape recorder, or use cunning software tools like Modem Spy (left) that will automatically record all your calls, date them, you can label them then they are stored for later playback. Modem Spy costs just $25 and you can download a free trial version from www.modemspy.com.

You can't use a recording (either on tape or computer) as evidence in court, but it will serve to jog your memory about everything that was said. You should also tell people you are recording the conversation, a fact that will inevitably put them in a different frame of mind. At the end of the day, if you are in dispute, you need to seek an agreement without the involvement of a solicitor, and certainly out of court . . . But then, in the words of my solicitor, 'some people are bonkers'.

Primary world film & TV markets

NATPE
Primarily US market, but some international. Host city changes (New Orleans most recent)
Late January
www.napte.org

Toronto Film Festival
Toronto, Canada
Festival, not a market but attended by buyers.
Early September
www.e.bell.ca/filmfest

London Screenings
London, England
Designed to catch traffic for MIFED and serves primarily European and US buyers.
Late October
www.londonscreenings.com

Berlin Film Festival
Berlin, Germany
Festival, not a market but attended by buyers.
Early February
www.berlinale.de

MIPCOM
Television market for world buyers.
Milan, Italy
Mid October

AFM – American Film Market
Los Angeles, USA
Primary feature film US market for world buyers.
Late February
www.afma.com

LA Screenings
Los Angeles, USA
Cannes competitor primarily for USA based sellers.
Mid May
www.videoageinternational.com

Sundance Film Festival
Utah, USA
Festival, not a market but attended by buyers.
Late January
www.sundance.org

Cannes Film Market and Festival
Cannes, France
Primary feature film Euro market for world buyers.
Mid May
www.cannesmarket.com

MIPTV
Television market for world buyers.
Cannes, France
Mid April
www.miptv.com

MIFED
Milan, Italy
Feature Euro market for world buyers.
Early November
www.mifed.com

Annually there are a number of markets where films are sold. As a film maker there isn't much point in attending these markets unless you are acting as your own sales agent. Having said that, if you do attend a market, you can help your sales agent doing any leg work needed (maybe even just getting coffee!). This experience of sales in the 'front line' is almost invaluable. Three days at the Cannes Film Market is worth its weight in gold in terms of making 'real' the business of buying and selling films, but repeated attendance to markets like MIPCOM will soon become dull as ditchwater.

Markets are split into two distinctive groups. Feature film markets and Television markets. Of course, there is enormous crossover and whilst you may have aspirations to do deals with feature film distributors, your film will probably attract more sales at the Television markets. The markets usually charge to attend as a way of keeping the public out. Contact the market organisers in advance so that you can arrange for a pass or badge that will allow you to get in. Don't wait until you get there to do this.

Film festivals are not markets, however they are often attended by distributors from the country in which the festival is located. Some festivals also have a significant but unofficial market-like quality (festivals like Sundance, Berlin and Toronto).

else on the planet will be. How to find that audience is the key to the success of your film.

Unfortunately, sales agents and distributors are not terribly discerning people, nor do they have much imagination. Ultimately, if the film is good, and when I say good I mean really good, you will find an audience. More than likely you will also find a contract on your desk for the next film that you want to make. This is perhaps the most important thing and the only true way to gauge the success of your first low-budget, independent film.

All your sales 'stuff' will just about fit into a small office archive box, the kind used for storing suspension files. Keep all your stuff in this box and never send out masters. Clone master tapes, duplicate disks and transparencies, photocopy paperwork ... and keep the masters some place safe.

Sales – Domestic Theatrical

Theatrical release is the Holy Grail for low/no budget feature films. It's where every film maker would love their audience to receive their film. It's also one of the fiercest market places in the world so understandably competition is high and glory, if any, is short lived. Commercial failure in the cinema, from a purely statistical perspective, is almost certainly assured.

Why you should release in the cinema

Because you want to do it.
Yes, it's an ego boost, but you probably deserve it. However, don't just do it to accommodate the wishes of cast, crew, friends, relatives or investors. You can have a special screening in pretty much any cinema on a Sunday morning that will carry a modest price tag.

Because it will help sell the film abroad.
Any theatrical release will generate some reviews and hopefully, some of these reviews will be good. But don't count on it. A theatrical review also means your sales agents will be able to say, *'yes it was released in cinemas in the UK . . . '* No matter how badly your film performs, this will sound good and boost sales and perceived value.

Because it will help sell the film to video, DVD, TV etc.
Your release will raise the profile of your film such that when it hits the shelves in Blockbuster, it will already be known. You might get some good quotes from reviews to put on the sleeve and Blockbuster and other video outlets will certainly have heard of the film. Ditto for TV and Satellite.

Because it will platform you as a film maker.
'So what have you done?' asks the executive, and you reply 'you can see my movie down at the Odeon . . .' It's always a great way to open a meeting as it says very loudly, I am serious and my film was taken seriously too. All those good reviews will also help your agent get you more work.

Because, damn it, it's why you did it in the first place!
Not logical, but at the end of the day, low budget independent film making is about as far as you can get from logical.

Why you shouldn't release in cinemas

Because it's a dog.
You might not like it but your movie, like my first movie *The Runner* just stinks. If you dare put it in front of critics, they may shred you and the movie. You will lose a lot of money and possibly even damage your video and TV prospects.

Because you will only post produce to videotape.
Shooting on video only, or post producing to video only means that the cost of making a 35mm blow up print is massive (around £20-30K depending on various factors) and you might not be able to make that commitment. There is a strong argument that making a genre film for TV only is a very smart business move, but it won't launch your career.

Because you can't afford to throw more money away.
Sadly, even over a great deal of time your film may not make much money back and now you feel like spending a further ten grand and upward isn't too smart. Sell to video; take the money and run.

Because your movie has already done its job.
You set out to carve a career and your movie has done just that. You already have a deal for a fully funded movie where other people will do all the hard work of releasing the film for you. Move on; don't spend time splashing in a puddle when you could be swimming in a lake. Do a great DVD transfer and be happy that most enthusiasts will see it at home on a widescreen TV and with great surround sound.

Domestic Theatrical

Let's assume . . . You've decided that you want to go the whole nine yards — a theatrical release, then video, DVD, Pay TV, free TV, Internet . . . and any other future possibilities . . . You have also decided, perhaps against better judgement, to decline working with an established distributor and release the film yourself.

Why you should self distribute . . .

Because any mistakes you make will be your own.

If this is your first movie, learning how a film is distributed is important. Most of it is dull, but if YOU release your film, at the least you'll fully appreciate how it works. If you screw up it will be your mistake and you won't be able to moan at anyone. Equally, if you get it right, and it's not that hard, you get the glory and the rewards.

Because you will get all the money.

If the film makes any money, you will not have to suffer the frustration of knowing that the distributor has taken all the money, paid themselves their percentages, paid off their expenses, and left nothing in the pot for you.

Because you probably won't get ripped off.

Sad but true, many distributors are less than honest. Not because they are crooks, mainly because distributing independent films is essentially an impossible job and they will end up cooking the books. Not all will do this, but a good few will.

Because a distributor may shelve your film.

You may sign what seems like a great deal, but the person you had a special relationship with moves on and you are left with a faceless distributor. Worse, they may not really care about your film and after showing it around, could just let it collect dust. What do they care if it makes no real money back, it's not like they are investors.

Because no one else will release it . . .

Ah, now we come to the one and only REAL reason you are self-distributing. No one will take your baby and give it the legs you feel it deserves. Be careful as distributors know their game, and if they pass then there is a good reason for that. But hey, everyone passed on your script so what do they know! Errr . . .

Why you shouldn't self distribute . . .

Because you hate your movie and want to move on.

Yes, that's probably the truth of the matter and is probably the smartest thing to do. However much you hate your movie as you complete it, over a short time you will grow to love it again and rekindle your romance. So chill directly after completing your film.

Because distributors know the game.

This is what they do day after day. They bring something beyond value to the table, they bring experience. They also bring contacts and personal relationships and in this game, it's not what you know, but who you know.

Because you should be onto the next thing.

When your film is released and if it is well received you will have a golden opportunity when the industry, both in the UK and LA, will view you with some interest. They may well ask the question, 'So if I gave you a million bucks.. what would you make?' In an ideal world you'd slap that great script on the table and scream, 'This, and it's going to be great . . . ' But if you have been embroiled in the distribution of your first film you probably won't have that great script waiting in the wings.

Because frankly, the movie stinks.

And not only should you not self distribute, but no one should distribute it. Bury it, chalk it up to experience and move onto your next film where you won't make as many mistakes and hopefully come away with a great movie.

The theatrical release is where you show your movie in cinemas, usually for the PR value for both you as a film maker, and the film . . . this may help with video, DVD, TV and international sales.

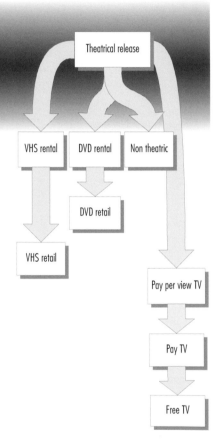

Small pond with BIG FISH . . .

And you are the tiddler . . . Theatrical distribution in the UK for indie pics is a very limited game. There are only a few players who would even consider your movie, and more often, new film makers opt to do it themselves. Whether you chose to use a distributor, or do it yourself, you will inevitably become very involved, so the two models, *distributor* or *self distribution*, are pretty much the same.

Self abuse

If you do self distribute, this is how to do it. In essence, what you will do is set up a new distribution company to handle the release of your movie. Think of it as a new arm of your existing production company. You don't need to set up a new limited company for this, just continue to use the one you set up for production. Thankfully there are no major legal issues to deal with either, as you are not going to assign your rights to anyone.

Book the booker

The first thing to do is cut a deal with a theatrical booker. This is the person who will physically manage the release, after all, you don't want to be bothered about moving a print from Scunthorpe to Brighton between the last screening on the Thursday night and the first screening at lunch time on a Friday. They do this day in, day out and know whom to use as a rock solid courier. There are currently two UK theatrical bookers (2003), Ratpack and Winstone Films. Show them your movie and see if they want to get involved. If they do it's up to you to cut the best deal you can, and for low budget films, it usually follows one of two routes – revenue split or up front fee.

Whichever deal you cut you will supply all the materials (prints and posters etc.) as well as handling the press and PR. They will manage the physical elements of the release such as ensuring prints, trailers and posters get to theatres on time. In the revenue split model you will share the returns after the booker has recouped their expenses. In the straight fee model you would pay an amount per print for them to manage the release. This is often something like £2500 for doing it, plus £500 per print, plus all courier fees (which usually aren't too much, say another couple of hundred). Obviously the revenue-split method is less risky but your film will need to be strong to convince them to become yet another investor in this ongoing and probably burgeoning project and more often than not they will quite sensibly require a straight fee.

So you cut the deal. The booker will then take a 35mm print to a preview theatre such as Mr Young's and show it to the exhibitors (exhibitors being the cinema owners) after which the booker will cut deals with one or more of the major chains, and with independent theatres. A launch date will be set some time in the future, probably about three to six months hence and the booker will report back to you. From then on much of the hard work will land

Theatrical Release Flow chart

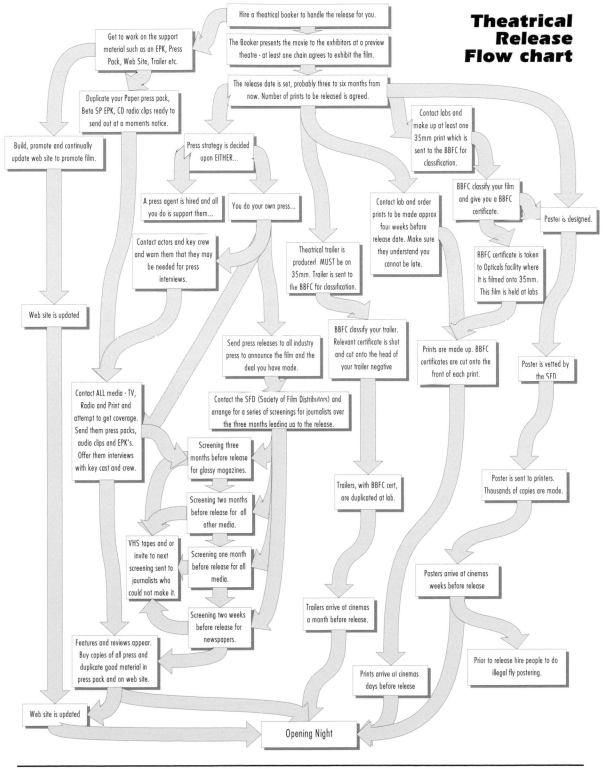

Hire a theatrical booker to handle the release for you.

The Booker presents the movie to the exhibitors at a preview theatre - at least one chain agrees to exhibit the film.

The release date is set, probably three to six months from now. Number of prints to be released is agreed.

Get to work on the support material such as an EPK, Press Pack, Web Site, Trailer etc.

Duplicate your Paper press pack, Beta SP EPK, CD radio clips ready to send out at a moments notice.

Build, promote and continually update web site to promote film.

Press strategy is decided upon EITHER...

Contact labs and make up at least one 35mm print which is sent to the BBFC for classification.

BBFC classify your film and give you a BBFC certificate.

Poster is designed.

A press agent is hired and all you do is support them...

You do your own press...

Contact lab and order prints to be made approx four weeks before release date. Make sure they understand you cannot be late.

RBFC certificate is taken to Opticals facility where It is filmed onto 35mm. This film is held at labs

Contact actors and key crew and warn them that they may be needed for press interviews.

Theatrical trailer is produced. MUST be on 35mm. Trailer is sent to the BBFC for classification.

Web site is updated

Send press releases to all industry press to announce the film and the deal you have made.

BBFC classify your trailer. Relevant certificate is shot and cut onto the head of your trailer negative

Prints are made up. BBFC certificates are cut onto the front of each print.

Poster is vetted by the SFD

Contact ALL media - TV, Radio and Print and attempt to get coverage. Send them press packs, audio clips and EPK's. Offer them interviews with key cast and crew.

Contact the SFD (Society of Film Distributors) and arrange for a series of screenings for journalists over the three months leading up to the release.

Screening three months before release for glossy magazines.

Trailers, with BBFC cert, are duplicated at lab.

Poster is sent to printers. Thousands of copies are made.

Screening two months before release for all other media.

VHS tapes and or invite to next screening sent to journalists who could not make it.

Screening one month before release for all media.

Posters arrive at cinemas weeks before release

Trailers arrive at cinemas a month before release.

Features and reviews appear. Buy copies of all press and duplicate good material in press pack and on web site.

Screening two weeks before release for newspapers.

Prior to release hire people to do illegal fly postering.

Web site is updated

Prints arrive at cinemas days before release

Opening Night

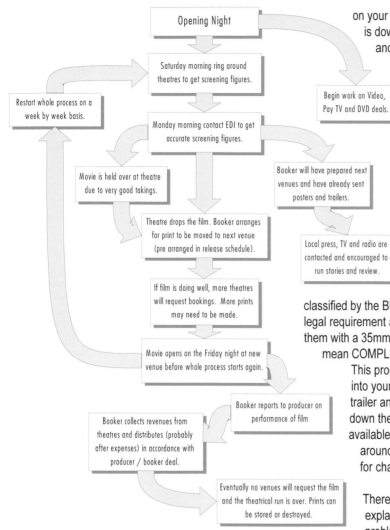

on your shoulders as much of the success of your film is down to press and elements such as the poster and trailer.

It's all in the name

A word about the movie title. Strong genre titles will always attract a crowd, especially from the less discerning multiplex audiences . . . *'That sounds like a good movie . . .'* is a phrase I have heard repeatedly. As if the title is any gauge of quality! *Urban Ghost Story* performed well in the provinces and I believe that it is largely due to the strong, simple, genre title.

Certifiable!

Every film in the UK screened in a commercial theatre needs to be classified by the BBFC (British Board of Film Classification), a legal requirement and unavoidable. You will need to supply them with a 35mm print of your film that is completed, and I mean COMPLETED. They will then screen it and classify it. This procedure can take a couple of months so build it into your schedule. They will also do this for your trailer and separately for your VHS/DVD release later down the line. The current cost of this classification is available from the BBFC website, but budget for around £1k. The BBFC provides a discounted rate for charitable organisations.

There are extensive guidelines on their site explaining what kind of material will cause problems. You'll have a good idea as to what certificate it will be awarded, and you'll also have a gut feeling if your movie may run into difficulties. The BBFC have relaxed considerably over recent years, so it's unlikely you will run into problems.

Once the BBFC have classified your film they will contact you and supply you with a small certificate. You will need to make sure this gets shot onto 35mm film and a good five seconds of that certificate is cut onto the head of each and every print. Sometimes the booker will take care of this for you but you'd better ask in case they assume you're doing it.

Flashback

Let's flashback to the moment when you've just cut the deal for your release. The number of prints has been decided so call the laboratory and

Theatrical release flow chart cont . . .

warn them that you're going to need the prints a few weeks before your release and ensure they can guarantee to hit your deadline. Obviously, you don't want to make a print until you have to, as each print will cost in the region of £1k. Remember to factor in that one print that the BBFC already has and is using to classify your film.

Doing your own release will mean you may well end up carrying prints between venues, screenings and festivals. Beware, even a short 80 minute feature film on 35mm is VERY heavy.

Poster perfection

All the way through the making of your film from conception to its recent completion, you'll have had poster image ideas. You can design the poster yourself or have a third party design company handle it on your behalf. It isn't too hard to design your own poster but there is a strong argument for involving a specialist designer who can look at your work and movie and perhaps come up with a new and exciting spin. Hopefully you have arrived at a strong and simple title, which should be large and bold on your poster and readable from a distance. Remember also that the

Distributor Theatrical Release

Micro Release Approximate Costs	
Two prints	£1,400.00
BBFC classification	£1,000.00
Trailers and prints	£1,500.00
Bookers fees	£3,000.00
PR agent (on the cheap!)	£3,000.00
Posters and printing (inc design)	£2,000.00
Fly postering	£1,000.00
Total approximate costs for micro release	£12,900.00

Micro Release Box Office Revenues	
Average ticket price	£5.00
Minus VAT at 17.5%	£4.26
Of which distributor gets 25%	£1.07
(house nut is not reached)	
Number of tickets sold in 1 week = 250	
Box office gross (after VAT deducted)	£1,065.00
Distributor gets	£266.25
Film plays for one week at 30 venues (and that's good!)	
Total net to distributor	£7,987.50
Distributor deducts their 35% commision leaving	£2,795.63
Distributor now deducts expenses leaving a balance of	-£10,104.38
Total theatrical release returns (or in this case loss)	-£10,104.38

DIY Theatrical Release

Micro Release Approximate Costs	
Two prints	£1,800.00
BBFC classification	£1,000.00
Trailers and prints	£1,500.00
Bookers fees	£3,000.00
PR agent (on the cheap!)	£3,000.00
Posters and printing (inc design)	£2,000.00
Fly postering	£1,000.00
Total approximate costs for micro release	£13,300.00

Micro Release Box Office Revenues	
Average ticket price	£5.00
Minus VAT at 17.5%	£4.26
Of which distributor gets 25%	£1.07
(house nut is not reached)	
Number of tickets sold in 1 week = 250	
Box office gross (after VAT deducted)	£1,065.00
Distributor gets	£266.25
Film plays for one week at 30 venues (and that's good!)	
Total net to distributor	£7,987.50
You now deduct your costs from returns	-£5,312.50
Total theatrical release returns (or in this case loss)	-£5,312.50

Scenerio #1 (Left pane) Film makers work with a distributor), Scenario #2 (right pane) Film makers act as their own distributor. It is worth noting that it is likely a film, if self distributed, will not perform as well as if it is released with a ditsributor who knows the ropes and already has relationships with other companies in the industry.

This release assumes that the film is really quite good and has an audience. The release takes place during a quiet time and goes out on two prints. It also assumes the film makers work for months on the PR and fully support it. In this breakdown it assumes the film will play for a total of 30 weeks, that's 15 weeks for each print at probably a total of 20 venues (remember some venues may hold it over for more than one week). Any losses will normally be deducted from Video, DVD and TV sales later on.

Title	Distributor	Country of origin	£Box office
About Adam	Metrodome	UK IE US	£76,333
Another Life	Winchester	UK	£11,316
Beautiful Creatures	UIP	UK	£203,619
Bloody Angels	ICA	UK NO	£5,267
Blow Dry	Buena Vista	UK US DL	£122,630
Born Romantic	Optimum	UK	£381,840
Bread And Roses	Film Four	UK DL ED IT FR	£223,574
Bridget Jones Diary	UIP	UK US FR	£42,007,008
Brother	Film Four	UK JP US FR	£97,024
Children's Midsummer…, The	Squirrel	UK	£1,615
Christmas Carol, A	Pathe	UK DL	£1,372,998
Claim, The	Pathe	UK CA FR	£214,243
Contender, The	Icon	UK US DL	£405,803
Cpt. Corelli's Mandolin	Buena Vista	UK US FR	£9,793,071
Croupier	Film Four	UK IE DL FR	£548,080
Dazzle	Peakviewing	UK	£3,056
Dead Babies	Helkon SK	UK	£3,821
Disco Pigs	Entertainment	UK IE	£116,578
Dog Eat Dog	Film Four	UK DL	£3,935
Enemy At The Gates	Pathe	UK US IE FR DL	£3,935,795
Enigma	Buena Vista	UK US DL NL	£4,747,440
Esther Kahn	Feature Film Co.	UK FR	£2,361
Filthy Earth, The	Film Four	UK	£3,737
Gabriel And Me	Pathe	UK	£21,374
Ghost World	Icon	UK US DL	£528,572
Goodbye Charlie Bright	Metrodome	UK	£82,665
Greenfingers	Winchester	UK US	£66,670
Harry Potter & The Philosopher's Stone	Warner	UK US	£57,496,638
High Heels And Low Lifes	Buena Vista	UK	£1,630,090
Hole, The	Pathe	UK FR	£2,292,804
Inbetweeners	Britpack	UK	£18,888
Intimacy	Pathe	UK FR	£370,501
Jump Tomorrow	Film Four	UK US	£20,109
Lara Croft: Tomb Raider	UIP	UK US DL FR	£12,822,883
Large	Pathe	UK	£16,242
Last Resort	Artificial Eye	UK	£141,770
Late Night Shopping	Film Four	UK DL	£104,286
Liam	Artificial Eye	UK DL IT	£60,791
Like Father	Amber	UK	£1,591
Little Otik	Film Four	UK CZR JP	£24,355
Lost Lover, The	Metrodome	UK IT	£2,700
Low Down, The	Film Four	UK	£42,947
Lucky Break	Film Four	UK US DL	£1,254,772
Man Who Wasn't There, The	Entertainment	UK US	£1,645,828
Martins, The	Icon	UK	£967,528
Me Without You	Momentum	UK DL	£126,710
Mean Machine, The	UIP	UK US	£3,006,463
Mike Bassett: England Manager	Entertainment	UK US	£3,536,652
My Brother Tom	Film Four	UK DL	£3,260
Navigators, The	bfi	UK ES IT FR	£8,748
New Year's Day	Optimum	UK FR	£10,959
Nine Lives Of Tomas Katz, The	NFT	UK DL	£4,451
On The Nose	Buena Vista	UK IE CA	£55,196
Out Of Depth	Steon	UK	£3,299
Pandaemonium	Optimum	UK US	£64,965
Parole Officer, The	UIP	UK	£3,283,870
Pasty Faces	Metrodome	UK	£9,763
Proof Of Life	Warner	UK US	£2,771,631
Rage	Metrodome	UK	£5,543
Room To Rent	Pathe	UK FR	£7,867
Saltwater	Artificial Eye	UK IE ES	£19,146
Sexy Beast	Film Four	UK US ES	£774,942
Shadow Of The Vampire	Metrodome	UK US LU	£245,294
Shiner	Momentum	UK	£34,499
Sorcerer's Apprentice, The	Peakviewing	UK	£6,927
South West 9	Fruitsalad	UK IE	£82,198
Strictly Sinatra	UIP	UK	£16,172
The 51st State	Momentum	UK CA	£3,492,423
The Criminal, The	Downtown	UK US	£40,565
Truth Game, The	NFT	UK	£3,568
Vory Annie Mary	Film Four	UK FR	£148,965
Weak At Denise	Guerilla	UK	£1,920
Wedding Planner, The	Pathe	UK US DL	£2,545,166
What's Cooking	Helkon	SK UK US	£200,059

UK box office gross for UK films in 2001

This chart is an alphabetical list of all UK films released in 2001 (excluding re-issues), be they big or small budget, UK only or international co-productions, even semi-Hollywood studio based. We can't print their budgets as we just don't know them, and even if we did research the numbers, it's unlikely we would ever get told the truth, which would then be simply misleading – producers just don't want their financial dirty laundry to be on display. Remember, these are the box office grosses, so from these figures you need to deduct 17.5% for VAT, the cinema would then on average (certainly for the smaller, non major films) take 75% of the remainder, the balance going to the distributor, who would then take their split (whatever deal the producer cut) the balance going toward their expenses. Take a long hard look at some of the indie films, look at their box office and do the simple maths . . . Even indie films that look like they did well, such as 'The Inbetweeners', were released on 30 prints or so (at around £800 each, never mind the cost of transport, advertising, etc.) It's a sobering chart.

Source The British Film Institute.

UK theatrical poster size is unique – it is called Quad (40" by 30"). Remember it also a legal requirement that the BBFC certificate appears on the poster. If certification does not take place in time you can manually place stickers on the posters at the eleventh hour. If you have a very small theatrical print release, you can also print off a few posters, maybe as few as 10. They are expensive, but much cheaper than running off 1000. Most good commercial colour printers can do you a deal on printing posters and as a guide should cost you £2k-ish for 1000 posters.

Once you have designed your poster, you will need to have it vetted by the SFD (Society of Film Distributors) and the BBFC. Part of their job is to ensure that artwork isn't offensive to the public and is a requirement of the industry – you cannot skip it. Once the posters are printed you'll undoubtedly frame the first one, put it on your production office wall and send the majority of the rest to the booker who will then co-ordinate sending them out to the cinemas in advance.

Stick 'em up!

In the week of the release, fly postering is essential. It's illegal to put posters up in public places without relevant licences, but it goes on all the time – no matter how big and supposedly legit a company is, they will dabble in illegal fly postering. It's essential that your name does not appear on the poster as this could lead back to you, so you will need to make a simple and generic poster with an image and movie title only, along with tag lines if you like.

Then cut a deal with a shady character who has a gang of people who go out at three in the morning and stick your posters up wherever you have paid for them to go. We can't tell you who these people are, for obvious legal reasons, but ask around and you'll soon make contact. It usually costs around £2k and you can fly poster pretty much any city you like – there's always someone ready to do it.

There are no guarantees either. You may get your poster up one night and the following night it's been fly postered over. There is no redress as the whole deal is dodgy in the first place. On our second film *White Angel*, we fly postered and the following night, Pink Floyd covered every poster we had paid to put up.

Press-ing matters

Flashback again, you've just cut your deal. You now need to make a decision about your press campaign. Are you going to do it or are you going to pay someone to do it on your behalf? PR agents aren't cheap but are excellent at what they do, namely placing you and your movie in high profile maga-zines, newspapers, radio, TV etc. If you decide to pay

During the theatrical release for Urban Ghost Story, venues that we felt would generate larger audiences were selected. One such venue was the cinema in Chris's home town of Wigan, where a series of articles written by sympathetic journalist Charles Graham forced a release. The first was 'SNUBBED' which ran the 'local boy does good but big business ignores talent' angle, followed by 'SUCCESS', where the cinema agreed to screen the film. The resulting full pages in the local press generated controversy and Urban Ghost Story ended up being the third biggest performer of the week (only beaten by 'American Pie 2' and Spielberg's AI).

Fly postering is illegal. The poster campaigns you see in the streets are put up by organised gangs that at best are on the edge of the criminal underworld. Don't think about driving around town at 3am with a bucket of paste, brush and 300 posters or you may find yourself in a very unpleasant position! Pay them or don't bother.

David Wilkinson
Guerilla Films

'I started as a self distributor and have been producing films for over 20 years. In the UK I am still the only real producer who is also a distributor and my advice to a new film maker would be to go this route.'

'When distributing yourself you must appreciate that you are NOT going to recoup much of your P&A spend from the cinema release. No self distributor over the last 15 years has managed to recoup their money from the cinema alone. They may claim that they have but I know who they are and I know the true figures. Most established distributors don't recoup their theatric P&A from the cinema so it's almost impossible that an "amateur" is going to. This is why hardly any established company can afford to take on a no budget film for the cinema.'

'If you self-distribute you are going to put more time, energy and enthusiasm into your film than any third party.'

'The real income for your film is going to come from video, DVD and all forms of TV. You must get all this sorted out and in place before you start your theatrical campaign. Most self distributors spend all their time on the cinema and forget these other markets which are far, far more important. One self distributor came to me to take on his film for release in the rental market – 18 months after the cinema opening! Of course it was too late.'

someone to do it, much of the hard work of the release will be taken care of by them. PR quotes are often in the range of £10-20k (ouch!), but we have had collaborative and excellent PR campaigns run by a small firm or individual for as little as £2k. Arguably, this is some of the the best money you can spend. Whether you do your own press or a PR agent handles it, this is what should happen.

First of all, contact all the key crew and cast members, warn them of the release and explain that they will be expected to help in the publicity. The SFD will be contacted and a number of screenings set up and staggered in such a way that every journalist will have a clear opportunity to see your film.

SFD

The SFD ensure that your film does not compete for press screening time with any other movie which means that if journalists don't turn up to see your film, it isn't because they're watching *Jurassic Park 4*, it's because they weren't told about the screening by either you or your press agents or the film isn't sufficiently interesting to get them to come and see it. There will be a number of these screenings, maybe as many as 7 leading up to the release of the film. Even then many journalists will not get to see it on the big screen and will end up watching it on a crummy VHS. God forbid!

Press pack

At all times you need to supply journalists with the materials they need to report or comment upon you or your film. Hopefully, months earlier you will have completed a professional and extensive press pack (see elsewhere in this book). You must ensure that all journalists get copies of your press pack, and where relevant, copies of the music, soundbites for the radio, or a BetaSP electronic press kit (EPK) for TV. Remember, if people don't know about your film, they're not going to come and see it. As press and reviews start to appear, a good agent will send you copies, but it's a good idea to start going to the newsagents on a regular basis to check magazines for reviews. Buy yourself a large scrapbook and a glue stick and start archiving your press cuttings. Integrate any particularly good reviews into the back of your press pack, offering the journalists the opportunity to read good reviews of your film. Don't go crazy and include 100 good reviews (like you're going to get 100 good reviews!), 2 or 3 will do.

Hopefully you have been managing a website throughout your production and now you can use it to announce the release of your film. In the weeks leading up to your release it is a good idea to update your website on an almost daily basis. On the opening night, take a digital stills camera, shoot some pics and get them on the website for Saturday morning, along with the *'successful low budget film'* story. Ideally you will have developed an extensive e-mail mailing list. Use this to announce all dates and venues for

CASE STUDY – Urban Ghost Story

UGC Wigan Box Office 12th - 18th October 2001

American Pie 2 (opening week)	£20,567
AI (week 5)	£1,739
Urban Ghost Story (opening week)	£1,423
Knights Tale (week 9)	£1,111
The Score (week3)	£812
Fast & Furious (week 5)	£779
Enigma (week3)	£773
South West Nine (opening week)	£266
Total weekly box office	£27,470

These figures are the total box office revenues for the UGC Wigan Multiplex (in the Northwest of England). You can clearly see why cinema chains favour popular American movies with American Pie 2 taking pretty much four times as much as all the other films combined. Even so, Urban Ghost Story performed well. A combination of good local PR and a strong simple genre title were probably responsible. South West Nine, another low budget UK film with a large press and ads spend performed poorly. We believe that it's title and Londoncentric theme were a turn off, especially for the average cinema goer in Wigan!

the release of the film. Also use your website as a dynamic and updateable press-pack, including all your good reviews and features.

For one week only!

One of the major problems with the theatrical release is that everyone gets very excited about it and says *'yes, I'm going to come and see it, but maybe I'll wait until the second week . . .'* Unfortunately, it is not uncommon for independent films to last only a matter of days at the box office, so it is imperative to ensure that every potential audience member understands that they must see the movie *this week* and not *next week*, or it will probably be gone.

Check in the ego in before you go . . .

It's inevitable that for the release of your first film your ego is going to require a countrywide release with a bigger PR spend than you can afford. Aside from being practically impossible, it may not be a good idea. Each print costs £1k, to move that print and service that print will cost more. And each extra screen in any one city on which your film plays will dilute the quantity of audience between venues.

One refreshing thought is that large or small, your release should generate pretty much the same amount of press coverage. In 95 out of 100 instances, a UK theatrical release in of itself is commercial suicide, but it is a wonderful ego brush and often very successful in marking you as a film maker. The trick is to get your ego massaged, get all the good press, but to risk as little as possible. The way to do this is to go out on as few prints as possible. Sure, this means you will not be a smash hit, but it also means you won't lose a fortune and you will still get all the value of a theatrical release. And if the film does well, it will continue to play as long as audiences come. There are examples of films running for months on one screen in London, in a few rare examples even years.

You have three days to make your mark - Friday, Saturday and Sunday. If you don't perform well then the exhibitors who last week were very enthusiastic, will dump you like a psychotic date. Draft in everyone you can to help you make as big a splash as possible. Call everyone you know, tell everyone you meet, hassle strangers on the streets . . . Tell them all to come and see your film over the weekend.

CASE STUDY – Urban Ghost Story

Our third movie, Urban Ghost Story, had what we feel was a successful yet considered release. We played only in very friendly theatres where we knew we would get good figures, often being held over for second weeks. We released only on two screens, but always managed to make it appear that we were doing something bigger.

Primarily we released in London (Odeon Panton St.) where the majority of cast and crew lived, along with thousands of film fans and low budget film makers. We also opened in Glasgow where the film was set and lead actress was from. In both instances we were held over. We played a number of other venues including my home town of Wigan in the North West where the film did exceptionally well, being moved to the premiere screen for week two, and even beating movies like The Fast and The Furious. The reviews and press were pretty much all good, fuelling DVD / VHS interest.

The release also platformed our company, Living Spirit Pictures, and in meetings whenever people ask about our films, we can say that we release theatrically and have the figures and reviews to prove it.

As an example, our second film *White Angel* went out on 16 prints and was a disaster. By contrast our following film, *Urban Ghost Story* went out on 2 prints, broke even and gained just as much press and industry attention. Plus we were not as stretched so we could focus more on the most important aspects of the release.

You must be Nuts!

The golden area to aim for with a theatrical release is to hit the house nut. What the hell is the house nut? This a figure, set by each and every cinema (and every one is different) where the revenue split inverts, from their favour to your favour. It's designed to reward the makers of extremely successful films.

As a rough guide . . . A cinema has 200 seats and the average figure for the house nut is set at £18.50 per seat. So the house nut is 200 x £18.50 = £3,700. That's what you have to take in a week to hit the house nut. For that first £3,800 there is a 75 / 25 split in the cinema's favour. After hitting the house nut, the figures begin to invert on a sliding scale and can end up at 90/10 in favour of the film makers (distributor). This goes some way to explain why on the opening weekends of blockbuster films, drinks and popcorn sales are so vital to cinemas – it's where they make the *real* money.

Showing in the smallest screens in cinemas is also a good idea because the house nut is lower for that screen. Your ego may love screening in a 400 seat theatre but you will never hit the house nut, but hitting the house nut in a screen that has say 75 seats is more possible.

In reality it's unlikely you will hit the house nut, unless you mount an extraordinary campaign to get every person you know, and every person they know, to come along on the opening weekend. This was echoed by a distributor friend who confided that in the 20 years he has been in the business he has never hit the house nut.

If you are going to have a cast and crew gathering at one of these screenings, do it in the opening weekend but in the afternoon. You don't want to pack out your screenings in the evening showings where 'real' customers who don't know you and just want to see the movie may turn up and get refused as the screen is sold out.

Act BIG but be small

Keeping the number of prints down has clear cost advantages, but if you are considering releasing your film in more than one screen in any major city, there are some things to consider. Let's assume there is a finite amount of people that will see your film, people that are interested in seeing independent, low-budget films. There aren't many of those people. So let's assume you're going to open in a city such as Glasgow, and let's assume there is a maximum of 1000 people who will brave a wet and cold February evening to see your micro-budget movie. If you are playing on two screens at either end of the city, they'll just go for the closest and they'll have cost you two prints to service that audience.

If you screened on only one print, they would all be forced to attend just the one cinema. These people are probably not casual moviegoers but hardcore, and will go the extra distance to see that non-Hollywoodised, low-budget, quirky, weird, off-the-wall, whatever your movie is. You may lose a few to the extra distance, but it will save you considerably more than the cost of the extra print and its servicing. When Monday morning comes and the cinema owners look at the weekend figures in order to decide which films stay for another week and which get axed, your figures could be £750 in each of two screens *'nah ditch it . . .'* or £1500 in one screen *'That's ok, let's keep it for another week . . .'* It's extraordinarily unlikely that your film will go over two weeks, unless it has hit a niche or is of exceptional quality. That second week is important because it doesn't cost you anything to be there, whereas moving to a new venue for another 'first week' will have cost you money to get there. So the second week is financial icing on the cake.

The decision as to whether you stay the second week in any one theatre will be made on a Monday morning by the exhibitors, (cinemas) and it's based wholly on the weekend's takings. If you hit the house nut, you'll stay. If you did well, you'll still probably stay. When you do eventually get bumped, the booker should have arranged a new venue for you to move to, and the print should be shipped to the new cinema probably in a new city and the whole process will begin again.

Ian Rattray
Ratpack Films

'The theatrical booker is the link in the chain between the 'creative' and the 'exhibition' sides of the industry. I organise everything required to get the film onto the screens in a cinema which usually starts with getting the film entered into the booker's bible, the EDI and SFD release schedules. These schedules inform anyone who is interested, just what will be released and when. This information is often accessed by other distributors and of course, the press and media.

The process usually starts with a meeting, then a viewing of the film, ideally on a big screen but more often than not on a VHS tape! I would then advise on the viability of the film in the cinema – not every film is suited, a fact many new film makers don't want to hear. If we decided to proceed I would cut a deal with the film makers and advise them on PR agencies and draw up a release budget. I do not pay for a release, they do, be they the distributors or the film makers directly. I then organise an exhibitor (cinema owners) screening after which I produce a booker's reaction sheet. Be warned these reports can be painful reading! From here we can work out the final release date, which is typically many months away, and then go through the physical steps of the release – moving prints, collecting royalties etc.

Distribution isn't rocket science, but it is an art, perhaps even a dark art. It requires an instinct for what is right for a film.'

In conclusion . . .

There are two sets of figures in this section. Study them well as they will give you a feel of just how little commercial value the release represents. You can draw your own conclusions from these figures.

Secondly, whilst it may be financial suicide in the short term, with a longer view, a theatrical release can pay back dividends. It should enhance video / DVD / TV deals domestically. But most important is the impact on international sales. A film has a one year shelf life for a sales agent before it becomes 'old news' and essentially part of their back catalogue. If a film is not released domestically within that one year window, it sends out a message to international buyers – *there is something wrong with this film*. Accordingly its value can drop, and possibly slip into the unsellable category.

Finally, books such as the Time Out and Halliwell's film guides only carry reviews of theatrically released movies.

Whilst its time-consuming and often soul-destroying, a long run travelling campaign with perhaps only two prints has in the past netted the distributors/ film makers hundreds of thousands of pounds (The Scarlet Tunic for instance). To make this type of release an enduring success and not just an effective PR exercise, will take months if not a year, and will require an extraordinary commitment to publicity at a grass roots level in every single venue attended. This means local newspapers, radio and TV and personal appearances wherever the film goes. Alternatively, you can opt to grab the PR value, screen only in the venues where you know and can guarantee you will do good business, get in and out as quickly and painlessly as you can, and grab the best video / TV deal you can get whilst riding high on any good PR and Box Office you can shout about.

If you go to a screening of your film in a commercial cinema, make yourself known to the manager. Usually, they will be happy to chat to you and give you all the figures for the week's takings.

How to make your own movie poster

Tag line text, prepared in a Word Processor, imported and laid out in Quark Express.

Movie logo prepared in Adobe Illustrator, and laid out in Quark Xpress.

Credit billing text, prepared in a Word Processor, imported and laid out in Quark Express.

Photographic background prepared in Photoshop, then laid out in Quark Express.

Additional logos prepared in Adobe Illustrator and laid out in Quark Express.

Producing your own artwork for posters and video sleeves is both fun and relatively easy, especially for those who like using computers and who have an eye for images. Don't get drawn into the Mac or PC debate, both can handle this type of work with little effort. There are three major software tools that you will need to use . . .

Bitmap 'photo' editor

First you will create and work with photographic images (bitmaps). These are things like a montage of photos of your actors, a fireball, or image of a hand holding a gun. Essentially photographs that you will manipulate and edit. For this kind of work you will need a photo editing program such as Adobe Photoshop. It's not hard to track down and buy cheap copies of either an LE version (light edition but still perfectly adequate) or a copy that is a few versions old (Photoshop 7 is currently the latest version, but I still use Photoshop 5 as it does everything I need).

Photoshop is THE industry leader, so stick with it. Images created with Photoshop are made of individual pixels, or dots. That means that if you make the image bigger, so the dots get bigger too. That's why you have to work at the very highest resolution you can possibly ask your computer to do – nowadays, this isn't really an issue as the cheapest computers have enough processor power, RAM and hard disk space to cope.

Photographic bitmaps do not fare well when increased in size if the original was too low resolution.

Vector 'graphics' editor

Second you will use a Vector editing program to handle graphical elements such as your movie logo, a Dolby logo, BBFC certificates etc. The industry leader here is Adobe Illustrator, but for most people this is a little over the top. There are a host of cheaper programs that will do the job more than adequately, even some freeware and shareware programs do a splendid job.

These vector based images are not made of pixels or dots, and if you make them bigger, the edges will look clean and sharp. It's a similar technology to the one used by fonts, that's why you can make a font as big as you want and print it out on your laser printer and it will still look crisp and sharp. The only bummer with vector art is that it can't be used for photo realistic images, for that you'll need Photoshop.

Vector graphics resize perfectly but are useless for photos and suitable only for logos and text style elements.

Layout software

With these two programs you will create photographic images (that are resolution dependent) and vector based images and logos (that are resolution independent). The two are combined in a layout program such as industry leader Quark Xpress. Again, there are a number of alternative packages that you can use, but Quark is THE industry leader and whatever files you create need to be accessed and printed by professional printers. And they don't want to untangle incompatibilities and weird file types . . . So they will almost certainly demand a Quark file (as will your sales agents and distributors in foreign territories.) Quark is NEVER cheap software to buy, so it's best to find a friend who owns a copy and ask them to do the work for you. Again, don't get fazed by the PC or Mac debate – both should be able to open files created on either system (although moving from Mac to PC is more problematic). Whilst there is no real reason to recommend it, I have the gut feeling that if you complete your work on a Mac, you will get less grief from the printers. It's not a limitation of the technology, more a limitation of the printers and their unwillingness to work with PC files. In essence, you could easily create all your elements on a PC – images in Photoshop, logos with your Vector editing program (maybe Illustrator) and text in MS Word – then take them all to a designer with Quark and a Mac, and ask them to lay it out, then save the file and burn a CD for sending off to the printers.

Before you can start any creative work, get all your elements together. Type out your credit block and tag lines in MS Word. You don't want to do this when laying out in Quark as you will make spelling mistakes that won't get noticed until 200 posters are plastered outside your premiere screening. Trawl your reviews for good lines you can pull out (if a magazine said that your movie is 'staggering in its awfulness . . .' that could be truncated to 'staggering . . .'), and type those into the Word file too. Get all your pictures together – they should have been scanned already, the key images having been scanned from the photographic negative or transparency, ideally at a professional scanning bureau (although desktop scanners are very good now).

Stage 1 – Create the background in Photoshop

Your poster is going to contain a photographic image as the background, with text and logos laid on top. First we need to create that photographic background. This isn't going to be a long tutorial on how to use Photoshop, you'll have to buy another book for that, or just play around. Assuming you know how to do basic photo editing in Photoshop, here's the unique bits to keep an eye on. The final UK theatrical poster is Quad sized (30" by 40" landscape). We don't need to work at that size for now as we can 'size it up' in our final layout in Quark. Now before you go off on your *'Ah but you said you shouldn't increase photo image files in size as they are made of bitmaps and the dots might start to show . . .'* just go and take a close look at a movie poster. You will see that all the logos and text are super crisp, but up close, the photo image quality is pretty rough. This is entirely normal as you are supposed to see a poster from a distance, not six inches!

Sizing up

Using *Photoshop*, from the file menu select *New* and the *New* dialogue box will pop up. This has all the image size and resolution figures. In *Width* and *Height* change the drop down boxes to *pixels* (unless they are already set to *pixels*). Put *4000* in the Width box and *3000* in the Height box. This will create a file that is 4000 x 3000 pixels (and therefore the correct dimensions for a 40" x 30" poster). In Resolution type *300 (pixels / inch)*. This sets the resolution of the file.

The 'new' dialogue box

Next, from the *Mode* drop down menu select *CMYK Color*. Most printers (but not all) will use CMYK colours and NOT RGB. The two are radically different and there are some colour limitations with CMYK so get it right now.

Finally, at the top is the *Name* box, delete Untitled-1 and name it *UK Theatrical Quad Poster*. Click *OK* and a blank image will be displayed in Photoshop.

Saving habit

Save it now by going to the *File Menu* then *Save As* and the *Save As* dialogue Box will appear. It's important to use Photoshop's own file format (PSD) for now as this will allow you to use layers. In the *Save As* drop down box select *Photoshop *.PSD*. In the *File name* box type *UK Theatrical Quad Poster* then save it to your hard drive (in a place where you will remember where you put it!) From now, and at regular intervals, hit the CTRL + S keys on the keyboard (at the same time) to perform a save. Computers crash, especially when being pushed. You don't want to lose hours of work do you?

The 'save' dialogue box

Now you will need to create your image – as said earlier, this isn't a 'how to use Photoshop guide', that would add 1000 pages! Go and buy a good, simple, book. It isn't that hard to use.

Keep in mind . . .

One thing to keep in mind is that of bleed. Bleed is an area outside the main image where the image continues, so that it can accommodate the small discrepancies encountered when cutting up your poster at the printers. The image should always be designed with an extra 10% around the edges to accommodate this. It probably won't appear in your final poster as the printers will likely get it spot on, but if they are out by half a centimeter, then you need to make sure there is something there to be printed!

Another consideration for your design is that of word and logo placement. You don't want to create a background image so busy that words and logos get lost in a jumble.

Think bold. The movie title will be big, so leave a space for it. There will be a credit block, so leave a space at the bottom for it. Look at other posters, examine how they make their impact, the size of actors, other images from the movie, all in relation to the size and placement of the movie title logo and other text.

Remember, you need people to take a passing glance and know what your movie is called, what kind of movie it is, and whether they are interested – if they are they may take a closer (but still very quick) look. This isn't art, this is marketing, and it's a VERY busy world out there. Be bold, be simple, be bright.

TIF save

When completed, and be sure you are done . . . Save your file. Now we need to 'flatten' it as you will have many layers that will vastly increase the file size. From the *Layer* menu select *Flatten*. The image will now flatten down to one layer. Now save the file, not as a PSD (Photoshop file) but as a TIF file. TIFs are high quality images that are both Mac and PC friendly. They are also lossless, unlike the commonly used JPEGs (do not use JPEGs!). During the save procedure for TIF files it will bring up a dialogue box with two options. First is *LZW Compression*, a form of lossless compression which will make a smaller file without dropping any quality (although some very old Macs may have problems opening files with LZW compression). Second is *Byte Order,* which refers to the way in which the file data is saved. You can select either *PC* or *Mac* as both Macs and PCs can read each type, although for safety's sake, you might as well save it as a Mac byte ordered file (unless you plan to complete everything on a PC).

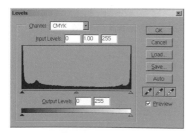

'Tiff Options' for saving a file

Legal levels

Finally, check your levels. The levels tool in Photoshop will help you check that you haven't made your image too dark or too bright. It might look fine on your monitor but have you set up your monitor correctly? It may look very different when printed. Colours are not so much a problem as contrast is. When printed out, images can often come out much darker or much lighter than expected, so set up your monitor correctly! Failing that, you can take a quick peek using the *Levels* tool. Go to the *Image* menu, then *Adjust*, then *Levels*. The *Levels* tool will appear. The graph shows the levels in the image, left is black, right is white. If you have any absolute black or white in your image, you need to make sure they are hitting their respective edges. You can adjust the highlights and dark areas with the left and right sliders, and the mid tones using the middle slider. You may also need to use the *Brightness and Contrast* tool (first close the *Levels* tool) to make the image punchier (by increasing contrast) or lighter / darker (by using the brightness slider).

Manipulating the levels in your file will tell you if you have true blacks and whites, and not mily grey blacks.

When you are done, re-save the image and close *Photoshop*. It's now time to start work on your logos.

Stage 2 – Create your vector artwork

Your Vector Artwork is stuff like th movie logo, certificates and other logos (like Dolby for instance). These all need to be prepared in a Vector Artwork program such as Adobe Illustrator. But there's no need to get quite so heavy and Illustrator is a bit of a monster for most people. There are heaps of good shareware programs to choose from as well as low cost competitors. A superb PC alternative is Xara and you can download a free demo version from www.xara.com. If you are quick, you can do all your work before the demo expires (although Xara is an extremely worthy purchase).

Commercial logos

All the logos, such as BBFC classification, Dolby logos etc., are surprisingly hard to come by (in easy to use formats). We have converted them all and saved them on our website (and will also be included in future editions of The Guerilla Film Makers Handbook CDRom*). They are saved in two formats,* Illustrator (.AI) *and* Windows Meta File (.WMF)*. On the whole, if you can use the* Windows Meta Files*, I would do so, they just seem to work better. Ironic huh?*

Tracking down vector art versions of logos is harder than you'd imagine.

This all leads me onto a philosophical point about computer software. Don't upgrade. Ever. Unless you absolutely must. You are just asking for problems. If it works, don't fix it. With regard to saving files . . . Most software offers you the option to save files in older formats. For instance, you might be using Word 2000, but your writer has Word 95 at home. They send you a Word 95 file, which you open in Word 2000, no problems. Then you do an edit, save it and send it back – but now they cannot open it – you have saved it as a Word 2000 file which is incompatible with Word 95! To get around this you could choose to save it as a Word 95 file instead of a Word 2000 file. The lesson – always save in older more compatible formats. The option to do this is often buried in the setup or simply a drop down menu in the Save As dialogue box that pops up when you tell your computer to save your work. This little tip could save you days of farting around with file incompatibilities. For example, on the BBFC website many of the certificates are saved as Illustrator files, version 10 that is, that won't open in version 9 . . . Grrrrr. Yet when saving in Illustrator, you can even save it as a version 1 Illustrator file! Why didn't they do that huh? OK, minor rant over.

Always save as the earliest compatible software version you are offered.

Your movie logo

It's important to create an identity for your movie, and that starts with the logo you design for the movie title. There are thousands of fonts available on the internet so there really is no excuse for failing to design an exciting and appropriate logo. You'll get a feel for how your logo should look, but keep it balanced, simple and above all BOLD! In your vector artwork software, type out your title, use your selected font, arrange and resize until you find a look that you like (play around with colours, drop shadows, bold, italic, different sizes, width and height etc . . .) Then select all the words and look for a command on one of the menus called 'group'. This will, er, group all the words into a single object. Lastly, go to the file menu, *and select* Export. *Hopefully, you'll have a number of options. On a PC select* Windows Meta Files (16bit) *and on a Mac select either* Adobe Illustrator *or* EPS. *Save the file to your hard drive. You can now use this logo in pretty much any software, even MS Word documents, as well as for your poster artwork.*

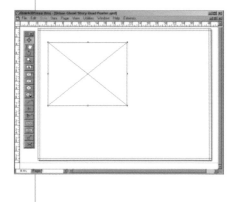

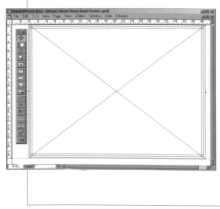

Stage 3 – Final layout

It's time to take all the elements that you have gathered and lay them out in Quark Xpress. It's not the most intuitive bit of software, but as long as you don't fear it, you'll get on just fine.

1. New Document

Start up Quark. Go to the *File* menu and select *New* and then *Document*. The *New Document* dialogue box will pop up. You can ignore most of it except for the *Page* section in which you should choose *Custom* from the *Size* drop down box, and enter *40"* in the width box and *30"* in the *Height* box. Finally ensure that *Landscape* is selected and hit OK. Your new and empty Quark document will appear. As the dimensions you just set equal Quad Poster size (40" by 30") it's a little big for the screen, so go to the *View* menu and select *Fit in Window*. The image will zoom out so that you can see the whole empty poster document. Save your file now so that you can periodically hit Ctrl+S to keep up to date with your saves. If you are offered a version number for your save, select the lowest – in this instance Version 3.3. Quark displays heaps of floating palettes by default but you won't need these just yet, so close them all except the *Tools Palette*. If you accidentally close it, you can easily get it back by hitting F8.

2. Boxed In

Quark uses boxes in which items – be it a bitmap picture, a vector graphic or just some text – are stored. These boxes are then dragged into the right place, and the items within them (text and pictures) are modified until the desired overall layout is achieved. Once you get the hang of it you'll see just how simple it is. Let's create our first empty box into which we will put the background image for the poster. From the floating *Tools Palette* on the left click on the *Rectangle Picture Box Tool (*it should be the sixth button down and looks like a square with an X in it). The mouse pointer will now have changed to a small cross. Click anywhere within your empty poster and, whilst holding down the mouse key, drag down and to the right. An empty Picture Box will appear. Release the mouse button and you have created your first empty box!

3. Picture Box

If you click anywhere within that empty *Picture Box*, the mouse will change to a funny icon, looking a little like the four directions of the compass. Click on the box and notice that if you keep the mouse button pressed, you can drag the empty picture box around the poster. Drag it to the top left of the Poster and just slightly over the edge of the poster (this will accommodate your bleed for the printers). Hover your mouse over the far bottom right corner of the empty *Picture Box* and you'll see the mouse changes to a hand with a pointing finger. Click on the bottom right, and whilst holding down the mouse key, drag it down and to the bottom right, making the empty *Picture Box* slightly larger than the poster. Release the mouse button and the empty *Picture Box* has now resized to be slightly larger than the empty poster.

4. Insert the image

Now it's time to insert the Photoshop artwork background you produced earlier. Go to the *File menu* and select *Get Picture* – the *Get Picture* dialogue box will pop up. Find the background image on your hard drive and click on it (you probably saved it as a TIF file remember). A small preview should appear in the bottom right of the dialogue box, along with some statistics about the file (yes it's a whopper and should be around 20mb!) Click on *Open* and the picture will be inserted in the top right of the *Picture Box*. It isn't full size yet but it is the correct aspect ratio (4:3).

5. Resize the pic

Now we have to resize the bitmap background image to cover the entire poster area. You will notice that now, when you hover the mouse anywhere within the empty poster, it turns into the compass icon. Click on the bitmap picture and press the *shift key, ctrl key* and *alt key* (all at the bottom left of the keyboard) and at the same time you can now press the < key to make the image smaller or the > key to make the image larger. We want to make it much bigger so use the > repeatedly until the image fills the poster. Now we have the beginnings of our poster!

6. Add the logo

Now it's time to add the logo. It's exactly the same process as we just did for the background image except you don't need to drag the new empty picture box to the top of the screen, or even resize it just yet. Create a new *Rectangular Picture Box*, click in the empty *Picture Box* then go to the *File Menu* and *Get Picture* and select the logo you created in your vector software. Your logo should appear, but this time you will see the box has remained white. You need to tell the box to be become transparent. Right click in the box and select *Modify* from the mouse drop down box (also available from the *Item menu*). The *Modify* box will pop up. Click on the *Box tab* and from the right side of the box where it says *Color*, select *None* from the drop down menu. Hit *OK* to close the *Modify Box* (note how the back-ground to the Logo has become transparent). You can still see the outline of the *Picture Box* but this won't be printed, it's there so you can see where all your items are placed. Now you can resize the *Picture Box*, drag it to a desired position and resize the logo (by using the Shift+Ctrl+Alt plus < or > keys . . . Phew!)

7. Add some text

Now we need to add the tag line for the movie, in this case it's 'She died . . . She Came Back . . . SOMETHING FOLLOWED . . .' On the floating *Tools Palette*, just above the *Rectangle Picture Box* button is the *Rectangle Text Box* button, it looks like a box with an A in it. Click on it and drag across part of your poster to create an empty *Text Box*. This is pretty much the same as placing images, except you are going to type some text into it. Again the box created will have a white background so you will need to *right click, Modify* and change the *Box Color* to *None*. Now we need to add the text. On the floating *Tool Palette*, the second button down is the *Content Tool*, it looks like a cursor key and a hand. Click on it, then click in the empty *Text Box* and start typing. At first you won't see anything as your poster is very large and the default text size is very small. Type a few words, then stop and press the *shift key* and the *left arrow* on the keyboard – this should highlight the text (if this fails you may need to fiddle around with your mouse to select the text). Once you have the text selected you can use the good old Shift+Ctrl+Alt plus > key to make the text bigger. By default the text will be black so it may still be hard to see. Once the text is bigger hit F12 to bring up the *Color Palette* and click on the middle top button (the one with an A in it) to select the *Text Color*, then select the colour you want from the list below (in our case it's white). The text will go white.

8. Format that text

Next we want to add a little spice to the text. To change the justification (whilst the text is still selected) press *shift+ctrl+L* for left, *shift+ctrl+R* for right and *shift+ctrl+C* for centre. You can also modify the text width by pressing the *shift+ctrl+[* (narrower) and *shift+ctrl+]* (wider) keys. You can toggle bold on and off with the *shift+ctrl+B* keys and itallic with the *shift+ctrl+I* keys. Cool! Finally, from the *Style Menu* at the top of the screen you can select a *Font*. You should have already isolated which fonts you will use on your poster, so go ahead and select it. A word of warning. Just because you have heaps of fonts installed, it doesn't mean you should use them. It's best to keep the number of fonts used to a minimum or your artwork will start to become a little cluttered. No more than three fonts overall, ideally only two. For *Urban Ghost Story* we used a freeware font called *Royal Pain*, a fairly distressed typewriter like font which was also used for the movie credits, all helping build a consistent image for the movie.

9. Add some more

Next we are going to add a *'presents'* and *'cast'* bit of text at the top of the poster, plus the credit block which you typed out earlier (you can cut and paste this text into a *Text Box*) and checked 100 times to ensure you've not forgotten anyone important or spelt a name wrong. Go ahead and do all this, using the same principles as before. We used a windows font called *Fujiyama Light* for these kind of text blocks. If you hit F9 you will bring up the *Measurements Palette* which you may find more convenient than the menus and keyboard shortcuts. Finally, add a few more *Picture Boxes* and import the extra bits such as Dolby logos, BBFC certificates, distribution company logos etc . . . If you need to get in close, you can use the magnifier tool from the floating *Tools Palette* – clicking on an area will zoom in, clicking on an area whilst pressing the alt key at the same time will zoom back out.

10. Final prep

Finally you need to save your document for the printer in a way that they can access everything you have laid out. From the *File Menu* select *Collect For Output*. Create a new folder called *File for printer*, click on it to go into the new folder and hit the *Collect* button. Quark will then save a number of files into this new directory, including all the hi-res images you created previously. It's a good idea to copy the font files for the fonts you used in the poster and put them into this directory too. Finally, burn a copy of the folder and all its contents to CD (or copy to a Zip disk) and send it to the printers. As you have never done this before, and printers often work with very experienced designers (so they won't be looking out for your mistakes) it's a good idea to work as closely as you can with them. At all stages go and see proofs of the artwork to ensure nothing weird has happened.

One into three –
video and DVD covers

Once you have all your elements prepared, you are going to have spend some time repositioning and rescaling for various different poster sizes and orientation, but also for the VHS (rental and retail) and DVD sleeve artwork (don't forget to allow for the bleed of the image at the printers). The artwork sizes are to the left. VHS stickers are produced at the VHS duplication facility but you will also need to prepare artwork for the actual DVD disk. Distributors often take care of this, but it may end up falling at your feet too.

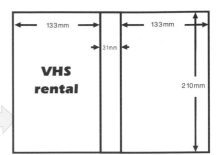

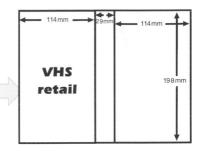

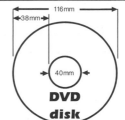

Don't forget to leave an appropriate space for your barcode. You can download fonts to create a barcode yourself, but it seems to be industry practice to get the duplication facility (who are creating the actual VHS or DVD copies) to create the barcodes for you. This barcode will contain information about the product and distributor so that shops and rental outlets can track what they sell or rent (assuming they use barcodes themselves!)

DVD 'on-body' artwork

Producing the *'on disk'* artwork is pretty much the same as the poster and video cover. Prepare a background in Photoshop then layout in Quark, dropping vector art on top for logos etc. The only thing to keep in mind is whether you are going to go to the expense of a producing full colour disks, single colour artwork, or simply just some text and a logo? When you consider that what is actually printed on the disk will not be seen by the customer until after they have bought or rented the disk, it begs the question why spend any money on this at all? If you can save money on duplication by just having text on the disk, it's money well saved.

Sales – Domestic Video, DVD and TV sales

The ILC Group – Video and DVD Distributors
48 Broadley Terrace, Marylebone, London NW1 6LG
Tel : +44 (0) 20 7258 0324 Fax: +44 (0) 20 723 9606
www.ilcdvd.com

Domestic Video, DVD & TV

Getting your movie into video shops for people to rent, and retail shops for people to buy . . .

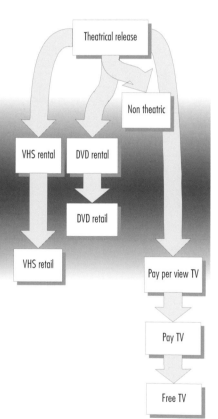

Theatrical release → Non theatric

VHS rental · DVD rental

DVD rental → DVD retail

VHS rental → VHS retail

Non theatric → Pay per view TV → Pay TV → Free TV

'You can rent it down at the video shop'

Your movie's been released at the cinemas, and whether its performance was good, bad or indifferent, the next step is to release on Video and DVD. We'll assume that by now you've already completed all your master videotapes and have the DVD production underway (see elsewhere in the book for information on this). The first thing to do is cut a deal with a distributor.

Done deal

You will probably have a deal in place with the same distributor as the one who handled your theatrical release as they will want to offset any losses from the theatrical release against video and DVD. If you did your own theatrical release, you may need to find a distributor. You may be tempted to think about self-distribution on video, but unlike theatrical distribution, this isn't necessarily a good idea, mainly because the people who work in video distribution like to work with people they know and people who can guarantee volume of product. You, having only one product, don't have volume.

Hot date

The first thing your distributor will do is set a release date. They will want this to be as close to the theatrical release as possible in order to minimise any losses they have made on the theatrical release and to maximise any public awareness your film generated during it.

It is industry practice to guarantee a window of 6 months from the theatrical release of a film – so if your film comes out in July, you would release video and DVD in December or January. Those distributors who ignore this industry practice are generally distributors who are very cash poor or on their way out. If the distributor breaks this unwritten rule, they will find cinemas unwilling to screen the next film they wish to release, and you don't want to be doing business with these kind of people. Trust me, they will go bankrupt and take your movie with them.

Rent or buy?

The video and DVD release has two threads – *Rental* and *Retail.* The rental happens first. This is where customers can go to their local video store and rent your movie on VHS or DVD for something like £3.75. There is a trend

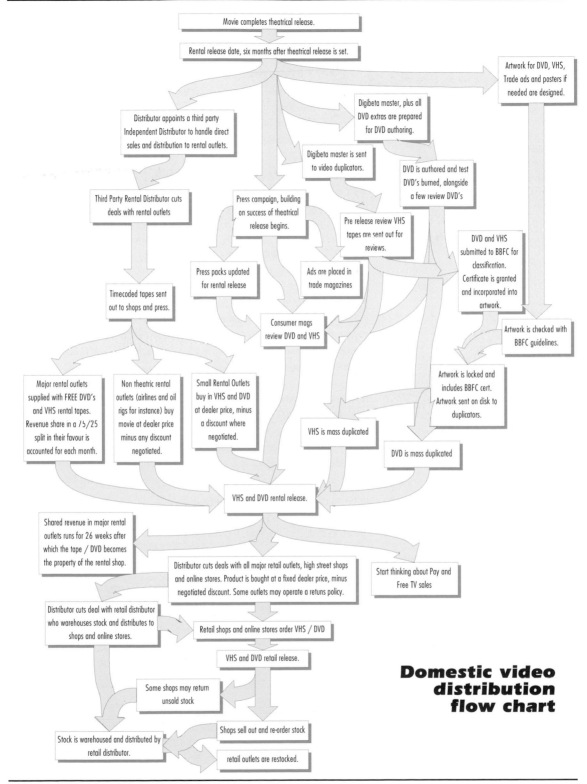

Movie completes theatrical release.

Rental release date, six months after theatrical release is set.

Artwork for DVD, VHS, Trade ads and posters if needed are designed.

Distributor appoints a third party Independent Distributor to handle direct sales and distribution to rental outlets.

Digibeta master, plus all DVD extras are prepared for DVD authoring.

Digibeta master is sent to video duplicators.

DVD is authored and test DVD's burned, alongside a few review DVD's

Third Party Rental Distributor cuts deals with rental outlets

Press campaign, building on success of theatrical release begins.

Pre release review VHS tapes are sent out for reviews.

DVD and VHS submitted to BBFC for classification. Certificate is granted and incorporated into artwork.

Press packs updated for rental release

Ads are placed in trade magazines

Timecoded tapes sent out to shops and press.

Consumer mags review DVD and VHS

Artwork is checked with BBFC guidelines.

Major rental outlets supplied with FREE DVD's and VHS rental tapes. Revenue share in a 75/25 split in their favour is accounted for each month.

Non theatric rental outlets (airlines and oil rigs for instance) buy movie at dealer price minus any discount negotiated.

Small Rental Outlets buy in VHS and DVD at dealer price, minus a discount where negotiated.

Artwork is locked and includes BBFC cert. Artwork sent on disk to duplicators.

VHS is mass duplicated

DVD is mass duplicated

VHS and DVD rental release.

Shared revenue in major rental outlets runs for 26 weeks after which the tape / DVD becomes the property of the rental shop.

Distributor cuts deals with all major retail outlets, high street shops and online stores. Product is bought at a fixed dealer price, minus negotiated discount. Some outlets may operate a retuns policy.

Start thinking about Pay and Free TV sales

Distributor cuts deal with retail distributor who warehouses stock and distributes to shops and online stores.

Retail shops and online stores order VHS / DVD

VHS and DVD retail release.

Some shops may return unsold stock

Domestic video distribution flow chart

Stock is warehoused and distributed by retail distributor.

Shops sell out and re-order stock

retail outlets are restocked.

When you cut a deal with a distributor make sure they agree to give you a number of VHS and DVD copies. Ask for at least 50 of each. It won't cost them too much and it means you can give them away to people who helped you make the film, and also people who could help your film / career in the future but need to see the movie. The distributor won't want to give you this stock but stand firm.

now to release DVD retail at the same time as DVD rental, but for now, let's ignore this for the purposes of this model.

A release date is set 6 months in the future. You may wish to spend as much time as you can on your video and DVD release but to compound things, much of your time will be spent dealing with the fallout from your theatrical release. The post-theatrical release is a golden opportunity where the industry at large will probably have heard of you, and even if they haven't, you can utter the magical phrase 'yeah, we were out at the cinema's last week, did you manage to catch the movie?' You should be spending as much time as possible promoting yourself and trying to get your next production off the ground.

Don't get down

The video and DVD release, following the euphoria of the theatrical release, will feel somewhat anti-climatic and you may be tempted to just do a deal with a distributor and let them figure it all out. Do not do this. You need, at the very least, to be consulted at all levels of the release. If you don't, you can guarantee you'll get a dreadful cover with a terrible tag line and a transfer that looks like it's been telecinied through bog paper (see elsewhere in the book for telecine and video mastering).

As a rule (and I know I will get in trouble with many of my distributor friends for saying this), distributors have no taste. Sorry. Where you have made just one movie and have spent years with it, to the distributor, your movie is simply the product they are handling this week, or this month. They do not have the same emotional investment as you, even if you have fallen out of love with your movie. So you need to be a creative force at all times and manage the project.

Video PR

Once the release date is set, from a publicity point of view, a similar process

Video rental and retail example balance sheet. Figures based on average to good performance for indie movie.

	Rentals/Units	Gross	Returns	Your cut	Dist Cut
VHS shared revenue generates 10,000 rentals at £3.19	10,000	£31,900.00	£7,975.00	£1,993.75	£5,981.25
VHS dealer purchase, 1500 tapes averaging £20 each	1,500	£30,000.00	£30,000.00	£7,500.00	£22,500.00
DVD shared revenue, 4000 rentals at £3.19	4,000	£12,760.00	£3,190.00	£797.50	£2,392.50
VHS sell through, RRP £8.99 (inc VAT) , av. dealer price of £4.80	1,500	£7,200.00	£7,200.00	£900.00	£6,300.00
DVD sell through, RRP £17.99 (inc VAT) , av. dealer price of £9.50	2,500	£23,750.00	£23,750.00	£2,968.75	£20,781.25

Revenues will take six months to filter through. Figures do not include VAT, except where stated. Remember the distributor should organise everything AND pay for all expenses.

	You make	They make
	£14,160.00	£57,955.00

Domestic Video Distribution Deal

What they will probably want . . .	*What you need to know . . .*
1. Term, – 5 to 15 years	1. Your share is from the gross and not the net – i.e. they cannot deduct expenses.
2. 75%-90% of rental income, either from direct sales or shared revenue.	2. How often they will account to you.
3. 80%-90% of retail income.	3. Full access to accounts (within reason).
4. Your involvement in PR, although this might be minimal.	4. Rights revert if they go under.
5. Stills and any existing artwork if available.	5. They cannot sub license without your consent.
6. They may or may not want TV. If they do they will probably do a 50-50 split.	6. Guarantee when they will release.
7. If they were the theatrical distributor, they will offset theatrical losses against video income.	7. Contact with another film maker whose film was handled by them so you can ask questions.
	8. TV window. How long they want between video release and when you can sell to TV.

to that of the theatrical release will be employed, but on a smaller scale. Much of the PR work boils down to sending review copies to newspapers and magazines along with a press pack. Also, prior to the release on VHS and DVD, ads should be placed in all the major trade magazines to alert the industry to the rental release on VHS and DVD. It's VERY tough to get any coverage outside of straight reviews for a film that goes straight to video, or indeed the video release of any film.

Revamped artwork

The Artwork for the VHS and DVD boxes, advertisements in trade maga zines, and small posters (should you decide you need them) will simply be a matter of resizing and adjusting the existing theatrical poster artwork that you have already designed. You also have the advantage of adding all the great quotes you (hopefully) got during the theatrical release.

Whilst the theatrical release poster needs to be passed through a board by law, the video doesn't. The BBFC publish content guidelines, and some stores may refuse to stock a title if the cover is contentious, but you do not need to have it classified by the BBFC.

Certification . . . again!

As with the theatrical release, the BBFC need to classify your film for VHS and DVD. At the relevant times you'll need to supply them with a BetaSP tape. Remember you can't lock down your artwork without knowing the relevant certificate for your film. This classification will cost you something like £1k. If your distributor is using your trailer on other rental titles, this will also need classification (as will DVD extras).

Masters

For now, we'll assume that you've already produced top quality telecines in both 16:9 anamorphic for DVD and 4:3 full screen for VHS (see elsewhere in this book for video mastering).

Like all businesses, the video trade has their own publications – View and Timecode

Steve O'Sullivan
Video Store Manager

'British films just don't perform. It's not first choice. If it doesn't have a Hollywood name, it doesn't have that initial appeal – unless, it had a lot of PR and people know and like it, like the "Full Monty", for example. It's not about how good the film is either. British films have a stigma about being boring. If I give my opinion to a customer and say it's a British film people get apprehensive and tend not to rent it. They need reassurance when renting a British film. Most of the time they end up going for what they know which is why a poor Hollywood movie like "XXX" gets heavily rented.

For all films, including small ones, we operate a revenue share deal. But the small British films tend to stay on the shelf unrented and after several weeks we end up selling them in our ex-rental bin. We have some films that don't do any business at all, like "My Kingdom". Got great reviews and rented 20 times. We totally over-estimated the rental on that title, and I hate seeing unrented titles filling my shelves. Sometimes I can't wait to sell my stock, but for that I need authorisation from head office.

In terms of what I watch as a consumer, I tend to stay away from small movies. I generally go with chart movies. Usually I won't go with small movies as I have my pick of the shop. Some Brit films seem to last, like "Shallow Grave" which is still renting. That, originally, was built up on word of mouth. But generally, we just know the British films aren't value for money. So many films seem to be made for the sake of it. I can just look at the cover and know if a film will rent or not. I advise you to put a lot of thought into the artwork.'

The 4:3 master should go to the VHS duplication company. These are the people with a warehouse of 1000s of video recorders, who will make the copies of your film. In the first instance, they will make up perhaps 20-50 VHS copies which will be sent to reviewers and journalists and also to the video trade shop owners who want to see the film before they decide on whether they should pass on it or take 10 copies for rental. The 16:9 anamorphic version should go, with all your DVD extras, to the DVD authoring company.

The production of the DVD is dealt with elsewhere in this book, but needless to say, it's essential you do a fantastic job and include as many extras as you possibly can. The production of the DVD will probably take longer than you think, especially if you are going to include extras. Most extras can be created using miniDV and post producing them on a home edit system such as Final Cut Pro, Adobe Premiere or Avid Xpress DV.

Ok, let's zap back in time to the point where you've cut the deal with the distributor.

Distribution Deals

What kind of deal should you look for? Probably what you will get is an 80/20 split of gross receipts for the rental release in their favour. The phrase they will use is "20% of dealer price less discounts". This means they will pay for all materials and duplication, take all the risk and take 80% of the pie leaving you with 20%. And the dealer price less discounts means that your movie may have a dealer price of £50, but when discounted this would drop to anywhere between £15 and £30 (this split will also be used for the gross receipts from shared revenue deals with the major video chains such as Blockbusters – see later).

This revenue split may drop to 15% or even 10% when it comes to retail sales (selling in shops such as HMV or online with Amazon.com). Of course, you may be lucky and have found a particularly generous distributor, or you may have a very hot film in which case you can probably increase these percentages.

Video rental is currently split between 2 practices. Shared revenue and dealer purchase.

Shared revenue

What is shared revenue and how does it work? Shared revenue is only employed by the major video chains and it works in a way that is probably going to get your hackles up, but as these guys are the big players and you have a small independent film, there's not a lot you can do. The distributor will make up a number of VHS and DVDs, say 2000 VHS tapes and 1500 DVDs, and then give them to Blockbuster for free. Blockbusters will then rent

Case study – The 13th Sign

After leaving film school, Adam Mason woke up one day and decided that he should make a feature. Following the tried and tested route of in your face horror being one of the forgiving genres for first time indie film makers he made 'The 13th Sign', shot on DV for £5k and ultimately costing only £25k.

Adam cut a deal with a distributor and to his surprise the movie made it into shops, in Block busters generating over 30,000 rentals and selling over 2000 DVDs in high street shops. Doing the maths, and we can't be sure exactly what the film did, we guess the revenue generated for his distributor was around £20k for retail and at least £25k for rentals. And what did Adam get? A very small fraction of that amount, certainly not what he deserved.

The success of his film in the rental and retail market place is down to a number of things. It is a film in a traditionally successful genre, with loyal and eager fans. It has a good title and artwork, all making it jump off the shelf. In fact, that's all it has when it comes to the customer. No recognisable director or cast, no reviews, nothing. Just a good title, good artwork, and it's existence within a strong genre. From the industry side, the first few minutes are very slick, as are the last five, ideal for the guys in the trade who will look at the opening and whizz through to the end to ensure it delivers. Adam has moved on to his second film, proud of his first effort but acutely aware of its weaknesses.

Check out www.paranoid-celluloid.co.uk to what these guys are doing now. And if you want to buy the DVD, buy it from him, that way he at least gets some of the revenues guaranteed.

these titles and split the revenue 75/25 in their favour. After 26 weeks, these VHSs and DVDs become the property of Blockbusters and they can then do what they like with them – sell them off cheap (which will inevitably cut into your retail business) or just chuck them in the bin!

There is no dispute that Blockbusters are an exceptionally reputable company and will report accurately and honestly to you, but some of the other chains could be accused of being economic with the truth, leading to you feeling very paranoid about whether you'll actually know how many rentals your film has made. There's nothing you can do about shared revenue, it's here to stay for the meantime at least, but there are rumours that it will bite the dust, especially as video on demand through digital TV becomes more prevalent.

Direct sales

Small independent shops and chains run the other half of the rental business. They do not have the might to enforce or manage shared revenue so the distributor will operate direct sales at the 'dealer price less discount rates'. For these sales the distributor will employ a sub-distributor. This relationship is much like that of the film booker in the theatrical release. This sub-distributor spends their days selling VHS and DVDs to the small, independent shops and chains.

If a distributor creates artwork for your DVD / VHS cover, try and get them to let you have a copy on disk (Quark Xpress file) so that you can add it to your arsenal for international sales. Often they will ask for a fee for this. Don't accept this. Make it a contractual obligation in the first place.

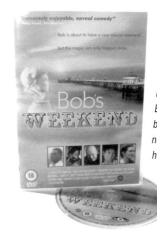

Case study – Bob's weekend

Jevon O'Neil, a successful director / producer of TV commercials, was in search of a career change. He decided to make a low budget film, Bob's Weekend. It was shot in Blackpool during October '95, costing £120k (with £245k deferred). The cash came mostly from Jevon's savings, friends and family.

It's about a man who, upon losing his job, and discovering that his wife is having an affair, goes to Blackpool to commit suicide. Whilst there he undergoes a dark night of the soul involving a series of bizarre encounters with a strange array of locals, resulting in self discovery and a realisation that life is not all that bad after all. In both the Edinburgh and London film festivals it received glowing reviews, however, by 1997 no sales agent or distributor had made an offer (indeed Jevon wasn't sure if anyone even bothered to watch the movie) and the movie sat on the shelf. Jevon persisted and turned every stone, with Guerilla Films originally making an offer (which Jevon declined), but ultimately resulting in Paramount TV's UK office expressing interest in the film for worldwide TV distribution – a first for Paramount TV. Their parent company produces so many feature films and TV movies of their own they rarely even consider taking third party programming.

Jevon then cut a deal with Guerilla Films and decided NOT to release in cinemas, but to go straight to video, rights which Paramount did not want. Meanwhile the BBC had already picked up the film (through Paramount as it was now being packaged with the likes of What Lies Beneath) and it was released on rental VHS in December 2001, five years after its first screening. It performed poorly in the rental market as many chains discovering its age via the imdb.com, assumed it must be a stinker if it's taken so long to be released. On DVD however it is doing well. Paramount started officially selling the film in late 2001 and to date it has sold to 11 territories, the cash cost of the film being more than covered by these sales.

By not releasing in cinemas and cutting a worldwide TV deal where his film would be packaged with extremely desirable films for broadcasters, Jevon has managed to secure an enviable position.

The key thing they have is existing relationships and volume. They know who to sell to, how many they will probably take and how much they can get away with. And because they shift hundreds of titles a year, they will work quickly and efficiently.

As stated earlier, typically, the dealer price will be £50 for a VHS and most shops will get a discount down to £25. Some of the smaller, less powerful shops will pay up to £30. Unfortunately there are Mafia like cartels operating in some areas, and they have the might to squeeze the price down to as little as £15 per VHS. Another problem is that as the majors often drop their prices to £15 per unit, it makes it very hard for indie distributors to remain competitive. Add to this that if a title performs less than well it will be discounted in a matter of weeks and be available to the trade for under a tenner. Get hold of copies of the video trade mags and there are heaps of ads for movies that were released recently and now available at silly discounts.

If you have offered your cast and crew deferred fees (and we advise you do not), get ready for a series of phone calls from irate cast and crew members who don't understand why you haven't made millions yet and why you can't pay them their deferred fees. "You must have made your money back 'cos I can rent it from Blockbuster!'

The sub-distributor gets paid in one of two ways. They'll either receive a fee for doing the job or more commonly receive a percentage of the sales. Typically, this is no more than 40% and should be considerably less, but this will depend upon the strength and relationships that your distributor has with the sub-distributor.

It is becoming horribly apparent that if your film were an apple pie, many other people are feeding heartily at your table before you're even invited to scrabble for the scraps.

Before you go

Prior to the release of the film 400-500 preview tapes with burnt in time code and the word SAMPLE printed across the artwork cover will be sent out, by the sub distributor, to the industry as preview tapes. Often these will find their way to journalists and video shop owners. Clearly there is a manufacturing and distribution cost here.

Non theatric rights

This sub-distributor may also deal with non-theatrical rights, the very peculiar practice of selling your movie to areas that don't fit within a given geographical territory such as airlines, ferries and oilrigs. Don't discount this revenue as it can be considerable. I have heard of at least one instance where a British, low-budget film recouped over $130k from these kind of deals (of course, this $130k went to the distributor, while the film makers only saw $52k). If a non theatric deal is cut, this usually happens in the window between the theatrical release and the VHS / DVD rental release.

Movement and delivery

Movement and delivery of all VHS and DVDs will be handled by yet another distributor, who specialises in warehousing and physical distribution. Again, they will be paid on either a fee or percentage basis. These are specialised companies who do nothing more than warehouse stock and send it out when an order is received.

So to recap, your distributor will probably cut deals with the major chains such as Blockbuster for the shared revenue. They will hire a sub-distributor who will cut deals with smaller video shops and chains and do direct sales 'at dealer price less discounts'. Your distributor will also hire a further company to handle warehousing and physical delivery of the stock.

Doing all this professionally will mean that on the date of your release you will be able to go down to your local video shop and rent a copy of your own movie, or hopefully not rent it because somebody else has already rented it!

Retail

Now the video rental part of your movie release is launched, you'll need to start spearheading two new directions. Firstly, the free TV and PAY-TV sales (which we discuss elsewhere in the book) and secondly, VHS and DVD

David Wilkinson
Guerilla Films

'Fifteen years ago a low budget film like Letter to Brezhnev *(£320k) would sell 17,000 rental copies at an average price of £32. Now a similar film would be lucky to ship 2500 at an average price £9-12. My best selling British production is a documentary and has sold more copies than all my fiction productions combined. It's sobering.*

If you do your own cinema distribution, unless you are going to have a number of titles, you will find it hard to set up accounts with rental and retail outlets. They look for volume and want a regular supplier of numerous titles. Everyone thinks that video and DVD will return huge amounts of money, if not for the producer, for the distributor. This is very rare. Typically I do deals where I offer a 50-50 split for producers after manufacturing and distribution expenses are deducted (charged at verifiable cost). This means that the producer can receive greater income but only after the video / DVD release has recovered its costs. In other words, if their film sells well.

I distribute more low/micro budget British films than any other UK distributor and in my opinion these films are going to go the way of foreign language films. Non English speaking films may be available in rental stores but they are bought at retail dealer prices. By 2003-4 I don't see a rental market for these low/micro budget British films.'

Domestic video distribution manufacturing costs

ITEM	Number	Cost	Total	Comment
VHS screening tapes with Time Code	600	£2.50	£1,500.00	Tapes sent out before the release to journalists and shops.
VHS and DVD artwork	1	£500.00	£500.00	You can do this yourself to save money.
VHS copies and packaging	2000	£1.50	£3,000.00	This is the VHS copy plus sleeve and box, all in price.
Trailer BBFC	1	£100.00	£100.00	BBFC need to certify a trailer of it is to go on other tapes.
Movie BBFC	1	£1,200.00	£1,200.00	BBFC need to certify the movie.
DVD Mastering	1	£700.00	£700.00	This is the making of the DVD master onto DLT tape.
DVD glass master	0	£0.00	£0.00	Should not be charged unless the quantity is very low.
DVD copies and packaging	2000	£1.00	£2,000.00	The duplication of the disk, packaging, and case.
Warehousing	1	£500.00	£500.00	Of course, there is your attic / garage.
Print advertment artwork	1	£1,000.00	£1,000.00	The artwork used in trade mags to advertise the video/DVD.
Advertising	1	£7,500.00	£7,500.00	The more you advertise, the more copies the shops will take.
PR campaign plus expenses	1	£4,000.00	£4,000.00	You could do this yourself.
Shipping of product	0	£0.00	£0.00	Probably part of a percentage deal with the sub-distributor.

Total potential outlay	**£22,000**

Costs for the rental / retail release can be considerable*. The time coded VHS tapes are to be sent to smaller rental shops so they can se the film to decide whether they want to buy copies. BBFC may need two sets of classification, not just for the widescreen DVD, but also the VHS pan and scan version. You may want to release widescreen on VHS to save £1200, but many rental stores will take a dim view of this. The glass master for the DVD should not be charged for now but be aware of its existence and ask about being charged for it. All the duplication costs include packaging (box and sleeve) as long as you supply appropriate masters. Advertising is essential in your quest to convince the major stores to take your product. The more you spend, the more stock you will sell to the stores. Of course, whilst they are happy to put your movie on their shelves, they will be just as happy to send it back to you twelve months later if it hasn't sold. The shipping of product to stores should be covered within the deal you have struck with the sub distributor, they take care of everything for their slice. Again, be aware that it is a cost.

The biggest hidden problem is that of returns. If you sell 2000 copies into stores such as Virgin and HMV, you might be very happy. Twelve months later however, they may return 1500 copies, some returns from customers, some unsold stock. You then have to give them their money back AND pay for the shipping back to you, then have to warehouse the stock! Return stock can be anywhere between 10-70%. All deals, as usual, are open to negotiation. Whever a major distributor can bring volume to a deal, they will ALWAYS get a better price.

* If you are working with a distributor, they should cover all these costs.

retail. This is where customers can buy a copy of your movie on either VHS or DVD and keep it, typically from video stores, high street retail shops and online stores.

Depending on the size of your distributor, they may handle sales to all retail outlets directly, or they may use a third party sub-distributor. In general though they should be handling the sales themselves, otherwise this whole process is starting to beg the question, *'What on earth am I using a distributor for? I should be doing this myself'*. The distributor will probably use the same distribution and warehousing company as the one used for the rental release and they will deal with the physical distribution of DVDs and VHS tapes to the shops.

Dominate. Don't rely on distributors to get it right. Treat them as your employee and manage the project youself. Keep on top of artwork, BBFC classification, mastering of the DVD and duplication. You act as quality control at all times and accept no compromise. Distributors are notorious for their disinterest in quality. They do not care that this is your baby of several years, and that your whole livelihood is wrapped up in it. This is just their release for next month, along with twelve other titles.

Volume

The amount of units you sell and the types of retail outlets that will take your movie depend largely on the film itself, its previous success and to some degree, the existing relationships between retailer and distributor. Another good reason for not self-distributing.

Never give your master videotapes to a distributor, they will lose them! Make clones and use them to make your VHS copies and DVD master.

How it works

The way the retail part of the business works is that your VHS and DVD will have a fixed dealer price. This is how it is calculated. If your DVD is going to cost say £15.99 in the shops, you minus the VAT element, taking it down to £13.61, then deduct 25% to take it down to £10.89. This is the dealer price and cannot be changed. However, each retail outlet will have their own discounts added, which could be anywhere between 0-40%, depending on relationships, volume of order and size of outlet. Some retail outlets will purchase discs or cassettes and if they don't sell, it's their tough luck, whereas others, especially the larger outlets such as HMV, will operate a sale or return policy. This means if the disc doesn't sell over a given amount of time, they will return it and deduct its value from future sales of other products that the distributor handles. The distributor will then have to back calculate how much to deduct from your royalty share, so that other film makers don't pay for your sale or return.

Once a retailer sells out of stock they will either re-order or at some point the distributor should contact the retailer asking if they want more stock. If they do, this will be shipped from the warehousing company.

Remember also that if you sell out you will need to produce more stock and generally this stock is manufactured in a minimum of 500 and more often by the 1000, all of which can carry an unwanted price tag, especially if sales have slumped and stock may end up collecting dust in the warehouse for some time.

TV sales

If the film maker used a distributor for the theatric and video / DVD releases, then that distributor will probably take TV rights to cover their inevitable losses (on the theatric and possibly even the video and DVD releases). If the film goes straight to video and the producer has secured a deal for video only, then the producer may have the rights to sell to a broadcaster direct. It all depends on the deal they cut.

In theory it should be very easy for a film maker to sell to a UK broadcaster, whether they be free TV, VOD (Video On Demand), cable or satellite. In some cases, the film maker may have already pulled in some cash from a broadcaster as production funding, which would then mean it is a co-production. For this, the broadcaster could provide anywhere up to perhaps

Broadcasters always need daytime programming more than night time programming. There are many more hours to fill and frankly, making kiddies' films is not seen to be as cool as making more adult themed movies, be it horror, action, erotic whatever . . . The smart producer would make a family film knowing that competition for that time slot is much less fierce.

£250k towards the budget (perhaps even as much as £750k) in return for either a few UK showings or the UK TV rights in perpetuity. However, if the film is completed without a co-production deal in place, it is a very different story. Then it becomes an acquisition.

Who buys?

There are only a few people who view films for the broadcasters and they always have an enormous backlog of 'screeners' (VHS tapes). These few people alone have the power to say 'yes' or 'no' to a TV sale. It's this simple, if they see it and they like it, you may get a deal. If they don't like it, they won't bite.

What every producer wants is the situation where two or more broadcast companies want the film so that they each try to outbid each other, although this doesn't happen often. Most UK broadcasters have all the British films they need from their own production divisions so there is no real requirement for them to screen any more. Occasionally they do license third party films, however these tend to be bought in packages from distributors. These companies will have long-term relationships with all the broadcasters and are able to better persuade a company to take a film.

Also, within broadcast companies, they change their programming ideas all the time. For instance, the director of programmes may suddenly decide they want a season of independent horror movies. The acquisitions department will then ring up the distributors asking what indie horror films they have, and if you're not in the loop, you don't get the call. The whole process from idea to final purchase could take less than a month.

This does not rule out a producer selling his or her own film.

If a broadcaster likes a film they will initially offer as little as possible and because you are in such a weak negotiating position, it's very hard to get that price up – I know of some low budget British films that have sold for as little as £5k for UK TV! There are also cases of independent films being licensed to TV having NOT had a cinema or video release. Some of these have sold for around $1m, but they usually have big Hollywood stars in the lead roles and are billed as premieres. This kind of deal is unlikely to be achieved by a producer, though it is possible.

It's always down to how badly someone wants the film, and more often then not, they just don't want low budget British Independent films. Why? If I were harsh, and I would include my own work in this, the films are usually average, to poor, and often just downright rubbish.

Steve Jenkins
Head of Film Acquisitions, BBC

'When it comes to getting your film onto a BBC channel, I wouldn't want to paint a completely gloomy picture, but there are an awful lot of films vying for our slots. Films that have recognisable faces, films that have received good reviews and achieved success theatrically stand the best chance of getting bought.

It is more difficult for British film makers to get their films shown on terrestrial channels if they have not received a theatrical release. If a film has failed to achieve that, you have to ask whether a BBC audience will want to watch it. There are too many films around that are about a group of 'twenty-somethings' living together, coming to terms with bad relationships and other problems. All too often the films are like TV drama pretending to be theatrical – they are like an episode of Cold Feet, but not as good. Many American films get onto the screens as part of package deals from distributors, but it is important to realise that even if an American film is formulaic, they often have larger budgets and therefore the luxury of grander production values. British films need to distinguish themselves from everything else that is already on, and think of the audience that you are making it for. I watch some films and can't see quite who the producers thought would watch them, apart from their friends. I buy only finished and completed feature films for the four BBC Channels. We tend to favour thrillers and action pictures for late nights on BBC1, and most of our big prime and holiday slots will be filled by box-office hits, many of which will come from the US majors. But our biggest film at Christmas 2002 was 'Billy Elliot', which came from BBC Films and was British. BBC4's current policy is to screen foreign language films – their interest in English language films is limited. At the moment there is little scope for film acquisition on BBC3. They are heavily committed to original production, and currently only show one mainstream film a week. As the channel develops there is the possibility that BBC3 will find slots for more innovative British films appealing to their target, mid-20s audience.

I do not pre-buy, unmade movies. If you are looking for funding to get the film made, you need to talk to David Thompson of BBC Films for instance. And needless to say, the quality of the script is crucial. I am looking for films that are character based and narrative led, it's really important to stop people changing channels, and I need to be sure that the films that I buy will keep viewers interested. While most films acquired will have big names as the leads, there are opportunities for films with television stars as well. The best way to get a film in front of me is to wait until it is completed and then e-mail or phone, we are very approachable! This is better than trying to track me down at Cannes or Toronto when I have a busy schedule. We always watch completed British films and are always on the look out for the next striking film from a breakout new director.'

Success?

What the distributor really brings to the equation is the ability to package. For instance, the low budget film 'Bob's Weekend' eventually secured a UK TV sale, eight years after it was made and solely because it was part of a package. Yes the broadcaster liked the film but on it's own it was not viable option.

A distributor will take a commission of anywhere from 25% – 50% for TV rights. The larger percentage will be for theatrical distributors whose only real earnings often come from TV. The TV is the icing on the cake and can make up for poor returns in the cinema and on video & DVD. Television is a hungry medium and it constantly needs to be fed with programming. Films are amongst the most popular programming watched. Although prices for films from UK broadcasters are not good at present, this may change.

However, the harsh truth is that unless you have the rights to 'Trainspotting' or 'Lock Stock' the chances of you as a producer selling your film, for a good price, or even at all, are slim.

What is Next?

So you've completed your first film. You are probably drifting around in a mixed state of elation at your success (you did it!), depression at your failure (its not as good as you hoped!), determination to do it again (but better), fear at how you will survive (financially), overwhelmed by possible opportunities (real or in your mind), and at some point you'll bump back down to earth. Welcome to the 'first film club'. Are you ready to apply for membership to 'the second film club'?

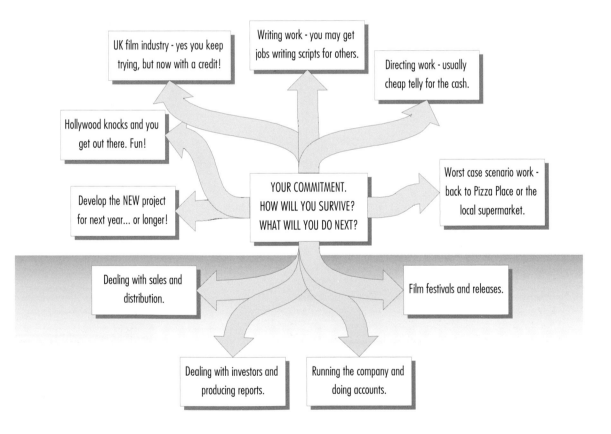

What is next?

A long time ago in a galaxy far, far away, you had this idea to make a film. It took much longer and cost much more than you expected, and it's not as good as you'd hoped, but hey, you've made it. You're a film maker!

It seems an age since you shot the film and even the buzz of the premiere is diminishing quickly. All the good stuff . . . that is the brainstorming and writing process, shooting, editing, sound mixing, screening etc . . . is done and dusted. What's left is a mixture of long term project management and a vast expanse of perceived opportunity. You are no longer an *'I want to make a movie'*, you're now an *'I've made a movie'*. You have a CV and your company has corporate kudos (but not that much). The questions in your mind will be *'how much work am I going to have to do to manage the long-term responsibilities of the project?'* and *'what on earth am I going to do next with the opportunity this film has created?'*

You spent so long determined to make the film, and now that you have done it, you will feel an anticlimax. You'll also have some tough choices to make. Do you do it again? How soon could you even do it? Who is going to manage the long term business? In short, what's next?

Join the club and network

Now you've made a film, you have the opportunity of joining *'the club'*. Film makers are divided into two groups. Those who have made a film and those who have not. Some people are good at faking it and look like they've made a film (you'll meet a lot of these people at parties, screenings and clubs and they will tell you all about the exciting projects they are about to make). And some people who have made a film are not very good at looking like they have (which can work against you in this elitist business).

There are a number of clubs and haunts where film makers hang out. I'm not suggesting you will make better films or even more films by joining this underworld, but it is a business of personalities and all too often jobs and money go to talented people who are known to the people with the cash, rather than talented people who are unknown to them. London, and more specifically Soho, is the heart of the UK film industry. So it makes sense to get to know the area, the clubs and bars and get used to networking.

Running accounts

Having made a film and having started a Limited Company, you are now obliged to keep that company

It can take years for your film to actually 'get out there' by which time you may have emotionally moved on to other things, and your film can become a bit of an albatross. Then when you consider all the accounts and reports that will also need to be produced, you can see why so many film makers take so long between their first and second films.

Kate Watson
Agent

'We recognise new talent, that's what we do, but selling it is tough and competitive. We are sent a lot of reels by first time film makers and we try to look at as many as we can. Writer/directors who come to us with only a short film or two can be tricky to market as there are so many new and young film makers out there.

The majority of short films we see are thin on character and storyline and overall disappointing. Remember, as a first time film maker, this is your calling card. This piece of work must say something unique about you, it also has to be professional. Yes it is a great achievement to have made any film, but that in itself is not enough, it must have substance. It's essential to remain constantly pro-active, do the festival rounds and preferably have another source of income, maybe even within the industry.

Film makers should have more of a realistic understanding of what that first film is going to achieve. Many of the film school graduates who contact us believe that they are now fully fledged directors, but this is not so, we all continue to learn with every job we do. The majority would benefit far quicker if they were prepared to work in other capacities while developing their own projects. The experience of being on other film makers sets is always invaluable.'

up and running for the life of the project. That means anywhere between a year or two and possibly a decade! It's a matter of tax really, and how the tax man might view your company assets (that means the film) should you decide to close the company. In essence, you have created an asset that has a value of at least the money you spent on it. So if you make the film for £100k, then immediately close the company, the asset will need to be sold to someone – and if no one is prepared to buy it for a fair market price, it will be passed on to the directors or it's value – £100k – which means you'll get hit with a 40% tax bill, that's a bill for something in the region of £40k! You can't just give the film away!

The value of the film will decrease over time, and personally, I have argued with the tax office that a film has no real value after five to seven years. I know film makers who have closed their company a year after production and I know film makers who are still running their accounts a decade after the fact. You need to take a view, speak to an accountant, and decide what you want to do. There are no rules. However, no matter how short a period, for some time you will need to produce full accounts and VAT returns.

Here's the rub. Who does the accounts? More than likely, it will be the producer but you cannot over estimate just how much long-term grief these accounts will cause. Think of it, you could be doing quarterly VAT returns for the next five years.

Investors

Let's assume that you financed your film from a group of private investors. For many years to come they are going to want regular reports on how their investment is performing. Wouldn't you? You may have say, thirty investors, a few of which move home every year (so you need to track their contact information), all of whom will need regular contact. Who is going to produce the reports? Who is going to pay for the reports to be sent? Again, it's likely this job will land at the foot of the producer. Don't kid yourself, as with the accounts, you'll come to loath all of this *'stuff'* that will regularly thwart your attempts to make another movie. On the whole, investors are very generous and pragmatic people who will accept almost any eventuality as long as they are kept informed. So keep the information flowing.

Managing sales

Let's assume you have cut a great deal with a sales agent who is now going to represent your film around the world. Do you think they are going to send you regular cheques? I can bet they won't. You are going to have to work very hard to give them everything they need to sell your film and then over the next few years, keep in regular contact, demanding reports, demanding payment (if you've made sales). Again, who does this? If sales are made and money comes flowing back in, who calculates the investor's share out? Who writes the cheques? As usual, it's going to be the producer.

Case Study – Chris Nolan and Following

Chris Nolan (and his wife Emma Nolan) made a movie called 'Following'. It was shot over weekends on a budget under £10k. It's a short film, perhaps even too short to be called a feature, but . . . It's very original and extremely well made. Critics loved it. Film makers loved it. The British public didn't really get a chance to see it because of the limited theatrical release and almost non existent video release (staggeringly it isn't even out on DVD in the UK, but there is a US region 1 release). But more than anything, it made a promise. It said 'I was made by an intelligent film maker who could, if given the chance, do something really amazing . . .' And that's what Chris Nolan did! He made 'Memento', one of the most original and exciting takes on a tried and tested formula ever made. Hear the pitch and you're hooked . . . 'It's about a guy who has short term memory loss, he can't remember anything that happens to him over fifteen minutes ago, and he's trying to figure out who killed his wife . . . and it's told backwards!' Wow! I mean WOW! I was so there, and so were Newmarket who financed it on a lowish Hollywood budget (around $5m). The movie was a massive success, not necessarily at the box office (as usual, UK distributors thought, incorrectly I believe, it was too complicated for 'stupid' mainstream audiences, and gave it a kind of art house release!) It doesn't really matter because the critics loved it, and again, so did the film makers. And so Chris Nolan found himself at the helm of a Hollywood monster sized production – 'Insomnia' – with Al Pacino, Robin Williams, Hilary Swank . . . all in the space of a few short years, and all because they made an intriguing and brilliantly executed micro budget movie.

Festivals

Your movie will regularly play at international festivals for the first year, and thereafter it will attend fewer and fewer. Almost certainly, the director will be invited to the festivals to help promote the film. The producer will stay at home. Don't underestimate how much time can be eaten up zipping around the world, visiting exotic countries, screening your movie to enthusiastic audiences, but not actually getting you any closer to that next movie.

The next project

After the premiere for your movie, you'll sit in a bar with the key players who made the film happen. For now you'll forget all the crap that's going to happen in the next year or two (such as your moral commitment to your investors to get their money back plus some) and consider the future as a wide open and exciting opportunity to make whatever you want to make next. There will be much patting on the back, good intentions, promises of properly paid jobs and a general feeling that you're going to be on set shooting another movie within the next twelve months. No one will bring up the fact that you don't have a script and that it's going to take you the best part of a year, perhaps even longer (because you now know how hard it is to write a great script) to get it down on paper. Nor will you consider that it's going to be hard to convince any investor to stump up some dosh without a successful track record from this film. Still it's your night so dream BIG!

Then there's the film industry. If your movie is exceptional, then the industry, perhaps even Hollywood, will start knocking on your door. But with horror, the producer will realise that the only opportunities on offer are for the director. There's no space or desire to accommodate anyone else.

The world is filled with film makers who manage to make a movie. But the process, for one reason or another, has put them off making a second. Almost anyone can make a movie. But not everyone can make a second, or a third . . .

Life after the movie

In 1998 Jonathan Newman set out to make a feature film for £10k. It was financed with a Video On Demand pre-sale to British Telecom (the first in the UK). With a strong cast, including James Dreyfus (Gimme Gimme Gimme) and Saeed Jaffrey, the film was shot over 21 days. 'Then came the hard part . . . ' says Jonathan, 'finishing the film. It was clear that I needed a considerable amount of cash to complete and deliver the film to a sales agent and UK distributor, both of which I had interest from. After a lot of searching and false offers, I finally partnered with Brighton based Spice Factory. I was grateful that they managed to secure a bank overdraft to complete the film, but this partnership proved a long-term and costly disappointment, and like so many other film makers I have been left with a very bitter taste in my mouth.

Nevertheless, we finished and delivered the film to our US based sales agent, ****, and UK distributor, Redbus. **** made some sales abroad, but it soon became clear that they were not the most efficient sales agency, and I felt, again very disappointed as they would never return my calls and I have still not managed to get specific information from them about my film. Redbus, though promising to release the film theatrically, sat on it and had difficulties. I decided it was time to cut my losses. Getting out of the UK theatrical contract, I managed to place it with a small video label and the film came out on rental and sell-through and actually performed quite well. I began this feature film actually intending to make a short film, but it somehow all escalated. While it definitely exceeded my expectations, it was far from perfect. Afterwards, I had the usual hopes and dreams of winning a major festival, making major sales and kick-starting my career.

While the film sold, and played a few festivals, it just didn't propel me into the place I hoped it might. It was a hard and uphill struggle – it still is – as the film has a life afterwards, and as the producer, I'm still shovelling other people's BS. Fundamentally, I found that the relationships between producer, co-producers, sales agents and distributors lacked integrity. The producer, rightly or wrongly, always feels like someone is screwing them. As a sales agent, it's just too easy to charge the producer for all your market expenses: nice restaurants, your lovely yacht, your suite at the Carlton and so on. This might not be what actually happens, but it's the eternal paranoia you feel when you relinquish control. On 'Being Considered', our sales agent still owes money to the delivery agent (who makes copies of the masters for each territory). As we speak, they just made a sale to Czech Republic but cannot deliver as the delivery agent is still owed money and as a result, the sales agent and co-producer are attempting to bypass the delivery agent and get the delivery items from me directly. Of course, if the integrity of everyone's relationship was intact to begin with, (i.e. people did not screw each other), these kind of things wouldn't happen!'

* Note, for legal reasons, names have been omitted.

If you are working in a producer / director team, as early as you can in to your relationship, have a discussion about what you will do if opportunity knocks, but for only one of you (and possibly at the exclusion of the other). Without a prior and sensible agreement, there will be tears, much gnashing of teeth and potential life-long friends can be lost.

And here's one I prepared earlier

Getting an agent will open many doors, but the agent will never get you the work, they will only get you through the door. It's then up to you to be dazzling.

Bernie Shultz
FOX

The smart film maker will of course already have that great script ready for when opportunity knocks. If you think of your low budget film as your one time only ticket to the big time, when you get that meeting with that executive, and they utter the knee trembling phrase *'So what would you do with $20m?'* you don't want to answer as I did, *'I'm not sure, can I get back to you?'*. What you want to do is drop onto their desk that great script that you wrote over the last couple of years, *'this is what I want to make, it's going to be great and it's going to make YOU a lot of money!'*.

In the industry, a low budget film is often perceived as a talent calling card and you'll be surprised just who will take your meeting because they don't know if you are the next Tarantino or Rodriguez.

Survival

During this long phase after the film is completed, the awful question of *'how will I survive?'* will raise it's ugly head. There is a good chance that the director could get work on cheap telly (prime time soaps often pay anywhere between £1-2k a week which to any cash strapped malnourished film maker is a veritable fortune). There are other obvious avenues such as corporate videos, wedding videos etc. but these can often be time consuming and demoralising. If your screenplay was very strong, you may even get writing assignments. And if push comes to shove, you could always go back to stocking shelves at the local super-market for a while. Either way, you'll probably find it tough to devote all your energies to that *'next project'*. Worse still, you'll see other film makers who have wealthy backgrounds, free to pursue their career as they have been taken care of by mummy and daddy. Whatever you have to do, stick with it and don't get disheartened. We all know the overnight success stories, but the truth is the vast majority of film makers will only achieve success toward the end of their career. It's a marathon and you need to stay the distance. Don't fall by the wayside. Never give up. If you feel like this, send me an e-mail (chris@livingspirit.com) and I will have a good yell at you!

Getting an agent

After your film is launched, the director and writer will have the opportunity to get themselves an agent (producers don't get agents). This agent can act like a portal through which you can pass to gain access to the *real film world* and better still you'll have the recommendation of a respected industry player. The best way to get an agent is to contact them and send them press clippings and the good reviews for your film, but crucially you must invite them to a screening (both the London Film Festival and Edinburgh Film Festivals are regularly attended by talent seeking agents). If they are interested, you'll go for a meeting to feel each other out. If everyone is happy, then they'll agree to represent you and take a fee for any jobs that you get (usually around 10%). It's important to understand that an agent will never get you a job. The best they can do is get you the meeting but it is up to you to deliver, and YOU must get the job. They'll cut the deal for you and almost certainly get you more money than you would on your own, which will more than compensate you for their 10% commission.

Agents are not psychic, you need to tell them what you want to do with your career, and what your strengths and weaknesses are. They need to know the truth if they are going to get you great jobs. Ideally, you should bond with your agent and become buddies. I would always advise asking them to try to get you meetings for cheap telly work straight away as cash flow is your enemy. Better to direct telly than deliver pizza, which is what it can so often turn into. Put your ego in a box for now and take the money.

Genevieve Jolliffe
British Filmmaker in L.A

'The No.1 consideration before moving is 'how do I get a visa to enable me to live and work in the US?' It isn't easy. There are a variety of visas to look at, as a visa exists for practically every letter of the alphabet! The two main temporary visas that can help lead to a green card (permanent residence) are the O-1 and the H-1. There's a lot to do to prepare for this and although you can do it yourself, I'd get a professional immigration lawyer. Once you have a visa and you're in the US, you can apply for a social security number. It's only then that you will be regarded as a normal person and be able to live a normal lifestyle, with things that you've always taken for granted.

First stop is to get a driving license. This is super important as this is used as ID and America is a place where you need to have ID on you at all times (a passport does not always work). A Cop once told me that if I had no ID on me, how could he identify my body? (!) Your next step should then be health insurance, or you'll find yourself paying $600 for each doctors visit, and then $thousands if an accident occurs. Also forget that great relationship you built up with your UK bank manager, as having moved country, it's as though you're 18 again, and you must start to build up your credit rating.

Once the practicalities are over, you'll find it easy. Americans are extremely friendly, they love the English and there are many ex-pats here who can give you advice. Plus, there are heaps of networking organizations out here for film makers. However, all this takes time, but it is 'totally' worth it. And if you ever feel a little homesick, there are plenty of British pubs and curry houses to keep you happy!

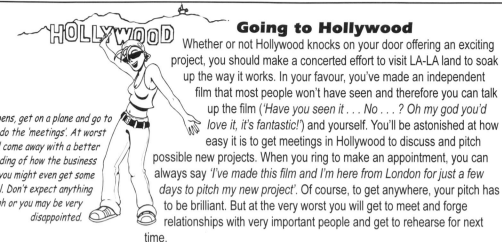

Going to Hollywood

Whether or not Hollywood knocks on your door offering an exciting project, you should make a concerted effort to visit LA-LA land to soak up the way it works. In your favour, you've made an independent film that most people won't have seen and therefore you can talk up the film (*'Have you seen it . . . No . . . ? Oh my god you'd love it, it's fantastic!'*) and yourself. You'll be astonished at how easy it is to get meetings in Hollywood to discuss and pitch possible new projects. When you ring to make an appointment, you can always say *'I've made this film and I'm here from London for just a few days to pitch my new project'*. Of course, to get anywhere, your pitch has to be brilliant. But at the very worst you will get to meet and forge relationships with very important people and get to rehearse for next time.

Whatever happens, get on a plane and go to Hollywood and do the 'meetings'. At worst you will come away with a better understanding of how the business works, at best, you might even get some kind of deal. Don't expect anything though or you may be very disappointed.

Ask around your film maker friends who have contacts in LA and you'll usually find someone who's willing to let you crash on their sofa for a few days. You also need to be able to drive and must rent a car as everyone drives in LA. The Americans are extremely professional and you may find yourself starting meetings at breakfast and working all the way through to the evening.

It's been a long time

It will seem an age since you started your film. Your hopes and dreams may not have been fully realised, but you are now a film maker. A player. And more important, you are experienced, so that next time you'll do a better job. This isn't a race. There are no winners. Just the movies you choose to make. Hopefully you'll be able to make the best movies you can, AND make a living out of it. That's all any of us can really ask for.

If you choose to continue making movies, it's important to get back on the horse straight away, keep that tunnel vision and make it happen! NOW! I myself have been dazzled by the side lights or life, exciting opportunities like *'writing god damn books!'* Great but it isn't getting my movie made! And so as I type the last few words of this book, I look to the future wondering what it holds . . . Aware that if I do make my next movie soon, it will be entirely because I invest a huge amount of time, energy and resources into making it happen. It doesn't get any easier and it certainly won't make itself . . . *but it is what I choose*. And if you choose it too, then I hope we meet up one time soon on this grand and exciting journey. So here's to success and, truly, I hope to see YOU at the Oscars sometime!

The new 'Guerilla Film Makers Handbook – US edition' is now completely updated and revised, specifically for the USA (so now there are two versions, the UK Edition 2 and USA edition 1). It covers the independent scene in America but also examines the Hollywood Studio system. It's an obvious first choice for film makers taking that trip across the pond, even if I say so myself! Case studies include 'The Good Girl', 'Donnie Darko', 'The Deep End', 'Roger Dodger' to name a few. It will be on the streets mid 2003.

Avid XpressDV Rough Guide

What is editing and how do you do it?

It is . . . Getting your shot material into an editing system, then cutting the pictures and sound together until it looks like your movie, then outputting it all back onto tape.

If you shot your movie on film, then the first thing to do is to get the laboratory that processed it, to telecine the footage and record it onto videotape (maybe with sound). If you are cutting on Avid ExpressDV, then get your telecine deliverer on DVCam (with timecode!)

The rough guide to how it works . . .

1. Take your tapes to an editing system. This can be anything from a home PC running editing software such as Avid ExpressDV, to a hired edit suite with an Avid Media Composer. You can either plug your camera straight into the computer, or a tape deck needs to be connected to the system. If you have used more than one tape format, then check that the edit suite has got decks for all of them.

These tapes are known as your 'media' and have to be copied or digitised into the editing system. They are stored on one or several hard disks. You play the tapes and the computer records them. Once they are on the system you can access any part of the media instantly, instead of having to play through the tape (which is why editing on a computer is known as nonlinear editing).

Every tape contains some extra information, known as timecode, which is passed on to the computer. This is a chronological unique reference to every frame on the tape (and the project). It is crucial for the computer to be able to reference from which tape or source the media comes, and exactly where on the tape. The only common videotape formats that do not use this are VHS and miniDV (miniDV has a kind of timecode but NOT one suitable for making an EDL and neg cutting list for instance). It's therefore highly advisable to copy any VHS media onto a digital tape like DVCam before digitising.

As soon as you start digitising your media, you also need to start organising it. On the Avid you have to start a system of named windows called bins. These are like folders on a PC. The standard method is to create a bin for each tape, and a bin for each scene in the film. The editing software will ask you to name each tape as you digitise it. It is a good idea to use the same name that is written on the tape. If your tapes are not already nicely named in order of shooting, then do it yourself before you digitise them. Go for a simple system like 001, 002, 003 (not 1,2,3 or 'Jimmy's tape from Tuesday') etc.

Avid XpressDV Rough Guide

You can either digitise each tape as a whole, or you can break it down into parts or clips. As a rule, it is much better to digitise everything you have, if you have the drive space, because it is very time consuming to go back and look through a tape for something later on.

Once everything is digitised, you need to organise the media into the scene bins. Long arbitrary clips can be broken down into shorter subclips. The idea is that you want to end up with every take separated and labelled according to the scene number, take number and shot description. Then copy each into its corresponding scene bin.

Avid XpressDV is a pro quality editing system that uses an industry standard interface and has wide compatibility. It is the tool I would choose if I were to make a low budget movie and couldn't afford a full blown system.

2. Start editing. This involves choosing parts of your clips and placing them together on a continuous track called the timeline, to create sequences. You decide which part of the source clips that you want to use and mark an in point at the start and an out point at the end. Then you lay that section onto the timeline. As you build up the sequence you make adjustments in the timeline and keep playing it through. A sequence can be treated in the same way as a clip, for instance you can mark them with in and out points. The sequence plays in a separate window from source clips, known as the record monitor. You can also put multiple sequences onto the timeline e.g. when you are putting together the scenes (which are currently separate and small scene by scene edits of your movie) into one long version.

As well as cutting together your shots, editing also includes the use of special effects, laying down music and sound effects, putting on titles and even colour grading the picture.

3. Put the edit onto tape. This is simply a case of playing the movie out of the computer and recording it onto tape. You can also create a list of all the timecode references used in your edit, known as an EDL (edit decision list). This can be taken to other editing systems and used to redigitise only the parts of the tapes that are used in the movie, or even used as a cutting list for a negative cutter.

Avid XpressDV – Creating a New Project

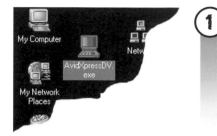

① Starting AvidXpressDVD

Double click the Avid icon on the desktop or on the start menu (on a PC), or via the applications folder in the extensions manager on the desktop (on a MAC) to start up the software. This will start up your AvidXpressDV software so you can start editing.

② First screen – Select Project

AvidXpressDV will now start and after a few initialisation windows, the Select Project *window pops up. As you are starting a new project, click on* New Project *and the* New Project *box will pop up.*

Projects are like folders on your hard drive, except they contain all the information about your film such as tapes, clips, edits etc. Unlike EDLs, projects are not interchangeable with other editing systems, so you can't take an AvidXpressDV project and open it in Adobe Premiere.

③ Creating your new project

Type the name of your project into the Project Name *box. Keep the project name short and to the point. Make sure* PAL *and not* NTSC *is selected (if you are editing in the UK and using PAL video). Click* OK. *Your new project will appear in the* Select a Project *window. Press* OK *to open your new project.*

PAL and NTSC are the two major tv formats used in the world. PAL works at 25 frames a second (or 50 fields) and NTSC works at 30 frames a second (or sixty fields). Practically, this means you will use PAL in the UK and NTSC in the USA. However, there are moves in the USA to shoot low budget DV features on PAL as its frame rate works better with cinema projection and the image is higher resolution.

④ The Project Window

The Project Window *has the title of the project you have created in the top left corner. There are 4 tabs:* Bins, Settings, Effects *(displayed as an effect icon), and* Info. *This setup is different to other versions of Avid software. Closing this window will close the whole project. This window is the centre from which all your major settings can be accessed, as well as your bins. It usually lives at the top left of your Avid screen(s).*

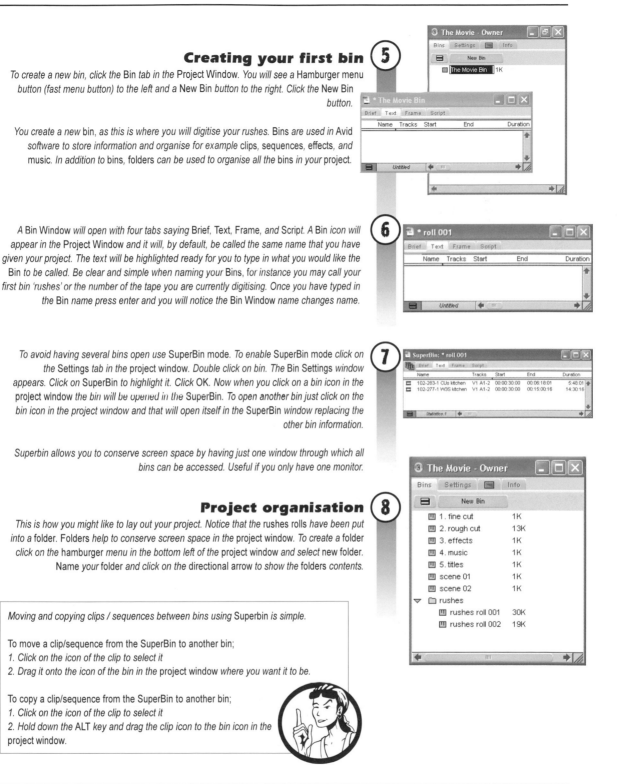

Creating your first bin (5)

To create a new bin, click the Bin *tab in the* Project Window. *You will see a* Hamburger menu *button (fast menu button) to the left and a* New Bin *button to the right. Click the* New Bin *button.*

You create a new bin, *as this is where you will digitise your rushes.* Bins *are used in* Avid *software to store information and organise for example clips, sequences, effects, and music. In addition to bins,* folders *can be used to organise all the* bins *in your* project.

A Bin Window will open with four tabs saying Brief, Text, Frame, *and* Script. *A Bin icon will appear in the* Project Window *and it will, by default, be called the same name that you have given your project. The text will be highlighted ready for you to type in what you would like the Bin to be called. Be clear and simple when naming your Bins, for instance you may call your first bin 'rushes' or the number of the tape you are currently digitising. Once you have typed in the Bin name press enter and you will notice the Bin Window name changes name.*

To avoid having several bins open use SuperBin *mode. To enable* SuperBin *mode click on the* Settings *tab in the* project window. *Double click on bin. The Bin Settings window appears. Click on SuperBin to highlight it. Click OK. Now when you click on a bin icon in the* project window *the bin will be opened in the* SuperBin. *To open another bin just click on the bin icon in the project window and that will open itself in the* SuperBin *window replacing the other bin information.*

Superbin allows you to conserve screen space by having just one window through which all bins can be accessed. Useful if you only have one monitor.

Project organisation (8)

This is how you might like to lay out your project. Notice that the rushes rolls have been put into a folder. Folders help to conserve screen space in the project window. To create a folder click on the hamburger menu in the bottom left of the project window and select new folder. Name your folder and click on the directional arrow to show the folders contents.

Moving and copying clips / sequences between bins using Superbin is simple.

To move a clip/sequence from the SuperBin to another bin;
1. Click on the icon of the clip to select it
2. Drag it onto the icon of the bin in the project window where you want it to be.

To copy a clip/sequence from the SuperBin to another bin;
1. Click on the icon of the clip to select it
2. Hold down the ALT key and drag the clip icon to the bin icon in the project window.

Bin views

There are different ways of viewing information contained within a bin. *The* Brief, Text, Frame, *and* Script *views are* default bin views. *Use the tabs in the* bin window *to switch between these* default views.

Brief view (right) has five columns conserving screen space in the bin *window.*

Text view (below) contains columns displaying a wider overview of information of the contents of the bin.

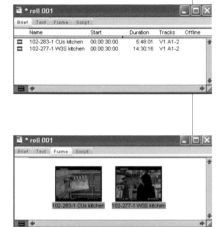

Frame view (right) displays a single frame of the clip *and the* name *below it. To* enlarge *the* frame, *click* Ctrl+L. *To* reduce *the size of the frame click* Ctrl+K. *You can also play the* clip *in the* bin. *Use this to cue up a frame that best resembles the contents of the* clip.

Script view (left) also enables you to view a single frame of the clip. The frames are set to appear on the left side of the bin view and columns to the right display detailed information about the clip. Use the comments box to type in notes about the clip. For example 'fluffed lines'.

To sort the contents of a column in a bin into alphanumeric order, select the column name. The column is highlighted, and then click Ctrl-E.

Customise bin view

You can customise your bin view to suit your needs (left). To change the headings in the bin you must first select text view. Click on the hamburger menu in the bin window and select headings. The Bin Column Selection window pops up. You can then select any of the headings listed for you to be able to view them in your bin. Below are some of the column headings and what they mean.

Audio – *the audio sample rate which should be 48000K.*

Audio Format – *Use AIFF as it is compatible with both Mac and PC.*

Creation Date – *the date the media file was created (digitised).*

Drive – *the location of the media file.*

Duration – *how long the clip lasts.*

End – *the time code of the end of the clip.*

IN-OUT – *the duration from the mark in to out on the clip.*

Mark IN – *the timecode of the point set as the in point.*

Mark OUT – *the timecode of the point set as the out point.*

Modified Date – *the last date and time the clip was used.*

Offline – *if media is offline it cannot be seen by the avid.*

Project – *the name of the project.*

Scene – *type in the scene number in this column.*

Start – *the timecode of the start of the clip.*

Take – *type in the take number in this column.*

Tape – *the tape number.*

Tracks – *will indicate the video and audio tracks digitised.*

Video – *the colour space (res) at which the clip was digitised.*

Bin headings

The bins in your project contain clips, audio clips, subclips, effects and sequences. These are all represented as icons in your bin.

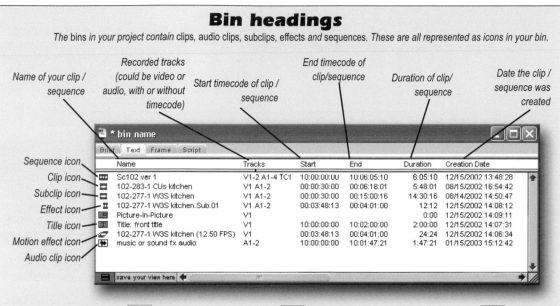

Name of your clip / sequence

Recorded tracks (could be video or audio, with or without timecode)

Start timecode of clip / sequence

End timecode of clip/sequence

Duration of clip/ sequence

Date the clip / sequence was created

Sequence icon
Clip icon
Subclip icon
Effect icon
Title icon
Motion effect icon
Audio clip icon

Name	Tracks	Start	End	Duration	Creation Date
Sc102 ver 1	V1-2 A1-4 TC1	10:00:00:00	10:06:05:10	6:05:10	12/15/2002 13:48:28
102-283-1 CUs kitchen	V1 A1-2	00:00:30:00	00:06:18:01	5:48:01	08/15/2002 16:54:42
102-277-1 W3S kitchen	V1 A1-2	00:00:30:00	00:15:00:16	14:30:16	08/14/2002 14:50:47
102-277-1 W3S kitchen.Sub.01	V1 A1-2	00:03:48:13	00:04:01:00	12:12	12/15/2002 14:08:12
Picture-In-Picture	V1			0:00	12/15/2002 14:09:11
Title: front tttle	V1	10:00:00:00	10:02:00:00	2:00:00	12/15/2002 14:07:31
102-277-1 W3S kitchen (12.50 FPS)	V1	00:03:48:13	00:04:01:00	24:24	12/15/2002 14:06:34
music or sound fx audio	A1-2	10:00:00:00	10:01:47:21	1:47:21	01/15/2003 15:12:42

save your view here

CLIPS

(also known as master clips*). These are video and or audio that have been cloned onto your hard drive during the recording (digitising on other Avids) process from your master DV tapes. The cllp Icon in the bin is connected to the media file in the OMFI media file folder on the hard drive. To view the clip, double click the icon in the bin. This loads the clip into the source monitor. Press play in the source monitor to view the clip.*

SEQUENCES

Sequences *consist of a selection of clips, subclips or other sequences, all strung together on the timeline. In essence, this is your edit. Again it's important that you do not delete the media files of clips that have been cut into your sequence. If you do, a media offline image will pop up when you play back the clip in the record monitor in the composer window. The media for this clip is offline. To get this back online you will need to batch record the offline clip.*

AUDIO CLIPS

The icon for the audio clip is displayed like a waveform. Clips with this icon only contain audio. Audio clips can be dialogue, music, sound effects (fx), voice over etc. They work in the same way as clips. The audio clip icon is also linked to a media file on the hard drive. To preview the audio clip, double click the icon in the bin.

EFFECTS

As you apply effects to your sequence they will appear in a bin. You can keep effects in a dedicated 'effects' bin should you need to re-use the effect more than once. To save an effect to a different bin, click and drag the effect icon from the effect editor window to the effects bin. To then apply this effect to your sequence, click and drag it onto the segment or transition you want to effect. When you render an effect, a media file called a precompute is created. The effect icon provides a link to this precompute which is located in the OMFI media file folder on the hard drive. Some effects are 'real-time' and do not need to be rendered during the offline edit.

SUBCLIPS

Subclips *are sections of either clips or sequences that you have extracted, kind of like mini edits or a part of a scene that you want to separate from the rest of the scene. For instance, you can use subclips to extract a section of a sequence which can then be worked on without changing the original sequence. To make a subclip mark an IN and an OUT point on a clip or sequence, hold down the Alt key (on a PC) or the Option key (on a mac) and drag the clip to the bin. Note that the subclip and clip from which it was extracted, are connected to the same media file. If you delete the original clip's media file, you will also be deleting your subclip's media.*

TITLES

The title icon represents media created when using the title tool to create title cards for your sequence. You can load these clips into your source monitor and then edit them into your sequence. You will use title cards to identify missing shots / scenes from your film as you create your assembly. You can also use the title tool to create front and end titles for your film.

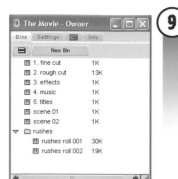

(9) Project organisation

This is how you might like to lay out your project. Notice that the rushes rolls *have been put into a folder. Folders* help to conserve screen space in the *project window. To create a folder click on the* hamburger *menu in the bottom left of the* project window and select *new folder. Name* your folder and click on the *directional arrow to* show the *folders* contents.

(10) Toolsets

It's easy to manage screen space in Avid XpressDV using Toolsets. *Using* Toolsets, *the windows you open can be arranged without overlap, and all tools needed to perform a certain task are opened automatically. Click on the* Toolset *drop down menu to reveal several* Toolset *views –* Basic *(the simplest setup),* Recording *(for when you want to transfer media from your DV tape to the computer),* Source Record Editing *(for when you are editing),* Audio Editing *(for when you are editing sound),* Effects Editing *(for when you are adding and editing effects) and* Colour Correction *(for when you are colour correcting the images). The* Toolsets *are most useful for people who have only one computer monitor.*

Cutting room chaos

The cutting room can become a minefield if you fail to set up an efficient system for organising all the material that gets sent to you from the outside world. You will be sent tapes, CDs, graphics, and endless paperwork from both the set and the lab. You need to organise all this material so that at any stage you are able to access it within seconds. You will need shelves to store all your tape stock and files. All tapes sent to the cutting room should be logged in and out of your tape log book. You will need to keep a contact list of names and addresses containing all production crew details and post production contacts.

As soon as paper work arrives it needs to be filed (mainly this will be paperwork from set and the lab), which will include sound reports, camera reports, tramline scripts, continuity logs, daily shoot reports, telecine reports, and call sheets etc. A tidy, well organised cutting room will give your the editor a clear head to concentrate on the cut.

Label tapes

I can't express how important it is to keep the cutting room exceptionally well organised, one aspect being that of labelling tapes. Label your tapes as soon as they are given to you (both the tape and the box) with the date, production title, tape number, slates shot, address and telephone number of the production. You are always going to be able to find shots quickly and efficiently if your tapes are correctly labelled. Be clear in your scrawling too, not only you need to be able to read your nasty handwriting.

Project settings

The settings *tab in the* project window (right) *reveals various options for adjusting project, user and site settings. Double click on any of the settings to open its window where you will be able to adjust the settings. You are most likely going to adjust the following settings.*

Audio setting *(above) allows you to select between audio scrub options, the default pan for your project's audio, and audio tools preload. Audio scrubbing is a term that refers to the process of scrubbing backwards and forwards listening for the best edit point in a piece of audio. Use the default setup for marking and trimming audio. The default pan option will change how you monitor and output audio from your computer. When alternating tracks L/R is selected tracks 1 and 3 will play out of the left speaker and 2 and 4 out of the right speaker. The audio pan is split between the left and right speakers for audio monitoring and output. If all tracks are centred then the audio will be monitored and output equally from both speakers (mono).*

Audio Project *(above) allows you to check the audio sample rate for your project. The sample rate you should use is 48kHz (for DV). You may later import audio from a CD, which has a sample rate of 44.1kHz, and Avid XpressDV will ask if you wish to convert the sample rate of the audio you are importing. All audio must be at the same rate (as that of the project) or you will not hear it. Your audio input source will automatically be set to OHCI (open host controller interface, your firewire card in your computer) through which it is receiving audio. Click on the input source and change it when you input audio from another source such as a CD player or microphone.*

General Settings *(above) is where you can adjust the default starting timecode for all new sequences you cut. The broadcast standard start timecode is 10:00:00:00 (hrs:mins:sec:frames). Just type the numbers into the box and it will automatically fill in the colons for you. Then click ok.*

The Video Display *Setting (above) is especially important for Avid XpressDV users. You want to check the box that says 'DV device supports digital video input' and select 'send video to DV device'. This will enable you to view your footage on a TV monitor to the side of your set-up (client monitor).*

Bin settings *(above) will allow you to ask your computer to auto-save your project at least every 15 minutes so that if your computer crashes you will only have lost a maximum of fifteen minutes work. The Attic is a special directory where Avid creates multiple backups of your project, handy to know if you ever suffer a catastrophe. The maximum files in attic should be set to 50 (depending on how big your project is). Increasing the number of files in the attic provides you with more insurance should your project become corrupt. The same applies to the number of versions of any bin open in your project. You should set this to 5. You can always back track should you need to.*

Project settings (cont . . .)

Desktop Play Delay – Current

Frames: 16
0   25

OK   Cancel

Desktop Play Delay *allows you to modify the delay between the video monitor on the desktop and the video monitor attached to your camera or deck that plays through your firewire card (which will lag slightly behind). Tiny adjustments to the offset will get your record monitor and viewing monitor in sync. You'll need several attempts before getting both in sync.*

General Settings – Current

PAL
Temporary File Directory:
D:\Program Files\Avid\Avid Xpress DV   Set
Default Starting TC
10:00:00:00

OK   Cancel

General Settings *is where you can adjust the default starting timecode for all new sequences you cut. The broadcast standard start timecode is 10:00:00:00 (hrs:mins:sec:frames). Just type the numbers into the box and it will automatically fill in the colons for you. Then click ok.*

Record Settings – Current

General   Batch   Edit   Media Files   DV Options

Stop deck after record
Pause deck after record

Preroll Method: Best Available

Force unique clip names
Activate bin window after record
Space bar stops record
Record across timecode breaks

Pause deck while logging

OK   Cancel

The Record Setting *is where you can determine how the computer interacts with your deck (camera), and how the media files are created. Click on the* batch tab *and select optimise for disk space. Select the* media files tab *and click on record to multiple files and increase the maximum recording time to 60 minutes. Click on switch to emptiest drive and select 6 minutes of disk space as the point at which media can be cloned onto the emptiest drive. You want to leave some space on your drive for the media databases to exist or your system may crash.*

Media Creation – Current

Drive Filtering   Record   Titles   Import   Mixdown   Motion Effects

Video Resolution: DV 25 420
Apply to All

Video Drive: →   FILES 2 (G:)
Audio Drive: →   FILES 2 (G:)
Apply to All

OK   Cancel

Use the Media Creation *setting to help set up your* drive management *options before you start cutting. Check both boxes in the* drive filtering *tab. This prevents Avid from storing media files on your system drive.*

If you are working in a PAL project *select* DV25 420 *as the video resolution in the* record tab. *Always leave around 6 minutes of free disk space on a drive to allow media databases to function.* Media databases *act as a directory listing all the media stored on that particular disk. As you create new media they update themselves.*

Media databases *also assist your computer with keeping track of where media is located*

(3) msmFMID.pmr
(3) msmMMOB.mdb

on hard disks. If the drive becomes too full these databases cannot update themselves.

Catherine Fletcher
Editor and Director

'In 1998, at the grand old age of 31, I was unemployed, broke, living at home and all I wanted to do was make movies. So I borrowed some money and made a short film. The film fell short of the mark so I shelved it – but it led to my brother asking me to edit an obscure internal BBC promo for a friend using Adobe Premiere and a mini DV camera. After my short I thought anything else would be easy. Guess what? It was. And fun. I then did a two day Avid course and persuaded a DP to let me cut his showreel for nothing. Then I spread the word that I was now an editor, heartily believing that I could be. I put adverts in the back of indie film newsletters and on film school noticeboards. I told people I had cut my short (which I hadn't), a BBC corporate and numerous promos etc. Finally someone needed an editor urgently, "It's short notice but for you I'll do it at the introductory rate of £100 per day" I said. It worked. At the edit I forgot how to use the Avid, asked the techies tons of questions, then crashed the computer and lost a day's work (very hard to do, but I can explain). I still got paid.

Then I cut my first drama, a graduate short for expenses. Straight after that I got a DV feature which led to a S16 feature for £200 a week. I worked on shorts and corporates for the next two years, learning lots about effects and technical stuff. I got my break on an ITV soap opera after a kind friend pretended to be my agent and the producer liked a short on my reel. A year later and I've cut a major drama series, a movie in Canada, got an agent and I'm not living at my Mum's anymore. So you really want to edit? Tell everyone you're an editor. Cut anything you can. Be prepared to work for nothing. Believe in your dream.'

*Skillset will subsidise the Avid course for anyone who is freelance. That means everyone.

Project settings

The settings tab in the project window (right) reveals various options for adjusting project, user and site settings. Double click on any of the settings to open its window where you will be able to adjust the settings. You are most likely going to adjust the following settings.

Audio setting *(above) allows you to select between* audio scrub *options, the* default pan *for your* project's *audio, and audio tools preload. Audio scrubbing is a term that refers to the process of scrubbing backwards and forwards listening for the best edit point in a piece of audio. Use the default setup for* marking *and trimming* audio. *The default pan option will change how you monitor and output audio from your computer. When alternating tracks L/R is selected tracks 1 and 3 will play out of the left speaker and 2 and 4 out of the right speaker. The audio pan is split between the left and right speakers for audio monitoring and output. If all tracks are centred then the audio will be monitored and output equally from both speakers (mono).*

Audio Project *(above) allows you to check the* audio sample rate *for your project. The sample rate you should use is 48kHz (for DV). You may later* import audio from a CD, which has a sample rate of *44.1kHz, and Avid XpressDV will ask if you wish to convert the sample rate of the audio you are importing. All audio must be at the same rate (as that of the project) or you will not hear it. Your audio input source will automatically be set to OHCI (open host controller interface, your firewire card in your computer) through which it is receiving audio. Click on the input source and change it when you input audio from another source such as a CD player or microphone.*

General Settings *(above) is where you can adjust the default starting timecode for all new sequences you cut. The broadcast standard start timecode is 10:00:00:00 (hrs:mins:sec:frames). Just type the numbers into the box and it will automatically fill in the colons for you. Then click ok.*

The Video Display *Setting (above) is especially important for Avid XpressDV users. You want to check the box that says 'DV device supports digital video input' and select 'send video to DV device'. This will enable you to view your footage on a TV monitor to the side of your set-up (client monitor).*

Bin settings *(above) will allow you to ask your computer to auto-save your project at least every 15 minutes so that if your computer crashes you will only have lost a maximum of fifteen minutes work. The Attic is a special directory where Avid creates multiple backups of your project, handy to know if you ever suffer a catastrophe. The maximum files in attic should be set to 50 (depending on how big your project is). Increasing the number of files in the attic provides you with more insurance should your project become corrupt. The same applies to the number of versions of any bin open in your project. You should set this to 5. You can always back track should you need to.*

Project settings (cont . . .)

Desktop Play Delay *allows you to modify the delay between the video monitor on the desktop and the video monitor attached to your camera or deck that plays through your firewire card (which will lag slightly behind). Tiny adjustments to the offset will get your record monitor and viewing monitor in sync. You'll need several attempts before getting both in sync.*

General Settings *is where you can adjust the default starting timecode for all new sequences you cut. The broadcast standard start timecode is 10:00:00:00 (hrs:mins:sec:frames). Just type the numbers into the box and it will automatically fill in the colons for you. Then click ok.*

The Record Setting *is where you can determine how the computer interacts with your deck (camera), and how the media files are created. Click on the* batch tab *and select optimise for disk space. Select the* media files tab *and click on* record to multiple files *and increase the maximum recording time to 60 minutes. Click on switch to emptiest drive and select 6 minutes of disk space as the point at which media can be cloned onto the emptiest drive. You want to leave some space on your drive for the media databases to exist or your system may crash.*

Use the Media Creation *setting to help set up your* drive management *options before you start cutting. Check both boxes in the* drive filtering *tab. This prevents Avid from storing media files on your system drive.*

If you are working in a PAL project select DV25 420 as the video resolution in the record tab. Always leave around 6 minutes of free disk space on a drive to allow media databases to function. Media databases act as a directory listing all the media stored on that particular disk. As you create new media they update themselves.

Media databases *also assist your computer with keeping track of where media is located*

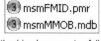

on hard disks. If the drive becomes too full these databases cannot update themselves.

Catherine Fletcher
Editor and Director

'In 1998, at the grand old age of 31, I was unemployed, broke, living at home and all I wanted to do was make movies. So I borrowed some money and made a short film. The film fell short of the mark so I shelved it – but it led to my brother asking me to edit an obscure internal BBC promo for a friend using Adobe Premiere and a mini DV camera. After my short I thought anything else would be easy. Guess what? It was. And fun. I then did a two day Avid course and persuaded a DP to let me cut his showreel for nothing. Then I spread the word that I was now an editor, heartily believing that I could be. I put adverts in the back of indie film newsletters and on film school noticeboards. I told people I had cut my short (which I hadn't), a BBC corporate and numerous promos etc. Finally someone needed an editor urgently, "It's short notice but for you I'll do it at the introductory rate of £100 per day" I said. It worked. At the edit I forgot how to use the Avid, asked the techies tons of questions, then crashed the computer and lost a day's work (very hard to do, but I can explain). I still got paid.

Then I cut my first drama, a graduate short for expenses. Straight after that I got a DV feature which led to a S16 feature for £200 a week. I worked on shorts and corporates for the next two years, learning lots about effects and technical stuff. I got my break on an ITV soap opera after a kind friend pretended to be my agent and the producer liked a short on my reel. A year later and I've cut a major drama series, a movie in Canada, got an agent and I'm not living at my Mum's anymore. So you really want to edit? Tell everyone you're an editor. Cut anything you can. Be prepared to work for nothing. Believe in your dream.'
*Skillset will subsidise the Avid course for anyone who is freelance. That means everyone.

Recording / capturing footage

In order to edit your footage, you will need to transfer it to the computer's hard drive. Avid XpressDV clones the video and audio from your DV tapes so there is no quality loss in the transfer. To transfer your footage you will need to connect your camera, or a DV deck to the computer via the Firewire port. Avid XpressDV will then control the camera / deck, with fast forward, rewind, record etc. You can record all your tapes, or just selected bits. Remember, you have a limited amount of storage space so it is best to digitise only what you need.

Go to the Toolset *menu at the top of the screen and select* Recording. *This will bring up the* Record Tool, *which you will now use to clone the digital video from the tape to the computer's hard disk.*

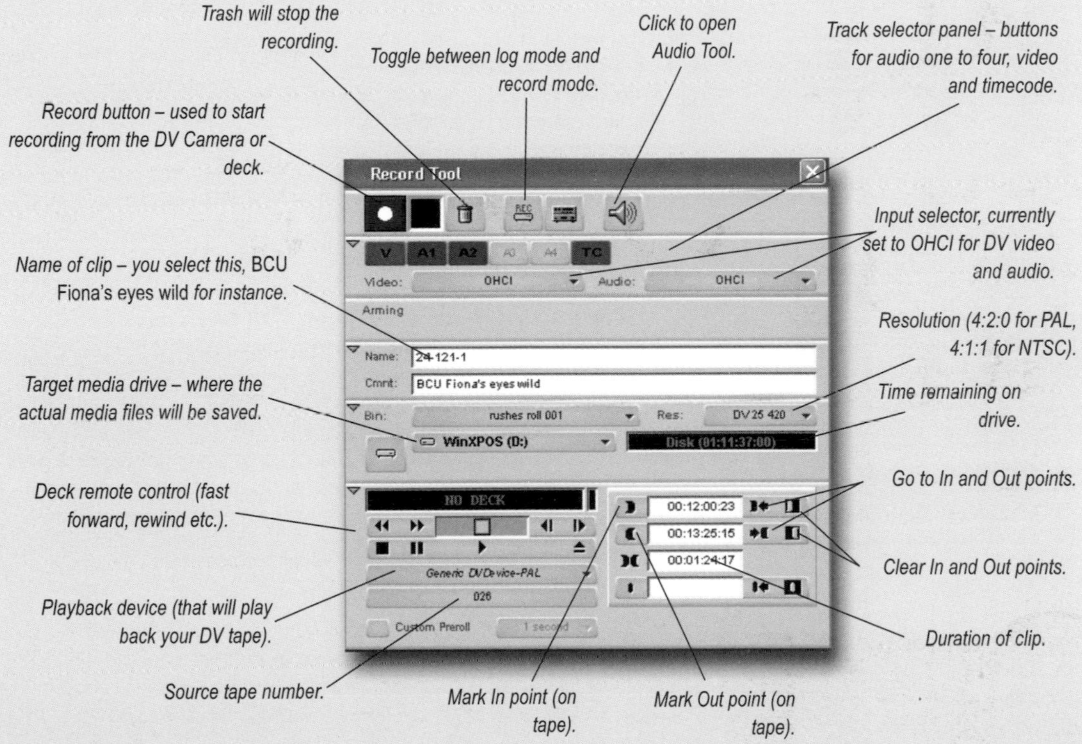

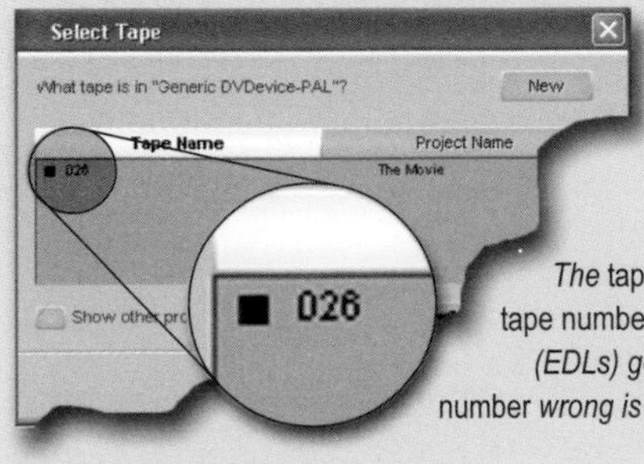

Trash will stop the recording.

Toggle between log mode and record mode.

Click to open Audio Tool.

Track selector panel – buttons for audio one to four, video and timecode.

Record button – used to start recording from the DV Camera or deck.

Name of clip – you select this, BCU Fiona's eyes wild *for instance.*

Target media drive – where the actual media files will be saved.

Deck remote control (fast forward, rewind etc.).

Playback device (that will play back your DV tape).

Source tape number.

Mark In point (on tape).

Mark Out point (on tape).

Input selector, currently set to OHCI for DV video and audio.

Resolution (4:2:0 for PAL, 4:1:1 for NTSC).

Time remaining on drive.

Go to In and Out points.

Clear In and Out points.

Duration of clip.

Record Tool

Video: OHCI   Audio: OHCI

Arming

Name: 24-121-1
Cmnt: BCU Fiona's eyes wild
Bin: rushes roll 001   Res: DV 25 420

WinXPOS (D:)   Disk (01:11:37:00)

NO DECK

Generic DVDevice-PAL
026
Custom Preroll   1 second

00:12:00:23
00:13:25:15
00:01:24:17

Select Tape

What tape is in "Generic DVDevice-PAL"?   New

Tape Name   Project Name
026   The Movie

Show other pro

Getting tape numbers wrong!
The tape number is the key link to the original tape or negative if shot on film. If the tape number is incorrectly typed into the Avid, then all the subsequent edit decision lists (EDLs) generated by the computer will not correspond to the original rushes. Getting a tape number wrong is a big no no! It is also important that tape numbers are unique to each and every tape for the project you are working on. No two can ever be the same.

Avid XpressDV – Quick Step Guide to Recording

(1) Naming the tape

To start recording you need to open the recording tool. Go to the Tools menu and then Record. The Recording Tool will then pop up. Avid will ask you which tape is in the camera, so name it now – it should be no more than a six figure number (001 for tape 1 and 026 for tape 26. Don't use names like graveyard scene when it should be a tape number). Click on the tape icon, the tape name will be highlighted in blue to show you have selected it, click OK. Check that the tape number in the Record Tool matches the tape number that you are about to record.

(2) Start recording

The quickest way to start recording is to cue (fast forward / rewind) your tape to the point at which you would like to digitise from. You can use the fast forward, rewind, stop and play buttons in the Record Tool as a remote for controlling your camera. Check the V1, A1, A2 buttons in the track selector panel in the record tool. Then simply hit the record button (red button), to begin digitising and click the record button again when you wish to stop. The clip you have just digitised will appear in the bin you selected in the record tool.

The clip will automatically be named with the tape number. You should rename the clip so that it makes sense. You can do this by typing in the space under the Name Column in the Bin Window. Remember, keep it short and simple e.g Sc102-24-3-CU John enters, poor dialogue (this refers to scene 102 in the screenplay which was slate 24 during the shoot and this clip is take 3. CU means close-up followed by a brief description followed by comments). You can also use the comments column for any additional comments.

Note that you can type in these comments during recording in the name and comments space in the Record Tool. To do so just start to type during recording and tab between the name and comments spaces. Repeat the above steps for the rest of the footage you would like to be recorded.

Avid XpressDV – Cutting Your First Sequence

(1) Creating a new sequence

A sequence is several clips spliced together. To view your first clip (that's the stuff you have just digitised), double click the clip icon in the bin. It appears in the source monitor.

The Source monitor is the left screen in the Composer Window when it functions as a dual monitor for source/record editing. You will view source material in the source monitor and view your cut sequence in the record monitor. Your settings may tell Avid XpressDV to open the clip in a source pop-up monitor. You can choose to view the source footage either way.

Play and rewind ②

Use the play *button under the source monitor to view the footage. Click the play button again to stop at a certain point in the clip. To scroll through the clip quickly point the cursor at the blue position indicator click and drag from left to right. The J-K-L keys on the keyboard can be used to play, pause, fast forward, and rewind your source footage. By hitting the 'J' or 'L' key more than once you increase the number of frames per second at which you view the footage. Hit the space bar at the point you want to stop playing.*

In and Out points ③

Mark an In *point where you want to start the clip and* mark an Out *point where you want the clip to end. Mark an In and Out by clicking the mark in/out buttons under the source pop-up or using the 'I' and 'O' keys on your keyboard respectively. To play your clip from the mark in to out points press '6' on your keyboard.*
(see box below)

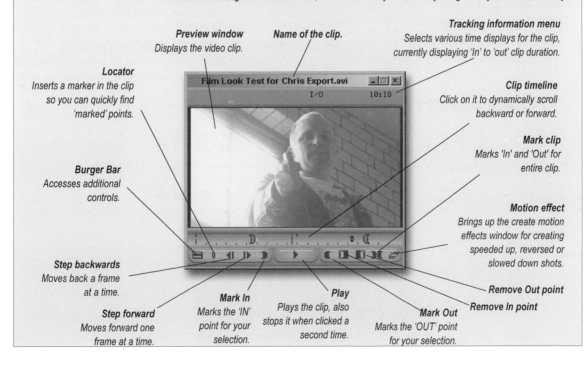

Anatomy of the 'source window'

To edit a clip onto the timeline, you need to tell *Avid XpressDV* what you want. The way you do this is by using IN and Out points. They are accessible through on screen buttons, or the fastest way to work is by using the keyboard short cut keys.

Preview window
Displays the video clip.

Name of the clip.

Tracking information menu
Selects various time displays for the clip, currently displaying 'In' to 'out' clip duration.

Locator
Inserts a marker in the clip so you can quickly find 'marked' points.

Clip timeline
Click on it to dynamically scroll backward or forward.

Mark clip
Marks 'In' and 'Out' for entire clip.

Burger Bar
Accesses additional controls.

Motion effect
Brings up the create motion effects window for creating speeded up, reversed or slowed down shots.

Step backwards
Moves back a frame at a time.

Remove Out point

Step forward
Moves forward one frame at a time.

Mark In
Marks the 'IN' point for your selection.

Play
Plays the clip, also stops it when clicked a second time.

Mark Out
Marks the 'OUT' point for your selection.

Remove In point

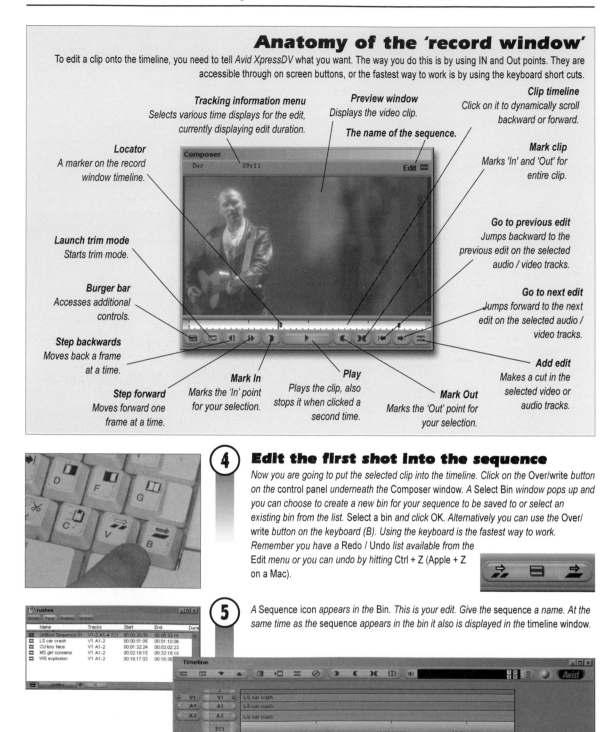

Anatomy of the 'record window'

To edit a clip onto the timeline, you need to tell *Avid XpressDV* what you want. The way you do this is by using IN and Out points. They are accessible through on screen buttons, or the fastest way to work is by using the keyboard short cuts.

Tracking information menu
Selects various time displays for the edit, currently displaying edit duration.

Preview window
Displays the video clip.

The name of the sequence.

Clip timeline
Click on it to dynamically scroll backward or forward.

Locator
A marker on the record window timeline.

Mark clip
Marks 'In' and 'Out' for entire clip.

Go to previous edit
Jumps backward to the previous edit on the selected audio / video tracks.

Launch trim mode
Starts trim mode.

Burger bar
Accesses additional controls.

Go to next edit
Jumps forward to the next edit on the selected audio / video tracks.

Step backwards
Moves back a frame at a time.

Add edit
Makes a cut in the selected video or audio tracks.

Step forward
Moves forward one frame at a time.

Mark In
Marks the 'In' point for your selection.

Play
Plays the clip, also stops it when clicked a second time.

Mark Out
Marks the 'Out' point for your selection.

Edit the first shot into the sequence

(4) *Now you are going to put the selected clip into the timeline. Click on the Over/write button on the control panel underneath the Composer window. A Select Bin window pops up and you can choose to create a new bin for your sequence to be saved to or select an existing bin from the list. Select a bin and click OK. Alternatively you can use the Over/write button on the keyboard (B). Using the keyboard is the fastest way to work. Remember you have a Redo / Undo list available from the Edit menu or you can undo by hitting Ctrl + Z (Apple + Z on a Mac).*

(5) *A Sequence icon appears in the Bin. This is your edit. Give the sequence a name. At the same time as the sequence appears in the bin it also is displayed in the timeline window.*

Anatomy of the timeline

The timeline is a visual representation of the clips you have cut together to make your sequence. Take a moment to really get your head around it 'cos it's kinda the heart of the edit.

Step out
Returns you to normal timeline mode.

Step in
Use to layer effects within a single video layer. This is called Nesting effects.

Audio tool
Displays the audio levels.

Toggle real-time effects
This is green when real-time effects are enabled and blue when disabled. When real-time effects are disabled, effect icons have no coloured dot in the Effect Palette and display a blue dot in the Timeline, indicating that they must be rendered before they will play in real time. When real-time effects are enabled, most effect icons have a green dot in both the Effect Palette and in the Timeline, indicating that they might play in real time, depending on the complexity of the effects and the sequence.

Trim mode
This will enter Trim Mode to adjust the incoming and outgoing frames at the head and tail of clips cut together.

Mute
Click to mute the audio playback.

Effect mode
This will open the Effect Editor window. This is where you can adjust effects you have applied to your sequence.

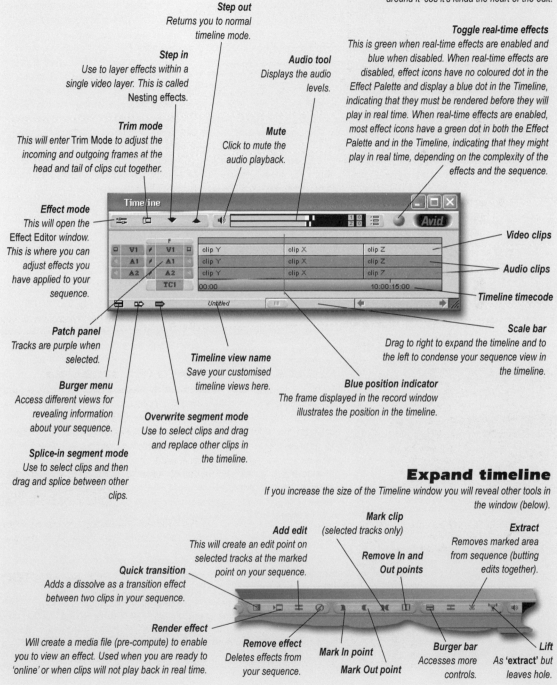

Video clips

Audio clips

Timeline timecode

Patch panel
Tracks are purple when selected.

Scale bar
Drag to right to expand the timeline and to the left to condense your sequence view in the timeline.

Timeline view name
Save your customised timeline views here.

Burger menu
Access different views for revealing information about your sequence.

Blue position indicator
The frame displayed in the record window illustrates the position in the timeline.

Overwrite segment mode
Use to select clips and drag and replace other clips in the timeline.

Splice-in segment mode
Use to select clips and then drag and splice between other clips.

Expand timeline

If you increase the size of the Timeline window you will reveal other tools in the window (below).

Mark clip
(selected tracks only)

Add edit
This will create an edit point on selected tracks at the marked point on your sequence.

Extract
Removes marked area from sequence (butting edits together).

Remove In and Out points

Quick transition
Adds a dissolve as a transition effect between two clips in your sequence.

Render effect
Will create a media file (pre-compute) to enable you to view an effect. Used when you are ready to 'online' or when clips will not play back in real time.

Remove effect
Deletes effects from your sequence.

Mark In point

Mark Out point

Burger bar
Accesses more controls.

Lift
As 'extract' but leaves hole.

The Timeline . . . in more detail

The timeline *is a linear visual representation of video and audio that you have cut into your sequence. Customising your* timeline *enables you to view different information about your sequence. Use either the* timeline *fast menu or the* timeline *settings to change the information displayed in the* timeline. *For example, selecting 'show marked waveforms' will give you instant aid when editing audio. You can also choose to display more information about the video clips that have been cut into the sequence. For example clip names and source names.*

I would recommend you use Auto-Patching *from the* timeline *settings as this will automatically patch enabled source tracks and record tracks that correspond in the* timeline *speeding up your editing process. To avoid slipping out of sync, it's advisable to have* sync locks *on (see patch panel boxout).*

Select dupe detection *in the timeline settings options. This will identify where you have duplicated the use of the same footage in the timeline. This will aid your editing decisions if you shot and are finishing on film. As you cannot cut the same frame of negative into your final sequence more than once,* dupe detection *will let you know when you make that mistake by colouring duplicated video clips.*

The position indicator *(blue vertical line on timeline or in position bar on both source and record monitors) can be used to quickly locate any part of the sequence for viewing. Simply click and drag the blue position indicator. Scroll up and down the timeline by clicking and dragging, or click at a specific point in the timeline. Then click play in the record monitor to play from this point.*

Use the scale bar *to stretch your sequence out to enable you to see your edits more clearly. You can increase the height of your video and audio tracks. This may be useful when for example you are adjusting audio levels. To enlarge the tracks (you have to select them in the patch panel) press Ctrl+L (windows) or apple+L (Mac). To reduce the track size click Ctrl+K (windows) or apple+K (mac).*

6 *You will notice the blue position indicator is placed at the very end of the sequence. If you are happy with the out point of the first clip Mark an In point on the sequence. The sequence is now ready for the next clip to be cut onto the timeline.*

Load the second clip into the source monitor *as before and mark an In point and an Out point. Check that you have selected the video and audio tracks in the patch panel on the timeline. Click the* Over/write *button and the second clip assembles itself after the first clip. You have now made your very first cut!*

Having made your first edits you can now continue to roughly assemble the rest of your sequence. Splicing a clip into your sequence will shunt all the clips after it down the timeline. Once you have a 'roughly assembled' sequence, go back and refine your edits using Trim Mode.

7 *The difference between* overwrite *and* splice-in *is that* overwrite *(B key) will replace footage in your sequence with the selected source clip, whereas* splice-in *(V key) will insert footage in between clips at the mark in point on the timeline.*

To splice-in, *load a clip into the source monitor and mark an 'In' and 'Out' point. Mark an 'In' point on the sequence in the timeline and hit the* splice-in *key (V key). The clip appears in the timeline at the mark in point. You will notice that all the clips after the mark in point have moved further down the timeline to make room for the new clip.*

Source tracks
In this case, one video and two audio tracks. The audio tracks have been mapped to go to A3 and A4 of the timeline, and the video track has been mapped to V2.

Sync locks
Currently the sync is locked on these tracks.

Record Tracks
This timeline has two video layers and four audio tracks into which you could edit your footage.

The patch panel is your friend

On the extreme left of the timeline is the patch panel. Essentially, you use this tool to tell Avid which layers on your source clips should go where in your edit.

To the left side of the patch panel, the layers of video and audio that make up the clip loaded into the source monitor are displayed. To the right of the patch panel the layers of video and audio that form the sequence you are cutting are displayed. You are able to select and deselect layers by clicking on them (and they will go purple).

You can use the patch panel to patch / map 'A1' in the source clip to be cut onto 'A2' in the sequence for instance. To do this, click on 'A1' in the source side of the patch panel, and while holding down the mouse click, drag the cursor to 'A2' on the record side of the patch panel. An arrow will appear as you do so. 'A1' is now patched to 'A2'.

If your clip does not appear in the timeline as you expected I would advise checking the patch panel to check that audio and video layers are selected and are patched. If you make a mistake or want to undo an action you have just performed simply click Ctrl-Z (for windows) or Apple-Z (for mac). You can undo / redo up to 32 actions via the edit menu.

Trim mode

Having completed your rough cut, it's now time to fine cut your film. Trim mode is used to refine your edits, adjusting the incoming and outgoing frames of the clips cut together in your sequence. Be warned, you need to pay particular attention to slipping out of sync whilst in trim mode. Avoid slipping out of sync by turning your sync locks on in the patch panel on the timeline.

To enter trim mode, click on the trim mode icon in the Record monitor, and also on the timeline (or { on the keyboard).

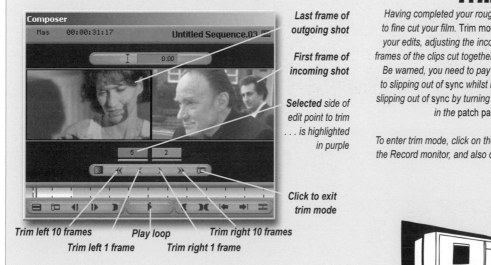

Last frame of outgoing shot

First frame of incoming shot

Selected *side of edit point to trim . . . is highlighted in purple*

Click to exit trim mode

Trim left 10 frames   Play loop   Trim right 10 frames
Trim left 1 frame   Trim right 1 frame

Whatever format of DV you plan to shoot, make sure you can play it back in the edit. For instance, all Sony DV cameras appear to be capable of playing back DVCam where, for instance, Canon cameras cannot.

Dual-roller trims *simultaneously adjust the incoming and outgoing frames of a cut on selected tracks. In this mode the sequence duration remains the same. To see how this works move the blue position indicator to an edit point in your timeline. Select V1 in the record side of your patch panel to only trim on this video track. Uncheck the audio tracks in the patch panel. Click on the* trim mode *button in the timeline. You will notice a pink* dual-roller *automatically appear at your edit point in the timeline and the composer window switches to* trim mode *view. Click the play loop button to play over your edit point. If caps lock is enabled you will also be able to hear the audio. If you cannot hear audio, check the speaker icon in the patch panel is enabled. Then click the trim frame buttons to change the position of your edit point. If you click trim right one frame you will add one frame to the clip Y and remove one frame from clip X. You can continue to fine tune your edit point adding and removing frames from the incoming and out going clips until you are happy with your cut. To exit trim mode press escape.*

Single-roller trims *subtract or add frames to one side of an edit point. This will change the duration of your sequence. Working with the same edit point as above let's see how this single-roller* trim *mode is different. Select* trim mode *in the timeline. Check V1 is selected in the patch panel. In the* trim mode *display in the composer monitor click on the right trim window to trim only that side of the clip. You will notice that the pink roller appears on the right side of the edit point only. Now click trim right one frame. You will notice one frame of clip X is removed without affecting clip Y. Press play loop to check your edit point. You will not be able to use* single trim mode *if sync locks are on and you have not selected all video and audio tracks in your timeline. You need to switch* sync locks *off if you only wish to trim one track in your timeline. Be careful, you are danger of slipping out of sync if you are careless.*

If you want to trim more than just the video track when in dual-roller trim *mode just select the tracks you want to trim in the patch panel on the timeline. To select additional tracks in* single-roller trim *mode shift+click the right/left side of the transition in the timeline. To quickly select more than one transition for trimming, shift+click and drag from left to right in the timeline to lasso the tracks you want to trim. The following diagram shows the effect trimming has on different sides of transitions on multiple tracks.*

The video track has the single-roller trim *on the right side of the transition. The audio tracks have the* single-roller trims *on the left side of the transition. Trimming right ten frames will remove ten frames of video from clip Y, and remove ten frames of audio from clip X. This will neatly tuck the incoming audio of clip Y under the video of clip X. This can sometimes help with making your transitions appear smoother.*

Trim mode *can also be a useful tool for slipping and sliding video and audio clips in your timeline. When you slip and slide in* trim mode *the duration of your sequence remains unchanged.*

Enter slip trim mode *by placing the blue position indicator on the clip you want to slip. Lasso the clip in the timeline clicking the mouse from right to left. The pink single roller trims will appear on the inside at the head and tail of the clip.*

Click trim right one frame. This will remove one frame at the head and reveal one frame at the tail as the clip slips in its position to show a different section of the original source clip in your cut sequence.

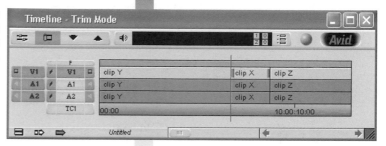

Sliding a clip changes the position of the clip in the timeline. To enter slide trim mode *click* shift+alt *(windows) or* option key *(mac) and lasso the clip from right to left using your mouse. The pink single trim rollers are on the outside of the clip you want to slide.*

The content of the clip X, which you are sliding stays the same. The clips either side of clip X will be altered as you trim frames in either direction. If you trim ten frames left, ten frames off the tail of clip Y are removed and ten frames at the head of clip Z are revealed.

Remember you can only trim, slip and slide for the number of frames that exist in the original digitised source for the clip cut into your timeline.

Importing audio from a CD

You may wish to add sound FX or music to your film to enhance the soundtrack. To import sound fx or music from a CD, put the CD in the CD-ROM of your computer. Open a bin in the project window or click on a bin that is already open to highlight it. Right click on the mouse in the bin, and select import from the pop-up menu. Go to the CD drive (in the select files to import window) and highlight the tracks you wish to import by Ctrl+clicking each track. Music on a CD is recorded at 44.1kHz and you will be asked if you want to perform a sample rate conversion when you import certain tracks. The computer has recognised that your audio settings for your project have been set to 48kHz (for most DV projects), and it is automatically offering to convert these files so that all audio files in your project will have the same sample rate. Click 'yes' to the sample rate conversion and the files you have selected will start importing. The files will appear as audio clips in the bin once they have finished importing. Name the clips, as you would do for master clips, by typing in the name column in the bin.

You can now edit these audio files (music or effects) into your timeline as you would with any normal video clip.

Creating titles

Titles can be created and cut into your sequence for opening/end credits, or simply as reminders (for example missing shots or scenes). When you create a title you create title media, which is stored on your media drive in the OMFI media files folder. The title appears in your bin as a title icon and can be cut into your sequence in exactly the same way as a master clip.

To create a title, open the title tool via the tools menu. The title tool window opens with a frame of video from your sequence. To change the frame of video over which you are creating your titles, move the blue position indicator to a point in your sequence over which you wish titles to appear. You can now design your title layout specifically for this clip in your film. If you want the title to be created with a black background click the 'V' button in the title tool window to deselect the transparent background.

Click on 'T' and click on the title window to show the cursor. You can start to type your text. Use the text formatting tools to change the font style and size. Add a shadow by clicking on the shadow box and typing in a number, for example 5. You can change the colour of the text or the shadow by clicking on the fill and shadow boxes. Click and hold down the mouse while you drag in the colour picker to the colour of your choice. To reposition your text within the frame click on the cursor button in the title tool window. Then click on the text, which will show a text box, and drag to reposition it.

To save your title select save from the file menu. Give your title a name and save it at the project resolution (DV 25 411 for NTSC and DV 25 420 PAL) in the bin of your choice. The title icon will appear in the bin and you can now cut it into your sequence.

To cut a title into your sequence you treat it in exactly the same way as a master clip. Load the title into the source monitor by double clicking on the title icon in the bin. If you have created a title to be cut on top of a video frame you must first create a new video layer. Create a new video layer by clicking Ctrl+Y (on a PC) or Apple+Y (on a MAC). Video layer two appears in the timeline. Click and drag source V1 to record V2 in the patch panel. Mark and IN and OUT on the title loaded in the source monitor. Click the red overwrite button in the composer window to cut the title onto video track 2 on your timeline. If you had created a title with a black background you will need to splice this into the sequence on video track 1. You would treat this exactly the same as a master clip being cut into your sequence.

Outputting your sequence

Avid XpressDV has different ways of outputting your sequence (edit). In this instance you will be outputting to tape via your camera. Load the sequence into the record monitor of the composer window. Select digital cut from the clip menu to open up the digital cut tool. You can choose to use remote or local deck control. You can only use remote deck control if you are using a tape which has already been striped with timecode (also known as blacked). Generally your striped tape will be set up in the following way,

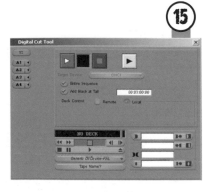

09:58:30:00 – bars and tone starts
09:59:30:00 – clock counts down
09:59:57:00 – 3 seconds of black
10:00:00:00 – programme starts

You will most probably be using a new tape which has not been striped. In this case set

Backing up your project

At the end of each day, your project must be backed up onto an external disk that you can walk away with, for example a zip disc (a feature project may not fit on a floppy disk). To back up your project, right click on My Computer on the desktop and select Explore. In the left hand window double click on the (C:) drive, then double click on the folder called Program Files, double click on the folder called Avid, then double click on the folder Avid XpressDV, double click on Avid Projects, right click on the folder with your project name and select copy. Put a floppy or zip disc in your drive and right click on the zip or floppy drive icon in the Explore window and select paste. Take the disc with you and keep it VERY safe.

the deck control in the digital cut tool to local (which means you will press record on your camera at the relevant time).

Open the audio tool via the tools menu. Select stereo mix in the setup options panel. This will output your sequence in stereo when completing a digital cut. Move the blue position indicator to the head of your sequence. Check all tracks are enabled in the patch panel. When selected they are purple and each enabled audio track will have a speaker icon. Then check that all selected tracks are also selected in the digital cut tool. Load a new tape into your camera. In the digital cut tool set the custom pre-roll to 30 seconds. To do this check the custom pre-roll button, then click and scroll down the duration menu. Make sure the entire sequence box is selected, and add black at tail for at least 30 seconds. Click record in the digital cut tool and when it begins the custom pre-roll press record in your camera. This will insert black at the head of your sequence. Monitor the digital cut on your monitor, and listen to the sound by connecting headphones to your camera (or speakers). Always check your tapes whenever you have completed a digital cut for picture and sound.

Managing Media

Once video and audio footage has been digitised it is called media. Digitising media onto your computers hard disk requires some management. Avid XpressDV will continue to create media files for any effects, graphics and music you create and import. When you use the record tool to digitise video and audio onto the hard disk of the computer the Avid XpressDV software compresses the files it creates. The digital video resolutions used in Avid XpressDV are DV25 4:1:1 for NTSC, and DV25 4:2:0 for PAL projects. DV (digital video) uses a 1/4-inch tape to record digital video. The video is sampled at 720 pixels per scan line. However the colour is sampled at 4:1:1 (NTSC) in 525-lines and 4:2:0 (PAL) 625-line formats.

In the record tool you can select that video and audio be saved to separate hard disks. To select different hard disks for audio and video click on the drive icon in the record tool. Click on the drop down menu next to the 'V' disk and select the disk you want video to be saved on. Click on the drop down menu next to the 'A' disk and select the disk you want audio to be saved on. Separating audio and video on different disks will improve the computer's performance when accessing files from these hard disks. You will be asked to select a drive upon which you wish to render your effects, for example as and when you create motion effects. If you can save these to the same disk you can manage these files more effectively

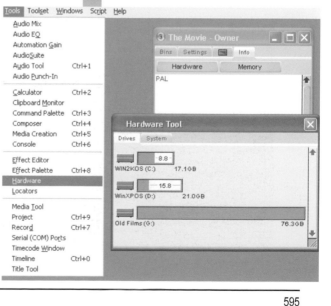

when disk space *becomes an issue later down the line. Managing* drive space *efficiently in the first place will help you trouble shoot problems in the future before they even happen. The* hardware tool *can also be used to display a visual representation of how much* drive space *is available on your drives. You can access the* hardware tool *via the* info tab *in the* project window *or by selecting* hardware *from the* tools menu. *Each drive upon which media is stored is represented by a drive icon to the left. The pink shaded area represents the amount of drive space that has been used. The figure in the white space within the box indicates how much drive space is available.*

The Media Tool *can be used to find the files stored on your hard drive that correspond to clips in your Avid project. You can select specific drives to be scanned in order to locate and manage media. You can delete files from the media tool freeing up drive space for new material. To delete a file simply select it and hit delete on the keyboard. You will be asked to confirm your selection. Only delete material you will not need as once it has been erased from the drives you have to re-digitise it if you want to use it again in your edit. You can open the media tool via the tools menu.*

(17) Creating an EDL

EDL manager *is an application that creates* edit decision lists. *An* edit decision list *contains details about all the clips that have been cut into your sequence. Your Avid XpressDV EDL is compatible with other programmes, as well as other Avid software such as Symphony. Your EDL is also a way of communicating with your negative cutter as to where all your picture edits exist if you shot on film. Always check with your negative cutter (or online editor) what their EDL requirements are. In this instance we will create a CMX 3600 EDL which creates an edit decision list for the picture cuts in your sequence.*

To create an EDL load a sequence into the record monitor. Select create EDL from your output menu. EDL manager opens up. Select get current sequence from the file menu. You will create a separate EDL for each video track. Make sure master is checked in your view list. Click on options and select CMX 3600. Select V1 in the track selector panel in the EDL manager window. Click update and the EDL for video track one appears in the EDL manager window. The list contains in/out points from the source tapes and in/out points indicating where each clip has been cut into your sequence. Save your EDL to a floppy disk. Select save from the file menu and name your EDL with no more than six characters. Navigate to the floppy disk drive. It is advisable to name it with the type of EDL it is and for what track it represents. For example 'v1cmx' and add the initials of your film to the end of the file name. Once you have saved your EDL to floppy you are ready to create the EDL for video track two (you would have a second video track for optical and title effects for instance, so that they are kept separate for the neg cutter). Select clear from the file menu to clear the EDL manager window. Then click on V1 in the track selector panel and drag down to select V2. As before, select get current sequence from the file menu. The EDL for video track two appears in the EDL manager window. It is advisable to print out your EDL as a back up.

Monitor set-up

If you decide that you want to set up your own home edit suite, you will need some way to accurately monitor what is actually 'in' the images that you are editing. Normally, you would use a graded broadcast monitor (a two 21" TV that costs £2k!), but you probably can't afford one. So a portable telly will have to do. What are you looking for? I would suggest that you blow £150 on a good Sony portable, ideally one with a flat tube. You may think that you should just go with the one you can borrow off your brother in law, but Sony TV's are excellent and there are a few hidden features that you can access.

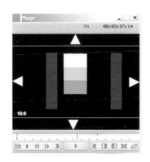

1. Setting Up

Before starting, you will need to download the set-up files from our website. Using your favourite video software, in this case Avid XpressDV, transfer the plug, colour bars and tests onto a DV tape.

2. DV to VHS

Next, connect your DV camera to a VHS video (DV Vvdeo out to VHS video in) so that you can monitor, through the VHS, what is recorded on the tape. The reason for this is that during set-up on some Sony TVs, you will need an RF signal going in to the TV and not a composite video signal (the only way out of your camera is composite, S-Video or Firewire and not RF). Plug the aerial cable from the back of your VHS into the back of your Sony TV. Set your VCR to AV1 (or whichever input your DV composite video is connected to) and play the DV tape, then tune the TV in so that you can see the video image. Store the video channel on the TV and you are ready for the advanced setup.

WARNING – This next bit could bugger your TV so be careful!

3. Access the menu

There are a number of keys you will need to press to get into the Service Mode screen of your Sony TV. You will have to try them all until you find one that works. The screen you will see when you access Service Screen will be something like this one (right).

a – First attempt, will probably fail . . . Turn off the TV and, whilst holding the + and – buttons on the front of the TV, switch it back on. Probably didn't work so try the next one . . .

b – Now you will need the remote. Press the power button (usually green and at the top of the remote) to put the TV in standby mode. Next press the Info / Display button (see diagram), next press the number 5 button, next press the Volume + button, and finally press the green power button again. Work? Nope, didn't with mine either . . .

c – OK, next go. Put the TV in standby (green power button), then the Info / Display button, then the number 5 button, and finally the green power button again. Work? Oh dear . . . Final go then . . .

d – Put the TV in standby (green button), then the Info / Display button, then the number 5 button, next press the Volume + button, and finally press the teletext off button (see diagram) . . . . Hoorah, worked for both my Sony monitor TVs too!

Generic Sony Remote

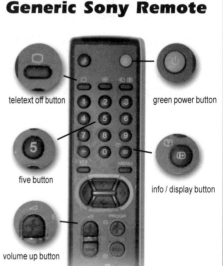

teletext off button

green power button

five button

info / display button

volume up button

4. You're in!

OK, so now you are in the Service Mode screen. You should see live video pictures in the background, you will need this so that you can set-up the picture size and aspect. Each TV has a variant on the set-up but here's a brief of the things you will need to modify.

5. Sub menus

Press the menu button on your remote and you will get to a sub menu (right) which will display a number of settings. You only need to worry about the first, Geometry. Go to this section and you'll be presented with a number of options which you can modify. Before doing anything, write down the settings so that if things go pear shaped, you can put everything back as it was.

Play the DV tape to bring up the various screens. Use the Pluge screen to set up the far top and bottom of the screen, and left and right of the screen with the arrows. The idea is to get the monitor to display the whole image without any cropping (or as little as possible). It will take you twenty minutes of farting around to get this right, and you will need to keep fast forwarding and rewinding your tape to check that your new settings will also display correctly with the colour bars.

6. Exit the menu

Once done, press the Menu button to take you back to the main Service Mode Screen and press 0 0 (zero twice). Your TV should exit the Service Mode.

7. B/C/C – Brightness, contrast and colour

Lastly, you'll want to set up the screen so that it knows when black is black. It's essential that you set-up your monitor for this so that you don't discover nasty problems further down the line. You can use the normal consumer setup for this as you'll just use brightness (with the Pluge screen off your DV tape), contrast (which should be set quite high), and colour (which should be set slightly lower than normal – most TVs are set too high). Play the pluge tape and adjust the brightness (you can set the contrast quite high too) so that it matches the diagram. Save your settings and exit the user set-up.

Depending on the TV there will be other features such as NR (noise reduction) which should be turned off and Colour Correction should also be turned off. However, some Sony TVs carry a Movie Mode which should help as it will reduce the effect of clamping – that is when a dark image is followed by a bright image (or vice versa) the image will jump and resize. This Movie Mode will help with this, but it might override your brightness/contrast/ colour settings. Do tests and take a view on which is best.

The main setup options in the Service Mode on a Sony TV.

The various parameters you have to play with in order to maximise the image for your home edit suite TV monitor.

If you have any problems with this one, don't call me, don't e-mail me, don't write. You have been WARNED!

Index

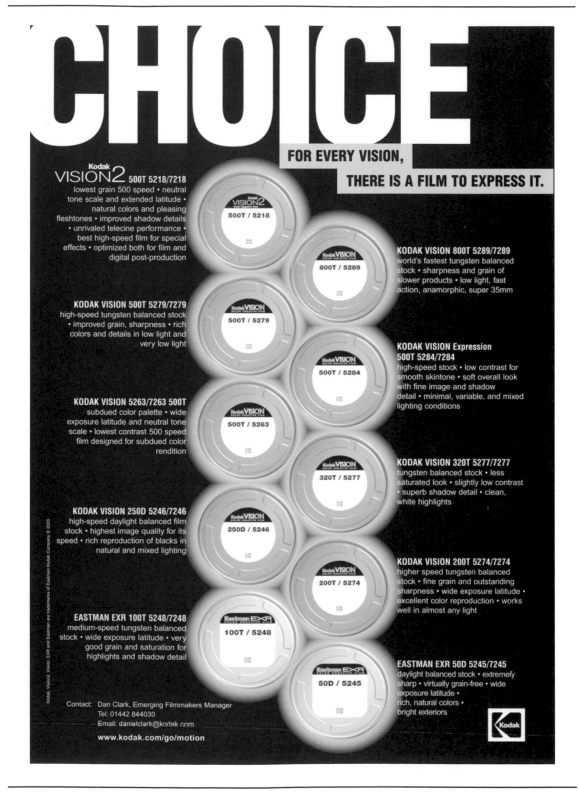

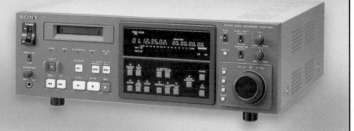